THE WORKS OF CHRISTOPHER MARLOWE

EDITED BY

C. F. TUCKER BROOKE

B.LITT. OXON. ; INSTRUCTOR IN ENGLISH IN YALE UNIVERSITY

OXFORD

AT THE CLARENDON PRESS

Oxford University Press, Ely House, London W. 1

GLASGOW NEW YORK TORONTO MELBOURNE WELLINGTON
CAPE TOWN SALISBURY IBADAN NAIROBI LUSAKA ADDIS ABABA
BOMBAY CALCUTTA MADRAS KARACHI LAHORE DACCA
KUALA LUMPUR SINGAPORE HONG KONG TOKYO

FIRST PUBLISHED 1910
REPRINTED 1925, 1929, 1941, 1946, 1953, 1957, 1962, 1964, 1966, 1969
PRINTED IN GREAT BRITAIN

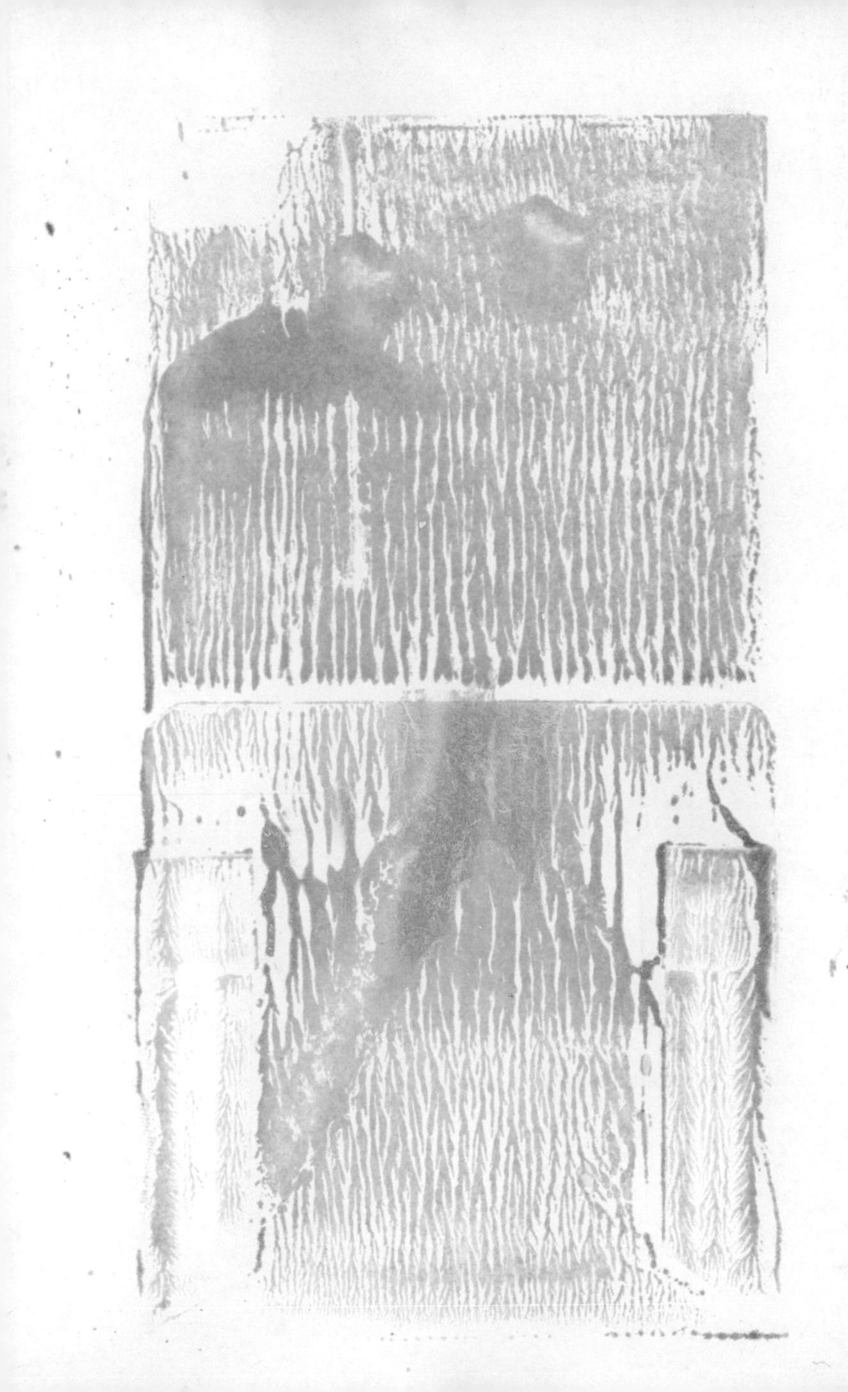

PREFACE

THIS volume is designed to furnish the student and the general reader with a serviceable edition of Marlowe's accepted writings. The text reproduces faithfully, it is believed, that of the most reliable version of each work, except as regards punctuation and capitalization. In the latter particulars it appears inconsistent with the requirements of conscientious editing to retain such errors as are due to the carelessness of the original compositor or to the limitations of the printer's fount used, but in making these necessary minor changes the text has in no sense been 'modernized'. Unmeaning irregularities in punctuation and in the use of capitals have been normalized, where the comfort of the enlightened reader seemed absolutely to demand it, but always in accordance with Elizabethan rather than Victorian principles. In many cases intelligibility clearly required the substitution of a full stop for a probably accidental comma, or the reverse; and it appeared unnecessary that the reader should be annoyed by such occasional, irregular spellings as 'tamburlaine' and 'zenocrate', merely because the printer of the first edition of the play in question was presumably insufficiently provided with capital T's and Z's.[1] No attempt has been made to introduce the modern symmetry and logical consistency in capitalization and pointing. Semicolons appear only in the rare cases where they are found in the old editions; the present-day distinctions between the uses of

[1] Every such deviation from the original has, however, been carefully noted by the editor and will be listed in the forthcoming *editio major* in an Appendix for the benefit of those who may wish to study the vagaries of Elizabethan typography. The matter does not in any way concern the appreciation of Marlowe.

commas and colons are not pressed too far; and the employment of the comma for elocutionary effect, to indicate a drop of the voice, has been retained. So, too, there has been no interference with the occasional practice of capitalizing common nouns or with the ordinary absence of capitals in proper adjectives. Errors in the division of lines have been corrected, but wherever the alteration amounts to much more than the mere substitution of a capital letter at the commencement of the line, the change is indicated in the critical apparatus. The long 's' is not retained, and black letter type is supplanted by roman. Words printed in roman in a black-letter setting are here given in italic. All further deviations from the *editio princeps* of each play or poem are recorded in the footnotes, which give also the variant readings of the other early editions, as well as a selection of the more valuable modern emendations.

The *apparatus criticus* is comparatively simple. Each separate division of the book is preceded by a list of *sigla*, enumerating chronologically first the early editions, which determine the text, and then the more modern versions, which possess in themselves no authority, and finally giving in alphabetical order the names and works of critics who have offered conjectural emendations. Bibliographical completeness is attempted in the case of the early editions alone. Only such modern reprints and critical writings are mentioned as there has been occasion to cite in the footnotes. The basis of the text is always the edition named first in the list of *sigla*, which, wherever the relative dates of editions can be ascertained, is the oldest except in the single case of the song of the *Passionate Shepherd*.

Certain well-known abbreviations are used throughout the critical apparatus: *Conj.* before the name of an editor or critic indicates that the change in question was merely suggested, without being introduced into the text. *Add.* means that the word or passage referred to was first inserted by the editor whose name follows ; when such new matter appears in the present text, it is enclosed in angular brackets. The abbreviation *etc.* after an editor's name signifies that the reading has been adopted in all later editions. *Exc.* stands for ' except '. The note ' thirst *Dyce to Bull.*' means that the reading ' thirst ' in place of ' thrust ' appears in all the editions from that of Dyce to that of Bullen inclusive.

This volume contains the plays and poems which must at present be regarded as making up Marlowe's extant works. The epigrams of Sir John Davies and Chapman's continuation of *Hero and Leander* are also included because of their close historical connexion with genuine poems. For the purpose of distinction these non-Marlovian pieces are printed in small type, and the same device is used to mark the supplementary portions of *Doctor Faustus* first found in the editions of 1616 and 1663 respectively, though it is possible, and even probable, that a portion of the new matter of the 1616 version represents Marlowe's own work.

Two inconsiderable poems, printed by Dyce in his edition of Marlowe, have been omitted because the evidence in favour of their authenticity seems inadequate. A fourteen-line Latin epitaph on Sir Roger Manwood († 1592) is written in manuscript on the back of the title-page of a copy [1] of the 1629 edition of *Hero and Leander*, whence Dyce incorporated it on the ground that Manwood, who was of Kentish origin, may have been a patron of Marlowe, and that the unknown scribe in copying the epitaph into a work of Marlowe's (and Chapman's) meant to imply the former poet's authorship. This reasoning is on the face of it rather weak, and the fact that the book containing the epitaph was not in existence till thirty-six years after Marlowe's death might cast doubt on much stronger evidence.

Dyce also inserted into his edition a *Dialogue in Verse*,

[1] Last heard of in the possession of Colonel W. F. Prideaux of Calcutta (1886).

consisting of about eighty lines, which Collier had first discovered and had printed in *The Alleyn Papers* (p. 8) from a single MS. folio at Dulwich College. This fragment, which is written in the MS. (Dulwich College MS. I. f 272) as prose and possesses neither any likeness to Marlowe's work nor any great poetic merit, has inscribed on the back in an unknown hand the words *Kitt Marlowe*. The folly of taking too seriously such vague hints, particularly in the case of suspected manuscripts like those at Dulwich, has often been made evident.

Only the most indispensable critical matter could be admitted into this volume. Each work is preceded by an introduction which sets forth briefly the facts of most importance and summarizes the editor's conclusions. For further details on all these points the reader must be referred to the library edition of Marlowe now in preparation. There will be found also the discussion of Marlowe's life and genius by Professor Raleigh, as well as the explanatory notes on the text and the investigation of Marlowe's claims to partial or complete authorship of *Henry VI*, *Titus Andronicus*, *The Taming of a Shrew*, *Lust's Dominion*, and the other supposititious works.

The editor feels himself greatly indebted for the loan of early Marlowe editions to the kindness of his Grace the Duke of Devonshire, the Earl of Ellesmere, and the directors of numerous public and private libraries. He owes particular thanks for critical help and assistance to Professor Walter Raleigh, Mr. Percy Simpson, and Mr. J. Le Gay Brereton. To all of these and to others who have been generous of assistance he begs to offer his sincere acknowledgements, while awaiting the opportunity of a specific statement of indebtedness, along with bibliographical and textual details, in the forthcoming larger edition.

C. F. T. B.

CORNELL UNIVERSITY,
1909.

CONTENTS

TAMBURLAINE

Date. The two parts of *Tamburlaine* are commonly ascribed to the years 1587 and 1588 respectively, and these dates are almost certainly correct, at least as regards theatrical presentation. It is possible that some portion of the first part may have been written during Marlowe's residence at Cambridge, but it can hardly have been acted on any stage before the poet came to London in 1586. The downward limit is fixed by a sneer of Robert Greene in the epistle 'to the gentlemen readers' of *Perimedes the Blacke-Smith,* where he ridicules the popular tragedy of the time, 'daring God out of heauen with that Atheist *Tamburlan,*' and goes on to speak of the 'mad and scoffing poets, that haue propheticall spirits, as bred of *Merlin's* race, if there be anye in England that set the end of schollarisme in an English blanck verse. . . .' The first allusion is pretty clearly to Tamburlaine's speech in Act v of the second part (ll. 4290–4313), while the words 'Merlin's race' are a punning reference to 'Marlin', the common Elizabethan variant of Marlowe's name.

Early editions and stage history. *Tamburlaine* was entered at Stationers' Hall in 1590. The entry reads as follows: 'xiiij^{to} die Augusti ⟨1590⟩ Richard Jones. Entred vnto him for his Copye *The twooe commicall discourses of* TOMBERLEIN *the Cithian shepparde* vnder the handes of Master Abraham Hartewell, and the Wardens. vj^{d}.' The two parts were issued together in octavo form in 1590, and again in 1592, the publisher in both cases being Jones, who takes occasion to announce in his epistle to the readers (cf. p. 7) that he has omitted 'some fond and friuolous Iestures'. How great these omissions were there is no likelihood of our learning. Certainly in their present form the two plays have little claim to the title of 'commicall discourses', even when we allow for Elizabethan roughness of definition.

Henslowe's diary records fifteen performances of Part I and seven performances of Part II between August 28,

1594, and November 13, 1595; the profits are in nearly every case large. From this and from the letter 'j' affixed to the notice of the first performance,[1] it may be assumed that *Tamburlaine* had been to some extent re-written for revival in 1594-5 by the same company which had originally produced it—the Lord Admiral's or Henslowe's. The revised text seems never to have been printed. In 1605-6 Edward White printed a third edition, based on that of 1590; the two parts are here for the first time given separate title pages, and they were published in successive years. There is no reason to believe that any other text of *Tamburlaine* existed until the beginning of the nineteenth century. Bibliographers' allusions to a *quarto* of 1590, and to editions of 1593, 1597, and 1600 respectively, are not supported by any discoverable evidence, and the statements of all modern editors previous to A. Wagner (1885) contain inaccuracies.

Authorship. The two parts of *Tamburlaine* differ from all the other works of Marlowe here printed, in that there is no documentary evidence to establish their authenticity. The title pages of the three early editions bear no author's name, and it so happens that among the myriad allusions to these plays prior to the Restoration we find no pronouncement on the subject of their origin. A reference in Henslowe's Diary[2] to 'Marloes tambelan' turns out to be a flat forgery, another mention in the 'Gorgon' poems suffixed to Gabriel Harvey's *New Letter of Notable Contents* (1593) is much too obscure to prove anything, and the lines in Heywood's second Prologue to the *Jew of Malta*,[3] once taken as a statement of Marlowe's authorship of *Tamburlaine*, make in fact no such assertion.

That a young poet's first experiment in a not very aristocratic species of literature should go publicly unclaimed and unheralded, even after it had achieved success, is, of course, in the Elizabethan age the reverse of surprising. The fact has for us no earthly significance except that it explains what would otherwise be almost inexplicable, namely, the way in which Milton's blundering nephew, Edward Phillips,[4] came to ascribe the plays to Thomas Newton, author of a prose history touching the same events; and the repudiation of Marlowe's authorship in

[1] Cf. *Henslowe's Diary*, ed W. W. Greg, Pt. II, pp. 167, 168.
[2] Ed. Greg, I, p. 38.
[3] Cf. p 239, ll. 5-8.
[4] *Theatrum Poetarum*, 1675.

later years by Malone, Broughton, and the compiler of the first [1] collected edition of the poet's works. The question has now settled itself beyond the imaginable possibility of change, and the two parts of *Tamburlaine* will continue to head the list of Marlowe's writings, until we are able to establish the chronological priority of some other work of the same poet—*Dido,* for instance, or the Ovid translations. For the Marlovian authorship of *Tamburlaine* an almost overwhelming case could be made out, if need were, from circumstantial evidence alone, but there is no reason for resorting to such proof. The personality of the writer is everywhere apparent in these plays. We are not merely assured that no poet except Marlowe was desirous or capable, about 1587, of starting the dramatic and stylistic revolution which *Tamburlaine* inaugurated. We perceive also that the individual artistic development which we can trace backwards from *Edward II* to *Dr. Faustus* must inevitably have had its rise in *Tamburlaine.*

The dominant trait of Marlowe's genius is its youthfulness; and we approach nowhere else so near to the essential character of the poet as in these two early plays, which, if they did not actually begin his career of authorship, certainly introduced him first to public notice. To a higher degree perhaps than is usually apprehended our conception of Marlowe as a personal influence in poetry is derived from the enthusiastic lyrism of *Tamburlaine,* and it remains a very open question whether the gain in form and objectivity in the later dramas brings with it an altogether sufficient compensation for the decrease in boyish ideality.

Source. The question of the sources whence Marlowe derived his material for *Tamburlaine* has been much discussed, and is still not entirely solved. For the first part it seems clear that the poet was indebted primarily to the fourteenth chapter of the second part of Fortescue's *Foreste,* published in 1571, and again in 1576. Fortescue's book is a translation of Pedro Mexia's *Silva de varia lecion* (1543), which in its turn is based largely, as regards the chapter in question, but by no means entirely, on the chronicle of Andreas Cambinus. A direct translation from the Italian of Cambinus by John Shute [2] appears to have been entirely ignored by Marlowe, and there is no reason for

[1] 1826.

[2] *Two very notable Commentaries the one of the Originall of the Tvrcks and Empire of the house of Ottomanno* . . . 1562.

assuming the poet's acquaintance with George Whetstone's condensed version of Fortescue in *The English Myrror*, 1586 (pp. 78–83). It would seem probable, however, that Thomas Newton's *Notable History of the Saracens*, 1575, furnished Marlowe with a number of proper names and suggested the story of Sigismund in Part II, while Messrs. Herford and Wagner [1] have shown that individual passages of Part I are taken in all probability from the Latin of Petrus Perondinus (1553).

The second part of *Tamburlaine* is confessedly an afterthought, not contemplated when the first part was written. It is mostly Marlowe's invention. The story of Olympia, however, was taken, as Collier first pointed out, from Ariosto (*Orlando Furioso*, Bk. XXIX). It would be of interest to determine the precise channel through which this tale reached the dramatist ; he may, of course, have known it in the Italian, but it is more likely that he read it in MS. in Sir John Harington's translation, which after years of preparation was published in 1591. A similar instance of borrowing from a MS. source occurs at the end of the fourth act of Part II (ll. 4098–4103), where six lines are copied from the as yet unpublished *Fairy Queen*, and copied so carelessly as to leave a tell-tale Alexandrine in the midst of the usual pentameters of dramatic verse.

[1] *Academy*, xxiv, pp. 265, 266.

Tamburlaine
the Great.

Who, from a Scythian Shephearde,
by his rare and woonderfull Conquests,
became a most puissant and mightye Monarque.
And (for his tyranny, and terrour in Warre) was tearmed,
The Scourge of God.

Deuided into two Tragicall Dis-
courses, as they were sundrie times
shewed vpon Stages in the Citie
of London.

By the right honorable the Lord
Admyrall, his seruantes.

Now first, and newlie published.

Benj Ayl[?]

LONDON.
Printed by Richard Ihones: at the signe
of the Rose and Crowne neere Holborne Bridge. 1590.

1590 = Octavo edition of that year. B.L.
1592 = ,, ,, ,, ,, B.L.
1605 = Quarto ,, ,, ,, B.L.

Rob. = (Robinson's) edition of Marlowe, 1826.

Dyce { *Dyce* [1] = Dyce's first edition of Marlowe, 1850.
Dyce [2] = ,, revised ,, ,, ,, 1858, etc.

Cunn. = Cunningham's ,, ,, ,, 1870, etc.
Bull. = Bullen's ,, ,, ,, 1885.
Wag. = A. Wagner's edition of *Tamburlaine*, 1885.
Ellis = 'Mermaid' edition of Marlowe's best plays, 1887, etc.
T. B. = The present editor.

Brennan = C. B.'s conjectures in '*Anglia*', *Beiblatt*, 1905, p. 207.
Brereton = J. Le Gay Brereton, (*a*) *Notes on the Text of Marlowe*, '*Anglia*', *Beiblatt*, 1905, pp. 203 ff.
(*b*) *Passages from the Works of Marlowe*, Sydney, 1902.
Broughton = J. B.'s MS. notes in copy of *Rob.* (Brit. Mus. 11771 d).
Coll. = J. P. Collier's MS. notes in copy of *Dyce*[1] (Brit. Mus. 11771 bbb 6).
Coll.[2] = J. P. C.'s Introduction to *Coleridge*, *Seven Lectures on Shakespeare*, 1856.
Cook = A. S. C. in *Modern Language Notes*, xxi. 112, 113.
Deighton = K. D., *The Old Dramatists: Conjectural Readings*, 1896.
Elze = K. E., *Notes on Elizabethan Dramatists*, 1889.
Fraser's Mag. = Unsigned article in *Fraser's Town and Country Magazine*, xlvii, pp. 221–34.
Mitford = J. M. in *Gentleman's Magazine*, Jan. 1841.
Schipper = J. S., *De Versu Marlovii.*

To the Gentlemen Readers: and others that take pleasure in reading Histories.

Gentlemen, and curteous Readers whosoeuer: I haue here published in print for your sakes, the two tragical Discourses of the Scythian Shepheard, Tamburlaine, *that became so great a Conquerour, and so mightie a Monarque: My hope is, that they wil be now no lesse acceptable vnto you to read* 5 *after your serious affaires and studies, then they haue bene (lately) delightfull for many of you to see, when the same were shewed in London vpon stages: I haue (purposely) omitted and left out some fond and friuolous Iestures, digressing (and in my poore opinion) far vnmeet for the matter, which* 10 *I thought, might seeme more tedious vnto the wise, than any way els to be regarded, though (happly) they haue bene of some vaine conceited fondlings greatly gaped at, what times they were shewed vpon the stage in their graced deformities: neuertheles now, to be mixtured in print with such matter* 15 *of worth, it wuld prooue a great disgrace to so honorable & stately a historie: Great folly were it in me, to commend vnto your wisedomes, either the eloquence of the Authour that writ them, or the worthinesse of the matter it selfe; I therefore leaue vnto your learned censures, both the one and* 20 *the other, and my selfe the poore printer of them vnto your most curteous and fauourable protection; which if you vouchsafe to accept, you shall euermore binde mee to imploy what trauell and seruice I can, to the aduauncing and pleasuring of your excellent degree.* 25

Yours, most humble at commaundement,
R. I. Printer

2 the two] this *1605* discourse *1605* 5 they] it *1605* 6 they haue] it hath *1605* 7 were] was *1605* 13 times] time *1592* 15 mixtured] mingled *1605* 19 them] it *1605* 20 leaue] leaue it *1605* 20, 21 both . . . other *om. 1605* 21 of them] therof *1605* 22 protections *1605* 23 accept] doe *1605* 26 humble *om. 1605*

⟨DRAMATIS PERSONAE

MYCETES, *King of Persia.*
COSROE, *his brother.*
MEANDER,
THERIDAMAS,
ORTYGIUS,
CENEUS,
MENAPHON, } *Persian lords.*
TAMBURLAINE, *a Scythian shepherd.*
TECHELLES,
USUMCASANE, } *his followers.*
BAJAZETH, *emperor of the Turks.*
KING OF FEZ.
KING OF MOROCCO
KING OF ARGIER.
KING OF ARABIA.
SOLDAN OF EGYPT.
GOVERNOR OF DAMASCUS.
AGYDAS,
MAGNETES, } *Median lords.*
CAPOLIN, *an Egyptian.*
PHILEMUS, *Bassoes, Lords, Citizens, Moors, Soldiers, and Attendants.*
ZENOCRATE, *daughter to the Soldan of Egypt.*
ANIPPE, *her maid.*
ZABINA, *wife to Bajazeth.*
EBEA, *her maid.*
Virgins of Damascus.⟩[1]

[1] *Add. Dyce.*

The Two Tragicall Discourses of Mighty Tamburlaine, the Scythian Shepheard, &c.

The Prologue.

From iygging vaines of riming mother wits,
And such conceits as clownage keepes in pay,
Weele lead you to the stately tent of War,
Where you shall heare the Scythian Tamburlaine
Threatning the world with high astounding tearms 5
And scourging kingdoms with his conquering sword.
View but his picture in this tragicke glasse,
And then applaud his fortunes as you please.

Actus 1. *Scæna* 1.

Mycetes, Cosroe, Meander, Theridamas, Ortygius, Ceneus, (Menaphon,) with others.

Mycetes.

Brother *Cosroe*, I find my selfe agreeu'd,
Yet insufficient to expresse the same: 10
For it requires a great and thundring speech:
Good brother tell the cause vnto my Lords,
I know you haue a better wit than I.
Cos. Vnhappie *Persea*, that in former age
Hast bene the seat of mightie Conquerors, 15
That in their prowesse and their pollicies,
Haue triumpht ouer *Affrike*, and the bounds
Of *Europe*, wher the Sun dares scarce appeare,
For freezing meteors and coniealed colde:
Now to be rulde and gouerned by a man, 20
At whose byrth-day *Cynthia* with *Saturne* ioinde,
And *Ioue*, the Sun and *Mercurie* denied

Heading The two . . . Tamburlaine *1590*: The first part of the two . . . Tamburlaine *1592*: The Tragicall Conquestes of Tamburlaine *1605* 8 you please] they passe *conj. Coll.* 17 Affrica *1605* 19 meteors] waters *conj. Coll.*

To shed their influence in his fickle braine,
Now Turkes and Tartars shake their swords at thee
Meaning to mangle all thy Prouinces. 25

Mycet. Brother, I see your meaning well enough.
And thorough your Planets I perceiue you thinke,
I am not wise enough to be a kinge,
But I refer me to my noble men,
That knowe my wit, and can be witnesses: 30
I might command you to be slaine for this,
Meander, might I not?

Meand. Not for so small a fault my soueraigne Lord.

Mycet. I meane it not, but yet I know I might,
Yet liue, yea, liue, *Mycetes* wils it so: 35
Meander, thou my faithfull Counsellor,
Declare the cause of my conceiued griefe,
Which is (God knowes) about that *Tamburlaine*,
That like a Foxe in midst of haruest time,
Dooth pray vppon my flockes of Passengers. 40
And as I heare, doth meane to pull my plumes,
Therefore tis good and meete for to be wise.

Meand. Oft haue I heard your Maiestie complain,
Of *Tamburlaine*, that sturdie Scythian thiefe,
That robs your merchants of *Persepolis*, 45
Treading by land vnto the Westerne Isles,
And in your confines with his lawlesse traine,
Daily commits inciuill outrages.
Hoping (misled by dreaming prophesies)
To raigne in *Asia*, and with barbarous Armes, 50
To make himselfe the Monarch of the East:
But ere he march in *Asia*, or display
His vagrant Ensigne in the Persean fields,
Your Grace hath taken order by *Theridimas*,
Chardg'd with a thousand horse, to apprehend 55
And bring him Captiue to your Highnesse throne.

Myce. Ful true thou speakst, & like thy selfe my lord
Whom I may tearme a *Damon* for thy loue.
Therefore tis best, if so it lik you all,
To send my thousand horse incontinent, 60
To apprehend that paltrie Scythian.
How like you this, my honorable Lords?
Is it not a kingly resolution?

23 their *Dyce etc.*: his *1590–1605* 46 Trading *1592* 48 vnciuill *1605*

Cosr. It cannot choose, because it comes from you.
Myce. Then heare thy charge, valiant *Theridimas* 65
The chiefest Captaine of *Mycetes* hoste,
The hope of *Persea,* and the verie legges
Whereon our state doth leane, as on a staffe,
That holds vs vp, and foiles our neighbour foes.
Thou shalt be leader of this thousand horse, 70
Whose foming galle with rage and high disdaine,
Haue sworne the death of wicked *Tamburlaine.*
Go frowning foorth, but come thou smyling home,
As did Sir *Paris* with the Grecian Dame,
Returne with speed, time passeth swift away, 75
Our life is fraile, and we may die to day.
Ther. Before the Moone renew her borrowed light,
Doubt not my Lord and gratious Soueraigne,
But *Tamburlaine,* and that Tartarian rout,
Shall either perish by our warlike hands, 80
Or plead for mercie at your highnesse feet.
Myce. Go, stout *Theridimas,* thy words are swords
And with thy lookes thou conquerest all thy foes:
I long to see thee backe returne from thence,
That I may view these milk-white steeds of mine, 85
All loden with the heads of killed men.
And from their knees, euen to their hoofes below,
Besmer'd with blood, that makes a dainty show.
The. Then now my Lord, I humbly take my leaue.
Myc. Therid⟨amas⟩ farewel ten thousand times. (*Exit.*
Ah, *Menaphon,* why staiest thou thus behind, 91
When other men prease forward for renowne:
Go *Menaphon,* go into *Scythia,*
And foot by foot follow *Theridamas.*
Cos. Nay, pray you let him stay, a greater ⟨task⟩ 95
Fits *Menaphon,* than warring with a Thiefe:
Create him Prorex of *Affrica,*
That he may win the Babylonians hearts,
Which will reuolt from Persean gouernment,
Vnlesse they haue a wiser king than you. 100
Myc. Vnlesse they haue a wiser king than you?
These are his words, *Meander* set them downe
Cos. And ad this to them, that all *Asia*
Lament to see the follie of their King.
Myc. Well here I sweare by this my royal seat— 105

66 chiefe *1605* 95 you *om. 1605* task *add. Rob. etc.*: feat *MS. note in Bodleian copy of ed. 1605* 97 of] of all *1605 etc.*

Cos. You may doe well to kisse it then.
Myc. Embost with silke as best beseemes my state,
To be reueng'd for these contemptuous words.
O where is dutie and allegeance now ?
Fled to the Caspean or the Ocean maine ? 110
What, shall I call thee brother ? No, a foe,
Monster of Nature, shame vnto thy stocke,
That dar'st presume thy Soueraigne for to mocke.
Meander come, I am abus'd *Meander*. *Exit.*

Manent Cosroe & Menaphon.

Mena. How now my Lord, what, mated and amaz'd
To heare the king thus thr⟨e⟩aten like himselfe ? 116
Cos. Ah *Menaphon*, I passe not for his threates,
The plot is laid by Persean Noble men,
And Captaines of the Medean garrisons,
To crowne me Emperour of *Asia*, 120
But this it is that doth excruciate
The verie substance of my vexed soule :
To see our neighbours that were woont to quake
And tremble at the Persean Monarkes name,
Now sits and laughs our regiment to scorne, 125
And that which might resolue me into teares :
Men from the farthest Equinoctiall line,
Haue swarm'd in troopes into the Easterne India :
Lading their shippes with golde and pretious stones :
And made their spoiles from all our prouinces. 130
Mena. This should intreat your highnesse to reioice,
Since Fortune giues you opportunity,
To gaine the tytle of a Conquerour,
By curing of this maimed Emperie.
Affrike and *Europe* bordering on your land, 135
And continent to your Dominions :
How easely may you with a mightie hoste,
Passe into *Græcia*, as did *Cyrus* once.
And cause them to withdraw their forces home,
Least you subdue the pride of Christendome ? 140
Cos. But Menaph⟨on⟩ what means this trumpets sound ?
Mena. Behold, my Lord *Ortigius*, and the rest,
Bringing the Crowne to make you Emperour.

106 then] then, Mycetes *conj. Elze*, *Wag.* 126 resolue] dissolue *1605* 129 shippe *1592* 138 Passe] Hast *1605* 140 you] they *1605*

Enter Ortigius & Ceneus bearing a Crowne with others.

Ort. Magnificent and mightie Prince *Cosroe*,
We in the name of other Persean states, 145
And commons of this mightie Monarchie,
Present thee with th' Emperiall Diadem.
Cene. The warlike Souldiers, & the Gentlemen,
That heretofore haue fild *Persepolis*
With *Affrike* Captaines, taken in the field: 150
Whose ransome made them martch in coates of gold,
With costlie iewels hanging at their eares,
And shining stones vpon their loftie Crestes,
Now liuing idle in the walled townes,
Wanting both pay and martiall discipline, 155
Begin in troopes to threaten ciuill warre,
And openly exclaime against the King.
Therefore to stay all sodaine mutinies,
We will inuest your Highnesse Emperour:
Whereat the Souldiers will conceiue more ioy, 160
Then did the Macedonians at the spoile
Of great *Darius* and his wealthy hoast.
Cosr. Wel, since I see the state of *Persea* droope,
And languish in my brothers gouernment:
I willingly receiue th'mperiall crowne, 165
And vow to weare it for my countries good:
In spight of them shall malice my estate.
Ortyg. And in assurance of desir'd successe,
We here doo crowne thee Monarch of the East,
Emperour of *Asia*, and of *Persea*, 170
Great Lord of *Medea* and *Armenia*:
Duke of *Affrica* and *Albania*,
Mesopotamia and of *Parthia*,
East *India* and the late discouered Isles,
Chiefe Lord of all the wide vast *Euxine* sea, 175
And of the euer raging Caspian Lake:
Long liue *Cosroe* mighty Emperour.
Cos. And *Ioue* may neuer let me longer liue,
Then I may seeke to gratifie your loue,
And cause the souldiers that thus honour me, 180
To triumph ouer many Prouinces.
By whose desires of discipline in Armes,

143 + S. D. Ceneus] Conerus *1590–1605* 157 the] their *1592* 170 and of] and *1592* 176 euer] riuer *1605* 177 *Prefix* All *before this line 1605* 182 of] and *conj. Coll.*

I doubt not shortly but to raigne sole king,
And with the Armie of *Theridamas*,
Whether we presently will flie (my Lords) 185
To rest secure against my brothers force.
Ortyg. We knew my Lord, before we brought the crowne,
Intending your inuestion so neere
The residence of your dispised brother,
The Lords would not be too exasperate, 190
To iniure or suppresse your woorthy tytle.
Or if they would, there are in readines
Ten thousand horse to carie you from hence,
In spite of all suspected enemies.
Cosr. I know it wel my Lord, & thanke you all. 195
Ortyg. Sound vp the trumpets then, God saue the King.
Exeunt.

Actus I. Scæna 2.

Tamburlaine leading *Zenocrate* : *Techelles, Vsumcasane,* other Lords and Souldiers loden with treasure.

Tam. Come lady, let not this appal your thoughts
The iewels and the treasure we haue tane
Shall be reseru'd, and you in better state,
Than if you were arriu'd in *Siria*. 200
Euen in the circle of your Fathers armes :
The mightie Souldan of *Egyptia*.
Zeno. Ah Shepheard, pity my distressed plight,
(If as thou seem'st, thou art so meane a man)
And seeke not to inrich thy followers, 205
By lawlesse rapine from a silly maide,
Who traueiling with these Medean Lords
To *Memphis*, from my vncles country of *Medea*,
Where all my youth I haue bene gouerned,
Haue past the armie of the mightie Turke : 210
Bearing his priuie signet and his hand :
To safe conduct vs thorow *Affrica*.
Mag⟨netes⟩. And since we haue arriu'd in *Scythia*,
Besides rich presents from the puisant *Cham*,
We haue his highnesse letters to command 215
Aide and assistance if we stand in need.

190 Lord *1590, 1592* 191 iniurie *1592, 1605 etc.* 196 *Prefix* All *before* God *1605* S.D. other] & other *1605*. 207 Medean] my uncle's *Cunn.* Medean Lords] Lords of Medea *conj. Brennan* 208 my vncles] his *Cunn.* of Medea *omit conj. Brennan.*

Tam. But now you see these letters & commandes
Are countermanded by a greater man :
And through my prouinces you must expect
Letters of conduct from my mightinesse, 220
If you intend to keep your treasure safe.
But since I loue to liue at liberty,
As easely may you get the Souldans crowne,
As any prizes out of my precinct.
For they are friends that help to weane my state, 225
Till men and kingdomes help to strengthen it :
And must maintaine my life exempt from seruitude.
But tell me Maddam, is your grace betroth'd ?
Zen. I am (my Lord,) for so you do import.
Tam. I am a Lord, for so my deeds shall prooue, 230
And yet a shepheard by my Parentage :
But Lady, this faire face and heauenly hew
Must grace his bed that conquers *Asia* :
And meanes to be a terrour to the world,
Measuring the limits of his Emperie 235
By East and west, as *Phœbus* doth his course :
Lie here ye weedes that I disdaine to weare,
This compleat armor, and this curtle-axe
Are adiuncts more beseeming *Tamburlaine.*
And Maddam, whatsoeuer you esteeme 240
Of this successe, and losse vnvallued,
Both may inuest you Empresse of the East :
And these that seeme but silly country Swaines,
May haue the leading of so great an host,
As with their waight shall make the mountains quake, 245
Euen as when windy exhalations,
Fighting for passage, tilt within the earth.
Tec. As princely Lions when they rouse themselues,
Stretching their pawes, and threatning heardes of Beastes.
So in his Armour looketh *Tamburlaine* : 250
Me thinks I see kings kneeling at his feet,
And he with frowning browes and fiery lookes,
Spurning their crownes from off their captiue heads.
Vsum. And making thee and me *Techelles,* kinges,
That euen to death will follow *Tamburlaine.* 255
Tam. Nobly resolu'd, sweet friends and followers,
These Lords (perhaps) do scorne our estimates :
And thinke we prattle with distempered spirits
But since they measure our deserts so meane,
That in conceit bear Empires on our speares, 260

Affecting thoughts coequall with the cloudes,
They shall be kept our forced followers,
Till with their eies they view vs Emperours.
Zen. The Gods, defenders of the innocent,
Will neuer prosper your intended driftes, 265
That thus oppresse poore friendles passengers.
Therefore at least admit vs libertie,
Euen as thou hop'st to be eternized,
By liuing *Asias* mightie Emperour.
Agid⟨as⟩. I hope our Ladies treasure and our owne,
May serue for ransome to our liberties : 271
Returne our Mules and emptie Camels backe,
That we may traueile into *Siria*,
Where her betrothed Lord *Alcidamus*,
Expects th' arriuall of her highnesse person. 275
Mag. And wheresoeuer we repose our selues,
We will report but well of *Tamburlaine*.
Tamb. Disdaines *Zenocrate* to liue with me ?
Or you my Lordes to be my followers ?
Thinke you I way this treasure more than you ? 280
Not all the Gold in *Indias* welthy armes,
Shall buy the meanest souldier in my traine.
Zenocrate, louelier than the Loue of *Ioue*,
Brighter than is the siluer Rhodope,
Fairer than whitest snow on Scythian hils, 285
Thy person is more woorth to *Tamburlaine*,
Than the possession of the Persean Crowne,
Which gratious starres haue promist at my birth.
A hundreth Tartars shall attend on thee,
Mounted on Steeds, swifter than *Pegasus*. 290
Thy Garments shall be made of Medean silke,
Enchast with precious iuelles of mine owne :
More rich and valurous than *Zenocrates*.
With milke-white Hartes vpon an Iuorie sled,
Thou shalt be drawen amidst the frosen Pooles, 295
And scale the ysie mountaines lofty tops :
Which with thy beautie will be soone resolu'd.
My martiall prises with fiue hundred men,
Wun on the fiftie headed *Vuolgas* waues,
Shall all we offer to *Zenocrate*, 300
And then my selfe to faire *Zenocrate*.

275 th'] the *1592* 283 Ioue] loue *1592* 284 Rhodope *Dyce etc.*: Rhodolfe *1590–1605* 297 desolu'd *1605* 300 Shall all we *1590*: Shall we *1592*: We all shall *1605*: Shall we all *Dyce to Bull.*

Tech. What now? In loue?
Tam. *Techelles,* women must be flatered.
But this is she with whom I am in loue.

Enter a Souldier.

Sould. Newes, newes. 305
Tamb. How now, what's the matter?
Sould. A thousand Persean horsmen are at hand,
Sent from the King to ouercome vs all.
Tam. How now my Lords of *Egypt* & *Zenocrate*?
Now must your iewels be restor'd againe: 310
And I that triumpht so be ouercome.
How say you Lordings, Is not this your hope?
Agid. We hope your selfe wil willingly restore them.
Tamb. Such hope, such fortune haue the thousand horse.
Soft ye my Lords and sweet *Zenocrate.* 315
You must be forced from me ere you goe:
A thousand horsmen? We fiue hundred foote?
An ods too great, for vs to stand against:
But are they rich? And is their armour good?
Sould. Their plumed helmes are wrought with beaten golde. 320
Their swords enameld, and about their neckes
Hangs massie chaines of golde downe to the waste,
In euery part exceeding braue and rich.
Tam. Then shall we fight couragiously with them,
Or looke you, I should play the Orator? 325
Tech. No: cowards and fainthearted runawaies,
Looke for orations when the foe is neere.
Our swordes shall play the Orators for vs.
Vsum. Come let vs meet them at the mountain foot,
And with a sodaine and an hot alarme 330
Driue all their horses headlong down the hill.
Tech. Come let vs martch.
Tam. Stay *Techelles*, aske a parlee first,

The Souldiers enter.

Open the Males, yet guard the treasure sure,
Lay out our golden wedges to the view, 335
That their reflexions may amaze the Perseans.
And looke we friendly on them when they come:

311 tryumph *1605* 329 foot] top *1605, Dyce to Bull.*

But if they offer word or violence,
Weele fight fiue hundred men at armes to one,
Before we part with our possession. 340
And gainst the Generall we will lift our swords,
And either lanch his greedy thirsting throat,
Or take him prisoner, and his chaine shall serue
For Manackles, till he be ransom'd home.
Tech. I heare them come, shal we encounter them ?
Tam. Keep all your standings, and not stir a foote, 346
My selfe will bide the danger of the brunt.

Enter Theridamas with others.

Ther. Where is this Scythian *Tamberlaine* ?
Tam. Whom seekst thou Persean ? I am *Tamburlain.*
Ther. Tamburlaine ? A Scythian Shepheard, so imbellished 350
With Natures pride, and richest furniture,
His looks do menace heauen and dare the Gods,
His fierie eies are fixt vpon the earth,
As if he now deuis'd some Stratageme :
Or meant to pierce *Auernas* darksome vaults, 355
To pull the triple headed dog from hell.
Tamb. Noble and milde this Persean seemes to be,
If outward habit iudge the inward man.
Tech. His deep affections make him passionate.
Tamb. With what a maiesty he rears his looks : 360
In thee (thou valiant man of Persea)
I see the folly of thy Emperour :
Art thou but Captaine of a thousand horse,
That by Characters grauen in thy browes,
And by thy martiall face and stout aspect, 365
Deseru'st to haue the leading of an hoste ?
Forsake thy king and do but ioine with me
And we will triumph ouer all the world.
I hold the Fates bound fast in yron chaines,
And with my hand turne Fortunes wheel about, 370
And sooner shall the Sun fall from his Spheare,
Than *Tamburlaine* be slaine or ouercome.
Draw foorth thy sword, thou mighty man at Armes,
Intending but to rase my charmed skin :
And *Ioue* himselfe will stretch his hand from heauen, 375

348 this] the *1605* Scythian] Scythian Shepherd *conj. Dyce*
362 thy] the *1605*

To ward the blow, and shield me safe from harme.
See how he raines down heaps of gold in showers,
As if he meant to giue my Souldiers pay,
And as a sure and grounded argument,
That I shall be the Monark of the East, 380
He sends this Souldans daughter rich and braue,
To be my Queen and portly Emperesse.
If thou wilt stay with me, renowmed man,
And lead thy thousand horse with my conduct,
Besides thy share of this Egyptian prise, 385
Those thousand horse shall sweat with martiall spoile
Of conquered kingdomes, and of Cities sackt.
Both we wil walke vpon the lofty clifts,
And Christian Merchants that with Russian stems
Plow vp huge furrowes in the Caspian sea, 390
Shall vaile to vs, as Lords of all the Lake.
Both we will raigne as Consuls of the earth,
And mightie kings shall be our Senators.
Ioue sometime masked in a Shepheards weed,
And by those steps that he hath scal'd the heauens, 395
May we become immortall like the Gods.
Ioine with me now in this my meane estate,
(I cal it meane, because being yet obscure,
The Nations far remoou'd admyre me not)
And when my name and honor shall be spread, 400
As far as *Boreas* claps his brazen wings,
Or faire *Bootes* sends his cheerefull light,
Then shalt thou be Competitor with me,
And sit with *Tamburlaine* in all his maiestie.

Ther. Not *Hermes* Prolocutor to the Gods, 405
Could vse perswasions more patheticall.

Tam. Nor are *Apollos* Oracles more true,
Then thou shalt find my vaunts substantiall.

Tec. We are his friends, and if the Persean king
Should offer present Dukedomes to our state, 410
We thinke it losse to make exchange for that,
We are assured of by our friends successe.

Vsum. And kingdomes at the least we all expect,
Besides the honor in assured conquestes:
Where kings shall crouch vnto our conquering swords, 415
And hostes of souldiers stand amaz'd at vs,
When with their fearfull tongues they shall confesse
Theise are the men that all the world admires.

388 cliffes *1592* 402 Botëes *1590*, *1592*: Boetes *1605*

Ther. What stronge enchantments tice my yeelding soule?
Ah, these resolued noble Scythians! 420
But shall I prooue a Traitor to my King?
Tam. No, but the trustie friend of *Tamburlaine.*
Ther. Won with thy words, & conquered with thy looks,
I yeeld my selfe, my men & horse to thee:
To be partaker of thy good or ill, 425
As long as life maintaines *Theridamas.*
Tam. Theridamas my friend, take here my hand.
Which is as much as if I swore by heauen,
And call'd the Gods to witnesse of my vow,
Thus shall my heart be still combinde with thine, 430
Vntill our bodies turne to Elements:
And both our soules aspire celestiall thrones.
Techelles, and *Casane,* welcome him.
Tech. Welcome renowmed Persean to vs all.
⟨*Vsum*⟩*Cas.* Long may *Theridamas* remaine with vs. 435
Tam. These are my friends in whom I more reioice,
Than dooth the King of Persea in his Crowne:
And by the loue of *Pyllades* and *Orestes,*
Whose statues we adore in Scythia,
Thy selfe and them shall neuer part from me, 440
Before I crowne you kings in *Asia.*
Make much of them gentle *Theridamas,*
And they will neuer leaue thee till the death.
Ther. Nor thee, nor them, thrice noble *Tamburlain*
Shal want my heart to be with gladnes pierc'd 445
To do you honor and securitie.
Tam. A thousand thankes worthy *Theridamas*:
And now faire Madam, and my noble Lords,
If you will willingly remaine with me,
You shall haue honors, as your merits be: 450
Or els you shall be forc'd with slauerie.
Agid. We yeeld vnto thee happie *Tamburlaine.*
Tamb. For you then Maddam, I am out of doubt.
Zeno. I must be pleasde perforce, wretched Zenocrate.
Exeunt.

419 tice] to *conj. Cook* 420 Ah *Brereton*: Are *1590–1605, Dyce*[1]: To *Rob, Dyce*[2], *Cunn.*: *Qy.*, As ? these] there *conj. Cook* 439 statues *1605*: statutes *1590, 1592* 441 King *1605* 444 Nor . . them] Nor they nor theirs *Rob.* 449 will *om. 1605*

Actus 2. *Scæna* 1.

Cosroe, Menaphon, Ortygius, Ceneus, with other Souldiers.

Cosroe. Thus farre are we towards *Theridamas,* 455
And valiant *Tamburlaine,* the man of fame,
The man that in the forhead of his fortune,
Beares figures of renowne and myracle:
But tell me, that hast seene him, *Menaphon,*
What stature wields he, and what personage? 460
Mena. Of stature tall, and straightly fashioned,
Like his desire, lift vpwards and diuine,
So large of lims, his ioints so strongly knit,
Such breadth of shoulders as might mainely beare
Olde *Atlas* burthen, twixt his manly pitch, 465
A pearle more worth, then all the world is plaste:
Wherein by curious soueraintie of Art,
Are fixt his piercing instruments of sight:
Whose fiery cyrcles beare encompassed
A heauen of heauenly bodies in their Spheares: 470
That guides his steps and actions to the throne,
Where honor sits inuested royally:
Pale of complexion: wrought in him with passion,
Thirsting with souerainty with loue of armes.
His lofty browes in foldes, do figure death, 475
And in their smoothnesse, amitie and life:
About them hangs a knot of Amber heire,
Wrapped in curles, as fierce *Achilles* was,
On which the breath of heauen delights to play,
Making it daunce with wanton maiestie: 480
His armes and fingers long and s⟨i⟩nowy,
Betokening valour and excesse of strength:
In euery part proportioned like the man,
Should make the world subdued to *Tamburlaine.*
Cos. Wel hast thou pourtraid in thy tearms of life, 485
The face and personage of a woondrous man:
Nature doth striue with Fortune and his stars
To make him famous in accomplisht woorth:
And well his merits show him to be made
His Fortunes maister, and the king of men, 490
That could perswade at such a sodaine pinch,

474 with loue *1590, 1592*: and loue *1605 etc.* 481 His armes long, his fingers snowy-white, *1605* sinewy *Dyce etc.*: snowy *1590, 1592*

With reasons of his valour and his life,
A thousand sworne and ouermatching foes:
Then when our powers in points of swords are ioin'd
And closde in compasse of the killing bullet, 495
Though straight the passage and the port be made,
That leads to Pallace of my brothers life,
Proud is his fortune if we pierce it not.
And when the princely Persean Diadem,
Shall ouerway his wearie witlesse head, 500
And fall like mellowed fruit, with shakes of death,
In faire *Persea* noble *Tamburlaine*
Shall be my Regent, and remaine as King.
Ort. In happy hower we haue set the Crowne
Vpon your kingly head, that seeks our honor, 505
In ioyning with the man, ordain'd by heauen
To further euery action to the best.
Cen. He that with Shepheards and a litle spoile,
Durst in disdaine of wrong and tyrannie,
Defend his freedome gainst a Monarchie: 510
What will he doe supported by a king?
Leading a troope of Gentlemen and Lords,
And stuft with tr⟨e⟩asure for his highest thoughts?
Cos. And such shall wait on worthy *Tamburlaine.*
Our army will be forty thousand strong, 515
When *Tamburlain* and braue *Theridamas*
Haue met vs by the riuer *Araris*:
And all conioin'd to meet the witlesse King,
That now is marching neer to Parthia,
And with vnwilling souldiers faintly arm'd, 520
To seeke reuenge on me and *Tamburlaine.*
To whom sweet *Menaphon*, direct me straight.
Mena. I will my Lord. *Exeunt.*

Act. 2. Scæna 2.

Mycetes, Meander, with other Lords and Souldiers.

Mycetes. Come my *Meander*, let vs to this geere,
I tel you true my heart is swolne with wrath, 525
On this same theeuish villaine *Tamburlaine.*
And of that false *Cosroe*, my traiterous brother.
Would it not grieue a King to be so abusde,
And haue a thousand horsmen tane away?

498 is] in *1605*

And which is worst to haue his Diadem 530
Sought for by such scalde knaues as loue him not ?
I thinke it would : wel then, by heauens I sweare,
Aurora shall not peepe out of her doores,
But I will haue *Cosroe* by the head,
And kill proud *Tamburlaine* with point of sword. 535
Tell you the rest (*Meander*) I haue said.
Mean. Then hauing past Armenian desarts now,
And pitcht our tents vnder the Georgean hilles,
Whose tops are couered with Tartarian thieues,
That lie in ambush, waiting for a pray : 540
What should we doe but bid them battaile straight,
And rid the world of those detested troopes ?
Least if we let them lynger here a while,
They gather strength by power of fresh supplies.
This countrie swarmes with vile outragious men, 545
That liue by rapine and by lawlesse spoile,
Fit Souldiers for the wicked *Tamburlaine.*
And he that could with giftes and promises
Inueigle him that lead a thousand horse,
And make him false his faith vnto his King, 550
Will quickly win such as are like himselfe.
Therefore cheere vp your mindes, prepare to fight.
He that can take or slaughter *Tamburlaine,*
Shall rule the Prouince of *Albania.*
Who brings that Traitors head *Theridamas,* 555
Shal haue a gouernment in *Medea,*
Beside the spoile of him and all his traine :
But if *Cosroe* (as our Spials say,
And as we know) remaines with *Tamburlaine,*
His Highnesse pleasure is that he should liue, 560
And be reclaim'd with princely lenitie.
A Spy. An hundred horsmen of my company
Scowting abroad vpon these champion plaines,
Haue view'd the army of the Scythians,
Which make reports it far exceeds the Kings. 565
Mean. Suppose they be in number infinit,
Yet being void of Martiall discipline,
All running headlong after greedy spoiles :

530 worse *1592, Dyce to Bull.* 538 pitcht *1592, 1605*: pitch *1590* 547 the] that *1605* 550 the King *1605* 551 are] be *1592, Dyce to Bull.* 557 Besides *1605* 561 S.D. Enter a Spy *add. Dyce* 565 makes *1605* report *1592, 1605 etc. exc. Wag.* 568 after greedy] greedy after *conj. Dyce* [1], *Dyce* [2]

And more regarding gaine than victory:
Like to the cruell brothers of the earth, 570
Sprong of the teeth of Dragons venomous,
Their carelesse swords shal lanch their fellowes throats
And make vs triumph in their ouerthrow.
Myc. Was there such brethren, sweet *Meander*, say
That sprong of teeth of Dragons venomous? 575
Meand. So Poets say, my Lord.
Myce. And tis a prety toy to be a Poet.
Wel, wel (*Meander*) thou art deeply read:
And hauing thee, I haue a iewell sure:
Go on my Lord, and giue your charge I say, 580
Thy wit will make vs Conquerors to day.
Mean. Then noble souldiors, to intrap these theeues,
That liue confounded in disordered troopes,
If wealth or riches may preuaile with them,
We haue our Cammels laden all with gold: 585
Which you that be but common souldiers,
Shall fling in euery corner of the field:
And while the base borne Tartars take it vp,
You fighting more for honor than for gold,
Shall massacre those greedy minded slaues. 590
And when their scattered armie is subdu'd:
And you march on their slaughtered carkasses,
Share equally the gold that bought their liues,
And liue like Gentlemen in *Persea*,
Strike vp the Drum and martch corragiously, 595
Fortune her selfe dooth sit vpon our Crests.
Myc. He tels you true, my maisters, so he does.
Drums, why sound ye not when *Meand⟨er⟩* speaks.
Exeunt.

Actus 2. Scæna 3.

Cosroe, Tamburlaine, Theridamas, Techelles, Vsumcasane, Ortygius, with others.

Cosroe. Now worthy Tamburlaine, haue I reposde,
In thy approoued Fortunes all my hope, 600
What thinkst thou man, shal come of our attemptes?
For euen as from assured oracle,
I take thy doome for satisfaction.
Tamb. And so mistake you not a whit my Lord.

571 teeth of *om. 1605* 595 the *om. 1605*

For Fates and Oracles ⟨of⟩ heauen haue sworne, 605
To roialise the deedes of *Tamburlaine*:
And make them blest that share in his attemptes.
And doubt you not, but if you fauour me,
And let my Fortunes and my valour sway
To some direction in your martiall deeds, 610
The world will striue with hostes of men at armes
To swarme vnto the Ensigne I support.
The host of *Xerxes*, which by fame is said
To drinke the mightie Parthian *Araris*,
Was but a handful to that we will haue. 615
Our quiuering Lances shaking in the aire,
And bullets like *Ioues* dreadfull Thunderbolts,
Enrolde in flames and fiery smoldering mistes,
Shall threat the Gods more than Cyclopian warres,
And with our Sun-bright armour as we march, 620
Weel chase the Stars from heauen, and dim their eies
That stand and muse at our admyred armes.
Therid. You see my Lord, what woorking woordes he hath.
But when you see his actions top his speech,
Your speech will stay, or so extol his worth, 625
As I shall be commended and excusde
For turning my poore charge to his direction.
And these his two renowmed friends my Lord,
Would make one thrust and striue to be retain'd
In such a great degree of amitie. 630
Tech. With dutie and with amitie we yeeld
Our vtmost seruice to the faire *Cosroe*.
Cos. Which I esteeme as portion of my crown.
Vsumcasane and *Techelles* both,
When she that rules in *Rhamnis* golden gates, 635
And makes a passage for all prosperous Armes:
Shall make me solely Emperour of *Asia*,
Then shall your meeds and vallours be aduaunst
To roomes of honour and Nobilitie.
Tam. Then haste *Cosroe* to be king alone, 640
That I with these my friends and all my men,
May triumph in our long expected Fate.
The King your Brother is now hard at hand,

605 of *add. Rob. etc.* 610 To some *1590*, *1605 etc.*: To scorne *1592*: Nor scorn *conj. Broughton* 611 will] shall *1605* 614 T' have drank *Rob.*: To have drank *Cunn.*, *Bull.* 624 top *Dyce*, *Wag.*: stop *1590–1605*, *Cunn.*, *Bull.* 629 thrust *1590*, *1592*: thrist *1605*: thirst *Dyce to Bull.* 631 and *1605*, *Dyce etc.*: not *1590*, *1592* 632 the] thee *1605* 638 meeds] deeds *1605*

Meete with the foole, and rid your royall shoulders
Of such a burthen, as outwaies the sands 645
And all the craggie rockes of Caspea.

⟨*Enter a Messenger.*⟩

Mess. My Lord, we haue discouered the enemie
Ready to chardge you with a mighty armie.
Cos. Come, *Tamburlain,* now whet thy winged sword
And lift thy lofty arme into the cloudes, 650
That it may reach the King of Perseas crowne,
And set it safe on my victorious head.
Tam. See where it is, the keenest Cutle-axe,
That ere made passage thorow Persean Armes.
These are the wings shall make it flie as swift, 655
As dooth the lightening: or the breath of heauen,
And kill as sure as it swiftly flies.
Cos. Thy words assure me of kind successe:
Go valiant Souldier, go before and charge
The fainting army of that foolish King. 660
Tamb. Vsumcasane and *Techelles* come,
We are enough to scarre the enemy,
And more than needes to make an Emperour. ⟨*Exeunt.*⟩

⟨*Scene IV.*⟩

To the Battaile, and Mycetes comes out alone with his Crowne in his hand, offering to hide it.

Myc. Accurst be he that first inuented war,
They knew not, ah, they knew not simple men, 665
How those were hit by pelting Cannon shot,
Stand staggering like a quiuering Aspen leafe,
Fearing the force of *Boreas* boistrous blasts.
In what a lamentable case were I,
If Nature had not giuen me wisedomes lore? 670
For Kings are clouts that euery man shoots at,
Our Crowne the pin that thousands seeke to cleaue.
Therefore in pollicie I thinke it good
To hide it close: a goodly Stratagem,
And far from any man that is a foole. 675

646 S.D. *add. Dyce* 656 or the breath] o'er the breadth *conj. Coll.* 662 enough *1590, 1605*: enow *1592* 663 S.D. *add. Rob.* Scene IV. *add. Dyce* 667 Stand] Stand those *1605*

So shall not I be knowen, or if I bee,
They cannot take away my crowne from me.
Here will I hide it in this simple hole.

Enter Tamburlain.

Tam. What fearful coward stragling from the camp
When Kings themselues are present in the field? 680
Myc. Thou liest.
Tam. Base villaine, darst thou giue the lie?
Myc. Away, I am the King: go, touch me not.
Thou breakst the law of Armes vnlesse thou kneele,
And cry me mercie, noble King. 685
Tam. Are you the witty King of *Persea*?
Myce. I marie am I: haue you any suite to me?
Tam. I would intreat you to speak but three wise wordes.
Myce. So I can when I see my time.
Tam. Is this your Crowne? 690
Myce. I, Didst thou euer see a fairer?
Tamb. You will not sell it, wil ye?
Myce. Such another word, and I will haue thee executed.
Come giue it me.
Tamb. No, I tooke it prisoner. 695
Myce. You lie, I gaue it you.
Tam. Then tis mine.
Myce. No, I meane, I let you keep it.
Tamb. Wel, I meane you shall haue it againe.
Here take it for a while, I lend it thee, 700
Till I may see thee hem'd with armed men.
Then shalt thou see me pull it from thy head:
Thou art no match for mightie *Tamburlaine.* ⟨*Exit.*⟩
Myce. O Gods, is this *Tamburlaine* the thiefe,
I marueile much he stole it not away. 705

Sound trumpets to the battell, and he runs in.

⟨*Scene V.*⟩

Cosroe, Tamburlaine, Theridamas, Menaphon, Meander, Ortygius, Techelles, Vsumcasane, with others.

Tamb. Holde thee *Cosroe*, weare two imperiall Crownes.
Thinke thee inuested now as royally,
Euen by the mighty hand of *Tamburlaine*,

682 giue *1590, 1592, Rob., Dyce*[1], *Bull, Wag.*: giue me *1605, Dyce*[2], *Cunn.* 703 S.D. *add. Dyce* Scene V. *add. Dyce*

As if as many kinges as could encompasse thee,
With greatest pompe had crown'd thee Emperour. 710
Cosr. So do I thrice renowmed man at armes,
And none shall keepe the crowne but *Tamburlaine*:
Thee doo I make my Regent of Persea,
And Generall Lieftenant of my Armies.
Meander, you that were our brothers Guide, 715
And chiefest Counsailor in all his acts,
Since he is yeelded to the stroke of War,
On your submission we with thanks excuse,
And giue you equall place in our affaires.
Mean. Most happy Emperour in humblest tearms 720
I vow my seruice to your Maiestie,
With vtmost vertue of my faith and dutie.
Cosr. Thanks good *Meander*, then *Cosroe* raign
And gouerne Persea in her former pomp:
Now send Ambassage to thy neighbor Kings, 725
And let them know the Persean King is chang'd:
From one that knew not what a King should do,
To one that can commaund what longs thereto:
And now we will to faire *Persepolis*,
With twenty thousand expert souldiers. 730
The Lords and Captaines of my brothers campe,
With litle slaughter take *Meanders* course,
And gladly yeeld them to my gracious rule:
Ortigius and *Menaphon*, my trustie friendes,
Now will I gratify your former good, 735
And grace your calling with a greater sway.
Ort. And as we euer aimd at your behoofe,
And sought your state all honor it deseru'd,
So will we with our powers and our liues,
Indeuor to preserue and prosper it. 740
Cos. I will not thank thee (sweet *Ortigius*)
Better replies shall prooue my purposes.
And now Lord *Tamburlaine*, my brothers Campe
I leaue to thee, and to *Theridamas*,
To follow me to faire *Persepolis*. 745
Then will we march to all those Indian Mines,
My witlesse brother to the Christians lost:
And ransome them with fame and vsurie.
And till thou ouertake me *Tamburlaine*,

716 chiefest] chiefe *1592* 720 happy] happiest *1605* 737 aimd *1605 etc.*: and *1590, 1592* 738 it] is *1592* 739 our liues] liues *1592* 746 we] I *1605*

(Staying to order all the scattered troopes) 750
Farewell Lord Regent, and his happie friends,
I long to sit vpon my brothers throne.
Mena. Your Maiestie shall shortly haue your wish,
And ride in triumph through *Persepolis.* *Exeunt.*

Manent Tamb. Tech. Ther. Vsum.

Tamb. And ride in triumph through *Persepolis?* 755
Is it not braue to be a King, *Techelles?*
Vsumcasane and *Theridamas,*
Is it not passing braue to be a King,
And ride in triumph through *Persepolis?*
Tech. O my Lord, tis sweet and full of pompe. 760
Vsum. To be a King, is halfe to be a God.
Ther. A God is not so glorious as a King:
I thinke the pleasure they enioy in heauen
Can not compare with kingly ioyes in earth.
To weare a Crowne enchac'd with pearle and golde, 765
Whose vertues carie with it life and death,
To aske, and haue: commaund, and be obeied:
When looks breed loue, with lookes to gaine the prize.
Such power attractiue shines in princes eies.
Tam. Why say *Theridamas,* wilt thou be a king? 770
Ther. Nay, though I praise it, I can liue without it.
Tam. What saies my other friends, wil you be kings?
Tec. I, if I could with all my heart my Lord.
Tam. Why, that's wel said *Techelles,* so would I,
And so would you my maisters, would you not? 775
Vsum. What then my Lord?
Tam. Why then *Casane* shall we wish for ought
The world affoords in greatest nouueltie,
And rest attemplesse faint and destitute?
Me thinks we should not, I am strongly moou'd, 780
That if I should desire the Persean Crowne,
I could attaine it with a woondrous ease,
And would not all our souldiers soone consent,
If we should aime at such a dignitie?
Ther. I know they would with our perswasions. 785
Tam. Why then *Theridamas,* Ile first assay,
To get the Persean Kingdome to my selfe:
Then thou for *Parthia,* they for *Scythia* and *Medea.*
And if I prosper, all shall be as sure,

753 *Prefix* Mean. *1592, Dyce to Bull.*

As if the Turke, the Pope, *Affrike* and *Greece*, 790
Came creeping to vs with their crownes apeece.
Tech. Then shall we send to this triumphing King,
And bid him battell for his nouell Crowne ?
Vsum. Nay quickly then, before his roome be hot.
Tam. Twil prooue a pretie iest (in faith) my friends.
The. A iest to chardge on twenty thousand men ? 796
I iudge the purchase more important far.
Tam. Iudge by thy selfe *Theridamas*, not me,
For presently *Techelles* here shal haste,
To bid him battaile ere he passe too farre, 800
And lose more labor than the gaine will quight.
Then shalt thou see the Scythian *Tamburlaine*,
Make but a iest to win the Persean crowne.
Techelles, take a thousand horse with thee,
And bid him turne his back to war with vs, 805
That onely made him King to make vs sport.
We will not steale vpon him cowardly,
But giue him warning and more warriours.
Haste the *Techelles*, we will follow thee.
What saith *Theridamas* ? 810
Ther. Goe on for me.

Exeunt.

Actus 2. *Scæna* 6.

Cosroe, Meander, Ortygius, Menaphon, with other Souldiers.

Cos. What means this diuelish shepheard to aspire
With such a Giantly presumption,
To cast vp hils against the face of heauen :
And dare the force of angrie *Iupiter*. 815
But as he thrust them vnderneath the hils,
And prest out fire from their burning iawes :
So will I send this monstrous slaue to hell,
Where flames shall euer feed vpon his soule.
Mean. Some powers diuine, or els infernall, mixt 820
Their angry seeds at his conception :
For he was neuer sprong of humaine race,
Since with the spirit of his fearefull pride,

791 apeece *1605, Dyce to Bull.*: apace *1590, 1592* 802 the] this *1592, Dyce to Wag.* 805 his] him *Rob. etc.* 808 and] with *1605* 809 + S.D. Exit Techelles *add. Dyce, Wag.*

He dares so doubtlesly resolue of rule,
And by profession be ambitious. 825
Ort. What God or Feend, or spirit of the earth,
Or Monster turned to a manly shape,
Or of what mould or mettel he be made,
What star or state soeuer gouerne him,
Let vs put on our meet incountring mindes, 830
And in detesting such a diuelish Thiefe,
In loue of honor & defence of right,
Be arm'd against the hate of such a foe,
Whether from earth, or hell, or heauen he grow.
Cos. Nobly resolu'd, my good *Ortygius.* 835
And since we all haue suckt one wholsome aire
And with the same proportion of Elements,
Resolue, I hope we are resembled,
Vowing our loues to equall death and life,
Let's cheere our souldiers to incounter him, 840
That grieuous image of ingratitude :
That fiery thirster after Soueraingtie :
And burne him in the fury of that flame,
That none can quence but blood and Emperie.
Resolue my Lords and louing souldiers now, 845
To saue your King and country from decay :
Then strike vp Drum, and all the Starres that make
The loathsome Circle of my dated life,
Direct my weapon to his barbarous heart,
That thus opposeth him against the Gods, 850
And scornes the Powers that gouerne *Persea.*
⟨*Exeunt.*⟩

Enter to the Battell, & after the battell, enter Cosroe wounded, Theridamas, Tamburlaine, Techelles, Vsumcasane, with others.

Cos. Barbarous and bloody *Tamburlaine,*
Thus to depriue me of my crowne and life.
Treacherous and false *Theridamas,*
Euen at the morning of my happy state, 855
Scarce being seated in my royall throne,
To worke my downfall and vntimely end.
An vncouth paine torments my grieued soule,
And death arrests the organe of my voice.

824 dare *1605* 829 state] fate *Dyce* 848 my] his *conj. Coll.* 851 *After this line* Scene VII. *add. Dyce* 852 Barbarous O barbarous *conj. Dyce*

Who entring at the breach thy sword hath made, 860
Sackes euery vaine and artier of my heart,
Bloody and insatiate *Tamburlain.*

Tam. The thirst of raigne and sweetnes of a crown,
That causde the eldest sonne of heauenly *Ops*,
To thrust his doting father from his chaire, 865
And place himselfe in the Emperiall heauen,
Moou'd me to manage armes against thy state.
What better president than mightie *Ioue*?
Nature that fram'd vs of foure Elements,
Warring within our breasts for regiment, 870
Doth teach vs all to haue aspyring minds:
Our soules, whose faculties can comprehend
The wondrous Architecture of the world:
And measure euery wandring plannets course,
Still climing after knowledge infinite, 875
And alwaies moouing as the restles Spheares,
Wils vs to weare our selues and neuer rest,
Vntill we reach the ripest fruit of all,
That perfect blisse and sole felicitie,
The sweet fruition of an earthly crowne. 880

Ther. And that made me to ioine with *Tamburlain*,
For he is grosse and like the massie earth,
That mooues not vpwards, nor by princely deeds
Doth meane to soare aboue the highest sort.

Tec. And that made vs the friends of *Tamburlaine*, 885
To lift our swords against the Persean King.

Vsum. For as when *Ioue* did thrust old *Saturn* down,
Neptune and *Dis* gain'd each of them a Crowne:
So do we hope to raign in *Asia*,
If *Tamburlain* be plac'd in Persea. 890

Cos. The strangest men that euer nature made,
I know not how to take their tyrannies.
My bloodlesse body waxeth chill and colde,
And with my blood my life slides through my wound.
My soule begins to take her flight to hell, 895
And sommons all my sences to depart:
The heat and moisture which did feed each other,
For want of nourishment to feed them both,
Is drie and cold, and now dooth gastly death
With greedy tallents gripe my bleeding hart, 900
And like a Harpye tires on my life.

861 Sackes] Sucks *conj. Coll.* 877 weare] weary *conj. Coll.* 878 fruites *1592* 901 Harpye *1592*: Harpyr *1590*: Harper *1605*

Theridamas and *Tamburlaine*, I die,
And fearefull vengeance light vpon you both.

Tamburlaine takes the Crowne and puts it on.

Tam. Not all the curses which the furies breathe,
Shall make me leaue so rich a prize as this: 905
Theridamas, *Techelles*, and the rest,
Who thinke you now is king of *Persea*?
All. *Tamburlaine*, *Tamburlaine.*
Tamb. Though *Mars* himselfe the angrie God of armes,
And all the earthly Potentates conspire, 910
To dispossesse me of this Diadem:
Yet will I weare it in despight of them,
As great commander of this Easterne world,
If you but say that *Tamburlaine* shall raigne.
Al. Long liue *Tamburlaine*, and raigne in *Asia*. 915
Tamb. So, now it is more surer on my head,
Than if the Gods had held a Parliament:
And all pronounst me king of Persea. ⟨*Exeunt.*⟩

Finis Actus 2.

Actus 3. Scæna 1.

Baiazeth, the kings of Fess, Moroco, and Argier, with others, in great pompe.

Baiazeth. Great Kings of *Barbary*, and my portly Bassoes,
We heare, the Tartars & the Easterne theeues 920
Vnder the conduct of one *Tamburlaine*,
Presume a bickering with your Emperour:
And thinks to rouse vs from our dreadful siege
Of the famous Grecian *Constantinople*.
You know our Armie is inuincible: 925
As many circumcised Turkes we haue,
And warlike bands of Christians renied,
As hath the Ocean or the Terrene sea
Small drops of water, when the Moon begins
To ioine in one her semi-circled hornes: 930
Yet would we not be brau'd with forrain power,
Nor raise our siege before the Gretians yeeld,
Or breathles lie before the citie walles.

903 + S.D. Tamburlaine *Dyce etc.*: He *1590–1605* 904 thy furies *1592* 918 + S.D. Exeunt *add. Rob. etc.* 927 Christians renegadens *or* Christian renegades *conj. Mitford*

Fess. Renowmed Emperour, and mighty Generall,
What if you sent the Bassoes of your guard, 935
To charge him to remaine in *Asia*,
Or els to threaten death and deadly armes,
As from the mouth of mighty *Baiazeth*.
Bai. Hie thee my Bassoe fast to *Persea*,
Tell him thy Lord the Turkish Emperour, 940
Dread Lord of *Affrike*, *Europe* and *Asia*,
Great King and conquerour of Grecia,
The Ocean, Terrene, and the cole-blacke sea,
The high and highest Monarke of the world,
Wils and commands (for say not I intreat) 945
Not once to set his foot in *Affrica*,
Or spread his collours in Grecia,
Least he incurre the furie of my wrath.
Tell him, I am content to take a truce,
Because I heare he beares a valiant mind. 950
But if presuming on his silly power,
He be so mad to manage Armes with me,
Then stay thou with him, say I bid thee so.
And if before the Sun haue measured heauen
With triple circuit thou regreet vs not, 955
We meane to take his mornings next arise
For messenger, he will not be reclaim'd,
And meane to fetch thee in despight of him.
Bass. Most great and puisant Monarke of the earth,
Your Bassoe will accomplish your behest : 960
And show your pleasure to the Persean,
As fits the Legate of the stately Turk. *Exit Bass.*
Arg. They say he is the King of *Persea*.
But if he dare attempt to stir your siege,
Twere requisite he should be ten times more, 965
For all flesh quakes at your magnificence.
Bai. True (*Argier*) and tremble at my lookes.
Moro. The spring is hindred by your smoothering host,
For neither rain can fall vpon the earth,
Nor Sun reflexe his vertuous beames thereon. 970
The ground is mantled with such multitudes.
Bai. All this is true as holy *Mahomet*,
And all the trees are blasted with our breathes.

939 Bassoe] Brother *1605* 944 higest *1590* 946 Not] Nor *1605* in] on *1605* 947 collours] colours forth *Cunn.* in] into *conj. Elze* : ouer *conj. Wag.* 954 heauen] the heauen *1605* 967 trembles *Dyce to Bull.*

Fess. What thinks your greatnes best to be atchieu'd
In pursuit of the Cities ouerthrow? 975
Bai. I wil the captiue Pioners of *Argier*,
Cut of the water, that by leaden pipes
Runs to the citie from the mountain *Carnon*,
Two thousand horse shall forrage vp and downe,
That no reliefe or succour come by Land. 980
And all the sea my Gallies countermaund.
Then shall our footmen lie within the trench,
And with their Cannons mouth'd like *Orcus* gulfe
Batter the walles, and we will enter in:
And thus the Grecians shall be conquered. 985
Exeunt.

Actus 3. *Scæna* 2.

Agidas, Zenocrate, Anippe, with others.

⟨*Agydas.*⟩ Madam *Zenocrate*, may I presume
To know the cause of these vnquiet fits:
That worke such trouble to your woonted rest?
Tis more then pitty such a heauenly face
Should by hearts sorrow wax so wan and pale, 990
When your offensiue rape by *Tamburlaine*,
(Which of your whole displeasures should be most)
Hath seem'd to be digested long agoe.
Zen. Although it be digested long agoe,
As his exceding fauours haue deseru'd, 995
And might content the Queene of heauen as well
As it hath chang'd my first conceiu'd disdaine.
Yet since a farther passion feeds my thoughts,
With ceaselesse and disconsolate conceits,
Which dies my lookes so liuelesse as they are, 1000
And might, if my extreams had full euents,
Make me the gastly counterfeit of death.
Agid. Eternall heauen sooner be dissolu'd,
And all that pierceth *Phœbes* siluer eie,
Before such hap fall to *Zenocrate*. 1005
Zen. Ah, life and soule, still houer in his Breast,
And leaue my body sencelesse as the earth.
Or els vnite you to his life and soule,
That I may liue and die with *Tamburlaine*.

999 ceaselesse] carelesse *1605* 1004 Phœbes] Phoebus *1605*, *Dyce to Bull.* 1006 his] the *1605* 1008 you] me *1605*

Enter Tamburlaine with Techelles and others.

Agid. With *Tamburlaine*? Ah faire *Zenocrate.* 1010
Let not a man so vile and barbarous,
That holds you from your father in despight,
And keeps you from the honors of a Queene,
Being supposde his worthlesse Concubine,
Be honored with your loue, but for necessity. 1015
So now the mighty Souldan heares of you,
Your Highnesse needs not doubt but in short time,
He will with *Tamburlaines* destruction
Redeeme you from this deadly seruitude.
Zen. ⟨Agydas,⟩ leaue to wound me with these words,
And speake of *Tamburlaine* as he deserues: 1021
The entertainment we haue had of him,
Is far from villanie or seruitude,
And might in noble minds be counted princely.
Agid. How can you fancie one that lookes so fierce,
Onelie disposed to martiall Stratagems? 1026
Who when he shall embrace you in his armes,
Will tell how many thousand men he slew,
And when you looke for amorous discourse,
Will rattle foorth his facts of war and blood, 1030
Too harsh a subiect for your dainty eares.
Zen. As looks the sun through *Nilus* flowing stream,
Or when the morning holds him in her armes,
So lookes my Lordly loue, faire *Tamburlaine*:
His talke much sweeter than the Muses song, 1035
They sung for honor gainst *Pierides.*
Or when *Minerua* did with *Neptune* striue,
And higher would I reare my estimate,
Than *Iuno* sister to the highest God,
If I were matcht with mightie *Tamburlaine.* 1040
Agid. Yet be not so inconstant in your loue,
But let the yong Arabian liue in hope,
After your rescue to e⟨n⟩ioy his choise.
You see though first the King of *Persea*
(Being a Shepheard) seem'd to loue you much, 1045
Now in his maiesty he leaues those lookes,
Those words of fauour, and those comfortings,
And giues no more than common courtesies.

1020 Agydas, leave *conj. Dyce, Bull.*: Leaue *1590–1605*: Leave, Agydas *Cunn.* 1035 much] more 1605

Zen. Thence rise the tears that so distain my cheeks,
Fearing his loue through my vnworthynesse. 1050

Tamburlaine goes to her, & takes her away louingly by the hand, looking wrathfully on Agidas, and sayes nothing.
⟨*Exeunt all except Agydas.*⟩

Agid. Betraide by fortune and suspitious loue,
Threatned with frowning wrath and iealousie,
Surpriz'd with feare of hideous reuenge,
I stand agast: but most astonied
To see his choller shut in secrete thoughtes, 1055
And wrapt in silence of his angry soule
Vpon his browes was pourtraid vgly death,
And in his eies the furie of his hart,
That shine as Comets, menacing reuenge,
And casts a pale complexion on his cheeks. 1060
As when the Sea-man sees the *Hyades*
Gather an armye of Cemerian clouds,
(*Auster* and *Aquilon* with winged Steads
All sweating, tilt about the watery heauens,
With shiuering speares enforcing thunderclaps, 1065
And from their shieldes strike flames of lightening)
All fearefull foldes his sailes, and sounds the maine,
Lifting his prayers to the heauens for aid,
Against the terrour of the winds and waues.
So fares *Agydas* for the late felt frownes 1070
That sent a tempest to my daunted thoughtes,
And makes my soule deuine her ouerthrow.

Enter Techelles with a naked dagger ⟨*and Vsumcasane*⟩.

Tech. See you *Agidas* how the King salutes you.
He bids you prophesie what it imports. *Exit.*
Agid. I prophecied before and now I prooue, 1075
The killing frownes of iealousie and loue.
He needed not with words confirme my feare,
For words are vaine where working tooles present
The naked action of my threatned end.
It saies, *Agydas*, thou shalt surely die, 1080
And of extremities elect the least.

1050 + S.D. Exeunt .. Agydas *add. Dyce* 1053 of] and *1592* 1058 furies *1592* 1059 shine] shone *conj. Dyce*[1], *Dyce*[2] 1071 sent] send *Dyce*[2] 1072 S.D. and Vsumcasane *add. Dyce* 1074 + S.D. *om. 1605, Dyce etc.*

More honor and lesse paine it may procure,
To dy by this resolued hand of thine,
Than stay the torments he and heauen haue sworne.
Then haste *Agydas*, and preuent the plagues: 1085
Which thy prolonged Fates may draw on thee:
Go wander free from feare of Tyrants rage,
Remooued from the Torments and the hell:
Wherewith he may excruciate thy soule.
And let *Agidas* by *Agidas* die. 1090
And with this stab slumber eternally.

⟨*Stabs himselfe.*⟩

Tech. *Vsumcasane*, see how right the man
Hath hit the meaning of my Lord the King.
Vsum. Faith, and *Techelles*, it was manly done.
And since he was so wise and honorable, 1095
Let vs affoord him now the bearing hence,
And craue his triple worthy buriall.
Tech. Agreed *Casane*, we wil honor him.

⟨*Exeunt, bearing out the body.*⟩

Act. 3. *Scæna* 3.

Tamburlain, Techelles, Vsumcasane, Theridamas, Bassoe, Zenocrate, with others.

Tamburlaine. Bassoe, by this thy Lord and maister knowes,
I meane to meet him in *Bithynia*: 1100
See how he comes! Tush. Turkes are ful of brags
And menace more than they can wel performe:
He meet me in the field and fetch thee hence?
Alas (poore Turke) his fortune is to weake,
T'incounter with the strength of *Tamburlaine*. 1105
View well my Camp, and speake indifferently,
Doo not my captaines and my souldiers looke
As if they meant to conquer *Affrica*.
Bass. Your men are valiant but their number few,
And cannot terrefie his mightie hoste. 1110
My Lord, the great Commander of the worlde,
Besides fifteene contributorie kings,
Hath now in armes ten thousand Ianisaries,
Mounted on lusty Mauritanian Steeds.
Brought to the war by men of *Tripoly*. 1115

1091 S.D. *add. 1605* 1098 + S.D. *add. Dyce* 1102 menace] meane *1605*

Two hundred thousand footmen that haue seru'd
In two set battels fought in Grecia :
And for the expedition of this war,
If he think good, can from his garrisons,
Withdraw as many more to follow him. 1120

Tech. The more he brings, the greater is the spoile,
For when they perish by our warlike hands,
We meane to seate our footmen on their Steeds,
And rifle all those stately Ianisars. 1124

Tam. But wil those Kings accompany your Lord ?

Bass. Such as his Highnesse please, but some must stay
To rule the prouinces he late subdude.

Tam. Then fight couragiously, their crowns are yours.
This hand shal set them on your conquering heads :
That made me Emperour of *Asia.* 1130

Vsum. Let him bring millions infinite of men,
Vnpeopling Westerne *Affrica* and *Greece* :
Yet we assure vs of the victorie.

Ther. Euen he that in a trice vanquisht two kings,
More mighty than the Turkish Emperour : 1135
Shall rouse him out of Europe, and pursue
His scattered armie til they yeeld or die.

Tamb. Wel said *Theridamas*, speake in that mood,
For Wil and Shall best fitteth *Tamburlain*,
Whose smiling stars giues him assured hope 1140
Of martiall triumph, ere he meete his foes :
I that am tearm'd the Scourge and Wrath of God,
The onely feare and terrour of the world,
Wil first subdue the Turke, and then inlarge
Those Christian Captiues, which you keep as slaues, 1145
Burdening their bodies with your heauie chaines,
And feeding them with thin and slender fare,
That naked rowe about the Terrene sea.
And when they chance to breath and rest a space,
Are punisht with Bastones so grieuously, 1150
That they lie panting on the Gallies side,
And striue for life at euery stroke they giue.
These are the cruell pirates of *Argeire*,
That damned traine, the scum of *Affrica*,
Inhabited with stragling Runnagates, 1155
That make quick hauock of the Christian blood.

1123 seate] set *1592*, *Dyce*, *Bull.* 1140 giue *1592*, *Dyce to Bull.* 1149 breath and rest *1590*, *1605*, *Wag.*: rest or breath *1592*, *Rob. to Bull.* 1151 they *om. 1605*

But as I liue that towne shall curse the time
That *Tamburlaine* set foot in Affrica.

Enter Baiazeth with his Bassoes and contributorie Kinges. ⟨*Zabina and Ebea.*⟩

Bai. Bassoes and Ianisaries of my Guard,
Attend vpon the person of your Lord, 1160
The greatest Potentate of *Affrica.*
Tam. Techelles, and the rest prepare your swordes.
I meane t'incounter with that *Baiazeth.*
Bai. Kings of *Fesse*, *Moroccus* and *Argier*,
He cals me *Baiazeth*, whom you call Lord. 1165
Note the presumption of this Scythian slaue :
I tell thee villaine, those that lead my horse
Haue to their names tytles of dignity,
And dar'st thou bluntly call me *Baiazeth* ?
Tam. And know thou Turke, that those which lead my horse, 1170
Shall lead thee Captiue thorow Affrica.
And dar'st thou bluntly call me *Tamburlaine* ?
Bai. By *Mahomet*, my Kinsmans sepulcher,
And by the holy *Alcaron* I sweare,
He shall be made a chast and lustlesse Eunuke, 1175
And in my Sarell tend my Concubines :
And all his Captaines that thus stoutly stand,
Shall draw the chariot of my Emperesse,
Whom I haue brought to see their ouerthrow.
Tamb. By this my sword that conquer'd *Persea*, 1180
Thy fall shall make me famous through the world :
I will not tell thee how Ile handle thee,
But euery common souldier of my Camp
Shall smile to see thy miserable state.
Fess. What meanes the mighty Turkish Emperor 1185
To talk with one so base as *Tamburlaine* ?
Moro. Ye Moores and valiant men of *Barbary*,
How can ye suffer these indignities ?
Arg. Leaue words and let them feele your lances pointes,
Which glided through the bowels of the Greekes. 1190
Bai. Wel said my stout contributory kings,
Your threefold armie and my hugie hoste,
Shall swallow vp these base borne Perseans.

1158 S.D. contributorie] his contributory *1605* Zabina and Ebea *add. Dyce* 1163 to encounter *1592* 1168 title *1605* 1182 Ile] I will *1605* 1185 the] this *1605* 1188 ye] you *1605*

Tech. Puissant, renowmed and mighty *Tamburlain*,
Why stay we thus prolonging all their liues ? 1195
Ther. I long to see those crownes won by our swords
That we may raigne as kings of Affrica.
Vsum. What Coward wold not fight for such a prize ?
Tamb. Fight all couragiously and be you kings.
I speake it, and my words are oracles. 1200
Bai. *Zabina*, mother of three brauer boies,
Than *Hercules*, that in his infancie
Did pash the iawes of Serpents venomous :
Whose hands are made to gripe a warlike Lance,
Their shoulders broad, for complet armour fit, 1205
Their lims more large and of a bigger size
Than all the brats ysprong from *Typhons* loins :
Who, when they come vnto their fathers age,
Will batter Turrets with their manly fists.
Sit here vpon this royal chaire of state, 1210
And on thy head weare my Emperiall crowne,
Vntill I bring this sturdy *Tamburlain*,
And all his Captains bound in captiue chaines.
Zab. Such good successe happen to *Baiazeth*.
Tam. *Zenocrate*, the loueliest Maide aliue, 1215
Fairer than rockes of pearle and pretious stone,
The onely Paragon of *Tamburlaine*,
Whose eies are brighter than the Lamps of heauen,
And speech more pleasant than sweet harmony :
That with thy lookes canst cleare the darkened Sky : 1220
And calme the rage of thundring *Iupiter* :
Sit downe by her : adorned with my Crowne,
As if thou wert the Empresse of the world.
Stir not *Zenocrate* vntill thou see
Me martch victoriously with all my men, 1225
Triumphing ouer him and these his kings,
Which I will bring as Vassals to thy feete.
Til then take thou my crowne, vaunt of my worth,
And manage words with her as we will armes.
Zen. And may my Loue, the king of *Persea* 1230
Returne with victorie, and free from wound.
Bai. Now shalt thou feel the force of Turkish arms,
Which lately made all Europe quake for feare :
I haue of Turkes, Arabians, Moores and Iewes
Enough to couer all *Bythinia*. 1235

1195 all *1590, 1605, Wag.* : of *1592, Rob. to Bull.* 1197 raigne *1590, 1605, Wag.* : rule *1592, Rob. to Bull.*

Let thousands die, their slaughtered Carkasses
Shal serue for walles and bulwarkes to the rest :
And as the heads of *Hydra*, so my power
Subdued, shall stand as mighty as before :
If they should yeeld their necks vnto the sword, 1240
Thy souldiers armes could not endure to strike
So many blowes as I haue heads for thee.
Thou knowest not (foolish hardy *Tamburlaine*)
What tis to meet me in the open field,
That leaue no ground for thee to martch vpon. 1245

Tam. Our conquering swords shall marshal vs the way
We vse to march vpon the slaughtered foe :
Trampling their bowels with our horses hooffes :
Braue horses, bred on the white Tartarian hils :
My Campe is like to *Iulius Cæsars* Hoste, 1250
That neuer fought but had the victorie :
Nor in *Pharsalia* was there such hot war,
As these my followers willingly would haue :
Legions of Spirits fleeting in the aire,
Direct our Bullets and our weapons pointes 1255
And make our strokes to wound the sencelesse aire,
And when she sees our bloody Collours spread,
Then Victorie begins to take her flight,
Resting her selfe vpon my milk-white Tent :
But come my Lords, to weapons let vs fall. 1260
The field is ours, the Turk, his wife and all.

Exit, with his followers.

Bai. Come Kings and Bassoes, let vs glut our swords
That thirst to drinke the feble Perseans blood.

Exit, with his followers.

Zab. Base Concubine, must thou be plac'd by me
That am the Empresse of the mighty Turke ? 1265

Zen. Disdainful Turkesse and vnreuerend Bosse,
Call'st thou me Concubine that am betroath'd
Vnto the great and mighty *Tamburlaine* ?

Zab. To *Tamburlaine* the great Tartarian thiefe ?

Zen. Thou wilt repent these lauish words of thine, 1270
When thy great Bassoe maister and thy selfe

1242 thee] them *Dyce*[2] 1249 the *omit conj. Dyce* : th' *Cunn.*, *Bull.* 1256 our] your *Dyce etc.* air *conj. Dyce*[2] : lure *1590, 1605* : lute *1592* : light *Rob. etc.* : wind *conj. Cunn.* : winds *conj. Wag.* 1266 Bosse] Bassa *conj. Mitford*

Must plead for mercie at his kingly feet,
And sue to me to be your Aduocates.
Zab. And sue to thee ? I tell thee shamelesse girle,
Thou shalt be Landresse to my waiting maid. 1275
How lik'st thou her *Ebea*, will she serue ?
Ebea. Madame, she thinks perhaps she is too fine.
But I shall turne her into other weedes,
And make her daintie fingers fall to woorke.
Zen. Hearst thou *Anippe*, how thy drudge doth talk,
And how my slaue, her mistresse menaceth. 1281
Both for their sausinesse shall be employed,
To dresse the common souldiers meat and drink.
For we will scorne they should come nere our selues.
Anip. Yet somtimes let your highnesse send for them
To do the work my chamber maid disdaines. 1286

They sound the battell within, and stay.

Zen. Ye Gods and powers that gouerne Persea :
And made my lordly Loue her worthy King :
Now strengthen him against the Turkish *Baiazeth*,
And let his foes like flockes of fearfull Roes, 1290
Pursude by hunters, flie his angrie lookes,
That I may see him issue Conquerour.
Zab. Now *Mahomet*, solicit God himselfe,
And make him raine down murthering shot from heauen
To dash the Scythians braines, and strike them dead,
That dare to manage armes with him, 1296
That offered iewels to thy sacred shrine,
When first he war'd against the Christians.

To the battell againe.

Zen. By this the Turks lie weltring in their blood
And *Tamburlaine* is Lord of *Affrica*. 1300
Zab. Thou art deceiu'd, I heard the Trumpets sound,
As when my Emperour ouerthrew the Greeks :
And led them Captiue into Affrica.
Straight will I vse thee as thy pride deserues :
Prepare thy selfe to liue and die my slaue. 1305
Zen. If *Mahomet* should come from heauen and sweare,
My royall Lord is slaine or conquered,
Yet should he not perswade me otherwise,
But that he liues and will be Conquerour.

1273 aduocate *1605*, *Dyce to Bull.* 1296 him] Baiazeth *Wag.*
1300 And] as *1605* 1302 As] and *1605*

Baiazeth flies, and he pursues him. The battell short, and they enter, Baiazeth is ouercome.

Tam. Now king of Bassoes, who is Conqueror? 1310
Bai. Thou, by the fortune of this damned foile,
Tam. Where are your stout contributorie kings?

Enter Techelles, Theridamas, Vsumcasane.

Tech. We haue their crownes their bodies strowe the fielde.
Tam. Each man a crown? why kingly fought ifaith.
Deliuer them into my treasurie. 1315
Zen. Now let me offer to my gracious Lord
His royall Crowne againe, so highly won.
Tam. Nay take the Turkish Crown from her, *Zen⟨ocrate⟩*
And crowne me Emperour of Affrica. 1319
Zab. No Tamburlain, though now thou gat the best
Thou shalt not yet be Lord of Affrica.
Ther. Giue her the Crowne Turkesse you wer best.

He takes it from her, and giues it Zenocrate.

Zab. Iniurious villaines, thieues, runnagates,
How dare you thus abuse my Maiesty?
Ther. Here Madam, you are Empresse, she is none. 1325
Tam. Not now *Theridamas*, her time is past:
The pillers that haue bolstered vp those tearmes,
Are falne in clusters at my conquering feet.
Zab. Though he be prisoner, he may be ransomed.
Tamb. Not all the world shall ransom *Baiazeth*. 1330
Bai. Ah faire *Zabina*, we haue lost the field.
And neuer had the Turkish Emperour
So great a foile by any forraine foe.
Now will the Christian miscreants be glad,
Ringing with ioy their superstitious belles: 1335
And making bonfires for my ouerthrow.
But ere I die those foule Idolaters
Shall make me bonfires with their filthy bones,
For though the glorie of this day be lost,
Affrik and *Greece* haue garrisons enough 1340
To make me Soueraigne of the earth againe.
Tam. Those walled garrisons wil I subdue,
And write my selfe great Lord of *Affrica*:
So from the East vnto the furthest West,

1309 S.D. short] is short *1605* 1311 foil *conj. Dyce*[1], *Dyce*[2] *etc.*: soile *1590–1605* 1344 farthest *1605*

Shall *Tamburlain* extend his puisant arme. 1345
The Galles and those pilling Briggandines,
That yeerely saile to the Venetian gulfe,
And houer in the straightes for Christians wracke,
Shall lie at anchor in the Isle *Asant*,
Vntill the Persean Fleete and men of war, 1350
Sailing along the Orientall sea,
Haue fetcht about the Indian continent:
Euen from *Persepolis* to *Mexico*,
And thence vnto the straightes of *Iubalter*:
Where they shall meete, and ioine their force in one, 1355
Keeping in aw the Bay of *Portingale*,
And all the Ocean by the British shore:
And by this meanes Ile win the world at last.
Bai. Yet set a ransome on me *Tamburlaine*.
Tam. What, thinkst thou *Tamburlain* esteems thy gold?
Ile make the kings of *India* ere I die, 1361
Offer their mines (to sew for peace) to me,
And dig for treasure to appease my wrath:
Come bind them both and one lead in the Turke.
The Turkesse let my Loues maid lead away. 1365

They bind them.

Bai. Ah villaines, dare ye touch my sacred armes.
O *Mahomet*, Oh sleepie *Mahomet*.
Zab. O cursed *Mahomet* that makest vs thus
The slaues to Scythians rude and barbarous.
Tam. Come bring them in, & for this happy conquest
Triumph, and solemnize a martiall feast. 1371

Exeunt. Finis Actus tertii.

Actus 4. *Scæna* 1.

Souldan of Egipt with three or four Lords, Capolin ⟨a Messenger.⟩

Souldan. Awake ye men of *Memphis*, heare the clange
Of Scythian trumpets, heare the Basiliskes,
That roaring, shake *Damascus* turrets downe.
The rogue of *Volga* holds *Zenocrate*, 1375
The Souldans daughter for his Concubine,
And with a troope of theeues and vagabondes,

1357 British] brightest *1592* 1366 ye] you *1592*, *Dyce*, *Wag.* 1368 makes *1605* 1371 martiall] materiall *1605* S.D. a Messenger *add. Dyce etc.*

Hath spread his collours to our high disgrace:
While you faint-hearted base Egyptians,
Lie slumbering on the flowrie bankes of *Nile*, 1380
As Crocodiles that vnaffrighted rest,
While thundring Cannons rattle on their Skins.
Mess. Nay (mightie Souldan) did your greatnes see
The frowning lookes of fiery *Tamburlaine*,
That with his terrour and imperious eies, 1385
Commandes the hearts of his associates,
It might amaze your royall maiesty.
Soul. Villain, I tell thee, were that *Tamburlaine*
As monstrous as *Gorgon*, prince of Hell,
The Souldane would not start a foot from him. 1390
But speake, what power hath he ?
Mess. Mightie Lord,
Three hundred thousand men in armour clad,
Vpon their pransing Steeds, disdainfully
With wanton paces trampling on the ground. 1395
Fiue hundred thousand footmen threatning shot,
Shaking their swords, their speares and yron bils,
Enuironing their Standard round, that stood
As bristle-pointed as a thorny wood.
Their warlike Engins and munition 1400
Exceed the forces of their martial men.
Soul. Nay could their numbers counteruail the stars
Or euer drisling drops of Aprill showers,
Or withered leaues that Autume shaketh downe:
Yet would the Souldane by his conquering power, 1405
So scatter and consume them in his rage,
That not a man should liue to rue their fall.
Cap. So might your highnesse, had you time to sort
Your fighting men, and raise your royall hoste.
But *Tamburlaine*, by expedition 1410
Aduantage takes of your vnreadinesse.
Soul. Let him take all th'aduantages he can,
Were all the world conspird to fight for him,
Nay, were he Deuill, as he is no man,
Yet in reuenge of faire *Zenocrate*, 1415
Whom he detaineth in despight of vs,
This arme should send him downe to *Erebus*,
To shroud his shame in darknes of the night.

1389 Gorgon] the Gorgon *Rob.* 1403 euer *om. 1592* 1407 should] shal *1592* 1412 th'] the *1605* 1414 Deuill *1590*: Deul *1592*: the deuill *1605*

Mess. Pleaseth your mightinesse to vnderstand,
His resolution far exceedeth all : 1420
The first day when he pitcheth downe his tentes,
White is their hew, and on his siluer crest
A snowy Feather spangled white he beares,
To signify the mildnesse of his minde,
That satiate with spoile refuseth blood : 1425
But when *Aurora* mounts the second time,
As red as scarlet is his furniture,
Then must his kindled wrath bee quencht with blood,
Not sparing any that can manage armes :
But if these threats mooue not submission, 1430
Black are his collours, blacke Pauilion,
His speare, his shield, his horse, his armour, plumes,
And Ietty Feathers menace death and hell.
Without respect of Sex, degree or age,
He raceth all his foes with fire and sword. 1435
Soul. Mercilesse villaine, Pesant ignorant,
Of lawfull armes, or martiall discipline :
Pillage and murder are his vsuall trades.
The slaue vsurps the glorious name of war.
See *Capolin* the faire Arabian king, 1440
That hath bene disapointed by this slaue
Of my faire daughter, and his princely Loue :
May haue fresh warning to go war with vs,
And be reueng'd for her dispar⟨a⟩dgement.
⟨*Exeunt.*⟩

Actus 4. Scæna 2.

Tamburlain, Techelles, Theridamas, Vsumcasane, Zenocrate, Anippe, two Moores drawing Baiazeth in his cage, and his wife following him.

Tamb. Bring out my foot-stoole. 1445
They take him out of the cage.

Bai. Ye holy Priests of heauenly *Mahomet*,
That sacrificing slice and cut your flesh,
Staining his Altars with your purple blood :
Make heauen to frowne and euery fixed starre
To sucke vp poison from the moorish Fens, 1450
And poure it in this glorious Tyrants throat.

1444 + S.D. *add. Dyce* 1445 S.D. him] Bajazeth *Dyce* 1451 it *om. 1592, Wag.*

Tam. The chiefest God first mouuer of that Spheare,
Enchac'd with thousands euer shining lamps,
Will sooner burne the glorious frame of Heauen,
Then it should so conspire my ouerthrow. 1455
But Villaine, thou that wishest this to me,
Fall prostrate on the lowe disdainefull earth,
And be the foot-stoole of great *Tamburlain*,
That I may rise into my royall throne.
Bai. First shalt thou rip my bowels with thy sword,
And sacrifice my heart to death and hell, 1461
Before I yeeld to such a slauery.
Tamb. Base villain, vassall, slaue to *Tamburlaine*:
Vnworthy to imbrace or touch the ground,
That beares the honor of my royall waight. 1465
Stoop villaine, stoope, stoope for so he bids,
That may command thee peecemeale to be torne,
Or scattered like the lofty Cedar trees,
Strooke with the voice of thundring *Iupiter*.
Bai. Then as I look downe to the damned Feends, 1470
Feends looke on me, and thou dread God of hell,
With Eban Scepter strike this hatefull earth,
And make it swallow both of vs at once.

He gets vp vpon him to his chaire.

Tamb. Now cleare the triple region of the aire,
And let the maiestie of heauen beholde 1475
Their Scourge and Terrour treade on Emperours.
Smile Stars that raign'd at my natiuity:
And dim the brightnesse of their neighbor Lamps,
Disdaine to borrow light of *Cynthia*,
For I the chiefest Lamp of all the earth, 1480
First rising in the East with milde aspect,
But fixed now in the Meridian line,
Will send vp fire to your turning Spheares,
And cause the Sun to borrowe light of you.
My sword stroke fire from his coat of steele, 1485
Euen in *Bythinia*, when I took this Turke:
As when a fiery exhalation
Wrapt in the bowels of a freezing cloude,
Fighting for passage, make⟨s⟩ the Welkin cracke,

1455 it should] should it *1592* 1456 this] it *1605* 1459 into] vnto *1592* 1461 heart *1590*, *1605*, *Dyce*[2], *Wag.*: soule *1592*, *Rob.*, *Dyce*[1], *Cunn.*, *Bull.* 1466 stoop, stoop, stoop; for *conj. Dyce* 1473 S.D. He] Tamburlaine *Dyce etc.* 1478 their] your *conj. Dyce*[1], *Dyce*[2] *etc.* 1489 makes *Dyce etc.*: make *1590–1605*

And casts a flash of lightning to the earth. 1490
But ere I martch to wealthy *Persea*,
Or leaue *Damascus* and th' Egyptian fields,
As was the fame of *Clymenes* brain-sicke sonne,
That almost brent the Axeltree of heauen,
So shall our swords, our lances and our shot 1495
Fill all the aire with fiery meteors.
Then when the Sky shal waxe as red as blood,
It shall be said, I made it red my selfe,
To make me think of nought but blood and war.
Zab. Vnworthy king, that by thy crueltie, 1500
Vnlawfully vsurpest the Persean seat:
Dar'st thou that neuer saw an Emperour,
Before thou met my husband in the field,
Being thy Captiue, thus abuse his state,
Keeping his kingly body in a Cage, 1505
That rooffes of golde, and sun-bright Pallaces,
Should haue prepar'd to entertaine his Grace?
And treading him beneath thy loathsome feet,
Whose feet the kings of *Affrica* haue kist.
Tech. You must deuise some torment worsse, my Lord
To make these captiues reine their lauish tongues. 1511
Tam. *Zenocrate*, looke better to your slaue.
Zen. She is my Handmaids slaue, and she shal looke
That these abuses flow not from her tongue:
Chide her *Anippe*. 1515
Anip. Let these be warnings for you then my slaue,
How you abuse the person of the king:
Or els I sweare to haue you whipt stark nak'd.
Bai. Great *Tamburlaine*, great in my ouerthrow,
Ambitious pride shall make thee fall as low, 1520
For treading on the back of *Baiazeth*,
That should be horsed on fower mightie kings.
Tam. Thy names and tytles, and thy dignities
Are fled from *Baiazeth*, and remaine with me,
That will maintaine it against a world of Kings. 1525
Put him in againe. ⟨*They put him into the cage.*⟩
Bai. Is this a place for mighty *Baiazeth*?
Confusion light on him that helps thee thus.
Tam. There whiles he liues, shal *Baiezeth* be kept,

1490 to] on *1605* 1493 Clymenes *1592, Dyce etc.*: Clymeus *1590, 1605* 1494 brent] burnt *1605* 1514 from] in *1592* 1516 for you then] then for you *1605, Dyce* 1523 dignitie *1605* 1526 S.D. *add. Dyce* 1529 while *1605*

And where I goe be thus in triumph drawne : 1530
And thou his wife shalt feed him with the scraps
My seruitures shall bring the from my boord.
For he that giues him other food than this :
Shall sit by him and starue to death himselfe.
This is my minde, and I will haue it so. 1535
Not all the Kings and Emperours of the Earth :
If they would lay their crownes before my feet,
Shall ransome him, or take him from his cage.
The ages that shall talk of *Tamburlain*,
Euen from this day to *Platoes* wondrous yeare, 1540
Shall talke how I haue handled *Baiazeth*.
These Mores that drew him from *Bythinia*,
To faire *Damascus*, where we now remaine,
Shall lead him with vs wheresoere we goe.
Techelles, and my louing followers, 1545
Now may we see *Damascus* lofty towers,
Like to the shadowes of *Pyramides*,
That with their beauties grac'd the Memphion fields :
The golden stature of their feathered bird
That spreads her wings vpon the citie wals, 1550
Shall not defend it from our battering shot.
The townes-men maske in silke and cloath of gold,
And euery house is as a treasurie.
The men, the treasure, and the towne is ours.
Ther. Your tentes of white now pitch'd before the gates
And gentle flags of amitie displaid, 1556
I doubt not but the Gouernour will yeeld,
Offering *Damascus* to your Maiesty.
Tam. So shall he haue his life, and all the rest.
But if he stay vntil the bloody flag 1560
Be once aduanc'd on my vermilion Tent,
He dies, and those that kept vs out so long.
And when they see me march in black aray,
With mournfull streamers hanging down their heads,
Were in that citie all the world contain'd, 1565
Not one should scape : but perish by our swords.
Zen. Yet would you haue some pitie for my sake,
Because it is my countries, and my Fathers.
Tam. Not for the world *Zenocrate*, if I haue sworn :
Come bring in the Turke. *Exeunt.* 1570

1531 shal *1592* 1548 grac'd] grace *Dyce to Wag.* 1549 stature] statue *1605*, *Cunn.* 1554 is] are *Rob. to Cunn.* 1568 country *Rob. to Bull.*

Act. 4. *Scæna* 3.

Souldane, Arabia, Capoline, with st⟨r⟩eaming collors and Souldiers.

Souldan. Me thinks we martch as *Meliager* did,
Enuironed with braue Argolian knightes:
To chace the sauage Cal⟨i⟩donian Boare,
Or *Cephalus* with lustie Thebane youths
Against the Woolfe that angrie *Themis* sent, 1575
To waste and spoile the sweet Aonian fieldes.
A monster of fiue hundred thousand heades,
Compact of Rapine, Pyracie, and spoile,
The Scum of men, the hate and Scourge of God,
Raues in *Egyptia*, and annoyeth vs. 1580
My Lord it is the bloody *Tamburlaine*,
A sturdy Felon and a base-bred Thiefe,
By murder raised to the Persean Crowne,
That dares controll vs in our Territories.
To tame the pride of this presumptuous Beast, 1585
Ioine your Arabians with the Souldans power:
Let vs vnite our royall bandes in one,
And hasten to remooue *Damascus* siege.
It is a blemish to the Maiestie
And high estate of mightie Emperours, 1590
That such a base vsurping vagabond
Should braue a king, or weare a princely crowne.
Ara. Renowmed Souldane, haue ye lately heard
The ouerthrow of mightie *Baiazeth*,
About the confines of *Bythinia*? 1595
The slauerie wherewith he persecutes
The noble Turke and his great Emperesse?
Soul. I haue, and sorrow for his bad successe:
But noble Lord of great *Arabia*,
Be so perswaded, that the Souldan is 1600
No more dismaide with tidings of his fall,
Than in the hauen when the Pilot stands
And viewes a strangers ship rent in the winds,
And shiuered against a craggie rocke,
Yet in compassion of his wretched state, 1605
A sacred vow to heauen and him I make,
Confirming it with *Ibis* holy name,

1570 + S.D. streaming *1605 etc.*: steaming *1590, 1592* 1573 Calcedonian *1605* 1574 lustie *om. 1605* 1582 and *om. 1592* 1587 bandes] handes *1605*

That *Tamburlaine* shall rue the day, the hower,
Wherein he wrought such ignominious wrong
Vnto the hallowed person of a prince, 1610
Or kept the faire *Zenocrate* so long,
As Concubine, I feare to feed his lust.

Ara. Let griefe and furie hasten on reuenge,
Let *Tamburlaine* for his offences feele
Such plagues as heauen and we can poure on him. 1615
I long to breake my speare vpon his crest,
And prooue the waight of his victorious arme:
For Fame I feare hath bene too prodigall
In sounding through the world his partiall praise.

Soul. *Capolin*, hast thou suruaid our powers. 1620

Cap. Great Emperours of *Egypt* and *Arabia*,
The number of your hostes vnited is,
A hundred and fifty thousand horse,
Two hundred thousand foot, braue men at armes,
Couragious and full of hardinesse: 1625
As frolike as the hunters in the chace
Of sauage beastes amid the desart woods.

Arab. My mind presageth fortunate successe,
And *Tamburlaine*, my spirit doth foresee
The vtter ruine of thy men and thee. 1630

Soul. Then reare your standardes, let your sounding Drummes
Direct our Souldiers to *Damascus* walles.
Now *Tamburlaine*, the mightie Souldane comes,
And leads with him the great *Arabian* King,
To dim thy basenesse and obscurity, 1635
Famous for nothing but for theft and spoile,
To race and scatter thy inglorious crue,
Of Scythians and slauish Persians.

Exeunt.

Actus 4. *Scæna* 4.

The Banquet, and to it commeth Tamburlain al in scarlet, Theridamas, Techelles, Vsumcasane, the Turke, with others.

Tamb. Now hang our bloody collours by *Damascus*,
Reflexing hewes of blood vpon their heads, 1640

1608 the hower] and houre *1605* 1625 and *om. 1605* 1635 thy basenesse and] the basnesse of *1605* Scena 4 *1605*: Scæna 5 *1590, 1592*

While they walke quiuering on their citie walles,
Halfe dead for feare before they feele my wrath:
Then let vs freely banquet and carouse
Full bowles of wine vnto the God of war,
That meanes to fill your helmets full of golde: 1645
And make *Damascus* spoiles as rich to you,
As was to *Iason Colchos* golden fleece.
And now *Baiazeth,* hast thou any stomacke?

Bai. I, such a stomacke (cruel Tamburlane) as I could willingly feed vpon thy blood-raw hart. 1650

Tam. Nay, thine owne is easier to come by, plucke out that, and twil serue thee and thy wife: Wel *Zenocrate,* Techelles, and the rest, fall to your victuals.

Bai. Fall to, and neuer may your meat digest.
Ye Furies that can maske inuisible, 1655
Diue to the bottome of *Auernas* poole,
And in your hands bring hellish poison vp,
And squease it in the cup of *Tamburlain.*
Or winged snakes of *Lerna* cast your stings,
And leaue your venoms in this Tyrants dish. 1660

Zab. And may this banquet prooue as omenous,
As *Prognes* to th' adulterous Thracian King,
That fed vpon the substance of his child.

Zen. My Lord, how can you suffer these
Outragious curses by these slaues of yours? 1665

Tam. To let them see (diuine *Zenocrate*)
I glorie in the curses of my foes,
Hauing the power from the Emperiall heauen,
To turne them al vpon their proper heades. 1669

Tech. I pray you give them leaue Madam, this speech is a goodly refreshing to them.

Ther. But if his highnesse would let them be fed, it would doe them more good.

Tam. Sirra, why fall you not too, are you so daintily brought vp, you cannot eat your owne flesh? 1675

Bai. First legions of deuils shall teare thee in peeces.

Vsum. Villain, knowest thou to whom thou speakest?

Tam. O let him alone: here, eat sir, take it from my swords point, or Ile thrust it to thy heart.

He takes it and stamps vpon it.

1655 maske] walke *1605* 1664 My Lord] My lord, my lord *Bull.*: My gracious Lord *conj. Wag.* suffer] tamely suffer *conj. Dyce, Ellis* 1671 goodly] good *1605* to] for *1592, Dyce* 1674 you not] ye not *1605* 1678 here] there *1605* from] vp from *1605*

Ther. He stamps it vnder his feet my Lord. 1680

Tam. Take it vp Villaine, and eat it, or I will make thee slice the brawnes of thy armes into carbonadoes, and eat them.

Vsu. Nay, twere better he kild his wife, & then she shall be sure not to be staru'd, & he be prouided for a moneths victuall before hand. 1686

Tam. Here is my dagger, dispatch her while she is fat, for if she liue but a while longer, shee will fall into a consumption with freatting, and then she will not bee woorth the eating. 1690

Ther. Doost thou think that *Mahomet* wil suffer this?

Tech. Tis like he wil, when he cannot let it.

Tam. Go to, fal to your meat: what not a bit? belike he hath not bene watered to day, giue him some drinke.

They giue him water to drinke, and he flings it on the ground.

Faste and welcome sir, while hunger make you eat. How now *Zenocrate*, dooth not the Turke and his wife make a goodly showe at a banquet? 1697

Zen. Yes, my Lord.

Ther. Me thinks, tis a great deale better than a consort of musicke. 1700

Tam. Yet musicke woulde doe well to cheare vp *Zenocrate*: pray thee tel, why art thou so sad? If thou wilt haue a song, the Turke shall straine his voice: but why is it?

Zen. My lord, to see my fathers towne besieg'd, 1705
The countrie wasted where my selfe was borne,
How can it but afflict my verie soule?
If any loue remaine in you my Lord,
Or if my loue vnto your maiesty
May merit fauour at your highnesse handes, 1710
Then raise your siege from faire *Damascus* walles,
And with my father take a frindly truce.

Tamb. *Zenocrate*, were Egypt *Ioues* owne land,
Yet would I with my sword make *Ioue* to stoope.
I will confute those blind Geographers 1715
That make a triple region in the world,
Excluding Regions which I meane to trace,
And with this pen reduce them to a Map,
Calling the Prouinces, Citties and townes
After my name and thine *Zenocrate*: 1720

1682 slice] fleece *1605* 1688 fall] not fall *1605*

Here at *Damascus* will I make the Point
That shall begin the Perpendicular.
And wouldst thou haue me buy thy Fathers loue
With such a losse ? Tell me *Zenocrate*?
Zen. Honor still waight on happy *Tamburlaine* : 1725
Yet giue me leaue to plead for him my Lord.
Tam. Content thy selfe, his person shall be safe,
And all the friendes of faire *Zenocrate*,
If with their liues they will be pleasde to yeeld,
Or may be forc'd to make me Emperour. 1730
For Egypt and Arabia must be mine.
Feed you slaue, thou maist thinke thy selfe happie to be fed from my trencher.
Bai. My empty stomacke ful of idle heat,
Drawes bloody humours from my feeble partes, 1735
Preseruing life, by hasting cruell death.
My vaines are pale, my sinowes hard and drie,
My iointes benumb'd, vnlesse I eat, I die.
Zab. Eat *Baiazeth*. Let vs liue in spite of them, looking some happie power will pitie and inlarge vs. 1740
Tam. Here Turk, wilt thou haue a cleane trencher ?
Bai. I Tyrant, and more meat.
Tam. Soft sir, you must be dieted, too much eating will make you surfeit.
Ther. So it would my lord, specially hauing so smal a walke, and so litle exercise. 1746

Enter a second course of Crownes.

Tam. Theridamas, Techelles and *Casane*, here are the cates you desire to finger, are they not ?
Ther. I (my Lord) but none saue kinges must feede with these. 1750
Tech. Tis enough for vs to see them, and for *Tamburlaine* onely to enioy them.
Tam. Wel, here is now to the Souldane of *Egypt*, the King of *Arabia*, and the Gouernour of *Damascus*. Now take these three crownes, and pledge me, my contributorie Kings. I crowne you here (*Theridamas*) King of *Argier* : *Techelles* King of *Fesse*, and *Vsumcasane*, King of *Morocus*. How say you to this (Turke) these are not your contributorie kings.
Bai. Nor shall they long be thine, I warrant them. 1760

1723 thy] my *1605* 1736 hastening *1605*, *Dyce*, *Cunn.* 1745 specially] especially *1605*, *Rob.*, *Cunn.*

Tam. Kings of *Argier, Morocus,* and of *Fesse*:
You that haue martcht with happy *Tamburlaine,*
As far as from the frozen place of heauen,
Vnto the watry mornings ruddy bower,
And thence by land vnto the Torrid Zone, 1765
Deserue these tytles I endow you with
By valour and by magnanimity.
Your byrthes shall be no blemish to your fame,
For vertue is the fount whence honor springs,
And they are worthy she inuesteth kings. 1770
Ther. And since your highnesse hath so well vouchsaft,
If we deserue them not with higher meeds
Then erst our states and actions haue retain'd,
Take them away againe and make vs slaues.
Tam. Wel said *Theridamas,* when holy Fates 1775
Shall stablish me in strong *Egyptia,*
We meane to traueile to th'Anta⟨r⟩tique Pole,
Conquering the people vnderneath our feet,
And be renowm'd, as neuer Emperours were.
Zenocrate, I will not crowne thee yet, 1780
Vntil with greater honors I be grac'd.

Finis Actus quarti.

Actus 5. *Scæna* 1.

The Gouernour of Damasco, with three or foure Citizens, and foure Virgins with branches of Laurell in their hands.

Gouernour. Stil dooth this man or rather God of war,
Batter our walles, and beat our Turrets downe.
And to resist with longer stubbornesse,
Or hope of rescue from the Souldans power, 1785
Were but to bring our wilfull ouerthrow,
And make vs desperate of our threatned liues:
We see his tents haue now bene altered,
With terrours to the last and cruelst hew:
His cole-blacke collours euery where aduaunst, 1790
Threaten our citie with a generall spoile:
And if we should with common rites of Armes,
Offer our safeties to his clemencie,

1763 place] plage *Dyce*[2] *to Bull.* 1764 bower *1605*: hower *1590, 1592* 1767 valour *Rob. etc.*: value *1590–1605* 1769 whence] where *1605* 1774 againe *om. 1605* 1777 th'] the *1605*

I feare the custome proper to his sword,
Which he obserues as parcell of his fame, 1795
Intending so to terrifie the world,
By any innouation or remorse,
Will neuer be dispenc'd with til our deaths.
Therfore, for these our harmlesse virgines sakes,
Whose honors and whose liues relie on him: 1800
Let vs haue hope that their vnspotted praiers
Their blubbered cheekes and hartie humble mones
Will melt his furie into some remorse:
And vse vs like a louing Conquerour.

Virg. If humble suites or imprecations, 1805
(Vttered with teares of wretchednesse and blood,
Shead from the heads and hearts of all our Sex,
Some made your wiues, and some your children)
Might haue intreated your obdurate breasts,
To entertaine some care of our securities, 1810
Whiles only danger beat vpon our walles,
These more than dangerous warrants of our death
Had neuer bene erected as they bee,
Nor you depend on such weake helps as we.

Go. Wel, louely Virgins, think our countries care, 1815
Our loue of honor loth to be enthral'd
To forraine powers, and rough imperious yokes:
Would not with too much cowardize or feare,
Before all hope of rescue were denied,
Submit your selues and vs to seruitude. 1820
Therefore in that your safeties and our owne,
Your honors, liberties and liues were weigh'd
In equall care and ballance with our owne,
Endure as we the malice of our stars,
The wrath of *Tamburlain*, and power of warres, 1825
Or be the means the ouerweighing heauens
Haue kept to quallifie these hot extreames.
And bring vs pardon in your chearfull lookes.

2. *Virg.* Then here before the maiesty of heauen,
And holy *Patrones* of *Egyptia*, 1830
With knees and hearts submissiue we intreate
Grace to our words and pitie to our lookes
That this deuise may prooue propitious,
And through the eies and eares of *Tamburlaine*,
Conuey euents of mercie to his heart: 1835

1799 sake *1605* 1810 cares *1592* 1814 help *1605* 1825 powers *1605*

Graunt that these signes of victorie we yeeld
May bind the temples of his conquering head,
To hide the folded furrowes of his browes,
And shadow his displeased countenance,
With happy looks of ruthe and lenity. 1840
Leaue vs my Lord, and louing countrimen,
What simple Virgins may perswade, we will.
Go. Farewell (sweet Virgins) on whose safe return
Depends our citie, libertie, and liues.
Exeunt ⟨*all except the Virgins.*⟩

Actus 5. *Scæna* 2.

Tamburlaine, Techelles, Theridamas, Vsumcasan, with others: Tamburlaine all in blacke, and verie melancholy.

Tamb. What, are the Turtles fraide out of their neastes?
Alas poore fooles, must you be first shal feele 1846
The sworne destruction of *Damascus.*
They know my custome: could they not as well
Haue sent ye out, when first my milkwhite flags
Through which sweet mercie threw her gentle beams 1850
Reflexing them on your disdainfull eies:
As now when furie and incensed hate
Flings slaughtering terrour from my coleblack tents,
And tels for trueth, submissions comes too late.
1\. *Virgin.* Most happy King and Emperour of the earth,
Image of Honor and Nobilitie, 1856
For whome the Powers diuine haue made the world,
And on whose throne the holy Graces sit,
In whose sweete person is compriz'd the Sum
Of natures Skill and heauenly maiestie, 1860
Pittie our plightes, O pitie poore *Damascus*:
Pitie olde age, within whose siluer haires
Honor and reuerence euermore haue raign'd,
Pitie the mariage bed, where many a Lord
In prime and glorie of his louing ioy 1865
Embraceth now with teares of ruth and blood,
The iealous bodie of his fearfull wife,

1844 S.D. all . . Virgins *add. Dyce* 1847 Damascus walls *Bull.* 1848 know] knew *1592, Dyce to Bull.* 1851 Reflexing] Reflexed *Rob. etc. exc. Bull.* your] their *conj. Dyce*[1], *Dyce*[2], *Wag.* 1852 As] and *1605* 1853 tent *1605* 1854 submission *Rob. etc. exc. Bull.* 1866 of ruth and] and ruth of *1605*

Whose cheekes and hearts so punisht with conceit,
To thinke thy puisant neuer staied arme
Will part their bodies, and preuent their soules 1870
From heauens of comfort, yet their age might beare,
Now waxe all pale and withered to the death,
As well for griefe our ruthlesse Gouernour
Haue thus refusde the mercie of thy hand,
(Whose scepter Angels kisse, and Furies dread) 1875
As for their liberties, their loues or liues.
O then for these, and such as we our selues,
For vs, for infants, and for all our bloods,
That neuer nourisht thought against thy rule,
Pitie, O pitie, (sacred Emperour) 1880
The prostrate seruice of this wretched towne.
And take in signe thereof this gilded wreath,
Whereto ech man of rule hath giuen his hand,
And wisht as worthy subiects happy meanes,
To be inuesters of thy royall browes, 1885
Euen with the true Egyptian Diadem.

Tam. Virgins, in vaine ye labour to preuent
That which mine honor sweares shal be perform'd:
Behold my sword, what see you at the point?

Virg. Nothing but feare and fatall steele my Lord. 1890

Tam. Your fearfull minds are thicke and mistie then,
For there sits Death, there sits imperious Death,
Keeping his circuit by the slicing edge.
But I am pleasde you shall not see him there,
He now is seated on my horsmens speares: 1895
And on their points his fleshlesse bodie feedes.
Techelles, straight goe charge a few of them
To chardge these Dames, and shew my seruant death,
Sitting in scarlet on their armed speares.

Omnes. O pitie vs. 1900

Tam. Away with them I say and shew them death.

They take them away.

I will not spare these proud Egyptians,
Nor change my Martiall obseruations,
For all the wealth of Gehons golden waues,
Or for the loue of *Venus*, would she leaue 1905
The angrie God of Armes, and lie with me.
They haue refusde the offer of their liues,

1874 Haue] Hath *1605, Dyce to Bull.*: Has *Rob.* 1879 nourish *1605* 1884 wisht] wish *1605* 1887 ye] you *1592, Rob. to Bull.*

And know my customes are as peremptory
As wrathfull Planets, death, or destinie.

Enter Techelles.

What, haue your horsmen shewen the virgins Death? 1910
Tech. They haue my Lord, and on *Damascus* wals
Haue hoisted vp their slaughtered carcases.
Tam. A sight as banefull to their soules I think
As are Thessalian drugs or Mithradate.
But goe my Lords, put the rest to the sword. 1915
Exeunt.

Ah faire *Zenocrate*, diuine *Zenocrate*,
Faire is too foule an Epithite for thee,
That in thy passion for thy countries loue,
And feare to see thy kingly Fathers harme,
With haire discheweld wip'st thy watery cheeks: 1920
And like to *Flora* in her mornings pride,
Shaking her siluer treshes in the aire,
Rain'st on the earth resolued pearle in showers,
And sprinklest Saphyrs on thy shining face,
Wher Beauty, mother to the Muses sits, 1925
And comments vollumes with her Yuory pen:
Taking instructions from thy flowing eies,
Eies when that *Ebena* steps to heauen,
In silence of thy solemn Euenings walk,
Making the mantle of the richest night, 1930
The Moone, the Planets, and the Meteors light.
There Angels in their christal armours fight
A doubtfull battell with my tempted thoughtes,
For Egypts freedom and the Souldans life:
His life that so consumes *Zenocrate*, 1935
Whose sorrowes lay more siege vnto my soule,
Than all my Army to *Damascus* walles.
And neither Perseans Soueraign, nor the Turk
Troubled my sences with conceit of foile,
So much by much, as dooth *Zenocrate*. 1940
What is beauty saith my sufferings then?
If all the pens that euer poets held,
Had fed the feeling of their maisters thoughts,
And euery sweetnes that inspir'd their harts,

1921 morning *Cunn.*, *Bull.* 1922 tresses *1592*, *Rob. etc.* 1928 when that] that when *Ellis*, *Bull.*: which when that *conj. Schipper*, *Wag.* 1930 Making] Make in *Ellis*, *Bull.* 1932 There] These *Cunn.*, *Bull.* fights *1605* 1938 Persia's *Rob. etc.*

Their minds, and muses on admyred theames : 1945
If all the heauenly Quintessence they still
From their immortall flowers of Poesy,
Wherein as in a myrrour we perceiue
The highest reaches of a humaine wit.
If these had made one Poems period 1950
And all combin'd in Beauties worthinesse,
Yet should ther houer in their restlesse heads,
One thought, one grace, one woonder at the least,
Which into words no vertue can digest :
But how vnseemly is it for my Sex 1955
My discipline of armes and Chiualrie,
My nature and the terrour of my name,
To harbour thoughts effeminate and faint ?
Saue onely that in Beauties iust applause,
With whose instinct the soule of man is toucht, 1960
And euery warriour that is rapt with loue,
Of fame, of valour, and of victory
Must needs haue beauty beat on his conceites,
I thus conceiuing and subduing both
That which hath st⟨o⟩opt the tempest of the Gods, 1965
Euen from the fiery spangled vaile of heauen,
To feele the louely warmth of shepheards flames,
And martch in cottages of strowed weeds,
Shal giue the world to note for all my byrth,
That Vertue solely is the sum of glorie, 1970
And fashions men with true nobility.
Who's within there ?

Enter two or three.

Hath *Baiazeth* bene fed to day ?
An. I, my Lord.
Tamb. Bring him forth, & let vs know if the towne be ransackt. 1976

1953 least] last *conj. Broughton* 1965–8 *Insert these lines between 1960 and 1961 conj. Mitford* 1965 stoopt *Dyce*[2] *etc.* : stopt *1590–1605* tempest *1590–1605* : temper *conj. Coll.* : tempers *conj. Fraser's Mag., Brereton* : chiefest *Dyce*[2] *to Wag.* : topmost *conj. Deighton* 1966 fiery spangled *1590, 1592* : spangled firie *1605* : fire-yspangled *conj. Coll., conj. Dyce*[2] vaile] vault *conj. Coll.* 1967 louely] lowly *conj. Coll., Cunn., Bull., Brereton* 1968 martch *1590–1605* : mask *conj. Broughton, Dyce to Wag.* : match *conj. Fraser's Mag., Brereton* cottages] coatches *1605* cottages of strowed] cottagers' off-strowed *conj. Broughton* of] on *conj. Cook* weeds] reeds *Dyce*[2] *etc.* 1974 *Prefix* An.] Attend. *Dyce*

Enter Techelles, Theridamas, Vsumcasan & others.

Tech. The town is ours my Lord, and fresh supply
Of conquest, and of spoile is offered vs.
Tam. Thats wel *Techelles*, what's the newes?
Tech. The Souldan and the Arabian king together 1980
Martch on vs with such eager violence,
As if there were no way but one with vs.
Tam. No more there is not I warrant thee *Techelles.*
They bring in the Turke.
Ther. We know the victorie is ours my Lord,
But let vs saue the reuerend Souldans life, 1985
For faire *Zenocrate*, that so laments his state.
Tamb. That will we chiefly see vnto, *Theridamas.*
For sweet *Zenocrate*, whose worthinesse
Deserues a conquest ouer euery hart:
And now my footstoole, if I loose the field, 1990
You hope of libertie and restitution:
Here let him stay my maysters from the tents,
Till we haue made vs ready for the field.
Pray for vs *Baiazeth*, we are going. *Exeunt.*
Bai. Go, neuer to returne with victorie: 1995
Millions of men encompasse thee about,
And gore thy body with as many wounds.
Sharpe forked arrowes light vpon thy horse:
Furies from the blacke *Cocitus* lake,
Breake vp the earth, and with their firebrands, 2000
Enforce thee run vpon the banefull pikes.
Volleyes of shot pierce through thy charmed Skin,
And euery bullet dipt in poisoned drugs,
Or roaring Cannons seuer all thy ioints,
Making thee mount as high as Eagles soare. 2005
Zab. Let all the swords and Lances in the field,
Stick in his breast, as in their proper roomes,
At euery pore let blood comme dropping foorth,
That lingring paines may massacre his heart,
And madnesse send his damned soule to hell. 2010
Bai. Ah faire *Zabina*, we may curse his power,
The heauens may frowne, the earth for anger quake,
But such a Star hath influence in his sword,

1976 S.D. & *1590*: and *1592*: with *1605* 1981 vs] with vs *1592* 1985 reuerent *1605* 1994 S.D. Exeunt all except Bajazeth and Zabina *Dyce* 1999 Furies] May Furies *conj. Broughton* 2008 pore] dore *1605*

As rules the Skies, and countermands the Gods,
More than Cymerian *Stix* or Distinie : 2015
And then shall we in this detested guyse,
With shame, with hungar, and with horror aie
Griping our bowels with retorqued thoughtes,
And haue no hope to end our extasies.
Zab. Then is there left no *Mahomet*, no God, 2020
No Feend, no Fortune, nor no hope of end
To our infamous monstrous slaueries?
Gape earth, and let the Feends infernall view
A hell, as hoplesse and as full of feare
As are the blasted banks of *Erebus* : 2025
Where shaking ghosts with euer howling grones,
Houer about the vgly Ferriman,
To get a passage to *Elisian*.
Why should we liue, O wretches, beggars, slaues,
Why liue we *Baiazeth*, and build vp neasts, 2030
So high within the region of the aire,
By liuing long in this oppression,
That all the world will see and laugh to scorne
The former triumphes of our mightines,
In this obscure infernall seruitude ? 2035
Bai. O life more loathsome to my vexed thoughts,
Than noisome parbreak of the Stygian Snakes,
Which fils the nookes of Hell with standing aire,
Infecting all the Ghosts with curelesse griefs :
O dreary Engines of my loathed sight, 2040
That sees my crowne, my honor and my name,
Thrust vnder yoke and thraldom of a thiefe.
Why feed ye still on daies accursed beams,
And sink not quite into my tortur'd soule?
You see my wife, my Queene and Emperesse, 2045
Brought vp and propped by the hand of fame,
Queen of fifteene contributory Queens,
Now throwen to roomes of blacke abiection,
Smear'd with blots of basest drudgery :
And Villanesse to shame, disdaine, and misery : 2050
Accursed *Baiazeth*, whose words of ruth,
That would with pity chear *Zabinas* heart :
And make our soules resolue in ceasles teares,

2017 aie] aye *1605*: live *Rob.*: stay *Dyce etc.* 2024 A *Rob. etc.*: As *1590–1605* 2028 Elysium *Rob. to Bull.* 2036 thought *1605* 2043 ye] you *1605* 2048 abiection *1590, Rob. etc.*: obiection *1592, 1605* 2051 ruth] truth *1605*

Sharp hunger bites vpon and gripes the root :
From whence the issues of my thoughts doe breake. 2055
O poore *Zabina*, O my Queen, my Queen,
Fetch me some water for my burning breast,
To coole and comfort me with longer date,
That in the shortned sequel of my life,
I may poure foorth my soule into thine armes, 2060
With words of loue : whose moaning entercourse
Hath hetherto bin staid, with wrath and hate
Of our expreslesse band inflictions.

Zab. Sweet *Baiazeth*, I will prolong thy life,
As long as any blood or sparke of breath 2065
Can quench or coole the torments of my griefe.

She goes out.

Bai. Now *Baiazeth*, abridge thy banefull daies,
And beat thy braines out of thy conquer'd head :
Since other meanes are all forbidden me,
That may be ministers of my decay. 2070
O highest Lamp of euerliuing *Ioue*,
Accursed day infected with my griefs,
Hide now thy stained face in endles night,
And shut the windowes of the lightsome heauens.
Let vgly darknesse with her rusty coach 2075
Engyrt with tempests wrapt in pitchy clouds,
Smother the earth with neuer fading mistes :
And let her horses from their nostrels breathe
Rebellious winds and dreadfull thunderclaps :
That in this terrour *Tamburlaine* may liue, 2080
And my pin'd soule resolu'd in liquid ay⟨re⟩,
May styl excruciat his tormented thoughts.
Then let the stony dart of sencelesse colde,
Pierce through the center of my withered heart,
And make a passage for my loathed life. 2085

He brains himself against the cage.

Enter Zabina.

Zab. What do mine eies behold, my husband dead ?
His Skul al riuin in twain, his braines dasht out ?
The braines of *Baiazeth*, my Lord and Soueraigne ?
O *Baiazeth*, my husband and my Lord, 2089

2068 thy braines *1590, 1592, Cunn. to Wag.* : the braines *1605, Rob., Dyce* 2071 euerlasting *1605* 2081 ayre *1605 etc.* : ay *1590, 1592*

O *Baiazet*, O Turk, O Emperor, giue him his liquor? Not I, bring milk and fire, and my blood I bring him againe, teare me in peeces, giue me the sworde with a ball of wildefire vpon it. Downe with him, downe with him. Goe to my child, away, away, away. Ah, saue that Infant, saue him, saue him. I, euen I speake to her, the Sun was downe. Streamers white, Red, Blacke, here, here, here. Fling the meat in his face. *Tamburlaine, Tamburlaine*, Let the souldiers be buried. Hel, death, *Tamburlain*, Hell, make ready my Coch, my chaire, my iewels, I come, I come, I come. 2100

She runs against the Cage and braines her selfe.

⟨*Enter*⟩ *Zenocrate wyth Anippe.*

⟨*Zen.*⟩ Wretched *Zenocrate*, that liuest to see,
Damascus walles di'd with Egyptian blood,
Thy Fathers subiects and thy countrimen:
Thy streetes strowed with disseuered iointes of men,
And wounded bodies gasping yet for life. 2105
But most accurst, to see the Sun-bright troope
Of heauenly vyrgins and vnspotted maides,
Whose lookes might make the angry God of armes,
To breake his sword, and mildly treat of loue,
On horsmens Lances to be hoisted vp, 2110
And guiltlesly endure a cruell death.
For euery fell and stout Tartarian Stead,
That stampt on others with their thundring hooues
When al their riders chardg'd their quiuering speares
Began to checke the ground, and rain themselues: 2115
Gazing vpon the beautie of their lookes:
Ah *Tamburlaine*, wert thou the cause of this
That tearm'st *Zenocrate* thy dearest loue?
Whose liues were dearer to *Zenocrate*
Than her owne life, or ought saue thine owne loue. 2120
But see another bloody spectacle.
Ah wretched eies, the enemies of my hart,
How are ye glutted with these grieuous obiects,
And tell my soule mor tales of bleeding ruth?
See, se *Anippe* if they breathe or no. 2125

Anip. No breath nor sence, nor motion in them both.

2092 giue] & giue *1592*, *Rob.* 2097-8 Let . . Tamburlain *om. 1605* 2098 buried] cursed *Rob.*: burned *Cunn.* 2100 I come *om. 1605* S.D. Enter *add. 1605* 2101 *Prefix* Zen. *add. 1605* 2104 Thy] The *Dyce etc.*

Ah Madam, this their slauery hath Enforc'd,
And ruthlesse cruelty of *Tamburlaine.*
Zen. Earth cast vp fountaines from thy entralles,
And wet thy cheeks for their vntimely deathes: 2130
Shake with their waight in signe of feare & griefe:
Blush heauen, that gaue them honor at their birth,
And let them die a death so barbarous.
Those that are proud of fickle Empery,
And place their chiefest good in earthly pompe: 2135
Behold the Turke and his great Emperesse.
Ah *Tamburlaine,* my loue, sweet *Tamburlaine,*
That fights for Scepters and for slippery crownes,
Behold the Turk and his great Emperesse,
Thou that in conduct of thy happy stars, 2140
Sleep'st euery night with conquest on thy browes,
And yet wouldst shun the wauering turnes of war.
In feare and feeling of the like distresse,
Behold the Turke and his great Emperesse.
Ah myghty *Ioue* and holy *Mahomet,* 2145
Pardon my Loue, oh pardon his contempt,
Of earthly fortune, and respect of pitie,
And let not conquest ruthlesly pursewde
Be equally against his life incenst,
In this great Turk and haplesse Emperesse. 2150
And pardon me that was not moou'd with ruthe,
To see them liue so long in misery:
Ah what may chance to thee *Zenocrate*?
Anip. Madam content your self and be resolu'd,
Your Loue hath fortune so at his command, 2155
That she shall stay and turne her wheele no more,
As long as life maintaines his mighty arme,
That fights for honor to adorne your head.
Enter a Messenger ⟨*Philemus*⟩.
Zen. What other heauie news now brings *Philemus*?
Phi. Madam, your father and th' *Arabian* king, 2160
The first affecter of your excellence,
Comes now as *Turnus* gainst *Eneas* did,
Armed with lance into the Egyptian fields,
Ready for battaile gainst my Lord the King.
Zen. Now shame and duty, loue and feare presents 2165
A thousand sorrowes to my martyred soule:

2129 thy] thine *1605* 2138 fightst *1605, Dyce etc.* 2142 warres *1605* 2147 respect of] respective *conj. Broughton* 2158 S.D. a Messenger] Philemus *Dyce etc.*

Whom should I wish the fatall victory,
When my poore pleasures are deuided thus,
And rackt by dutie from my cursed heart:
My father and my first betrothed loue, 2170
Must fight against my life and present loue:
Wherin the change I vse condemns my faith,
And makes my deeds infamous through the world.
But as the Gods to end the Troyans toile,
Preuented *Turnus* of *Lauinia*, 2175
And fatally enricht *Eneas* loue,
So for a finall Issue to my griefes,
To pacifie my countrie and my loue,
Must *Tamburlaine* by their resistlesse powers,
With vertue of a gentle victorie, 2180
Conclude a league of honor to my hope,
Then as the powers deuine haue preordainde,
With happy safty of my fathers life,
Send like defence of faire *Arabia*.

They sound to the battaile. And Tamburlaine enioyes the victory, after Arabia enters wounded.

Ar. What cursed power guides the murthering hands,
Of this infamous Tyrants souldiers, 2186
That no escape may saue their enemies:
Nor fortune keep them selues from victory.
Lye down *Arabia*, wounded to the death,
And let *Zenocrates* faire eies beholde 2190
That as for her thou bearst these wretched armes,
Euen so for her thou diest in these armes:
Leauing thy blood for witnesse of thy loue.
Zen. Too deare a witnesse for such loue my Lord.
Behold *Zenocrate*, the cursed obiect 2195
Whose Fortunes neuer mastered her griefs:
Behold her wounded in conceit for thee,
As much as thy faire body is for me.
Ar. Then shal I die with full contented heart,
Hauing beheld deuine *Zenocrate*, 2200
Whose sight with ioy would take away my life,
As now it bringeth sweetnesse to my wound,
If I had not bin wounded as I am.
Ah that the deadly panges I suffer now,
Would lend an howers license to my tongue: 2205
To make discourse of some sweet accidents

2177 finall] small *1592* 2193 thy blood] my blood *1592*

Haue chanc'd thy merits in this worthles bondage.
And that I might be priuy to the state,
Of thy deseru'd contentment and thy loue :
But making now a vertue of thy sight, 2210
To driue all sorrow from my fainting soule :
Since Death denies me further cause of ioy,
Depriu'd of care, my heart with comfort dies,
Since thy desired hand shall close mine eies.

Enter Tamburlain leading the Souldane, Techelles, Theridamas, Vsumcasane, with others.

Tam. Come happy Father of *Zenocrate,* 2215
A title higher than thy Souldans name :
Though my right hand haue thus enthralled thee
Thy princely daughter here shall set thee free,
She that hath calmde the furie of my sword,
Which had ere this bin bathde in streames of blood, 2220
As vast and deep as *Euphrates* or *Nile.*
Zen: O sight thrice welcome to my ioiful soule,
To see the king my Father issue safe,
From dangerous battel of my conquering Loue.
Soul. Wel met my only deare *Zenocrate,* 2225
Though with the losse of Egypt and my Crown.
Tam. Twas I my lord that gat the victory,
And therfore grieue not at your ouerthrow,
Since I shall render all into your hands,
And ad more strength to your dominions 2230
Than euer yet confirm'd th' Egyptian Crown.
The God of war resignes his roume to me,
Meaning to make me Generall of the world,
Ioue viewing me in armes, lookes pale and wan,
Fearing my power should pull him from his throne. 2235
Where ere I come the fatall sisters sweat,
And griesly death by running to and fro,
To doo their ceassles homag to my sword :
And here in Affrick where it seldom raines,
Since I arriu'd with my triumphant hoste, 2240
Haue swelling cloudes drawen from wide gasping woundes,
Bene oft resolu'd in bloody purple showers,
A meteor that might terrify the earth,
And make it quake at euery drop it drinks :
Millions of soules sit on the bankes of *Styx,* 2245

2217 haue] hath *1605* 2235 should] shall *1605* 2241 wide-gaping *Dyce*

Waiting the back returne of *Charons* boat,
Hell and *Elisian* swarme with ghosts of men,
That I haue sent from sundry foughten fields,
To spread my fame through hell and vp to heauen:
And see my Lord, a sight of strange import, 2250
Emperours and kings lie breathlesse at my feet,
The Turk and his great Emperesse as it seems,
Left to themselues while we were at the fight,
Haue desperatly dispatcht their slauish liues:
With them *Arabia* too hath left his life, 2255
Al sights of power to grace my victory:
And such are obiects fit for *Tamburlaine*,
Wherein as in a mirrour may be seene,
His honor, that consists in sheading blood,
When men presume to manage armes with him. 2260
Soul. Mighty hath God & *Mahomet* made thy hand
(Renowmed *Tamburlain*) to whom all kings
Of force must yeeld their crownes and Emperies,
And I am pleasde with this my ouerthrow:
If as beseemes a person of thy state, 2265
Thou hast with honor vsde *Zenocrate*.
Tamb. Her state and person wants no pomp you see,
And for all blot of foule inchastity,
I record heauen, her heauenly selfe is cleare:
Then let me find no further time to grace 2270
Her princely Temples with the Persean crowne:
But here these kings that on my fortunes wait:
And haue bene crown'd for prooued worthynesse,
Euen by this hand that shall establish them,
Shal now, adioining al their hands with mine, 2275
Inuest her here my Queene of *Persea*.
What saith the noble Souldane and *Zenocrate*?
Soul. I yeeld with thanks and protestations
Of endlesse honor to thee for her loue.
Tamb. Then doubt I not but faire *Zenocrate* 2280
Will soone consent to satisfy vs both.
Zen. Els should I much forget my self, my Lord.
Ther. Then let vs set the crowne vpon her head,
That long hath lingred for so high a seat.
Tech. My hand is ready to performe the deed, 2285
For now her mariage time shall worke vs rest.
Vsum. And her's the crown my Lord, help set it on.

2247 Elysium *Rob. to Bull.* 2276 my] the *1592*, *Rob.*, *Dyce*, *Bull.*
2280 I not] not I *1605* 2282 Els] Then *1592* 2287 on *om. 1592*

Tam. Then sit thou downe diuine *Zenocrate,*
And here we crowne thee Queene of *Persea,*
And all the kingdomes and dominions 2290
That late the power of *Tamburlaine* subdewed :
As *Iuno,* when the Giants were supprest,
That darted mountaines at her brother *Ioue* :
So lookes my Loue, shadowing in her browes
Triumphes and Trophees for my victories : 2295
Or as *Latonas* daughter bent to armes,
Adding more courage to my conquering mind.
To gratify the sweet *Zenocrate,*
Egyptians, Moores and men of Asia,
From *Barbary* vnto the Westerne *Indie,* 2300
Shall pay a yearly tribute to thy Syre.
And from the boundes of *Affrick* to the banks
Of *Ganges,* shall his mighty arme extend.
And now my Lords and louing followers,
That purchac'd kingdomes by your ma⟨r⟩tiall deeds, 2305
Cast off your armor, put on scarlet roabes.
Mount vp your royall places of estate,
Enuironed with troopes of noble men,
And there make lawes to rule your prouinces:
Hang vp your weapons on *Alcides* poste, 2310
For *Tamburlaine* takes truce with al the world.
Thy first betrothed Loue, *Arabia,*
Shall we with honor (as beseemes) entombe,
With this great Turke and his faire Emperesse:
Then after all these solemne Exequies, 2315
We wil our rites of mariage solemnize.

Finis Actus quinti & vltimi huius primae partis.

2298 the] thee *Dyce*[2] 2310 poste] posts *Dyce, Cunn., Wag.* 2313 as] as best *1592* 2316 rites *conj. Mitford, Dyce etc.*: celebrated rites *1590–1605, Rob.* + Finis . . partis] Finis *1605*

Tamburlaine the Greate.

VVith his impaßionate furie, for the death of his Lady and Loue faire Zenocrate: his forme of exhortation and discipline *to his three Sonnes, and the manner of his owne death.*

The second part.

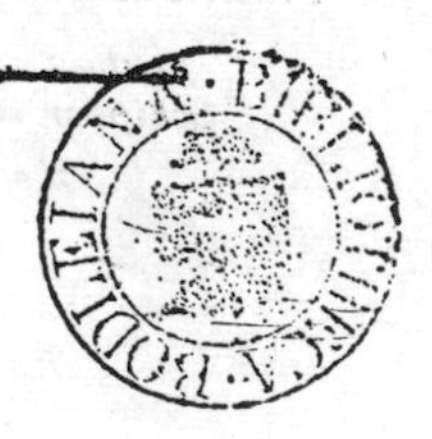

LONDON

Printed by E. A, *for* Ed. White, *and are to be solde* at his Shop neere the little North doore of Saint Paules Church at the Signe of the Gun.

1606.

1590 = Octavo edition of that year. B. L.
1592 = ,, ,, ,, ,, B. L.
1606 = Quarto ,, ,, ,, B. L.

Rob. = (Robinson's) edition of Marlowe, 1826.
Dyce { *Dyce*[1] = Dyce's first edition of Marlowe, 1850.
Dyce[2] = ,, revised ,, ,, ,, 1858, etc.
Cunn. = Cunningham's ,, ,, ,, 1870, etc.
Bull. = Bullen's ,, ,, ,, 1885.
Wag. = A. Wagner's edition of *Tamburlaine*, 1885.
Ellis = 'Mermaid' edition of Marlowe's best plays, 1887, etc.
T. B. = The present editor.

Brereton = J. Le Gay B., (*a*) 'Notes on the Text of Marlowe,' *Anglia*, Beiblatt, 1905, pp. 203 ff.
(*b*) *Passages from the Works of Marlowe* (Sydney, 1902).
Broughton = J. B.'s MS. notes in copy of *Rob.* (Brit. Mus. 11771 d).
Coll. = J. P. Collier's MS. notes in copy of *Dyce*[1] (Brit. Mus. 11771 bbb 6).
Coll.[2] = J. P. C.'s Introduction to *Coleridge*, *Seven Lectures on Shakespeare*, 1856.
Cook = A. S. C. in *Modern Language Notes*, xxi. 112, 113.
Deighton = K. D., *The Old Dramatists*: *Conjectural Readings*, 1896.
Elze = K. E., *Notes on Elizabethan Dramatists*, 1889.
Fraser's Mag. = Unsigned article in *Fraser's Town and Country Magazine*, xlvii, pp. 221–34.
Mitford = J. M. in *Gentleman's Magazine*, Jan. 1841.
Schipper = J. S., *De Versu Marlovii*.

⟨DRAMATIS PERSONAE

TAMBURLAINE, *king of Persia.*
CALYPHAS, AMYRAS, CELEBINUS, *his sons.*
THERIDAMAS, *king of Argier.*
TECHELLES, *king of Fez.*
USUMCASANE, *king of Morocco.*
ORCANES, *king of Natolia.*
KING OF TREBIZON.
KING OF SORIA.
KING OF JERUSALEM.
KING OF AMASIA.
GAZELLUS, *viceroy of Byron.*
URIBASSA.
SIGISMUND, *king of Hungary.*
FREDERICK, BALDWIN, *Lords of Buda and Bohemia.*
CALLAPINE, *son to Bajazeth, and prisoner to Tamburlaine.*
ALMEDA, *his keeper.*
GOVERNOR OF BABYLON.
CAPTAIN OF BALSERA.
HIS SON.
MAXIMUS, PERDICAS, *Physicians, Lords, Citizens, Messengers, Soldiers, and Attendants.*

ZENOCRATE, *wife to Tamburlaine.*
OLYMPIA, *wife to the Captain of Balsera.*
Turkish Concubines.⟩[1]

[1] *Add. Dyce.*

THE SECOND PART OF

The bloody Conquests

of mighty Tamburlaine.

With his impassionate fury, for the death of *his Lady and loue, faire Zenocrate:* his fourme of exhortation and discipline to his three *sons, and the maner of his own death.*

The Prologue.

The generall welcomes Tamburlain receiu'd,
When he arriued last vpon our stage,
Hath made our Poet pen his second part,
Wher death cuts off the progres of his pomp, 2320

Heading. With his . . maner of his own death *om. 1606* *Prologue* 2318 our] the *1606*

And murdrous Fates throwes al his triumphs down.
But what became of faire Zenocrate,
And with how manie cities sacrifice
He celebrated her sad funerall,
Himselfe in presence shal vnfold at large. 2325

Actus I. *Scæna* I.

Orcanes, king of Natolia, Gazellus, vice-roy of Byron, Vribassa, and their traine, with drums and trumpets.

Orcanes.

Egregious Viceroyes of these Eastern parts
Plac'd by the issue of great *Baiazeth*
And sacred Lord the mighty *Calapine*:
Who liues in *Egypt*, prisoner to that slaue,
Which kept his father in an yron cage: 2330
Now haue we martcht from faire *Natolia*
Two hundred leagues, and on *Danubius* banks,
Our warlike hoste in compleat armour rest,
Where *Sigismond* the king of *Hungary*
Should meet our person to conclude a truce. 2335
What? Shall we parle with the Christian,
Or crosse the streame, and meet him in the field?
Byr. King of *Natolia*, let vs treat of peace,
We all are glutted with the Christians blood,
And haue a greater foe to fight against, 2340
Proud *Tamburlaine*, that now in *Asia*,
Neere *Guyrons* head doth set his conquering feet,
And means to fire Turky as he goes:
Gainst him my Lord must you addresse your power.
Vribas. Besides, king *Sigismond* hath brought from Christendome, 2345
More then his Camp of stout Hungarians,
Sclauonians, Almans, Rutters, Muffes, and Danes,
That with the Holbard, Lance, and murthering Axe,
Will hazard that we might with surety hold.
⟨*Orc.*⟩ Though from the shortest Northren Paralell, 2350
Vast *Gruntland* compast with the frozen sea,

2321 tryumph *1606, Rob.* 2324 sad *Rob. to Bull.*: said *1590–1606, Wag.* 2344 must you] you must *1592, Rob. to Bull.* 2347 Almans, Rutters] Almain Rutters *conj. Coll.* Muffes] Russ *conj. Coll.* 2350 *Prefix om. 1590–1606* 2351 Grantland *1606, Rob. to Bull.*

Inhabited with tall and sturdy men,
Gyants as big as hugie *Polypheme*:
Millions of Souldiers cut the Artick line,
Bringing the strength of *Europe* to these Armes, 2355
Our Turky blades shal glide through al their throats,
And make this champion mead a bloody Fen.
Danubius stream that runs to *Trebizon*,
Shall carie wrapt within his scarlet waues,
As martiall presents to our friends at home 2360
The slaughtered bodies of these Christians.
The Terrene main wherin *Danubius* fals,
Shall by this battell be the bloody Sea.
The wandring Sailers of proud *Italy*,
Shall meet those Christians fleeting with the tyde, 2365
Beating in heaps against their Argoses,
And make faire *Europe* mounted on her bull,
Trapt with the wealth and riches of the world,
Alight and weare a woful mourning weed.
Byr. Yet stout *Orcanes*, Prorex of the world, 2370
Since *Tamburlaine* hath mustred all his men,
Marching from *Cairon* northward with his camp,
To *Alexandria*, and the frontier townes,
Meaning to make a conquest of our land:
Tis requisit to parle for a peace 2375
With *Sigismond* the king of *Hungary*:
And saue our forces for the hot assaults
Proud *Tamburlaine* intends *Natolia*.
Orc. Viceroy of *Byron*, wisely hast thou said:
My realme, the Center of our Empery 2380
Once lost, All Turkie would be ouerthrowne:
And for that cause the Christians shall haue peace.
Slauonians, Almains, Rutters, Muffes, and Danes
Feare not *Orcanes*, but great *Tamburlaine*,
Nor he but Fortune that hath made him great. 2385
We haue reuolted Grecians, Albanees,
Cicilians, Iewes, Arabians, Turks, and Moors,
Natolians, Sorians, blacke Egyptians,
Illirians, Thracians, and Bythinians,
Enough to swallow forcelesse *Sigismond* 2390

2354 cut the] out of *1606* 2383 Almain Rutters, Russ *conj. Coll.* 2387 Cicilians] *Qy.* Cilicians 2388 Sorians] Syrians *1592* blacke] and black *1606* 2389 Illirians *1606*: Illicians *1590, 1592* *Between 2388 and 2389 ed. 1606 inserts*: FRED. And we from Europe to the same intent *which is really l. 2443 and is there missing in ed. 1606*

Yet scarse enough t'encounter *Tamburlaine*.
He brings a world of people to the field,
From *Scythia* to the Orientall Plage
Of *India*, wher raging *Lantchidol*
Beates on the regions with his boysterous blowes, 2395
That neuer sea-man yet discouered :
All *Asia* is in Armes with *Tamburlaine*,
Euen from the midst of fiery *Cancers* Tropick,
To *Amazonia* vnder *Capricorne*.
And thence as far as *Archipellago*, 2400
All *Affrike* is in Armes with *Tamburlaine*.
Therefore Viceroies the Christians must haue peace.

Act. 1. *Scæna* 2.

Sigismond, Fredericke, Baldwine, and their traine with drums and trumpets.

Sigis. *Orcanes* (as our Legates promist thee)
Wee with our Peeres haue crost *Danubius* stream
To treat of friendly peace or deadly war : 2405
Take which thou wilt, for as the Romans vsde
I here present thee with a naked sword.
Wilt thou haue war, then shake this blade at me,
If peace, restore it to my hands againe:
And I wil sheath it to confirme the same. 2410
Orc. Stay *Sigismond*, forgetst thou I am he
That with the Cannon shooke *Vienna* walles,
And made it dance vpon the Continent :
As when the massy substance of the earth,
Quiuer about the Axeltree of heauen. 2415
Forgetst thou that I sent a shower of dartes
Mingled with powdered shot and fethered steele
So thick vpon the blink-ei'd Burghers heads,
That thou thy self, then County-Pallatine,
The king of *Boheme*, and the *Austrich* Duke, 2420
Sent Herralds out, which basely on their knees
In all your names desirde a truce of me ?
Forgetst thou, that to haue me raise my siege,
Wagons of gold were set before my tent :
Stampt with the princely Foule that in her wings 2425

2393 Plage] Place *1606* 2402 Viceroie *1592*, *Dyce to Bull.* 2415 Quivers *Rob. to Bull.*

Caries the fearfull thunderbolts of *Ioue*,
How canst thou think of this and offer war?
Sig. *Vienna* was besieg'd, and I was there,
Then County-Pallatine, but now a king:
And what we did, was in extremity: 2430
But now *Orcanes*, view my royall hoste,
That hides these plaines, and seems as vast and wide,
As dooth the Desart of *Arabia*
To those that stand on *Badgeths* lofty Tower,
Or as the Ocean to the Traueiler 2435
That restes vpon the snowy Appenines:
And tell me whether I should stoope so low,
Or treat of peace with the Natolian king?
Byr. Kings of *Natolia* and of *Hungarie*,
We came from Turky to confirme a league, 2440
And not to dare ech other to the field:
A friendly parle might become ye both.
Fred. And we from *Europe* to the same intent,
Which if your General refuse or scorne,
Our Tents are pitcht, our men stand in array, 2445
Ready to charge you ere you stir your feet.
Nat. So prest are we, but yet if *Sigismond*
Speake as a friend, and stand not vpon tearmes,
Here is his sword, let peace be ratified
On these conditions specified before, 2450
Drawen with aduise of our Ambassadors.
Sig. Then here I sheath it, and giue thee my hand,
Neuer to draw it out, or manage armes
Against thy selfe or thy confederates:
But whilst I liue will be at truce with thee. 2455
Nat. But (*Sigismond*) confirme it with an oath,
And sweare in sight of heauen and by thy Christ.
Sig. By him that made the world and sau'd my soule
The sonne of God and issue of a Mayd,
Sweet Iesus Christ, I sollemnly protest, 2460
And vow to keepe this peace inuiolable.
Nat. By sacred *Mahomet*, the friend of God,
Whose holy Alcaron remaines with vs,
Whose glorious body when he left the world,
Closde in a coffyn mounted vp the aire, 2465
And hung on stately *Mecas* Temple roofe,

2438 Or] As *Rob*., *Cunn*. 2442 ye] you *1592*, *Dyce to Bull*.
2443 *Here missing in ed. 1606, being wrongly inserted after* 2388
2445 stand] are *1606* 2453 or] and *1606*

I sweare to keepe this truce inuiolable:
Of whose conditions, and our solemne othes
Sign'd with our handes, each shal retaine a scrowle:
As memorable witnesse of our league. 2470
Now *Sigismond*, if any Christian King
Encroche vpon the confines of thy realme,
Send woord, *Orcanes* of *Natolia*
Confirm'd this league beyond *Danubius* streame,
And they will (trembling) sound a quicke retreat, 2475
So am I fear'd among all Nations.

Sig. If any heathen potentate or king
Inuade *Natolia*, *Sigismond* will send
A hundred thousand horse train'd to the war,
And backt by stout Lanceres of *Germany*, 2480
The strength and sinewes of the imperiall seat.

Nat. I thank thee *Sigismond*, but when I war
All *Asia Minor*, *Affrica*, and *Greece*
Follow my Standard and my thundring Drums:
Come let vs goe and banquet in our tents: 2485
I will dispatch chiefe of my army hence
To faire *Natolia*, and to *Trebizon*,
To stay my comming gainst proud *Tamburlaine*.
Freend *Sigismond*, and peeres of *Hungary*,
Come banquet and carouse with vs a while, 2490
And then depart we to our territories.

Exeunt.

Actus 1. *Scæna* 3.

Callapine with Almeda, his keeper.

Callap. Sweet *Almeda*, pity the ruthfull plight
Of *Callapine*, the sonne of *Baiazeth*,
Born to be Monarch of the Western world:
Yet here detain'd by cruell *Tamburlaine*. 2495

Alm. My Lord I pitie it, and with my heart
Wish your release, but he whose wrath is death,
My soueraigne Lord, renowmed *Tamburlain*,
Forbids you further liberty than this.

Cal. Ah were I now but halfe so eloquent 2500
To paint in woords, what Ile perfourme in deeds,
I know thou wouldst depart from hence with me.

Al. Not for all *Affrike*, therefore mooue me not.

Cal. Yet heare me speake my gentle *Almeda*.

2480 by] with *1606*

Al. No speach to that end, by your fauour sir. 2505
Cal. By *Cario* runs.
Al. No talke of running, I tell you sir.
Cal. A litle further, gentle *Almeda.*
Al. Wel sir, what of this?
Cal. By *Cario* runs to *Alexandria* Bay, 2510
Darotes streames, wherin at anchor lies
A Turkish Gally of my royall fleet,
Waiting my comming to the riuer side,
Hoping by some means I shall be releast,
Which when I come aboord will hoist vp saile, 2515
And soon put foorth into the Terrene sea:
Where twixt the Isles of *Cyprus* and of *Creete,*
We quickly may in Turkish seas arriue.
Then shalt thou see a hundred kings and more
Vpon their knees, all bid me welcome home. 2520
Amongst so many crownes of burnisht gold,
Choose which thou wilt, all are at thy command,
A thousand Gallies mann'd with Christian slaues
I freely giue thee, which shall cut the straights,
And bring Armados from the coasts of Spaine, 2525
Fraughted with golde of rich *America*:
The Grecian virgins shall attend on thee,
Skilful in musicke and in amorous laies:
As faire as was *Pigmalions* Iuory gyrle,
Or louely *Io* metamorphosed. 2530
With naked Negros shall thy coach be drawen,
And as thou rid'st in triumph through the streets,
The pauement vnderneath thy chariot wheels
With Turky Carpets shall be couered:
And cloath of Arras hung about the walles, 2535
Fit obiects for thy princely eie to pierce.
A hundred Bassoes cloath'd in crimson silk
Shall ride before the on Barbarian Steeds:
And when thou goest, a golden Canapie
Enchac'd with pretious stones, which shine as bright 2540
As that faire vail that couers all the world:
When *Phœbus* leaping from his Hemi-Spheare,
Discendeth downward to th' Antipodes.
And more than this, for all I cannot tell.
Alm. How far hence lies the Galley, say you? 2545
Cal. Sweet *Almeda,* scarse halfe a league from hence.

2506, 2510 Cario] Cairo *Rob. to Bull.* 2511 stream *Dyce*[2] 2525 from] to *1592*

Alm. But need we not be spied going aboord?
Cal. Betwixt the hollow hanging of a hill
And crooked bending of a craggy rock,
The sailes wrapt vp, the mast and tacklings downe, 2550
She lies so close that none can find her out.
Alm. I like that well: but tel me my Lord, if I should let you goe, would you bee as good as your word? Shall I be made a king for my labour?
Cal. As I am *Callapine* the Emperour, 2555
And by the hand of *Mahomet* I sweare,
Thou shalt be crown'd a king and be my mate.
Alm. Then here I sweare, as I am *Almeda*,
Your Keeper vnder *Tamburlaine* the great,
(For that's the style and tytle I haue yet) 2560
Although he sent a thousand armed men
To intercept this haughty enterprize,
Yet would I venture to conduct your Grace,
And die before I brought you backe again.
Cal. Thanks gentle *Almeda*, then let vs haste, 2565
Least time be past, and lingring let vs both.
Al. When you will my Lord, I am ready.
Cal. Euen straight: and farewell cursed *Tamburlaine*.
Now goe I to reuenge my fathers death.
Exeunt.

Actus 1. *Scæna* 4.

Tamburlaine with Zenocrate, and his three sonnes, Calyphas, Amyras, and Celebinus, with drummes and trumpets.

Tamb. Now, bright *Zenocrate*, the worlds faire eie, 2570
Whose beames illuminate the lamps of heauen,
Whose chearful looks do cleare the clowdy aire
And cloath it in a christall liuerie,
Now rest thee here on faire *Larissa* Plaines,
Where Egypt and the Turkish Empire parts, 2575
Betweene thy sons that shall be Emperours,
And euery one Commander of a world.
Zen. Sweet *Tamburlain*, when wilt thou leaue these armes
And saue thy sacred person free from scathe:
And dangerous chances of the wrathfull war. 2580
Tam. When heauen shal cease to mooue on both the poles
& when the ground wheron my souldiers march
Shal rise aloft and touch the horned Moon,

And not before my sweet *Zenocrate*:
Sit vp and rest thee like a louely Queene. 2585
So, now she sits in pompe and maiestie:
When these my sonnes, more precious in mine eies
Than all the wealthy kingdomes I subdewed:
Plac'd by her side, looke on their mothers face.
But yet me thinks their looks are amorous, 2590
Not martiall as the sons of *Tamburlaine*.
Water and ayre being simbolisde in one
Argue their want of courage and of wit,
Their haire as white as milke and soft as Downe,
Which should be like the quilles of Porcupines, 2595
As blacke as Ieat, and hard as Iron or steel,
Bewraies they are too dainty for the wars.
Their fingers made to quauer on a Lute,
Their armes to hang about a Ladies necke:
Their legs to dance and caper in the aire: 2600
Would make me thinke them Bastards, not my sons,
But that I know they issued from thy wombe,
That neuer look'd on man but *Tamburlaine*.

Zen. My gratious Lord, they haue their mothers looks
But when they list, their conquering fathers hart: 2605
This louely boy the yongest of the three,
Not long agoe bestrid a Scythian Steed:
Trotting the ring, and tilting at a gloue:
Which when he tainted with his slender rod,
He raign'd him straight and made him so curuet, 2610
As I cried out for feare he should haue falne.

Tam. Wel done my boy, thou shalt haue shield and lance
Armour of proofe, horse, helme, & Curtle-axe
And I will teach thee how to charge thy foe,
And harmelesse run among the deadly pikes. 2615
If thou wilt loue the warres and follow me,
Thou shalt be made a King and raigne with me,
Keeping in yron cages Emperours.
If thou exceed thy elder Brothers worth,
And shine in compleat vertue more than they, 2620
Thou shalt be king before them, and thy seed
Shall issue crowned from their mothers wombe.

Cel. Yes father, you shal see me if I liue,
Haue vnder me as many kings as you,
And martch with such a multitude of men, 2625
As all the world shall tremble at their view.

2594 and] as *1606* 2626 shall] should *1606*

Tam. These words assure me boy, thou art my sonne.
When I am old and cannot mannage armes,
Be thou the scourge and terrour of the world.
Amy. Why may not I my Lord, as wel as he, 2630
Be tearm'd the scourge and terrour of the world?
Tam. Be al a scourge and terror to the world,
Or els you are not sons of *Tamburlaine*.
Cal. But while my brothers follow armes my lord
Let me accompany my gratious mother, 2635
They are enough to conquer all the world
And you haue won enough for me to keep.
Tam. Bastardly boy, sprong from some cowards loins:
And not the issue of great *Tamburlaine*,
Of all the prouinces I haue subdued 2640
Thou shalt not haue a foot, vnlesse thou beare
A mind corragious and inuincible:
For he shall weare the crowne of *Persea*,
Whose head hath deepest scarres, whose breast most woundes,
Which being wroth, sends lightning from his eies, 2645
And in the furrowes of his frowning browes,
Harbors reuenge, war, death and cruelty:
For in a field whose superficies
Is couered with a liquid purple veile,
And sprinkled with the braines of slaughtered men, 2650
My royal chaire of state shall be aduanc'd:
And he that meanes to place himselfe therein
Must armed wade vp to the chin in blood.
Zen. My Lord, such speeches to our princely sonnes,
Dismaies their mindes before they come to prooue 2655
The wounding troubles angry war affoords.
Cel. No Madam, these are speeches fit for vs,
For if his chaire were in a sea of blood,
I would prepare a ship and saile to it,
Ere I would loose the tytle of a king. 2660
Amy. And I would striue to swim through pooles of blood,
Or make a bridge of murthered Carcases,
Whose arches should be fram'd with bones of Turks,
Ere I would loose the tytle of a king.
Tam. Wel louely boies, you shal be Emperours both 2665

2631 of] to *1606* 2632 to] of *1606* 2648 superficies *Rob. etc.*: superfluities *1590–1606* 2665 you *1590*: ye, *1592*, *1606*, *Rob. to Bull.*

Stretching your conquering armes from east to west:
And sirha, if you meane to weare a crowne,
When we shall meet the Turkish Deputie
And all his Viceroies, snatch it from his head,
And cleaue his Pericranion with thy sword. 2670
Cal. If any man will hold him, I will strike,
And cleaue him to the channell with my sword.
Tamb. Hold him, and cleaue him too, or Ile cleaue thee
For we will martch against them presently.
Theridamas, Techelles, and *Casane* 2675
Promist to meet me on *Larissa* plaines
With hostes apeece against this Turkish crue,
For I haue sworne by sacred *Mahomet,*
To make it parcel of my Empery,
The trumpets sound *Zenocrate,* they come. 2680

Actus I. *Scæna* 5.

Enter Theridamas, and his traine with Drums and Trumpets.

Tamb. Welcome *Theridamas,* king of *Argier.*
Ther. My Lord the great and mighty *Tamburlain,*
Arch-Monarke of the world, I offer here,
My crowne, my selfe, and all the power I haue,
In all affection at thy kingly feet. 2685
Tam. Thanks good *Theridamas.*
Ther. Vnder my collors march ten thousand Greeks
And of *Argier* and *Affriks* frontier townes,
Twise twenty thousand valiant men at armes,
All which haue sworne to sacke *Natolia*: 2690
Fiue hundred Briggandines are vnder saile,
Meet for your seruice on the sea, my Lord,
That lanching from *Argier* to *Tripoly,*
Will quickly ride before *Natolia*:
And batter downe the castles on the shore. 2695
Tam. Wel said *Argier,* receiue thy crowne againe.

Actus I. *Scæna* 6.

Enter Techelles and Vsumcasane together.

Tamb. Kings of *Morocus* and of *Fesse,* welcome
Vsu. Magnificent & peerlesse *Tamburlaine,*
I and my neighbor King of *Fesse* haue brought

To aide thee in this Turkish expedition, 2700
A hundred thousand expert souldiers:
From *Azamor* to *Tunys* neare the sea,
Is *Barbary* vnpeopled for thy sake,
And all the men in armour vnder me,
Which with my crowne I gladly offer thee. 2705
Tam. Thanks king of *Morocus*, take your crown again.
Tech. And mighty *Tamburlaine*, our earthly God,
Whose lookes make this inferiour world to quake,
I here present thee with the crowne of *Fesse*,
And with an hoste of Moores trainde to the war, 2710
Whose coleblacke faces make their foes retire,
And quake for feare, as if infernall *Ioue*
Meaning to aid thee in these Turkish armes,
Should pierce the blacke circumference of hell,
With vgly Furies bearing fiery flags, 2715
And millions of his strong tormenting spirits:
From strong *Tesella* vnto *Biledull*,
All *Barbary* is vnpeopled for thy sake.
Tam. Thanks king of *Fesse*, take here thy crowne again.
Your presence (louing friends and fellow kings) 2720
Makes me to surfet in conceiuing ioy,
If all the christall gates of *Ioues* high court
Were opened wide, and I might enter in
To see the state and maiesty of heauen,
It could not more delight me than your sight. 2725
Now will we banquet on these plaines a while,
And after martch to Turky with our Campe,
In number more than are the drops that fall
When *Boreas* rents a thousand swelling cloudes.
And proud *Orcanes* of *Natolia*, 2730
With all his viceroies shall be so affraide,
That though the stones, as at *Deucalions* flood,
Were turnde to men, he should be ouercome:
Such lauish will I make of Turkish blood,
That *Ioue* shall send his winged Messenger 2735
To bid me sheath my sword, and leaue the field:
The Sun vnable to sustaine the sight,
Shall hide his head in *Thetis* watery lap,
And leaue his steeds to faire Bootes charge:
For halfe the world shall perish in this fight: 2740

2710 warres *1606* 2712 if] if the *1606* 2713 thee *Rob.*: them *1590–1606* these *1606 etc.*: this *1590, 1592*

But now my friends, let me examine ye,
How haue ye spent your absent time from me?
Vsum. My Lord our men of *Barbary* haue martcht
Foure hundred miles with armour on their backes,
And laine in leagre fifteene moneths and more, 2745
For since we left you at the Souldans court,
We haue subdude the Southerne Guallatia,
And all the land vnto the coast of Spaine.
We kept the narrow straight of *Gibralter*,
And made *Canarea* cal vs kings and Lords, 2750
Yet neuer did they recreate themselues,
Or cease one day from war and hot alarms,
And therefore let them rest a while my Lord.
Tam. They shal *Casane*, and tis time yfaith.
Tech. And I haue martch'd along the riuer *Nile*, 2755
To *Machda*, where the mighty Christian Priest
Cal'd *Iohn* the great, sits in a milk-white robe,
Whose triple Myter I did take by force,
And made him sweare obedience to my crowne.
From thence vnto *Cazates* did I martch, 2760
Wher Amazonians met me in the field:
With whom (being women) I vouchsaft a league,
And with my power did march to *Zansibar*
The Westerne part of *Affrike*, where I view'd
The Ethiopian sea, riuers and lakes: 2765
But neither man nor child in al the land:
Therfore I tooke my course to *Manico*,
Where vnresisted I remoou'd my campe:
And by the coast of *Byather* at last,
I came to *Cubar*, where the Negros dwell, 2770
And conquering that, made haste to *Nubia*,
There hauing sackt *Borno* the Kingly seat,
I took the king, and lead him bound in chaines
Vnto *Damasco*, where I staid before.
Tamb. Well done *Techelles*: what saith *Theridamas*?
Ther. I left the confines and the bounds of *Affrike* 2776
And made a voyage into *Europe*,
Where by the riuer *Tyros* I subdew'd
Stoka, Padalia, and *Codemia*.
Then crost the sea and came to *Oblia*, 2780
And *Nigra Silua*, where the Deuils dance,

2764 Westerne] eastern *conj. Broughton, Cunn., Bull.* 2774 Damascus *Dyce, Cunn.* 2777 made] thence I made *Cunn., Bull.* Europa *conj. Elze, Wag.*

Which in despight of them I set on fire :
From thence I crost the Gulfe, call'd by the name
Mare magiore, of th' inhabitantes :
Yet shall my souldiers make no period 2785
Vntill *Natolia* kneele before your feet.
Tamb. Then wil we triumph, banquet and carouse,
Cookes shall haue pensions to prouide vs cates,
And glut vs with the dainties of the world,
Lachrima Christi and Calabrian wines 2790
Shall common Souldiers drink in quaffing boules,
I, liquid golde when we haue conquer'd him,
Mingled with corrall and with orient pearle :
Come let vs banquet and carrouse the whiles. *Exeunt.*

Finis Actus primi.

Actus 2. Scæna 1.

Sigismond, Fredericke, Baldwine, with their traine

Sigis. Now say my Lords of *Buda* and *Bohemia*, 2795
What motion is it that inflames your thoughts,
And stirs your valures to such soddaine armes ?
Fred. Your Maiesty remembers I am sure
What cruell slaughter of our Christian bloods,
These heathnish Turks and Pagans lately made, 2800
Betwixt the citie *Zula* and *Danubius*,
How through the midst of *Verna* and *Bulgaria*
And almost to the very walles of *Rome*,
They haue not long since massacred our Camp.
It resteth now then that your Maiesty 2805
Take all aduantages of time and power,
And worke reuenge vpon these Infidels :
Your Highnesse knowes for *Tamburlaines* repaire,
That strikes a terrour to all Turkish hearts,
Natolia hath dismist the greatest part 2810
Of all his armie, pitcht against our power
Betwixt *Cutheia* and *Orminius* mount :
And sent them marching vp to *Belgasar*,
Acantha, *Antioch*, and *Cæsaria*,
To aid the kings of *Soria* and *Ierusalem*. 2815
Now then my Lord, aduantage take hereof,
And issue sodainly vpon the rest :

2793 orient *Rob. etc.* : orientall *1590-1606* 2816 hereof] thereof *1592, Rob. to Bull.*

That in the fortune of their ouerthrow,
We may discourage all the pagan troope,
That dare attempt to war with Christians. 2820
Sig. But cals not then your Grace to memorie
The league we lately made with king *Orcanes*,
Confirm'd by oth and Articles of peace,
And calling Christ for record of our trueths ?
This should be treacherie and violence, 2825
Against the grace of our profession.
Bald. No whit my Lord : for with such Infidels,
In whom no faith nor true religion rests,
We are not bound to those accomplishments,
The holy lawes of Christendome inioine : 2830
But as the faith which they prophanely plight
Is not by necessary pollycy,
To be esteem'd assurance for our selues,
So what we vow to them should not infringe
Our liberty of armes and victory. 2835
Sig. Though I confesse the othes they vndertake,
Breed litle strength to our securitie,
Yet those infirmities that thus defame
Their faiths, their honors, and their religion,
Should not giue vs presumption to the like. 2840
Our faiths are sound, and must be consumate,
Religious, righteous, and inuiolate.
Fred. Assure your Grace tis superstition
To stand so strictly on dispensiue faith :
And should we lose the opportunity 2845
That God hath giuen to venge our Christians death
And scourge their foule blasphemous Paganisme,
As fell to *Saule*, to *Balaam*, and the rest,
That would not kill and curse at Gods command,
So surely will the vengeance of the highest 2850
And iealous anger of his fearefull arme
Be pour'd with rigour on our sinfull heads,
If we neglect this offered victory.
Sig. Then arme my Lords, and issue sodainly,
Giuing commandement to our generall hoste, 2855
With expedition to assaile the Pagan,
And take the victorie our God hath giuen. *Exeunt*.

2834 what we *1590*, *1606* : that we *1592*, *Dyce to Bull.* : we that *Rob.* 2839 faiths] fame *1606* and their] their *Rob.* : and *Dyce to Bull.* 2841 consummate *Dyce*² *etc.* : consinuate *1590*-*1606* : continuate *Rob.*, *Dyce*¹ : continent *conj. Mitford* 2853 this] the *1606*

Actus 2. *Scæna* 2.

Orcanes, Gazellus, Vribassa with their traine.

Orcanes. *Gazellus, Vribassa,* and the rest,
Now will we march from proud *Orminus* mount
To faire *Natolia,* where our neighbour kings 2860
Expect our power and our royall presence,
T'incounter with the cruell *Tamburlain,*
That nigh *Larissa* swaies a mighty hoste,
And with the thunder of his martial tooles
Makes Earthquakes in the hearts of men and heauen. 2865
Gaz. And now come we to make his sinowes shake,
With greater power than erst his pride hath felt,
An hundred kings by scores wil bid him armes,
And hundred thousands subiects to each score :
Which if a shower of wounding thunderbolts 2870
Should breake out off the bowels of the clowdes
And fall as thick as haile vpon our heads,
In partiall aid of that proud Scythian,
Yet should our courages and steeled crestes,
And numbers more than infinit of men, 2875
Be able to withstand and conquer him.
Vrib. Me thinks I see how glad the christian King
Is made, for ioy of your admitted truce :
That could not but before be terrified:
With vnacquainted power of our hoste. 2880

Enter a messenger.

Mess. Arme dread Soueraign and my noble Lords.
The treacherous army of the Christians,
Taking aduantage of your slender power,
Comes marching on us, and determines straight,
To bid vs battaile for our dearest liues. 2885
Orc. Traitors, villaines, damned Christians.
Haue I not here the articles of peace,
And solemne couenants we haue both confirm'd,
He by his Christ, and I by *Mahomet* ?
Gaz. Hel and confusion light vpon their heads, 2890
That with such treason seek our ouerthrow,
And cares so litle for their prophet Christ.

2864 martial] materiall *1592* 2869 And] An *Cunn.* thousand *Cunn., Wag.* 2878 your] our *1606, Dyce*

Orc. Can there be such deceit in Christians,
Or treason in the fleshly heart of man,
Whose shape is figure of the highest God? 2895
Then if there be a Christ, as Christians say,
But in their deeds deny him for their Christ:
If he be son to euerliuing *Ioue*,
And hath the power of his outstretched arme,
If he be iealous of his name and honor, 2900
As is our holy prophet *Mahomet*,
Take here these papers as our sacrifice
And witnesse of thy seruants periury.
Open thou shining vaile of *Cynthia*
And make a passage from the imperiall heauen 2905
That he that sits on high and neuer sleeps,
Nor in one place is circumscriptible,
But euery where fils euery Continent,
With strange infusion of his sacred vigor,
May in his endlesse power and puritie 2910
Behold and venge this Traitors periury.
Thou Christ that art esteem'd omnipotent,
If thou wilt prooue thy selfe a perfect God,
Worthy the worship of all faithfull hearts,
Be now reueng'd vpon this Traitors soule, 2915
And make the power I haue left behind
(Too litle to defend our guiltlesse liues)
Sufficient to discomfort and confound
The trustlesse force of those false Christians.
To armes my Lords, on Christ still let vs crie, 2920
If there be Christ, we shall haue victorie.

⟨*Exeunt.*⟩

Sound to the battell, and Sigismond comes out wounded.

Sig. Discomfited is all the Christian hoste,
And God hath thundered vengeance from on high,
For my accurst and hatefull periurie.
O iust and dreadfull punisher of sinne, 2925
Let the dishonor of the paines I feele,
In this my mortall well deserued wound,
End all my penance in my sodaine death,
And let this death wherein to sinne I die,
Conceiue a second life in endlesse mercie. 2930

2903 + S.D. He tears to pieces the articles of peace *add. Dyce* 2920 Lord *1606* 2921 S.D. Exeunt *add. Rob.* Scene III *inserted here Rob. to Bull.* 2922 Christians *1606*

Enter Orcanes, Gazellus, Vribassa, with others.

Or. Now lie the Christians bathing in their bloods,
And Christ or *Mahomet* hath bene my friend.
Gaz. See here the periur'd traitor *Hungary*,
Bloody and breathlesse for his villany.
Orc. Now shall his barbarous body be a pray 2935
To beasts and foules, and al the winds shall breath
Through shady leaues of euery sencelesse tree,
Murmures and hisses for his hainous sin.
Now scaldes his soule in the Tartarian streames,
And feeds vpon the banefull tree of hell, 2940
That *zoacum*, that fruit of bytternesse,
That in the midst of fire is ingraft,
Yet flourisheth as *Flora* in her pride,
With apples like the heads of damned Feends,
The Dyuils there in chaines of quencelesse flame, 2945
Shall lead his soule through *Orcus* burning gulfe:
From paine to paine, whose change shal neuer end:
What saiest thou yet *Gazellus* to his foile:
Which we referd to iustice of his Christ,
And to his power, which here appeares as full 2950
As raies of *Cynthia* to the clearest sight?
Gaz. Tis but the fortune of the wars my Lord,
Whose power is often proou'd a myracle.
Orc. Yet in my thoughts shall Christ be honoured,
Not dooing *Mahomet* an iniurie, 2955
Whose power had share in this our victory:
And since this miscreant hath disgrac'd his faith,
And died a traitor both to heauen and earth,
We wil both watch and ward shall keepe his trunke
Amidst these plaines, for Foules to pray vpon. 2960
Go *Vribassa*, giue it straight in charge.
Vri. I will my Lord. *Exit Vrib.*
Orc. And now *Gazellus*, let vs haste and meete
Our Army and our brother of *Ierusalem*,
Of *Soria*, *Trebizon* and *Amasia*, 2965
And happily with full Natolian bowles
Of Greekish wine now let vs celebrate
Our happy conquest, and his angry fate.
Exeunt.

2955 an] any *1606* 2959 shall] and *1606* 2961 giue] and giue *1592*

Actus 2. Scæna vltima.

The Arras is drawen, and Zenocrate lies in her bed of state, Tamburlaine sitting by her: three Phisitians about her bed, tempering potions. Theridamas, Techelles, Vsumcasane, and the three sonnes.

Tamburlaine.

Blacke is the beauty of the brightest day,
The golden balle of heauens eternal fire, 2970
That danc'd with glorie on the siluer waues:
Now wants the fewell that enflamde his beames
And all with faintnesse and for foule disgrace,
He bindes his temples with a frowning cloude,
Ready to darken earth with endlesse night: 2975
Zenocrate that gaue him light and life,
Whose eies shot fire from their Iuory bowers,
And tempered euery soule with liuely heat,
Now by the malice of the angry Skies,
Whose iealousie admits no second Mate, 2980
Drawes in the comfort of her latest breath
All dasled with the hellish mists of death.
Now walk the angels on the walles of heauen,
As Centinels to warne th' immortall soules,
To entertaine deuine *Zenocrate.* 2985
Apollo, Cynthia, and the ceaslesse lamps
That gently look'd vpon this loathsome earth,
Shine downwards now no more, but deck the heauens
To entertaine diuine *Zenocrate.*
The christall springs whose taste illuminates 2990
Refined eies with an eternall sight,
Like tried siluer runs through Paradice
To entertaine diuine *Zenocrate.*
The Cherubins and holy Seraphins
That sing and play before the king of kings, 2995
Vse all their voices and their instruments
To entertaine diuine *Zenocrate.*
And in this sweet and currious harmony,
The God that tunes this musicke to our soules:
Holds out his hand in highest maiesty 3000
To entertaine diuine *Zenocrate.*
Then let some holy trance conuay my thoughts,

2977 their *om. 1592* bowers] brows *Dyce* 2987 this] the *1606*

Vp to the pallace of th'imperiall heauen:
That this my life may be as short to me
As are the daies of sweet *Zenocrate*: 3005
Phisitions, wil no phisicke do her good?
Phis. My Lord, your Maiesty shall soone perceiue:
And if she passe this fit, the worst is past.
Tam. Tell me, how fares my faire *Zenocrate*?
Zen. I fare my Lord, as other Emperesses, 3010
That when this fraile and transitory flesh
Hath suckt the measure of that vitall aire
That feeds the body with his dated health,
Wanes with enforst and necessary change.
Tam. May neuer such a change transfourme my loue 3015
In whose sweet being I repose my life,
Whose heauenly presence beautified with health,
Giues light to *Phœbus* and the fixed stars,
Whose absence makes the sun and Moone as darke
As when opposde in one Diamiter 3020
Their Spheares are mounted on the serpents head,
Or els discended to his winding traine:
Liue still my Loue and so conserue my life,
Or dieng, be the author of my death.
Zen. Liue still my Lord, O let my soueraigne liue, 3025
And sooner let the fiery Element
Dissolue, and make your kingdome in the Sky,
Than this base earth should shroud your maiesty:
For should I but suspect your death by mine,
The comfort of my future happinesse 3030
And hope to meet your highnesse in the heauens,
Turn'd to dispaire, would break my wretched breast,
And furie would confound my present rest.
But let me die my Loue, yet let me die,
With loue and patience let your true loue die: 3035
Your griefe and furie hurtes my second life,
Yet let me kisse my Lord before I die,
And let me die with kissing of my Lord.
But since my life is lengthened yet a while,
Let me take leaue of these my louing sonnes, 3040
And of my Lords whose true nobilitie
Haue merited my latest memorie:
Sweet sons farewell, in death resemble me,

3006 no] not *1592* 3011 and] a *1592* 3024 author *1606*, *Dyce to Bull.*: anchor *1590*, *1592*, *Wag.* 3034 yet] yes *Rob.*, *Dyce*

And in your liues your fathers excellency.
Some musicke, and my fit wil cease my Lord. 3045

They call musicke.

Tam. Proud furie and intollorable fit,
That dares torment the body of my Loue,
And scourge the Scourge of the immortall God :
Now are those Spheares where *Cupid* vsde to sit,
Wounding the world with woonder and with loue, 3050
Sadly supplied with pale and ghastly death :
Whose darts do pierce the Center of my soule.
Her sacred beauty hath enchaunted heauen,
And had she liu'd before the siege of *Troy*,
Hellen, whose beauty sommond Greece to armes, 3055
And drew a thousand ships to *Tenedos*,
Had not bene nam'd in *Homers* Iliads :
Her name had bene in euery line he wrote :
Or had those wanton Poets, for whose byrth
Olde *Rome* was proud, but gasde a while on her, 3060
Nor *Lesbia*, nor *Corrinna* had bene nam'd,
Zenocrate had bene the argument
Of euery Epigram or Eligie.

The musicke sounds, and she dies.

Tam. What, is she dead? *Techelles*, draw thy sword,
And wound the earth, that it may cleaue in twaine, 3065
And we discend into th'infernall vaults,
To haile the fatall Sisters by the haire,
And throw them in the triple mote of Hell,
For taking hence my faire *Zenocrate*.
Casane and *Theridamas* to armes, 3070
Raise Caualieros higher than the cloudes,
And with the cannon breake the frame of heauen,
Batter the shining pallace of the Sun,
And shiuer all the starry firmament :
For amorous *Ioue* hath snatcht my loue from hence, 3075
Meaning to make her stately Queene of heauen.
What God so euer holds thee in his armes,
Giuing thee Nectar and Ambrosia,
Behold me here diuine *Zenocrate*,
Rauing, impatient, desperate and mad, 3080
Breaking my steeled lance, with which I burst
The rusty beames of *Ianus* Temple doores,

3044 excellence *1606*, *Dyce to Bull.* 3045 S.D. call] call for *1606*

Letting out death and tyrannising war:
To martch with me vnder this bloody flag,
And if thou pitiest *Tamburlain* the great, 3085
Come downe from heauen and liue with me againe.
Ther. Ah good my Lord be patient, she is dead,
And all this raging cannot make her liue,
If woords might serue, our voice hath rent the aire,
If teares, our eies haue watered all the earth : 3090
If griefe, our murthered harts haue straind forth blood.
Nothing preuailes, for she is dead my Lord.
Tam. For she is dead? thy words doo pierce my soule.
Ah sweet *Theridamas*, say so no more,
Though she be dead, yet let me think she liues, 3095
And feed my mind that dies for want of her :
Where ere her soule be, thou shalt stay with me
Embalm'd with Cassia, Amber Greece and Myrre,
Not lapt in lead but in a sheet of gold,
And till I die thou shalt not be interr'd. 3100
Then in as rich a tombe as *Mausolus*,
We both will rest and haue one Epitaph
Writ in as many seuerall languages,
As I haue conquered kingdomes with my sword.
This cursed towne will I consume with fire, 3105
Because this place bereft me of my Loue :
The houses burnt, wil looke as if they mourn'd
And here will I set vp her stature,
And martch about it with my mourning campe,
Drooping and pining for *Zenocrate*. 3110
The Arras is drawen.

Actus 3. *Scæna* 1.

Enter the kings of Trebisond and Soria, one bringing a sword, & another a scepter : Next Natolia and Ierusalem with the Emperiall crowne : After Calapine, and after him other Lordes : Orcanes and Ierusalem crowne him and the other giue him the scepter.

Orca. *Calepinus Cyricelibes*, otherwise *Cybelius*, son and successiue heire to the late mighty Emperour *Baiazeth*, by

3097 S.D. To the body *add. Dyce after* thou 3100 shall *1606*
3102 one *1590*, *Dyce*, *Wag.*: on *1592*: our *1606*, *Rob.*, *Cunn.*, *Bull.*
3108 stature *1590*, *1592*, *Wag.*: statue *1606*, *Rob.*: statua *conj. Dyce*, *Cunn.*, *Bull.* Actus 3 *etc.* S.D. Lordes] Lords and Almeda *Dyce etc.* crowne him] crown Callapine *Dyce*

the aid of God and his friend *Mahomet*, Emperour of *Natolia, Ierusalem, Trebizon, Soria, Amasia, Thracia, Illyria, Carmonia* and al the hundred and thirty Kingdomes late contributory to his mighty father. Long liue *Callepinus*, Emperour of Turky. 3117

Cal. Thrice worthy kings of *Natolia*, and the rest,
I will requite your royall gratitudes
With all the benefits my Empire yeelds: 3120
And were the sinowes of th'imperiall seat
So knit and strengthned, as when *Baiazeth*
My royall Lord and father fild the throne,
Whose cursed fate hath so dismembred it,
Then should you see this Thiefe of *Scythia*, 3125
This proud vsurping king of *Persea*,
Do vs such honor and supremacie,
Bearing the vengeance of our fathers wrongs,
As all the world should blot our dignities
Out of the booke of base borne infamies. 3130
And now I doubt not but your royall cares
Hath so prouided for this cursed foe,
That since the heire of mighty *Baiazeth*
(An Emperour so honoured for his vertues)
Reuiues the spirits of true Turkish heartes, 3135
In grieuous memorie of his fathers shame,
We shall not need to nourish any doubt,
But that proud Fortune, who hath followed long
The martiall sword of mighty *Tamburlaine*,
Will now retaine her olde inconstancie, 3140
And raise our honors to as high a pitch
In this our strong and fortunate encounter.
For so hath heauen prouided my escape,
From al the crueltie my soule sustaind,
By this my friendly keepers happy meanes, 3145
That *Ioue* surchardg'd with pity of our wrongs,
Will poure it downe in showers on our heads:
Scourging the pride of cursed *Tamburlain*.

Orc. I haue a hundred thousand men in armes,
Some, that in conquest of the periur'd Christian, 3150
Being a handfull to a mighty hoste,
Thinke them in number yet sufficient,
To drinke the riuer *Nile* or *Euphrates*,
And for their power, ynow to win the world.

3124 Fates *1606* 3129 our] his *Dyce, Bull.* 3135 of] of all *1592, Dyce to Bull.* 3141 honour *1606* 3150 in] in the *1592*

Ier. And I as many from *Ierusalem*, 3155
Iudæa, Gaza, and *Scalonians* bounds,
That on mount *Sinay* with their ensignes spread,
Looke like the parti-coloured cloudes of heauen,
That shew faire weather to the neighbor morne.
Treb. And I as many bring from *Trebizon*, 3160
Chio, Famastro, and *Amasia*,
All bordring on the *Mare-maior* sea:
Riso, Sancina, and the bordering townes,
That touch the end of famous *Euphrates*,
Whose courages are kindled with the flames, 3165
The cursed Scythian sets on all their townes,
And vow to burne the villaines cruell heart.
Sor. From *Soria* with seuenty thousand strong,
Tane from *Aleppo, Soldino, Tripoly*,
And so vnto my citie of *Damasco*, 3170
I march to meet and aide my neigbor kings,
All which will ioine against this *Tamburlain*,
And bring him captiue to your highnesse feet.
Orc. Our battaile then in martiall maner pitcht,
According to our ancient vse, shall beare 3175
The figure of the semi-circled Moone:
Whose hornes shall sprinkle through the tainted aire,
The poisoned braines of this proud Scythian.
Cal. Wel then my noble Lords, for this my friend,
That freed me from the bondage of my foe: 3180
I thinke it requisite and honorable,
To keep my promise, and to make him king,
That is a Gentleman (I know) at least.
Alm. That's no matter sir, for being a king, for *Tamburlain* came vp of nothing. 3185
Ier. Your Maiesty may choose some pointed time,
Perfourming all your promise to the full:
Tis nought for your maiesty to giue a kingdome.
Cal. Then wil I shortly keep my promise *Almeda*.
Alm. Why, I thank your Maiesty. 3190
Exeunt.

3156 Iuda *1606* Scalonians] Sclauonians *1606*: Sclavonia's *Rob. etc.*

Actus 3. *Scæna* 2.

Tamburlaine with Vsumcasane, and his three sons, foure bearing the hearse of Zenocrate, and the drums sounding a dolefull martch, the Towne burning.

Tamb. So, burne the turrets of this cursed towne,
Flame to the highest region of the aire:
And kindle heaps of exhalations,
That being fiery meteors, may presage,
Death and destruction to th'inhabitants. 3195
Ouer my Zenith hang a blazing star,
That may endure till heauen be dissolu'd,
Fed with the fresh supply of earthly dregs,
Threatning a death and famine to this land,
Flieng Dragons, lightning, fearfull thunderclaps, 3200
Sindge these fair plaines, and make them seeme as black
As is the Island where the Furies maske
Compast with *Lethe*, *Styx* and *Phlegeton*,
Because my deare *Zenocrate* is dead.
Cal⟨yphas⟩. This Piller plac'd in memorie of her, 3205
Where in Arabian, Hebrew, Greek, is writ
This towne being burnt by Tamburlaine the great,
Forbids the world to build it vp againe.
Amy⟨ras⟩. And here this mournful streamer shal be plac'd
Wrought with the Persean and Egyptian armes 3210
To signifie she was a princesse borne,
And wife vnto the Monarke of the East.
Celib⟨inus⟩. And here this table as a Register
Of all her vertues and perfections.
Tam. And here the picture of *Zenocrate*, 3215
To shew her beautie, which the world admyr'd,
Sweet picture of diuine *Zenocrate*,
That hanging here, wil draw the Gods from heauen:
And cause the stars fixt in the Southern arke,
Whose louely faces neuer any viewed, 3220
That haue not past the Centers latitude,
As Pilgrimes traueile to our Hemi-spheare,
Onely to gaze vpon *Zenocrate*.
Thou shalt not beautifie *Larissa* plaines,
But keep within the circle of mine armes. 3225
At euery towne and castle I besiege,

3199 death *1590–1606*, *Rob.*: dearth *Dyce etc.* 3207 being] was *conj. Brereton* 3210 and *1590*, *1606*, *Wag.*: and the *1592*

Thou shalt be set vpon my royall tent.
And when I meet an armie in the field,
Those looks will shed such influence in my campe,
As if *Bellona*, Goddesse of the war 3230
Threw naked swords and sulphur bals of fire,
Vpon the heads of all our enemies.
And now my Lords, aduance your speares againe,
Sorrow no more my sweet *Casane* now :
Boyes leaue to mourne, this towne shall euer mourne, 3235
Being burnt to cynders for your mothers death.
Cal. If I had wept a sea of teares for her,
It would not ease the sorrow I sustaine.
Amy. As is that towne, so is my heart consum'd,
With griefe and sorrow for my mothers death. 3240
Cel. My mothers death hath mortified my mind,
And sorrow stops the passage of my speech.
Tamb. But now my boies, leaue off, and list to me,
That meane to teach you rudiments of war :
Ile haue you learne to sleepe vpon the ground, 3245
March in your armour throwe watery Fens,
Sustaine the scortching heat and freezing cold,
Hunger and thirst right adiuncts of the war.
And after this, to scale a castle wal,
Besiege a fort, to vndermine a towne, 3250
And make whole cyties caper in the aire.
Then next, the way to fortifie your men,
In champion grounds, what figure serues you best,
For which the *quinque*-angle fourme is meet,
Because the corners there may fall more flat : 3255
Whereas the Fort may fittest be assailde,
And sharpest where th'assault is desperate.
The ditches must be deepe, the Counterscarps
Narrow and steepe, the wals made high and broad,
The Bulwarks and the rampiers large and strong, 3260
With Caualieros and thicke counterforts,
And roome within to lodge sixe thousand men
It must haue priuy ditches, countermines,
And secret issuings to defend the ditch.
It must haue high Argins and couered waies 3265
To keep the bulwark fronts from battery,
And Parapets to hide the Muscatters :

3229 Those *Dyce etc.*: Whose *1590–1606* 3238 sorrows *1592, Rob. to Bull.* 3248 thirst *1606 etc.*: cold *1590, 1592* 3254 which *Rob. etc.*: with *1590–1606* 3258 the] and *1606*

Casemates to place the great Artillery,
And store of ordinance that from euery flanke
May scoure the outward curtaines of the Fort, 3270
Dismount the Cannon of the aduerse part,
Murther the Foe and saue their walles from breach.
When this is learn'd for seruice on the land,
By plaine and easie demonstration,
Ile teach you how to make the water mount, 3275
That you may dryfoot martch through lakes & pooles,
Deep riuers, hauens, creekes, and litle seas,
And make a Fortresse in the raging waues,
Fenc'd with the concaue of a monstrous rocke,
Inuincible by nature of the place. 3280
When this is done, then are ye souldiers,
And worthy sonnes of *Tamburlain* the great.
Cal. My Lord, but this is dangerous to be done,
We may be slaine or wounded ere we learne.
Tam. Villain, art thou the sonne of *Tamburlaine*, 3285
And fear'st to die, or with a Curtle-axe
To hew thy flesh and make a gaping wound?
Hast thou beheld a peale of ordinance strike
A ring of pikes, mingled with shot and horse,
Whose shattered lims, being tost as high as heauen, 3290
Hang in the aire as thicke as sunny motes,
And canst thou Coward stand in feare of death?
Hast thou not seene my horsmen charge the foe,
Shot through the armes, cut ouerthwart the hands,
Dieng their lances with their streaming blood, 3295
And yet at night carrouse within my tent,
Filling their empty vaines with aiery wine,
That being concocted, turnes to crimson blood,
And wilt thou shun the field for feare of woundes?
View me thy father that hath conquered kings, 3300
And with his hoste martch round about the earth,
Quite voide of skars, and cleare from any wound,
That by the warres lost not a dram of blood,
And see him lance his flesh to teach you all.

He cuts his arme.

3268 great] greatst *1606* 3272 their] the *Dyce etc.* 3280 by] by the *1606* 3281 ye] you *1606* 3286 a] the *1592, Rob., Bull.* 3289 shot] foot *conj. Dyce* mingled . . horse] and horse, mangled with shot *conj. Mitford*: of mingled foot and horse *conj. Cunn.* 3301 his] this *1606* marcht *1606 etc.* 3303 dram] drop *1592, Rob. to Bull.*

A wound is nothing be it nere so deepe, 3309
Blood is the God of Wars rich liuery.
Now look I like a souldier, and this wound
As great a grace and maiesty to me,
As if a chaire of gold enamiled,
Enchac'd with Diamondes, Saphyres, Rubies 3310
And fairest pearle of welthie *India*
Were mounted here vnder a Canapie :
And I sat downe, cloth'd with the massie robe,
That late adorn'd the Affrike Potentate,
Whom I brought bound vnto *Damascus* walles. 3315
Come boyes and with your fingers search my wound,
And in my blood wash all your hands at once,
While I sit smiling to behold the sight.
Now my boyes, what think you of a wound?

Cal. I know not what I should think of it. Me thinks tis a pitifull sight. 3321

Cel. Tis nothing: giue me a wound father.

Amy. And me another my Lord.

Tam. Come sirra, giue me your arme.

Cel. Here father, cut it brauely as you did your own. 3325

Tam. It shall suffice thou darst abide a wound.
My boy, thou shalt not loose a drop of blood,
Before we meet the armie of the Turke.
But then run desperate through the thickest throngs,
Dreadlesse of blowes, of bloody wounds and death: 3330
And let the burning of *Larissa* wals,
My speech of war, and this my wound you see
Teach you my boyes to beare couragious minds,
Fit for the followers of great *Tamburlaine*.
Vsumcasane now come let vs martch 3335
Towards *Techelles* and *Theridamas*,
That we haue sent before to fire the townes,
The towers and cities of these hatefull Turks,
And hunt that Coward, faintheart, runaway,
With that accursed traitor *Almeda*, 3340
Til fire and sword haue found them at a bay.

Vsu. I long to pierce his bowels with my sword,
That hath betraied my gracious Soueraigne,
That curst and damned Traitor *Almeda*.

Tam. Then let vs see if coward *Calapine* 3345
Dare leuie armes against our puissance,

3313 the] a *1592, 1606, Rob. to Bull.* 3319 you] ye *1592, Dyce to Bull.* 3340 accursed] cursed *1592* 3342 his] the *1592*

That we may tread vpon his captiue necke,
And treble all his fathers slaueries. *Exeunt.*

Actus 3. Scæna 3.

Techelles, Theridamas and their traine.

Therid. Thus haue wee martcht Northwarde from *Tamburlaine,*
Vnto the frontier point of *Soria* : 3350
And this is *Balsera* their chiefest hold,
Wherein is all the treasure of the land.
Tech. Then let vs bring our light Artilery,
Minions, Fauknets, and Sakars to the trench,
Filling the ditches with the walles wide breach, 3355
And enter in, to seaze vpon the gold :
How say ye Souldiers, Shal we not ?
Soul. Yes, my Lord, yes, come lets about it.
Ther. But stay a while, summon a parle, Drum,
It may be they will yeeld it quietly, 3360
Knowing two kings, the friends to *Tamburlain,*
Stand at the walles, with such a mighty power.

Summon the battell. Captaine with his wife and sonne.

Cap. What requier you my maisters ?
Ther. Captaine, that thou yeeld vp thy hold to vs.
Cap. To you ? Why, do you thinke me weary of it ?
Tech. Nay Captain, thou art weary of thy life, 3366
If thou withstand the friends of *Tamburlain.*
Ther. These Pioners of *Argier* in Affrica,
Euen in the cannons face shall raise a hill
Of earth and fagots higher than thy Fort, 3370
And ouer thy Argins and couered waies
Shal play vpon the bulwarks of thy hold
Volleies of ordinance til the breach be made,
That with his ruine fils vp all the trench.
And when we enter in, not heauen it selfe 3375
Shall ransome thee, thy wife and family.
Tech. Captaine, these Moores shall cut the leaden pipes,

3349 Northwarde] southward *conj. Cunn.* 3350 point] port *1606, Rob., Cunn.* 3356 gold *1590–1606, Rob., Cunn., Bull.* : hold *Dyce, Wag.* 3357 we] we or *Bull.* 3360 quietly] quickely *1606* 3361 friend *1590, 1592* 3365 do you] do thou *1592* 3369 in] to *1606*

That bring fresh water to thy men and thee,
And lie in trench before thy castle walles :
That no supply of victuall shall come in, 3380
Nor ⟨any⟩ issue foorth, but they shall die :
And therefore Captaine, yeeld it quietly.

Cap. Were you that are the friends of *Tamburlain*
Brothers to holy *Mahomet* himselfe,
I would not yeeld it : therefore doo your worst. 3385
Raise mounts, batter, intrench, and vndermine,
Cut off the water, all conuoies that can,
Yet I am resolute, and so farewell. ⟨*Exeunt.*⟩

Ther. Pioners away, and where I stuck the stake,
Intrench with those dimensions I prescribed : 3390
Cast vp the earth towards the castle wall,
Which til it may defend you, labour low :
And few or none shall perish by their shot.

Pion. We will my Lord. *Exeunt.*

Tech. A hundred horse shall scout about the plaines
To spie what force comes to relieue the holde. 3396
Both we (*Theridamas*) wil intrench our men,
And with the Iacobs staffe measure the height
And distance of the castle from the trench,
That we may know if our artillery 3400
Will carie full point blancke vnto their wals

Ther. Then see the bringing of our ordinance
Along the trench into the battery,
Where we will haue Gabions of sixe foot broad,
To saue our Cannoniers from musket shot, 3405
Betwixt which, shall our ordinance thunder foorth,
And with the breaches fall. smoake, fire, and dust,
The cracke, the Ecchoe and the souldiers crie
Make deafe the aire, and dim the Christall Sky.

Tech. Trumpets and drums, alarum presently, 3410
And souldiers play the men, the hold is yours.
⟨*Exeunt.*⟩

3381 any *add. Rob.* 3382 quietly] quickely *1606* 3383 you . . the] all you that are *1606* 3384 to] of *1592*, *Rob.*, *Dyce*, *Bull.* 3387 that can] that come *Rob.* : you can *Cunn.* 3388 I am] am I *1606* S.D. *add. Rob.* 3403 into] vnto *1606* 3404 gabions *conj. Broughton*, *conj. Coll.*, *Cunn.*, *Bull.* : Galions *1590–1606* 3411 hold] holds, *1590*, *1592* S.D. *add. Rob.*

⟨*Scene* 4.⟩

Enter the Captaine with ⟨*Olympia*⟩ *his wife and sonne.*

Olym. Come good my Lord, & let vs haste from hence
Along the caue that leads beyond the foe,
No hope is left to saue this conquered hold.
Cap. A deadly bullet gliding through my side, 3415
Lies heauy on my heart, I cannot liue.
I feele my liuer pierc'd and all my vaines,
That there begin and nourish euery part,
Mangled and torne, and all my entrals bath'd
In blood that straineth from their orifex. 3420
Farewell sweet wife, sweet son farewell, I die.
Olym. Death, whether art thou gone that both we liue?
Come back again (sweet death) & strike vs both:
One minute end our daies, and one sepulcher
Containe our bodies: death, why comm'st thou not? 3425
Wel, this must be the messenger for thee.
Now vgly death stretch out thy Sable wings,
And carie both our soules, where his remaines.
Tell me sweet boie, art thou content to die?
These barbarous Scythians full of cruelty, 3430
And Moores, in whom was neuer pitie found,
Will hew vs peecemeale, put vs to the wheele,
Or els inuent some torture worse than that,
Therefore die by thy louing mothers hand,
Who gently now wil lance thy Iuory throat, 3435
And quickly rid thee both of paine and life.
Son. Mother dispatch me, or Ile kil my selfe,
For think ye I can liue, and see him dead?
Giue me your knife, (good mother) or strike home:
The Scythians shall not tyrannise on me. 3440
Sweet mother strike, that I may meet my father.

She stabs him.

Olym. Ah sacred *Mahomet*, if this be sin,
Intreat a pardon of the God of heauen,
And purge my soule before it come to thee.

Scene 4] Scene 3 *continued 1590–1606, Rob.* S.D. Enter the] Enter *1606* Olympia *add. Dyce* 3420 straineth] staineth *1592* orifex] orifice *Rob.*

Enter Theridamas, Techelles and all their traine.

Ther. How now Madam, what are you doing? 3445
Olim. Killing my selfe, as I haue done my sonne,
Whose body with his fathers I haue burnt,
Least cruell Scythians should dismember him.
Tech. Twas brauely done, and like a souldiers wife.
Thou shalt with vs to *Tamburlaine* the great, 3450
Who when he heares how resolute thou wert,
Wil match thee with a viceroy or a king.
Olym. My Lord deceast, was dearer vnto me,
Than any Viceroy, King or Emperour,
And for his sake here will I end my daies. 3455
Ther. But Lady goe with vs to *Tamburlaine*,
And thou shalt see a man greater than *Mahomet*,
In whose high lookes is much more maiesty
Than from the Concaue superficies
Of *Ioues* vast pallace the imperiall Orbe, 3460
Vnto the shining bower where *Cynthia* sits,
Like louely *Thetis* in a Christall robe:
That treadeth Fortune vnderneath his feete,
And makes the mighty God of armes his slaue:
On whom death and the fatall sisters waite, 3465
With naked swords and scarlet liueries:
Before whom (mounted on a Lions backe)
Rhamnusia beares a helmet ful of blood,
And strowes the way with braines of slaughtered men:
By whose proud side the vgly furies run, 3470
Harkening when he shall bid them plague the world.
Ouer whose Zenith cloth'd in windy aire,
And Eagles wings ioin'd to her feathered breast,
Fame houereth, sounding of her golden Trumpe:
That to the aduerse poles of that straight line, 3475
Which measureth the glorious frame of heauen,
The name of mightie *Tamburlain* is spread:
And him faire Lady shall thy eies behold.
Come.
Olim. Take pitie of a Ladies ruthfull teares, 3480
That humbly craues vpon her knees to stay,
And cast her bodie in the burning flame,
That feeds vpon her sonnes and husbands flesh.
Tech. Madam, sooner shall fire consume vs both,

3451 wert] art *1606, Rob., Cunn., Bull.* 3457 *Qy. omit* man?
3473 ioin'd] inioin'd *1592* 3474 of] in *1606, Cunn.*

Then scortch a face so beautiful as this, 3485
In frame of which, Nature hath shewed more skill,
Than when she gaue eternall *Chaos* forme,
Drawing from it the shining Lamps of heauen.
Ther. Madam, I am so far in loue with you,
That you must goe with vs, no remedy. 3490
Olim. Then carie me I care not where you will,
And let the end of this my fatall iourney,
Be likewise end to my accursed life.
Tech. No Madam, but the beginning of your ioy,
Come willinglie, therfore. 3495
Ther. Souldiers now let vs meet the Generall,
Who by this time is at *Natolia*,
Ready to charge the army of the Turke.
The gold, the siluer, and the pearle ye got,
Rifling this Fort, deuide in equall shares: 3500
This Lady shall haue twice so much againe,
Out of the coffers of our treasurie.
Exeunt.

Actus 3. *Scæna* 5.

Callepine, Orcanes, Ierusalem, Trebizon, Soria, Almeda, with their traine ⟨*and Messenger*⟩.

Messenger. Renowmed Emperour, mighty *Callepine*,
Gods great lieftenant ouer all the world:
Here at *Alepo* with an hoste of men 3505
Lies *Tamburlaine*, this king of *Persea*:
In number more than are the quyuering leaues
Of *Idas* forrest, where your highnesse hounds,
With open crie pursues the wounded Stag:
Who meanes to gyrt *Natolias* walles with siege, 3510
Fire the towne and ouerrun the land.
Cal. My royal army is as great as his,
That from the bounds of *Phrigia* to the sea
Which washeth *Cyprus* with his brinish waues,
Couers the hils, the valleies and the plaines. 3515
Viceroies and Peeres of Turky play the men,
Whet all your swords to mangle *Tamburlain*,

3494 the *om. Cunn., Bull.* 3499 the siluer] and siluer *1592, Rob. to Bull.* ye] we *Bull.* 3502 S.D. and a Messenger *add. Dyce.* 3503 and mighty *1606* 3517 your] our *1606*

His sonnes, his Captaines and his followers,
By *Mahomet* not one of them shal liue.
The field wherin this battaile shall be fought, 3520
For euer terme, the Perseans sepulchre,
In memorie of this our victory.
Orc. Now, he that cals himself the scourge of *Ioue,*
The Emperour of the world, and earthly God,
Shal end the warlike progresse he intends, 3525
And traueile hedlong to the lake of hell:
Where legions of deuils (knowing he must die
Here in *Natolia*, by your highnesse hands)
All brandishing their brands of quenchlesse fire,
Streching their monstrous pawes, grin with their teeth,
And guard the gates to entertaine his soule. 3531
Cal. Tel me Viceroies the number of your men,
And what our Army royall is esteem'd.
Ier. From *Palestina* and *Ierusalem*,
Of Hebrewes, three score thousand fighting men 3535
Are come since last we shewed your maiesty.
Orc. So from *Arabia* desart, and the bounds
Of that sweet land, whose braue Metropolis
Reedified the faire *Semyramis*,
Came forty thousand warlike foot and horse, 3540
Since last we numbred to your Maiesty.
Treb. From *Trebizon* in *Asia* the lesse,
Naturalized Turks and stout Bythinians
Came to my bands full fifty thousand more,
That fighting, knowes not what retreat doth meane, 3545
Nor ere returne but with the victory,
Since last we numbred to your maiesty.
Sor. Of Sorians from *Halla* is repair'd
And neighbor cities of your highnesse land,
Ten thousand horse, and thirty thousand foot, 3550
Since last we numbred to your maiestie:
So that the Army royall is esteem'd
Six hundred thousand valiant fighting men.
Callep. Then welcome *Tamburlaine* vnto thy death.
Come puissant Viceroies, let vs to the field, 3555
(The Perseans Sepulchre) and sacrifice
Mountaines of breathlesse men to *Mahomet*,

3521 terme] term'd *conj. Dyce*[1], *Dyce*[2] 3523 the *om. 1592* 3528 your] our *1606* 3529 their] in their *1592* 3530 pawes] jaws *Cunn.* with *om. 1592* 3536 your] to your *1606*, *Rob.* 3548 repair'd] prepar'd *1606* 3549 *om. 1606*

Who now with *Ioue* opens the firmament,
To see the slaughter of our enemies.

Tamburlaine with his three sonnes, Vsumcasane with other.

Tam. How now *Casane*? See a knot of kings, 3560
Sitting as if they were a telling ridles.
Vsu. My Lord, your presence makes them pale and wan.
Poore soules they looke as if their deaths were neere.
Tamb. Why, so he is *Casane*, I am here,
But yet Ile saue their liues and make them slaues. 3565
Ye petty kings of Turkye I am come,
As *Hector* did into the Grecian campe,
To ouerdare the pride of *Græcia*,
And set his warlike person to the view
Of fierce *Achilles*, riuall of his fame. 3570
I doe you honor in the *simile*,
For if I should as *Hector* did *Achilles*,
(The worthiest knight that euer brandisht sword)
Challenge in combat any of you all,
I see how fearfully ye would refuse, 3575
And fly my gloue as from a Scorpion.
Orc. Now thou art fearfull of thy armies strength,
Thou wouldst with ouermatch of person fight,
But Shepheards issue, base borne *Tamburlaine*,
Thinke of thy end, this sword shall lance thy throat. 3580
Tamb. Villain, the shepheards issue, at whose byrth
Heauen did affoord a gratious aspect,
And ioin'd those stars that shall be opposite,
Euen till the dissolution of the world,
And neuer meant to make a Conquerour, 3585
So famous as is mighty *Tamburlain*:
Shall so torment thee and that *Callapine*,
That like a roguish runnaway, suborn'd
That villaine there, that slaue, that Turkish dog,
To false his seruice to his Soueraigne, 3590
As ye shal curse the byrth of *Tamburlaine*.
Cal. Raile not proud Scythian, I shall now reuenge
My fathers vile abuses and mine owne.
Ier. By *Mahomet* he shal be tied in chaines,
Rowing with Christians in a Brigandine, 3595
About the Grecian Isles to rob and spoile:

3559 S.D. others *1592* 3563 death *Cunn.* 3564 Why] And *Rob., Cunn., Bull* he] it *1606, Rob.* 3586 is] the *1606*

And turne him to his ancient trade againe.
Me thinks the slaue should make a lusty theefe.

Cal. Nay, when the battaile ends, al we wil meet,
And sit in councell to inuent some paine, 3600
That most may vex his body and his soule.

Tam. Sirha, *Callapine,* Ile hang a clogge about your necke for running away againe, you shall not trouble me thus to come and fetch you.
But as for you (Viceroy) you shal haue bits, 3605
And harnest like my horses, draw my coch:
And when ye stay, be lasht with whips of wier,
Ile haue you learne to feed on prouander,
And in a stable lie vpon the planks.

Orc. But *Tamburlaine,* first thou shalt kneele to vs
And humbly craue a pardon for thy life. 3611

Treb. The common souldiers of our mighty hoste
Shal bring thee bound vnto the Generals tent.

Sor. And all haue iointly sworne thy cruell death,
Or bind thee in eternall torments wrath. 3615

Tam. Wel sirs, diet your selues, you knowe I shall haue occasion shortly to iourney you.

Cel. See father, how *Almeda* the Iaylor lookes vpon vs.

Tam. Villaine, traitor, damned fugitiue,
Ile make thee wish the earth had swallowed thee: 3620
Seest thou not death within my wrathfull looks.
Goe villaine, cast thee headlong from a rock,
Or rip thy bowels, and rend out thy heart,
T' appease my wrath, or els Ile torture thee,
Searing thy hatefull flesh with burning yrons, 3625
And drops of scalding lead, while all thy ioints
Be rackt and beat asunder with the wheele,
For if thou liuest, not any Element
Shal shrowde thee from the wrath of *Tamburlaine.*

Cal. Wel, in despight of thee he shall be king: 3630
Come *Almeda,* receiue this crowne of me.
I here inuest thee king of *Ariadan,*
Bordering on *Mare Roso* neere to *Meca.*

Or. What, take it man.

Al. Good my Lord, let me take it. 3635

Cal. Doost thou aske him leaue? Here, take it.

3608 on] with *1592* 3610 thou shalt] shalt thou *1606* 3613 the] our *1606, Rob., Cunn., Bull* 3623 and rend *1590, Rob., Wag.*: and rent *1592, Dyce to Bull*: or rend *1606* 3627 beat] rent *conj. Coll.*

Tam. Go too sirha, take your crown, and make vp the halfe dozen. So sirha, now you are a king you must giue armes.

Or. So he shal, and weare thy head in his Scutchion.

Tamb. No, let him hang a bunch of keies on his standerd, to put him in remembrance he was a Iailor, that when I take him, I may knocke out his braines with them, and lock you in the stable, when you shall come sweating from my chariot.

Treb. Away, let vs to the field, that the villaine may be slaine. 3646

Tamb. Sirha, prepare whips, and bring my chariot to my Tent: For as soone as the battaile is done, Ile ride in triumph through the Camp.

Enter Theridamas, Techelles, and their traine.

How now ye pety kings, loe, here are Bugges 3650
Wil make the haire stand vpright on your heads,
And cast your crownes in slauery at their feet.
Welcome *Theridamas* and *Techelles* both,
See ye this rout, and know ye this same king?

Ther. I, my Lord, he was *Calapines* keeper. 3655

Tam. Wel, now you see hee is a king, looke to him *Theridamas*, when we are fighting, least hee hide his crowne as the foolish king of *Persea* did.

Sor. No *Tamburlaine*, hee shall not be put to that Exigent, I warrant thee. 3660

Tam. You knowe not sir:
But now my followers and my louing friends,
Fight as you euer did, like Conquerours,
The glorie of this happy day is yours:
My sterne aspect shall make faire Victory, 3665
Houering betwixt our armies, light on me,
Loden with Lawrell wreathes to crowne vs all.

Tech. I smile to think, how when this field is fought,
And rich *Natolia* ours, our men shall sweat
With carrieng pearle and treasure on their backes. 3670

Tamb. You shall be princes all immediatly:
Come fight ye Turks, or yeeld vs victory.

Or. No, we wil meet thee slauish *Tamburlain.*

Exeunt.

3637 too *om.* *1606* 3640 No] Go 1592 3654 know ye] know you *1606* 3656 you] ye *1592, Rob. to Bull.* 3665 aspects *1606* 3667 Laden *1606*

Actus 4. Scæna 1.

Alarme: Amyras and Celebinus issues from the tent where Caliphas sits a sleepe.

⟨*Amyras.*⟩ Now in their glories shine the golden crownes
Of these proud Turks, much like so many suns 3675
That halfe dismay the maiesty of heauen:
Now brother, follow we our fathers sword,
That flies with fury swifter than our thoughts,
And cuts down armies with his conquering swings.
Cel. Call foorth our laisie brother from the tent, 3680
For if my father misse him in the field,
Wrath kindled in the furnace of his breast,
Wil send a deadly lightening to his heart.
Amy. Brother, ho, what, giuen so much to sleep
You cannot leaue it, when our enemies drums 3685
And ratling cannons thunder in our eares
Our proper ruine, and our fathers foile?
Cal. Away ye fools, my father needs not me,
Nor you in faith, but that you wil be thought
More childish valourous than manly wise: 3690
If halfe our campe should sit and sleepe with me,
My father were enough to scar the foe:
You doo dishonor to his maiesty,
To think our helps will doe him any good.
Amy. What, dar'st thou then be absent from the fight,
Knowing my father hates thy cowardise, 3696
And oft hath warn'd thee to be stil in field,
When he himselfe amidst the thickest troopes
Beats downe our foes to flesh our taintlesse swords.
Cal. I know sir, what it is to kil a man, 3700
It works remorse of conscience in me,
I take no pleasure to be murtherous,
Nor care for blood when wine wil quench my thirst.
Cel. O cowardly boy, fie for shame, come foorth.
Thou doost dishonor manhood, and thy house. 3705
Cal. Goe, goe tall stripling, fight you for vs both,
And take my other toward brother here,
For person like to prooue a second *Mars*,

3674 *Prefix om. 1590, 1606* 3679 conquering swings *Wag.*: conquerings wings *1590*: conquering wings *1592, 1606, Rob. to Bull.* 3685 You cannot] Can you not *1606* 3687 ruine] ruins *Rob., Cunn.*

Twill please my mind as wel to heare both you
Haue won a heape of honor in the field, 3710
And left your slender carkasses behind,
As if I lay with you for company.
Amy. You wil not goe then?
Cal. You say true.
Amy. Were all the lofty mounts of *Zona mundi,* 3715
That fill the midst of farthest *Tartary,*
Turn'd into pearle and proffered for my stay,
I would not bide the furie of my father:
When made a victor in these hautie arms,
He comes and findes his sonnes haue had no shares 3720
In all the honors he proposde for vs.
Cal. Take you the honor, I will take my ease,
My wisedome shall excuse my cowardise:
I goe into the field before I need?

Alarme, and Amy. and Celeb. run in.

The bullets fly at random where they list. 3725
And should I goe and kill a thousand men,
I were as soone rewarded with a shot,
And sooner far than he that neuer fights.
And should I goe and do nor harme nor good,
I might haue harme, which all the good I haue 3730
Ioin'd with my fathers crowne would neuer cure.
Ile to cardes: *Perdicas.*

⟨*Enter Perdicas.*⟩

Perd. Here my Lord.
Cal. Come, thou and I wil goe to cardes to driue away the time. 3735
Per. Content my Lord, but what shal we play for?
Cal. Who shal kisse the fairest of the Turkes Concubines first, when my father hath conquered them.
Per. Agreed yfaith. 3739

They play.

Cal. They say I am a coward, (*Perdicas*) and I feare as litle their *tara, tantaras,* their swordes or their cannons, as I doe a naked Lady in a net of golde, and for feare I should be affraid, would put it off and come to bed with me.

3709 both you] you both *1606, Cunn., Bull.* 3719 arms] aims *conj. Coll.* 3726 should I] I should *1606* 3729 nor harme *1590, Wag.*: no harme *1592, 1606, Rob. to Bull.* 3734 goe] go away *Rob., Cunn.*

Per. Such a feare (my Lord) would neuer make yee retire. 3745

Cal. I would my father would let me be put in the front of such a battaile once, to trie my valour.

Alarme.

What a coyle they keepe, I beleeue there will be some hurt done anon amongst them.

⟨*Exeunt.*⟩

Enter Tamburlain, Theridamas, Techelles, Vsumcasane, Amyras, Celebinus, leading the Turkish kings.

Tam. See now ye slaues, my children stoops your pride
And leads your glories sheep-like to the sword. 3751
Bring them my boyes, and tel me if the warres
Be not a life that may illustrate Gods,
And tickle not your Spirits with desire
Stil to be train'd in armes and chiualry ? 3755

Amy. Shal we let goe these kings again my Lord
To gather greater numbers gainst our power,
That they may say, it is not chance doth this,
But matchlesse strength and magnanimity ?

Tamb. No, no *Amyras*, tempt not Fortune so, 3760
Cherish thy valour stil with fresh supplies :
And glut it not with stale and daunted foes.
But wher's this coward, villaine, not my sonne,
But traitor to my name and maiesty.

He goes in and brings him out.

Image of sloth, and picture of a slaue, 3765
The obloquie and skorne of my renowne,
How may my hart, thus fired with mine eies,
Wounded with shame, and kill'd with discontent,
Shrowd any thought may holde my striuing hands
From martiall iustice on thy wretched soule. 3770

Ther. Yet pardon him I pray your Maiesty.

Tech. & Vsu. Let al of vs intreat your highnesse pardon.

Tam. Stand vp, ye base vnworthy souldiers,
Know ye not yet the argument of Armes ?

Amy. Good my Lord, let him be forgiuen for once, 3775
And we wil force him to the field hereafter.

Tam. Stand vp my boyes, and I wil teach ye arms,

3750 ye] my *1606* 3751 glories *1590, 1606, Wag.*: bodies *1592, Rob. to Bull.* 3757 against *1606* 3767 mine] my *1592* 3775 once] one *1592* 3777 ye] you *1606*

And what the iealousie of warres must doe.
O *Samarcanda,* where I breathed first,
And ioy'd the fire of this martiall flesh, 3780
Blush, blush faire citie, at thine honors foile,
And shame of nature which *Iaertis* streame,
Embracing thee with deepest of his loue,
Can neuer wash from thy distained browes.
Here *Ioue,* receiue his fainting soule againe, 3785
A Forme not meet to giue that subiect essence,
Whose matter is the flesh of *Tamburlain,*
Wherein an incorporeall spirit mooues,
Made of the mould whereof thy selfe consists,
Which makes me valiant, proud, ambitious, 3790
Ready to leuie power against thy throne,
That I might mooue the turning Spheares of heauen,
For earth and al this aery region
Cannot containe the state of *Tamburlaine.*
⟨*Stabs Calyphas.*⟩
By *Mahomet,* thy mighty friend I sweare, 3795
In sending to my issue such a soule,
Created of the massy dregges of earth,
The scum and tartar of the Elements,
Wherein was neither corrage, strength or wit,
But follie, sloth, and damned idlenesse: 3800
Thou hast procur'd a greater enemie,
Than he that darted mountaines at thy head,
Shaking the burthen mighty *Atlas* beares:
Whereat thou trembling hid'st thee in the aire,
Cloth'd with a pitchy cloud for being seene. 3805
And now ye cankred curres of *Asia,*
That will not see the strength of *Tamburlaine,*
Although it shine as brightly as the Sun.
Now you shal feele the strength of *Tamburlain,*
And by the state of his supremacie, 3810
Approoue the difference twixt himself and you.
Orc. Thou shewest the difference twixt our selues and thee
In this thy barbarous damned tyranny.
Ier. Thy victories are growne so violent,
That shortly heauen, fild with the meteors 3815
Of blood and fire thy tyrannies haue made,

3780 martiall] materiall *1606* 3781 thine] thy *1606* 3782 which *Rob. etc.*: with *1590–1606* 3788 incorporall *1606* 3794 S.D. *add. Dyce* 3809 you shal] shall ye *1606* feele] see *Rob., Cunn.*

Will poure down blood and fire on thy head:
Whose scalding drops wil pierce thy seething braines,
And with our bloods, reuenge our bloods on thee.
Tamb. Villaines, these terrours and these tyrannies
(If tyrannies wars iustice ye repute) 3821
I execute, enioin'd me from aboue:
To scourge the pride of such as heauen abhors,
Nor am I made Arch-monark of the world,
Crown'd and inuested by the hand of *Ioue*, 3825
For deeds of bounty or nobility:
But since I exercise a greater name,
The Scourge of God and terrour of the world,
I must apply my selfe to fit those tearmes,
In war, in blood, in death, in crueltie, 3830
And plague such Pesants as resist in me
The power of heauens eternall maiesty.
Theridamas, Techelles, and *Casane*,
Ransacke the tents and the pauilions
Of these proud Turks, and take their Concubines, 3835
Making them burie this effeminate brat,
For not a common Souldier shall defile
His manly fingers with so faint a boy.
Then bring those Turkish harlots to my tent,
And Ile dispose them as it likes me best, 3840
Meane while take him in.
Soul. We will my Lord.
⟨*Exeunt with the body of Calyphas.*⟩
Ier. O damned monster, nay a Feend of Hell,
Whose cruelties are not so harsh as thine,
Nor yet imposd with such a bitter hate. 3845
Orc. Reuenge it *Radamanth* and *Eacus*,
And let your hates extended in his paines,
Expell the hate wherewith he paines our soules.
Treb. May neuer day giue vertue to his eies,
Whose sight composde of furie and of fire 3850
Doth send such sterne affections to his heart.
Sor. May neuer spirit, vaine or Artier feed
The cursed substance of that cruel heart,
But (wanting moisture and remorsefull blood)
Drie vp with anger, and consume with heat. 3855

3819 blood on *1592, Rob.* 3820 Villaine *1606* 3831 resist in *conj. Broughton, Dyce etc.*: resisting *1590–1606, Rob.* 3832 The] Resist the *Rob.* 3842 S.D. *add. Dyce* 3846 it *om. 1606* 3848 Expell] Excel *Dyce etc.*

Tam. Wel, bark ye dogs. Ile bridle al your tongues
And bind them close with bits of burnisht steele,
Downe to the channels of your hatefull throats,
And with the paines my rigour shall inflict,
Ile make ye roare, that earth may eccho foorth 3860
The far resounding torments ye sustaine,
As when an heard of lusty Cymbrian Buls,
Run mourning round about the Femals misse,
And stung with furie of their following,
Fill all the aire with troublous bellowing: 3865
I will with Engines, neuer exercisde,
Conquer, sacke, and vtterly consume
Your cities and your golden pallaces,
And with the flames that beat against the clowdes
Incense the heauens, and make the starres to melt, 3870
As if they were the teares of *Mahomet*
For hot consumption of his countries pride:
And til by vision, or by speach I heare
Immortall *Ioue* say, Cease my *Tamburlaine*,
I will persist a terrour to the world, 3875
Making the Meteors, that like armed men
Are seene to march vpon the towers of heauen,
Run tilting round about the firmament,
And breake their burning Lances in the aire,
For honor of my woondrous victories. 3880
Come bring them in to our Pauilion.

Exeunt.

Actus 4. *Scæna* 2.

Olympia alone.

⟨*Olympia.*⟩ Distrest *Olympia*, whose weeping eies
Since thy arriuall here beheld no Sun,
But closde within the compasse of a tent,
Hath stain'd thy cheekes, & made thee look like death,
Deuise some meanes to rid thee of thy life, 3886
Rather than yeeld to his detested suit,
Whose drift is onely to dishonor thee.
And since this earth, dew'd with thy brinish teares,
Affoords no hearbs, whose taste may poison thee, 3890
Nor yet this aier, beat often with thy sighes,

3860 ye] you *1606* 3881 into *1606* 3883 beheld *1590*, *Rob.*, *conj. Dyce*, *Wag.*: beholde *1592*, *1606*, *Dyce to Bull.* 3884 a] the *1592*, *Rob.*, *Cunn.*

Contagious smels, and vapors to infect thee,
Nor thy close Caue a sword to murther thee,
Let this inuention be the instrument.

Enter Theridamas.

The. Wel met *Olympia*, I sought thee in my tent 3895
But when I saw the place obscure and darke,
Which with thy beauty thou wast woont to light,
Enrag'd, I ran about the fields for thee,
Supposing amorous *Ioue* had sent his sonne,
The winged *Hermes*, to conuay thee hence: 3900
But now I finde thee, and that feare is past.
Tell me *Olympia*, wilt thou graunt my suit?
Olym. My Lord and husbandes death, with my sweete sons,
With whom I buried al affections,
Saue griefe and sorrow which torment my heart, 3905
Forbids my mind to entertaine a thought
That tends to loue, but meditate on death,
A fitter subiect for a pensiue soule.
Ther. *Olympia*, pitie him, in whom thy looks
Haue greater operation and more force 3910
Than *Cynthias* in the watery wildernes,
For with thy view my ioyes are at the full,
And eb againe, as thou departst from me.
Olim. Ah, pity me my Lord, and draw your sword,
Making a passage for my troubled soule, 3915
Which beates against this prison to get out,
And meet my husband and my louing sonne.
Ther. Nothing, but stil thy husband and thy sonne?
Leaue this my Loue, and listen more to me,
Thou shalt be stately Queene of faire *Argier*, 3920
And cloth'd in costly cloath of massy gold,
Vpon the marble turrets of my Court
Sit like to *Venus* in her chaire of state,
Commanding all thy princely eie desires,
And I will cast off armes and sit with thee, 3925
Spending my life in sweet discourse of loue.
Olym. No such discourse is pleasant in mine eares,
But that where euery period ends with death,
And euery line begins with death againe:
I cannot loue to be an Emperesse. 3930

3897 wast] was *1592* 3903 Sonne *1606* 3925 and] to *1592*, *Rob. to Bull.* 3927 in] to *1606*

Ther. Nay Lady, then if nothing wil preuaile,
Ile vse some other means to make you yeeld,
Such is the sodaine fury of my loue,
I must and wil be pleasde, and you shall yeeld:
Come to the tent againe. 3935

Olym. Stay good my Lord, and wil you saue my honor,
Ile giue your Grace a present of such price,
As all the world cannot affoord the like.

Ther. What is it?

Olym. An ointment which a cunning Alcumist 3940
Distilled from the purest Balsamum,
And simplest extracts of all Minerals,
In which the essentiall fourme of Marble stone,
Tempered by science metaphisicall,
And Spels of magicke from the mouthes of spirits, 3945
With which if you but noint your tender Skin,
Nor Pistol, Sword, nor Lance can pierce your flesh.

Ther. Why Madam, thinke ye to mocke me thus palpably?

Olim. To prooue it, I wil noint my naked throat,
Which when you stab, looke on your weapons point, 3950
And you shall se't rebated with the blow.

Ther. Why gaue you not your husband some of it,
If you loued him, and it so precious?

Olym. My purpose was (my Lord) to spend it so,
But was preuented by his sodaine end. 3955
And for a present easie proofe hereof,
That I dissemble not, trie it on me.

Ther. I wil *Olympia*, and will keep it for
The richest present of this Easterne world.

She noints her throat.

Olym. Now stab my Lord, and mark your weapons point
That wil be blunted if the blow be great. 3961

Ther. Here then *Olympia*.

⟨*Stabs her.*⟩

What, haue I slaine her? Villaine, stab thy selfe:
Cut off this arme that murthered my Loue:
In whom the learned Rabies of this age 3965
Might find as many woondrous myracles,

3936 good] now *1592*, *Rob. to Bull.* and wil you] if you will *1606*, *Rob.* 3945 mouthes] mother *1592* 3948 ye] you *1606*, *Rob. to Bull.* 3956 hereof] thereof *1592*, *Rob. to Bull.* 3958 and will] and I will *1592*: and I'll *Rob.*, *Cunn.* 3962 S.D. *add. Dyce* 3964 my] thy *Rob.*, *Cunn.*, *Bull.*

As in the Theoria of the world.
Now Hell is fairer than *Elisian*,
A greater Lamp than that bright eie of heauen,
From whence the starres doo borrow all their light, 3970
Wanders about the black circumference,
And now the damned soules are free from paine,
For euery Fury gazeth on her lookes :
Infernall *Dis* is courting of my Loue,
Inuenting maskes and stately showes for her, 3975
Opening the doores of his rich treasurie,
To entertaine this Queene of chastitie,
Whose body shall be tomb'd with all the pompe
The treasure of my kingdome may affoord.
Exit, taking her away.

Actus 4. *Scæna* 3.

Tamburlaine drawen in his chariot by Trebizon and Soria with bittes in their mouthes, reines in his left hand, in his right hand a whip, with which he scourgeth them. Techelles, Theridamas, Vsumcasane, Amyras, Celebinus: Natolia, and Ierusalem led by with fiue or six common souldiers.

Tam. Holla, ye pampered Iades of *Asia* : 3980
What, can ye draw but twenty miles a day,
And haue so proud a chariot at your heeles,
And such a Coachman as great *Tamburlaine* ?
But from *Asphaltis*, where I conquer'd you,
To *Byron* here where thus I honor you ? 3985
The horse that guide the golden eie of heauen,
And blow the morning from their nosterils,
Making their fiery gate aboue the cloudes,
Are not so honoured in their Gouernour,
As you (ye slaues) in mighty *Tamburlain*. 3990
The headstrong Iades of *Thrace*, *Alcides* tam'd,
That King *Egeus* fed with humaine flesh,
And made so wanton that they knew their strengths,
Were not subdew'd with valour more diuine,
Than you by this vnconquered arme of mine. 3995
To make you fierce, and fit my appetite,
You shal be fed with flesh as raw as blood,

3979 my] thy *1592* : this *Rob.* 3989 in] as *1606*

And drinke in pailes the strongest Muscadell:
If you can liue with it, then liue, and draw
My chariot swifter than the racking cloudes: 4000
If not, then dy like beasts, and fit for nought
But perches for the black and fatall Rauens.
Thus am I right the Scourge of highest *Ioue*,
And see the figure of my dignitie,
By which I hold my name and maiesty. 4005

Ami. Let me haue coach my Lord, that I may ride,
And thus be drawen with these two idle kings.

Tam. Thy youth forbids such ease my kingly boy,
They shall to morrow draw my chariot,
While these their fellow kings may be refresht. 4010

Orc. O thou that swaiest the region vnder earth,
And art a king as absolute as *Ioue*,
Come as thou didst in fruitfull *Scicilie*,
Suruaieng all the glories of the land:
And as thou took'st the faire *Proserpina*, 4015
Ioying the fruit of *Ceres* garden plot,
For loue, for honor, and to make her Queene,
So for iust hate, for shame, and to subdew
This proud contemner of thy dreadfull power,
Come once in furie and suruay his pride, 4020
Haling him headlong to the lowest hell.

Ther. Your Maiesty must get some byts for these,
To bridle their contemptuous cursing tongues,
That like vnruly neuer broken Iades,
Breake through the hedges of their hateful mouthes, 4025
And passe their fixed boundes exceedingly.

Tech. Nay, we wil break the hedges of their mouths
And pul their kicking colts out of their pastures.

Vsu. Your Maiesty already hath deuisde
A meane, as fit as may be to restraine 4030
These coltish coach-horse tongues from blasphemy.

Cel. How like you that sir king? why speak you not?

Ier. Ah cruel Brat, sprung from a tyrants loines,
How like his cursed father he begins,
To practize tauntes and bitter tyrannies? 4035

Tam. I Turke, I tel thee, this same Boy is he,
That must (aduaunst in higher pompe than this)
Rifle the kingdomes I shall leaue vnsackt.

4006 coach] a coach *1606* 4007 with] by *1606*, *Rob. to Cunn.*
4016 garden] garded *1592* 4032 speake ye *1592*, *Rob.*, *Cunn.*
4036 same *om. 1606*

If *Ioue* esteeming me too good for earth,
Raise me to match the faire *Aldeboran*, 4040
Aboue the threefold Astracisme of heauen,
Before I conquere all the triple world.
Now fetch me out the Turkish Concubines,
I will prefer them for the funerall
They haue bestowed on my abortiue sonne. 4045

The Concubines are brought in.

Where are my common souldiers now that fought
So Lion-like vpon *Asphaltis* plaines?
Soul. Here my Lord.
Tam. Hold ye tal souldiers, take ye Queens apeece
(I meane such Queens as were kings Concubines) 4050
Take them, deuide them and their iewels too,
And let them equally serue all your turnes.
Soul. We thank your maiesty.
Tam. Brawle not (I warne you) for your lechery,
For euery man that so offends shall die. 4055
Orc. Iniurious tyrant, wilt thou so defame
The hatefull fortunes of thy victory,
To exercise vpon such guiltlesse Dames
The violence of thy common Souldiours lust?
Tam. Liue continent then (ye slaues) and meet not me
With troopes of harlots at your sloothful heeles. 4061
Lad. O pity vs my Lord, and saue our honours.
Tam. Are ye not gone ye villaines with your spoiles?

They run away with the Ladies.

Ier. O mercilesse infernall cruelty.
Tam. Saue your honours? twere but time indeed, 4065
Lost long before you knew what honour meant.
Ther. It seemes they meant to conquer vs my Lord,
And make vs ieasting Pageants for their Trulles.
Tam. And now themselues shal make our Pageant,
And common souldiers iest with all their Truls, 4070
Let them take pleasure soundly in their spoiles,
Till we prepare our martch to *Babylon*,
Whether we next make expedition.
Tech. Let vs not be idle then my Lord,
But presently be prest to conquer it. 4075
Tam. We wil *Techelles*, forward then ye Iades:
Now crowch ye kings of greatest *Asia*,

4041 Aboue] about *1606* 4051 their *om. 1592* 4060 continent *Rob. to Wag.*: content *1590–1606* 4066 you] ye *1592*, *Rob. to Bull.*

And tremble when ye heare this Scourge wil come,
That whips downe cities, and controwleth crownes,
Adding their wealth and treasure to my store. 4080
The Euxine sea North to *Natolia*,
The Terrene west, the Caspian north north-east,
And on the south *Senus Arabicus*,
Shal al be loden with the martiall spoiles
We will conuay with vs to *Persea*. 4085
Then shal my natiue city *Samarcanda*
And christall waues of fresh *Iaertis* streame,
The pride and beautie of her princely seat,
Be famous through the furthest continents,
For there my Pallace royal shal be plac'd : 4090
Whose shyning Turrets shal dismay the heauens,
And cast the fame of *Ilions* Tower to hell.
Thorow the streets with troops of conquered kings,
Ile ride in golden armour like the Sun,
And in my helme a triple plume shal spring, 4095
Spangled with Diamonds dancing in the aire,
To note me Emperour of the three fold world,
Like to an almond tree ymounted high,
Vpon the lofty and celestiall mount,
Of euer greene *Selinus* queintly dect 4100
With bloomes more white than *Hericinas* browes,
Whose tender blossoms tremble euery one,
At euery little breath that thorow heauen is blowen :
Then in my coach like *Saturnes* royal son,
Mounted his shining chariot, gilt with fire, 4105
And drawen with princely Eagles through the path,
Pau'd with bright Christall, and enchac'd with starres,
When all the Gods stand gazing at his pomp.
So will I ride through *Samarcanda* streets,
Vntil my soule disseuered from this flesh, 4110
Shall mount the milk-white way and meet him there.
To *Babylon* my Lords, to *Babylon*.

Exeunt.

Finis Actus quarti.

4084 al *om. 1606* 4093 Thorow] & through *1606* 4100 euer *Rob. etc.*: euery *1590–1606* 4101 browes] bowes *1592* 4103 that thorow] from *1606* : through *Cunn., Bull.* 4105 chariot *Dyce etc.*: chariots *1590–1606*

Actus 5. *Scæna* 1.

Enter the Gouernour of Babylon vpon the walles with ⟨Maximus and⟩ others.

Gouer. What saith *Maximus*?
Max. My Lord, the breach the enimie hath made
Giues such assurance of our ouerthrow, 4115
That litle hope is left to saue our liues,
Or hold our citie from the Conquerours hands.
Then hang out flagges (my Lord) of humble truce,
And satisfie the peoples generall praiers,
That *Tamburlains* intollorable wrath 4120
May be suppress by our submission.
Gou. Villaine, respects thou more thy slauish life,
Than honor of thy countrie or thy name?
Is not my life and state as deere to me,
The citie and my natiue countries weale, 4125
As any thing of price with thy conceit?
Haue we not hope, for all our battered walles,
To liue secure, and keep his forces out,
When this our famous lake of *Limnasphaltis*
Makes walles a fresh with euery thing that falles 4130
Into the liquid substance of his streame,
More strong than are the gates of death or hel?
What faintnesse should dismay our courages,
When we are thus defenc'd against our Foe,
And haue no terrour but his threatning lookes? 4135

Enter another, kneeling to the Gouernour.

⟨*Citizen.*⟩ My Lord, if euer you did deed of ruth,
And now will work a refuge to our liues,
Offer submission, hang vp flags of truce,
That *Tamburlaine* may pitie our distresse,
And vse vs like a louing Conquerour, 4140
Though this be held his last daies dreadfull siege,
Wherein he spareth neither man nor child,
Yet are there Christians of *Georgia* here,
Whose state he euer pitied and relieu'd:
Wil get his pardon if your grace would send. 4145

4118 out] our *1592*, *1606* 4126 of] in *1606* with] in *Rob.*, *Cunn.* 4135 S.D. another] another Citizen *Wag.* 4136 *Prefix* Cit. *add. Dyce* 4144 he] was *1592*, *Rob.*, *Dyce* [1], *Cunn.*, *Bull.* 4145 Wil] Would *Rob.*, *Cunn.*, *Bull.*

Gouer. How is my soule enuironed,
And this eternisde citie *Babylon,*
Fill'd with a packe of faintheart Fugitiues,
That thus intreat their shame and seruitude ?
Another. My Lord, if euer you wil win our hearts, 4150
Yeeld vp the towne, saue our wiues and children :
For I wil cast my selfe from off these walles,
Or die some death of quickest violence,
Before I bide the wrath of *Tamburlaine.*
Gouer. Villaines, cowards, Traitors to our state, 4155
Fall to the earth, and pierce the pit of Hel,
That legions of tormenting spirits may vex
Your slauish bosomes with continuall paines,
I care not, nor the towne will neuer yeeld
As long as any life is in my breast. 4160

Enter Theridamas and Techelles, with other souldiers.

⟨*Theridamas.*⟩ Thou desperate Gouernour of *Babylon,*
To saue thy life, and vs a litle labour,
Yeeld speedily the citie to our hands,
Or els be sure thou shalt be forc'd with paines,
More exquisite than euer Traitor felt. 4165
Gou. Tyrant, I turne the traitor in thy throat,
And wil defend it in despight of thee.
Call vp the souldiers to defend these wals.
Tech. Yeeld foolish Gouernour, we offer more
Than euer yet we did to such proud slaues, 4170
As durst resist vs till our third daies siege :
Thou seest vs prest to giue the last assault,
And that shal bide no more regard of parlie.
Gou. Assault and spare not, we wil neuer yeeld.

Alarme, and they scale the walles.

Enter Tamburlain, ⟨drawn in his chariot by the kings of Trebizon and Soria ; Amyras, Celebinus, Usumcasane ; Orcanes king of Natolia, and the king of Ierusalem, led by soldiers ; and others.⟩

Tam. The stately buildings of faire *Babylon,* 4175

4146 How] Alas (*or* Ay me) how *conj. Wag.* environed with cares *conj. Broughton, Bull.* : environed with grief *conj. Dyce*[1] 4150 *Prefix* Sec. Cit. *Dyce* you] ye *1592, Rob., Cunn.* 4151 saue] and saue *1606 etc.* 4161 *Prefix add. Rob.* 4168–4224 *These lines are missing from the Bodleian copy of 1590, owing to the loss of leaf* 'K 3'. *Text follows Chatsworth copy.* 4174 S.D. drawn . . and others *Dyce etc.*: with Vsumcasane, Amyras, and Celebinus, with others, the two spare kings *1590–1606*

Whose lofty Pillers, higher than the cloudes,
Were woont to guide the seaman in the deepe,
Being caried thither by the cannons force,
Now fil the mouth of *Limnasphaltes* lake,
And make a bridge vnto the battered walles. 4180
Where *Belus, Ninus* and great *Alexander*
Haue rode in triumph, triumphs *Tamburlaine,*
Whose chariot wheeles haue burst th' Assirians bones,
Drawen with these kings on heaps of carkasses,
Now in the place where faire *Semiramis,* 4185
Courted by kings and peeres of *Asia,*
Hath trode the Meisures, do my souldiers martch,
And in the streets, where braue Assirian Dames
Haue rid in pompe like rich *Saturnia,*
With furious words and frowning visages, 4190
My horsmen brandish their vnruly blades.

Enter Theridamas and Techelles bringing the Gouernor of Babylon.

Who haue ye there my Lordes ?
Ther. The sturdy Gouernour of *Babylon,*
That made vs all the labour for the towne,
And vsde such slender reckning of your maiesty. 4195
Tam. Go bind the villaine, he shall hang in chaines,
Vpon the ruines of this conquered towne.
Sirha, the view of our vermillion tents,
Which threatned more than if the region
Next vnderneath the Element of fire, 4200
Were full of Commets and of blazing stars,
Whose flaming traines should reach down to the earth
Could not affright you, no, nor I my selfe,
The wrathfull messenger of mighty *Ioue,*
That with his sword hath quail'd all earthly kings, 4205
Could not perswade you to submission,
But stil the ports were shut : villaine I say,
Should I but touch the rusty gates of hell,
The triple headed *Cerberus* would howle,
And wake blacke *Ioue* to crouch and kneele to me, 4210
But I haue sent volleies of shot to you,
Yet could not enter till the breach was made.
Gou. Nor if my body could haue stopt the breach,
Shouldst thou haue entred, cruel *Tamburlaine* :

4195 of] for *1606* 4205 quell'd *Rob.* 4210 wake] make *1606, Dyce*[2], *Wag.*

Tis not thy bloody tents can make me yeeld, 4215
Nor yet thy selfe, the anger of the highest,
For though thy cannon shooke the citie walles,
My heart did neuer quake, or corrage faint.
Tam. Wel, now Ile make it quake, go draw him vp,
Hang him vp in chaines vpon the citie walles, 4220
And let my souldiers shoot the slaue to death.
Gouern. Vile monster, borne of some infernal hag,
And sent from hell to tyrannise on earth,
Do all thy wurst, nor death nor *Tamburlaine*,
Torture or paine can daunt my dreadlesse minde. 4225
Tam. Vp with him then, his body shalbe scard.
Gou. But *Tamburlain*, in *Lymnasphaltis* lake,
There lies more gold than *Babylon* is worth,
Which when the citie was besieg'd I hid,
Saue but my life and I wil giue it thee. 4230
Tam. Then for all your valour, you would saue your life.
Where about lies it ?
Gou. Vnder a hollow bank, right opposite
Against the Westerne gate of *Babylon*.
Tam. Go thither some of you and take his gold, 4235
The rest forward with execution.
Away with him hence, let him speake no more :
I think I make your courage something quaile.
When this is done, we'll martch from *Babylon*,
And make our greatest haste to *Persea* : 4240
These Iades are broken winded, and halfe tyr'd,
Vnharnesse them, and let me haue fresh horse :
So, now their best is done to honour me,
Take them, and hang them both vp presently.
Tre. Vild Tyrant, barbarous bloody *Tamburlain*. 4245
Tamb. Take them away *Theridamas*, see them dispatcht.
Ther. I will my Lord.

⟨*Exit with the Kings of Trebizon and Soria.*⟩

Tam. Come Asian Viceroies, to your taskes a while
And take such fortune as your fellowes felt.
Orc. First let thy Scythyan horse teare both our limmes
Rather then we should draw thy chariot, 4251
And like base slaues abiect our princely mindes
To vile and ignominious seruitude.
Ier. Rather lend me thy weapon *Tamburlain*,

4217 citie *om. 1606* 4219 him] it *1592* 4220 vp *om. Rob.*, *Dyce*[2] *etc.* 4226 scard] seard *1606*, *Rob.* 4247 S.D. *add. Dyce*

That I may sheath it in this breast of mine, 4255
A thousand deathes could not torment our hearts
More than the thought of this dooth vexe our soules.

Amy. They will talk still my Lord, if you doe not bridle them.

Tam. Bridle them, and let me to my coach.

They bridle them.

⟨*The Governor of Babylon appears hanging in chains on the walls. Re-enter Theridamas.*⟩

Amy. See now my Lord how braue the Captaine hangs.

Tam. Tis braue indeed my boy, wel done, 4261
Shoot first my Lord, and then the rest shall follow.

Ther. Then haue at him to begin withall.

Theridamas shootes.

Gou. Yet saue my life, and let this wound appease
The mortall furie of great *Tamburlain*. 4265

Tam. No, though *Asphaltis* lake were liquid gold,
And offer'd me as ransome for thy life,
Yet shouldst thou die, shoot at him all at once.

They shoote.

So now he hangs like *Bagdets* Gouernour,
Hauing as many bullets in his flesh, 4270
As there be breaches in her battered wall.
Goe now and bind the Burghers hand and foot,
And cast them headlong in the cities lake:
Tartars and Perseans shall inhabit there,
And to command the citie, I will build 4275
A Cytadell, that all Affrica
Which hath bene subiect to the Persean king,
Shall pay me tribute for, in *Babylon*.

Tech. What shal be done with their wiues and children my Lord. 4280

Tam. *Techelles*, drowne them all, man, woman, and child,
Leaue not a Babylonian in the towne.

Tech. I will about it straight, come Souldiers. *Exit.*

Tam. Now *Casane*, wher's the Turkish *Alcaron*,
And all the heapes of supersticious bookes, 4285
Found in the Temples of that *Mahomet*,
Whom I haue thought a God? they shal be burnt.

4259+S.D. The . . Theridamas *add. Dyce.* 4276 Cytadell] lofty citadel *Bull.* Affrica] Arabia *conj. Broughton*

Cas. Here they are my Lord.

Tam. Wel said, let there be a fire presently.

⟨*They light a fire.*⟩

In vaine I see men worship *Mahomet.* 4290
My sword hath sent millions of Turks to hell,
Slew all his Priests, his kinsmen, and his friends,
And yet I liue vntoucht by *Mahomet*:
There is a God full of reuenging wrath,
From whom the thunder and the lightning breaks, 4295
Whose Scourge I am, and him will I obey
So *Casane*, fling them in the fire.

⟨*They burn the books.*⟩

Now *Mahomet*, if thou haue any power,
Come downe thy selfe and worke a myracle,
Thou art not woorthy to be worshipped, 4300
That suffers flames of fire to burne the writ
Wherein the sum of thy religion rests.
Why send'st thou not a furious whyrlwind downe,
To blow thy Alcaron vp to thy throne,
Where men report, thou sitt'st by God himselfe, 4305
Or vengeance on the head of *Tamburlain*,
That shakes his sword against thy maiesty,
And spurns the Abstracts of thy foolish lawes.
Wel souldiers, *Mahomet* remaines in hell,
He cannot heare the voice of *Tamburlain*, 4310
Seeke out another Godhead to adore,
The God that sits in heauen, if any God,
For he is God alone, and none but he.

⟨*Re-enter Techelles.*⟩

Tech. I haue fulfil'd your highnes wil, my Lord,
Thousands of men drown'd in *Asphaltis* Lake, 4315
Haue made the water swell aboue the bankes,
And fishes fed by humaine carkasses,
Amasde, swim vp and downe vpon the waues,
As when they swallow *Assafitida*,
Which makes them fleet aloft and gaspe for aire. 4320

Tam. Wel then my friendly Lordes, what now remaines
But that we leaue sufficient garrison

4289 S.D. *add. Dyce* 4292 Slew] Slain *Rob., Cunn., Bull.* 4296 will I] I will *1606* 4297 S.D. *add. Dyce* 4303 sends *1606* 4305 sits *1606* 4306 head] blood *1606* 4313 S.D. *add. Dyce* 4317 fed *Rob. etc.*: feed *1590–1606* 4318 vpon *om. 1606* 4320 gaspe] gape *1592, Rob. to Bull.*

And presently depart to *Persea*,
To triumph after all our victories.
Ther. I, good my Lord, let vs in hast to *Persea*, 4325
And let this Captaine be remoou'd the walles,
To some high hill about the citie here.
Tam. Let it be so, about it souldiers :
But stay, I feele my selfe distempered sudainly.
Tech. What is it dares distemper *Tamburlain* ? 4330
Tam. Something Techelles, but I know not what,
But foorth ye vassals, what so ere it be,
Sicknes or death can neuer conquer me.

Exeunt.

Actus 5. *Scæna* 2.

Enter Callapine, Amasia, with drums and trumpets.

Callap. King of *Amasia*, now our mighty hoste,
Marcheth in *Asia maior*, where the streames, 4335
Of *Euphrates* and *Tigris* swiftly runs,
And here may we behold great Babylon,
Circled about with *Limnasphaltis* Lake,
Where *Tamburlaine* with all his armie lies,
Which being faint and weary with the siege, 4340
Wee may lie ready to encounter him,
Before his hoste be full from *Babylon*,
And so reuenge our latest grieuous losse,
If God or *Mahomet* send any aide.
Ama. Doubt not my lord, but we shal conquer him.
The Monster that hath drunke a sea of blood, 4346
And yet gapes stil for more to quench his thirst,
Our Turkish swords shal headlong send to hell,
And that vile Carkasse drawne by warlike kings,
The Foules shall eate, for neuer sepulchre 4350
Shall grace that base-borne Tyrant *Tamburlaine*.
Cal. When I record my Parents slauish life,
Their cruel death, mine owne captiuity,
My Viceroies bondage vnder *Tamburlaine*,
Me thinks I could sustaine a thousand deaths, 4355
To be reueng'd of all his Villanie.
Ah sacred *Mahomet*, thou that hast seene
Millions of Turkes perish by *Tamburlaine*,
Kingdomes made waste, braue cities sackt & burnt,

4325 in *om. 1606* 4332 so ere] soeuer *1606* 4337 may we] we may *1606, Rob., Cunn.* 4351 that] this *1592, Dyce to Bull.*

And but one hoste is left to honor thee: 4360
Aid thy obedient seruant *Callapine*,
And make him after all these ouerthrowes,
To triumph ouer cursed *Tamburlaine*.
Ama. Feare not my Lord, I see great *Mahomet*
Clothed in purple clowdes, and on his head 4365
A Chaplet brighter than *Apollos* crowne,
Marching about the ayer with armed men,
To ioine with you against this *Tamburlaine*.
Renowmed Generall, mighty *Callapine*,
Though God himselfe and holy *Mahomet*, 4370
Should come in person to resist your power,
Yet might your mighty hoste incounter all,
And pull proud *Tamburlaine* vpon his knees,
To sue for mercie at your highnesse feete.
Cal. Captaine, the force of *Tamburlaine* is great, 4375
His fortune greater, and the victories
Wherewith he hath so sore dismaide the world,
Are greatest to discourage all our drifts,
Yet when the pride of *Cynthia* is at full,
She waines againe, and so shall his I hope, 4380
For we haue here the chiefe selected men
Of twenty seuerall kingdomes at the least:
Nor plowman, Priest, nor Merchant staies at home,
All Turkie is in armes with *Callapine*,
And neuer wil we sunder camps and armes, 4385
Before himselfe or his be conquered.
This is the time that must eternize me,
For conquering the Tyrant of the world.
Come Souldiers, let vs lie in wait for him
And if we find him absent from his campe, 4390
Or that it be reioin'd again at full,
Assaile it and be sure of victorie.
Exeunt.

Actus 5. *Scæna* 3.

Theridamas, Techelles, Vsumcasane.

⟨*Theridamas.*⟩ Weepe heauens, and vanish into liquid teares,
Fal starres that gouerne his natiuity,
And sommon al the shining lamps of heauen 4395
To cast their bootlesse fires to the earth,

4393 *Prefix om. 1590–1606*

And shed their feble influence in the aire.
Muffle your beauties with eternall clowdes,
For hell and darknesse pitch their pitchy tentes,
And Death with armies of Cymerian spirits 4400
Giues battile gainst the heart of *Tamburlaine*.
Now in defiance of that woonted loue,
Your sacred vertues pour'd vpon his throne,
And made his state an honor to the heauens,
These cowards inuisiblie assaile hys soule, 4405
And threaten conquest on our Soueraigne:
But if he die, your glories are disgrac'd,
Earth droopes and saies, that hell in heauen is plac'd.
Tech. O then ye Powers that sway eternal seates,
And guide this massy substance of the earthe, 4410
If you retaine desert of holinesse,
As your supreame estates instruct our thoughtes,
Be not inconstant, carelesse of your fame,
Beare not the burthen of your enemies ioyes,
Triumphing in his fall whom you aduaunst, 4415
But as his birth, life, health and maiesty
Were strangely blest and gouerned by heauen,
So honour heauen til heauen dissolued be,
His byrth, his life, his health and maiesty.
Cas. Blush heauen to loose the honor of thy name,
To see thy foot-stoole set vpon thy head, 4421
And let no basenesse in thy haughty breast,
Sustaine a shame of such inexcellence:
To see the deuils mount in Angels throanes,
And Angels diue into the pooles of hell. 4425
And though they think their painfull date is out,
And that their power is puissant as *Ioues*,
Which makes them manage armes against thy state,
Yet make them feele the strength of *Tamburlain*,
Thy instrument and note of Maiesty, 4430
Is greater far, than they can thus subdue,
For if he die, thy glorie is disgrac'd,
Earth droopes and saies that hel in heauen is plac'd.

⟨*Enter Tamburlaine, drawn by the captive kings; Amyras, Celebinus, Physicians.*⟩

Tam. What daring God torments my body thus,

4405 inuisiblie] inuincible *1592*: invisible *Rob., Cunn., Bull.* 4415 whom you] you most *Rob.* 4423 inexcellencie *1592* 4433 S.D. add. *Wag.*

And seeks to conquer mighty *Tamburlaine*, 4435
Shall sicknesse prooue me now to be a man,
That haue bene tearm'd the terrour of the world ?
Techelles and the rest, come take your swords,
And threaten him whose hand afflicts my soul,
Come let vs march against the powers of heauen, 4440
And set blacke streamers in the firmament,
To signifie the slaughter of the Gods.
Ah friends, what shal I doe ? I cannot stand,
Come carie me to war against the Gods,
That thus inuie the health of *Tamburlaine*. 4445
Ther. Ah good my Lord, leaue these impatient words,
Which ad much danger to your malladie.
Tam. Why shal I sit and languish in this paine?
No, strike the drums, and in reuenge of this,
Come let vs chardge our speares and pierce his breast, 4450
Whose shoulders beare the Axis of the world,
That if I perish, heauen and earth may fade.
Theridamas, haste to the court of *Ioue*,
Will him to send *Apollo* hether straight,
To cure me, or Ile fetch him downe my selfe. 4455
Tech. Sit stil my gratious Lord, this griefe wil cease,
And cannot last, it is so violent.
Tam. Not last *Techelles*, no, for I shall die.
See where my slaue, the vglie monster death
Shaking and quiuering, pale and wan for feare, 4460
Stands aiming at me with his murthering dart,
Who flies away at euery glance I giue,
And when I look away, comes stealing on :
Villaine away, and hie thee to the field,
I and myne armie come to lode thy barke 4465
With soules of thousand mangled carkasses.
Looke where he goes, but see, he comes againe
Because I stay. *Techelles* let vs march,
And weary Death with bearing soules to hell.
Phi. Pleaseth your Maiesty to drink this potion, 4470
Which wil abate the furie of your fit,
And cause some milder spirits gouerne you.
Tam. Tel me, what think you of my sicknes now ?
Phi. I view'd your vrine, and the hypostasis
Thick and obscure doth make your danger great, 4475
Your vaines are full of accidentall heat,

4465 barke] backe *1606, Rob. to Bull.* 4474 hypostasis *Rob., etc.* : Hipostates *1590–1606*

Whereby the moisture of your blood is dried,
The *Humidum* and *Calor*, which some holde
Is not a parcell of the Elements,
But of a substance more diuine and pure, 4480
Is almost cleane extinguished and spent,
Which being the cause of life, imports your death.
Besides my Lord, this day is Criticall,
Dangerous to those, whose Chrisis is as yours :
Your Artiers which alongst the vaines conuey 4485
The liuely spirits which the heart ingenders
Are partcht and void of spirit, that the soule
Wanting those Organnons by which it mooues,
Can not indure by argument of art,
Yet if your maiesty may escape this day, 4490
No doubt, but you shal soone recouer all.

Tam. Then will I comfort all my vital parts,
And liue in spight of death aboue a day.

Alarme within.

⟨*Enter a Messenger.*⟩

Mess. My Lord, yong *Callapine* that lately fled from your maiesty, hath nowe gathered a fresh Armie, and hearing your absence in the field, offers to set vpon vs presently. 4497

Tam. See my Phisitions now, how *Ioue* hath sent
A present medicine to recure my paine :
My looks shall make them flie, and might I follow, 4500
There should not one of all the villaines power
Liue to giue offer of another fight.

Vsum. I ioy my Lord, your highnesse is so strong,
That can endure so well your royall presence,
Which onely will dismay the enemy. 4505

Tam. I know it wil *Casane* : draw you slaues,
In spight of death I will goe show my face.

Alarme, Tamb. goes in, and comes out againe with al the rest.

Thus are the villaines, cowards fled for feare,
Like Summers vapours, vanisht by the Sun,
And could I but a while pursue the field, 4510
That *Callapine* should be my slaue againe.

4488 those Organnons] these organisms *Rob.* 4493 S.D. Enter a Messenger *add. Dyce* 4496 vpon] on *1592* 4508 villain *Rob.*, *Dyce*[2] *to Bull.*

But I perceiue my martial strength is spent,
In vaine I striue and raile against those powers,
That meane t'inuest me in a higher throane,
As much too high for this disdainfull earth. 4515
Giue me a Map, then let me see how much
Is left for me to conquer all the world,
That these my boies may finish all my wantes.

One brings a Map.

Here I began to martch towards *Persea,*
Along *Armenia* and the Caspian sea, 4520
And thence vnto *Bythinia*, where I tooke
The Turke and his great Empresse prisoners,
Then martcht I into *Egypt* and *Arabia*,
And here not far from *Alexandria*,
Whereas the Terren and the red sea meet, 4525
Being distant lesse than ful a hundred leagues,
I meant to cut a channell to them both,
That men might quickly saile to *India*.
From thence to *Nubia* neere *Borno* Lake,
And so along the Ethiopian sea, 4530
Cutting the Tropicke line of *Capricorne*,
I conquered all as far as *Zansibar*.
Then by the Northerne part of *Affrica*,
I came at last to *Græcia*, and from thence
To *Asia*, where I stay against my will, 4535
Which is from *Scythia*, where I first began,
Backeward and forwards nere fiue thousand leagues.
Looke here my boies, see what a world of ground
Lies westward from the midst of *Cancers* line,
Vnto the rising of this earthly globe, 4540
Whereas the Sun declining from our sight,
Begins the day with our Antypodes:
And shall I die, and this vnconquered?
Loe here my sonnes, are all the golden Mines,
Inestimable drugs and precious stones, 4545
More worth than *Asia*, and the world beside,
And from th' Antartique Pole, Eastward behold
As much more land, which neuer was descried,
Wherein are rockes of Pearle, that shine as bright
As all the Lamps that beautifie the Sky, 4550
And shal I die, and this vnconquered?

4519 to] my *Ellis* 4521 vnto] to *1606* 4536 begun *1606*
4540 this] the *1606*, *Rob.*

Here louely boies, what death forbids my life,
That let your liues commaund in spight of death.
Amy. Alas my Lord, how should our bleeding harts
Wounded and broken with your Highnesse griefe, 4555
Retaine a thought of ioy, or sparke of life ?
Your soul giues essence to our wretched subiects,
Whose matter is incorporoat in your flesh.
Cel. Your paines do pierce our soules, no hope suruiues,
For by your life we entertaine our liues. 4560
Tam. But sons, this subiect not of force enough,
To hold the fiery spirit it containes,
Must part, imparting his impressions,
By equall portions into both your breasts :
My flesh deuided in your precious shapes, 4565
Shal still retaine my spirit, though I die,
And liue in all your seedes immortally :
Then now remooue me, that I may resigne
My place and proper tytle to my sonne :
First take my Scourge and my imperiall Crowne, 4570
And mount my royall chariot of estate,
That I may see thee crown'd before I die.
Help me (my Lords) to make my last remooue.
Ther. A woful change my Lord, that daunts our thoughts,
More than the ruine of our proper soules. 4575
Tam. Sit vp my sonne, let me see how well
Thou wilt become thy fathers maiestie.

They crowne him.

Ami. With what a flinty bosome should I ioy
The breath of life, and burthen of my soule,
If not resolu'd into resolued paines, 4580
My bodies mortified lineaments
Should exercise the motions of my heart,
Pierc'd with the ioy of any dignity ?
O father, if the vnrelenting eares
Of death and hell be shut against my praiers, 4585
And that the spightfull influence of heauen
Denie my soule fruition of her ioy,
How should I step or stir my hatefull feete,
Against the inward powers of my heart,

4557 subiects] substance *conj. Coll.* 4561 subiect] substance *conj. Coll.* 4564 into] vnto *1606, Rob.* 4567 your] our 1606 4576 let] and let *Rob. etc.* 4581 lineaments] laments *1606, Rob.* 4583 Piec'd *conj. Coll.*

Leading a life that onely striues to die, 4590
And plead in vaine, vnpleasing souerainty.
Tam. Let not thy loue exceed thyne honor sonne,
Nor bar thy mind that magnanimitie,
That nobly must admit necessity:
Sit vp my boy, and with those silken raines, 4595
Bridle the steeled stomackes of those Iades.
Ther. My Lord, you must obey his maiesty,
Since Fate commands, and proud necessity.
Amy. Heauens witnes me, with what a broken hart
And damned spirit I ascend this seat, 4600
And send my soule before my father die,
His anguish and his burning agony.
Tam. Now fetch the hearse of faire *Zenocrate*,
Let it be plac'd by this my fatall chaire,
And serue as parcell of my funerall. 4605
Cas. Then feeles your maiesty no soueraigne ease,
Nor may our hearts all drown'd in teares of blood,
Ioy any hope of your recouery?
Tamb. Casane no, the Monarke of the earth,
And eielesse Monster that torments my soule, 4610
Cannot behold the teares ye shed for me,
And therefore stil augments his cruelty.
Tech. Then let some God oppose his holy power,
Against the wrath and tyranny of death,
That his teare-thyrsty and vnquenched hate 4615
May be vpon himselfe reuerberate.

They bring in the hearse.

Tam. Now eies, inioy your latest benefite,
And when my soule hath vertue of your sight,
Pierce through the coffin and the sheet of gold,
And glut your longings with a heauen of ioy. 4620
So, raigne my sonne, scourge and controlle those slaues
Guiding thy chariot with thy Fathers hand.
As precious is the charge thou vndertak'st
As that which *Clymenes* brainsicke sonne did guide,
When wandring *Phœbes* Iuory cheeks were scortcht 4625
And all the earth like *Ætna* breathing fire:
Be warn'd by him, then learne with awfull eie
To sway a throane as dangerous as his:
For if thy body thriue not full of thoughtes

4595 those] these *1606, Rob. to Cunn.* 4596 those] these *1606, Rob. to Cunn.* 4624 Clymenes] Clymeus *1590, 1606* 4625 Phœbus *1606, Rob.*

As pure and fiery as *Phyteus* beames, 4630
The nature of these proud rebelling Iades
Wil take occasion by the slenderest haire,
And draw thee peecemeale like *Hyppolitus*,
Through rocks more steepe and sharp than Caspian cliftes.
The nature of thy chariot wil not beare 4635
A guide of baser temper than my selfe,
More then heauens coach, the pride of *Phaeton*
Farewel my boies, my dearest friends, farewel,
My body feeles, my soule dooth weepe to see
Your sweet desires depriu'd my company, 4640
For *Tamburlaine*, the Scourge of God must die.
Amy. Meet heauen & earth, & here let al things end,
For earth hath spent the pride of all her fruit,
And heauen consum'd his choisest liuing fire.
Let earth and heauen his timelesse death deplore, 4645
For both their woorths wil equall him no more.

FINIS

4633 thee] mee *1606* 4634 cliftes] cliffs *Dyce to Bull.*: clefts *conj. Coll.*

DOCTOR FAUSTUS

Date. The position of *Doctor Faustus* as the immediate successor of *Tamburlaine* in the series of Marlowe's works is well established by the testimony of metre and dramatic structure. External evidence verifies the conclusions of literary criticism and points with tolerable certainty to the winter of 1588/9 as the date of the play's completion. The allusions to the 'fiery keele at *Antwarpes* bridge' (l. 124) and to the Duke of Parma as oppressor of the Netherlands (l. 121) determine the extreme limits of composition—1585 and 1590 respectively. A more exact *terminus a quo* is furnished by the date of the second part of *Tamburlaine*, which belongs almost certainly to 1588, and presumably to the earlier part of the year. On the other hand, it is probable from what we know of the procedure of ballad writers of the time that the 'ballad of the life and deathe of Doctor Ffaustus the great Cungerer', which was licensed on the last day of February, 1588/9 was inspired by the successful production of the play, and it is practically certain that the latter must have been acted before November 6, 1589, when the company which produced it had been silenced by the Lord Mayor on complaint of the Master of the Revels.[1]

Stage history and early editions. Henslowe's Diary mentions twenty-four performances of *Doctor Faustus* by the Lord Admiral's Company between September 30, 1594, and January 5, 1596/7. In October, 1597, it was produced once again by the Lord Admiral's and Lord Pembroke's players in conjunction, this time apparently without any profits. The first recorded presentation, however, brought Henslowe in the unusually large sum of £3 12*s*., from which, as well as from the number of performances, it must be inferred that the piece was then a novelty, though Henslowe does not mark it as a 'new' play. The probability is that it had been acted during 1589, till the inhibition of the players, and was next brought before the public five

[1] Cf. Collier, *Hist. Eng. Dram. Poetry*, 1879, I, 264, 5.

years later, when the Admiral's men reappeared in London, in 1594, with Henslowe as their manager.

On January 7, 1600/1, 'a booke called *the plaie of Doctor Faustus*' was entered for publication by Thomas Bushell, and it is likely that an edition was issued the same year, though no copy is apparently extant. All the early editions of *Faustus* are of excessive rarity. The oldest now known was published by Bushell in 1604, a unique copy being preserved in the Bodleian. Under date of September 13, 1610, the Stationers' Register records the transfer of copyright in *Doctor Faustus* from Bushell to John Wright, who had already in 1609 published an edition of the play, now known from two exemplars, and who issued the next six editions, dated respectively 1611, 1616, 1619, 1620, 1624, 1631. Of the last-named texts all except that of 1631 appear to exist in unique copies. In 1663 the play was again published, this time in an excessively maimed and corrupted state.

Text and Authorship. The quartos of 1604-31 present *Faustus* in two very different shapes. The more original type is represented by the editions of 1604, 1609, and 1611; those of 1616 to 1631 offer a text which has been amplified to the extent of one-half the original, while the old matter has been in some cases omitted, and in others completely recast. With the question of the relation of the two texts is bound up the further question, What part of each version is to be ascribed to Marlowe? Both points have been much discussed, and the credible evidence is too scanty to justify dogmatic assertion. There seems, however, at present to be small warrant for the belief that the 1616 edition contains any matter by Marlowe not found in the earlier versions, with the exception of a few single lines (e.g. 835, 836), which may have been in the problematical 1601 text, and were possibly omitted by the negligence of the compositor of the 1604 edition. The other changes of the later texts—which consist in the bowdlerizing of certain 'atheistical' passages, the addition of a number of crude scenes taken mostly from the prose *Faustbook*, and the expansion of a few brief speeches into longer passages of tolerable blank verse—all these changes are sufficiently accounted for by Henslowe's memorandum of the payment of £4 on November 22, 1602, to William Birde and Samuel Rowley 'for ther adicyones in doctor fostes'. Four pounds is most ample payment, at Henslowe's rate, for all the new passages in the 1616 edition, and there appears to be nothing in any of these passages, with the exception of the few scattered lines already referred to,[1] which is beyond the capacity of Rowley, or suggests the authorship of Marlowe.

The text of 1604–11 is almost certainly that prepared for publication, and perhaps published, by Thomas Bushell in 1601, before Birde and Rowley's alterations had been made. The views of nearly all critics concerning this earlier text appear to have been coloured, perhaps unconsciously, by the well-known forgery in Henslowe's Diary, which professes to record a payment to Dekker in 1597 for additions to *Faustus*. It is morally certain that no such additions were made at that time, and there seems no reason to imagine that the 1604 text is anything else than Marlowe's original version of 1588/9, debased by a dozen years of theatrical manipulation and by careless printing. The blank verse is occasionally faulty, and it is very likely that some of the comic matter, like that omitted by the publisher of *Tamburlaine* (cf. p. 7, ll. 8 ff.), represents the improvisation of the company's clown. It is evident enough, for example, that the author of ll. 994–6 totally failed to understand Marlowe's conception of the effects of conjuring as Mephistopheles explains it in ll. 281–9. Yet with all its corruptions the text of 1604 is probably the most faithful representative extant of Marlowe's manuscript, and it is the principle of the present editor to follow that edition, relegating to an Appendix the probably spurious additions and revisions of 1616.

The edition of 1663 varies greatly from all the others, and has no authority. Several weak comic insertions appear, the most notable being in large measure plagiarized from the *Jew of Malta*.[2] This edition carries to a ridiculous degree the prudery of the version of 1616–31. Lines and phrases alluding to the deity, to eternal punishment, or to religious scepticism are ruthlessly expunged. It may well be that the text was prepared for acting by strolling companies during the Commonwealth period. We know that *Mucedorus* and other plays were so acted in defiance of Puritan regulations, and such an origin would account for the extraordinary efforts of the editor to remove all moral grounds of offence.

[1] For proof of the occasional superiority of the 1616 readings, cf. F. S. Boas, *Taming of a Shrew*, (1908), pp. 91, 92.

[2] Cf. pp. 198–202.

Source. The material out of which Marlowe constructed his tragedy of *Doctor Faustus* comes ultimately from the German *Faustbuch*, or 'Historia von D. Johann Fausten', published at Frankfort-on-the-Main by Johann Spies in 1587. The particular channel through which Marlowe became acquainted with the story has been the subject of much debate; it has been argued both that he knew the original German text and that his information was drawn from the verbal reports of actors newly returned from theatrical tours in Germany. It seems now certain, however, that Marlowe's only source was an English translation of the 1587 *Faustbuch*, published probably in 1588. It is true that no copy of so early an edition of the translation has so far been discovered, but the earliest extant issue—that of 1592—bears a very close resemblance to Marlowe's text, and is shown not to be the *editio princeps* by the words on the title page: 'Newly imprinted, and in conuenient places imperfect matter amended.' Further proof of the same point has been collected by Dr. H. Logeman.[1]

The English translation was used not only by Marlowe himself, but also by the elaborators of the 1616 text. The play, however, contains much for which the translation furnished no suggestion. Thus the good and evil angels are an addition of Marlowe, and only the barest hint for the mask of the seven deadly sins can be found in the prose history.

The Stationers' Register, under date of October 16, 1609, records the transfer of copyright in a work called 'Doctor Ffaustus the 2 parte' from Mistress Burby to Master Welby. Nothing appears to be known of the book in question. As a sequel to the play of *Faustus* is hardly imaginable, it is probable that the title is that of one of the numerous continuations of the Faustus-Wagner history.

[1] *The English Faust-Book of 1592*, Introduction, p. xv.

THE TRAGICALL

Hiſtory of D. Fauſtus.

As it hath bene Acted by the Right Honorable the Earle of Nottingham his ſeruants.

Written by Ch. Marl.

LONDON

Printed by V. S. for Thomas Buſhell. 1604.

1604 = Quarto edition of that year. B.L.
1609 = „ „ „ „ „ B.L.
1611 = „ „ „ „ „ B.L.
1616 = „ „ „ „ „ B.L.
1619 = „ „ „ „ „ B.L.
1620 = „ „ „ „ „ B.L.
1624 = „ „ „ „ „ B.L.
1631 = „ „ „ „ „ B.L.
1663 = „ „ „ „ „ B.L.

Dilke = Text of *Doctor Faustus* in *Old English Plays*, vol. i, 1814 (ed. C. W. Dilke).
Rob. = G. Robinson's edition of Marlowe, 1826.
Dyce { *Dyce* [1] = Dyce's first edition of Marlowe, 1850.
Dyce { *Dyce* [2] = Dyce's revised edition of Marlowe, 1858, etc.
Cunn. = Cunningham's edition of Marlowe, 1870, etc.
Wag. = W. Wagner's edition of *Doctor Faustus*, 1877.
Ward = Ward's edition of *Doctor Faustus*, 1878, etc.
Bull. = Bullen's edition of Marlowe, 1885.
Ellis = 'Mermaid' edition of Marlowe's best plays, 1887, etc.
Brey. = Breymann's edition of *Doctor Faustus*, 1889.
Gollancz = 'Temple Dramatists' edition of *Doctor Faustus*, 1897.
T. B. = The present editor.

Albers = J. H. A. in *Jahrbuch f. rom. u. engl. Lit.*, 1876, 369 ff.
Baker = H. T. B. in *Modern Language Notes*, xxi. 86, 87.
Brennan = C. B. in *Anglia*, Beiblatt 1905, 208.
Brereton = J. Le G. B. „ „ „ 204.
Broughton = J. B.'s MS. notes in copy of *Rob.* B.M. 11771 d.
Cook = A. S. C. in *Modern Language Notes*, xxi. 145–7.
Crossley = J. C., quoted by *Dyce.*
Düntzer = H. D. in *Anglia*, i. 44–54.
Koeppel = E. K.'s conjectures, quoted by *Brey.*
Logeman = H. L., *Faustus Notes*, 1898.
Mitford = J. M. in *Gentleman's Magazine*, Jan., 1841.
Schröer = K. J. S. in *Anglia*, v. 134–6.
Tancock = O. W. T. in *Notes and Queries*, 5th Series, xi. 324, 325.

The tragicall Historie of Doctor Faustus

⟨The ACTORS Names

Faustus.
Mephostophilis.
Good Angell.
Bad Angell.
Three Scholers.
Seven Deadlie Sinnes.
Lucipher, Belzebub, three Divels more.

Duke and Dutches of Saxonie.
Emperour of Jarmany.
Frederick., *Mertino.*, *Benvolio.* } *Three Gentlemen.*
Solamaine the Emperour and Empery.

Mustapher., *Caleph.* } *Two Bashawes.*
Robin the Clowne.
Dick an Hostler.
Carter.
Horse-courser.
Hostie. (sic)
Majecane.⟩ [1]

⟨DRAMATIS PERSONÆ (for the text of 1604)

The Pope.
Cardinal of Lorrain.
The Emperor of Germany.
Duke of Vanholt.
Faustus.
Valdes, Cornelius, } *friends to Faustus.*
Wagner, *servant to Faustus.*
Clown.

Robin.
Ralph.
Vintner.
Horse-courser.
A Knight.
An Old Man.
Scholars, Friars, and Attendants.
Duchess of Vanholt.
Lucifer.
Belzebub.

Mephistophilis.
Good Angel.
Evil Angel.
The Seven Deadly Sins.
Devils.
Spirits in the shapes of Alexander the Great, of his paramour, and of Helen.
Chorus.⟩ [2]

⟨DRAMATIS PERSONÆ (for the text of 1616)

The Pope.
The Emperor of Germany.
Raymond, *king of Hungary.*
Duke of Saxony.
Bruno.
Duke of Vanholt.
Martino, Frederick, Benvolio, } *gentlemen.*
Faustus.
Valdes, Cornelius, } *friends to Faustus.*

Wagner, *servant to Faustus.*
Clown. Robin.
Dick. Vintner.
Horse-courser.
Carter.
An Old Man.
Scholars, Cardinals, Archbishop of Rheims, Bishops, Monks, Friars, Soldiers, and Attendants.
Duchess of Vanholt.

Hostess.
Lucifer.
Belzebub.
Mephistophilis.
Good Angel.
Evil Angel.
The Seven Deadly Sins.
Devils.
Spirits in the shapes of Alexander the Great, of his paramour, of Darius, and of Helen.
Chorus.⟩ [2]

[1] *Add. 1663.* [2] *Add. Dyce.*

The tragicall Historie of Doctor Faustus

Enter Chorus.

⟨*Chor.*⟩ Not marching now in fields of *Thracimene,*
Where *Mars* did mate the Carthaginians,
Nor sporting in the dalliance of loue,
In courts of Kings where state is ouerturnd,
Nor in the pompe of prowd audacious deedes, 5
Intends our Muse to daunt his heauenly verse:
Onely this (Gentlemen) we must performe,
The forme of *Faustus* fortunes good or bad.
To patient Iudgements we appeale our plaude,
And speake for *Faustus* in his infancie: 10
Now is he borne, his parents base of stocke,
In *Germany*, within a towne calld *Rhodes*:
Of riper yeeres to *Wertenberg* he went,
Whereas his kinsmen chiefly brought him vp.
So soone hee profites in Diuinitie, 15
The fruitfull plot of Scholerisme grac't,
That shortly he was grac't with Doctors name,
Excelling all, whose sweete delight disputes
In heauenly matters of *Theologie*,
Till swolne with cunning, of a selfe conceit, 20
His waxen wings did mount aboue his reach,
And melting heauens conspirde his ouerthrow.
For falling to a diuelish exercise,
And glutted now with learnings golden gifts,

Heading tragicall Historie *1604–11*: Tragedie *1616–63* 1 *Prefix om. 1604–63* now *om. 1616–63* in] in the *1616–63* 2 the] the warlicke (warlike) *1616–63* Carthagens *1616–24*: Carthagen *1631, 1663* 6 daunt] vaunt *1616–63*: vent *Logeman* his] her *Dyce, Cunn.* 7 Gentlemen] Gentles *1616–63* must] must now *1616–63* 9 To] And now to *1616–63* our plaude *om. 1616–63* our] for *Brey.* 11 his] of *1616–63* 13 Of] At *1616–63* Wertenberg *1604, 1609*: Wittenberg *1611–63* 15 soone] much *1616–63* 16 *om. 1616–63* 18 whose . . disputes] and sweetly can dispute *1616–63*: whose sweete disputes delight *conj. Koeppel, Brey.*: who sweetly like disputes *conj. Brey.* 19 In] In th' *1616–63* 20 cunning] coming *conj. Brennan* of a] and a *1619–63* 22 conspirde] became *1663* 24 now *1616 etc.*: more *1604–11*

He surffets vpon cursed Negromancy. 25
Nothing so sweete as magicke is to him
Which he preferres before his chiefest blisse,
And this the man that in his study sits. *Exit.*

Enter Faustus in his Study.

Faustus. Settle thy studies *Faustus*, and beginne
To sound the deapth of that thou wilt professe : 30
Hauing commencde, be a Diuine in shew,
Yet leuell at the end of euery Art,
And liue and die in *Aristotles* workes :
Sweete *Analutikes* tis thou hast rauisht me,
Bene disserere est finis logices, 35
Is to dispute well, Logickes chiefest end,
Affoords this Art no greater myracle ?
Then reade no more, thou hast attaind the end :
A greater subiect fitteth *Faustus* wit,
Bid *on cai me on* farewell, *Galen* come : 40
Seeing, *vbi desinit philosophus, ibi incipit medicus.*
Be a physition *Faustus*, heape vp golde,
And be eternizde for some wondrous cure.
Summum bonum medicinæ sanitas,
The end of physicke is our bodies health : 45
Why *Faustus*, hast thou not attaind that end ?
Is not thy common talke sound Aphorismes ?
Are not thy billes hung vp as monuments,
Whereby whole Citties haue escapt the plague,
And thousand desprate maladies beene easde, 50
Yet art thou still but *Faustus*, and a man.
Wouldst thou make man to liue eternally ?
Or being dead, raise them to life againe ?
Then this profession were to be esteemd.
Physicke farewell, where is *Iustinian* ? 55
Si vna eademq⟨ue⟩ res legatur duobus,
Alter rem, alter valorem rei, &c.
A pretty case of paltry legacies :

25 vpon] on the *1619–63* 28 + Act the First. Scene I. *add. Rob.* : Scene I *Ward, Bull.* 34 Anulatikes *1604* : Analytic *conj. Dyce* 38 the] that *1616–63* 40 on cai me on *Bull. etc.* : Oncaymaeon *1604* : Oeconomy *1609–31* : Orconomy *1663* Galen] and Galen *1616–63* 41 *om. 1616–63* 47 *om. 1616–63* sound] found *Dyce, Cunn., Bull.* 50 thousand] diuers *1619–63* easde] cur'd *1616–63* 52 Couldst *1616–63* man] men *1611–63* 53 them] men *1620–63* 55 + S.D. Reads *add. Dyce* 58 pretty] petty *1616–63* 58 + S.D. Reads *add. Dyce*

Exhaereditare filium non potest pater nisi :
Such is the subiect of the institute 60
And vniuersall body of the law :
His study fittes a mercenary drudge,
Who aimes at nothing but externall trash,
Too seruile and illiberall for me :
When all is done, Diuinitie is best. 65
Ieromes Bible, *Faustus*, view it well.
Stipendium peccati mors est : ha, *Stipendium*, *&c*.
The reward of sinne is death : thats hard.
Si peccasse negamus, fallimur, & nulla est in nobis veritas.
If we say that we haue no sinne, 70
We deceiue our selues, and theres no truth in vs.
Why then belike
We must sinne, and so consequently die.
I, we must die an euerlasting death :
What doctrine call you this, *Che sera, sera*, 75
What wil be, shall be ? Diuinitie, adieu,
These Metaphisickes of Magicians,
And Negromantike bookes are heauenly :
Lines, circles, sceanes, letters and characters :
I, these are those that *Faustus* most desires. 80
O what a world of profit and delight,
Of power, of honor, of omnipotence
Is promised to the studious Artizan ?
All things that mooue betweene the quiet poles
Shalbe at my commaund, Emperours and Kings 85
Are but obeyd in their seuerall prouinces :
Nor can they raise the winde, or rend the cloudes :
But his dominion that exceedes in this,
Stretcheth as farre as doth the minde of man.
A sound Magician is a mighty god : 90
Heere *Faustus* trie thy braines to gaine a deitie.

Enter Wagner.

Wagner, commend me to my deerest friends,

59 nisi] nisi &c. *1620–31* 61 law *1616 etc.* : Church *1604–11* 62 His] This *1616–63* 63 externall] eternal *1663* 64 Too seruile *1616, etc.* : The deuill *1604–11* 66 +, 68 + S.D. Reads *add. Dyce* 70 that *om. 1663* 71 there is *1616–63* 76 wil] shall *1663* 79 sceanes *om. 1616–63* and *om. 1616–63* 82 and omnipotence *1616–63* 87 *om. 1616–63* 90 mighty] Demi- *1616–63* 91 Faustus *om. 1616–63* trie thy *1604–11* : tire my *1616–63* : tire thy *Dyce, Bull.* gaine] get *1616, 1663*

The Germaine *Valdes*, and *Cornelius*,
Request them earnestly to visite me.
Wag. I wil sir. *Exit.*
Fau. Their conference will be a greater help to me, 96
Than all my labours, plodde I nere so fast.

Enter the good Angell and the euill Angell.

Good A. O *Faustus*, lay that damned booke aside,
And gaze not on it, lest it tempt thy soule,
And heape Gods heauy wrath vpon thy head. 100
Reade, reade the scriptures, that is blasphemy.
Euill An. Go forward *Faustus* in that famous art,
Wherein all natures treasury is containd:
Be thou on earth as *Ioue* is in the skie,
Lord and commaunder of these Elements. *Exeunt.*
Fau. How am I glutted with conceit of this? 106
Shall I make spirits fetch me what I please,
Resolue me of all ambiguities,
Performe what desperate enterprise I will?
Ile haue them flye to *India* for gold, 110
Ransacke the Ocean for orient pearle,
And search all corners of the new found world
For pleasant fruites and princely delicates:
Ile haue them reade mee straunge philosophie,
And tell the secrets of all forraine kings, 115
Ile haue them wall all *Iermany* with brasse,
And make swift *Rhine* circle faire *Wertenberge.*
Ile haue them fill the publike schooles with silk,
Wherewith the students shalbe brauely clad:
Ile leuy souldiers with the coyne they bring, 120
And chase the Prince of *Parma* from our land,
And raigne sole king of all our prouinces:
Yea stranger engines for the brunt of warre,
Then was the fiery keele at *Antwarpes* bridge,
Ile make my seruile spirits to inuent: 125
Come *Germaine Valdes* and *Cornelius*,
And make me blest with your sage conference.

93 Germaine Valdes] Grimoaldus *conj. Düntzer* 97 + S.D. Enter *etc.*] Enter the Angell and Spirit *1616–63* 99–101 tempt thy soule . . blasphemy] tempt thy heart to blasphemy *1663* 100 wrath] rod *1609, 1611* 103 treasury *1604*: treasure *1609–63, Dyce, Bull., Wag* 109 enterprises *1624–63* 117 make *1604–16*: with *1619–63* faire] all *1624–63* Wittenberge *1616–63* 118 silk *Dyce etc.*: skill *1604–63* 122 our *1604, Bull., Brey.*: the *1609–63, Rob. to Wag.* 126 Germaine Valdes] Grimoaldus *conj. Düntzer* 127 blest] wise *1620–63*

Enter Valdes and Cornelius.

Valdes, sweete *Valdes*, and *Cornelius*,
Know that your words haue woon me at the last,
To practise Magicke and concealed arts : 130
Yet not your words onely, but mine owne fantasie,
That will receiue no obiect for my head,
But ruminates on Negromantique skill.
Philosophy is odious and obscure,
Both Law and Phisicke are for pettie wits, 135
Diuinitie is basest of the three,
Vnpleasant, harsh, contemptible and vilde,
Tis Magicke, Magicke that hath rauisht mee.
Then gentle friends ayde me in this attempt,
And I that haue with concise sylogismes 140
Graueld the Pastors of the Germaine Church,
And made the flowring pride of *Wertenberge*
Swarme to my Problemes as the infernall spirits
On sweet *Musæus* when he came to hell,
Will be as cunning as *Agrippa* was, 145
Whose shadowes made all *Europe* honor him.
Vald. Faustus,
These bookes, thy wit and our experience
Shall make all nations to canonize vs,
As Indian Moores obey their Spanish Lords, 150
So shall the subiects of euery element
Be alwaies seruiceable to vs three.
Like Lyons shall they guard vs when we please,
Like *Almaine* Rutters with their horsemens staues,
Or Lapland Gyants trotting by our sides, 155
Sometimes like women, or vnwedded maides,
Shadowing more beautie in their ayrie browes,
Then has the white breasts of the queene of Loue :
From *Venice* shall they dregge huge Argoces,
And from *America* the golden fleece, 160
That yearely stuffes olde *Philips* treasury,
If learned *Faustus* will be resolute.

128 Valdes, sweete Valdes] sweet Grimoaldus *conj. Düntzer* 131–3 *om. 1616–63* 131 onely] alone *conj. Dyce* 136–7 *om. 1616–63* 140 Consissylogismes *1604, 1609* : subtile sylogismes *1611–63* 142 Wittenberg *1616–63* 146 shadow *1616–63, Dyce* 149 to *om. 1620–63* 151 subiects] spirits *1616–63, Dyce to Bull.* 158 has the *1616, Brey.* : in their *1604–11* : haue the *1619–63, Rob., Dyce, Cunn., Bull.* : 's in the *Wag.* 159 From *1609–63 etc.* : For *1604* shall they *1604, 1611–19*: shall the *1609*: they shall *1620–63* dragge *1609 etc.* huge] whole *1620–63, Rob.* 161 stuff'd *1616, 1619*

Fau. *Valdes* as resolute am I in this
As thou to liue, therefore obiect it not.
Corn. The myracles that Magicke will performe, 165
Will make thee vow to studie nothing else.
He that is grounded in Astrologie,
Inricht with tongues, well seene in minerals,
Hath all the principles Magicke doth require,
Then doubt not (*Faustus*) but to be renowmd, 170
And more frequented for this mystery,
Then heretofore the Delphian Oracle.
The spirits tell me they can drie the sea,
And fetch the treasure of all forraine wrackes,
I, all the wealth that our forefathers hid 175
Within the massie entrailes of the earth.
Then tell me *Faustus*, what shal we three want?
Fau. Nothing *Cornelius*. O this cheares my soule,
Come shewe me some demonstrations magicall,
That I may coniure in some lustie groue, 180
And haue these ioyes in full possession.
Val. Then haste thee to some solitary groue,
And beare wise *Bacons* and *Albanus* workes,
The Hebrew Psalter, and new Testament,
And whatsoeuer else is requisit 185
Wee will enforme thee ere our conference cease.
Cor. *Valdes*, first let him know the words of art,
And then all other ceremonies learnd,
Faustus may trie his cunning by himselfe.
Val. First Ile instruct thee in the rudiments, 190
And then wilt thou be perfecter then I.
Fau. Then come and dyne with me, and after meate
Weele canuas euery quidditie thereof:
For ere I sleepe Ile trie what I can do,
This night Ile coniure though I die therefore. *Exeunt.*

Enter two Schollers.

1\. *Sch.* I wonder whats become of *Faustus*, that was wont to make our schooles ring with *sic probo.* 197
2\. *Sch.* That shall we know, for see here comes his boy.

168 in *om. 1604* 172 heretofore] hetherto *1609, 1611* 180 lustie *1604*: little *1609, 1611*: bushy *1616–63, Rob., Cunn., Bull.*: hidden *Wag.* 183 Albanus] Albertus *conj. Mitford, Dyce, Cunn., Wag., Bull.* 195 + Scene II. *add. Cunn. etc. exc. Dyce* 198 we] we presently *1616–63* for see *om. 1616–63*

Enter Wagner.

1. *Sch.* How now sirra, wheres thy maister ?
Wag. God in heauen knowes. 200
2. Why, dost not thou know ?
Wag. Yes I know, but that followes not.
1. Go too sirra, leaue your ieasting, and tell vs where hee is.
Wag. That follows not necessary by force of argument, that you being licentiate should stand vpon't, therefore acknowledge your error, and be attentiue. 207
2. Why, didst thou not say thou knewst ?
Wag. Haue you any witnesse on't ?
1. Yes sirra, I heard you. 210
Wag. Aske my fellow if I be a thiefe.
2. Well, you will not tell vs.
Wag. Yes sir, I will tell you, yet if you were not dunces you would neuer aske me such a question, for is not he *corpus naturale*, and is not that *mobile* ? then wherefore should you aske me such a question ? but that I am by nature flegmaticke, slowe to wrath, and prone to leachery (to loue I would say), it were not for you to come within fortie foote of the place of execution, although I do not doubt to see you both hang'd the next Sessions. Thus hauing triumpht ouer you, I will set my countnance like a precisian, and begin to speake thus : truly my deare brethren, my maister is within at dinner with *Valdes* and *Cornelius*, as this wine if it could speake, it would enforme your worships, and so the Lord blesse you, preserue you, and keepe you my deare brethren, my deare brethren. 226
Exit.

1. Nay then I feare he is falne into that damned art, for which they two are infamous through the world.
2. Were he a stranger, and not alied to me, yet should I grieue for him : but come let vs go and informe the

201 know] know then *1616–63* 205 necessary *om. 1616–63* 206 that] which *1616–63* Licentiats *1616–63* vpon't *1604* : vpon it *1609, 1611* : vpon *1616–63* 208–11 *om. 1616–63* 212 Well] Then *1616–63* 213 Yes sir] You are deceiu'd, for *1616–63* 214 not he] he not *1616–63* 220 to] but to *1616–63* 224 it would] would *1616–63, Dyce, Bull.* 226 my deere brethren *once 1616–63* 227 Nay . . he is] O Faustus, then I feare that (the *1624–63*) which I haue long suspected That thou art *1616–63* the damned *1631, 1663* 229 and *om. 1616–1663* 229–30 yet . . for him] The danger of his soule would make me mourne *1616–63*

Rector, and see if hee by his graue counsaile can reclaime him. 232

1. O but I feare me nothing can reclaime him.
2. Yet let vs trie what we can do. *Exeunt.*

Enter Faustus to coniure.

Fau. Now that the gloomy shadow of the earth, 235
Longing to view *Orions* drisling looke,
Leapes from th' antartike world vnto the skie,
And dimmes the welkin with her pitchy breath:
Faustus, begin thine incantations,
And trie if diuels will obey thy hest, 240
Seeing thou hast prayde and sacrific'd to them.
Within this circle is *Iehouahs* name,
Forward and backward anagrammatiz'd
The breuiated names of holy Saints,
Figures of euery adiunct to the heauens, 245
And characters of signes and erring starres,
By which the spirits are inforst to rise,
Then feare not *Faustus*, but be resolute,
And trie the vttermost Magicke can performe. 249

Sint mihi dei acherontis propitij, valeat numen triplex Iehouæ, ignei, aërij, aquatici spiritus saluete, Orientis princeps Belsibub, inferni ardentis monarcha & demigorgon, propitiamus vos, vt appareat & surgat Mephastophilis: quid tu moraris? per Iehouam, gehennam & consecratam aquam quam nunc spargo, signúmque crucis quod nunc facio, & per vota nostra ipse nunc surgat nobis dicatus Mephastophilis. 257

231 and see . . by] It may be *1616–63* can] may *1616–63* 232 him *om. 1619–63* 233 O but *om. 1616–63* can] will *1616–63* him] him now *1616–63* 234 trie] see *1616–63* 234+ Scene III. *add. Rob. etc. exc. Dyce* S.D. Enter . . coniure *1604–11*: Thunder. Enter Lucifer and 4 deuils, Faustus to them with this speech *1616–63* 235 earth] night *1616–63* 238 her] his *1620–63* 242–45 *Condensed in ed. 1663 to* Within this circle is the names of all infernal spirits 243 Anagramatis'd *1616–31*: and Agramithist *1604–11* 244 Th' abreuiated *1616–63* 246 erring] euening *1616*: crying *1663* 248 but] to *1616–63* 249 vttermost] vtmost *1616–63* 249 + S.D. Thunder *add. 1616–63* 251 ignei . . aquatici] Ignis, aëris, aquæ, terræ *conj. Schröer, Gollancz, Brey.* aquatici *T.B.*: Aquatani *Qq* 253 Mephastophilis] Mephostophilis Dragon *1616–63* 254 quid tu moraris *conj. Schroer, conj. Bull., Gollancz, Brey.*: quod tumeraris *Qq, Rob. to Bull.*: quod tu mandares *conj. Crossley*: per Dragon (*or* Dagon) quod numen est aëris *conj. Mitford*: qui arbiter est aëris *conj. Wag.*: quod nominaris *conj. Düntzer*

Enter a Diuell.

I charge thee to returne and chaunge thy shape,
Thou art too vgly to attend on me,
Goe and returne an old Franciscan Frier, 260
That holy shape becomes a diuell best. *Exit diuell.*
I see theres vertue in my heauenly words,
Who would not be proficient in this art?
How pliant is this *Mephastophilis*?
Full of obedience and humilitie, 265
Such is the force of Magicke and my spels.
No *Faustus*, thou art Coniurer laureate
That canst commaund great *Mephastophilis*,
Quin regis Mephastophilis fratris imagine.

Enter Mephostophilis.

Me. Now *Faustus*, what wouldst thou haue me do? 270
Fau. I charge thee wait vpon me whilst I liue,
To do what euer *Faustus* shall commaund,
Be it to make the Moone drop from her spheare,
Or the Ocean to ouerwhelme the world.
Me. I am a seruant to great *Lucifer*, 275
And may not follow thee without his leaue,
No more then he commaunds must we performe.
Fau. Did not he charge thee to appeare to mee?
Me. No, I came now hither of mine owne accord.
Fau. Did not my coniuring speeches raise thee? speake.
Me. That was the cause, but yet per accident, 281
For when we heare one racke the name of God,
Abiure the scriptures, and his Sauiour Christ,
Wee flye, in hope to get his glorious soule,
Nor will we come, vnlesse he vse such meanes 285
Whereby he is in danger to be damnd:
Therefore the shortest cut for coniuring
Is stoutly to abiure the Trinitie,
And pray deuoutly to the prince of hell.
Fau. So *Faustus* hath 290

257 S.D. a *om. 1624–63* 267–9 *om. 1616–63* 267 No] Now *conj. Albers, Wag., Bull* 270 do] to do *Bull.* 279 now *om. 1620–63, Rob. to Bull.* 280 speeches *1604, Dyce etc.*: spirits *1609, 1611*: *om. 1616–63* 281 accident *1604–20*: accidens *1624–63, Rob. etc.* 282–4 *Contracted 1663 to* For when we hear one swear, We flye, in hope to get him 286 damnd] lost *1663* 288 the Trinitie *1604–11*: all godlinesse *1616–63*

Already done, & holds this principle,
There is no chiefe but onely *Belsibub*,
To whom *Faustus* doth dedicate himselfe,
This word damnation terrifies not him,
For he confounds hell in *Elizium*. 295
His ghost be with the olde Philosophers,
But leauing these vaine trifles of mens soules,
Tell me what is that *Lucifer* thy Lord?

Me. Arch-regent and commaunder of all spirits.

Fau. Was not that *Lucifer* an Angell once? 300

Me. Yes *Faustus*, and most dearely lou'd of God.

Fau. How comes it then that he is prince of diuels?

Me. O by aspiring pride and insolence,
For which God threw him from the face of heauen.

Fau. And what are you that liue with *Lucifer*? 305

Me. Vnhappy spirits that fell with *Lucifer*,
Conspir'd against our God with *Lucifer*,
And are for euer damnd with *Lucifer*.

Fau. Where are you damn'd?

Me. In hell. 310

Fau. How comes it then that thou art out of hel?

Me. Why this is hel, nor am I out of it:
Thinkst thou that I who saw the face of God,
And tasted the eternal ioyes of heauen,
Am not tormented with ten thousand hels, 315
In being depriv'd of euerlasting blisse?
O *Faustus*, leaue these friuolous demaunds,
Which strike a terror to my fainting soule.

Fau. What, is great *Mephastophilis* so passionate,
For being deprivd of the ioyes of heauen? 320
Learne thou of *Faustus* manly fortitude,
And scorne those ioyes thou neuer shalt possesse.
Go beare those tidings to great *Lucifer*,
Seeing *Faustus* hath incurrd eternall death,
By desprate thoughts against *Ioues* deitie: 325
Say, he surrenders vp to him his soule,

294 damnation] being lost *1663* him] me *1616–63* 295, 296 *om. 1663* 295 he confounds] I confound *1616–31* 296 His] My *1616–31* 297 of . . soules *om. 1663* 299 all *om. 1631, 1663* 301 and . . God *om. 1663* 304 God threw him] he was thrown *1663* 306 fell *1604, Dyce etc.*: liue *1609–63, Rob.* 307 our God] heaven *1663* 308 damnd] lost *1663* 313 who] that *1609–63* 313, 314 saw . . And *om. 1663* 318 strikes *1609–24* 323 those] these *1616–63, Dyce etc.* 326 vp *om. 1609. 1611* soule] self *1663*

So he will spare him 24. yeeres,
Letting him liue in al voluptuousnesse,
Hauing thee euer to attend on me,
To giue me whatsoeuer I shal aske, 330
To tel me whatsoeuer I demaund,
To slay mine enemies, and ayde my friends,
And alwayes be obedient to my wil:
Goe and returne to mighty *Lucifer*,
And meete mee in my study at midnight, 335
And then resolue me of thy maisters minde.

Me. I will *Faustus*. *Exit.*

Fau. Had I as many soules as there be starres,
Ide giue them al for *Mephastophilis*:
By him Ile be great Emprour of the world, 340
And make a bridge through the moouing ayre,
To passe the *Ocean* with a band of men,
Ile ioyne the hils that binde the *Affricke* shore,
And make that land continent to *Spaine*,
And both contributory to my crowne: 345
The Emprour shal not liue but by my leaue,
Nor any Potentate of *Germany*:
Now that I haue obtaind what I desire,
Ile liue in speculation of this Art,
Til *Mephastophilis* returne againe. *Exit.*

Enter Wagner and the Clowne.

Wag. Sirra boy, come hither. 351

Clo. How, boy? swowns boy, I hope you haue seene many boyes with such pickadevaunts as I haue. Boy, quotha?

Wag. Tel me sirra, hast thou any commings in? 355

Clo. I, and goings out too, you may see else.

Wag. Alas poore slaue, see how pouerty iesteth in his nakednesse, the vilaine is bare, and out of seruice, and so hungry, that I know he would giue his soule to the Diuel for a shoulder of mutton, though it were blood rawe. 361

Clo. How, my soule to the Diuel for a shoulder of

327 24. *1604*: four and twenty *1609–63* 330 me *om. 1609, 1611* 332 and *1604, Dyce, Bull., Ward*: and to *1609–63, Rob., Cunn., Wag.* 344 land] country *1616–63, Dyce, Bull., Ward, Wag.* 348 desire] desir'd *1616–63, Dyce, Ward* 350 + Scene IV *add. Cunn. etc.* 351–432 *Qq 1616–63 give this scene in a considerably altered form. For the text as there found cf. Appendix, pp.* 195, 196

mutton though twere blood rawe? not so good friend, burladie I had neede haue it wel roasted, and good sawce to it, if I pay so deere. 365

Wag. Wel, wilt thou serue me, and Ile make thee go like *Qui mihi discipulus?*

Clo. How, in verse?

Wag. No sirra, in beaten silke and staues acre.

Clo. How, how, knaues acre? I, I thought that was al the land his father left him: Doe yee heare, I would be sorie to robbe you of your liuing 372

Wag. Sirra, I say in staues acre.

Clo. Oho, oho, staues acre, why then belike, if I were your man, I should be ful of vermine. 375

Wag. So thou shalt, whether thou beest with me, or no: but sirra, leaue your iesting, and binde your selfe presently vnto me for seauen yeeres, or Ile turne al the lice about thee into familiars, and they shal teare thee in peeces. 380

Clo. Doe you heare sir? you may saue that labour, they are too familiar with me already, swowns they are as bolde with my flesh, as if they had payd for my meate and drinke.

Wag. Wel, do you heare sirra? holde, take these gilders.

Clo. Gridyrons, what be they? 386

Wag. Why french crownes.

Clo. Mas but for the name of french crownes a man were as good haue as many english counters, and what should I do with these? 390

Wag. Why now sirra thou art at an houres warning whensoeuer or wheresoeuer the diuell shall fetch thee.

Clo. No, no, here take your gridirons againe.

Wag. Truly Ile none of them.

Clo. Truly but you shall. 395

Wag. Beare witnesse I gaue them him.

Clo. Beare witnesse I giue them you againe.

Wag. Well, I will cause two diuels presently to fetch thee away. *Baliol* and *Belcher*. 399

Clo. Let your *Balio* and your *Belcher* come here, and Ile knocke them, they were neuer so knockt since they were diuels. Say I should kill one of them what would

369 staues acre] stauracin *or* stauracia *conj. Tancock* 377 your *1604–11*: thy *Brey.* your *1604–11*: thy *Brey.* 383 my meate *1604–11*: their meat *Dyce, Bull.* 385 + S.D. Gives money *add. Dyce*

folkes say? do ye see yonder tall fellow in the round slop, hee has kild the diuell: so I should be cald kill diuell all the parish ouer. 405

Enter two diuells, and the clowne runnes vp and downe crying.

Wag. *Balioll* and *Belcher*, spirits away. *Exeunt.*

Clow. What, are they gone? a vengeance on them, they haue vilde long nailes: there was a hee diuell and a shee diuell. Ile tell you how you shall know them: all hee diuels has hornes, and all shee diuels has clifts and clouen feete. 411

Wag. Well sirra follow me.

Clo. But do you hear? if I should serue you, would you teach me to raise vp *Banios* and *Belcheos*?

Wag. I will teach thee to turne thy selfe to any thing, to a dogge, or a catte, or a mouse, or a ratte, or any thing. 417

Clo. How? a Christian fellow to a dogge or a catte, a mouse or a ratte? no, no sir, if you turne me into any thing, let it be in the likenesse of a little pretie frisking flea, that I may be here and there and euery where. O Ile tickle the pretie wenches plackets, Ile be amongst them ifaith.

Wag. Wel sirra, come.

Clo. But doe you heare *Wagner*? 425

Wag. How *Balioll* and *Belcher*.

Clo. O Lord, I pray sir, let *Banio* and *Belcher* go sleepe.

Wag. Vilaine, call me Maister *Wagner*, and let thy left eye be diametarily fixt vpon my right heele, with *quasi vestigias nostras insistere.* *Exit.*

Clo: God forgiue me, he speakes Dutch fustian: 431 well, Ile folow him, Ile serue him, thats flat. *Exit.*

Enter Faustus in his Study.

Fau. Now Faustus must thou needes be damnd,
And canst thou not be saued?
What bootes it then to thinke of God or heauen? 435

404 the diuell] that diuell *1611* 405 S.D. crying *1604*: the Stage *1609*, *1611* 420 little *om.* *1609*, *1611* 430 vestigiis nostris *Dyce*[2], *Wag.* 432 + Act II. *add.* *1663*: Act the Second, Scene I. *Rob.*, *Cunn.*, *Wag.*: Scene V. *Ward*, *Bull.*, *Brey.* 433 damnd] lost *1663* 434 And *om.* *1616–63* 435 of] on *1616–63* God or *om.* *1663*

Away with such vaine fancies and despaire,
Despaire in God, and trust in Belsabub:
Now go not backeward: no Faustus, be resolute,
Why wauerest thou? O something soundeth in mine eares:
Abiure this Magicke, turne to God againe. 440
I and Faustus wil turne to God againe.
To God? he loues thee not,
The god thou seruest is thine owne appetite,
Wherein is fixt the loue of Belsabub.
To him Ile build an altare and a church, 445
And offer luke warme blood of new borne babes.

Enter good Angell, and Euill.

Good Angel. Sweet Faustus, leaue that execrable art.
Fau. Contrition, prayer, repentance: what of them?
Good Angel. O they are meanes to bring thee vnto heauen.
Euill Angel. Rather illusions, fruites of lunacy, 450
That makes men foolish that do trust them most.
Good Angel. Sweet Faustus, thinke of heauen, and heauenly things.
Euill Angel. No Faustus, thinke of honor and ⟨of⟩ wealth. *Exeunt.*
Fau. Of wealth,
Why the signory of Emden shalbe mine, 455
When *Mephastophilus* shal stand by me,
What God can hurt thee Faustus? thou art safe,
Cast no more doubts: come *Mephastophilus*,
And bring glad tidings from great *Lucifer*:
Ist not midnight? come *Mephastophilus*, 460
Veni, veni Mephastophile.

437 in God] of God *conj. Brey.* God] heaven *1663* 438 backeward] backe *1620–63, Cunn.* no *om. 1616–63* 439 Why *om. 1624–63* soundeth] roundeth *conj. Broughton* eares] eare *1616–63* 440–6 *Ed. 1663 contracts to* Abjure this Magick heaven and repent 441 *om. 1616–31* 442 To God] Why *1616–31* 442, 443 *one line 1616–31* 446 S.D. Enter . . Euill *1604–11*: Enter the two Angels *1616–63* 447 *Before this line Qq 1616–63 add* EUILL AN. Go forward Faustus in that famous (most famous *1619–63*) Art 448 of them *1604–11*: of these *1616*: be these *1619–63* 451 makes men *1604, 1609*: makee men *1611*: make them *1616–63* trust] vse *1616–63* 453 of wealth *1609–63*: wealth *1604* 453 + S.D. Ex. An. *1616–63* 454 Of *om. 1616–63* 457 God] power *1616–63* thee] me *1616–63* 458 Cast] Come *1611* come Mephastophilus] Mepho: come *1616–63* 461 Mephostophilis *1620–63*

Enter Meph:

Now tel ⟨me⟩, what sayes *Lucifer* thy Lord?
Me: That I shal waite on Faustus whilst he liues,
So he wil buy my seruice with his soule.
Fau: Already Faustus hath hazarded that for thee. 465
Me: But Faustus, thou must bequeathe it solemnely,
And write a deede of gift with thine owne blood,
For that security craues great *Lucifer*:
If thou deny it, I wil backe to hel.
Fau: Stay *Mephastophilus*, and tel me, what good 470
Wil my soule do thy Lord?
Me: Inlarge his kingdome.
Fau: Is that the reason he tempts vs thus?
Me: *Solamen miseris socios habuisse doloris.*
Fau: ⟨Why,⟩ haue you any paine that tortures others?
Me: As great as haue the humane soules of men: 476
But tel me Faustus, shal I haue thy soule,
And I wil be thy slaue, and waite on thee,
And giue thee more than thou hast wit to aske.
Fau: I *Mephastophilus*, I giue it thee. 480
Me: Then stabbe thine arme couragiously,
And binde thy soule, that at some certaine day
Great *Lucifer* may claime it as his owne,
And then be thou as great as *Lucifer*.
Fau: Loe *Mephastophilus*, for loue of thee, 485
I cut mine arme, and with my proper blood
Assure my soule to be great *Lucifers*,
Chiefe Lord and regent of perpetual night.
View heere the blood that trickles from mine arme,
And let it be propitious for my wish. 490

462 me *add.* *1616–63* sayes] saith *1616–63* 463 he liues *1616–63*: I liue *1604–11* 464 he] thou *1663* my] his *1663* his soule] thy blood *1663* 466 Faustus] now *1616–63*, *Wag.* 467 thine owne blood] it *1663* 468 great *om.* *1616–63* 469 wil] must *1616–63* 470 *Ends* tell me *1616–63* 471 my soule] that *1663* 473 he *1604–11*: why he *1616–63*, *Dyce*, *Wag.*, *Bull.*, *Ward* 475 Why *add.* *1616–63* torture *1616–63* other *1616–20* 476 soules] spirits *1663* 480 I'le giue *1616–63* thee] him *1616–63* 481 Then] Then Faustus *1616–63* thine] thy *1616*, *1619* 484 And *om.* *1620–63* 485 + S.D. Stabbing his arm *add.* *Dyce* 485 *Ends* arme *1616–63* 486 I cut mine] Faustus hath cut his *1616–63* my] his *1616–63* 487 Assure my soule *1604–11*: assures his soule *1616–31*: assures himself *1663* 489 the] this *1616–63* 490 my] thy *1624–63*

Meph: But Faustus, thou must
Write it in manner of a deede of gift.

Fau. I, so I will, but *Mephastophilis*,
My bloud conieales and I can write no more.

Me. Ile fetch thee fier to dissolue it straight. *Exit.*

Fau. What might the staying of my bloud portend?
Is it vnwilling I should write this bill? 497
Why streames it not, that I may write afresh?
Faustus giues to thee his soule: ah there it stayde,
Why shouldst thou not? is not thy soule thine owne?
Then write againe, Faustus giues to thee his soule. 501

Enter Mephastophilis with a chafer of coles.

Me. Heres fier, come Faustus, set it on.

Fau. So now the bloud begins to cleare againe,
Now will I make an ende immediately.

Me. O what will not I do to obtaine his soule? 505

Fau. *Consummatum est*, this Bill is ended,
And Faustus hath bequeath'd his soule to *Lucifer*.
But what is this inscription on mine arme?
Homo fuge, whither should I flie?
If vnto God hee'le throwe thee downe to hell, 510
My sences are deceiu'd, here's nothing writ.
I see it plaine, here in this place is writ,
Homo fuge, yet shall not *Faustus* flye.

Me. Ile fetch him somewhat to delight his minde. *Exit.*

Enter ⟨Mephastophilis⟩ with diuels, giuing crownes and rich apparell to Faustus, and daunce, and then depart.

Fau. Speake Mephastophilis, what meanes this shewe?

491 thou must *om. 1616–63* 492 Write it] write it down *Wag.*, *ending* l. 491 493 will] do *1616–63* S.D. Writes *add. Dyce after* will 497 this] the *1663* 499 ah] O *1616–63* 500 not thy soule] it not *1663* 501 soule *om. 1624–63* 501 S.D. a chafer of coles] the Chafer of Fire *1616–63* 502 Heres fier, come Faustus *1604–11*: See Faustus here is fire *1616–63*: Come Faustus, here is fier *Brey.* 504 + S.D. Writes *add. Dyce* 505 O *om. 1616–63* not I] I not *1609, 1611* obtaine] attaine *1619* his soule] this man *1663* S.D. Aside *add. Dyce* 507 his soule] himself *1663* 508 mine] my *1609, 1611* 509 should] shall *1631, 1663* 510 God] heauen *1616–63* thee *1604–11*: me *1616–63, Dyce etc.* 512 I see] O yes, I see *1616–63* here in this place] euen heere *1616–63* 514 + S.D. Aside and then exit *Dyce* Mephastophilis *add. Dyce* with diuels] Deuils *1616–63* and daunce] they dance *1616–63* S.D. Enter Mephostophilis *add. 1616–63 after* depart 515 What meanes this shew? speake Mephostophilis *1616–63*

Me. Nothing Faustus, but to delight thy minde withall,
And to shewe thee what Magicke can performe. 517
Fau. But may I raise vp spirits when I please?
Me. I Faustus, and do greater things then these.
Fau. Then theres inough for a thousand soules. 520
Here Mephastophilis receiue this scrowle.
A deede of gift of body and of soule:
But yet conditionally, that thou performe
All articles prescrib'd betweene vs both.
Me. Faustus, I sweare by hel and *Lucifer* 525
To effect all promises betweene vs made.
Fau. Then heare me reade them: on these conditions following.

First, that Faustus may be a spirit in forme and substance.
Secondly, that Mephastophilis shall be his seruant, and at his commaund. 530
Thirdly, that Mephastophilis shall do for him, and bring him whatsoeuer.
Fourthly, that hee shall be in his chamber or house inuisible.
Lastly, that hee shall appeare to the said Iohn Faustus, at all times, in what forme or shape soeuer he please. 535
I Iohn Faustus of Wertenberge, Doctor, by these presents, do giue both body and soule to Lucifer prince of the East, and his minister Mephastophilis, and furthermore graunt vnto them, that 24. yeares being expired, the articles aboue written inuiolate, full power to fetch or carry the said Iohn Faustus body and soule, flesh, bloud, or goods, into their habitation wheresoeuer. 542
By me Iohn Faustus.
Me. Speake *Faustus*, do you deliuer this as your deede?

516 withall *om. 1616–63, Wag., Brey.* 517 to shewe thee] let thee see *1616–63* 518 vp] such *1616–63* 520 *om. 1616–63* 521 Here] Then *1616–63* this scrowle *om. 1624–63* 522 A] This *1663* of body . . soule *om. 1663* 524 articles prescrib'd *1604–11*: Couenants and Articles *1616–63* 526 made] both *1616–63* 527 *Prefix* Fau.] Meph. Faustus *1663* them] it Mephostophilis *1616–63* S.D. Reads *add. Dyce after* them 529, 530 at his commaund] be by him commanded *1616–63* 532 whatsoeuer] whatsoever he requireth *1663, Rob., Cunn.*: whatsoever he desires *Dyce, Bull., Ward* 533 his chamber or house] house or chamber *1663* 535 forme or shape *1604*: forme and shape *1609, 1611*: shape and forme *1616–63* 536 Wittenberg *1616–63* 537 both body and soule] my self *1663* 539 24.] foure and twentie *1616–63* the] and these *1616–63* 540 written] written being *1616–63* 541 body and soule *om. 1663* flesh, bloud, or goods *1604–11*: flesh, bloud *1616, 1619*: flesh and blood *1620–63*

Fau. I, take it, and the diuell giue thee good on't.
Me. Now Faustus aske what thou wilt.
Fau. First will I question with thee about hell,
Tel me, where is the place that men call hell?
Me. Vnder the heauens.
Fau. I, but where about? 550
Me. Within the bowels of these elements,
Where we are tortur'd and remaine for euer.
Hell hath no limits, nor is circumscrib'd
In one selfe place, for where we are is hell,
And where hell is, must we euer be: 555
And to conclude, when all the world dissolues,
And euery creature shalbe purified,
All places shall be hell that is not heauen.
Fau. Come, I thinke hell's a fable.
Me. I, thinke so still, till experience change thy minde.
Fau. Why? thinkst thou then that Faustus shall bee damn'd? 561
Me. I, of necessitie, for here's the scrowle,
Wherein thou hast giuen thy soule to *Lucifer.*
Fau. I, and body too, but what of that?
Thinkst thou that Faustus is so fond, to imagine, 565
That after this life there is any paine?
Tush, these are trifles and meere olde wiues tales.
Me. But Faustus, I am an instance to proue the contrary,
For I am damnd, and am now in hell. 569
Fau. How? now in hell? nay and this be hell,
Ile willingly be damnd here: what walking, disputing, &c.
But leauing off this, let me haue a wife, the fairest maid

545 thee *om. 1663* on't] of it *1616–63* 546 Now] So, now *1616–63* aske *1604–11, 1663*: aske me *1616–31* 547 will I] I will *1616–63* with *om. 1609–63* 548 the] that *1620–63* 550 I] I, so are all things else *1616–63* whereabouts *1616–63* 554 for] but *1616–63* 555 must] there must *1616–63 Dyce, Ward, Bull., Brey.* euer] for ever *Wag.* 556 conclude] be short *1616–63* 558 is] are *1620–63, Dyce, Wag., Ward.* 559 Come *om. 1616–63* a] a meere *1619–63* 560 still *om. Brey., Gollancz* 561 thinkest thou then] dost thou think *1616–63* damn'd] lost *1663* 563 Wherein] In which *1616–63* soule] spirit *1663* 564 too, but] and *1663* 567 Tush] No *1616–63* meere *om. 1609, 1611* 568 Faustus *om. 1616–63, Wag.* 569 For] For I tell thee *1616–63* and now *1616–63* 570 How? now in hell *om. 1616–63* 571 here *om. 1616–63, Wag.* what walking, disputing, &c. *1604–11*: What sleeping, eating, walking and disputing *1616–63* 572 off *om. 1616–63*

in *Germany*, for I am wanton and lasciuious, and can not liue without a wife. 574

Me. How, a wife? I prithee *Faustus* talke not of a wife.

Fau. Nay sweete *Mephastophilis* fetch me one, for I will haue one.

Me. Well thou wilt haue one, sit there till I come, Ile fetch thee a wife in the diuels name. ⟨*Exit.*⟩

Enter ⟨Mephastophilis⟩ with a diuell drest like a woman, with fier workes.

Me: Tel ⟨me⟩ Faustus, how dost thou like thy wife?

Fau: A plague on her for a hote whore. 581

Me: Tut Faustus,
Marriage is but a ceremoniall toy,
If thou louest me, thinke ⟨no⟩ more of it.
Ile cull thee out the fairest curtezans, 585
And bring them eu'ry morning to thy bed.
She whome thine eie shall like, thy heart shal haue,
Be she as chaste as was *Penelope*,
As wise as *Saba*, or as beautiful
As was bright *Lucifer* before his fall. 590
Hold, take this booke, peruse it thorowly,
The iterating of these lines brings golde,
The framing of this circle on the ground,
Brings whirlewindes, tempests, thunder and lightning.
Pronounce this thrice deuoutly to thy selfe, 595
And men in armour shal appeare to thee,
Ready to execute what thou desirst.

Fau: Thankes *Mephastophilus*, yet faine would I haue

575–7 *om 1616–63* 578, 579 *Replaced by single line in 1616–63* Well Faustus, thou shalt have a wife 578 sit *1604*: stay *1609, 1611* 579 + S.D. Exit *add. Dyce* Enter . . fier workes] He fetches in a woman deuill *1616–63* 579 + + *Qq 1616–63 add the line* FAUST. What sight is this? 580 Tel . . wife?] Now Faustus wilt thou haue a wife? *1616–63* Tell me *Dyce etc.*: Tel *1604–11* 581 A plague . . whore] Here's a hot whore indeed; no, I'le no wife *1616–63* 582 Tut Faustus *om. 1616–63* 582–4 *Two lines 1604, div. after* if 584 If] And if *1616–63* no *add. 1609–63* 587 thy eye *1609, 1611, 1631, 1663* thy heart] thine heart *1619–24* 588 Be] Were *1616–63* was] were *1620–63* 591 Hold] Here *1616–63* booke] booke, and *1616–63* thorowly] well *1616–63* 591 + S.D. Gives book *add. Dyce* 594 whirlewindes . . lightning] Thunder, Whirle-winds, Storme and Lightning *1616–63* 596 armour] harnesse *1616–63* 597 desirst] commandst *1616–63* 598–611 *Recast as verse Wag. These lines are omitted in Qq 1616–63, which have instead* FAUST. Thankes Mephostophilis for this sweete booke. This will I keepe as chary

a booke wherein I might beholde al spels and incantations, that I might raise vp spirits when I please. 600

Me: Here they are in this booke. *There turne to them.*

Fau: Now would I haue a booke where I might see al characters and planets of the heauens, that I might knowe their motions and dispositions.

Me: Heere they are too. *Turne to them.*

Fau: Nay let me haue one booke more, and then I haue done, wherein I might see al plants, hearbes and trees that grow vpon the earth.

Me: Here they be.

Fau: O thou art deceiued. 610

Me: Tut I warrant thee. *Turne to them.* ⟨*Exeunt.*⟩

⟨*Enter Faustus in his Study, and Mephostophilis.*⟩

Fau: When I behold the heauens, then I repent,
And curse thee wicked *Mephastophilus*,
Because thou hast depriu'd me of those ioyes.

Me: Why Faustus, 615
Thinkst thou heauen is such a glorious thing?
I tel thee tis not halfe so faire as thou,
Or any man that breathes on earth.

Fau: How proouest thou that?

Me: It was made for man, therefore is man more excellent.

Fau: If it were made for man, twas made for me: 621
I wil renounce this magicke, and repent.

Enter good Angel, and euill Angel.

Good An: Faustus, repent, yet God wil pitty thee.

as my life. Exeunt; *after which Qq 1616–63 erroneously insert lines* 791 S.D. *to* 802 S.D. Enter Wagner solus *to* That to this day is highly solemnized. Exit Wagner. *This same speech, which here varies only slightly from the text of Qq 1604–11* (cf. p. 172), *occurs again in its proper place in Qq 1616–63 with the addition of 14 new lines.*

599 might *1604, Dyce*: may *1609, 1611* 611 + S.D. Exeunt *add. Bull.* 611 + [Act II] Scene II *add. Cunn., Wag.*: Scene VI. *Ward, Bull., Brey.* S.D. *add. 1616–63* 613 thee] the *1663* 614 those] these *1663* 615 Why Faustus] 'Twas thine (thy *1631, 1663*) own seeking Faustus, thanke thy selfe *1616–63* 616 Thinkst] But think'st *1616–63* is *om. 1609, 1611, 1619–63* 617 thee] thee Faustus *1616–63* tis] it is *1616–63* *Line ends at* faire *1616–63* 618 breathe *1616* 620 It was] 'Twas *1616–63* therefore is man] then he's *1616–63* 621 it were] Heauen was *1616–63* 622 S.D. Enter . . Angel *1604–9*: Enter good Angell and euill *1611*: Enter the two Angels *1616–63* 623 God] heaven *1663*

Euill An: Thou art a spirite, God cannot pitty thee.
Fau: Who buzzeth in mine eares I am a spirite? 625
Be I a diuel, yet God may pitty me,
I God wil pitty me, if I repent.
Euill An: I but Faustus neuer shal repent.
Exeunt ⟨*Angels.*⟩
Fau: My hearts so hardned I cannot repent,
Scarse can I name saluation, faith, or heauen, 630
But feareful ecchoes thunders in mine eares,
Faustus, thou art damn'd, then swordes and kniues,
Poyson, gunnes, halters, and invenomd steele
Are layde before me to dispatch my selfe,
And long ere this I should haue slaine my selfe, 635
Had not sweete pleasure conquerd deepe dispaire.
Haue not I made blinde *Homer* sing to me
Of *Alexanders* loue, and *Enons* death,
And hath not he that built the walles of *Thebes*,
With rauishing sound of his melodious harp 640
Made musicke with my *Mephastophilis*?
Why should I dye then, or basely dispaire?
I am resolu'd *Faustus* shal nere repent.
Come Mephastophilis, let vs dispute againe,
And argue of diuine *Astrologie*. 645
Tel me, are there many heauens aboue the Moone?
Are all celestiall bodies but one globe,
As is the substance of this centricke earth?
Me: As are the elements, such are the spheares,
Mutually folded in each others orbe, 650
And *Faustus*,
All iointly moue vpon one axletree,
Whose terminine is tearmd the worlds wide pole,
Nor are the names of *Saturne*, *Mars*, or *Iupiter*
Faind, but are erring starres. 655

624 God] it *1663* 626 God] heaven *1663* 627 I] Yea *1616–63* God] it *1663* 628 S.D. Angels *add. 1616–63* 629 hearts so] heart is *1616–63* 631–33 *So 1604–11*: *One line 1616–63*, Swords, poyson (poysons *1620–63*), halters and inuenomb'd steele 635 slaine my selfe] done the deed *1616–63* 638 Enons] Oenus *1663* 643 nere] not *1616–63* 645 argue] reason *1616–63* 646 Tel me] Speake *1616–63*, *Brey.* heauens] Spheares *1616–63* 649 spheares] heauens *1616–63* 649+*Qq 1616–63 add the line* Euen from the Moone vnto the Emperiall Orbe, 650 orbe] Spheares *1616–63* 651, 652 *One line Qq*: *div. Dyce* And Faustus all] And *1616–63* 653 terminine *1604–11*: termine *1616–63*: terminus *Cunn.* 655 erring] euening *1616–63*, *Rob.*

Fau. But tell me, haue they all one motion? both *situ & tempore.*

Me. All ioyntly moue from East to West in 24. houres vpon the poles of the world, but differ in their motion vpon the poles of the Zodiake. 660

Fau. Tush, these slender trifles *Wagner* can decide,
Hath *Mephastophilus* no greater skill?
Who knowes not the double motion of the plannets?
The first is finisht in a naturall day,
The second thus, as *Saturne* in 30. yeares, *Iupiter* in 12., *Mars* in 4., the Sunne, *Venus*, and Mercury in a yeare: the Moone in 28. dayes. Tush, these are fresh mens suppositions, but tell me, hath euery spheare a dominion or *Intelligentia*?

Me. I. 670

Fau. How many heauens or spheares are there?

Me. Nine, the seuen planets, the firmament, and the imperiall heauen.

Fau. Well, resolue me in this question, why haue wee not coniunctions, oppositions, aspects, eclipsis, all at one time, but in some yeares we haue more, in some lesse?

Me. *Per inæqualem motum respectu totius.*

Fau. Well, I am answered, tell me who made the world?

Me. I will not.

Fau. Sweete Mephastophilus, tell me. 680

Me. Moue me not, for I will not tell thee.

Fau. Villaine, haue I not bound thee to tel me any thing?

Me. I, that is not against our kingdome, but this is.
Thinke thou on hell *Faustus,* for thou art damnd. 685

Fau. Thinke Faustus vpon God that made the world.

656 tell me *om. 1616–63* 658 ioyntly *om. 1616–63* 24.] foure and twenty *1616–63* 659 motion] motions *1616–63* 660 poles] place *1663* 661 Tush *om. 1616–63* trifles] questions *1616–63* 664 The] That the *1616–63* 665 as *om. 1616–63* 667 Tush *om. 1616–63* suppositions] questions *1616–63* 669 Intelligentij *1604*: Intelligentii *1609, 1611*: *corr. 1616–63* 673+ *Qq 1616–63 add.* FAUST. But is there not Coelum igneum & Christalinum? MEPH. No Faustus they be but Fables. 674 Well *om. 1616–63* me] me then *1616–63* in *om. 1663* this *1604–11, 1663*: this one *1616–31* haue wee] are *1616–63* 676 more, some *1609, 1611* 678 tell] now tell *1616–63* 681 for . . thee] Faustus *1616–63* 682 I not *1604*: not I *1609–63* 684 I *om. 1620–63* but *om. 1616–63* 685 Thinke . . damnd] Thou art damn'd (lost *1663*), think thou of hell *1616–63* 686 *This speech given to* Good Angel *Ward* God] him *1663*

Me. Remember this. *Exit.*
Fau. I, goe accursed spirit to vgly hell,
Tis thou hast damn'd distressed *Faustus* soule:
Ist not too late? 690

Enter good Angell and euill.

Euill A. Too late.
Good A. Neuer too late, if Faustus can repent.
Euill A. If thou repent diuels shall teare thee in peeces.
Good A. Repent, & they shal neuer race thy skin.
Exeunt ⟨*Angels*⟩.
Fau. Ah Christ my Sauiour, 695
Seeke to saue distressed Faustus soule.

Enter Lucifer, Belsabub, and Mephastophilus.

Lu. Christ cannot saue thy soule, for he is iust,
Theres none but I haue intrest in the same.
Fau: O who art thou that lookst so terrible?
Lu: I am *Lucifer*, 700
And this is my companion Prince in hel.
Fau: O Faustus, they are come to fetch away thy soule.
Lu: We come to tell thee thou dost iniure vs.
Thou talkst of Christ, contrary to thy promise:
Thou shouldst not thinke of God, thinke of the deuil, 705
And of his dame too.
Fau: Nor will I henceforth: pardon me in this,
And Faustus vowes neuer to looke to heauen,
Neuer to name God, or to pray to him,
To burne his Scriptures, slay his Ministers, 710
And make my spirites pull his churches downe.

690 S.D. *follows* 685 *Ward* Enter good Angel and euil Angel *1611*: Enter the two Angels *1616–63* 692 can] will *1616–63* 693 shall] will *1616–63* 694 race *1604–11*: raise *1616–20*: raze *1624, Dyce to Bull.*: rase *1631, 1663* 695 Ah] O *1616–63* my Sauiour *repeated 1616–63* 696 Seeke] Helpe *1616–31*: Seek thou *conj. Dyce* 695, 696 Christ . . soule] help distressed Faustus *1663* 697 Christ] He *1663* 699 terribly *1616–63* 702 away *om. 1616–63, Wag., Brey.* thy soule] thee *1663* 703–6 *This speech is divided in Qq 1616–63 into five; thus,* BELZ. We are come to tell thee thou dost iniure vs. LUCIF. Thou calst on Christ (heaven *1663*) contrary to thy promise. BELS. Thou should'st not thinke on God (heaven *1663*). LUCIF. Thinke on the deuill. BELZ. And his dam to. 705 of . . of *1604, 1609*: of . . on *1611* 707 I] Faustus *1616–63*: he *Dilke*: *om. Rob.* me in] him for *1616–63* 709–11 *om. 1616–63*

Lu: Do so, and we will highly gratifie thee:
Faustus, we are come from hel to shew thee some pastime: sit downe, and thou shalt see al the seauen deadly sinnes appeare in their proper shapes. 715

Fau: That sight will be as pleasing vnto me,
As paradise was to *Adam*, the first day
Of his creation.

Lu: Talke not of paradise, nor creation, but marke this shew: talke of the diuel, and nothing else: come away. 720

Enter the seauen deadly sinnes.

Now Faustus, examine them of their seueral names and dispositions.

Fau: What art thou? the first.

Pride. I am Pride, I disdaine to haue any parents, I am like to *Ouids* flea, I can creepe into euery corner of a wench, sometimes like a periwig, I sit vpon her brow, or like a fan of feathers, I kisse her lippes, indeede I doe, what doe I not? but fie, what a scent is here? Ile not speake an other worde, except the ground were perfumde and couered with cloth of arras. 730

Fau: What art thou? the second.

Coue: I am *Couetousnes*, begotten of an olde churle, in an olde leatherne bag: and might I haue my wish, I would desire, that this house, and all the people in it were turnd to golde, that I might locke you vppe in my good chest: O my sweete golde. 736

712 Do so . . thee] So shalt thou shew thy selfe an obedient seruant, And we will highly gratify thee for it. *1616–63* 713–15 *Given to* Belz. *1616–63* 713 hel] hell in person *1616–63* 714 see al] behold *1616–63* 715 in] to thee in *1616–63* shapes] shapes and likenesse *1616–63* 716 pleasing] pleasant *1616–63* vnto] to *1616–19* 719 nor] or *1616–63* 719 this] the *1616–63* 720 talke . . away] go Mephostoph. fetch (and fetch *1631*, *1663*) them in. *1616–63* 721, 722 *Given to* Belz. *1616–63* 721 examine] question *1616–63* seueral *om.* *1616–63* 723 What] That shall I soone: What *1616–63* 726 brow] Brow: next, like a Necke-lace I hang about her Necke *1616–63* or] Then *1616–63* 727 her lippes] her *1616–63* indeed . . doe I not] And then turning my selfe to a wrought Smocke do what I list *1616–63* 728 scent] smell *1616–63* 728–9 an other worde, except] a word more for a Kings ransome, vnlesse *1616–63* 729 were] be *1616–63* 731 What] Thou art a proud knaue indeed: What *1616–63* 733 an olde leatherne] a leather *1616–63* haue] now obtaine *1616–63* 733–4 I would desire, that *om.* *1616–63* 734 and all . . were turnd] you and all, should turne *1616–63* 735 vppe in] safe into *1616–63* good *om.* *1616–63*

Fau: What art thou? the third.

Wrath: I am *Wrath*, I had neither father nor mother, I leapt out of a lions mouth, when I was scarce half an houre olde, and euer since I haue runne vp and downe the worlde, with this case of rapiers wounding my selfe, when I had no body to fight withal: I was borne in hel, and looke to it, for some of you shalbe my father. 743

Fau: What art thou? the fourth.

Enuy. I am *Enuy*, begotten of a Chimney-sweeper, and an Oyster wife: I cannot reade, and therefore wish al bookes were burnt: I am leane with seeing others eate. O that there would come a famine through all the worlde, that all might die, and I liue alone, then thou shouldst see how fatt I would be: but must thou sit and I stand? come downe with a vengeance. 751

Fau: Away enuious rascall: what art thou? the fift.

Glut: Who I sir? I am *Gluttony*: my parents are al dead, and the diuel a peny they haue left me, but a bare pention, and that is 30. meales a day, and tenne beauers, a small trifle to suffice nature. O I come of a royall parentage, my grandfather was a gammon of bacon, my grandmother a hogs head of Claret-wine: My godfathers were these, Peter Pickle-herring, and Martin Martlemas-biefe. O but my godmother she was a iolly gentlewoman, and welbeloued in euery good towne and Citie: her name was mistresse Margery March-beere: now *Faustus*, thou hast heard all my Progeny, wilt thou bid me to supper? 763

Fau. No, Ile see thee hanged, thou wilt eat vp all my victualls.

737 What] And what *1616–63* 738–52 *Qq. 1616–63 transpose the speeches of Wrath and Envy, so that the lines answering to* 738–44 *in these editions follow those corresponding to* 745–52 739 half *om. 1616–63* 740 euer since I haue *1604–11*: euer since haue *1616, 1619*: haue euer since *1620–63* 741 this] these *1616–63* 742 had no body] could get none *1616–63* 744 What] And what *1616–63* fourth] fift *1616–63* 747 were burnt] burn'd *1616–63* 748 through] ouer *1616–63* 749 I would] I'de *1616–63* 752 Away] Out *1616–63* rascall] wretch *1616–63* what] But what *1616–63* fift] fourth *1616–63* 753 Who I sir *om. 1616–63* 754 bare] small *1616–63* 755 is] buyes me *1616–63* 756 O *om. 1616–63* come *1604–19*: came *1620–31*: am *1663* parentage] Pedigree *1616–63* 757 grandfather] father *1616–63* grandmother] mother was *1616–63* 759 Pickeld- *1616–63* O *om. 1616–63* 760 she] O she *1616–63* a iolly] an ancient *1616–63* 760–1 and . . Citie *om. 1616–63* 761 mistresse *om. 1616–63* 764–5 No . . victualls] Not I *1616–63* 764 hanged *1604*: hang'd first *1609, 1611, Wag.*

Glut. Then the diuell choake thee.
Fau. Choake thy selfe glutton : what art thou ? the sixt. 768
Sloath. I am sloath, I was begotten on a sunny banke, where I haue laine euer since, and you haue done me great iniury to bring me from thence : let me be carried thither againe by Gluttony and Leachery. Ile not speake an other word for a Kings raunsome.
Fau. What are you mistresse minkes ? the seauenth and last. 775
Lechery. Who I sir ? I am one that loues an inch of raw Mutton better then an ell of fride stock-fish, and the first letter of my name beginnes with leachery.
Lu. Away, to hel, to hel. *Exeunt the sinnes.*
Now Faustus, how dost thou like this ? 780
Fau: O this feedes my soule.
Lu. Tut Faustus, in hel is al manner of delight.
Fau. O might I see hel, and returne againe, how happy were I then ? 784
Lu. Thou shalt, I wil send for thee at midnight, in mean time take this booke, peruse it throwly, and thou shalt turne thy selfe into what shape thou wilt.
Fau. Great thankes mighty Lucifer,
This wil I keepe as chary as my life.
Lu. Farewel Faustus, and thinke on the diuel. 790
Fau. Farewel great *Lucifer*: come *Mephastophilis*.
Exeunt omnes.

769 I am] Hey ho ; I am *1616–63* 770–2 where . . Leachery] hey ho *1616–63* 772–3 an other word] a word more *1616–63* 774 What] And what *1616–63* 776 I sir] I I sir *1616* 778 leachery] L *conj. Coll., Dyce*[2], *Cunn., Bull.* 779 *Prefix* Lu. *precedes* 780 *1604–11* *Dyce gives* 779 *to* Faustus 779–80 Away . . like this] Away to hell, away, on piper *1616–63* 779 S.D. the] the 7 *1616–63* 781 this feedes] how this sight doth delight *1616–63* 782 Tut] But *1616–63* 783 againe] againe safe *1616–63* 785 Thou] Faustus, thou *1616–63* I wil . . midnight] at midnight I will send for thee *1616–63* 785–6 in mean time . . peruse] Meane while peruse this booke, and view *1616–63* 787 thy self *omit conj. Bull.* 788 Great *om. 1616–63* 790 Farewel . . diuel] Now Faustus farewell *1616–63* 791 S.D. Exeunt omnes, seuerall waies *1616–31* : *om. 1663* *After this* S.D. *Qq 1616–63 add a new scene* (Act II. Scene III. *Cunn.*, Scene VII. *Brey.*). *Cf. Appendix, pp.* 196, 7.

Enter Wagner solus.

Wag. Learned Faustus,
To know the secrets of *Astronomy*,
Grauen in the booke of *Ioues* hie firmament,
Did mount himselfe to scale *Olympus* top, 795
Being seated in a chariot burning bright,
Drawne by the strength of yoky dragons neckes:
He now is gone to prooue *Cosmography*,
And as I guesse, wil first ariue at *Rome*,
To see the Pope, and manner of his court, 800
And take some part of holy *Peters* feast,
That to this day is highly solemnizd. *Exit Wagner*

Enter Faustus and Mephastophilus.

Fau. Hauing now, my good Mephastophilus,
Past with delight the stately towne of *Trier*,
Inuirond round with ayrie mountaine tops, 805
With walles of flint, and deepe intrenched lakes,
Not to be wonne by any conquering prince,
From *Paris* next coasting the Realme of France,
Wee sawe the riuer *Maine* fall into *Rhine*,
Whose bankes are set with groues of fruitful vines. 810
Then vp to *Naples*, rich *Campania*,
Whose buildings faire and gorgeous to the eye,
The streetes straight forth, and pau'd with finest bricke,
Quarters the towne in foure equiuolence.

792–802 *This passage occurs twice in Qq 1616–63: once by mistake before l.* 612 (*cf. note to ll.* 598–611) *and again in this place, with the addition of 14 new lines. For the elaborated version cf. Appendix, pp.* 197, 8 S.D. enter Wagner solus *1604–11, 1616–63, first draft*: Enter the Chorus *1616–24, second draft*: Enter Chorus *1631, 1663, second draft*: Act the Third. Enter Chorus *Rob., Cunn.* 792 Learned *om. Wag.* 792–3 *one line 1616–63, Wag.* 793 know] find *1616–63, second draft* 795 himselfe] him vp *1616–24, second draft*: vp *1631, second draft*: *om. 1663, second draft* 796 Being seated] Where sitting *1616–63, second draft* 797 yoky] yoaked *1624, first draft, 1616–63, second draft* 797 + *Thirteen lines inserted 1616–63, second draft* 798 + That measures costs, and kingdomes of the earth *add. 1616–63, second draft* 802 That to *1604–11, 1616, first draft*: That on *1619–63, first draft*: The which *1616–63, second draft* highly *om. 1631, 1663, first draft* 802 S.D. Wagner *om. 1616–63, second draft* 802 + Act III. *add. 1663*: Act the Third. Scene I. *Rob., Cunn., Wag.*: Scene VII. *Ward, Bull., Brey. The entire scene to l.* 904 *has been rewritten by the editor of ed. 1663. For the scene as it there appears cf. Appendix, pp.* 198–202. 805 round *om. 1624, 1631* 811 vp to] vnto *1620–31* 814 *om. 1616–31* foure equiuolence *1604, 1609*: forme equiuolent *1611*

There sawe we learned *Maroes* golden tombe, 815
The way he cut an English mile in length,
Thorough a rocke of stone in one nights space.
From thence to *Venice*, *Padua*, and the rest,
In one of which a sumptuous Temple stands,
That threats the starres with her aspiring toppe. 820
Thus hitherto hath Faustus spent his time,
But tell me now, what resting place is this?
Hast thou as erst I did commaund,
Conducted me within the walles of *Rome*?

Me. Faustus, I haue, and because we wil not be vnprouided, I haue taken vp his holinesse priuy chamber for our vse. 827

Fau. I hope his holinesse will bid vs welcome.

Me. Tut, tis no matter man, weele be bold with his goode cheare, 830
And now my Faustus, that thou maist perceiue
What *Rome* containeth to delight thee with,
Know that this Citie stands vpon seuen hilles
That vnderprops the groundworke of the same,
⟨Iust through the midst runnes flowing *Tybers* streame,
With winding bankes that cut it in two parts,⟩ 836
Ouer the which foure stately bridges leane,
That makes safe passage to each part of *Rome*.
Vpon the bridge call'd *Ponto Angelo*,
Erected is a Castle passing strong, 840
Within whose walles such store of ordonance are,
And double Canons, fram'd of carued brasse,
As match the dayes within one compleate yeare,
Besides the gates and high piramides,
Which *Iulius Caesar* brought from *Affrica*. 845

818 rest] East *1616–31* 819 one *1616–31, Rob. etc.*: midst *1604–11*: *Qy.*, most? 820 + *Qq 1616–31 add two lines*, Whose frame is paued with sundry coloured stones, And roof't aloft with curious worke in gold 822 me *om. 1624* 825–7 *Rewritten as verse 1616–31* 828 vs] you *1620–31, Rob.* 829 Tut . . man] All's one, for *1616–31* 830 good cheare] Venson *1616–31* 831 And] But *1616–31* 832 containeth] containes for *1616–31* thee with] thine eyes *1616–31* 834 vnderprop *1616–31* 835–6 *add. 1616–31, Rob., Dyce etc.* 837 foure] two *1616–31* leane] leade *Brey.* 838 make *1616–31* 839 Ponte *Dyce etc.* 841 Within . . walles] Where thou shalt (shall *1624*) see *1616–31* are *om. 1616–31* 842 And] As that the *1616–31* fram'd of carued] forg'd of *1616–31* 843 *expanded into two lines 1616–31* As] Doe *1616–31* match] watch *1616* the] the number of the *1616–31* within] contain'd Within the compasse of *1616–31* 844 Beside *1616–31*

Fau. Now by the kingdomes of infernall rule,
Of *Styx, Acheron,* and the fiery lake
Of euer-burning *Phlegiton* I sweare,
That I do long to see the monuments
And scituation of bright splendant *Rome,* 850
Come therefore, lets away.
Me. Nay Faustus stay, I know youd faine see the Pope,
And take some part of holy *Peters* feast,
Where thou shalt see a troupe of bald-pate Friers,
Whose *summum bonum* is in belly-cheare. 855
Fau. Well, I am content, to compasse then some sport,
And by their folly make vs merriment.
Then charme me that I may be inuisible, to do what I please,
Vnseene of any whilst I stay in Rome. 860
Me. So Faustus, now
Do what thou wilt, thou shalt not be discerned.

Sound a Sonnet, enter the Pope and the Cardinall of Lorraine to the banket, with Friers attending.

Pope. My Lord of *Lorraine,* wilt please you draw neare.
Fau. Fall too, and the diuel choake you and you spare.
Pope. How now, whose that which spake? Friers looke about. 865
Fri. Heere's no body, if it like your Holynesse.
Pope. My Lord, here is a daintie dish was sent me from the Bishop of *Millaine.*
Fau. I thanke you sir. *Snatch it.*
Pope. How now, whose that which snatcht the meate

847 Acheron *1604–11*: of Acheron *1616–31*: *Dyce, Ward to Brey.*: and Acheron *Wag.* 849 the] those *1619–31* 852 Faustus stay] stay my Faustus *1616–31* faine *om. 1616–31, Bull., Brey.* 854–62 *In place of this passage Qq 1616–31 add. 205 new lines*; *cf. Appendix, pp. 202–7* 856 then *1604–11*: them *Bull., Brey.* 858 me] me, Mephistophilis *Bull., Brey.* 860 of] by *Ward* 860+s.d. Mephistophilis charms him *add. Dyce* 862 s.d. Sonnet *1604*: Sinet *1609, 1611* and the] and *1611* 863 My Lord . . neare] *Two lines 1616–31*, Lord Archbishop of Reames, sit downe with vs. Bish. I thanke your Holinesse. 864 and the] the *1616–31, Brey.* choake you] choake *1620–31* 865 How now *om. 1616–31* which spake] spoke *1616–31* 866 *om. 1616–31* 867–8 Pope . . . Millaine.] Lord Raymond pray fall too, I am beholding (beholden *1620–31*) To the Bishop of Millaine, for this so rare a present. 869 s.d. *om. 1616–31* 870 whose that which] who *1616–31*

from me ? will no man looke ? My Lord, this dish was sent me from the Cardinall of Florence. 872

Fau. You say true, Ile hate. ⟨*Snatches the dish.*⟩

Pope. What againe ? my Lord Ile drinke to your grace.

Fau. Ile pledge your grace. ⟨*Snatches the cup.*⟩

Lor. My Lord, it may be some ghost newly crept out of Purgatory come to begge a pardon of your holinesse.

Pope. It may be so, Friers prepare a dirge to lay the fury of this ghost: once againe my Lord fall too.

The Pope crosseth himselfe.

Fau. What, are you crossing of your selfe ? 880
Well vse that tricke no more, I would aduise you

Crosse againe.

Fau. Well, theres the second time, aware the third.
I giue you faire warning.

Crosse againe, and Faustus hits him a boxe of the eare, and they all runne away.

Fau: Come on Mephastophilis, what shall we do ?

Me. Nay I know not, we shalbe curst with bell, booke, and candle. 886

Fau. How ? bell, booke, and candle, candle, booke, and bell,
Forward and backward, to curse *Faustus* to hell.
Anon you shal heare a hogge grunt, a calfe bleate, and an asse braye, because it is S. *Peters* holy day. 890

871 will . . looke] Villaines why speake you (ye *1619–31*) not *1616–31* My Lord, this] My good Lord Archbishop, heres a most daintie *1616–31* 872 the] a *1616–31* of Florence] in France *1616–31* 873 You . . true *om. 1616–31* hate] haue that too *1616–31* 873 + S.D. *add. Dyce* 873 + *Two* speeches *add. 1616–31* 874 What . . drinke to] Lord Raymond, I drink vnto *1616–31* 875 Ile] I *1616–31* 875 + S.D. *add. Dyce* 875 + *Five lines add. 1616–31* 876 Lor. . . it may] Bish. Please it (it *om. 1619–31*) your holinesse, I thinke it *1616–31* newly *om. 1616–31* 877 come . . holinesse] and now is come vnto your holinesse for his pardon. *1616–31* 878 Friers prepare] Go then command our Priests to sing *1616–31* 879 this] this same trouble-some *1616–31* once . . fall too *om. 1616–31* 880–885 Nay I know not] *Quite different 1616–31* 883 S.D. of] on *1609, 1611, Wag.* 885 we shalbe] you'le be *1616–31* 887 How *om. 1616–31* 899–90 *om. 1616–31*

Enter all the Friers to sing the Dirge.

Frier. Come brethren, lets about our businesse with good deuotion.

Sing this. Cursed be hee that stole away his holinesse meate from the table.—maledicat dominus. 895

Cursed be hee that strooke his holinesse a blowe on the face. maledicat dominus.

Cursed be he that tooke Frier Sandelo a blow on the pate. male, &c.

Cursed be he that disturbeth our holy Dirge. male, &c. 901

Cursed be he that tooke away his holinesse wine. maledicat dominus.

Et omnes sancti, Amen.

⟨Mephistophilis and Faustus⟩ beate the Friers, and fling fier-workes among them, and so Exeunt.

Enter Chorus.

When Faustus had with pleasure tane the view 905
Of rarest things, and royal courts of kings,
Hee stayde his course, and so returned home,
Where such as beare his absence, but with griefe,
I meane his friends and nearest companions,
Did gratulate his safetie with kinde words, 910
And in their conference of what befell,
Touching his iourney through the world and ayre,
They put forth questions of Astrologie,
Which *Faustus* answerd with such learned skill,
As they admirde and wondred at his wit. 915
Now is his fame spread forth in euery land,
Amongst the rest the Emperour is one,
Carolus the fift, at whose pallace now
Faustus is feasted mongst his noble men.

890 S.D. all *om. 1616–31* to sing] with Bell, Booke, and Candle, for *1616–31* the Dirge] dirge *1609, 1611* 891 *Prefix* I. Frier *1616–31* 893 S.D. Sing this *om. 1616–31* away *om. 1609–31* 897 on *om. 1616* 898 tooke] strucke *1616–31* 899, 901 Maledicat Dom. *1616–31* 903 male, etc. *1609, 1611*: Maledicat Dom. *1616–31* 904 Et . . Amen *om. 1616–31* 904 + S.D. Mephistophilis and Faustus *add. Dyce* and fling] fling *1616–31* fire worke *1616* so *om. 1616–31* Exeunt *repeated 1616–31* S.D. Enter Chorus *to l. 957 om. 1616–31* Act the Fourth. Enter Chorus *Wag.* 916 his] the *1611* 919 amongst *1609, 1611*

What there he did in triall of his art, 920
I leaue vntold, your eyes shall see performd. *Exit.*

Enter Robin the Ostler with a booke in his hand.

Robin. O this is admirable! here I ha stolne one of doctor Faustus coniuring books, and ifaith I meane to search some circles for my owne vse: now wil I make al the maidens in our parish dance at my pleasure starke naked before me, and so by that meanes I shal see more than ere I felt, or saw yet. 927

Enter Rafe calling Robin.

Rafe. Robin, prethee come away, theres a Gentleman tarries to haue his horse, and he would haue his things rubd and made cleane: he keepes such a chafing with my mistris about it, and she has sent me to looke thee out: prethee come away. 932

Robin. Keepe out, keep out, or else you are blowne vp, you are dismembred *Rafe*: keepe out, for I am about a roaring peece of worke. 935

Rafe. Come, what doest thou with that same booke thou canst not reade?

Robin. Yes, my maister and mistris shal finde that I can reade, he for his forehead, she for her priuate study: shee's borne to beare with me, or else my Art failes. 940

Rafe. Why *Robin* what booke is that?

Robin. What booke? why the most intollerable booke for coniuring that ere was inuented by any brimstone diuel.

Rafe. Canst thou coniure with it? 944

Robin. I can do al these things easily with it: first, I can make thee druncke with ipocrase at any taberne in Europe for nothing, thats one of my coniuring workes.

Rafe. Our maister Parson sayes thats nothing.

Robin. True *Rafe,* and more *Rafe,* if thou hast any mind to *Nan Spit,* our kitchin maide, then turne her and wind hir to thy owne vse, as often as thou wilt, and at midnight.

Rafe. O braue *Robin,* shal I haue *Nan Spit,* and to mine owne vse? On that condition Ile feede thy diuel with horse-bread as long as he liues, of free cost. 954

Robin. No more sweete *Rafe,* letts goe and make cleane

920 *om. 1609, 1611* 921 see] see't *Dyce*[2], *Wag., Ward* 921 + Scene VIII. *add. Ward, Bull.* 924 my *1604*: mine *1609, 1611* wil I] I will *1611* 936 that] the *1609, 1611* 946 Tauerne *1609, 1611* 950 her and *1604*: and *1609, 1611* 951 thy *1604*: thine *1609–11*

our bootes which lie foule vpon our handes, and then to our coniuring in the diuels name. *Exeunt.*

Enter Robin and Rafe with a siluer Goblet.

Robin. Come *Rafe,* did not I tell thee, we were for euer made by this doctor Faustus booke ? *ecce signum,* heeres a simple purchase for horse-keepers, our horses shal eate no hay as long as this lasts. 961

Enter the Vintner.

Rafe. But *Robin,* here comes the vintner.

Robin. Hush, Ile gul him supernaturally : Drawer, I hope al is payd, God be with you : come *Rafe.*

Vintn. Soft sir, a word with you, I must yet haue a goblet payde from you ere you goe. 966

Robin. I a goblet *Rafe,* I a goblet ? I scorne you : and you are but a &c. I a goblet ? search me.

Vintn. I meane so sir, with your fauor. 〈*Searches Robin.*〉

Robin. How say you now ? 970

Vintner. I must say somewhat to your felow, you sir.

Rafe. Me sir, me sir, search your fill :

〈*Vintner searches him.*〉

now sir, you may be ashamed to burden honest men with a matter of truth. 974

Vintner. Wel, tone of you hath this goblet about you.

Ro. You lie Drawer, tis afore me 〈*Aside*〉: sirra you, Ile teach ye to impeach honest men : stand by, Ile scowre you for a goblet, stand aside you had best, I charge you in the name of Belzabub : looke to the goblet *Rafe.* 〈*Aside to Ralph.*〉

Vintner. What meane you sirra ? 980

Robin. Ile tell you what I meane. *He reades.*
Sanctobulorum Periphrasticon : nay Ile tickle you Vintner, looke to the goblet *Rafe. Polypragmos Belseborams framanto pacostiphos tostu Mephastophilis, &c.*

Enter Mephostophilis : sets squibs at their backes : they runne about.

Vintner. O nomine Domine, what meanst thou *Robin* ? thou hast no goblet. 986

957 + Scene IX. *Ward, Bull. In Qq 1616–63 this scene to l.* 1006 *is entirely rewritten. No verbal resemblance except at ll.* 994–6. *For the version of 1616–63 cf. Appendix, pp.* 208, 209 961 S.D. the *om. 1616–63, Dyce to Bull.* S.D. *follows* supernaturally *Dyce to Bull.* 969 +, 972 +, 976 +, 979 + S.DD. *add. Dyce* 984 S.D. backes] backs, and then exit *Dyce*

Rafe. Peccatum peccatorum, heeres thy goblet, good Vintner. ⟨*Gives the goblet to Vintner, who exit.*⟩

Robin. Misericordia pro nobis, what shal I doe? good diuel, forgiue me now, and Ile neuer rob thy Library more.

Enter to them Meph.

Meph. Monarch of hel, vnder whose blacke suruey 991
Great Potentates do kneele with awful feare,
Vpon whose altars thousand soules do lie,
How am I vexed with these vilaines charmes?
From *Constantinople* am I hither come, 995
Onely for pleasure of these damned slaues.

Robin. How, from *Constantinople*? you haue had a great iourney, wil you take sixe pence in your purse to pay for your supper, and be gone? 999

Me. Wel villaines, for your presumption, I transforme thee into an Ape, and thee into a Dog, and so be gone. *Exit.*

Rob. How, into an Ape? thats braue, Ile haue fine sport with the boyes, Ile get nuts and apples enow.

Rafe. And I must be a Dogge. 1004

Robin. Ifaith thy head wil neuer be out of the potage pot. *Exeunt.*

Enter Emperour, Faustus, and a Knight, with Attendants.

Em. Maister doctor Faustus, I haue heard strange report of thy knowledge in the blacke Arte, how that none in my Empire, nor in the whole world can compare with thee, for the rare effects of Magicke: they say thou hast a familiar spirit, by whome thou canst accomplish what thou list: this therefore is my request, that thou let me see some proofe of thy skil, that mine eies may be witnesses to confirme what mine eares haue heard reported, and here I sweare to thee, by the honor of mine Imperial

988 S.D. *add. Dyce* 991 Monarch] *Before this line Qq 1604–11 wrongly insert two lines of prose, which all editors omit,* Vanish vilaines, th'one like an Ape, an other like a Beare, the third an Asse, for doing this enterprise. 994 with *1604–11*: by *1616–63* these *1604, 1616–63*: this *1609–11* 995 am . . come] haue they brought me now *1616–63* 1005 be *om. 1609, 1611* 1006+ *Qq 1616–63 add. a new scene of 49 lines* ⟨Act III⟩ Scene IV. *Rob., Cunn. Cf. Appendix, pp.* 210, 211 (*ll.* 1007–1055) 1006++Act the Fourth. Scene I. *Rob., Cunn.*: Scene X *Ward, Bull., Brey.* 1007–1105 *Rewritten and expanded Qq 1616–63. Cf. Appendix, pp.* 211–214 (*ll.* 1056–1178). *No verbal similarity between the two texts except at ll.* 1094–1101 1007 reports *1609, 1611* 1014 my eares *1609, 1611*

crowne, that what euer thou doest, thou shalt be no wayes preiudiced or indamaged. 1017

Knight Ifaith he lookes much like a coniurer. *Aside.*

Fau. My gratious Soueraigne, though I must confesse my selfe farre inferior to the report men haue published, and nothing answerable to the honor of your Imperial maiesty, yet for that loue and duety bindes me therevnto, I am content to do whatsoeuer your maiesty shall command me.

Em. Then doctor Faustus, marke what I shall say. 1025
As I was sometime solitary set,
Within my Closet, sundry thoughts arose,
About the honour of mine auncestors,
Howe they had wonne by prowesse such exploits,
Gote such riches, subdued so many kingdomes, 1030
As we that do succeede, or they that shal
Hereafter possesse our throne, shal
(I feare me) neuer attaine to that degree
Of high renowne and great authoritie,
Amongest which kings is *Alexander* the great, 1035
Chiefe spectacle of the worldes preheminence,
The bright shining of whose glorious actes
Lightens the world with his reflecting beames,
As when I heare but motion made of him,
It grieues my soule I neuer saw the man: 1040
If therefore thou, by cunning of thine Art,
Canst raise this man from hollow vaults below,
Where lies intombde this famous Conquerour,
And bring with him his beauteous Paramour,
Both in their right shapes, gesture, and attire 1045
They vsde to weare during their time of life,
Thou shalt both satisfie my iust desire,
And giue me cause to praise thee whilst I liue.

Fau: My gratious Lord, I am ready to accomplish your request, so farre forth as by art and power of my spirit I am able to performe. 1051

Knight. Ifaith thats iust nothing at all. *Aside.*

Fau But if it like your Grace, it is not in my abilitie to present before your eyes the true substantiall bodies of those two deceased princes which long since are consumed to dust. 1056

1020 report of men *1611* 1023 whatsoeuer] what *1609, 1611* 1029 wonne] done *conj. Dyce*[2] 1038 *om. 1609–1611* 1044 *om. 1609, 1611*

Knight. I mary, master doctor, now theres a signe of grace in you, when you wil confesse the trueth. *Aside.*

Fau: But such spirites as can liuely resemble *Alexander* and his Paramour, shal appeare before your Grace, in that manner that they best liu'd in, in their most florishing estate, which I doubt not shal sufficiently content your Imperiall maiesty. 1063

Em. Go to, maister Doctor, let me see them presently.

Kn. Do you heare maister Doctor? you bring *Alexander* and his paramour before the emperor? 1066

Fau. How then sir?

Kn. Ifaith thats as true as *Diana* turnd me to a stag.

Fau: No sir, but when *Acteon* died, he left the hornes for you: *Mephastophilis* be gone. *Exit Meph.*

Kn. Nay, and you go to coniuring, Ile be gone. *Exit Kn:*

Fau. Ile meete with you anone for interrupting me so: heere they are, my gratious Lord. 1073

Enter Meph: with Alexander and his paramour.

Emp. Maister Doctor, I heard this Lady while she liu'd had a wart or moale in her necke, how shal I know whether it be so or no?

Fau: Your highnes may boldly go and see. *Exit Alex:*

Emp: Sure these are no spirites, but the true substantiall bodies of those two deceased princes. 1079

Fau: Wilt please your highnes now to send for the knight that was so pleasant with me here of late?

Emp: One of you call him foorth.

Enter the Knight with a paire of hornes on his head.

Emp. How now sir Knight? why I had thought thou hadst beene a batcheler, but now I see thou hast a wife, that not only giues thee hornes, but makes thee weare them: feele on thy head. 1086

Kn: Thou damned wretch, and execrable dogge,
Bred in the concaue of some monstrous rocke:
How darst thou thus abuse a Gentleman?
Vilaine I say, vndo what thou hast done. 1090

Fau: O not so fast sir, theres no haste: but good, are you remembred how you crossed me in my conference with the emperour? I thinke I haue met with you for it.

1061 best *1604–11*: both *conj. Dyce*[1], *Dyce*[2] *etc.* 1075 wart or moale *1604*: moale or wart *1609, 1611* 1077 + S.D. Exit Alex.] Exeunt Spirits *Dyce, after* 1079 1079 those *1604*: these *1609, 1611* 1081 here *om. 1609, 1611* 1082 + S.D. Exit Attendant *add. Dyce*

Emp: Good Maister Doctor, at my intreaty release him, he hath done penance sufficient. 1095

Fau: My Gratious Lord, not so much for the iniury hee offred me heere in your presence, as to delight you with some mirth, hath *Faustus* worthily requited this iniurious knight, which being all I desire, I am content to release him of his hornes : and sir knight, hereafter speake well of Scholers : *Mephastophilis,* transforme him strait. Now my good Lord hauing done my duety, I humbly take my leaue. 1103

Emp: Farewel maister Doctor, yet ere you goe,
Expect from me a bounteous reward. *Exit Emperour.*

Fau: Now Mephastophilis, the restlesse course
That time doth runne with calme and silent foote,
Shortning my dayes and thred of vitall life,
Calls for the payment of my latest yeares,
Therefore sweet Mephastophilis, let vs 1110
Make haste to *Wertenberge.*

Me: What, wil you goe on horse backe, or on foote ?

Fau: Nay, til I am past this faire and pleasant greene, ile walke on foote.

Enter a Horse-courser

Hors: I haue beene al this day seeking one maister Fustian : masse, see where he is. God saue you maister doctor. 1117

Fau: What horse-courser, you are wel met.

Hors: Do you heare sir ? I haue brought you forty dollers for your horse. 1120

Fau: I cannot sel him so : if thou likst him for fifty, take him.

Hors: Alas sir, I haue no more, I pray you speake for me.

1094 Good] Then good *1616–63* at . . him] Let me intreate you to remoue his hornes *1616–63* 1095 he hath] He has *1616* sufficient] now sufficiently *1616–63* 1096 the *om. 1616–63* 1096–7 hee . . presence] done to me *1616–63* 1097 you] your Maiesty *1616–63* 1098 worthily] iustly *1616–63* 1099–1100 release him of] remoue *1616–63* 1100 sir . . hereafter] hereafter sir *1616–20, 1631, 1663* : hereafter *1624* speake] looke you speake *1616–63* 1101 Mephastophilis, transforme him *interpolated between* hornes *and* and (*l.* 1100) *1616–63* strait *om. 1616–63* S.D. Mephistophilis removes the horns *add Dyce after* strait 1105 + *New scene of 136 lines add. 1616–63*; *cf. Appendix, pp.* 214 (*l.* 1179)–217 1105+ Scene XI. *add. Ward, Bull., Brey.*: (Act IV.) Scene II. *Wag.* 1111–1198] *Abridged version of 54 lines in Qq 1616–63. No verbal resemblance except at ll.* 1127–33, 1142–8, *and* 1193–8 ; *cf. Appendix, pp.* 218, 219

Me: I pray you let him haue him, he is an honest felow, and he has a great charge, neither wife nor childe. 1126

Fau: Wel, come giue me your money, my boy wil deliuer him to you : but I must tel you one thing before you haue him, ride him not into the water at any hand.

Hors: Why sir, wil he not drinke of all waters ? 1130

Fau: O yes, he wil drinke of al waters, but ride him not into the water, ride him ouer hedge or ditch, or where thou wilt, but not into the water. 1133

Hors: Wel sir, Now am I made man for euer, Ile not leaue my horse for fortie : if he had but the qualitie of hey ding, ding, hey, ding, ding, Ide make a braue liuing on him ; hee has a buttocke as slicke as an Ele : wel god buy sir, your boy wil deliuer him me : but hark ye sir, if my horse be sick, or ill at ease, if I bring his water to you, youle tel me what it is ? *Exit Horsecourser.*

Fau. Away you villaine : what, doost thinke I am a horsedoctor ? What art thou Faustus but a man condemnd to die ? 1143
Thy fatall time doth drawe to finall ende,
Dispaire doth driue distrust vnto my thoughts,
Confound these passions with a quiet sleepe :
Tush, Christ did call the thiefe vpon the Crosse,
Then rest thee Faustus quiet in conceit. 1148
Sleepe in his chaire.

Enter Horsecourser all wet, crying.

Hors. Alas, alas, Doctor Fustian quoth a, mas, Doctor *Lopus* was neuer such a Doctor, has giuen me a purgation, has purg'd me of fortie Dollers, I shall neuer see them more : but yet like an asse as I was, I would not be ruled by him, for he bade me I should ride him into no water ; now,

1127 come *1604–11* : I will not stand with thee *1616–63* your] the *1616–63* S.D. Horse-courser gives Faustus the money *add. Dyce after* money 1127–8 my boy . . to you *om. 1616–63* 1128 but] now sirra *1616–63* one . . haue him] that you may ride him o're hedge and ditch, and spare him not ; but do you heare ? in any case *1616–63* 1129 at any hand *om. 1616–63* 1130 Why sir] How sir, not into the water ? why *1616–63* 1131 O *om. 1616–63* 1132 ride him ouer] o're *1616–63* or ditch] and ditch *1616–63* 1134 am I *1604* : I am a *1609, 1611* 1135 fortie] twice forty dollars *conj. Dyce* : twice forty *Wag., Bull.* 1137 buy] b'wi'ye *Dyce* 1138 ye *1604* : you *1609, 1611* 1144 doth drawe] *1604–11* : drawes *1616–63* to] to a *1616–63* 1145 vnto] into *1616–63, Dyce* 1147 *om. 1663* 1148 S.D. He sits to sleepe *1616–63*

I thinking my horse had had some rare qualitie that he would not haue had me knowne of, I like a ventrous youth, rid him into the deepe pond at the townes ende. I was no sooner in the middle of the pond, but my horse vanisht away, and I sat vpon a bottle of hey, neuer so neare drowning in my life : but Ile seeke out my Doctor, and haue my fortie dollers againe, or Ile make it the dearest horse : O yonder is his snipper snapper : do you heare ? you, hey, passe, where's your maister ? 1162

Me. Why sir, what would you ? you cannot speake with him.

Hors. But I wil speake with him.

Me. Why hee's fast asleepe, come some other time.

Hors. Ile speake with him now, or Ile breake his glasse-windowes about his eares. 1168

Me. I tell thee he has not slept this eight nights.

Hors. And he haue not slept this eight weekes Ile speake with him.

Me. See where he is fast asleepe.

Hors. I, this is he. God saue ye maister doctor, maister doctor, maister doctor Fustian, fortie dollers, fortie dollers for a bottle of hey. 1175

Me. Why, thou seest he heares thee not.

Hors. So, ho, ho : so, ho, ho. *Hallow in his eare.* No, will you not wake ? Ile make you wake ere I goe.

Pull him by the legge, and pull it away.

Alas, I am vndone, what shall I do ?

Fau. O my legge, my legge, helpe *Mephastophilis*, call the Officers, my legge, my legge. 1181

Me. Come villaine to the Constable.

Hors. O Lord sir, let me goe, and Ile giue you fortie dollers more.

Me. Where be they ? 1185

Hors. I haue none about me, come to my Oastrie, and Ile giue them you.

Me. Be gone quickly. *Horsecourser runnes away.*

Fau. What is he gone ? farwel he, Faustus has his legge againe, and the Horsecourser, I take it, a bottle of hey for his labour ; wel, this tricke shal cost him fortie dollers more. 1192

1159 in my] in al my *1609, 1611* 1169 this *1604, 1611* : these *1609* 1170 this *1604, 1611* : these *1609* 1173 ye] you *1611* 1177 S.D. eare] eares *1611* 1178 No] Now *Wag., Brey.*

Enter Wagner.

How now *Wagner*, what's the newes with thee ?

Wag. Sir, the Duke of *Vanholt* doth earnestly entreate your company. 1195

Fau. The Duke of *Vanholt* ! an honourable gentleman, to whom I must be no niggard of my cunning, come *Mephastophilis*, let's away to him. *Exeunt.*

Enter to them the Duke, and the Dutches, the Duke speakes.

Du: Beleeue me maister Doctor, this merriment hath much pleased me. 1200

Fau: My gratious Lord, I am glad it contents you so wel : but it may be Madame, you take no delight in this. I haue heard that great bellied women do long for some dainties or other, what is it Madame ? tell me, and you shal haue it. 1205

Dutch. Thankes, good maister doctor,

And for I see your curteous intent to pleasure me, I wil not hide from you the thing my heart desires, and were it nowe summer, as it is Ianuary, and the dead time of the winter, I would desire no better meate then a dish of ripe grapes. 1211

Fau: Alas Madame, thats nothing, *Mephastophilis*, be gone. *Exit Meph.*

Were it a greater thing then this, so it would content you, you should haue it. 1215

Enter Mephasto: with the grapes.

Here they be madam, wilt please you taste on them ?

Du: Beleeue me master Doctor, this makes me wonder aboue the rest, that being in the dead time of winter, and in the month of Ianuary, how you shuld come by these grapes.

Fau: If it like your grace, the yeere is diuided into twoo circles ouer the whole worlde, that when it is heere winter with vs, in the contrary circle it is summer with them, as

1193 what's the *1604–11* : what *1616–63* 1194 Sir] If it please you *1616–63* 1195 *After* company *1616–63 add* and hath sent some of his men to attend you with prouision fit for your iourney 1196 Vanholt's *1616–63* 1197 to] and one to *1616–63* 1198 Mephastophilis, let's *om. 1616–63* to him *om. 1616–63* 1198+ *New scene of 56 lines add. 1616–63; cf. Appendix, pp.* 219–220 (*l.* 1255) 1198++Scene XII *add. Ward, Bull., Brey.* 1199–1237 *Expanded 1616–63 to 124 lines. Occasional verbal resemblance between the two texts. For version of 1616–63 cf. Appendix, pp.* 220 (*l.* 1256)–224 1210 ripe *om. 1609, 1611*

in *India*, *Saba*, and farther countries in the East, and by means of a swift spirit that I haue, I had them brought hither, as ye see: how do you like them Madame, be they good? 1226

Dut: Beleeue me Maister doctor, they be the best grapes that ere I tasted in my life before.

Fau: I am glad they content you so Madam. 1229

Du: Come Madame, let vs in, where you must wel reward this learned man for the great kindnes he hath shewd to you.

Dut: And so I wil my Lord, and whilst I liue,
Rest beholding for this curtesie.

Fau: I humbly thanke your Grace. 1235

Du: Come, maister Doctor follow vs, and receiue your reward. *Exeunt.*

Enter Wagner solus.

Wag. I thinke my maister meanes to die shortly,
For he hath giuen to me al his goodes,
And yet me thinkes, if that death were neere, 1240
He would not banquet, and carowse, and swill
Amongst the Students, as euen now he doth,
Who are at supper with such belly-cheere,
As *Wagner* nere beheld in all his life.
See where they come: belike the feast is ended. ⟨*Exit.*⟩

Enter Faustus with two or three Schollers ⟨and Mephistophilis⟩.

1. *Sch.* Maister Doctor *Faustus*, since our conference about faire Ladies, which was the beutifulst in all the world, we haue determined with our selues, that *Helen of Greece* was the admirablest Lady that euer liued: therefore master Doctor, if you wil do vs that fauor, as to let vs see that peerelesse Dame of *Greece*, whome al the world admires for maiesty, wee should thinke our selues much beholding vnto you. 1253

1237+Scene XIII. *add. Ward, Bull., Brey.*: Act the Fifth *add. 1663 after* S.D.: Act the Fifth. Scene I. *Wag.* S.D. Thunder and lightning: Enter deuils with couer'd dishes: Mephostophilis leades them into Faustus Study: Then enter Wagner *1616–63* 1238–1284 *Retouched and in places rewritten 1616–63*; *cf. Appendix, pp.* 225, 226 1238 meanes . . shortly *1604–63*: shortly means to die *Cunn. Bull.* 1239–44 *Rewritten as prose 1616–63* 1240 neere] so near *Bull.* 1245 See] and see *1616–63* ended] done *1616–63* S.D. Exit *add. 1616–63* Scene XIV. *add. Bull.* S.D. and Mephistophilis *add. Dyce* 1250 that *1604–11*: so much *1616–63*

Fau. Gentlemen,
For that I know your friendship is vnfained,
And Faustus custome is not to denie
The iust requests of those that wish him well,
You shall behold that pearelesse dame of *Greece*,
No otherwaies for pompe and maiestie,
Then when sir *Paris* crost the seas with her, 1260
And brought the spoiles to rich *Dardania*.
Be silent then, for danger is in words.

Musicke sounds, and Helen passeth ouer the Stage.

2. *Sch.* Too simple is my wit to tell her praise,
Whom all the world admires for maiestie.
3. *Sch.* No maruel tho the angry Greekes pursude 1265
With tenne yeares warre the rape of such a queene,
Whose heauenly beauty passeth all compare.
1. Since we haue seene the pride of natures workes,
And onely Paragon of excellence,

Enter an old man.

Let vs depart, and for this glorious deed 1270
Happy and blest be Faustus euermore.
Fau. Gentlemen farwel, the same I wish to you.

Exeunt Schollers.

Old. Ah Doctor Faustus, that I might preuaile,
To guide thy steps vnto the way of life,
By which sweete path thou maist attaine the gole 1275
That shall conduct thee to celestial rest.
Breake heart, drop bloud, and mingle it with teares,
Teares falling from repentant heauinesse

1254–62 *Prose 1604–11* : *corr. 1616–63* 1254–5 *One line 1616–63*: *corr. Dyce* 1256 And *1604*: *om. 1609, 1611*: It is not *1616–63* is not *om. 1616–63* 1257 request *1609–63, Wag.* 1259 other-wise *1616–63* and] or *1616–63* 1262 S.D. sounds . . Helen] sound, Mephosto. brings in Hellen, she *1616–63* 1263 *Before this speech Qq 1616–63 insert*, 2. Was this faire Hellen, whose admired worth Made Greece with ten yeares warres afflict poore Troy? *Prefix* 2. Sch.] 3. *1616–63* wit] will *1631, 1663* praise] worth *1616–63* 1265–7 *om. 1616–63* 1268 Since] Now *1616–63* worke *1616–63* 1269 *om. 1616–63* 1270 Let . . depart] Wee'l take our leaues *1616–63* glorious deed] blessed sight *1616–63* 1272 I wish] wish I *1616–63* 1273–84 *Entirely rewritten 1616–63*; *cf. p.* 226 1277–84 *Baker suggests that these lines be given to Faustus*

Of thy most vilde and loathsome filthinesse,
The stench whereof corrupts the inward soule 1280
With such flagitious crimes of hainous sinnes,
As no commiseration may expel,
But mercie Faustus of thy Sauiour sweete,
Whose bloud alone must wash away thy guilt.
Fau. Where art thou Faustus ? wretch what hast thou done ? 1285
Damnd art thou Faustus, damnd, dispaire and die.
Hell calls for right, and with a roaring voyce
Sayes, Faustus come, thine houre is come,
And Faustus will come to do thee right.

Mepha. giues him a dagger.

Old. Ah stay good Faustus, stay thy desperate steps,
I see an Angell houers ore thy head, 1291
And with a violl full of precious grace,
Offers to powre the same into thy soule,
Then call for mercie and auoyd dispaire.
Fau. Ah my sweete friend, I feele 1295
Thy words to comfort my distressed soule,
Leaue me a while to ponder on my sinnes.
Old. I goe sweete Faustus, but with heauy cheare,
Fearing the ruine of thy hopelesse soule. ⟨*Exit.*⟩
Fau. Accursed Faustus, where is mercie now ? 1300
I do repent, and yet I do dispaire :
Hell striues with grace for conquest in my breast,
What shal I do to shun the snares of death ?
Me. Thou traitor Faustus, I arrest thy soule
For disobedience to my soueraigne Lord, 1305
Reuolt, or Ile in peece-meale teare thy flesh.
Fau: Sweete *Mephastophilis*, intreate thy Lord
To pardon my vniust presumption,

1281 sin *Dyce, Cunn., Wag.* 1286 *om. 1616–63* 1287 calls for] claimes his *1616–63* 1288 is] is almost *1616–63, Dyce etc. exc. Wag.* 1289 will] now will *1616–63, Dyce etc.* 1289+S.D. *on margin 1604–11* : *follows* 1285 *1616–63* 1290 Ah] O *1616–63* steps] stabs *Wag.* 1291 houer *1616–63* 1291–3 *om. 1663* 1294 Then *om. 1663* 1295 Ah . . sweete] O *1616–63* 1298 I . . Faustus] Faustus I leaue thee *1616–63* heauy cheare] griefe of heart *1616–63* 1299 ruine] enemy *1616–63* hopelesse *1604–11* : haplesse *1616–31* hopelesse soule] better part *1663* S.D. *add. 1616–63* 1300 where . . now] wretch what hast thou done *1616–63* 1304 thy soule] thee *1663* 1307 *Before this line Qq 1616–63 add*, I do repent I ere offended him,

And with my blood againe I wil confirme
My former vow I made to *Lucifer*. 1310
Me. Do it then quickely, with vnfained heart,
Lest greater danger do attend thy drift.
Fau: Torment sweete friend, that base and crooked age,
That durst disswade me from thy *Lucifer*,
With greatest torments that our hel affoords. 1315
Me: His faith is great, I cannot touch his soule,
But what I may afflict his body with,
I wil attempt, which is but little worth.
Fau: One thing, good seruant, let me craue of thee,
To glut the longing of my hearts desire, 1320
That I might haue vnto my paramour,
That heauenly *Helen* which I saw of late,
Whose sweete imbracings may extinguish cleane
These thoughts that do disswade me from my vow,
And keepe mine oath I made to *Lucifer*. 1325
Me. Faustus, this, or what else thou shalt desire,
Shalbe performde in twinckling of an eie.

Enter Helen.

Fau: Was this the face that lancht a thousand shippes?
And burnt the toplesse Towres of *Ilium*?
Sweete *Helen*, make me immortall with a kisse: 1330
⟨*Kisses her.*⟩
Her lips suckes forth my soule, see where it flies:
Come *Helen*, come giue mee my soule againe.
Here wil I dwel, for heauen be in these lips,
And all is drosse that is not *Helena*: *Enter old man.*
I wil be *Paris*, and for loue of thee, 1335
Insteede of *Troy* shal *Wertenberge* be sackt,
And I wil combate with weake *Menelaus*,
And weare thy colours on my plumed Crest:
Yea I wil wound *Achillis* in the heele,

1310 My] The *1616–63* 1311, 1313 *Prefixes om. 1616–31* 1311 quickely *1604–11*: Faustus *1616–63* 1312 dangers *1616–63* 1313 crooked age] aged man *1616–63* 1315 torment *1616, 1619* 1317 may *1604–16*: *om. 1619–24*: can *1631, 1663* 1321 might] may *1616–63* 1323 embraces *1616–63* cleane] cleare *1616–63* 1324 These] Those *1616–63, Dyce* 1325 mine *1604*: my *1609–63* oath *1604–11*: vow *1616–63* 1326 Faustus *om. 1616–63* thou shalt] my Faustus shall *1616–63* 1327 + S.D. Enter Hellen againe, passing ouer betweene two Cupids *1616–63* 1330+S.D. *add. 1663* 1331 sucke *1616–63* flees *Ward* 1333 be] is *1616–63* 1334 S.D. *om. 1616–63*: *follows* 1347 *Dyce to Bull*, 1336 Wittenberg *1616–63*

And then returne to *Helen* for a kisse. 1340
O thou art fairer then the euening aire,
Clad in the beauty of a thousand starres,
Brighter art thou then flaming *Iupiter*,
When he appeard to haplesse *Semele*,
More louely then the monarke of the skie 1345
In wanton *Arethusaes* azurde armes,
And none but thou shalt be my paramour. *Exeunt.*

Old man. Accursed *Faustus*, miserable man,
That from thy soule excludst the grace of heauen,
And fliest the throne of his tribunall seate. 1350

Enter the Diuelles.

Sathan begins to sift me with his pride:
As in this furnace God shal try my faith,
My faith, vile hel, shal triumph ouer thee.
Ambitious fiends, see how the heauens smiles
At your repulse, and laughs your state to scorne. 1355
Hence hel, for hence I flie vnto my God. *Exeunt.*

Enter Faustus with the Schollers.

Fau: Ah Gentlemen!

1. *Sch:* What ailes Faustus?

Fau: Ah my sweete chamber-fellow! had I liued with thee, then had I liued stil, but now I die eternally: looke, comes he not? comes he not? 1361

2. *Sch:* What meanes Faustus?

3. *Scholler.* Belike he is growne into some sickenesse by being ouer solitary.

1. *Sch:* If it be so, weele haue Physitians to cure him: tis but a surffet, neuer feare man. 1366

Fau: A surffet of deadly sinne that hath damnd both body and soule.

1341 euenings *1616–63* 1345 skie] sea *conj. Cook* 1346 Arethusaes] Amymone's *conj. Cook* azure *1616* 1347 + Scene XV *add. Bull.* 1348–56 *om. 1616–63, which insert instead 27 new lines*; *cf. p. 227* 1350 S.D. the *om. Dyce to Bull.* 1356 + Scene XIV. *add. Ward, Brey.*: Scene XVI. *Bull.* 1357 Ah] O *1616–63* 1360 I die] must dye *1616–63* looke] Looke sirs *1616–63* 1362 *Instead of this line Qq 1616–63 have,* 1. O my deere Faustus what imports this feare? 2. Is all our pleasure turn'd to melancholy? 1363 Belike . . by] He is not well with *1616–63* 1365 to cure him] and Faustus shall bee cur'd *1616–63* 1366 tis but *etc.*] *Given to* 3. *1616–63* neuer feare man] sir, feare nothing *1616–63* 1367–8 damnd . . soule] undone me *1663*

2. *Sch.* Yet Faustus, looke vp to heauen, remember gods mercies are infinite. 1370

Fau. But Faustus offence can nere be pardoned. The Serpent that tempted *Eue* may be sau'd, but not Faustus: Ah Gentlemen, heare me with patience, and tremble not at my speeches. Though my heart pants and quiuers to remember that I haue beene a student here these thirty yeeres, O would I had neuer seene *Wertenberge*, neuer read booke: and what wonders I haue done, al *Germany* can witnes, yea all the world, for which Faustus hath lost both *Germany*, and the world, yea heauen it selfe, heauen the seate of God, the throne of the blessed, the kingdome of ioy, and must remaine in hel for euer, hel, ah hel for euer, sweete friends, what shall become of Faustus, being in hel for euer? 1383

3. *Sch.* Yet Faustus call on God.

Fau. On God whome Faustus hath abiurde, on God, whome Faustus hath blasphemed: ah my God, I woulde weepe, but the diuel drawes in my teares. Gush foorth bloud, insteade of teares, yea life and soule. Oh he stayes my tong, I would lift vp my hands, but see, they hold them, they hold them. 1390

All. Who Faustus?

Fau. *Lucifer* and *Mephastophilis*.
Ah Gentlemen! I gaue them my soule for my cunning.

All. God forbid. 1394

Fau. God forbade it indeede, but Faustus hath done it: for vaine pleasure of 24. yeares hath Faustus lost eternall ioy and felicitie. I writ them a bill with mine owne bloud, the date is expired, the time wil come, and he wil fetch mee.

1. *Schol.* Why did not Faustus tel vs of this before, that Diuines might haue prayed for thee? 1401

Fau. Oft haue I thought to haue done so, but the diuell

1369–70 remember . . are] and remember mercy is *1616–63* 1371–2 The . . Faustus *om. 1663* 1373 Ah] O *1616–63* me *om. 1616* 1374 pant & quiuer *1616–63* 1376 neuer] nere *1619–63* Wittenberg *1616–63* 1379–81 heauen the seate . . ioy *om. 1663* 1381 ah] O *1616–63* 1384 *Prefix* 2. *1616–63* God] Heaven *1663* 1385 On God *om. 1663* on God *om. 1663* 1386 ah] O *1616–31* ah . . God *om. 1663* 1388 yea . . soule *om. 1663* 1389–90 them . . them] 'em . . 'em *1616–63* 1392 Lucifer] Why Lucifer *1616–63* 1393 Ah] O *1616–63* 1394 God *1604–11*: O God *1616–31*: Heaven *1663* 1395 God] Heaven *1663* 1396 for] for the *1616–63* 24.] foure and twenty *1616–63* 1398 the time wil come] this is the time *1616–63*

threatned to teare mee in peeces, if I namde God, to fetch both body and soule, if I once gaue eare to diuinitie: and now tis too late: Gentlemen away, lest you perish with me.

2. *Sch.* O what shal we do to ⟨saue⟩ Faustus? 1406

Faustus. Talke not of me, but saue your selues, and depart.

3. *Sch.* God wil strengthen me, I wil stay with Faustus.

1. *Sch.* Tempt not God, sweete friend, but let vs into the next roome, and there pray for him. 1411

Fau. I, pray for me, pray for me, and what noyse soeuer yee heare, come not vnto me, for nothing can rescue me.

2. *Sch.* Pray thou, and we wil pray that God may haue mercy vpon thee. 1415

Fau. Gentlemen farewel, if I liue til morning, Ile visite you: if not, Faustus is gone to hel.

All. Faustus, farewel.

Exeunt Sch.

The clocke strikes eleauen.

Fau. Ah Faustus,
Now hast thou but one bare hower to liue, 1420
And then thou must be damnd perpetually:
Stand stil you euer moouing spheres of heauen,
That time may cease, and midnight neuer come:
Faire Natures eie, rise, rise againe, and make
Perpetuall day, or let this houre be but 1425
A yeere, a moneth, a weeke, a naturall day,
That Faustus may repent, and saue his soule,
O lente, lente curite noctis equi:
The starres mooue stil, time runs, the clocke wil strike,
The diuel wil come, and Faustus must be damnd. 1430
O Ile leape vp to my God: who pulles me downe?
See see where Christs blood streames in the firmament.
One drop would saue my soule, halfe a drop, ah my Christ.
Ah rend not my heart for naming of my Christ,
Yet wil I call on him: oh spare me *Lucifer*! 1435

1403 God] Heaven *1663* 1404 both] me *1616–63* 1405 tis] 'ts *1616*: it is *1620–63* 1406 shal] may *1616–63* saue *add. 1616–63, Dyce etc.* 1411 there *om. 1611–63* 1413 yee] you *1616–63* 1418+*New passage of 48 lines add. 1616–63*; *cf. Appendix, pp.* 227–9 1419 Ah *1604–11*: O *1616–63* 1430 damnd] lost *1663* 1431 to my God *1604*: vnto my God *1609, 1611*: to God *Brey.*: to heauen *1616–63* 1432 *om. 1616* 1432–4 *om. 1663* 1433 would . . ah] of bloud will saue me; oh *1616–31* 1434 Ah *om. 1616–31, Wag., Brey.* 1435 him] it *1663* Lucifer *om. 1663*

Where is it now? tis gone: And see where God
Stretcheth out his arme, and bends his irefull browes:
Mountaines and hilles, come, come, and fall on me,
And hide me from the heauy wrath of God.
No, no. 1440
Then wil I headlong runne into the earth:
Earth gape. O no, it wil not harbour me:
You starres that raignd at my natiuitie,
Whose influence hath alotted death and hel,
Now draw vp Faustus like a foggy mist, 1445
Into the intrailes of yon labring cloude,
That when you vomite foorth into the ayre,
My limbes may issue from your smoaky mouthes,
So that my soule may but ascend to heauen:
Ah, halfe the houre is past: *The watch strikes.*
Twil all be past anone: 1451
Oh God,
If thou wilt not haue mercy on my soule,
Yet for Christs sake, whose bloud hath ransomd me,
Impose some end to my incessant paine. 1455
Let Faustus liue in hel a thousand yeeres,
A hundred thousand, and at last be sau'd.
O no end is limited to damned soules,
Why wert thou not a creature wanting soule?
Or, why is this immortall that thou hast? 1460
Ah *Pythagoras metemsucosis*, were that true,
This soule should flie from me, and I be changde
Vnto some brutish beast: al beasts are happy,
For when they die,
Their soules are soone dissolud in elements, 1465
But mine must liue still to be plagde in hel:
Curst be the parents that ingendred me:
No Faustus, curse thy selfe, curse *Lucifer*,
That hath depriude thee of the ioyes of heauen:
The clocke striketh twelue.

1436–7 And see . . browes *1604–11*: And see a threatning Arme, an (and *1624, 1631*) angry Brow *1616–31*: *om. 1663* 1437 out *1604*: forth *1609, 1611* 1439 God] heauen *1616–63* 1440 no *om. 1616–63* 1442 Earth gape] Gape earth *1616–63* 1444 hath] haue *1619–31* 1446 intrailes] entrance *1611* yon] your *1620–63* clouds *1663, Dyce, Ward* 1447 you] they *conj. Dyce* 1448 your] their *conj. Dyce* 1449 So . . but] But let my soule mount, and *1616–63* 1450 S.D. The clock strikes the half-hour *Dyce* 1450 Ah] O *1616–63* 1452–4 *Instead of these lines Qq 1616–63 have* O. if my soule must suffer for my sinne, 1458 O *om. 1616–63, Wag., Brey.* 1462 I] Ile *1663* 1463 Vnto] Into *1616–63* 1469 S.D. clooke *1604* striketh] strikes *1611–63*

O it strikes, it strikes: now body turne to ayre, 1470
Or *Lucifer* wil beare thee quicke to hel:

Thunder and lightning.

O soule, be changde into little water drops,
And fal into the *Ocean*, nere be found:
My God, my God, looke not so fierce on me:

Enter diuels.

Adders, and Serpents, let me breathe a while: 1475
Vgly hell gape not, come not *Lucifer*,
Ile burne my bookes, ah *Mephastophilis.* ⟨*Exeunt with him.*

Enter Chorus.

⟨*Chor.*⟩ Cut is the branch that might haue growne ful straight,
And burned is *Apolloes* Laurel bough,
That sometime grew within this learned man: 1480
Faustus is gone, regard his hellish fall,
Whose fiendful fortune may exhort the wise,
Onely to wonder at vnlawful things,
Whose deepenesse doth intise such forward wits,
To practise more than heauenly power permits. 1485

Terminat hora diem, Terminat Author opus.

1470 O *om. 1616–63* 1471 S.D. *om. 1616–63* 1472 little] small *1616–63* 1474 My God, my God] O mercy heauen *1616–63* 1474 S.D. Thunder, and enter the deuils *after* 1473 *1616–63* 1477 ah] Oh *1616–63* 1477 S.D. Exeunt *1616*: *om. 1619–63* 1477 *+18 new lines add. 1616–63*; *cf. Appendix, p. 229* 1485 + FINIS *add. 1611–63*

APPENDIX TO DR. FAUSTUS

Instead of ll. 351–432, the quartos of 1616–63 have the following:

Enter Wagner and the Clowne.

Wag. Come hither sirra boy. 351
Clo. Boy ? O disgrace to my person : Zounds boy in your face, you haue seene many boyes with beards, I am sure.
Wag. Sirra, hast thou no commings in ?
Clow. Yes, and goings out too, you may see sir. 355
Wag. Alas poore slaue, see how pouerty iests in his nakednesse, I know the Villaines out of seruice, and so hungry, that I know he would giue his soule to the deuill for a shoulder of Mutton, tho it were bloud raw.
Clo. Not so neither ; I had need to haue it well rosted, and good sauce to it, if I pay so deere, I can tell you. 361
Wag. Sirra, wilt thou be my man and waite on me ? and I will make thee go, like *Qui mihi discipulus.*
Clow. What, in Verse ?
Wag. No slaue, in beaten silke, and staues-aker. 365
Clow. Staues-aker ? that's good to kill Vermine : then, belike if I serue you, I shall be lousy.
Wag. Why so thou shalt be, whether thou dost it or no : for sirra, if thou dost not presently bind thy selfe to me for seuen yeares, I'le turne all the lice about thee into Familiars, and make them tare thee in peeces. 371
Clow. Nay sir, you may saue your selfe a labour, for they are as familiar with me, as if they payd for their meate and drinke, I can tell you.
Wag. Well sirra, leaue your iesting, and take these Guilders. ⟨*Gives money.*⟩
Clow. Yes marry sir, and I thanke you to. 376
Wag. So, now thou art to bee at an howres warning, whensoeuer, and wheresoeuer the deuill shall fetch thee.
Clow. Here, take your Guilders, I'le none of 'em.
Wag. Not I, thou art prest, prepare thy selfe, for I will presently raise vp two deuils to carry thee away : *Banio, Belcher.*

354 Sirra *om. 1620–63* 355 Yes *om. 1663* 365 staues-aker] stauracin *or* stauracia *conj. Tancock* 369 not *om. 1663* 372 saue] spare *1631, 1663* 379 Guilders *1616* : Guilders againe *1619–63* 380 for] or *Dyce*[1]

Clow. *Belcher?* and *Belcher* come here, I'le belch him: I am not afraid of a deuill. 384

Enter 2 deuils.

Wag. How now sir, will you serue me now?
Clow. I good *Wagner*, take away the deuill then.
Wag. Spirits away; now sirra follow me.
Clow. I will sir; but hearke you Maister, will you teach me this coniuring Occupation?
Wag. I sirra, I'le teach thee to turne thy selfe to a Dog, or a Cat, or a Mouse, or a Rat, or any thing. 391
Clow. A Dog, or a Cat, or a Mouse, or a Rat? O braue *Wagner*.
Wag. Villaine, call me Maister *Wagner*, and see that you walke attentiuely, and let your right eye be alwaies *Diametrally* fixt vpon my left heele, that thou maist, *Quasi vestigias nostras insistere.* 397
Clow. Well sir, I warrant you. *Exeunt.*

After line 791, Qq 1616–63 insert the following scene not found in Qq 1604–11:

Enter the Clowne.

⟨*Clown.*⟩ What *Dick*, looke to the horses there till I come againe. I haue gotten one of Doctor *Faustus* coniuring bookes, and now we'le haue such knauery, as't passes.

Enter Dick.

Dick. What *Robin*, you must come away & walk the horses. 796
Rob. I walke the horses? I scorn't 'faith, I haue other matters in hand, let the horses walk themselues and they will. ⟨*Reads*⟩ *A perse a, t. h. e the: o per se o deny orgon, gorgon:* keepe further from me O thou illiterate, and vnlearned Hostler.
Dick. 'Snayles, what hast thou got there, a book? why thou canst not tell ne're a word on't. 802
Rob. That thou shalt see presently: keep out of the circle, I say, least I send you into the Ostry with a vengeance.
Dick. That's like 'faith: you had best leaue your foolery, for an my Maister come, he'le coniure you 'faith. 806
Rob. My Maister coniure me? I'le tell thee what, an my Maister come here, I'le clap as faire a paire of hornes on's head as e're thou sawest in thy life.

386 devils *Dyce*[2], *Cunn.* 387+S.D. Exeunt Devils *add. Dyce after* away 396–7 vestigiis nostris *Dyce*[2], *Cunn.*
791 S.D. Enter the Clowne] Enter Robin with a book *Dyce* 797 'faith *1616*: ifaith *1619–63* 799 S.D. Reads *add. Dyce* o deny] o per he e, veni *1663* 802 not *om. 1619* not tell *om. 1620–63* 806 ifaith *1619–63* 808 as faire a *1616*: a fayre *1619–63*

Dick. Thou needst not do that, for my Mistresse hath done it. 811

Rob. I, there be of vs here, that haue waded as deepe into matters, as other men, if they were disposed to talke.

Dick. A plague take you, I thought you did not sneake vp and downe after her for nothing. But I prethee tell me, in good sadnesse *Robin*, is that a coniuring booke? 816

Rob. Do but speake what thou't haue me to do, and I'le do't: If thou't dance naked, put off thy cloathes, and I'le coniure thee about presently: Or if thou't go but to the Tauerne with me, I'le giue thee white wine, red wine, claret wine Sacke, Muskadine, Malmesey and Whippincrust, hold belly hold, and wee'le not pay one peny for it. 822

Dick. O braue, prethee let's to it presently, for I am as dry as a dog.

Rob. Come then let's away. *Exeunt.*

Immediately after the last line above (825), Qq 1616–63 print the following expanded version of the Chorus's (or Wagner's) speech. For the briefer form in which the speech occurs in Qq 1604–11 and, by mistake, at an earlier point in Qq 1616–63, cf. p. 172.

Enter the Chorus.

⟨*Chorus.*⟩ Learned *Faustus* to find the secrets of Astronomy,
Grauen in the booke of *Ioues* high firmament, 827
Did mount him vp to scale *Olimpus* top.
Where sitting in a Chariot burning bright,
Drawne by the strength of yoked Dragons neckes; 830
He viewes the cloudes, the Planets, and the Starres,
The Tropick Zones, and quarters of the skye,
From the bright circle of the horned Moone,
Euen to the height of *Primum Mobile*:
And whirling round with this circumference, 835
Within the concaue compasse of the Pole,
From East to West his Dragons swiftly glide,
And in eight daies did bring him home againe.
Not long he stayed within his quiet house,
To rest his bones after his weary toyle, 840
But new exploits do hale him out agen,
And mounted then vpon a Dragons backe,
That with his wings did part the subtle aire:
He now is gone to proue *Cosmography*,
That measures costs, and kingdomes of the earth: 845
And as I guesse will first arriue at *Rome*,

810 needs *1631–63* that] it *1663* 823 prethee *1616*: I prethee *1619–63* 825 let's *1616*: let vs *1619–63* S.D. the *om. 1631, 1663* 828 him *om. 1631, 1663* vp *om. 1663* 831 He viewes *1616, 1619*: To view *1620–63* 835 this] his *1624* 839 his] this *1663*

To see the Pope and manner of his Court,
And take some part of holy *Peters* feast,
The which this day is highly solemnized. *Exit.*

Instead of ll. 803–904, the edition of 1663 inserts the following new scene, partly plagiarized from the *Jew of Malta*:

ACT. III.

Enter Faustus *and* Mephostophilis.

Faust. Now,
Mephostophilis
Having past with delight the famous 805
Town of *Tyre*, environ'd round with Aiery
Mountain tops: we came to *Rome*, where
There is a Bridge cal'd *Ponto Angelo*, upon which
There is erected as many Cannons as there is
Days in a compleat year, besides the Gates 810
And high *Piramedes*, which *Julius Cæsar*
Brought from *Affrica*.
Meph. Having now *Faustus* past with delight
The famous City of *Rome*, and all the
Monuments of Antiquity: our next shall be 815
To see the *Sultans* Court, and what
Delight great *Babylon* affords. This day
The *Soldan* with his *Bashawes* holds a
Solemne Feast for his late Victory,
Obtain'd against the Christians: wee'l be 820
His guests, and though unbidden, bring no
Stooles with us: come stand by,
And thou shalt ⟨see⟩ the⟨m⟩ come immediately.
Faust. Thou knowst my good *Mephostophilis*,
Within eight dayes we view'd the face of 825
Heaven, Earth, and Hell, so high our dragons
Sord into the skie, that looking downwards,
The Earth appear'd to me in quantity
No bigger then my hand.
Then in this shew let me an actor be, 830
That the proud *Turk* may *Faustus* cunning see.
Meph. Faustus I will, but first stay
And view their triumphs as they passe this way,
And then devise what mischief best contents
Thy mind: be cunning in thy art to crosse 835
Their mirth, or dash the pride of their
Solemnity, to clap huge horns upon his
Bashawes head, or any villany thou canst
Devise, and I'le perform it *Faustus*. Hark they come,
This day shall make thee admir'd in *Babylon*. 840
Faust. One thing more my good *Mephostophilis*.
Let me intreat of thee that *Faustus* may
Delight his mind, and through their follies cause

827 Sword *1663*

Some mirth: so charm me, I may appear
Invisible to all are here, and doe 845
What ere I please, unseen of any.
Meph. Faustus I will kneel down,
Whilst on thy head I lay my hand,
And charm thee with this Magick wand.
Take this girdle, thou shalt appear 850
Invisible to all are here;
The Planets seven, and the gloomy Air,
Hell, and the furies forked haer,
Pluto's blew fire, and *Heccats* tree,
With Magick charmes so compasse thee, 855
That no eye may thy body see.

Now *Faustus* for all their tricks, do what
Thou wilt, thou shalt not be deceiv'd of any.
Faust. Thanks *Mephostophilis.*
Now *Bashawes* take heed 860
Lest *Faustus* make your shaven pates to bleed.

Enter Salomaine and two Bashawes.

Solo. Welcome *Mephostophilis* from the siege of *Malta,*
And though we use no great familiarity
Towards our Vassals, but with severe looks
Maintain the reverence due to the *Ottoman* 865
Family, and so strike terrour in our subjects
Hearts: yet since the fates have so much
Favour'd us, as we have gain'd that proud
Rebellious town, that refus'd payment of our
Yearly tribute: we will recreate your wearied 870
Limbs: and pass the time with you my Lords in
Mirth, and to increase our joyes the more, *Caleph* from
You, let us here the story of *Malta's* siege.
Ca. Dread Soveraigne,
We no sooner there arrived, but of the 875
Governour, in your most Royal name, we
Demanded the ten months tribute left
Vnpaid: they desir'd time to make collection
Amongst the inhabitants of the *Malta* for it.
A moneth we granted, in which time 880
They seis'd on half the Estates of all
The Jews amongst them;
The time for truce alotted, scarce expir'd,
Arriv'd *Martine Belbosco* out of *Spaine,* who
With great promises of his Masters aid, 885
Incourag'd those of *Malta* not to render
Their promis'd tribute, but defend themselves:
They follow'd his advice, and made him general,
Who with those *Malta* Knights and lusty Seamen,
So valiantly the Sea and Coast defended, 890
That all our force in vain had been employ'd,
Had not an unexpected chance reliev'd us.

Mustapha may it please you finish the story,
For I was sent upon another design,
You know it better. 895
Mus. One morning as our scouts reliev'd our watch,
Hard by the City walls they found a body
Senceless, and speechless, yet gave some sign
Of life remaining in it: after some time
Spent in recovering to himself, he did 900
Confesse he was a Jew o'th town, who
To revenge some wrongs done him by
The Christians, would shew us how to
Enter to the town, and in short time
Make us masters of it: he therefore led our 905
Scouts through a vault, and rose with them in the
Middle of the town, open'd the gates for us to
Enter in, and by that means the place
Became our own.
Solo. Most grateful news. 910
Calph. Go call the Emperesse.
In the mean time prepare a banquet,
She shall partake with us in our joy and mirth,
It is too solitary to be alwaies pind up
In the *Saralious* solentary lodgings: 915
The greatest Princes are of humane mold,
No bow so good, but if still bent *En. Emp.*
Will break.——Welcome my dearest,
Whose soft embraces my wearied limbs refresh,
The pleasures we have receiv'd through this 920
The Christians overthrow, invites us sweet
To make a day of joy and triumph, which
Caus'd us, dearest, desire thy company.
Emp. Great *Solomaine*,
The glory of the *Ottomans*, 925
My dear and honoured Lord,
Thus low your handmaid returns your
Highnesse thanks, that you wo'd be pleas'd to
Admit your humble Vassal to partake
Of your Joies, and the cause on't. 930
Mahomet preserve your Majesty,
And grant you may obtain
Many such victories.
Faust. An excellent beautie this *Mephostophilis*,
I must needs have a touch at her lips. 935
Mep. Do *Faustus*, enjoy thy wish, glut thy selfe
With pleasure whilst time and occasion permits.
Emp. *Mahomet* defend me.
What's that, that wisht to touch me?
Faust. Only a friend of yours inamour'd with 940
Your beautie Ladie.

906 Scouts *T.B.*: Stote *1663* 917 still] steel *1663* 920 this *T.B.*: the *1663*

Solo. You seem discontented, or else amaz'd
At some strange accident: what i'st
Offends you sweet? come drink of this Cordial
To revive thee. 945

Faust. Though I must confess I have no great need
Of cordial waters, yet i'le drink it, because
It came from an Empresses hand:
Here *Solomaine*, here's to thee, and all thy mens
Confusion. 950

Solo. Hell, Furies, traytors look about,
See what tis that thus disturbs our mirth, and tell me
Dogs, or by our holy Prophets tomb I swear
Ye all shall die the miserablest death, that
Ever witty cruelty invented: how my soul is 955
Tortur'd with these villianous charms: some
Musick there to moderate these passions in
My breast: ha! do devils haunt my Palace,
Or are they come to celebrate such meetings
As the Christians use? 960
I'le find the cause of all these strange events,
And by our counter charmes cross their intents.
Call our Majecian forth, and let him bring
Such necessaries as his Art requires, to force
An answer from this infernal fiend, 965
That does disturb our mirth.

Meph. Faustus stand by, and give me leave to act
My part: we spirits take no pleasure in wine,
Or women, all our delights to hurt and torture
Men, which i'le perform on his majecian. 970
Vnless he serve a power above me, as we
Have order in our confusion, and different degrees
Amongst us, I'le carry him away out of
His circle, and throw him down into some
Stinking puddle. 975

Faust. Why, but tell me *Mephostophilis*, dar'st thou
Attempt to venter on a man in his circle?

Meph. Because thou art ours and sold to Lucifer, and I
Have promis'd to serve thee faithfully, I'le not
Conceal the secrets of our state from thee, thou darling 980
Of great *Lucifer*: know all those rights and
Spells which mortals use to make us rise,
Appear visible, answer to their demands,
Fullfill their wills, and execute their malice on
Their enemies, are very fables, forg'd at first 985
In hell, and thrust on credulous mortals
To deceive 'm.
Nor is there such a power in signes and words, to
Make us to obey, that rule the elements, and in a
Moment, if we had but leave, would turn the 990
World to a confus'd nothing. 'Tis true we seem

To come constrain'd, and by the power of their
Charmes: but are more willing to be imploy'd to
Hurt and kill mankind, then they are willing to engage
Vs in their service, and wheresoe'r we find one bent to our
Familiarity, we fly then willingly to catch him. 996

Faust. Thanks good *Mephostophilis* for this discovering
Of your misery. *Enter Conjurer.*

Solo. *Majecian* shew thy skill, and by thy art inquire
What it is that thus disturbs our mirth, and then 1000
Command it forthwith to depart.

Conju. I obey your Royal pleasure.

Within my circle here I stand,
And in my hand, this silver wand
Arm'd with the potent hell gods names 1005
At which fiends tremble midst the flames.
By fat of infants newly kill'd,
And blood by cruel mothers spill'd,
By *Pluto's* love to *Proserpine*,
Which made his Hell-hood sigh and whine, 1010
By *Minos* and by *Æ⟨a⟩cus*,
By *Radament* and *Serberus*,
I do conjure you hellish spirits,
That the infernal vaul⟨t⟩es inherits;
Send from your sootty palace hither, 1015
One of your train to tell me whether
He that disturbs the Emperours feast,
Be a Devil, or a Ghost from hell releast.

Meph. A devil.

Conju. Thy name? who sent for thee? why dost not
Shew thy self? scornst thou my charmes, 1021
Which heretofore made thee fly as swift
As lightning to obey my hest? i'le torture thee
For this contempt of me, and sink thee to the
Bottom of the Seas, or bind thee in the deserts of 1025
Arrabia a thousand years to punish thy disobedience.

Meph. Will you so aud⟨ac⟩ious mortal? nay now you move
Me, and because your fears have made you stone cold,
I'le warm you for your threatning me with water,
And for fear you should get a Feavour by this 1030
Vnwonted fire, in the next pond you come at,
I quench your heat.

Conju. Help, help, help. *Exit.*

Sollo. Come my dearest, thy life is worth all ours. *Exeunt.*

For ll. 854–904 in Qq 1604–11, the editions of 1616–31 substitute the following greatly expanded passage:

The which, in state and high solemnity,
This day is held through *Rome* and *Italy*, 855

1009 Plato's *1663* 1025 bind thee *T.B.*: blind them *1663*
854 in state and *1619–31*: this day with *1616*

In honour of the Popes triumphant victory.
Faust. Sweete *Mephosto⟨philis,⟩* thou pleasest me:
Whilst I am here on earth, let me be cloyd
With all things that delight the heart of man.
My foure and twenty yeares of liberty 860
I'le spend in pleasure and in daliance,
That *Faustus* name, whilst this bright frame doth stand,
May be admired through the furthest Land.
Meph. 'Tis well said *Faustus*, come then stand by me
And thou shalt see them come immediately. 865
Faust. Nay stay my gentle *Mephostophilis*,
And grant me my request, and then I go.
Thou know'st within the compasse of eight daies,
We view'd the face of heauen, of earth and hell.
So high our Dragons soar'd into the aire, 870
That looking downe the earth appear'd to me,
No bigger then my hand in quantity.
There did we view the Kingdomes of the world,
And what might please mine eye, I there beheld.
Then in this shew let me an Actor be, 875
That this proud Pope may *Faustus* cunning see.
Meph. Let it be so my *Faustus*, but first stay,
And view their triumphs, as they passe this way.
And then deuise what best contents thy minde,
By cunning in thine Art to crosse the Pope, 880
Or dash the pride of this solemnity;
To make his Monkes and Abbots stand like Apes,
And point like Antiques at his triple Crowne:
To beate the beades about the Friers Pates,
Or clap huge hornes, vpon the Cardinals heads: 885
Or any villany thou canst deuise,
And I'le performe it *Faustus*: heark they come:
This day shall make thee be admir'd in *Rome*.

Enter the Cardinals and Bishops, some bearing Crosiers, some the Pillars, Monkes and Friers, singing their Procession: Then the Pope, and Raymond King of Hungary, with Bruno led in chaines.

Pope. Cast downe our Foot-stoole.
Ray. Saxon *Bruno* stoope, 890
Whilst on thy backe his hollinesse ascends
Saint *Peters* Chaire and State Pontificall.
Bru. Proud *Lucifer*, that State belongs to me:
But thus I fall to *Peter*, not to thee.
Pope. To me and *Peter*, shalt thou groueling lie, 895

867 my] one *conj. Dyce* 876 cunning *1624, 1631*: comming *1616–20* 880 cunning *1624, 1631*: comming *1616–20* 881 this *1616–20*: his *1624, 1631* 883 at *1616–20*: to *1624–31* 887 it *om. 1619–31* 888 S.D. Enter the *1616*: Enter *1619–31*

And crouch before the Papall dignity:
Sound Trumpets then, for thus Saint *Peters* Heire,
From *Bruno's* backe, ascends Saint *Peters* Chaire.

A Flourish while he ascends.

Thus, as the Gods creepe on with feete of wool,
Long ere with Iron hands they punish men, 900
So shall our sleeping vengeance now arise,
And smite with death thy hated enterprise.
Lord Cardinals of *France* and *Padua*,
Go forth-with to our holy Consistory,
And read amongst the Statutes Decretall, 905
What by the holy Councell held at *Trent*,
The sacred Sinod hath decreed for him,
That doth assume the Papall gouernment,
Without election, and a true consent:
Away and bring vs word with speed. 910

1 *Card.* We go my Lord. *Exeunt Cardinals.*

Pope. Lord *Raymond.*

Faust. Go hast thee gentle *Mephostophilis*,
Follow the Cardinals to the Consistory;
And as they turne their superstitious Bookes, 915
Strike them with sloth, and drowsy idlenesse;
And make them sleepe so sound, that in their shapes,
Thy selfe and I, may parly with this Pope:
This proud confronter of the Emperour,
And in despite of all his Holinesse 920
Restore this *Bruno* to his liberty,
And beare him to the States of *Germany*.

Meph. *Faustus*, I goe.

Faust. Dispatch it soone,
The Pope shall curse that *Faustus* came to *Rome*. 925

Exit Faustus and Meph.

Bruno. Pope *Adrian* let me haue some right of Law,
I was elected by the Emperour.

Pope. We will depose the Emperour for that deed,
And curse the people that submit to him;
Both he and thou shalt stand excommunicate, 930
And interdict from Churches priuiledge,
And all society of holy men:
He growes to prowd in his authority,
Lifting his loftie head aboue the clouds,
And like a Steeple ouer-peeres the Church. 935
But wee'le pul downe his haughty insolence:
And as Pope *Alexander* our Progenitour,
Trode on the neck of *Germane Fredericke*,
Adding this golden sentence to our praise;

902 *om.* *1619–31* 904 our] the *1619–31* 918 this *1616*: the *1619–31* 926 some *om.* *1620–31* 930 shalt *1616*, *1619*: shall *1620–31*

That *Peters* heires should tread on Emperours, 940
And walke vpon the dreadfull Adders backe,
Treading the Lyon, and the Dragon downe,
And fearelesse spurne the killing Basiliske:
So will we quell that haughty Schismatique;
And by authority Apostolicall 945
Depose him from his Regall Gouernment.
Bru. Pope *Iulius* swore to Princely *Sigismond*,
For him, and the succeeding Popes of *Rome*,
To hold the Emperours their lawfull Lords.
Pope. Pope *Iulius* did abuse the Churches Rites, 950
And therefore none of his Decrees can stand.
Is not all power on earth bestowed on vs?
And therefore tho we would we cannot erre.
Behold this Siluer Belt whereto is fixt
Seuen golden seales fast sealed with seuen seales, 955
In token of our seuen-fold power from heauen,
To binde or loose, lock fast, condemne, or iudge,
Resigne, or seale, or what so pleaseth vs.
Then he and thou, and all the world shall stoope,
Or be assured of our dreadfull curse, 960
To light as heauy as the paines of hell.

Enter Faustus and Mephosto. like the Cardinals.

Meph. Now tell me *Faustus*, are we not fitted well?
Faust. Yes *Mephosto.* and two such Cardinals
Ne're seru'd a holy Pope, as we shall do.
But whilst they sleepe within the Consistory, 965
Let vs salute his reuerend Father-hood.
Ray. Behold my Lord, the Cardinals are return'd.
Pope. Welcome graue Fathers, answere presently,
What haue our holy Councell there decreed,
Concerning *Bruno* and the Emperour, 970
In quittance of their late conspiracie
Against our State, and Papall dignitie?
Faust. Most sacred Patron of the Church of Rome,
By full consent of all the Synod
Of Priests and Prelates, it is thus decreed: 975
That *Bruno*, and the Germane Emperour
Be held as Lollords, and bold Schismatiques,
And proud disturbers of the Churches peace.
And if that *Bruno* by his owne assent,
Without inforcement of the German Peeres, 980
Did seeke to weare the triple Dyadem,
And by your death to clime S. *Peters* Chaire,
The Statutes Decretall haue thus decreed,
He shall be streight condemn'd of heresie,
And on a pile of Fagots burnt to death. 985

955 golden Lockes *conj. Brereton* 963 Mephostophilis *1620–31*
969 hath *1620–31* 974 Syncd] holy Synod *conj. Dyce*

Pope. It is enough: here, take him to your charge,
And beare him streight to *Ponto Angelo*,
And in the strongest Tower inclose him fast.
To morrow, sitting in our Consistory,
With all our Colledge of graue Cardinals, 990
We will determine of his life or death.
Here, take his triple Crowne along with you,
And leaue it in the Churches treasury.
Make haste againe, my good Lord Cardinalls,
And take our blessing Apostolicall. 995

Meph. So, so, was neuer Diuell thus blest before.

Faust. Away sweet *Mephosto*, be gone,
The Cardinals will be plagu'd for this anon.

Ex. Fa. & Mep. ⟨*with Bruno.*⟩

Pope. Go presently, and bring a banket forth,
That we may solemnize S. *Peters* feast, 1000
And with Lord *Raymond*, King of Hungary,
Drinke to our late and happy victory. *Exeunt.*

A Senit while the Banquet is brought in; and then Enter Faustus and Mephastophilis in their owne shapes.

Meph. Now *Faustus*, come prepare thy selfe for mirth,
The sleepy Cardinals are hard at hand,
To censure *Bruno*, that is posted hence, 1005
And on a proud pac'd Steed, as swift as thought,
Flies ore the Alpes to fruitfull Germany,
There to salute the wofull Emperour.

Faust. The Pope will curse them for their sloth to day,
That slept both *Bruno* and his crowne away, 1010
But now, that *Faustus* may delight his minde,
And by their folly make some merriment,
Sweet *Mephasto*⟨*philis*,⟩ so charme me here,
That I may walke inuisible to all,
And doe what ere I please, vnseene of any. 1015

Meph. Faustus thou shalt, then kneele downe presently,
Whilst on thy head I lay my hand,
And charme thee with this Magicke wand,
First weare this girdle, then appeare
Inuisible to all are here: 1020
The Planets seuen, the gloomy aire,
Hell and the Furies forked haire,
Pluto's blew fire, and Hecat's tree
With Magicke spels so compasse thee,
That no eye may thy body see. 1025

So *Faustus*, now for all their holinesse,
Do what thou wilt, thou shalt not be discern'd.

987 Ponte *Dyce etc.* 992 his] this *1620–31* 997 Mephostophilis *1631* 998 S.D. with Bruno *add. Dyce* 1002+⟨Act III.⟩ Scene II. *add. Rob.* S.D. Senit] Sinit *1620*: Sonet *1624*, *1631* 1006 on] one *1631* 1013 Mephostophilis *1620–31*

Faust. Thankes *Mephasto⟨philis,⟩* now Friers take heed,
Lest *Faustus* make your shauen crownes to bleed.
Meph. *Faustus* no more: see where the Cardinals come. 1030

Enter Pope and all the Lords. Enter the Cardinals with a Booke

Pope. Welcome Lord Cardinals: come sit downe.
Lord *Raymond*, take your seate, Friers attend,
And see that all things be in readinesse,
As best beseemes this solemne festiuall.
1. *Card.* First, may it please your sacred Holinesse, 1035
To view the sentence of the reuerend Synod,
Concerning *Bruno* and the Emperour.
Pope. What needs this question? Did I not tell you,
To morrow we would sit i'th Consistory,
And there determine of his punishment? 1040
You brought vs word euen now, it was decreed,
That *Bruno* and the cursed Emperour
Were by the holy Councell both condemn'd
For lothed Lollords, and base Schismatiques:
Then wherefore would you haue me view that booke? 1045
1. *Card.* Your Grace mistakes, you gaue vs no such charge.
Ray. Deny it not, we all are witnesses
That *Bruno* here was late deliuered you,
With his rich triple crowne to be reseru'd,
And put into the Churches treasury. 1050
Amb. Card. By holy *Paul* we saw them not.
Pope. By *Peter* you shall dye,
Vnlesse you bring them forth immediatly:
Hale them to prison, lade their limbes with gyues:
False Prelates, for this hatefull treachery, 1055
Curst be your soules to hellish misery.
⟨*Exeunt Attendants with the two Cardinals.*⟩
Faust. So, they are safe: now *Faustus* to the feast,
The Pope had neuer such a frolicke guest.
Pope. Lord Archbishop of *Reames*, sit downe with vs.
Bish. I thanke your Holinesse. 1060
Faust. Fall to, the Diuell choke you an you spare.
Pope. Who 's that spoke? Friers looke about,
Lord *Raymond* pray fall too, I am beholding
To the Bishop of Millaine, for this so rare a present.
Faust. I thanke you sir. ⟨*Snatches the dish.*⟩
Pope. How now? who snatch't the meat from me! 1066
Villaines why speake you not?
My good Lord Archbishop, heres a most daintie dish,
Was sent me from a Cardinall in France.

1028 Mephostophilis *1631* 1033 be] are *1631* 1052 you] ye *1631* 1054 to] forth to *1620–31* 1056 S.D. *add. Dyce* 1059–1096 *These lines are a free adaptation of Qq 1604–11, ll.* 863–890

Faust. I'le haue that too. ⟨*Snatches the dish.*⟩

Pope. What Lollards do attend our Hollinesse, 1071
That we receiue such great indignity? fetch me some wine.

Faust. I, pray do, for *Faustus* is a dry.

Pope. Lord *Raymond*, I drink vnto your grace.

Faust. I pledge your grace. ⟨*Snatches the cup.*⟩

Pope. My wine gone too? yee Lubbers look about 1076
And find the man that doth this villany,
Or by our sanctitude you all shall die.
I pray my Lords haue patience at this
Troublesome banquet. 1080

Bish. Please it your holinesse, I thinke it be some Ghost crept out of Purgatory, and now is come vnto your holinesse for his pardon.

Pope. It may be so:
Go then command our Priests to sing a Dirge, 1085
To lay the fury of this same troublesome ghost.

⟨*Exit an Attendant.—The Pope crosses himself.*⟩

Faust. How now?
Must euery bit be spiced with a Crosse?
Nay then take that. ⟨*Strikes the Pope.*⟩

Pope. O I am slaine, help me my Lords: 1090
O come and help to beare my body hence:
Damb'd be this soule for euer for this deed.

Exeunt the Pope and his traine.

Me. Now *Faustus*, what will you do now? for I can tell you you'le be curst with Bell, Booke, and Candle.

Faust. Bell, Booke, and Candle; Candle, Booke, and Bell,
Forward and backward, to curse *Faustus* to hell. 1096

Qq 1616–63 print the following amended version of ll. 957–1006:

Enter Clowne and Dicke, with a Cup.

Dick. Sirra *Robin*, we were best looke that your deuill can answere the stealing of this same cup, for the Vintners boy followes vs at the hard heeles. 959

Rob. 'Tis no matter, let him come; an he follow vs, I'le so coniure him, as he was neuer coniur'd in his life, I warrant him: let me see the cup.

Enter Vintner.

Dick. Here 'tis: Yonder he comes: Now *Robin*, now or neuer shew thy cunning. 964

1072 such *1616–20, 1631*: this *1624* 1078 you *1616*: ye *1619–31* 1086 S.D. *add. Dyce* 1089 S.D. *add. Dyce* 1092 this soule *1616*: his soule *1619–31*, *Dyce etc.* 1092 S.D. the *om. 1619–31*
958 same *om. 1631, 1663*

Vint. O, are you here? I am glad I haue found you, you are a couple of fine companions: pray where's the cup you stole from the Tauerne? 967

Rob. How, how? we steale a cup? take heed what you say, we looke not like cup-stealers I can tell you.

Vint. Neuer deny't, for I know you haue it, and I'le search you. 971

Rob. Search me? I and spare not: hold the cup *Dick*, come, come, search me, search me.

Vint. Come on sirra, let me search you now.

Dick. I, I, do, do, hold the cup *Robin*, I feare not your searching; we scorne to steale your cups I can tell you. 976

Vint. Neuer out face me for the matter, for sure the cup is betweene you two.

Rob. Nay there you lie, 'tis beyond vs both.

Vint. A plague take you, I thought 'twas your knauery to take it away: Come, giue it me againe. 981

Rob. I much, when can you tell: *Dick*, make me a circle, and stand close at my backe, and stir not for thy life, *Vintner* you shall haue your cup anon, say nothing *Dick*: *O per se o demogorgon, Belcher* and *Mephostophilis.* 985

Enter Mephostophilis.

Meph. You Princely Legions of infernall Rule,
How am I vexed by these villaines Charmes?
From *Constantinople* haue they brought me now,
Onely for pleasure of these damned slaues. 989

Rob. By Lady sir, you haue had a shroud iourney of it, will it please you to take a shoulder of Mutton to supper, and a Tester in your purse, and go backe againe.

Dick. I, I pray you heartily sir; for wee cal'd you but in ieast I promise you.

Meph. To purge the rashnesse of this cursed deed, 995
First, be thou turned to this vgly shape,
For Apish deeds transformed to an Ape.

Rob. O braue, an Ape? I pray sir, let me haue the carrying of him about to shew some trickes.

Meph. And so thou shalt: be thou transform'd to a dog, and carry him vpon thy backe; away be gone. 1001

Rob. A dog? that's excellent: let the Maids looke well to their porridge-pots, for I'le into the Kitchin presently: come *Dick*, come. *Exeunt the two Clownes.*

Meph. Now with the flames of euer-burning fire, 1005
I'le wing my selfe and forth-with flie amaine
Vnto my *Faustus* to the great Turkes Court. *Exit.*

972 + S.D. Aside to Dick, giving him the cup *add. Dyce after* Dick 973 +, 976 + S.D. Vintner searches him *add. Dyce* 975 + S.D. Aside to Robin giving him the cup *add. Dyce after* Robin 976 your *om. 1624* 983 at] to *1663* 989 + S.D. Exit Vintner *add. Dyce* 991 to take *1616–24*: take *1631, 1663* 1007 + ⟨Act III⟩ Scene IV. *add. Rob., Cunn.*

ll. 1007–1105 in Qq 1604–11 are thus elaborated in Qq 1616–63:

Enter Martino, and Frederick at seuerall dores.

Mart. What ho, Officers, Gentlemen,
Hye to the presence to attend the Emperour,
Good *Fredericke* see the roomes be voyded straight,
His Maiesty is comming to the Hall; 1010
Go backe, and see the State in readinesse.
Fre. But where is *Bruno* our elected Pope,
That on a furies back came post from *Rome*,
Will not his grace consort the Emperour? 1014
Mart. O yes, and with him comes the *Germane* Coniurer,
The learned *Faustus*, fame of *Wittenberge*,
The wonder of the world for Magick Art;
And he intends to shew great *Carolus*,
The race of all his stout progenitors;
And bring in presence of his Maiesty, 1020
The royall shapes and warlike semblances
Of *Alexander* and his beauteous Paramour.
Fre. Where is *Benuolio?*
Mart. Fast a sleepe I warrant you,
He took his rouse with stopes of Rhennish wine, 1025
So kindly yesternight to *Bruno's* health,
That all this day the sluggard keepes his bed.
Fre. See, see his window's ope, we'l call to him.
Mart. What hoe, *Benuolio.*

Enter Benuolio aboue at a window, in his nightcap: buttoning.

Benu. What a deuill ayle you two? 1030
Mar. Speak softly sir, least the deuil heare you:
For *Faustus* at the Court is late arriu'd,
And at his heeles a thousand furies waite,
To accomplish what soeuer the Doctor please.
Benu. What of this? 1035
Mar. Come leaue thy chamber first, and thou shalt see
This Coniurer performe such rare exploits,
Before the Pope and royall Emperour,
As neuer yet was seene in *Germany.*
Benu. Has not the Pope enough of coniuring yet? 1040
He was vpon the deuils backe late enough;
And if he be so farre in loue with him,
I would he would post with him to *Rome* againe.
Fred. Speake, wilt thou come and see this sport?
Ben. Not I. 1045
Mart. Wilt thou stand in thy Window, and see it then?
Ben. I, and I fall not asleepe i'th meane time.

1014 consort] comfort *1620*, *1624* 1021 warlike *1616*, *Rob.*, *Brey.*: perfect *1619–63*, *Dyce* 1030 ails *Rob.*, *Cunn.*

Mar. The Emperour is at hand, who comes to see
What wonders by blacke spels may compast be. 1049

Ben. Well, go you attend the Emperour: I am content for this once to thrust my head out at a window: for they say, if a man be drunke ouer night, the Diuell cannot hurt him in the morning: if that bee true, I haue a charme in my head, shall controule him as well as the Coniurer, I warrant you. 1055

Exit ⟨*Frederick and Martino.*⟩

A Senit. Charles the Germane Emperour, Bruno, Saxony, Faustus, Mephostophilis, Fredericke, Martino, and Attendants.

Emp. Wonder of men, renown'd Magitian,
Thrice learned *Faustus*, welcome to our Court.
This deed of thine, in setting *Bruno* free
From his and our professed enemy,
Shall adde more excellence vnto thine Art, 1060
Then if by powerfull Necromantick spels,
Thou couldst command the worlds obedience:
For euer be belou'd of *Carolus*.
And if this *Bruno* thou hast late redeem'd,
In peace possesse the triple Diadem, 1065
And sit in *Peters* Chaire, despite of chance,
Thou shalt be famous through all *Italy*,
And honour'd of the Germane Emperour.

Faust. These gracious words, most royall *Carolus*,
Shall make poore *Faustus* to his vtmost power, 1070
Both loue and serue the Germane Emperour,
And lay his life at holy *Bruno's* feet.
For proofe whereof, if so your Grace be pleas'd,
The Doctor stands prepar'd, by power of Art,
To cast his Magicke charmes, that shall pierce through 1075
The Ebon gates of euer-burning hell,
And hale the stubborne Furies from their caues,
To compasse whatsoere your grace commands.

Ben. Bloud he speakes terribly: but for all that, I doe not greatly beleeue him, he lookes as like ⟨a⟩ Coniurer as the Pope to a Coster-monger. ⟨*Aside.*⟩

Emp. Then *Faustus* as thou late didst promise vs, 1082
We would behold that famous Conquerour,
Great *Alexander*, and his Paramour,
In their true shapes, and state Maiesticall, 1085
That we may wonder at their excellence.

Faust. Your Maiesty shall see them presently.

1051 at a] at the *1631, 1663* 1055 + Act the Fourth. Scene I. *Rob., Cunn.*: Scene X *Brey.* S.D. Charles] Enter Charles *1620, 1624* 1069 These *1616*: Those *1619–63* 1078 whatsoere *1616–20*: whatsoeuer *1624*: wheresoere *1631, 1663* 1080 a *add. 1620–63*

Mephosto away,
And with a solemne noyse of trumpets sound,
Present before this royall Emperour, 1090
Great *Alexander* and his beauteous Paramour.

Meph. Faustus I will. ⟨*Exit.*⟩

Ben. Well M. Doctor, an your Diuels come not away quickly, you shall haue me asleepe presently : zounds I could eate my selfe for anger, to thinke I haue beene such an Asse all this while, to stand gaping after the diuels Gouernor, and can see nothing.

Faust. Ile make you feele something anon, if my Art faile me not.
My Lord, I must forewarne your Maiesty, 1100
That when my Spirits present the royall shapes
Of *Alexander* and his Paramour,
Your grace demand no questions of the King,
But in dumbe silence let them come and goe.

Emp. Be it as *Faustus* please, we are content. 1105

Ben. I, I, and I am content too : and thou bring *Alexander* and his Paramour before the Emperour, I'le be *Acteon*, and turne my selfe to a Stagge.

Faust. And Ile play *Diana*, and send you the hornes presently. 1110

Senit. *Enter at one ⟨dore⟩ the Emperour Alexander, at the other Darius ; they meete, Darius is throwne downe, Alexander kils him ; takes off his Crowne, and offering to goe out, his Paramour meetes him, he embraceth her, and sets Darius Crowne vpon her head ; and comming backe, both salute the Emperour, who leauing his State, offers to embrace them, which Faustus seeing, suddenly staies him. Then trumpets cease, and Musicke sounds.*

My gracious Lord, you doe forget your selfe,
These are but shadowes, not substantiall.

Emp. O pardon me, my thoughts are so rauished
With sight of this renowned Emperour,
That in mine armes I would haue compast him. 1115
But *Faustus*, since I may not speake to them,
To satisfie my longing thoughts at full,
Let me this tell thee : I haue heard it said,
That this faire Lady, whilest she liu'd on earth,
Had on her necke a little wart, or mole ; 1120
How may I proue that saying to be true ?

1088 Mephostophilis *1619–63* 1090 this *1616* : the *1619–63* 1093 an *1616* : and *1619–63* 1101 the] their *1663* 1103 demands *1624* 1110 S.D. dore *add. 1619–63* State] Seate *1620, 1624* 1112 These *1616* : They *1619–63* 1117 thought *1624* 1119 while *1619–63*

Faust. Your Maiesty may boldly goe and see.
Emp. Faustus I see it plaine,
And in this sight thou better pleasest me,
Then if I gain'd another Monarchie. 1125
Faust. Away, be gone. *Exit Show.*
See, see, my gracious Lord, what strange beast is yon, that thrusts his head out at window.
Emp. O wondrous sight: see Duke of *Saxony*,
Two spreading hornes most strangely fastened 1130
Vpon the head of yong *Benvolio*.
Sax. What is he asleepe, or dead ?
Faust. He sleeps my Lord, but dreames not of his hornes.
Emp. This sport is excellent: wee'l call and wake him.
What ho, *Benvolio*. 1135
Ben. A plague vpon you, let me sleepe a while.
Emp. I blame thee not to sleepe much, hauing such a head of thine owne.
Sax. Looke vp *Benvolio*, tis the Emperour calls.
Ben. The Emperour ? where ? O zounds my head. 1140
Emp. Nay, and thy hornes hold, tis no matter for thy head, for that's arm'd sufficiently.
Faust. Why how now sir Knight, what hang'd by the hornes ? this ⟨is⟩ most horrible: fie, fie, pull in your head for shame, let not all the world wonder at you. 1145
Ben. Zounds Doctor, is this your villany ?
Faust. O say not so sir: the Doctor has no skill,
No Art, no cunning, to present these Lords,
Or bring before this royall Emperour
The mightie Monarch, warlicke *Alexander*. 1150
If *Faustus* do it, you are streight resolu'd,
In bold *Acteons* shape to turne a Stagge.
And therefore my Lord, so please your Maiesty,
Il'e raise a kennell of Hounds shall hunt him so,
As all his footmanship shall scarce preuaile, 1155
To keepe his Carkasse from their bloudy phangs.
Ho, *Belimote, Argiron, Asterote.*
Ben. Hold, hold: zounds hee'l raise vp a kennell of Diuels I thinke anon: good my Lord intreate for me: 'sbloud I am neuer able to endure these torments. 1160
Emp. Then good M. Doctor,
Let me intreate you to remoue his hornes,
He has done penance now sufficiently.
Faust. My gracious Lord, not so much for iniury done to

1125 gain'd] had gain'd *1620, 1624* 1128 at] at the *1619–63* 1129 wondrous] wonderful *1663* 1130 strangely] stately *1663* 1140 O zounds] my head *1663* 1143 how *om. 1663* 1144 is *add. 1619–63* 1146 Zounds *om. 1663* is this] this is *1624, Dyce, Cunn., Brey.* 1153 so] to *1663* 1155 As *1616*: And *1619, 1631, 1663*: That *1620, 1624* 1158 zounds *om. 1663* 1159 'sbloud *om. 1663* 1163 has] hath *1619–63*

me, as to delight your Maiesty with some mirth : hath *Faustus* iustly requited this iniurious knight, which being all I desire, I am content to remoue his hornes. *Mephastophilis*, transforme him ; and hereafter sir, looke you speake well of Schollers. 1169

Ben. Speake well of yee ? 'sbloud and Schollers be such Cuckold-makers to clap hornes of honest mens heades o' this order Il'e nere trust smooth faces, and small ruffes more. But an I be not reueng'd for this, would I might be turn'd to a gaping Oyster, and drinke nothing but salt water.

Emp. Come *Faustus* while the Emperour liues, 1175
In recompence of this thy high desert,
Thou shalt command the state of *Germany*,
And liue belou'd of mightie *Carolus*. *Exeunt omnes.*

Enter Benvolio, Martino, Fredericke, and Souldiers.

Mar. Nay sweet *Benvolio*, let vs sway thy thoughts
From this attempt against the Coniurer. 1180

Ben. Away, you loue me not, to vrge me thus,
Shall I let slip so great an iniury,
When euery seruile groome ieasts at my wrongs,
And in their rusticke gambals proudly say,
Benvolio's head was grac't with hornes to day ? 1185
O may these eye-lids neuer close againe,
Till with my sword I haue that Coniurer slaine.
If you will aid me in this enterprise,
Then draw your weapons, and be resolute :
If not, depart : here will *Benvolio* die, 1190
But *Faustus* death shall quit my infamie.

Fred. Nay, we will stay with thee, betide what may,
And kill that Doctor if he come this way.

Ben. Then gentle *Fredericke* hie thee to the groue,
And place our seruants, and our followers 1195
Close in an ambush there behinde the trees,
By this, (I know) the Coniurer is neere,
I saw him kneele, and kisse the Emperours hand,
And take his leaue, laden with rich rewards.
Then Souldiers boldly fight ; if *Faustus* die, 1200
Take you the wealth, leaue vs the victorie.

Fred. Come souldiers, follow me vnto the groue,
Who kils him shall haue gold, and endlesse loue.
Exit Frederick with the Souldiers.

Ben. My head is lighter then it was by th'hornes,

1167 horne *1624* 1168 + S.D. Mephistophilis removes the horns *add. Dyce after* him 1168 sir *om. 1624* 1170 'sbloud] 's foot *1663* 1171 of] upon *1663* 1172 ruffes] bands *1663* 1176 thy *om. 1663* 1178 + ⟨Act IV⟩ Scene II *Rob., Cunn.* : Scene X[a] *Brey.* 1179 sway] stay *1624* 1187 that] the *1620–63* 1191 quite *1624* my *1616* : thy *1619–63* 1193 that] the *1620–63* 1196 an *om. 1619–63* 1200 boldly] brauely *1620–63*

But yet my heart more ponderous then my head, 1205
And pants vntill I see that Coniurer dead.
Mar. Where shall we place our selues *Benvolio?*
Ben. Here will we stay to bide the first assault.
O were that damned Hell-hound but in place,
Thou soone shouldst see me quit my foule disgrace. 1210

Enter Fredericke.

Fred. Close, close, the Coniurer is at hand,
And all alone, comes walking in his gowne;
Be ready then, and strike the Peasant downe.
Ben. Mine be that honour then: now sword strike home,
For hornes he gaue, Il'e haue his head anone. 1215

Enter Faustus with the false head

Mar. See, see, he comes.
Ben. No words: this blow ends all,
Hell take his soule, his body thus must fall.
Faust. Oh.
Fred. Grone you Master Doctor? 1220
Ben. Breake may his heart with grones: deere *Frederik* see
Thus will I end his griefes immediatly.
Man. Strike with a willing hand, his head is off.
Ben. The Diuel's dead, the Furies now may laugh.
Fred. Was this that sterne aspect, that awfull frowne,
Made the grim monarch of infernall spirits, 1226
Tremble and quake at his commanding charmes?
Mar. Was this that damned head, whose heart conspir'd
Benvolio's shame before the Emperour.
Ben. I, that's the head, and here the body lies, 1230
Iustly rewarded for his villanies.
Fred. Come, let's deuise how we may adde more shame
To the blacke scandall of his hated name.
Ben. First, on his head, in quittance of my wrongs,
I'le naile huge forked hornes, and let them hang 1235
Within the window where he yoak'd me first,
That all the world may see my iust reuenge.
Mar. What vse shall we put his beard to?
Ben. Wee'l sell it to a Chimny-sweeper: it will weare out ten birchin broomes I warrant you. 1240
Fred. What shall ⟨his⟩ eyes doe?
Ben. Wee'l put out his eyes, and they shall serue for buttons to his lips, to keepe his tongue from catching cold.

1205 heart's *1619–63* 1206 that] the *1619–63* 1213 the] that *1619–63* 1215 S.D. the *1616*: his *1619–63*: a *Rob.*, *Dyce*, *Cunn.* 1218+S.D. Stabs Faustus *add. Dyce* 1223 Struck *1663* 1223+S.D. Benvolio strikes off Faustus' head *add. Dyce* 1224 now *om. 1620–31* 1228 heart] art *Rob.*, *Dyce*, *Cunn.* 1230 here] there *1620–63* 1241 his *add. 1619–63* 1242 put *1616*, *1619*: pull *1620–63*

Mar. An excellent policie: and now sirs, hauing diuided him, what shall the body doe? ⟨*Faustus rises.*⟩ 1245

Ben. Zounds the Diuel's aliue agen.

Fred. Giue him his head for Gods sake.

Faust. Nay keepe it: *Faustus* will haue heads and hands,
I call your hearts to recompence this deed.
Knew you not Traytors, I was limitted 1250
For foure and twenty yeares, to breathe on earth?
And had you cut my body with your swords,
Or hew'd this flesh and bones as small as sand,
Yet in a minute had my spirit return'd,
And I had breath'd a man made free from harme. 1255
But wherefore doe I dally my reuenge?
Asteroth, Belimoth, Mephostophilis, { *Ent. Meph. & other Diuels.*
Go horse these traytors on your fiery backes,
And mount aloft with them as high as heauen,
Thence pitch them headlong to the lowest hell: 1260
Yet stay, the world shall see their miserie,
And hell shall after plague their treacherie.
Go *Belimothe*, and take this caitife hence,
And hurle him in some lake of mud and durt:
Take thou this other, dragge him through the woods, 1265
Amongst the pricking thornes, and sharpest briers,
Whilst with my gentle *Mephostophilis*,
This Traytor flies vnto some steepie rocke,
That rowling downe, may breake the villaines bones,
As he intended to dismember me. 1270
Fly hence, dispatch my charge immediatly.

Fred. Pitie vs gentle *Faustus*, saue our liues.

Faust. Away.

Fred. He must needs goe that the Diuell driues.

Exeunt Spirits with the knights.

Enter the ambusht Souldiers.

1 *Sold.* Come sirs, prepare your selues in readinesse, 1275
Make hast to help these noble Gentlemen,
I heard them parly with the Coniurer.

2 *Sold.* See where he comes, dispatch, and kill the slaue.

Faust. What's here? an ambush to betray my life:
Then *Faustus* try thy skill: base pesants stand, 1280
For loe these Trees remoue at my command,
And stand as Bulwarkes twixt your selues and me,
To sheild me from your hated treachery:

1245 S.D. Faustus rises *add. Dyce* 1246 Zounds *om. 1663* 1247 Gods] heavens *1663* 1249 I call *1616–63*, *ed. 1814*: And all *Rob.*, *Cunn.*: Ay, call *Dyce*[1]: Ay, all *Dyce*[2], *Brey.* 1250 you] Ye *1619–63* 1260 Thence *1616*: Then *1619–63* 1266 Among *1619–63* 1274+Scene III. *Rob.*, *Cunn.* 1281 these] the *1620–63*

Yet to encounter this your weake attempt,
Behold an Army comes incontinent. 1285

Faustus strikes the dore, and enter a deuill playing on a Drum, after him another bearing an Ensigne: and diuers with weapons, Mephostophilis with fire-workes; they set vpon the Souldiers and driue them out.

Enter at seuerall dores, Benuolio, Fredericke, and Martino, their heads and faces bloudy, and besmear'd with mud and durt; all hauing hornes on their heads.

Mart. What ho, *Benuolio.*
Benu. Here, what *Frederick*, ho.
Fred. O help me gentle friend; where is *Martino*?
Mart. Deere *Frederick* here,
Halfe smother'd in a Lake of mud and durt, 1290
Through which the Furies drag'd me by the heeles.
Fred. *Martino* see, *Benuolio's* hornes againe.
Mart. O misery, how now *Benuolio*?
Benu. Defend me heauen, shall I be haunted still? 1294
Mart. Nay feare not man, they haue no power to kill.
Benu. My friends transformed thus: O hellish spite,
Your heads are all set with hornes.
Fred. You hit it right,
It is your owne you meane, feele on your head.
Benu. 'Zons, hornes againe. 1300
Mart. Nay chafe not man, we all are sped.
Benu. What deuill attends this damn'd Magician,
That spite of spite, our wrongs are doubled?
Fred. What may we do, that we may hide our shames?
Benu. If we should follow him to worke reuenge, 1305
He'd ioyne long Asses eares to these huge hornes,
And make vs laughing stockes to all the world.
Mart. What shall we then do deere *Benuolio*?
Benu. I haue a Castle ioyning neere these woods,
And thither wee'le repaire and liue obscure, 1310
Till time shall alter this our brutish shapes:
Sith blacke disgrace hath thus eclipst our fame,
We'le rather die with griefe, then liue with shame.
Exeunt omnes.

1285 S.D. on a] upon a *1663* ⟨Act IV.⟩ Scene IV. *add. Rob., Cunn.* S.D. all hauing] hauing all *1619–63* 1289 *om 1663, thus giving ll.* 1290–1 *to Fred.* 1291 drag *1663* 1295 they *Cunn.*: we *1616–63* 1300 'Zons *1616*: Zounds *1619–31*: What *1663* 1311 this *1616*: these *1619–63* 1313+⟨Act IV.⟩ Scene V. *Rob., Cunn.*

ll. 1111–98 of Qq 1604–11 are in Qq 1616–63 condensed to the following:

Enter Faustus, and the Horse-courser, and Mephostophilis.

Horse. I beseech your Worship accept of these forty Dollors. 1112

Faust. Friend, thou canst not buy so good a horse, for so small a price: I haue no great need to sell him, but if thou likest him for ten Dollors more, take him, because I see thou hast a good minde to him. 1116

Horse. I beseech you sir accept of this; I am a very poore man, and haue lost very much of late by horse flesh, and this bargaine will set me vp againe.

Faust. Well, I will not stand with thee, giue me the money: now sirra I must tell you, that you may ride him o're hedge and ditch, and spare him not; but do you heare? in any case, ride him not into the water. 1123

Horse. How sir, not into the water? why will he not drink of all waters?

Faust. Yes, he will drinke of all waters, but ride him not into the water; o're hedge and ditch, or where thou wilt, but not into the water: Go bid the Hostler deliuer him vnto you, and remember what I say. 1129

Horse. I warrant you sir; O ioyfull day: Now am I a made man for euer. *Exit.*

Faust. What art thou *Faustus* but a man condemn'd to die?
Thy fatall time drawes to a finall end;
Despaire doth driue distrust into my thoughts.
Confound these passions with a quiet sleepe: 1135
Tush, Christ did call the Theefe vpon the Crosse,
Then rest thee *Faustus* quiet in conceit.

He sits to sleepe.

Enter the Horse-courser wet.

Horse. O what a cosening Doctor was this? I riding my horse into the water, thinking some hidden mystery had beene in the horse, I had nothing vnder me but a little straw, and had much ado to escape drowning: Well I'le go rouse him, and make him giue me my forty Dollors againe. Ho sirra Doctor, you cosoning scab; Maister Doctor awake, and rise, and giue me my mony againe, for your horse is turned to a bottle of Hay,—Maister Doctor. *He puls off his leg.*
Alas I am vndone, what shall I do? I haue puld off his leg.

Faust. O help, help, the villaine hath murder'd me. 1147

1110 S.D. and the] and a *Dyce* 1137 S.D. wet *om. 1663* 1141 scape *1624* 1145 Doctor] *After this word Q 1663 adds* S 'foot I think hee's rotten. 1147 hath] has *1631, 1663*

Horse. Murder or not murder, now he has but one leg, I'le out-run him, and cast this leg into some ditch or other.

Faust. Stop him, stop him, stop him—ha, ha, ha, *Faustus* hath his leg againe, and the Horse-courser a bundle of hay for his forty Dollors. 1152

Enter Wagner.

How now *Wagner* what newes with thee ?

Wag. If it please you, the Duke of *Vanholt* doth earnestly entreate your company, and hath sent some of his men to attend you with prouision fit for your iourney. 1156

Faust. The Duke of *Vanholt's* an honourable Gentleman, and one to whom I must be no niggard of my cunning : Come away. *Exeunt.*

ll. 1199–1237 of Qq 1604–11 are expanded as follows in Qq. 1616–31 :

Enter Clowne, Dick, Horse-courser, and a Carter.

Cart. Come my Maisters, I'le bring you to the best beere in Europe, what ho, Hostis ; where be these Whores ? 1200

Enter Hostis.

Host. How now, what lacke you ? What my old Guesse, welcome.

Clow. Sirra *Dick*, dost thou know why I stand so mute ?

Dick. No *Robin*, why is't ?

Clow. I am eighteene pence on the score, but say nothing, see if she haue forgotten me. 1206

Host. Who's this, that stands so solemnly by himselfe : what my old Guest ?

Clo. O Hostisse how do you ? I hope my score stands still.

Host. I there's no doubt of that, for me thinkes you make no hast to wipe it out. 1211

Dick. Why Hostesse, I say, fetch vs some Beere. (*Exit.*

Host. You shall presently : looke vp into th' hall there ho.

Dick. Come sirs, what shall we do now till mine Hostesse comes ? 1215

Cart. Marry sir, I'le tell you the brauest tale how a Coniurer seru'd me ; you know Doctor *Fauster.*

Horse. I, a plague take him, heere's some on's haue cause to know him ; did he coniure thee too ? 1219

Cart. I'le tell you how he seru'd me : As I was going to *Wittenberge* t'other day, with a loade of Hay, he met me,

1148 has] hath *1631, 1663* 1149 this] his *Brey.* 1149+S.D. Aside, and then runs out *add. Dyce* 1156 you *om. 1620–63* 1159+⟨Act IV.⟩ Scene VI. *add. Rob., Cunn.*: Scene XI[a] *Brey.*

1198 S.D. Clowne] Robin *Dyce etc.* 1203 thou *om. 1620–63* 1214 now *om. 1619–63* 1216 sirs *conj. Dyce* 1217 Faustus *1619–63* 1218 plague] pox *1663*

and asked me what he should giue me for as much Hay as he could eate ; now sir, I thinking that a little would serue his turne, bad him take as much as he would for three-farthings ; so he presently gaue me my mony, and fell to eating ; and as I am a cursen man, he neuer left eating, till he had eate vp all my loade of hay. 1227

All. O monstrous, eate a whole load of Hay !

Clow. Yes, yes, that may be ; for I haue heard of one, that has eate a load of logges. 1230

Horse. Now sirs, you shall heare how villanously he seru'd mee : I went to him yesterday to buy a horse of him, and he would by no meanes sell him vnder 40 Dollors ; so sir, because I knew him to be such a horse, as would run ouer hedge and ditch, and neuer tyre, I gaue him his money ; so when I had my horse, Doctor *Fauster* bad me ride him night and day, and spare him no time ; but, quoth he, in any case ride him not into the water. Now sir, I thinking the horse had had some quality that he would not haue me know of, what did I but rid him into a great riuer, and when I came iust in the midst my horse vanisht away, and I sate straddling vpon a bottle of Hay. 1242

All. O braue Doctor.

Horse. But you shall heare how brauely I seru'd him for it ; I went me home to his house, and there I found him a sleepe ; I kept a hallowing and whooping in his eares, but all could not wake him : I seeing that, tooke him by the leg, and neuer rested pulling, till I had pul'd me his leg quite off, and now 'tis at home in mine Hostry. 1249

Clow. And has the Doctor but one leg then ? that's excellent, for one of his deuils turn'd me into the likenesse of an Apes face.

Cart. Some more drinke Hostesse. 1253

Clow. Hearke you, we'le into another roome and drinke a while, and then we'le go seeke out the Doctor. *Exeunt omnes.*

Enter the Duke of Vanholt ; his Dutches, Faustus, and Mephostophilis.

Duke. Thankes Maister Doctor, for these pleasant sights. Nor know I how sufficiently to recompence your great deserts

1225 my *om. 1619–63* 1226 cursen] cursten *1663* 1229–30 heard . . has] an Uncle that did *1663* 1229 of *om. 1619, 1620* 1230 a] a whole *1663* 1236 Faustus *1619–63* bad] bid *1663* 1237 no time] not *1663* 1239 some *1616* : some rare *1619–63* 1240 ride *1624–63* 1241 in] into *1663* 1246 kept . . whooping] Whoop'd and hallowed *1663* all *om. 1663* 1248 me *om. 1663* 1249 mine] my *1663* 1251 for] then, for *1663* 1253 *After this line, instead of* 1254–5, *Q 1663 adds a new passage of 65 lines. Cf. Appendix, pp.* 224, 225. 1255 + Act the Fifth. Scene I. *add. Rob., Cunn.* : Scene XII. *Brey.*

in erecting that inchanted Castle in the Aire: the Sight whereof so delighted me,
As nothing in the world could please me more. 1260

Faust. I do thinke my selfe my good Lord, highly recompenced, in that it pleaseth your grace to thinke but well of that which *Faustus* hath performed. But gratious Lady, it may be, that you haue taken no pleasure in those sights; therefor I pray you tell me, what is the thing you most desire to haue, be it in the world, it shall be yours: I haue heard that great bellyed women do long for things, are rare and dainty. 1268

Lady. True Maister Doctor, and since I finde you so kind I will make knowne vnto you what my heart desires to haue, and were it now Summer, as it is Ianuary, a dead time of the Winter, I would request no better meate, then a dish of ripe grapes.

Fau. This is but a small matter: Go *Mephostophilis*, away. *Exit Mephosto.*
Madam, I will do more then this for your content. 1275

Enter Mepho. agen with the grapes.

Here, now taste yee these, they should be good
For they come from a farre Country I can tell you.

Duke. This makes me wonder more then all the rest, that at this time of the yeare, when euery Tree is barren of his fruite, from whence you had these ripe grapes. 1280

Faust. Please it your grace, the yeare is diuided into two circles ouer the whole world, so that when it is Winter with vs, in the contrary circle it is likewise Summer with them, as in *India*, *Saba*, and such Countries that lye farre East, where they haue fruit twice a yeare. From whence, by meanes of a swift spirit that I haue, I had these grapes brought as you see. 1287

Lady. And trust me, they are the sweetest grapes that e're I tasted.

The Clowne bounce at the gate, within.

Duke. What rude disturbers haue we at the gate? 1290
Go pacifie their fury set it ope,
And then demand of them, what they would haue.

They knocke againe, and call out to talke with Faustus.

A Seruant. Why how now Maisters, what a coyle is there?
What is the reason you disturbe the Duke?

Dick. We haue no reason for it, therefore a fig for him.

Ser. Why saucy varlets, dare you be so bold. 1296

1259 delighteth *1619–63* 1262 pleaseth] hath pleased *1620–63* 1277 come] came *1620–63* 1280 ripe *om. 1620–63* 1289 S.D. Clowns *Dyce* bounceth *1620–63, Cunn.*

Horsc. I hope sir, we haue wit enough to be more bold then welcome.

Ser. It appeares so, pray be bold else-where,
And trouble not the Duke. 1300

Duke. What would they haue?

Ser. They all cry out to speake with Doctor *Faustus.*

Cart. I, and we will speake with him.

Duke. Will you sir? Commit the Rascals.

Dick. Commit with vs, he were as good commit with his father, as commit with vs. 1306

Faust. I do beseech your grace let them come in,
They are good subiect for a merriment.

Duke. Do as thou wilt *Faustus,* I giue thee leaue.

Faust. I thanke your grace: 1310

Enter the Clowne, Dick, Carter, and Horse-courser.

Why, how now my good friends?
'Faith you are too outragious, but come neere,
I haue procur'd your pardons: welcome all.

Clow. Nay sir, we will be wellcome for our mony, and we will pay for what we take: What ho, giue's halfe a dosen of Beere here, and be hang'd. 1316

Faust. Nay, hearke you, can you tell me where you are?

Cart. I marry can I, we are vnder heauen.

Ser. I but sir sauce box, know you in what place?

Horsc. I, I, the house is good enough to drink in: Zons fill vs some Beere, or we'll breake all the barrels in the house, and dash out all your braines with your Bottles. 1322

Faust. Be not so furious: come, you shall haue Beere.
My Lord, beseech you giue me leaue a while,
I'le gage my credit, 'twill content your grace. 1325

Duke. With all my heart kind Doctor, please thy selfe,
Our seruants, and our Courts at thy command.

Faust. I humbly thanke your grace: then fetch some Beere.

Horsc. I mary, there spake a Doctor indeed, and 'faith Ile drinke a health to thy woodden leg for that word. 1330

Faust. My woodden leg? what dost thou meane by that?

Cart. Ha, ha, ha, dost heare him *Dick,* he has forgot his legge.

Horsc. I, I, he does not stand much vpon that.

Faust. No faith, not much vpon a woodden leg. 1335

Cart. Good Lord, that flesh and bloud should be so fraile with your Worship: Do not you remember a Horse-courser you sold a horse to?

1308 subjects *1663* for *1616*: to *1619–63* a *om. 1663* 1313 pardon *1624* 1317 me *om. 1620–63* 1320 Zons] come *1663* 1329 spoke *1624* 1332 dost *1616, 1663*: dost thou *1619–31* him] me *1624* 1336 Good Lord] O *1663* 1337 not *om. 1663*

Faust. Yes, I remember I sold one a horse.
Cart. And do you remember you bid he should not ride into the water? 1341
Faust. Yes, I do verie well remember that.
Cart. And do you remember nothing of your leg?
Faust. No in good sooth.
Cart. Then I pray remember your curtesie. 1345
Faust. I thank you sir.
Car. 'Tis not so much worth; I pray you tel me one thing.
Faust. What's that?
Cart. Be both your legs bedfellowes euery night together?
Faust. Wouldst thou make a *Colossus* of me, that thou askest me such questions? 1351
Cart. No truelie sir, I would make nothing of you, but I would faine know that.

Enter Hostesse with drinke.

Faust. Then I assure thee certainelie they are.
Cart. I thanke you, I am fully satisfied. 1355
Faust. But wherefore dost thou aske?
Cart. For nothing sir: but me thinkes you should haue a wooden bedfellow of one of 'em.
Horsc. Why do you heare sir, did not I pull off one of your legs when you were asleepe? 1360
Faust. But I haue it againe now I am awake: looke you heere sir.
All. O horrible, had the Doctor three legs.
Cart. Do you remember sir, how you cosened me and eat vp my load of — 1365

Faustus charmes him dumb.

Dick. Do you remember how you made me weare an Apes —
Horsc. You whoreson coniuring scab, do you remember how you cosened me with a ho — 1369
Clow. Ha' you forgotten me? you thinke to carry it away with your *Hey-passe*, and *Re-passe:* do you remember the dogs fa — *Exeunt Clownes.*
Host. Who payes for the Ale? heare you Maister Doctor, now you haue sent away my guesse, I pray who shall pay me for my A — ? *Exit Hostesse.*

1340 do you .. should *1616–31*: how you bid him *1663* 1345 pray *1616, 1619*: pray you *1620–31*: *om. 1663* 1346 I *om. 1620–63* 1347 you *om. 1663* 1357 thinke *1631, 1663* 1359 not I] I not *1624, 1663* 1361 I am awake *om. 1663* 1362 *After this line Q 1663 inserts* OM. How let's feel. HORSE. Tother leg. CLOW. Both together. 1365 load of —] load of — — hay, a, a, a *1663* S.D. him] them *Dyce* 1367 Apes —] Apes — — fa, a, a, a *1663* 1369 you] yo *1616* ho —] ho — — ho, ho, ho *1663* 1372 fa —] fa — — fa, fa, fa *1663*

Lady. My Lord, 1376
We are much beholding to this learned man.
Duke. So are we Madam, which we will recompence
With all the loue and kindnesse that we may. 1379
His Artfull sport, driues all sad thoughts away. *Exeunt.*

The text of 1663 agrees in the main with that of 1616–31 above, except that in place of ll. 1254–5 it adds the following:

Dic. Hostess, will you not give us a Song?
You sung us a fine Song 1255
When we were here last.
Host. Talk of Songs as soon as y' come into a house?
Let's see what Guests you'l be first, you do not call
For drink fast enough, I am a cup too low yet.
Clow. Where are you, Lick-spiget? fill us six Cans. 1260
Host. I marry, I know you can call apase, but have
You any money to pay for them?
Clow. O yes Hostess, money in both pockets. *Enter boy*
Host. Come then, give me a Can. *with Beer.*
Horse. Here's to you Hostess. 1265
Host. I thank ye, what song shall I sing?
Cart. Good sweet Hostess sing my song.
Host. What's that?
Cart. The Chimney high.
Dick. No, no, a Swallows nest. 1270
Host. All you that will look for a Swallows nest, a Swallows nest,
Must look in the Chimney high.
Dick. Now pray Hostess Sing my song too.
Host. Prethee what is't? 1274
Dick. You know, the song you sung when we were last here.
Clow. Now Hostess you know *She sings again.*
I owe you eighteen pence.
Host. I know you do.
Clow. Sing me but one song more, and Ile give you
Eighteen pence more for it, which is just five shillings. 1280
Host. Three shillings you fool.
Clow. Why, three and five is all one to me.
Cart. *Robin*, *Robin*, you say you have monie in both
Pockets: pay this reckoning, wee'l pay the next.
We paid for you last. 1285
Clow. Who I, Ile pay for none of you, I have none for my self.
Host. I thought so, you that cal'd and cal'd so fast,

1377 beholden *1620, 1631, 1663* 1380 sport *1616*: sports *1619–63* driue *1631, 1663*
1288 *Prefix* Host.] *Qy.*, Cart. ?

Would shrink your head out of the coller at last,
But I hope, as you brought us on, you'l bring us off. 1290
Clow. I warrant you lads, let me alone to conjure her.
Get me a piece of Chalk.
Host. What to do?
Clow. Pish, let me alone. *She sings.*
Host. Come now, where is my reckoning? 1295
Clow. Here, here Hostess, here, what's this? I I Chalks a Can.
Host. Two pence.
Clow. What's this, I I I I?
Host. A Groat.
Clow. And this, C? 1300
Host. Six pence.
Clow. And this, O?
Host. Why, a shilling.
Clow. And this, C?
Host. 'Tis six pence. 1305
Clow. What comes it all too?
Host. Three shillings.
Clow. Here take it Hostess, take it, ha, ha, ha.
Cart. O brave *Robin*, ha, ha, ha.
Host. I hope you don't mean to pay me thus, 1310
Why this is but chalk.
Clow. Chalk and Cheese is all one to us, for truely we
Have no monie Lanladie, but wee'l pay you
Very honestly, when we come again. *Exeunt.*
Host. Look you do. 1315
Well, I am deeply in my Brewers score,
But the best on't is, he durst as well be hang'd
As tell his wife. *Exeunt omnes.*

Lines 1238–84 are given thus in Qq 1616–63:

Thunder and lightning: Enter deuils with couer'd dishes: Mephostophilis leades them into Faustus Study: Then enter Wagner.

Wag. I think my Maister means to die shortly, he has made his will, & giuen me his wealth, his house, his goods, & store of golden plate; besides two thousand duckets ready coin'd: I wonder what he meanes, if death were nie, he would not frolick thus: hee's now at supper with the schollers, where ther's such belly-cheere, as *Wagner* in his life nere saw the like: and see where they come, belike the feast is done. *Exit.*

Enter Faustus, Mephostophilis, and two or three Schollers.

1 *Schol.* M. Doctor *Faustus*, since our conference about faire Ladies, which was the beautifullest in all the world,

we haue determin'd with our selues, that *Hellen* of Greece was the admirablest Lady that euer liu'd : therefore M. Doctor, if you will doe vs so much fauour, as to let vs see that peerelesse dame of Greece, whom all the world admires for Maiesty, we should thinke our selues much beholding vnto you. 1251

Faust. Gentlemen, for y^t I know your friendship is vnfain'd,
It is not *Faustus* custome to deny
The iust request of those that wish him well:
You shall behold that peerelesse dame of Greece, 1255
No otherwise for pompe or Maiesty,
Then when sir *Paris* crost the seas with her,
And brought the spoyles to rich *Dardania* :
Be silent then, for danger is in words.

Musicke sound, Mephosto brings in Hellen, she passeth ouer the stage.

2. Was this faire *Hellen*, whose admired worth 1260
Made *Greece* with ten yeares warres afflict poore *Troy?*
3. Too simple is my wit to tell her worth,
Whom all the world admires for maiesty.
1. Now we haue seene the pride of Natures worke,
Wee'l take our leaues, and for this blessed sight 1265
Happy and blest be *Faustus* euermore. *Exeunt Schollers.*
Faust. Gentlemen farewell : the same wish I to you.

Enter an old Man.

Old Man. O gentle *Faustus* leaue this damned Art,
This Magicke, that will charme thy soule to hell,
And quite bereaue thee of saluation. 1270
Though thou hast now offended like a man,
Doe not perseuer in it like a Diuell ;
Yet, yet, thou hast an amiable soule,
If sin by custome grow not into nature :
Then *Faustus*, will repentance come too late, 1275
Then thou art banisht from the sight of heauen ;
No mortall can expresse the paines of hell.
It may be this my exhortation
Seemes harsh, and all vnpleasant ; let it not,
For gentle sonne, I speake it not in wrath, 1280
Or enuy of thee, but in tender loue,
And pitty of thy future miserie.
And so haue hope, that this my kinde rebuke,
Checking thy body, may amend thy soule.

1281 enuv of *1616, 1619* : of enuy to *1620–63*

For the speech of the Old Man in Qq 1604–11 (ll. 1348–56), **Qq 1616–63 insert the following:**

Thunder. Enter Lucifer, Belzebub, and Mephostophilis.

Lucif. Thus from infernall *Dis* do we ascend
To view the subiects of our Monarchy, 1349
Those soules which sinne seales the blacke sonnes of hell,
'Mong which as chiefe, *Faustus* we come to thee,
Bringing with vs lasting damnation,
To wait vpon thy soule; the time is come
Which makes it forfeit.
Meph. And this gloomy night, 1355
Here in this roome will wretched *Faustus* be.
Bels. And here wee'l stay,
To marke him how he doth demeane himselfe.
Meph. How should he, but in desperate lunacie.
Fond worldling, now his heart bloud dries with griefe; 1360
His conscience kils it, and his labouring braine,
Begets a world of idle fantasies,
To ouer-reach the Diuell; but all in vaine,
His store of pleasures must be sauc'd with paine.
He and his seruant *Wagner* are at hand, 1365
Both come from drawing *Faustus* latest will.
See where they come.

Enter Faustus and Wagner.

Faust. Say *Wagner*, thou hast perus'd my will,
How dost thou like it?
Wag. Sir, so wondrous well, 1370
As in all humble dutie, I do yeeld
My life and lasting seruice for your loue.
Enter the scholers.
Faust. Gramercies *Wagner*. Welcome gentlemen.
1. Now worthy *Faustus*: me thinks your looks are chang'd.

Between lines 1418 and 1419 of Qq 1604–11, the later quartos add this passage:

Meph. I *Faustus*, now thou hast no hope of heauen,
Therefore despaire, thinke onely vpon hell; 1420
For that must be thy mansion, there to dwell.
Faust. O thou bewitching fiend, 'twas thy temptation,
Hath rob'd me of eternall happinesse.

1347+⟨Act V.⟩ Scene IV. *add. Rob., Cunn.*: Scene XIII^a *Brey.* 1349–51 *om. 1663* 1352 lasting damnation] the Deed *1663* 1353 To . . soule *om. 1663* 1361 and his] and *1624* 1367+ Scene XIV. *add. Brey.* 1372 your] you *1663* 1373 Gramercy *1619–63* 1373+S.D. Exit Wagner *add. Dyce*
1419 I] Ah *Cunn.* hopes *1663*

Meph. I doe confesse it *Faustus,* and reioyce;
'Twas I, that when thou wert i'the way to heauen, 1425
Damb'd vp thy passage, when thou took'st the booke,
To view the Scriptures, then I turn'd the leaues
And led thine eye.
What, weep'st thou? 'tis too late, despaire, farewell,
Fooles that will laugh on earth, must weepe in hell. *Exit.*

Enter the good Angell, and the bad Angell at seuerall doores.

Good. Oh *Faustus,* if thou hadst giuen eare to me, 1431
Innumerable ioyes had followed thee.
But thou didst loue the world.
Bad. Gaue eare to me,
And now must taste hels paines perpetually. 1435
Good. O what will all thy riches, pleasures, pompes,
Auaile thee now?
Bad. Nothing but vexe thee more,
To want in hell, that had on earth such store.

Musicke while the Throne descends.

Good. O thou hast lost celestiall happinesse, 1440
Pleasures vnspeakeable, blisse without end.
Hadst thou affected sweet diuinitie,
Hell, or the Diuell, had had no power on thee.
Hadst thou kept on that way, *Faustus* behold,
In what resplendant glory thou hadst set 1445
In yonder throne, like those bright shining Saints,
And triumpht ouer hell: that hast thou lost,
And now poore soule must thy good Angell leaue thee,
The iawes of hell are open to receiue thee. *Exit.*

Hell is discouered.

Bad. Now *Faustus* let thine eyes with horror stare 1450
Into that vaste perpetuall torture-house.
There are the Furies tossing damned soules,
On burning forkes: their bodies broyle in lead.
There are liue quarters broyling on the coles,
That ner'e can die: this euer-burning chaire 1455
Is for ore-tortur'd soules to rest them in.
These, that are fed with soppes of flaming fire,
Were gluttons, and lou'd only delicates,

1430 must *1619–63*: most *1616* 1430 S.D. bad Angell *1616*: Bad *1619–63* 1434 Gauest *Brey.* 1439 S.D. the *om. 1663* S.D. *follows* 1444 *Dyce, Cunn.* 1441 blisse . . end *om. 1663* 1443 had had no power] had no dower *1663* 1445 hadst] had *1663* set *1616*: sit *1619–63, Dyce, Brey.*: sat *Cunn.* 1449 are open *1616, 1619*: is ready *1620–63* 1453 broyle *1616, 1619, Brey.*: boyle *1620–63, Rob., Dyce, Cunn.* 1458 and *1616*: that *1620–63*

And laught to see the poore starue at their gates:
But yet all these are nothing, thou shalt see 1460
Ten thousand tortures that more horrid be.
Faust. O, I haue seene enough to torture me.
Bad. Nay, thou must feele them, taste the smart of all.
He that loues pleasure, must for pleasure fall:
And so I leaue thee *Faustus* till anon, 1465
Then wilt thou tumble in confusion. *Exit.*
The Clock strikes eleuen.

Between l. 1477 and the Chorus, Qq 1616–63 insert the following new scene:

Enter the Schollers.

1. Come Gentlemen, let vs go visit *Faustus*,
For such a dreadfull night, was neuer seene,
Since first the worlds creation did begin. 1480
Such fearefull shrikes, and cries, were neuer heard,
Pray heauen the Doctor haue escapt the danger.
2. O help vs heauen, see, here are *Faustus* limbs,
All torne asunder by the hand of death.
3. The deuils whom *Faustus* seru'd haue torne him thus:
For twixt the houres of twelue and one, me thought 1486
I heard him shreeke and call aloud for helpe:
At which selfe time the house seem'd all on fire,
With dreadfull horror of these damned fiends.
2. Well Gentlemen, tho *Faustus* end be such 1490
As euery Christian heart laments to thinke on:
Yet for he was a Scholler, once admired
For wondrous knowledge in our *Germane* schooles,
We'll giue his mangled limbs due buryall:
And all the Students clothed in mourning blacke, 1495
Shall waite vpon his heauy funerall. *Exeunt.*

1477 S.D. the *om.* *1619–63* 1482 haue] has *1619* 1483 Heauens *1620–63* 1485 Diuell *1619–63* hath *1620–63* 1488 selfe] same *1624–63*

THE JEW OF MALTA

Date. There is no evidence on which to determine very accurately the date of *The Jew of Malta.* The allusion to the death of the Duke of Guise in line 3 points to a period subsequent to December 23, 1588, for the composition of at least that part of the play. It is quite true, as Wagner has argued, that this Prologue of Macheuil may possibly have been written after the rest of the piece, but considerations of dramatic structure and versification make it well-nigh impossible to refer the play as a whole to an earlier year than 1589. It seems certainly to have been written and performed between the period of the composition of *Doctor Faustus* (? 1588–9) and February 26, 1591/2, when an entry in Henslowe's *Diary* shows it to be already an old play. The year 1590 cannot be far wrong.

Stage history and the early edition. The earliest mention of *The Jew of Malta* is that already referred to, which occurs very near the beginning of Henslowe's *Diary*: 'Rd. at the Jewe of malltuse the 26 of febrearye 1591 [1592, N.S.] l^s^.' The play belonged apparently to Henslowe and was acted by each of the many companies with which he was connected during the next five years. It was one of the most popular pieces in the manager's repertoire: the *Diary* notes thirty-six representations, the last being on June 21, 1596. This record exceeds that of any other of Marlowe's plays,[1] even the very popular *Doctor Faustus* having only twenty-five certified performances.

In 1601 *The Jew of Malta* was certainly revived, probably in a somewhat altered form. Unfortunately the *Diary* does not mention the individual performances for this period, but it contains the following notes of expenditure: 'Lent vnto Robart shawe & mr. Jube the 19 of Maye 1601 to bye divers thinges for the Jewe of malta the some of . . . v^li^.

[1] We have, however, no information concerning the number of performances of *Edward II* and *Dido*, which did not belong to Henslowe.

lent mor to the littell tayller the same daye for more thinges for the Jewe of malta some of . . x^s.' Later—at some time before the end of 1633—as we learn from the extant text, the play was presented at Court and at the Cockpit Theatre with prologues and epilogues on both occasions by Thomas Heywood.

On the seventeenth of May, 1594, Nicholas Linge and Thomas Millington entered for publication on the Stationers' Register *the famouse tragedie of the Riche Jewe of Malta.* On the previous day John Danter had licensed 'a ballad intituled the murtherous life and terrible death of the riche Jew of Malta', very obviously a piece inspired by the play.

It is peculiarly unfortunate that no copy of Linge and Millington's contemplated edition has come down to us. Instead, all editors have had to base their texts on the faulty and unauthoritative version published in 1633. It is, of course, possible that Linge and Millington were by some accident prevented from bringing out the edition which they had already licensed, but this seems, on the whole, improbable. It is certainly not easy to believe that this one play of Marlowe—apparently the most popular of all on the stage—should have remained forty years and more unprinted after a text was already in publishers' hands. Moreover, Heywood's adverb in the Epistle Dedicatory to the 1633 edition, 'now being *newly* brought to the Presse' (p. 237), would normally indicate that there existed an earlier edition.[1]

Text and authorship. It has been said that our only text of *The Jew of Malta* is that preserved in the 1633 version. There is no evidence that any one has seen an earlier edition, and we can hardly do more than hope that some happy accident may reveal a hitherto unknown and relatively correct text. Undoubtedly the 1633 quarto presents the tragedy in a form sadly corrupted and altered from that in which it left the hands of Marlowe. Besides the incidental impurities due to very bad printing and to the casual changes of actors during many decades, it is probable that the extant text incorporates the results of at least two separate revisions; the first carried out before the revival in 1601, to which Henslowe alludes, the second that which

[1] Cf. the phrase 'Newly imprinted' on the title-page of the 1592 *Faustbook* and discussion, *supra*, p. 142. But see, on the other hand, the title-page of *Tamburlaine*, 1590, 'Now *first*, and *newlie* published.'

must have been necessary before so old a work could be presented at Court and at the Cock-pit. The author of the prologues and epilogues on these last occasions and of the dedicatory epistle of 1633 is Thomas Heywood, the dramatist. It is not improbable that he likewise altered the play for performance at Court. Mr. Fleay[1] has pointed out the close similarity between the last friars' scene (ll. 1623–1715) and the underplot in Heywood's newly discovered comedy, *The Captives.*[2] The relationship, however, cannot be held to prove that Heywood is author of the passage in *The Jew of Malta,* which is evidently earlier and less carefully worked out than the other version. In the part of *The Captives* alluded to, Heywood *may* be elaborating an earlier conception of his own, but he may equally well be plagiarizing from Marlowe.

All critics of the play have noticed with regret the failure of the last half of *The Jew of Malta* to fulfil the splendid promise of the first two acts. It is beyond question that the vigorous flow of tragic interest and character portrayal with which the play opens wastes away amid what, for the modern reader, is a wilderness of melodrama and farce. The change is so marked as to suggest grave doubt whether the tragedy as we have it can represent even remotely the conception of a single man. And yet, after recognizing the practical certainty that the 1633 text gives an extremely corrupt version of Marlowe's work, and that the elaborators here, as in the case of *Doctor Faustus,* found far greater opportunity for revision and expansion in the latter half of the drama than in the earlier part, we do not appear justified by the facts in denying that the thread of the plot is probably throughout Marlowe's contribution. There is, indeed, hardly any explanation short of insanity which in a modern dramatist would account for the sudden change from the vivid realization of Barabas's character, as indicated in the first two acts, to the complete absence of sympathetic insight which marks the last three. In the present case, however, it must be considered that we are dealing confessedly[3] with a unique form of drama governed by rules of its own—the Machiavellian tragedy.

Machiavellianism was, on the Elizabethan stage, an avocation rather than a psychological necessity. In *The Jew of Malta,* as in *Titus Andronicus* and *Richard III,* the

[1] *Biog. Chron. Eng. Dr.*, ii. 61, 62

[2] *Old Plays*, ed. Bullen, vol. iv.

[3] Cf. ll. 1–35.

melodrama belongs to the first conception of the play; the deep humanity enters, as it were, by accidental inspiration. I believe that the heterogeneous character of *The Jew of Malta* is fundamental, not due in any essential degree either to excessive haste of composition or to plurality of authorship. The first two acts, as we have them, probably represent with moderate fidelity the deep study of a human passion with which Marlowe was inspired to preface, and partly to overlay, his drama of 'blood and thunder'. Few playwrights have ever shown such power in conceiving states of intense feeling, and surely none of comparable greatness has ever been less skilful than Marlowe in blending this lyric fabric with the structural framework of a tragedy. The last three acts appear to represent, though inaccurately, with possible interpolations and occasional changes, the original sensational plot of Marlowe, bare of the imaginative humanizing which the earlier acts received. I see little reason to believe that the poet's general design has anywhere been very seriously tampered with, and to the very end of the play there occur, among obvious corruptions, verses which it seems all but impossible to deny to Marlowe.[1]

Source. A direct source of *The Jew of Malta* has not been discovered. Many of the incidents are undoubtedly based on history, though in each case the poet has allowed himself considerable licence. Malta was several times besieged by the Turks, notably in 1565, but unsuccessfully. L. Kellner (*Englische Studien*, x. 80 ff.) has drawn attention to the interesting parallel between the career of Barabas in the play and that of Juan Miques (Michesius), a Portuguese Jew who flourished during the middle of the sixteenth century. After enduring persecution in his own country, in Antwerp, and in Venice, Miques took refuge with the Turks in Constantinople, and there employed his enormous wealth and his influence over the Sultan Selim to the disadvantage of the Christians. He was made Duke of Naxos and the Cyclades, and caused the Turkish attack on Cyprus in 1570. This notorious foe to Christendom is mentioned by the historians Foglietta,[2] Strada,[3] and others,

[1] e.g. 1330–5, 1399–1408, 1431–56, 1509–15, 1570–85, 1806–16, 1858–66, 2066–7 (cf. *Doctor Faustus*, 710, 711), 2230–7, 2361–73, 2405–8.

[2] *De Sacro Foedere in Selimum*, 1587.

[3] *De Bello Belgico*, 1632 ff.

but no such accounts known can claim to have done more than suggest in the vaguest way the character of Barabas.

A play called 'The Jew', of which we know nothing further, is mentioned in Stephen Gosson's *School of Abuse* as early as 1579, and a Viennese manuscript preserves the bare outlines of a comedy performed by English actors in which the plots of *The Jew of Malta* and *The Merchant of Venice* seem to be blended with some independent matter from the history of Michesius.[1]

[1] Cf. Meissner, *Die Englischen Comoedianten zur Zeit Shakespeare's in Oesterreich*, p. 131 ff.

The Famous

TRAGEDY

OF

THE RICH IEVV

OF *MALTA*.

AS IT VVAS PLAYD
BEFORE THE KING AND
QVEENE, IN HIS MAJESTIES
Theatre at *White-Hall*, by her Majesties
Servants at the *Cock-pit*.

Written by CHRISTOPHER MARLO.

LONDON;
Printed by *I. B.* for *Nichelas Vavasour*, and are to be sold
at his Shop in the Inner-Temple, neere the
Church. 1633.

1633	=	Quarto edition of that year.
Reed	=	Dodsley's *Select Old Plays*, second edition, ed. I. Reed, 1780, vol. viii.
Oxberry	=	W. O.'s edition of the play, 1818.
Coll.	=	Dodsley, third edition, ed. J. P. Collier, 1825, vol. viii.
Rob.	=	Robinson's edition of Marlowe, 1826.
Dyce { *Dyce*[1]	=	Dyce's first edition of Marlowe, 1850.
Dyce { *Dyce*[2]	=	Dyce's revised edition of Marlowe, 1858, &c.
Cunn.	=	Cunningham's edition of Marlowe, 1870, &c.
Bull.	=	Bullen's edition of Marlowe, 1885.
Ellis.	=	'Mermaid' Marlowe, ed. H. Ellis, 1887.
Wag.	=	A. Wagner's edition of the play, 1889.
T. B.	=	The present editor.
Brennan	=	C. B.'s conjectures *Anglia*, Beiblatt 1905, 208.
Brereton	=	J. Le G. B.'s conjectures, *Anglia*, Beiblatt 1905, 205.
Deighton	=	K. D., *The Old Dramatists*. Conjectural Readings, 1896.
Elze	=	K. E., *Notes on Elizabethan Dramatists*, 1889.
Gilchrist	=	G.'s conjectures quoted by *Coll.*
Mitford	=	J. M.'s conjectures quoted by *Dyce*.
Steevens	=	G. S.'s conjectures quoted by *Reed*.

⟨The Epistle Dedicatory⟩[1]

TO

MY WORTHY

FRIEND, MR THOMAS

HAMMON, OF GRAYES

INNE, &c.

This Play, composed by so worthy an Authour as Mr. *Marlo*; and the part of the Jew presented by so vnimitable an Actor as Mr. *Allin*, being in this later Age commended to the Stage: As I vsher'd it unto the Court, and presented it to the Cock-pit, with these Prologues 5 and Epilogues here inserted, so now being newly brought to the Presse, I was loath it should be published without the ornament of an Epistle; making choyce of you vnto whom to deuote it; then whom (of all those Gentlemen and acquaintance, within the compasse of my long know- 10 ledge) there is none more able to taxe Ignorance, or attribute right to merit. Sir, you haue bin pleased to grace some of mine owne workes with your curteous patronage; I hope this will not be the worse accepted, because commended by mee; ouer whom none can clayme more power or 15 priuilege than your selfe. I had no better a New-yeares gift to present you with; receiue it therefore as a continuance of that inuiolable obliegement, by which he rests still ingaged; who as he euer hath, shall alwayes remaine,

Tuissimus: 20

THO. HEYWOOD.

[1] From the top of page A 3r.

The Prologue spoken at Court.

Gracious and Great, that we so boldly dare,
('Mongst other Playes that now in fashion are)
To present this; writ many yeares agone,
And in that Age, thought second vnto none;
We humbly crave your pardon: we pursue 5
The story of a rich and famous Jew
Who liu'd in Malta*: you shall find him still,*
In all his proiects, a sound Macheuill;
And that's his Character: He that hath past
So many Censures, is now come at last 10
To haue your princely Eares: grace you him; then
You crowne the Action, and renowne the pen.

Epilogue.

It is our feare (dread Soueraigne) we haue bin
Too tedious; neither can't be lesse than sinne
To wrong your Princely patience: If we haue,
(Thus low deiected) we your pardon craue:
And if ought here offend your eare or sight, 5
We onely Act, and Speake, what others write.

The Prologue to the Stage, at the Cocke-pit.

We know not how our Play may passe this Stage,
But by the best of Poets in that age* * Marlo.
The Malta Jew *had being, and was made ;*
And He, then by the best of Actors play'd :* * Allin.
In Hero *and* Leander, *one did gaine* 5
A lasting memorie ; in Tamberlaine,
This Jew, *with others many : th' other wan*
The Attribute of peerelesse, being a man
Whom we may ranke with (*doing no one wrong*)
Proteus *for shapes, and* Roscius *for a tongue,* 10
So could he speake, so vary ; nor is't hate
To merit in him who doth personate* * Perkins.
Our Jew *this day, nor is it his ambition*
To exceed, or equall, being of condition
More modest ; this is all that he intends, 15
(And that too, at the vrgence of some friends)
To proue his best, and if none here gaine-say it,
The part he hath studied, and intends to play it.

Epilogue.

In Graving, with Pigmalion *to contend ;*
Or Painting, with Apelles ; *doubtlesse the end*
Must be disgrace : our Actor did not so,
He onely aym'd to goe, but not out-goe.
Nor thinke that this day any prize was plaid, 5
Here were no betts at all, no wagers laid ;
All the ambition that his mind doth swell,
Is but to heare from you, (*by me*) *'twas well.*

⟨The Ghost of Machivel.
Farneze Governer of Malta.
Lodowick his son } both in love
Mathias } with Abigal.
Selim Calymath, the Turkish Prince.
A Turkish Bashaw.
Martin Del bosco, a spanish Captain.
Barabas the rich Iew.
Ithimer his Man.
Pilio Borza, the Curtizans Man.
3 Fryers.
2 Marchants.

Mater, Mother to Mathias.
Abegal the Jews daughter.
The Courtizan.
2 Nuns⟩.[1]

⟨DRAMATIS PERSONÆ

MACHIAVEL, *the Prologue.*
BARABAS, *the Jew.*
FERNEZE, *Governor of Malta.*
CALYMATH, *Son to the Grand Signior.*
DON LODOWICK, *the Governor's son.*
DON MATHIAS.
ITHAMORE, *a Turkish Slave.*
DEL BOSCO, *the Spanish Vice Admiral.*
JACOMO, } *Friars.*
BARNARDINO, }
PILIA BORZA.[2]
TWO MERCHANTS.
Three JEWS.
KNIGHTS.
BASHAWS.
OFFICERS.
READER.

ABIGAIL, *Daughter to Barabas.*
⟨KATHERINE, *Mother to Mathias.*⟩[3]
TWO NUNS.
ABBESS.
BELLAMIRA, *a Courtezan.*⟩[4]

[1] Add. in hand of about 1750 on the back of title-page of a copy of ed. 1633 (Bodleian : Malone 915).
[2] Philia Borzo *Reed* [3] *Add. Coll.* [4] *Dramatis Personae add. Reed.*

THE
IEW OF
MALTA

Macheuil.

Albeit the world thinke *Macheuill* is dead,
Yet was his soule but flowne beyond the *Alpes*,
And now the *Guize* is dead, is come from *France*
To view this Land, and frolicke with his friends.
To some perhaps my name is odious, 5
But such as loue me, gard me from their tongues,
And let them know that I am *Macheuill*,
And weigh not men, and therefore not mens words:
Admir'd I am of those that hate me most.
Though some speake openly against my bookes, 10
Yet will they reade me, and thereby attaine
To *Peters* Chayre: And when they cast me off,
Are poyson'd by my climing followers.
I count Religion but a childish Toy,
And hold there is no sinne but Ignorance. 15
Birds of the Aire will tell of murders past;
I am asham'd to heare such fooleries:
Many will talke of Title to a Crowne.
What right had *Cæsar* to the Empire?
Might first made Kings, and Lawes were then most sure
When like the *Dracos* they were writ in blood. 21
Hence comes it, that a strong built Citadell
Commands much more then letters can import:
Which maxime had *Phaleris* obseru'd,
H' had neuer bellowed in a brasen Bull 25

S.D. Act I. Enter Machiavel *Reed to Coll.*: Enter Machiavel *Dyce to Bull.*: The Prologue. Enter Machiavel *Ellis* 19 Empire] empery *Reed etc. exc. Cunn.* 21 Dracos] Drancus *1633* 24 had] had but *conj. Dyce, Cunn. etc.*

Of great ones enuy; o'th poore petty wites,
Let me be enuy'd and not pittied!
But whither am I bound, I come not, I,
To reade a lecture here in *Britaine*,
But to present the Tragedy of a Iew, 30
Who smiles to see how full his bags are cramb'd,
Which mony was not got without my meanes.
I craue but this, Grace him as he deserues,
And let him not be entertain'd the worse 34
Because he fauours me. ⟨*Exit.*⟩

⟨*Actus Primus.*⟩

Enter Barabas in his Counting-house, with heapes of gold before him.

Iew. So that of thus much that returne was made:
And of the third part of the *Persian* ships,
There was the venture summ'd and satisfied.
As for those *Samintes*, and the men of *Vzz*,
That bought my *Spanish* Oyles, and Wines of *Greece*, 40
Here haue I purst their paltry siluerlings.
Fye; what a trouble tis to count this trash.
Well fare the *Arabians*, who so richly pay
The things they traffique for with wedge of gold,
Whereof a man may easily in a day 45
Tell that which may maintaine him all his life.
The needy groome that neuer fingred groat,
Would make a miracle of thus much coyne:
But he whose steele-bard coffers are cramb'd full,
And all his life time hath bin tired, 50
Wearying his fingers ends with telling it,
Would in his age be loath to labour so,
And for a pound to sweat himselfe to death:
Giue me the Merchants of the *Indian* Mynes,
That trade in mettall of the purest mould; 55
The wealthy *Moore*, that in the *Easterne* rockes
Without controule can picke his riches vp,

29 here] to you here *conj. Dyce*[2] Brittany *Bull.* 35 S.D. Exit *add. Dyce* Actus Primus *om. 1633, Reed, Coll.* 39 Samintes *1633, Reed*: Samnites *Coll., Dyce, Cunn.*: Sabans *Bull. to Wag.*: Samarites *conj. Deighton*: Samiotes *conj. Brennan* 41 siluerbings *1633, Reed, Coll.* 50 And] And he who *Bull.*

And in his house heape pearle like pibble-stones ;
Receiue them free, and sell them by the weight,
Bags of fiery *Opals, Saphires, Amatists,* 60
Iacints, hard *Topas,* grasse-greene *Emeraulds,*
Beauteous *Rubyes,* sparkling *Diamonds,*
And seildsene costly stones of so great price,
As one of them indifferently rated,
And of a Carrect of this quantity, 65
May serue in perill of calamity
To ransome great Kings from captiuity.
This is the ware wherein consists my wealth :
And thus me thinkes should men of iudgement frame
Their meanes of traffique from the vulgar trade, 70
And as their wealth increaseth, so inclose
Infinite riches in a little roome.
But now how stands the wind ?
Into what corner peeres my *Halcions* bill ?
Ha, to the *East* ? yes : See how stands the Vanes ? 75
East and by-*South* : why then I hope my ships
I sent for *Egypt* and the bordering Iles
Are gotten vp by *Nilus* winding bankes :
Mine Argosie from *Alexandria,*
Loaden with Spice and Silkes, now vnder saile, 80
Are smoothly gliding downe by *Candie* shoare
To *Malta,* through our Mediterranean sea.
But who comes heare ? How now.

Enter a Merchant.

Merch. *Barabas,* thy ships are safe,
Riding in *Malta* Rhode : And all the Merchants 85
With other Merchandize are safe arriu'd,
And haue sent me to know whether your selfe
Will come and custome them.
Iew. The ships are safe thou saist, and richly fraught.
Merch. They are. 90
Iew. Why then goe bid them come ashore,
And bring with them their bils of entry :
I hope our credit in the Custome-house
Will serue as well as I were present there.
Goe send 'vm threescore Camels, thirty Mules, 95
And twenty Waggons to bring vp the ware.

65 Carrect] caract *Dyce*[1] : carat *Dyce*[2] *to Ellis* 83 S.D. *precedes* How now *Dyce, Ellis* 84 Barabas *om. Wag.*

But art thou master in a ship of mine,
And is thy credit not enough for that ?
Merch. The very Custome barely comes to more
Then many Merchants of the Towne are worth, 100
And therefore farre exceeds my credit, Sir.
Iew. Goe tell 'em the Iew of *Malta* sent thee, man :
Tush, who amongst 'em knowes not *Barrabas* ?
Merch. I goe.
Iew. So then, there's somewhat come. 105
Sirra, which of my ships art thou Master of ?
Merch. Of the *Speranza*, Sir.
Iew. And saw'st thou not
Mine Argosie at *Alexandria* ?
Thou couldst not come from *Egypt*, or by Caire 110
But at the entry there into the sea,
Where *Nilus* payes his tribute to the maine,
Thou needs must saile by *Alexandria*.
Merch. I neither saw them, nor inquir'd of them.
But this we heard some of our sea-men say, 115
They wondred how you durst with so much wealth
Trust such a crazed Vessell, and so farre.
Iew. Tush ; they are wise, I know her and her strength :
But goe, goe thou thy wayes, discharge thy Ship,
And bid my Factor bring his loading in. 120
⟨*Exit* 1*st. Merchant.*⟩
And yet I wonder at this Argosie.

Enter a second Merchant.

2. *Merch.* Thine Argosie from *Alexandria*,
Know *Barabas*, doth ride in *Malta* Rhode,
Laden with riches, and exceeding store
Of *Persian* silkes, of gold, and Orient Perle. 125
Iew. How chance you came not with those other ships
That sail'd by *Egypt* ?
2. *Merch.* Sir we saw 'em not.
Iew. Belike they coasted round by *Candie* shoare
About their Oyles, or other businesses. 130
But 'twas ill done of you to come so farre
Without the ayd or conduct of their ships.
2. *Merch.* Sir, we were wafted by a Spanish Fleet
That neuer left vs till within a league,
That had the Gallies of the *Turke* in chase. 135

106 of] off *1633* 119 But *Dyce etc.* : By *1633* : Bye *Reed, Coll.* 120 S.D. *add. Reed*

Iew. Oh they were going vp to *Sicily*:
Well, goe
And bid the Merchants and my men dispatch
And come ashore, and see the fraught discharg'd.
Merch. I goe. *Exit.*
Iew. Thus trowles our fortune in by land and Sea, 141
And thus are wee on euery side inrich'd:
These are the Blessings promis'd to the Iewes,
And herein was old *Abrams* happinesse:
What more may Heaven doe for earthly man 145
Then thus to powre out plenty in their laps,
Ripping the bowels of the earth for them,
Making the Sea their seruant, and the winds
To driue their substance with successefull blasts?
Who hateth me but for my happinesse? 150
Or who is honour'd now but for his wealth?
Rather had I a Iew be hated thus,
Then pittied in a Christian pouerty:
For I can see no fruits in all their faith,
But malice, falshood, and excessiue pride, 155
Which me thinkes fits not their profession.
Happily some haplesse man hath conscience,
And for his conscience liues in beggery.
They say we are a scatter'd Nation:
I cannot tell, but we haue scambled vp 160
More wealth by farre then those that brag of faith.
There's *Kirriah Iairim,* the great Iew of *Greece,*
Obed in *Bairseth, Nones* in *Portugall,*
My selfe in *Malta*, some in *Italy*,
Many in *France,* and wealthy euery one: 165
I, wealthier farre then any Christian.
I must confesse we come not to be Kings:
That's not our fault: Alas, our number's few,
And Crownes come either by succession,
Or vrg'd by force; and nothing violent, 170
Oft haue I heard tell, can be permanent.
Giue vs a peacefull rule, make Christians Kings,
That thirst so much for Principality.
I haue no charge, nor many children,
But one sole Daughter, whom I hold as deare 175
As *Agamemnon* did his *Iphigen*:
And all I haue is hers. But who comes here?

139 freight *Reed, Coll.* 148 Sea] seas *Dyce to Bull.* seruant *Wag.*: seruants *1633 to Bull.*

Enter three Iewes.

1. Tush, tell not me, 'twas done of policie.
2. Come therefore let vs goe to *Barrabas*;
For he can counsell best in these affaires; 180
And here he comes.
Iew. Why, how now, Countrymen?
Why flocke you thus to me in multitudes?
What accident's betided to the Iewes?
1. A Fleet of warlike Gallyes, *Barabas*, 185
Are come from *Turkey*, and lye in our Rhode:
And they this day sit in the Counsell-house
To entertaine them and their Embassie.
Iew. Why, let 'em come, so they come not to warre;
Or let 'em warre, so we be conquerors: 190
Nay, let 'em combat, conquer, and kill all, *Aside.*
So they spare me, my daughter, and my wealth.
1. Were it for confirmation of a League,
They would not come in warlike manner thus.
2. I feare their comming will afflict vs all. 195
Iew. Fond men, what dreame you of their multitudes?
What need they treat of peace that are in league?
The *Turkes* and those of *Malta* are in league.
Tut, tut, there is some other matter in't.
1. Why, *Barabas*, they come for peace or warre. 200
Iew. Happily for neither, but to passe along
Towards *Venice* by the *Adriatick* Sea;
With whom they haue attempted many times,
But neuer could effect their Stratagem.
3. And very wisely sayd, it may be so. 205
2. But there's a meeting in the Senate-house,
And all the Iewes in *Malta* must be there.
Iew. Vmh; All the Iewes in *Malta* must be there?
I, like enough, why then let euery man
Prouide him, and be there for fashion-sake. 210
If any thing shall there concerne our state
Assure your selues I'le looke vnto my selfe. *Aside.*
1. I know you will; well brethren let vs goe.
2. Let's take our leaues; Farewell good *Barabas.*
Iew. Doe so; Farewell *Zaareth*, farewell *Temainte.* 215
⟨*Exeunt.*⟩
And *Barabas* now search this secret out.

212 vnto] unto't *conj. Coll.* 212 S.D. *om. Coll.* 215 Doe so *om. Dyce*[2] *to Bull.* 215 S.D. Exeunt Jews *add. Reed*

Summon thy sences, call thy wits togethre:
These silly men mistake the matter cleane.
Long to the *Turke* did *Malta* contribute ;
Which Tribute all in policie, I feare, 220
The *Turkes* haue let increase to such a summe,
As all the wealth of *Malta* cannot pay ;
And now by that aduantage thinkes, belike,
To seize vpon the Towne : I, that he seekes.
How ere the world goe, I'le make sure for one, 225
And seeke in time to intercept the worst,
Warily garding that which I ha got
Ego mihimet sum semper proximus.
Why let 'em enter, let 'em take the Towne. (*Exit.*)

Enter Gouernor of Malta, Knights met by Bassoes of the Turke ; Calymath.

Gouer. Now Bassoes, what demand you at our hands?
Bass. Know Knights of Malta, that we came from *Rhodes*, 231
From *Cyprus*, *Candy*, and those other Iles
That lye betwixt the Mediterranean seas.
Gov. What's *Cyprus*, *Candy*, and those other Iles
To vs, or *Malta* ? What at our hands demand ye ? 235
Calim. The ten yeares tribute that remaines vnpaid.
Gov. Alas, my Lord, the summe is ouergreat,
I hope your Highnesse will consider vs.
Calim. I wish, graue Gouernour 'twere in my power
To fauour you, but 'tis my fathers cause, 240
Wherein I may not, nay I dare not dally.
Gov. Then giue vs leaue, great *Selim-Calymath.*
Caly. Stand all aside, and let the Knights determine,
And send to keepe our Gallies vnder-saile,
For happily we shall not tarry here : 245
Now Gouernour, how are you resolu'd ?
Gov. Thus : Since your hard conditions are such
That you will needs haue ten yeares tribute past,
We may haue time to make collection
Amongst the Inhabitants of *Malta* for't. 250
Bass. That's more then is in our Commission.

221 Turk has *Rob. to Cunn.* 229+Scene II. *add. Cunn., Bull.* 229 S.D. Gouernors *1633, Reed, Coll.* 239, 246, 256, 262 Gouernours *1633, Reed, Coll., Cunn.* 242+S.D. Consults apart *add. Cunn.* 246 how] say how *Bull.*

Caly. What Callapine, a little curtesie.
Let's know their time, perhaps it is not long;
And 'tis more Kingly to obtaine by peace
Then to enforce conditions by constraint. 255
What respit aske you Gouernour?
Gov. But a month.
Caly. We grant a month, but see you keep your promise.
Now lanch our Gallies backe againe to Sea,
Where wee'll attend the respit you haue tane, 260
And for the mony send our messenger.
Farewell great Gouernor, and braue Knights of *Malta.*
Exeunt.
Gov. And all good fortune wait on *Calymath.*
Goe one and call those Iewes of *Malta* hither:
Were they not summon'd to appeare to day? 265
Officer. They were, my Lord, and here they come.

Enter Barabas, and three Iewes.

1. *Knight.* Haue you determin'd what to say to them?
Gov. Yes, giue me leaue, and *Hebrewes* now come neare.
From the Emperour of *Turkey* is arriu'd
Great *Selim-Calymath,* his Highnesse sonne, 270
To leuie of vs ten yeares tribute past,
Now then here know that it concerneth vs.
Bar. Then good my Lord, to keepe your quiet still,
Your Lordship shall doe well to let them haue it.
Gov. Soft *Barabas,* there's more longs too't than so.
To what this ten yeares tribute will amount 276
That we haue cast, but cannot compasse it
By reason of the warres, that robb'd our store;
And therefore are we to request your ayd.
Bar. Alas, my Lord, we are no souldiers: 280
And what's our aid against so great a Prince?
1. *Kni.* Tut, Iew, we know thou art no souldier;
Thou art a Merchant, and a monied man,
And 'tis thy mony, *Barabas,* we seeke.
Bar. How, my Lord, my mony? 285
Gov. Thine and the rest.
For, to be short, amongst you 'tmust be had.
Iew. Alas, my Lord, the most of vs are poore!
Gov. Then let the rich increase your portions.
Bar. Are strangers with your tribute to be tax'd? 290

262 S.D. *om. Dyce to Bull.* 263 + S.D. Exeunt Calymath and Bassoes *add. Dyce to Bull.*

2. *Kni.* Haue strangers leaue with vs to get their wealth?
Then let them with vs contribute.
Bar. How, equally?
Gov. No, Iew, like infidels.
For through our sufferance of your hatefull liues, 295
Who stand accursed in the sight of heauen,
These taxes and afflictions are befal'ne,
And therefore thus we are determined;
Reade there the Articles of our decrees. 299
Reader. First, the tribute mony of the *Turkes* shall all be leuyed amongst the *Iewes*, and each of them to pay one Halfe of his estate.
Bar. How, halfe his estate? I hope you meane not mine.
Gov. Read on.
Read. Secondly, hee that denies to pay, shal straight become a Christian. 306
Bar. How, a Christian? Hum, what's here to doe?
Read. Lastly, he that denies this, shall absolutely lose al he has.
All 3 *Iewes.* Oh my Lord we will giue halfe. 310
Bar. Oh earth-mettall'd villaines, and no *Hebrews* born!
And will you basely thus submit your selues
To leaue your goods to their arbitrament?
Gov. Why *Barabas* wilt thou be christned?
Bar. No, Gouernour, I will be no conuertite. 315
Gov. Then pay thy halfe.
Bar. Why know you what you did by this deuice?
Halfe of my substance is a Cities wealth.
Governour, it was not got so easily;
Nor will I part so slightly therewithall. 320
Gov. Sir, halfe is the penalty of our decree,
Either pay that, or we will seize on all.
Bar. *Corpo di deo*; stay, you shall haue halfe,
Let me be vs'd but as my brethren are.
Gov. No, Iew, thou hast denied the Articles, 325
And now it cannot be recall'd.
Bar. Will you then steale my goods?
Is theft the ground of your Religion?
Gov. No, Iew, we take particularly thine
To saue the ruine of a multitude: 330
And better one want for a common good,

300, 305, 308 *Prefix* Officer [reads] *Dyce* 303+S.D. Aside *add. Dyce to Bull.* 326 And now *om. Wag.* 326+S.D. Exeunt Officers, on a sign from Ferneze *add. Dyce*

Then many perish for a priuate man :
Yet *Barrabas* we will not banish thee,
But here in *Malta*, where thou gotst thy wealth,
Liue still ; and if thou canst, get more. 335
Bar. Christians ; what, or how can I multiply ?
Of nought is nothing made.
1. *Knight.* From nought at first thou camst to little welth,
From little vnto more, from more to most :
If your first curse fall heauy on thy head, 340
And make thee poore and scornd of all the world,
'Tis not our fault, but thy inherent sinne.
Bar. What ? bring you Scripture to confirm your wrongs ?
Preach me not out of my possessions.
Some Iewes are wicked, as all Christians are : 345
But say the Tribe that I descended of
Were all in generall cast away for sinne,
Shall I be tryed by their transgression ?
The man that dealeth righteously shall liue :
And which of you can charge me otherwise ? 350
Gov. Out, wretched *Barabas*,
Sham'st thou not thus to iustifie thy selfe,
As if we knew not thy profession ?
If thou rely vpon thy righteousnesse,
Be patient and thy riches will increase. 355
Excesse of wealth is cause of couetousnesse :
And couetousnesse, oh 'tis a monstrous sinne.
Bar. I, but theft is worse : tush, take not from me then,
For that is theft ; and if you rob me thus,
I must be forc'd to steale and compasse more. 360
1. *Kni.* Graue Gouernor, list not to his exclames :
Conuert his mansion to a Nunnery, *Enter Officers.*
His house will harbour many holy Nuns.
Gov. It shall be so : now Officers haue you done ?
Offic. I, my Lord, we haue seiz'd vpon the goods 365
And wares of *Barabas*, which being valued
Amount to more then all the wealth in *Malta*.
And of the other we haue seized halfe.
⟨*Gov.*⟩ Then wee'll take order for the residue.
Bar. Well then my Lord, say, are you satisfied ? 370
You haue my goods, my mony, and my wealth,

361 Gouernors *1633*, Reed list] listen *Cunn.*, *Bull.* 369 *Prefix om. 1633* : Fern. *add. Dyce* : Gov. *add. Cunn.*

My ships, my store, and all that I enioy'd ;
And hauing all, you can request no more ;
Vnlesse your vnrelenting flinty hearts
Suppresse all pitty in your stony breasts, 375
And now shall move you to bereave my life.

Gov. No, *Barabas,* to staine our hands with blood
Is farre from vs and our profession.

Bar. Why I esteeme the iniury farre lesse,
To take the liues of miserable men, 380
Then be the causers of their misery.
You haue my wealth, the labour of my life,
The comfort of mine age, my childrens hope,
And therefore ne're distinguish of the wrong.

Gov. Content thee, *Barabas,* thou hast nought but right.

Bar. Your extreme right does me exceeding wrong: 386
But take it to you i'th deuils name.

Gov. Come, let vs in, and gather of these goods
The mony for this tribute of the *Turke.*

1. *Knight.* 'Tis necessary that be look'd vnto : 390
For if we breake our day, we breake the league,
And that will proue but simple policie.

Exeunt, ⟨*all except Barabas and the Three Iews.*⟩

Bar. I, policie ? that's their profession,
And not simplicity, as they suggest.
The plagues of *Egypt,* and the curse of heauen, 395
Earths barrennesse, and all mens hatred
Inflict vpon them, thou great *Primus Motor.*
And here vpon my knees, striking the earth,
I banne their soules to everlasting paines
And extreme tortures of the fiery deepe, 400
That thus haue dealt with me in my distresse.

1. *Iew.* Oh yet be patient, gentle *Barabas.*

Bar. Oh silly brethren, borne to see this day !
Why stand you thus vnmou'd with my laments ?
Why weepe you not to thinke vpon my wrongs ? 405
Why pine not I, and dye in this distresse ?

1. *Iew.* Why, *Barabas,* as hardly can we brooke
The cruell handling of our selues in this :
Thou seest they haue taken halfe our goods.

Bar. Why did you yeeld to their extortion ? 410
You were a multitude, and I but one,
And of me onely haue they taken all.

392 S.D. all . . Iews *add. Dyce*

1. *Iew.* Yet brother *Barabas* remember *Iob.*
Bar. What tell you me of *Iob*? I wot his wealth
Was written thus: he had seuen thousand sheepe, 415
Three thousand Camels, and two hundred yoake
Of labouring Oxen, and fiue hundred
Shee Asses: but for euery one of those,
Had they beene valued at indifferent rate,
I had at home, and in mine Argosie 420
And other ships that came from *Egypt* last,
As much as would haue bought his beasts and him,
And yet haue kept enough to liue vpon;
So that not he, but I may curse the day,
Thy fatall birth-day, forlorne *Barabas*; 425
And henceforth wish for an eternall night,
That clouds of darkenesse may inclose my flesh,
And hide these extreme sorrowes from mine eyes:
For onely I haue toyl'd to inherit here
The months of vanity and losse of time, 430
And painefull nights haue bin appointed me.
2. *Iew.* Good *Barabas* be patient.
Bar. I, I pray leave me in my patience.
You that were ne're possest of wealth, are pleas'd with want.
But giue him liberty at least to mourne, 435
That in a field amidst his enemies,
Doth see his souldiers slaine, himselfe disarm'd,
And knowes no meanes of his recouerie:
I, let me sorrow for this sudden chance,
'Tis in the trouble of my spirit I speake; 440
Great iniuries are not so soone forgot.
1. *Iew.* Come, let vs leaue him in his irefull mood,
Our words will but increase his extasie.
2. *Iew.* On, then: but trust me 'tis a misery
To see a man in such affliction: 445
Farewell *Barabas.* *Exeunt.*
Bar. I, fare you well.
See the simplicitie of these base slaues,
Who for the villaines haue no wit themselues,
Thinke me to be a senselesse lumpe of clay 450
That will with euery water wash to dirt:
No, *Barabas* is borne to better chance,

433 I, I] Aye, I *Reed to Cunn.* 434 that were *omit conj. Bull*: that *om. Ellis* 446 S.D. Exeunt three Jews *Dyce, after* well

And fram'd of finer mold then common men,
That measure nought but by the present time.
A reaching thought will search his deepest wits, 455
And cast with cunning for the time to come:
For euils are apt to happen euery day.
But whither wends my beauteous *Abigall*?

Enter Abigall the Iewes daughter.

Oh what has made my louely daughter sad?
What? woman, moane not for a little losse: 460
Thy father has enough in store for thee.

Abig. Not for my selfe, but aged *Barabas*:
Father, for thee lamenteth *Abigaile*:
But I will learne to leaue these fruitlesse teares,
And vrg'd thereto with my afflictions, 465
With fierce exclaimes run to the Senate-house,
And in the Senate reprehend them all,
And rent their hearts with tearing of my haire,
Till they reduce the wrongs done to my father.

Bar. No, *Abigail*, things past recouery 470
Are hardly cur'd with exclamations.
Be silent, Daughter, sufferance breeds ease,
And time may yeeld vs an occasion
Which on the sudden cannot serue the turne.
Besides, my girle, thinke me not all so fond 475
As negligently to forgoe so much
Without prouision for thy selfe and me.
Ten thousand *Portagues*, besides great Perles,
Rich costly Iewels, and Stones infinite,
Fearing the worst of this before it fell, 480
I closely hid.

Abig. Where father?

Bar. In my house, my girle.

Abig. Then shall they ne're be seene of *Barrabas*:
For they haue seiz'd vpon thy house and wares. 485

Bar. But they will giue me leaue once more, I trow,
To goe into my house.

Abig. That may they not:
For there I left the Gouernour placing Nunnes,
Displacing me; and of thy house they meane 490
To make a Nunnery, where none but their owne sect
Must enter in; men generally barr'd.

468 rend *Reed, Coll., Bull.* 469 reduce] redress *conj. Dyce*[2]
482 father *om. Wag.*

Bar. My gold, my gold, and all my wealth is gone.
You partiall heauens, haue I deseru'd this plague?
What will you thus oppose me, lucklesse Starres, 495
To make me desperate in my pouerty?
And knowing me impatient in distresse
Thinke me so mad as I will hang my selfe.
That I may vanish ore the earth in ayre,
And leaue no memory that e're I was. 500
No, I will liue; nor loath I this my life:
And since you leaue me in the Ocean thus
To sinke or swim, and put me to my shifts,
I'le rouse my senses, and awake my selfe.
Daughter, I haue it: thou perceiu'st the plight 505
Wherein these Christians haue oppressed me:
Be rul'd by me, for in extremitie
We ought to make barre of no policie.
Abig. Father, what e're it be to iniure them
That haue so manifestly wronged vs, 510
What will not *Abigall* attempt?
Bar. Why so;
Then thus, thou toldst me they haue turn'd my house
Into a Nunnery, and some Nuns are there.
Abig. I did. 515
Bar. Then *Abigall*, there must my girle
Intreat the Abbasse to be entertain'd.
Abig. How, as a Nunne?
Bar. I, Daughter, for Religion
Hides many mischiefes from suspition. 520
Abig. I, but father, they will suspect me there.
Bar. Let 'em suspect, but be thou so precise
As they may thinke it done of Holinesse.
Intreat 'em faire, and giue them friendly speech,
And seeme to them as if thy sinnes were great, 525
Till thou hast gotten to be entertain'd.
Abig. Thus, father, shall I much dissemble.
Bar. Tush,
As good dissemble that thou neuer mean'st
As first meane truth, and then dissemble it, 530
A counterfet profession is better
Then vnseene hypocrisie.
Abig. Well father, say I be entertain'd,
What then shall follow?

519 Daughter *omit conj. Wag.* 529 meant'st *Cunn.* 532 vnseene] unforeseen *Cunn.*: unseeing *conj. Brereton.* 533 say] say that *Bull.*

Bar. This shall follow then ; 535
There haue I hid close underneath the plancke
That runs along the vpper chamber floore,
The gold and Iewels which I kept for thee.
But here they come ; be cunning *Abigall.*
Abig. Then father, goe with me. 540
Bar. No, *Abigall,* in this
It is not necessary I be seene.
For I will seeme offended with thee for't.
Be close, my girle, for this must fetch my gold.

Enter three Fryars and two Nuns.

1. *Fry.* Sisters, 545
We now are almost at the new made Nunnery.
1. *Nun.* The better ; for we loue not to be seene :
'Tis 30 winters long since some of vs
Did stray so farre amongst the multitude.
1. *Fry.* But, Madam, this house 550
And quarters of this new made Nunnery
Will much delight you.
Nun. It may be so : but who comes here ?
Abig. Grave Abbasse, and you, happy Virgins guide,
Pitty the state of a distressed Maid. 555
Abb. What art thou, daughter ?
Abig. The hopelesse daughter of a haplesse Iew,
The Iew of *Malta,* wretched *Barabas* ;
Sometimes the owner of a goodly house,
Which they haue now turn'd to a Nunnery. 560
Abb. Well, daughter, say, what is thy suit with vs ?
Abig. Fearing the afflictions which my father feeles,
Proceed from sinne, or want of faith in vs,
I'de passe away my life in penitence,
And be a Nouice in your Nunnery, 565
To make attonement for my labouring soule.
1. *Fry.* No doubt, brother, but this proceedeth of the spirit.
2. *Fry.* I,
And of a moving spirit too, brother ; but come,
Let vs intreat she may be entertain'd. 570

540 *Ends* Abigall *conj. Elze* : Abigall *omit conj. Wag.* 544+ S.D. They retire *add. Dyce* 551 quarters *Wag.* : waters *1633* : cloisters *conj. Bull.* 553 *After* so S.D. Abigall comes forward *add. Dyce to Bull.* 559 Sometime *Cunn.* 567, 569 brother *om. Wag.*

Abb. Well, daughter, we admit you for a Nun.
Abig. First let me as a Nouice learne to frame
My solitary life to your streight lawes,
And let me lodge where I was wont to lye.
I doe not doubt by your diuine precepts 575
And mine owne industry, but to profit much.
Bar. As much I hope as all I hid is worth. *Aside.*
Abb. Come daughter, follow vs.
Bar. Why how now *Abigall*, what mak'st thou
Amongst these hateful Christians? 580
1. *Fry.* Hinder her not, thou man of little faith,
For she has mortified her selfe.
Bar. How, mortified!
1. *Fry.* And is admitted to the Sister-hood.
Bar. Child of perdition, and thy fathers shame, 585
What wilt thou doe among these hatefull fiends?
I charge thee on my blessing that thou leaue
These diuels, and their damned heresie.
Abig. Father, giue me—
Bar. Nay backe, *Abigall*, 590
And thinke vpon the Iewels and the gold, { *Whispers*
The boord is marked thus that couers it. { *to her.*
Away accursed from thy fathers sight.
1. *Fry.* *Barabas*, although thou art in mis-beleefe,
And wilt not see thine owne afflictions, 595
Yet let thy daughter be no longer blinde.
Bar. Blind, Fryer, I wrecke not thy perswasions.
The boord is marked thus † that couers it,
For I had rather dye, then see her thus.
Wilt thou forsake mee too in my distresse, 600
Seduced Daughter, *Goe forget not* *Aside to her.*
Becomes it Iewes to be so credulous,
To morrow early Il'e be at the doore. *Aside to her.*
No come not at me, if thou wilt be damn'd,
Forget me, see me not, and so be gone. 605
Farewell, Remember to morrow morning. *Aside.*
Out, out thou wretch.
⟨*Exeunt.*⟩

579 *Prefix* Bar.] Bar. [coming forward] *Dyce* 589 giue] forgiue *Dyce, Wag.* 589+S.D. She goes to him *add. Cunn., Bull.* 601 forget] forget it *conj. Dyce*[2], *Wag.* not] net *1633*: not, go *Bull.* 607 *om. Cunn.* 607 S.D. Exeunt *add. Reed*: Exit on one side Barabas. Exeunt, on the other side, Friars, Abbess, and Nun: and as they are going out, *add. Dyce*

Enter Mathias.

Math. Whose this? Faire *Abigall* the rich Iewes daughter
Become a Nun? her fathers sudden fall
Has humbled her and brought her downe to this: 610
Tut, she were fitter for a tale of loue
Then to be tired out with Orizons:
And better would she farre become a bed
Embraced in a friendly louers armes,
Then rise at midnight to a solemne masse. 615

Enter Lodowicke.

Lod. Why how now Don *Mathias*, in a dump?
Math. Beleeue me, Noble *Lodowicke*, I haue seene
The strangest sight, in my opinion,
That euer I beheld.
Lod. What wast I prethe? 620
Math. A faire young maid scarce 14 yeares of age,
The sweetest flower in *Citherea's* field,
Cropt from the pleasures of the fruitfull earth,
And strangely metamorphis'd Nun.
Lod. But say, What was she? 625
Math. Why, the rich Iewes daughter.
Lod. What, *Barabas*, whose goods were lately seiz'd?
Is she so faire?
Math. And matchlesse beautifull;
As had you seene her 'twould haue mou'd your heart, 630
Tho countermin'd with walls of brasse, to loue
Or at the least to pitty.
Lod. And if she be so faire as you report,
'Twere time well spent to goe and visit her:
How say you, shall we? 635
Math. I must and will, Sir, there's no remedy.
Lod. And so will I too, or it shall goe hard.
Farewell *Mathias*.
Math. Farewell *Lodowicke* *Exeunt.*

624 Nun] to a Nun *Dyce, Bull., Wag.*: a nun *Cunn.* 628 Is . . faire] She is so faire *Wag., who adds the words to Math.'s speech below* 631 countermin'd] countermured *conj. Deighton* 639 S.D. Exeunt] Exeunt severally *Dyce, Bull.*

Actus Secundus.

Enter Barabas with a light.

Bar. Thus like the sad presaging Rauen that tolls 640
The sicke mans passeport in her hollow beake,
And in the shadow of the silent night
Doth shake contagion from her sable wings;
Vex'd and tormented runnes poore *Barabas*
With fatall curses towards these Christians. 645
The incertaine pleasures of swift-footed time
Haue tane their flight, and left me in despaire;
And of my former riches rests no more
But bare remembrance; like a souldiers skarre,
That has no further comfort for his maime. 650
Oh thou that with a fiery piller led'st
The sonnes of *Israel* through the dismall shades,
Light *Abrahams* off-spring; and direct the hand
Of *Abigall* this night; or let the day
Turne to eternall darkenesse after this: 655
No sleepe can fasten on my watchfull eyes,
Nor quiet enter my distemper'd thoughts,
Till I haue answer of my *Abigall.*

Enter Abigall aboue.

Abig. Now haue I happily espy'd a time
To search the plancke my father did appoint; 660
And here behold (vnseene) where I haue found
The gold, the perles, and Iewels which he hid.
Bar. Now I remember those old womens words,
Who in my wealth wud tell me winters tales,
And speake of spirits and ghosts that glide by night 665
About the place where Treasure hath bin hid:
And now me thinkes that I am one of those:
For whilst I liue, here liues my soules sole hope,
And when I dye, here shall my spirit walke.
Abig. Now that my fathers fortune were so good 670
As but to be about this happy place;
'Tis not so happy: yet when we parted last,
He said he wud attend me in the morne.
Then, gentle sleepe, where e're his bodie rests,
Give charge to *Morpheus* that he may dreame 675

646 uncertain *Cunn., Bull.* 664 wealth] youth *conj. Bull.*

A golden dreame, and of the sudden walke,
Come and receiue the Treasure I haue found.

Bar. Bueno para todos mi ganado no era:
As good goe on, as sit so sadly thus.
But stay, what starre shines yonder in the *East*? 680
The Loadstarre of my life, if *Abigall.*
Who's there?

Abig. Who's that?

Bar. Peace, *Abigal*, 'tis I.

Abig. Then father here receiue thy happinesse. 685

Bar. Hast thou't? *Throwes downe bags.*

Abig. Here, Hast thou't? There's more, and more, and more.

Bar. Oh my girle,
My gold, my fortune, my felicity;
Strength to my soule, death to mine enemy; 690
Welcome the first beginner of my blisse:
Oh *A⟨b⟩igal, Abigal*, that I had thee here too,
Then my desires were fully satisfied,
But I will practise thy enlargement thence:
Oh girle, oh gold, oh beauty, oh my blisse! 695
Hugs his bags.

Abig. Father, it draweth towards midnight now,
And 'bout this time the Nuns begin to wake;
To shun suspition, therefore, let vs part.

Bar. Farewell my ioy, and by my fingers take
A kisse from him that sends it from his soule. 700
Now *Phœbus* ope the eye-lids of the day,
And for the Rauen wake the morning Larke,
That I may houer with her in the Ayre,
Singing ore these, as she does ore her young.
Hermoso placer de los dineros. 705
Exeunt.

Enter Governor, Martin del Bosco, the knights.

Gov. Now Captaine tell vs whither thou art bound?
Whence is thy ship that anchors in our Rhoad?
And why thou cam'st ashore without our leaue?

676 walke] wake *Dyce to Bull.* 678 Birn para todos, my ga nada no er *1633*: *corr. Dyce* Bueno] Buen *Coll.* 686 Hast thou't *add to Abigail's speech below conj. Deighton* 686+S.D. *after* Here *in* 687 *Dyce to Bull* 692 Oh Aigal, Abigal *1633, Wag.* 700+S.D. Exit Abigail above *add. Dyce to Bull.* 705 Hermoso Piarer, de les Denirch *1633*: *corr. Dyce* placer] parecer *conj. Coll.* 705+Scene II *add. Cunn., Bull.*

Bosc. Governor of *Malta*, hither am I bound:
My Ship, *the flying Dragon*, is of *Spaine*, 710
And so am I, *Delbosco* is my name;
Vizadmirall vnto the Catholike King.
1. *Kni.* 'Tis true, my Lord, therefore intreat him well.
Bosc. Our fraught is *Grecians, Turks*, and *Africk Moores*.
For late vpon the coast of *Corsica*, 715
Because we vail'd not to the *Turkish* Fleet,
Their creeping Gallyes had vs in the chase:
But suddenly the wind began to rise,
And then we luff'd, and tack'd, and fought at ease:
Some have we fir'd, and many haue we sunke; 720
But one amongst the rest became our prize:
The Captain's slaine, the rest remaine our slaues,
Of whom we would make sale in *Malta* here.
Gov. Martin del Bosco, I haue heard of thee;
Welcome to *Malta*, and to all of vs; 725
But to admit a sale of these thy *Turkes*
We may not, nay we dare not giue consent
By reason of a Tributary league.
1. *Kni. Delbosco*, as thou louest and honour'st vs,
Perswade our Gouernor against the *Turke*; 730
This truce we haue is but in hope of gold,
And with that summe he craues might we wage warre.
Bosc. Will Knights of *Malta* be in league with *Turkes*,
And buy it basely too for summes of gold?
My Lord, remember that to *Europ's* shame, 735
The Christian Ile of *Rhodes*, from whence you came,
Was lately lost, and you were stated here
To be at deadly enmity with *Turkes*.
Gov. Captaine we know it, but our force is small.
Bosc. What is the summe that *Calymath* requires? 740
Gov. A hundred thousand Crownes.
Bosc. My Lord and King hath title to this Isle,
And he meanes quickly to expell you hence;
Therefore be rul'd by me, and keepe the gold:
I'le write unto his Maiesty for ayd, 745
And not depart vntill I see you free.
Gov. On this condition shall thy *Turkes* be sold.
Goe Officers and set them straight in shew.

714 fraught] freight *Reed, Coll.* 716 Turkish *conj. Gilchrist, Dyce etc.*: Spanish *1633* 719 luff'd and tack'd *Dyce etc.*: left, and tooke *1633* 737 stated] stationed *Wag.* 748 + S.D. Exeunt Officers *add. Dyce, Bull.*

Bosco, thou shalt be *Malta's* Generall;
We and our warlike Knights will follow thee 750
Against these barbarous mis-beleeuing *Turkes*.
Bosc. So shall you imitate those you succeed:
For when their hideous force inuiron'd *Rhodes*,
Small though the number was that kept the Towne,
They fought it out, and not a man suruiu'd 755
To bring the haplesse newes to Christendome.
Gov. So will we fight it out; come, let's away:
Proud-daring *Calymath*, instead of gold,
Wee'll send thee bullets wrapt in smoake and fire:
Claime tribute where thou wilt, we are resolu'd, 760
Honor is bought with bloud and not with gold.
Exeunt.

Enter Officers with slaues.

1. *Off.* This is the Market-place, here let 'em stand:
Feare not their sale, for they'll be quickly bought.
2. *Off.* Euery ones price is written on his backe,
And so much must they yeeld or not be sold. *Ent. Bar.*
1. *Off.* Here comes the Iew, had not his goods bin seiz'd,
He 'de giue vs present mony for them all. 767

Enter Barabas.

Bar. In spite of these swine-eating Christians,
(Vnchosen Nation, neuer circumciz'd;
Such as, poore villaines, were ne're thought vpon 770
Till *Titus* and *Vespasian* conquer'd vs,)
Am I become as wealthy as I was:
They hop'd my daughter would ha bin a Nun;
But she's at home, and I haue bought a house
As great and faire as is the Gouernors; 775
And there in spite of *Malta* will I dwell:
Hauing *Fernezes* hand, whose heart I'le haue;
I, and his sonnes too, or it shall goe hard.
I am not of the Tribe of *Levy*, I,
That can so soone forget an iniury. 780
We Iewes can fawne like Spaniels when we please;
And when we grin we bite, yet are our lookes
As innocent and harmelesse as a Lambes.
I learn'd in *Florence* how to kisse my hand,

759 thee] the *1633* 761 + Scene III *add. Bull.* S.D. slaues] Ithamore and other Slaves *Dyce to Bull.* 767 giue] given *Cunn.*, *Bull.* 770 as, poore villaines] poor villains as *Reed, Coll.* 773 have *Reed, Coll., Cunn.*

Heave vp my shoulders when they call me dogge, 785
And ducke as low as any bare-foot Fryar,
Hoping to see them starue vpon a stall,
Or else be gather'd for in our Synagogue ;
That when the offering-Bason comes to me,
Euen for charity I may spit intoo't. 790
Here comes Don *Lodowicke* the Gouernor's sonne,
One that I loue for his good fathers sake.

Enter Lodowicke.

Lod. I heare the wealthy Iew walked this way ;
I'le seeke him out, and so insinuate,
That I may haue a sight of *Abigall* ; 795
For Don *Mathias* tels me she is faire.

Bar. Now will I shew my selfe to haue more of the Serpent
Then the Doue ; that is, more knaue than foole.

Lod. Yond walks the Iew, now for faire *Abigall.*

Bar. I, I, no doubt but shee's at your command. 800

Lod. *Barabas,* thou know'st I am the Gouernors sonne.

Bar. I wud you were his father too, Sir, that's al the harm
I wish you : the slaue looks like a hogs cheek new sindg'd.

Lod. Whither walk'st thou, *Barobas* ?

Bar. No further : 'tis a custome held with vs, 805
That when we speake with *Gentiles* like to you,
We turne into the Ayre to purge our selues :
For vnto vs the Promise doth belong.

Lod. Well, *Barabas,* canst helpe me to a Diamond ?

Bar. Oh, Sir, your father had my Diamonds. 810
Yet I haue one left that will serve your turne :—
I meane my daughter : but e're he shall haue her
I'le sacrifice her on a pile of wood.
I ha the poyson of the City for him,
And the white leprosie. *Aside.*

Lod. What sparkle does it give without a foile ? 816

Bar. The Diamond that I talke of, ne'r was foild :—
But when he touches it, it will be foild :—
Lord *Lodowicke,* it sparkles bright and faire.

Lod. Is it square or pointed ? pray let me know. 820

797–8 *Verse Cunn., Bull., div. after* myself, dove 798 + S.D. Aside *add. Dyce* 802–3 *Verse Cunn., Bull., div. after* sir, looks 803 + S.D. Aside *add. Dyce* 807 into] unto *Dyce*[1] 815 S.D. *follows* 813 *1633, Wag.* 818 it will] he will *Cunn., Bull.* 818 + S.D. Aside *add. Coll.*

Bar. Pointed it is, good Sir,—but not for you. *Aside.*
Lod. I like it much the better.
Bar. So doe I too.
Lod. How showes it by night?
Bar. Outshines *Cinthia's* rayes: 825
You'le like it better farre a nights than dayes. *Aside.*
Lod. And what's the price?
Bar. Your life and if you haue it.—Oh my Lord
We will not iarre about the price; come to my house
And I will giu't your honour—with a vengeance. *Aside.*
Lod. No, *Barabas*, I will deserue it first. 831
Bar. Good Sir,
Your father has deseru'd it at my hands,
Who of meere charity and Christian ruth,
To bring me to religious purity, 835
And as it were in Catechising sort,
To make me mindfull of my mortall sinnes,
Against my will, and whether I would or no,
Seiz'd all I had, and thrust me out a doores,
And made my house a place for Nuns most chast. 840
Lod. No doubt your soule shall reape the fruit of it.
Bar. I, but my Lord, the haruest is farre off:
And yet I know the prayers of those Nuns
And holy Fryers, hauing mony for their paines,
Are wondrous; *and indeed doe no man good:* Aside.
And seeing they are not idle, but still doing, 846
'Tis likely they in time may reape some fruit,
I meane in fulnesse of perfection.
Lod. Good *Barabas* glance not at our holy Nuns.
Bar. No, but I doe it through a burning zeale, 850
Hoping ere long to set the house a fire;
For though they doe a while increase and multiply, Aside.
I'le haue a saying to that Nunnery.
As for the Diamond, Sir, I told you of,
Come home and there's no price shall make vs part, 855
Euen for your Honourable fathers sake.
It shall goe hard but I will see your death. Aside.
But now I must be gone to buy a slaue.
Lod. And, *Barabas*, I'le beare thee company. 859
Bar. Come then, here's the marketplace; whats the

826 a] o' *Dyce*[1] *to Bull.* 828+S.D. Aside *add. Coll. after* haue it
839 a] o' *Dyce*[2] *to Bull.* 853 saying] savin *Dyce*[1] 860–1
whats . . of] What price is on *Cunn.* 860–2 *Verse Cunn.*, *div. after* market-place, crowns

price of this slaue, 200 Crowns? Do the *Turks* weigh so much?

Off. Sir, that's his price.

Bar. What, can he steale that you demand so much?
Belike he has some new tricke for a purse; 865
And if he has, he is worth 300 plats.
So that, being bought, the Towne-seale might be got
To keepe him for his life time from the gallowes.
The Sessions day is criticall to theeues,
And few or none scape but by being purg'd. 870

Lod. Ratest thou this *Moore* but at 200 plats?

1. *Off.* No more, my Lord.

Bar. Why should this *Turke* be dearer then that *Moore*?

Off. Because he is young and has more qualities.

Bar. What, hast the Philosophers stone? and thou hast, breake my head with it, I'le forgiue thee. 876

Slave. No Sir, I can cut and shaue.

Bar. Let me see, sirra, are you not an old shauer?

Slave. Alas, Sir, I am a very youth.

Bar. A youth? I'le buy you, and marry you to Lady vanity, if you doe well. 881

Slave. I will serue you, Sir.

Bar. Some wicked trick or other. It may be vnder colour of shauing, thou'lt cut my throat for my goods. Tell me, hast thou thy health well? 885

Slave. I, passing well.

Bar. So much the worse; I must haue one that's sickly, and be but for sparing vittles: 'tis not a stone of beef a day will maintaine you in these chops; let me see one that's somewhat leaner. 890

1. *Off.* Here's a leaner, how like you him?

Bar. Where was thou borne?

Itha. In *Trace*; brought vp in *Arabia*.

Bar. So much the better, thou art for my turne.
An hundred Crownes, I'le haue him; there's the coyne.

1. *Off.* Then marke him, Sir, and take him hence. 896

Bar. I, marke him, you were best, for this is he
That by my helpe shall doe much villanie.
My Lord farewell: Come Sirra you are mine.

861 Turke *1633* 877 *Prefix* Slave *Reed etc.*: Itha. *1633* 879, 882, 886 *Prefix* Slave *Reed etc.*: Ith. *1633* 888 and] And't *Reed, Coll.*: An't *Dyce, Wag.* 892 was] wast *Reed, Coll., Dyce*[2] *etc.* 896 Sir] Barabas *Wag.* 898+S.D. Aside *add. Dyce to Bull.*

As for the Diamond it shall be yours ; 900
I pray, Sir, be no stranger at my house,
All that I haue shall be at your command.

Enter Mathias, Mater.

Math. What makes the Iew and *Lodowicke* so priuate ?
I feare me 'tis about faire *Abigall.*
Bar. Yonder comes Don *Mathias,* let vs stay ; 905
He loues my daughter, and she holds him deare :
But I haue sworne to frustrate both their hopes,
And be reveng'd upon the — Gouernor. (*Exit* Lod.)
Mater. This Moore is comeliest, is he not ? speake son.
Math. No, this is the better, mother, view this well.
Bar. Seeme not to know me here before your mother
Lest she mistrust the match that is in hand : 912
When you haue brought her home, come to my house ;
Thinke of me as thy father ; Sonne, farewell.
Math. But wherefore talk'd Don *Lodowick* with you ?
Bar. Tush man, we talk'd of Diamonds, not of *Abigal.*
Mater. Tell me, *Mathias,* is not that the Iew? 917
Bar. As for the Comment on the *Machabees*
I haue it, Sir, and 'tis at your command.
Math. Yes, Madam, and my talke with him was 920
About the borrowing of a booke or two.
Mater. Conuerse not with him, he is cast off from heauen.
Thou hast thy Crownes, fellow, come let's away. *Exeunt.*
Math. Sirra, Iew, remember the booke.
Bar. Marry will I, Sir. 925
Off. Come, I haue made
A reasonable market, let's away.
Bar. Now let me know thy name, and therewithall
Thy birth, condition, and profession.
Ithi. Faith, Sir, my birth is but meane, my name's
Ithimer, my profession what you please. 931
Bar. Hast thou no Trade ? then listen to my words,
And I will teach that shall sticke by thee :
First be thou voyd of these affections,
Compassion, loue, vaine hope, and hartlesse feare, 935

902+S.D. Exit Lodowick *add. Bull.* 908+S.D. Aside *add. Dyce* 920 was] was but *conj. Dyce, Bull., Wag.* 924 books *Reed, Coll.* 927 A *om. Ellis* 927+S.D. Exit *add. Reed* : Exeunt Officers with Slaves *add. Dyce* 933 teach *1633* : teach thee *Reed etc.*

Be mou'd at nothing, see thou pitty none,
But to thy selfe smile when the Christians moane.
Ithi. Oh braue, master, I worship your nose for this.
Bar. As for my selfe, I walke abroad a nights
And kill sicke people groaning under walls : 940
Sometimes I goe about and poyson wells ;
And now and then, to cherish Christian theeves,
I am content to lose some of my Crownes ;
That I may, walking in my Gallery,
See 'em goe pinion'd along by my doore. 945
Being young, I studied Physicke, and began
To practise first vpon the *Italian* ;
There I enric⟨h⟩'d the Priests with burials,
And alwayes kept the Sexton's armes in vre
With digging graues and ringing dead mens knels : 950
And after that was I an Engineere,
And in the warres 'twixt *France* and *Germanie*,
Vnder pretence of helping *Charles* the fifth,
Slew friend and enemy with my stratagems.
Then after that was I an Vsurer, 955
And with extorting, cozening, forfeiting,
And tricks belonging vnto Brokery,
I fill'd the Iailes with Bankrouts in a yeare,
And with young Orphans planted Hospitals,
And euery Moone made some or other mad, 960
And now and then one hang himselfe for griefe,
Pinning vpon his breast a long great Scrowle
How I with interest tormented him.
But marke how I am blest for plaguing them,
I haue as much coyne as will buy the Towne. 965
But tell me now, how hast thou spent thy time ?
Ithi. Faith, Master,
In setting Christian villages on fire,
Chaining of Eunuches, binding gally-slaues.
One time I was an Hostler in an Inne, 970
And in the night time secretly would I steale
To trauellers Chambers, and there cut their throats :
Once at *Ierusalem*, where the pilgrims kneel'd,
I strowed powder on the Marble stones,
And therewithall their knees would ranckle, so 975
That I haue laugh'd agood to see the cripples
Goe limping home to Christendome on stilts.

939 a] o' *Dyce*[2] *to Bull.* 945 pinion'd along] along pinion'd *conj. Elze* 971 I *om. Coll., Cunn.*

Bar. Why this is something: make account of me
As of thy fellow; we are villaines both:
Both circumcized, we hate Christians both: 980
Be true and secret, thou shalt want no gold.
But stand aside, here comes Don *Lodowicke.*

Enter Lodowicke.

Lod. Oh *Barabas* well met;
Where is the Diamond you told me of?
Bar. I haue it for you, Sir; please you walke in with me:
What, ho, *Abigall*; open the doore I say. 986

Enter Abigall.

Abig. In good time, father, here are letters come
From *Ormus*, and the Post stayes here within.
Bar. Giue me the letters, daughter, doe you heare?
Entertaine *Lodowicke* the Gouernors sonne 990
With all the curtesie you can affoord;
Prouided, that you keepe your Maiden-head.
Vse him as if he were a *Philistine.* *Aside.*
Dissemble, sweare, protest, vow to loue him,
He is not of the seed of Abraham. 995
I am a little busie, Sir, pray pardon me.
Abigall, bid him welcome for my sake.
Abig. For your sake and his own he's welcome hither.
Bar. Daughter, a word more; kisse him, speake him faire,
And like a cunning Iew so cast about, 1000
That ye be both made sure e're you come out.
Abig. Oh father, Don *Mathias* is my loue.
Bar. I know it: yet I say make loue to him;
Doe, it is requisite it should be so.
Nay on my life it is my Factors hand, 1005
But goe you in, I'le thinke vpon the account:—
The account is made, for *Lodowicke* dyes.
My Factor sends me word a Merchant's fled
That owes me for a hundred Tun of Wine:
I weigh it thus much; I haue wealth enough. 1010

985 please you] please *Wag.* 993 S.D. aside *follows* 995 *Coll. to Cunn.*: *follows* 997 *Bull.* 994 to loue] love to *conj. Dyce*[1], *Dyce*[2], *Bull.*, *Wag.* 999+S.D. Aside *add. Cunn.* 1001+S.D. Aside to her *add. Dyce* 1004+S.D. Aside to her *add. Dyce* 1006+S.D. Exeunt Lodowick and Abigail *add. Reed* 1007 Lodowicke] Ludovico *Dyce*: Lodowick he *Cunn.*, *Bull.* 1010 *After* much S.D. Snapping his fingers *add. Dyce to Bull.*

For now by this has he kist *Abigall* ;
And she vowes loue to him, and hee to her.
As sure as heauen rain'd *Manna* for the *Iewes*,
So sure shall he and Don *Mathias* dye :
His father was my chiefest enemie.— 1015
Whither goes Don *Mathias* ? stay a while.

Enter Mathias.

Math. Whither but to my faire loue *Abigall* ?
Bar. Thou know'st, and heauen can witnesse it is true,
That I intend my daughter shall be thine. 1019
Math. I, *Barabas*, or else thou wrong'st me much.
Bar. Oh, heauen forbid I should haue such a thought.
Pardon me though I weepe ; the Gouernors sonne
Will, whether I will or no, haue *Abigall* :
He sends her letters, bracelets, jewels, rings.
Math. Does she receiue them ? 1025
Bar. Shee ? No, *Mathias*, no, but sends them backe,
And when he comes, she lockes her selfe vp fast ;
Yet through the key-hole will he talke to her,
While she runs to the window looking out
When you should come and hale him from the doore.
Math. Oh treacherous *Lodowicke* ! 1031
Bar. Even now as I came home, he slipt me in,
And I am sure he is with *Abigall*.
Math. I'le rouze him thence.
Bar. Not for all *Malta*, therefore sheath your sword ;
If you loue me, no quarrels in my house ; 1036
But steale you in, and seeme to see him not ;
I'le giue him such a warning e're he goes
As he shall haue small hopes of *Abigall*.
Away, for here they come. 1040

Enter Lodowicke, Abigall.

Math. What, hand in hand, I cannot suffer this.
Bar. *Mathias*, as thou lou'st me, not a word.
Math. Well, let it passe, another time shall serue.
Exit.
Lod. *Barabas*, is not that the widowes sonne ? 1044
Bar. I, and take heed, for he hath sworne your death.
Lod. My death ? what, is the base borne peasant mad ?

1016 S.D. *precedes* 1016 *Dyce to Bull.* 1018 it] this *Cunn.*, *Bull.* 1045, 1046 *om. Reed, Coll.*

Bar No, no, but happily he stands in feare
Of that which you, I thinke, ne're dreame vpon,
My daughter here, a paltry silly girle.
Lod. Why, loues she Don *Mathias*? 1050
Bar. Doth she not with her smiling answer you?
Abig. He has my heart, I smile against my will.
(*Aside.*)
Lod. *Barabas*, thou know'st I haue lou'd thy daughter long.
Bar. And so has she done you, euen from a child.
Lod. And now I can no longer hold my minde. 1055
Bar. Nor I the affection that I beare to you.
Lod. This is thy Diamond, tell me, shall I haue it?
Bar. Win it, and weare it, it is yet vnsoyl'd.
Oh but I know your Lordship wud disdaine
To marry with the daughter of a Iew: 1060
And yet I'le giue her many a golden crosse
With Christian posies round about the ring.
Lod. 'Tis not thy wealth, but her that I esteeme,
Yet craue I thy consent.
Bar. And mine you haue, yet let me talke to her;—
This off-spring of *Cain*, this *Iebusite* 1066
That neuer tasted of the Passeouer,
Nor e're shall see the land of *Canaan*,
Nor our *Messias* that is yet to come, *Aside.*
This gentle Magot *Lodowicke* I meane, 1070
Must be deluded: let him haue thy hand,
But keepe thy heart till Don *Mathias* comes.
Abig. What shall I be betroth'd to *Lodowicke*?
Bar. It's no sinne to deceiue a Christian;
For they themselues hold it a principle, 1075
Faith is not to be held with Heretickes;
But all are Hereticks that are not Iewes;
This followes well, and therefore daughter feare not.—
I haue intreated her, and she will grant.
Lod. Then gentle *Abigal* plight thy faith to me. 1080
Abig. I cannot chuse, seeing my father bids:
Nothing but death shall part my loue and me.
Lod. Now haue I that for which my soule hath long'd.
Bar. So haue not I, but yet I hope I shall. *Aside.*

1052 S.D. *add. Dyce* 1058 vnsoyl'd] unfoil'd *conj. Coll., Wag.* 1069 S.D. *follows* 1072 *Reed to Bull.* 1078 + S.D. Aside to her *add. Dyce* 1079 + S.D. To Lodowick *add. Cunn.* 1082 + S.D. Aside *add. Cunn., Bull.*

Abig. Oh wretched *Abigal*, what hast thee done ? 1085
Lod. Why on the sudden is your colour chang'd ?
Abig. I know not, but farewell, I must be gone.
Bar. Stay her, but let her not speake one word more.
Lod. Mute a the sudden ; here's a sudden change.
Bar. Oh muse not at it, 'tis the *Hebrewes* guize, 1090
That maidens new betroth'd should weepe a while :
Trouble her not, sweet *Lodowicke* depart :
Shee is thy wife, and thou shalt be mine heire.
Lod. Oh, is't the custome, then I am resolu'd :
But rathe⟨r⟩ let the brightsome heauens be dim, 1095
And Natures beauty choake with stifeling clouds,
Then my faire *Abigal* should frowne on me.
There comes the villaine, now I'le be reueng'd.

Enter Mathias.

Bar. Be quiet *Lodowicke*, it is enough
That I haue made thee sure to *Abigal.* 1100
Lod. Well, let him goe. *Exit.*
Bar. Well, but for me, as you went in at dores
You had bin stab'd, but not a word on't now ;
Here must no speeches passe, nor swords be drawne.
Math. Suffer me, *Barabas*, but to follow him. 1105
Bar. No ; so shall I, if any hurt be done,
Be made an accessary of your deeds ;
Reuenge it on him when you meet him next.
Math. For this I'le haue his heart.
Bar. Doe so ; loe here I giue thee *Abigall.* 1110
Math. What greater gift can poore *Mathias* haue ?
Shall *Lodowicke* rob me of so faire a loue ?
My life is not so deare as *Abigall.*
Bar. My heart misgiues me, that to crosse your loue,
Hee's with your mother, therefore after him. 1115
Math. What, is he gone vnto my mother ?
Bar. Nay, if you will, stay till she comes her selfe.
Math. I cannot stay ; for if my mother come,
Shee 'll dye with griefe. *Exit.*
Abig. I cannot take my leaue of him for teares : 1120
Father, why haue you thus incenst them both ?
Bar. What's that to thee ?
Abig. I'le make 'em friends againe.

1085 thee] thou *Coll. to Bull.* 1085 + S.D. Aside *add. Dyce*
1089 a the] o' the *Reed to Bull.*

Bar. You'll make 'em friends? are there not Iewes enow
In *Malta*, but thou must dote vpon a Christian? 1125
Abig. I will haue Don *Mathias*, he is my loue.
Bar. Yes, you shall haue him: Goe put her in.
Ith. I, I'le put her in.
Bar. Now tell me, *Ithimore*, how lik'st thou this?
Ith. Faith Master, I thinke by this 1130
You purchase both their liues; is it not so?
Bar. True; and it shall be cunningly perform'd.
Ith. Oh, master, that I might haue a hand in this.
Bar. I, so thou shalt, 'tis thou must doe the deed:
Take this and beare it to *Mathias* streight, 1135
And tell him that it comes from *Lodowicke*.
Ith. 'Tis poyson'd, is it not?
Bar. No, no, and yet it might be done that way:
It is a challenge feign'd from *Lodowicke*.
Ith. Feare not, I'le so set his heart a fire, 1140
That he shall verily thinke it comes from him.
Bar. I cannot choose but like thy readinesse:
Yet be not rash, but doe it cunningly.
Ith. As I behaue my selfe in this, imploy me hereafter. *Exit.* 1145
Bar. Away then.
So, now will I goe in to *Lodowicke*,
And like a cunning spirit feigne some lye,
Till I haue set 'em both at enmitie.
Exit.

Actus Tertius.

Enter a Curtezane.

Since this Towne was besieg'd, my gaine growes cold: 1150
The time has bin, that but for one bare night
A hundred Duckets haue bin freely giuen:
But now against my will I must be chast.
And yet I know my beauty doth not faile.
From *Venice* Merchants, and from *Padua*, 1155
Were wont to come rare witted Gentlemen,
Schollers I meane, learned and liberall;
And now, saue *Pilia-borza*, comes there none,

1124 enow] enough *Reed, Coll., Cunn., Bull.* 1128+S.D. Exit Abigail *add. Reed* 1135+S.D. Giving a letter *add. Dyce* 1140 I'le] I will *Dyce to Bull.* 1145 S.D. *follows* 1146 *Reed to Bull.* 1147 in to] unto *Dyce*[1]

And he is very seldome from my house;
And here he comes. 1160

Enter Pilia-borza.

Pilia. Hold thee, wench, there's something for thee to spend.
Curt. 'Tis siluer, I disdaine it.
Pilia. I, but the Iew has gold,
And I will haue it or it shall goe hard.
Curt. Tell me, how cam'st thou by this? 1165
Pilia. Faith, walking the backe lanes through the Gardens I chanc'd to cast mine eye vp to the Iewes counting-house, where I saw some bags of mony, and in the night I clamber'd vp with my hooks, and as I was taking my choyce, I heard a rumbling in the house; so I tooke onely this, and runne my way: but here's the Iews man. 1172

Enter Ithimore.

Curt. Hide the bagge.
Pilia. Looke not towards him, let's away: zoon's what a looking thou keep'st, thou'lt betraye's anon. 1175
Ith. O the sweetest face that euer I beheld! I know she is a Curtezane by her attire: now would I giue a hundred of the Iewes Crownes that I had such a Concubine.
Well, I haue deliuer'd the challenge in such sort, 1180
As meet they will, and fighting dye; braue sport. *Exit.*

Enter Mathias.

Math. This is the place, now *Abigall* shall see
Whether *Mathias* holds her deare or no.

Enter Lodow. reading.

Math. What, dares the villain write in such base terms?
Lod. I did it, and reuenge it if thou dar'st. 1185

Fight: Enter Barabas aboue.

1161+S.D. Shewing a bag of silver *add. Dyce* 1175 betray us *Reed, Coll., Cunn.* 1175+S.D. Exeunt Bellamira and Pilia Borza *add. Dyce* 1181+Scene II *add. Cunn.* 1183 S.D. reading *om. Dyce, Bull., Wag.* 1184 *Prefix om. Dyce, Bull., Wag.*: Lod. *Cunn.* 1184+S.D. Looking at a letter *add. Dyce* 1185 *Prefix* Lod.] Math. *Cunn.*

Bar. Oh brauely fought, and yet they thrust not home.
Now *Lodowicke*, now *Mathias*, so;
So now they haue shew'd themselues to be tall fellowes.
Within. Part 'em, part 'em. 1189
Bar. I, part 'em now they are dead: Farewell, farewell.
Exit.

Enter Gouernor, Mater.

Gov. What sight is this? my *Lodowicke* slaine!
These armes of mine shall be thy Sepulchre.
Mater. Who is this? my sonne *Mathias* slaine!
Gov. Oh *Lodowicke*! hadst thou perish'd by the Turke,
Wretched *Ferneze* might haue veng'd thy death. 1195
Mater. Thy sonne slew mine, and I'le reuenge his death.
Gov. Looke, *Katherin*, looke, thy sonne gaue mine these wounds.
Mat. O leaue to griue me, I am grieu'd enough.
Gov. Oh that my sighs could turne to liuely breath;
And these my teares to blood, that he might liue. 1200
Mater. Who made them enemies?
Gov. I know not, and that grieues me most of all.
Mat. My sonne lou'd thine.
Gov. And so did *Lodowicke* him.
Mat. Lend me that weapon that did kill my sonne,
And it shall murder me. 1206
Gov. Nay Madem stay, that weapon was my son's,
And on that rather should *Ferneze* dye.
Mat. Hold, let's inquire the causers of their deaths,
That we may venge their blood vpon their heads. 1210
Gov. Then take them vp, and let them be interr'd
Within one sacred monument of stone;
Vpon which Altar I will offer vp
My daily sacrifice of sighes and teares,
And with my prayers pierce impartiall heauens, 1215
Till they ⟨reveal⟩ the causers of our smarts,
Which forc'd their hands diuide vnited hearts:
Come, *Katherina*, our losses equall are,
Then of true griefe let vs take equall share. *Exeunt.*

Enter Ithimore.

Ith. Why, was there euer seene such villany. 1220

1187, 1191 Ludovico *Dyce* 1187+S.D. Both fall *add. Dyce* 1216 they reveal *Dyce etc.*: they *1633*: they disclose *conj. Coll.* 1218 Katherine *Reed etc.*

So neatly plotted, and so well perform'd ?
Both held in hand, and flatly both beguil'd ?

Enter Abigall.

Abig. Why, how now *Ithimore*, why laugh'st thou so?
Ith. Oh, Mistresse, ha ha ha.
Abig. Why what ayl'st thou ? 1225
Ith. Oh my master.
Abig. Ha.
Ith. Oh Mistris ! I haue the brauest, grauest, secret, subtil, bottle-nos'd knaue to my Master, that euer Gentleman had. 1230
Abig. Say, knaue, why rail'st vpon my father thus ?
Ith. Oh, my master has the brauest policy.
Abig. Wherein ?
Ith. Why, know you not ?
Abig. Why, no. 1235
Ith. Know you not of *Mathias* & Don *Lodowick's* disaster ?
Abig. No, what was it ?
Ith. Why the deuil inuented a challenge, my Mr. writ it, and I carried it, first to *Lodowicke*, and *imprimis* to *Mathias*. 1241
And then they met, ⟨and⟩, as the story sayes,
In dolefull wise they ended both their dayes.
Abig. And was my father furtherer of their deaths ?
Ith. Am I *Ithimore* ? 1245
Abig. Yes.
Ith. So sure did your father write, & I cary the chalenge.
Abig. Well, *Ithimore*, let me request thee this,
Goe to the new made Nunnery, and inquire
For any of the Fryars of St. Iaques, 1250
And say, I pray them come and speake with me.
Ith. I pray, mistris, wil you answer me to one question ?
Abig. Well, sirra, what is't ?
Ith. A very feeling one ; haue not the Nuns fine sport with the Fryars now and then ? 1255
Abig. Go to, sirra sauce, is this your question ? get ye gon.
Ith. I will forsooth, Mistris. *Exit.*
Abig. Hard-hearted Father, unkind *Barabas*,

1236 Mathia and Don Lodowick *1633* 1241 Mathia *1633* 1242 and *add. Dyce* 1250 Iaques *Coll. etc.* : Iaynes *1633, Reed* : James *conj. Coll.* 1252 to] but *Cunn.*, *Bull.*

Was this the pursuit of thy policie? 1260
To make me shew them fauour seuerally,
That by my fauour they should both be slaine?
Admit thou lou'dst not *Lodowicke* for his sire,
Yet Don *Mathias* ne're offended thee:
But thou wert set vpon extreme reuenge, 1265
Because the Sire dispossest thee once,
And couldst not venge it, but vpon his sonne,
Nor on his sonne, but by *Mathias* meanes;
Nor on *Mathias*, but by murdering me.
But I perceiue there is no loue on earth, 1270
Pitty in Iewes, nor piety in Turkes.
But here comes cursed *Ithimore* with the Fryar.

Enter Ithimore, Fryar.

Fry. *Virgo, salve.*
Ith. When, ducke you?
Abig. Welcome graue Fryar; *Ithamore* begon, *Exit.*
Know, holy Sir, I am bold to sollicite thee. 1276
Fry. Wherein?
Abig. To get me be admitted for a Nun.
Fry. Why *Abigal* it is not yet long since
That I did labour thy admition, 1280
And then thou didst not like that holy life.
Abig. Then were my thoughts so fraile & vnconfirm'd,
And I was chain'd to follies of the world:
But now experience, purchased with griefe,
Has made me see the difference of things. 1285
My sinfull soule, alas, hath pac'd too long
The fatall Labyrinth of misbeleefe,
Farre from the Sonne that giues eternall life.
Fry. Who taught thee this?
Abig. The Abbasse of the house, 1290
Whose zealous admonition I embrace:
Oh therefore, *Iacomi*, let me be one,
Although unworthy of that Sister-hood.
Fry. *Abigal* I will, but see thou change no more,
For that will be most heauy to thy soule. 1295
Abig. That was my father's fault.
Fry. Thy father's, how?

1263 sire *Dyce etc.*: sinne *1633*, *Reed*, *Coll.* 1266 Sire *T. B.*: Pryor *1633*: Gouernor *Cunn.*, *Wag.* 1271 nor] or *Cunn.*, *Bull.* 1275 S.D. Exit Ithamore *Coll. to Bull.* 1288 Sonne] son *Reed to Dyce*[1]: sun *Dyce*[2] *to Bull.*

Abig. Nay, you shall pardon me: oh *Barabas,*
Though thou deseruest hardly at my hands,
Yet neuer shall these lips bewray thy life. 1300
Fry. Come, shall we goe?
Abig. My duty waits on you. *Exeunt.*

Enter Barabas reading a letter.

Bar. What, *Abigall* become a Nunne againe?
False, and vnkinde; what, hast thou lost thy father?
And all vnknowne, and vnconstrain'd of me, 1305
Art thou againe got to the Nunnery?
Now here she writes, and wils me to repent.
Repentance? *Spurca*: what pretendeth this?
I feare she knowes ('tis so) of my deuice
In Don *Mathias* and *Lodovicoes* deaths: 1310
If so, 'tis time that it be seene into:
For she that varies from me in beleefe
Giues great presumption that she loues me not;
Or louing, doth dislike of something done.
But who comes here? Oh *Ithimore* come neere; 1315
Come neere, my loue, come neere thy masters life,
My trusty seruant, nay, my second self;
For I haue now no hope but euen in thee;
And on that hope my happinesse is built:
When saw'st thou *Abigall*? 1320
Ith. To day.
Bar. With whom?
Ith. A Fryar.
Bar. A Fryar? false villaine, he hath done the deed.
Ith. How, Sir? 1325
Bar. Why made mine *Abigall* a Nunne.
Ith. That's no lye, for she sent me for him.
Bar. Oh vnhappy day,
False, credulous, inconstant *Abigall*!
But let 'em goe: And *Ithimore*, from hence 1330
Ne're shall she grieue me more with her disgrace;
Ne're shall she liue to inherit ought of mine,
Be blest of me, nor come within my gates,
But perish vnderneath my bitter curse
Like *Cain* by *Adam*, for his brother's death. 1335
Ith. Oh master.

1300+S.D. Aside *add. Dyce* 1308 portendeth *Reed* 1310 Mathias's and Lodowick's *Coll., Cunn.* 1314+S.D. Enter Ithamore *add. Reed* 1317 self *conj. Dyce*[1], *Dyce*[2] *etc.*: life *1633*

Bar. *Ithimore*, intreat not for her, I am mou'd,
And she is hatefull to my soule and me:
And least thou yeeld to this that I intreat,
I cannot thinke but that thou hat'st my life. 1340
Ith. Who I, master? Why I'le run to some rocke
And throw my selfe headlong into the sea;
Why I'le doe any thing for your sweet sake.
Bar. Oh trusty *Ithimore*; no seruant, but my friend;
I here adopt thee for mine onely heire, 1345
All that I haue is thine when I am dead,
And whilst I liue vse halfe; spend as my selfe;
Here take my keyes, I'le giue 'em thee anon:
Goe buy thee garments: but thou shalt not want:
Onely know this, that thus thou art to doe: 1350
But first goe fetch me in the pot of Rice
That for our supper stands vpon the fire.
Ith. I hold my head my master's hungry: I goe Sir.
Exit.
Bar. Thus euery villaine ambles after wealth
Although he ne're be richer then in hope: 1355
But, hush't.

Enter Ithimore with the pot.

Ith. Here 'tis, Master.
Bar. Well said, *Ithimore*;
What, hast thou brought the Ladle with thee too? 1359
Ith. Yes, Sir, the prouerb saies, he that eats with the deuil had need of a long spoone. I haue brought you a Ladle.
Bar. Very well, *Ithimore*, then now be secret,
And for thy sake, whom I so dearely loue,
Now shalt thou see the death of *Abigall*, 1365
That thou mayst freely liue to be my heire.
Ith. Why, master, wil you poison her with a messe of rice Porredge that wil preserue life, make her round & plump, and batten more then you are aware.
Bar. I but *Ithimore* seest thou this? 1370
It is a precious powder that I bought
Of an *Italian* in *Ancona* once,
Whose operation is to binde, infect,
And poyson deeply: yet not appeare
In forty houres after it is tane. 1375

1339 least] less *conj. Coll.*, *Dyce etc.* 1341 rocke] huge rock *Cunn.* 1353+S.D. Aside *add. after* hungry *Dyce*

Ith. How master?
Bar. Thus *Ithimore*:
This Euen they vse in *Malta* here ('tis call'd
Saint *Iaques* Euen) and then I say they vse
To send their Almes vnto the Nunneries: 1380
Among the rest beare this, and set it there;
There's a darke entry where they take it in,
Where they must neither see the messenger,
Nor make enquiry who hath sent it them.
Ith. How so? 1385
Bar. Belike there is some Ceremony in't.
There *Ithimore* must thou goe place this pot:
Stay, let me spice it first.
Ith. Pray doe, and let me help you, Mr. Pray let me taste first. 1390
Bar. Prethe doe: what saist thou now?
Ith. Troth Mr. I'm loth such a pot of pottage should be spoyld.
Bar. Peace, *Ithimore*, 'tis better so then spar'd.
Assure thy selfe thou shalt haue broth by the eye. 1395
My purse, my Coffer, and my selfe is thine.
Ith. Well, master, I goe.
Bar. Stay, first let me stirre it *Ithimore*.
As fatall be it to her as the draught
Of which great *Alexander* drunke, and dyed: 1400
And with her let it worke like *Borgias* wine,
Whereof his sire, the Pope, was poyson'd.
In few, the blood of *Hydra*, Lerna's bane;
The iouyce of *Hebon*, and *Cocitus* breath,
And all the poysons of the Stygian poole 1405
Breake from the fiery kingdome; and in this
Vomit your venome, and inuenome her
That like a fiend hath left her father thus.
Ith. What a blessing has he giu'nt? was euer pot of Rice porredge so sauc't? what shall I doe with it? 1410
Bar. Oh my sweet *Ithimore* goe set it downe
And come againe so soone as thou hast done,
For I haue other businesse for thee.
Ith. Here's a drench to poyson a whole stable of Flanders mares: I'le carry't to the Nuns with a powder. 1415

1379 Iagues *1633, Reed* 1387 pot *Reed etc.*: plot *1633* 1391 *After* doe S.D. Ithamore tastes *add. Dyce* 1394 + S.D. Puts the powder into the pot *add. Dyce* 1410 *After* sauc't S.D. Aside *add. Dyce*

Bar. And the horse pestilence to boot ; away.
Ith. I am gone.
Pay me my wages for my worke is done. *Exit.*
Bar. Ile pay thee with a vengeance *Ithamore.* *Exit.*

Enter Govern. Bosco. Knights. Bashaw.

Gov. Welcome, great *Bashaws,* how fares *Callymath,* 1420
What wind drives you thus into *Malta* rhode ?
Bash. The wind that bloweth all the world besides,
Desire of gold.
Gov. Desire of gold, great Sir ?
That's to be gotten in the Westerne *Inde* : 1425
In *Malta* are no golden Minerals.
Bash. To you of *Malta* thus saith *Calymath* :
The time you tooke for respite, is at hand,
For the performance of your promise past ;
And for the Tribute-mony I am sent. 1430
Gov. *Bashaw,* in briefe, shalt haue no tribute here,
Nor shall the Heathens liue vpon our spoyle :
First will we race the City wals our selues,
Lay waste the Iland, hew the Temples downe,
And shipping of our goods to *Sicily,* 1435
Open an entrance for the wastfull sea,
Whose billowes beating the resistlesse bankes,
Shall ouerflow it with their refluence.
Bash. Well, Gouernor, since thou hast broke the league
By flat denyall of the promis'd Tribute, 1440
Talke not of racing downe your City wals,
You shall not need trouble your selues so farre,
For *Selim-Calymath* shall come himselfe,
And with brasse-bullets batter downe your Towers,
And turne proud *Malta* to a wildernesse 1445
For these intolerable wrongs of yours ;
And so farewell.
Gov. Farewell :
And now you men of *Malta* looke about,
And let's prouide to welcome *Calymath* : 1450
Close your Port-cullise, charge your Basiliskes,
And as you profitably take vp Armes,
So now couragiously encounter them ;
For by this Answer, broken is the league,

1419+Scene V. *add. Bull.* 1421 drives you thus] thus drives you *Cunn., Bull.* 1435 of] off *Reed to Bull.* 1447 +S.D. Exit *add. Reed*

And nought is to be look'd for now but warres, 1455
And nought to vs more welcome is then wars.
Exeunt.

Enter two Fryars.

1. *Fry.* Oh brother, brother, all the Nuns are sicke,
And Physicke will not helpe them; they must dye.
2. *Fry.* The Abbasse sent for me to be confest:
Oh what a sad confession will there be? 1460
1. *Fry.* And so did faire *Maria* send for me:
I'le to her lodging; hereabouts she lyes. *Exit.*

Enter Abigall.

2. *Fry.* What, all dead saue onely *Abigall*?
Abig. And I shall dye too, for I feele death comming.
Where is the Fryar that conuerst with me? 1465
2. *Fry.* Oh he is gone to see the other Nuns.
Abig. I sent for him, but seeing you are come
Be you my ghostly father; and first know,
That in this house I liu'd religiously,
Chast, and deuout, much sorrowing for my sinnes, 1470
But e're I came—
2. *Fry.* What then?
Abig. I did offend high heauen so grieuously,
As I am almost desperate for my sinnes:
And one offence torments me more then all. 1475
You knew *Mathias* and Don *Lodowicke*?
2. *Fry.* Yes, what of them?
Abig. My father did contract me to 'em both:
First to Don *Lodowicke*, him I neuer lou'd;
Mathias was the man that I held deare, 1480
And for his sake did I become a Nunne.
2. *Fry.* So, say how was their end?
Abig. Both iealous of my loue, enuied each other:
And by my father's practice, which is there
Set downe at large, the Gallants were both slaine. 1485
2. *Fry.* Oh monstrous villany.
Abig. To worke my peace, this I confesse to thee;
Reueale it not, for then my father dyes.
2. *Fry.* Know that Confession must not be reueal'd,
The Canon Law forbids it, and the Priest 1490
That makes it knowne, being degraded first,
Shall be condemn'd, and then sent to the fire.

1456+Scene V *add. Cunn.*: Scene VI *add. Bull.* S.D. Fryars] Friars and Abigall *1633* 1484+S.D. Gives writing *add. Dyce*

Abig. So I haue heard; pray therefore keepe it close.
Death seizeth on my heart: ah gentle Fryar,
Conuert my father that he may be sau'd, 1495
And witnesse that I dye a Christian. ⟨*Dies.*⟩
2. *Fry.* I, and a Virgin too, that grieues me most:
But I must to the Iew and exclaime on him,
And make him stand in feare of me.

Enter 1. *Fryar.*

1. *Fry.* Oh brother, all the Nuns are dead, let's bury them. 1500
2. *Fry.* First helpe to bury this, then goe with me
And helpe me to exclaime against the Iew.
1. *Fry.* Why? what has he done?
2. *Fry.* A thing that makes me tremble to vnfold.
1. *Fry.* What, has he crucified a child? 1505
2. *Fry.* No, but a worse thing: 'twas told me in shrift,
Thou know'st 'tis death and if it be reueal'd.
Come let's away.

Exeunt.

Actus Quartus.

Enter Barabas, Itha. Bells within.

Bar. There is no musicke to a Christians knell:
How sweet the Bels ring now the Nuns are dead 1510
That sound at other times like Tinkers pans?
I was afraid the poyson had not wrought;
Or though it wrought, it would haue done no good,
For euery yeare they swell, and yet they liue;
Now all are dead, not one remaines aliue. 1515
Ith. That's braue, Mr. but think you it wil not be known?
Bar. How can it if we two be secret.
Ith. For my part feare you not.
Bar. I 'de cut thy throat if I did.
Ith. And reason too; 1520
But here's a royall Monastry hard by,
Good master let me poyson all the Monks.
Bar. Thou shalt not need, for now the Nuns are dead,
They'll dye with griefe. 1524
Ith. Doe you not sorrow for your daughters death?

1496 S.D. *add. Reed Cunn., Bull.* 1508 + Act the Fourth. Scene I. *add.*

Bar. No, but I grieue because she liu'd so long.
An *Hebrew* borne, and would become a Christian.
Cazzo, diabolo.

Enter the two Fryars.

Ith. Look, look, Mr. here come two religious Caterpillers.
Bar. I smelt 'em e're they came. 1530
Ith. God-a-mercy nose ; come let's begone.
2. *Fry.* Stay wicked Iew, repent, I say, and stay.
1. *Fry.* Thou hast offended, therefore must be damn'd.
Bar. I feare they know we sent the poyson'd broth.
Ith. And so doe I, master, therefore speake 'em faire.
2. *Barabas,* thou hast — 1536
1. I, that thou hast —
Bar. True, I haue mony, what though I haue ?
2. Thou art a —
1. I, that thou art a — 1540
Bar. What needs all this ? I know I am a Iew.
2. Thy daughter —
1. I, thy daughter, —
Bar. Oh speake not of her, then I dye with griefe.
2. Remember that — 1545
1. I, remember that —
Bar. I must needs say that I haue beene a great usurer.
2. Thou hast committed —
Bar. Fornication ? but that was in another Country :
And besides, the Wench is dead. 1551
2. I, but *Barabas,* remember *Mathias* and Don *Lodowick.*
Bar. Why, what of them ?
2. I will not say that by a forged challenge they met.
Bar. She has confest, and we are both vndone ; 1555
My bosome in⟨ti⟩mates, *but I must dissemble.* *Aside.*
Oh holy Fryars, the burthen of my sinnes
Lye heauy on my soule ; then pray you tell me,
Is 't not too late now to turne Christian ?
I haue beene zealous in the Iewish faith, 1560
Hard harted to the poore, a couetous wretch,
That would for Lucars sake haue sold my soule.
A hundred for a hundred I haue tane ;
And now for store of wealth may I compare
With all the Iewes in *Malta* ; but what is wealth ? 1565

1528 Catho diabola *1633* : *corr. Dyce* 1556 intimates *T. B.* : inmates *1633* : inmate *Dyce to Wag.* 1558 Lye] Lies *Rob.*

I am a Iew, and therefore am I lost.
Would pennance serue for this my sinne,
I could afford to whip my selfe to death.
Ith. And so could I; but pennance will not serue.
Bar. To fast, to pray, and weare a shirt of haire, 1570
And on my knees creepe to *Ierusalem.*
Cellers of Wine, and Sollers full of Wheat,
Ware-houses stuft with spices and with drugs,
Whole Chests of Gold, in *Bulloine,* and in Coyne,
Besides I know not how much weight in Pearle 1575
Orient and round, haue I within my house;
At *Alexandria,* Merchandize vnsold:
But yesterday two ships went from this Towne,
Their voyage will be worth ten thousand Crownes.
In *Florence, Venice, Antwerpe, London, Ciuill,* 1580
Frankeford, Lubecke, Mosco, and where not,
Haue I debts owing; and in most of these,
Great summes of mony lying in the bancho;
All this I'le giue to some religious house
So I may be baptiz'd and liue therein. 1585
1. Oh good *Barabas,* come to our house.
2. Oh no, good *Barabas,* come to our house.
And *Barabas,* you know —
Bar. I know that I haue highly sinn'd,
You shall conuert me, you shall haue all my wealth. 1590
1. Oh *Barabas,* their Lawes are strict.
Bar. I know they are, and I will be with you.
1. They weare no shirts, and they goe bare-foot too.
Bar. Then 'tis not for me; and I am resolu'd
You shall confesse me, and haue all my goods. 1595
1. Good *Barabas,* come to me.
Bar. You see I answer him, and yet he stayes;
Rid him away, and goe you home with me.
2. I'le be with you to night.
Bar. Come to my house at one a clocke this night.
1. You heare your answer, and you may be gone. 1601
2. Why, goe get you away.
1. I will not goe for thee.
2. Not, then I'le make thee, rogue. 1604
1. How, dost call me rogue? *Fight.*
Ith. Part 'em, master, part 'em.

1567 pennance] any penance *Cunn.* serue] serve to atone *Dyce, Wag.* 1577 vnsold] untold *Dyce* 1598 Rid] Bid *Reed, Coll.* 1604 rogue *T. B.*: goe *1633*

Bar. This is meere frailty, brethren, be content.
Fryar *Barnardine* goe you with *Ithimore.*
You know my mind, let me alone with him. 1609
⟨I.⟩ Why does he goe to thy house? let him begone.
Bar. I'le giue him something and so stop his mouth.
Exit.

I neuer heard of any man but he
Malign'd the order of the *Iacobines*:
But doe you thinke that I beleeue his words?
Why, Brother, you conuerted *Abigall*; 1615
And I am bound in charitie to requite it,
And so I will, oh *Iocome*, faile not but come.
Fry. But *Barabas*, who shall be your godfathers,
For presently you shall be shriu'd.
Bar. Marry, the *Turke* shall be one of my godfathers,
But not a word to any of your Couent. 1621
Fry. I warrant thee, *Barabas.* *Exit.*
Bar. So now the feare is past, and I am safe:
For he that shriu'd her is within my house.
What if I murder'd him e're *Iocoma* comes? 1625
Now I haue such a plot for both their liues,
As neuer Iew nor Christian knew the like:
One turn'd my daughter, therefore he shall dye;
The other knowes enough to haue my life,
Therefore 'tis not requisite he should liue. 1630
But are not both these wise men to suppose
That I will leaue my house, my goods, and all,
To fast and be well whipt; I'le none of that.
Now Fryar *Bernardine* I come to you,
I'le feast you, lodge you, giue you faire words, 1635
And after that, I and my trusty Turke—
No more but so: it must and shall be done.
Ithimore, tell me, is the Fryar asleepe?

Enter Ithimore.

Ith. Yes; and I know not what the reason is:
Doe what I can he will not strip himselfe, 1640
Nor goe to bed, but sleepes in his owne clothes;
I feare me he mistrusts what we intend.

1609 *Prefix* Ith. *before this line 1633, Reed, Coll.* 1609 + S.D. Aside to F. Barn. *add. Cunn., Bull.* 1610 *Prefix om. 1633, Reed, Coll.* 1621 convent *Reed, Coll., Cunn.* 1625 Jacomo *Reed to Bull.* 1630 'tis requisite he should not *conj. Deighton* 1637 + S.D. Exit *add. Cunn., Bull.* Scene II. Enter Barabas and Ithamore *add. Cunn., Bull.* 1638 S.D. *om. Cunn., Bull.*

Bar. No, 'tis an order which the Fryars vse:
Yet if he knew our meanings, could he scape?
Ith. No, none can heare him, cry he ne're so loud. 1645
Bar. Why, true, therefore did I place him there:
The other Chambers open towards the street.
Ith. You loyter, master, wherefore stay we thus?
Oh how I long to see him shake his heeles.
Bar. Come on, sirra, 1650
Off with your girdle, make a hansom noose;
Fryar, awake.
Fry. What, doe you meane to strangle me?
Ith. Yes, 'cause you vse to confesse.
Bar. Blame not vs but the prouerb, Confes & be hang'd.
Pull hard. 1656
Fry. What, will you haue my life?
Bar. Pull hard, I say, you would haue had my goods.
Ith. I, and our liues too, therefore pull amaine.
'Tis neatly done, Sir, here's no print at all. 1660
Bar. Then is it as it should be, take him vp.
Ith. Nay, Mr. be rul'd by me a little; so, let him leane vpon his staffe; excellent, he stands as if he were begging of Bacon.
Bar. Who would not thinke but that this Fryar liu'd?
What time a night is't now, sweet *Ithimore*? 1666
Ith. Towards one.

Enter Iocoma.

Bar. Then will not *Iocoma* be long from hence.
Ioco. This is the houre wherein I shall proceed;
Oh happy houre, wherein I shall conuert 1670
An Infidell, and bring his gold into
Our treasury.
But soft, is not this *Bernardine*? it is;
And vnderstanding I should come this way,
Stands here a purpose, meaning me some wrong, 1675
And intercept my going to the Iew;
Bernardine;

1651 + S.D. Ithamore takes off his girdle and ties a noose on it *add. Dyce* 1652 + S.D. They put the noose round the Friar's neck *add. Dyce* 1657 haue *conj. Reed, Dyce*: saue *1633* 1658 + S.D. They strangle the Friar *add. Dyce* 1662 *After* little S.D. Takes the body, sets it upright against the wall, and puts a staff in its hand *add. Dyce* 1667 S.D. *after* 1668 *Reed etc.* 1668 + S.D. Exeunt Barabas and Ithamore *add. Reed* Scene III *add. Cunn., Bull.* 1670 Oh happy houre *om. Wag.* *Line ends* Infidell *Wag.*

Wilt thou not speake? thou think'st I see thee not;
Away, I 'de wish thee, and let me goe by:
No, wilt thou not? nay then I'le force my way; 1680
And see, a staffe stands ready for the purpose:
As thou lik'st that, stop me another time.

Strike him, he fals. Enter Barabas ⟨*and Ithamore*⟩.

Bar. Why, how now *Iocoma*, what hast thou done?
Ioco. Why, stricken him that would haue stroke at me.
Bar. Who is it? *Bernardine*? now out alas, 1685
He is slaine.
Ith. I, Mr. he 's slain; look how his brains drop out on's nose.
Ioco. Good sirs I haue don't, but no body knowes it but you two, I may escape. 1690
Bar. So might my man and I hang with you for company.
Ith. No, let vs beare him to the Magistrates.
Ioco. Good *Barabas,* let me goe.
Bar. No, pardon me, the Law must haue his course.
I must be forc'd to giue in euidence, 1696
That being importun'd by this *Bernardine*
To be a Christian, I shut him out,
And there he sate: now I to keepe my word,
And giue my goods and substance to your house, 1700
Was vp thus early with intent to goe
Vnto your Friery, because you staid.
Ith. Fie vpon 'em, Mr.: will you turne Christian, when holy Friars turne deuils and murder one another.
Bar. No, for this example I'le remaine a Iew: 1705
Heauen blesse me; what, a Fryar a murderer?
When shall you see a Iew commit the like?
Ith. Why, a Turke could ha done no more.
Bar. To morrow is the Sessions; you shall to it.
Come *Ithimore*, let's helpe to take him hence. 1710
Ioco. Villaines, I am a sacred person, touch me not.
Bar. The Law shall touch you, we'll but lead you, we:
'Las, I could weepe at your calamity.
Take in the staffe too, for that must be showne:
Law wils that each particular be knowne. 1715
Exeunt.

1682 S.D. and Ithamore *add. Reed* 1715+Scene IV *add. Cunn., Bull.*

Enter Curtezant, and Pilia-borza.

Curt. *Pilia-borza,* didst thou meet with *Ithimore?*

Pil. I did.

Curt. And didst thou deliuer my letter?

Pil. I did.

Curt. And what think'st thou, will he come? 1720

Pil. I think so, and yet I cannot tell, for at the reading of the letter he look'd like a man of another world.

Curt. Why so?

Pil. That such a base slaue as he should be saluted by such a tall man as I am, from such a beautifull dame as you. 1726

Curt. And what said he?

Pil. Not a wise word, only gaue me a nod, as who shold say, Is it euen so; and so I left him, being driuen to a *Non-plus* at the critical aspect of my terrible countenance. 1730

Curt. And where didst meet him?

Pil. Vpon mine owne free-hold within 40 foot of the Gallowes, conning his neck-verse I take it, looking of a Fryars Execution, whom I saluted with an old hempen prouerb, *Hodie tibi, cras mihi,* and so I left him to the mercy of the Hangman: but the Exercise being done, see where he comes. 1737

Enter Ithimore.

Ith. I neuer knew a man take his death so patiently as this Fryar; he was ready to leape off e're the halter was about his necke; and when the Hangman had put on his Hempen Tippet, he made such haste to his prayers, as if hee had had another Cure to serue; well, goe whither he will, I'le be none of his followers in haste: And now I thinke on't, going to the execution, a fellow met me with a muschatoes like a Rauens wing, and a Dagger with a hilt like a warming-pan, and he gaue me a letter from one Madam *Bellamira,* saluting me in such sort as if he had meant to make cleane my Boots with his lips; the effect was, that I should come to her house. I wonder what the reason is. It may be she sees more in me than I can find in my selfe: for she writes further, that she loues me euer since she saw me, and who would not requite such loue? here's her house, and here she comes, and now would I were gone, I am not worthy to looke vpon her.

Pilia. This is the Gentleman you writ to. 1755

744 a mustachios *Reed*: mustachios *Coll., Cunn.*

Ith. Gentleman, he flouts me, what gentry can be in a poore Turke of ten pence? I'le be gone.

Curt. Is't not a sweet fac'd youth, *Pilia*?

Ith. Agen, sweet youth; did not you, Sir, bring the sweet youth a letter? 1760

Pilia. I did Sir, and from this Gentlewoman, who as my selfe, & the rest of the family, stand or fall at your seruice.

Curt. Though womans modesty should hale me backe, I can with-hold no longer; welcome sweet loue. 1765

Ith. Now am I cleane, or rather fouly out of the way.

Curt. Whither so soone?

Ith. I'le goe steale some mony from my Master to make me hansome: Pray pardon me, I must goe see a ship discharg'd. 1770

Curt. Canst thou be so vnkind to leaue me thus?

Pilia. And ye did but know how she loues you, Sir.

Ith. Nay, I care not how much she loues me; Sweet *Allamira*, would I had my Masters wealth for thy sake.

Pilia. And you can haue it, Sir, and if you please. 1775

Ith. If 'twere aboue ground I could, and would haue it; But hee hides and buries it vp as Partridges doe their egges, vnder the earth.

Pil. And is't not possible to find it out?

Ith. By no meanes possible. 1780

Curt. What shall we doe with this base villaine then?
⟨*Aside to Pilia Borza.*⟩

Pil. Let me alone, doe but you speake him faire:
But you know some secrets of the Iew,
Which if they were reueal'd, would doe him harme. 1784

Ith. I, and such as—Goe to, no more, I'le make him send me half he has, & glad he scapes so too. Pen and Inke: I'le write vnto him, we'le haue mony strait.

Pil. Send for a hundred Crownes at least.

He writes.

Ith. Ten hundred thousand crownes,—M[r]. *Barabas.*

Pil. Write not so submissiuely, but threatning him. 1790

1757+S.D. Aside *add. Dyce, Bull.* 1759 *After* youth S.D. Aside *add. Dyce to Bull.* 1766+S.D. Aside *add. Dyce, Bull.* 1769 *After* hansome S.D. Aside *add. Dyce etc.* 1772 And] An *Dyce, Cunn.* ye] you *Dyce* 1774 Allamira *1633*: Bellamira *Reed etc.* 1775 an if *Dyce to Bull.* 1781 S.D *add. Dyce* 1782+S.D. Aside to her *add. Dyce* 1783 But] But, sir *Cunn., Bull.* know] know, sir *conj. Dyce* 1786 Pen and Inke *om. Dyce*: *printed as* S.D. *Cunn., Bull.* 1790 threaten *Reed, Coll.*

Ith. Sirra *Barabas*, send me a hundred crownes.
Pil. Put in two hundred at least.
Ith. I charge thee send me 300 by this bearer, and this shall be your warrant; if you doe not, no more but so.
Pil. Tell him you will confesse. 1795
Ith. Otherwise I'le confesse all: vanish and returne in a Twinckle.
Pil. Let me alone, I'le vse him in his kinde. ⟨*Exit.*⟩
Ith. Hang him Iew.
Curt. Now, gentle *Ithimore*, lye in my lap. 1800
Where are my Maids? prouide a running Banquet;
Send to the Merchant, bid him bring me silkes.
Shall *Ithimore* my loue goe in such rags?
Ith. And bid the Ieweller come hither too.
Curt. I haue no husband, sweet, I'le marry thee. 1805
Ith. Content, but we will leaue this paltry land,
And saile from hence to *Greece*, to louely *Greece*,
I'le be thy *Iason*, thou my golden Fleece;
Where painted Carpets o're the meads are hurl'd,
And *Bacchus* vineyards ore-spread the world: 1810
Where Woods and Forrests goe in goodly greene,
I'le be *Adonis*, thou shalt be Loues Queene.
The Meads, the Orchards, and the Primrose lanes,
Instead of Sedge and Reed, beare Sugar Canes:
Thou in those Groues, by *Dis* aboue, 1815
Shalt liue with me and be my loue.
Curt. Whither will I not goe with gentle *Ithimore*?

Enter Pilea-borza.

Ith. How now? hast thou the gold?
Pil. Yes.
Ith. But came it freely, did the Cow giue down her milk freely? 1821
Pil. At reading of the letter, he star'd & stamp'd, & turnd aside. I tooke him by the beard, and look'd vpon him thus; told him he were best to send it. Then he hug'd & imbrac'd me. 1825
Ith. Rather for feare then loue.
Pil. Then like a Iew he laugh'd & jeer'd, and told me

1791, 1793, 1796 S.D. Writing *add. Dyce after Prefix* 1798 + S.D. Exit Pilia Borza with the letter *add. Dyce after* 1799 1801 running] cunning *Dyce*[2], *Cunn.* 1810 over-spread *Reed to Bull.* 1823 beard] sterd *1633*: *corr. Reed*

he lou'd me for your sake, & said what a faithfull seruant you had bin.

Ith. The more villaine he to keep me thus. Here's goodly 'parrell, is there not ? 1831

Pil. To conclude, he gaue me ten crownes.

Ith. But ten ? I'le not leaue him worth a gray groat. Giue me a Reame of paper, we'll haue a kingdome of gold for't.

Pil. Write for 500 Crownes. 1835

Ith. Sirra Iew, as you loue your life send me 500 crowns, and giue the Bearer 100. Tell him I must hau't.

Pil. I warrant your worship shall hau't.

Ith. And if he aske why I demand so much, tell him, I scorne to write a line vnder a hundred crownes. 1840

Pil. You'd make a rich Poet, Sir. I am gone. *Exit.*

Ith. Take thou the mony, spend it for my sake.

Curt. 'Tis not thy mony, but thy selfe I weigh :
Thus *Bellamira* esteemes of gold ; ⟨*Throws it aside.*⟩
But thus of thee.— *Kisse him.*

Ith. That kisse againe ; she runs diuision of my lips.
What an eye she casts on me ? It twinckles like a Starre.

Curt. Come my deare loue, let's in and sleepe together.

Ith. Oh that ten thousand nights were put in one,
That wee might sleepe seuen yeeres together 1850
Afore we wake.

Curt. Come Amorous wag, first banquet and then sleep.
⟨*Exeunt.*⟩

Enter Barabas, reading a letter.

Bar. *Barabas* send me 300 Crownes.
Plaine *Barabas* : oh that wicked *Curtezane* !
He was not wont to call me *Barabas*. 1855
Or else I will confesse : I, there it goes :
But if I get him, *Coupe de Gorge* for that.
He sent a shaggy totter'd staring slaue,
That when he speakes, drawes out his grisly beard,
And winds it twice or thrice about his eare ; 1860
Whose face has bin a grind-stone for mens swords,
His hands are hackt, some fingers cut quite off ;
Who when he speakes, grunts like a hog, and looks
Like one that is imploy'd in Catzerie

1832+S.D. Delivers the money to Ithamore *add. Dyce* 1836 +S.D. Writing *add. Dyce after Prefix* 1844 S.D. *add. Dyce* 1847+S.D. Aside *add. Dyce* 1850 together *om. Wag.* 1852 S.D. Exeunt *add. Reed* Scene V *add. Cunn., Bull.*

And crosbiting, such a Rogue 1865
As is the husband to a hundred whores:
And I by him must send three hundred crownes.
Well, my hope is, he will not stay there still;
And when he comes: Oh that he were but here!

Enter Pilia-borza.

Pil. Iew, I must ha more gold. 1870
Bar. Why wantst thou any of thy tale?
Pil. No; but 300 will not serue his turne.
Bar. Not serue his turne, Sir?
Pil. No Sir; and therefore I must haue 500 more.
Bar. I'le rather — 1875
Pil. Oh good words, Sir, and send it you were best; see, there's his letter.
Bar. Might he not as well come as send; pray bid him come & fetch it: what hee writes for you, ye shall haue straight. 1880
Pil. I, and the rest too, or else —
Bar. I must make this villaine away: please you dine with me, Sir, & you shal be most hartily poyson'd. *Aside.*
Pil. No, god-a-mercy, shall I haue these crownes?
Bar. I cannot doe it, I haue lost my keyes. 1885
Pil. Oh, if that be all, I can picke ope your locks.
Bar. Or climbe vp to my Counting-house window. You know my meaning.
Pil. I knowenough, and therfore talke not to me of your Counting-house: the gold, or know Iew it is in my power to hang thee. 1891
Bar. I am betraid.
'Tis not 500 Crownes that I esteeme,
I am not mou'd at that: this angers me,
That he who knowes I loue him as my selfe 1895
Should write in this imperious vaine? why Sir,
You know I haue no childe, and vnto whom
Should I leaue all but vnto *Ithimore*?
Pil. Here's many words but no crownes; the crownes.
Bar. Commend me to him, Sir, most humbly, 1900
And vnto your good mistris as vnknowne.
Pil. Speake, shall I haue 'vm, Sir?
Bar. Sir, here they are.

1865 a] a sort of *Cunn.* 1877+S.D. Gives letter *add. Dyce* 1882 *After* away S.D Aside *add. Dyce* 1892+S.D. Aside *add. Dyce* 1903+S.D. Gives money *add. Dyce*

Oh that I should part with so much gold!
Here take 'em, fellow, with as good a will— 1905
As I wud see thee hang'd; oh, loue stops my breath:
Neuer lou'd man seruant as I doe *Ithimore.*

Pil. I know it, Sir.

Bar. Pray when, Sir, shall I see you at my house? 1909

Pil. Soone enough to your cost, Sir: Fare you well.

Exit.

Bar. Nay to thine owne cost, villaine, if thou com'st.
Was euer Iew tormented as I am?
To haue a shag-rag knaue to come
300 Crownes, and then 500 Crownes?
Well, I must seeke a meanes to rid 'em all, 1915
And presently: for in his villany
He will tell all he knowes and I shall dye for't.
I haue it.
I will in some disguize goe see the slaue,
And how the villaine reuels with my gold. 1920

Exit.

Enter Curtezane, Ithimore, Pilia-borza.

Curt. I'le pledge thee, loue, and therefore drinke it off.

Ith. Saist thou me so? haue at it; and doe you heare?

⟨*Whispers to her.*⟩

Curt. Goe to, it shall be so.

Ith. Of that condition I wil drink it vp; here's to thee.

Curt. Nay, I'le haue all or none. 1925

Ith. There, if thou lou'st me doe not leaue a drop.

Curt. Loue thee, fill me three glasses.

Ith. Three and fifty dozen, I'le pledge thee.

Pil. Knauely spoke, and like a Knight at Armes.

Ith. Hey *Riuo Castiliano,* a man's a man. 1930

Curt. Now to the Iew.

Ith. Ha to the Iew, and send me mony you were best.

Pil. What wudst thou doe if he should send thee none?

Ith. Doe nothing; but I know what I know. He's a murderer. 1935

Curt. I had not thought he had been so braue a man.

1904 I] I e'er *conj. Dyce* 1904+S.D. Aside *add. Dyce* 1906 hang'd *omit conj. Brereton.* *After* hang'd S.D. Aside *add. Dyce* oh *om. Wag.* 1907 lou'd man seruant] man servant loved *Ellis, Wag.* 1911 to *om. Reed, Coll.* 1913 *After* come, *Dyce*[1] *adds* and force from me: force from me *add. Dyce*[2], *Ellis* 1920+Scene VI *add. Bull., Ellis* 1922 S.D. *add. Dyce* 1925 *Prefix* Curt.] Pil. *1633, Reed, Coll.* 1932 you] he *Dyce*[2] *etc.*

Ith. You knew *Mathias* and the Gouernors son : he and I kild 'em both, and yet neuer touch'd 'em.

Pil. Oh brauely done.

Ith. I carried the broth that poyson'd the Nuns, and he and I, snicle hand too fast, strangled a Fryar. 1941

Curt. You two alone ?

Ith. We two, and 'twas neuer knowne, nor neuer shall be for me.

Pil. This shall with me vnto the Gouernor. 1945
⟨*Aside to Bellamira.*⟩

Curt. And fit it should : but first let's ha more gold.
⟨*Aside to Pilia-Borza.*⟩
Come gentle *Ithimore,* lye in my lap.

Ith. Loue me little, loue me long, let musicke rumble,
Whilst I in thy incony lap doe tumble. 1949

Enter Barabas with a Lute, disguis'd.

Curt. A French Musician, come let's heare your skill ?

Bar. Must tuna my Lute for sound, twang twang first.

Ith. Wilt drinke French-man, here's to thee with a — Pox on this drunken hick-vp.

Bar. Gramercy Mounsier.

Curt. Prethe, *Pilia-borza,* bid the Fidler giue me the posey in his hat there. 1956

Pil. Sirra, you must giue my mistris your posey.

Bar. *A voustre commandemente Madam.*

Curt. How sweet, my *Ithimore,* the flowers smell.

Ith. Like thy breath, sweet-hart, no violet like 'em.

Pil. Foh, me thinkes they stinke like a Holly-Hoke. 1961

Bar. So, now I am reueng'd vpon 'em all.
The scent thereof was death, I poyson'd it. ⟨*Aside.*⟩

Ith. Play, Fidler, or I'le cut your cats guts into chitterlins.

⟨*Bar.*⟩ Pardona moy, be no in tune yet ; so now, now all be in. 1966

Ith. Giue him a crowne, and fill me out more wine.

Pil. There's two crownes for thee, play.

1941 snicle . . strangled] PILIA. Two hands snickle-fast— ITHA. Strangled *conj. Mitford* hand too fast] hand to fist *conj. Steevens* : hard and fast *conj. Cunn.* 1945 S.D. *add. Dyce* 1946 S.D. *add. Dyce* 1949 incoomy *1633* : *corr. Reed* 1958 + S.D. Giving nosegay *add. Dyce* 1963 S.D. *add. Dyce* 1965 *Prefix* Bar. *given as catch-word, but omitted at top of page* H4ᵛ Pardonnez *Coll. to Bull.* 1968 + S.D. Giving money *add. Dyce*

Bar. How liberally the villain giues me mine own gold. *Aside.*

Pil. Me thinkes he fingers very well. 1970

Bar. So did you when you stole my gold. *Aside.*

Pil. How swift he runnes.

Bar. You run swifter when you threw my gold out of my Window. *Aside.*

Curt. Musician, hast beene in *Malta* long? 1975

Bar. Two, three, foure month Madam.

Ith. Dost not know a Iew, one *Barabas*?

Bar. Very mush, Mounsier, you no be his man?

Pil: His man?

Ith. I scorne the Peasant, tell him so. 1980

Bar. He knowes it already. ⟨*Aside.*⟩

Ith. 'Tis a strange thing of that Iew, he liues vpon pickled Grashoppers, and sauc'd Mushrumbs.

Bar. What a slaue's this? The Gouernour feeds not as I doe. *Aside.*

Ith. He neuer put on cleane shirt since he was circumcis'd.

Bar. Oh raskall! I change my selfe twice a day. *Aside.*

Ith. The Hat he weares, *Iudas* left vnder the Elder when he hang'd himselfe. 1989

Bar. 'Twas sent me for a present from the great *Cham.* *Aside.*

Pil. A masty slaue he is. Whether now, Fidler?

Bar. Pardona moy, Mounsier, me be no well. *Exit.*

Pil. Farewell Fidler: One letter more to the Iew.

Curt. Prethe sweet loue, one more, and write it sharp.

Ith. No, I'le send by word of mouth now; bid him deliuer thee a thousand Crownes, by the same token, that the Nuns lou'd Rice, that Fryar *Bernardine* slept in his owne clothes. Any of 'em will doe it.

Pil. Let me alone to vrge it now I know the meaning.

Ith. The meaning has a meaning; come let's in: 2000
To vndoe a Iew is charity, and not sinne.

Exeunt.

1969 S.D. Aside, and then plays *Dyce* 1981 S.D. *add. Dyce* 1991 masty *1633*: nasty *Reed to Cunn.*: musty *Bull. to Wag.* 1992 Pardonnez *Coll. to Bull.* me *Reed etc.*: we *1633*

Actus Quintus.

Enter Gouernor. Knights. Martin Del-Bosco.

Gov. Now, Gentlemen, betake you to your Armes,
And see that *Malta* be well fortifi'd;
And it behoues you to be resolute;
For *Calymath* hauing houer'd here so long, 2005
Will winne the Towne, or dye before the wals.
Kni. And dye he shall, for we will neuer yeeld.

Enter Curtezane, Pilia-borza.

Curt. Oh bring vs to the Gouernor.
Gov. Away with her, she is a Curtezane.
Curt. What e're I am, yet Gouernor heare me speake;
I bring thee newes by whom thy sonne was slaine: 2011
Mathias did it not, it was the Iew.
Pil. Who, besides the slaughter of these Gentlemen,
Poyson'd his owne daughter and the Nuns,
Strangled a Fryar, and I know not what 2015
Mischiefe beside.
Gov. Had we but proofe of this.
Curt. Strong proofe, my Lord, his man's now at my Lodging
That was his Agent, he'll confesse it all. 2019
Gov. Goe fetch him straight, I alwayes fear'd that Iew.

Enter Iew, Ithimore.

Bar. I'le goe alone, dogs, do not hale me thus.
Ith. Nor me neither, I cannot out-run you, Constable.
Oh my belly.
Bar. One dram of powder more had made all sure.
What a damn'd slaue was I? 2025
Gov. Make fires, heat irons, let the racke be fetch'd.
Kni. Nay stay, my Lord, 'tmay be he will confesse.
Bar. Confesse; what meane you, Lords, who should confesse?
Gov. Thou and thy Turk; 'twas you that slew my son.
Ith. Gilty, my Lord, I confesse; your sonne and *Mathias* were both contracted vnto *Abigall*: ⟨he⟩ forg'd a counterfeit challenge. 2032

Actus Quintus] Scene I *add. Cunn., Bull.* 2014 Poisonéd *Dyce* 2020 *After* straight S.D. Exeunt Officers *add. Dyce* 2020 S.D. Re-enter Officers with Barabas and Ithamore *Dyce* 2021 alone] along *Wag.* 2025 + S.D. Aside *add. Dyce* 2031 he *add. Reed etc.*

Iew. Who carried that challenge ?
Ith. I carried it, I confesse, but who writ it ? Marry, euen he that strangled *Bernardine*, poyson'd the Nuns, and his owne daughter. 2036
Gov. Away with him, his sight is death to me.
Bar. For what ? you men of *Malta*, heare me speake ;
Shee is a Curtezane and he a theefe,
And he my bondman, let me haue law, 2040
For none of this can preiudice my life.
Gov. Once more away with him ; you shall haue law.
Bar. Deuils doe your worst, I liue in spite of you.
⟨*Aside.*⟩
As these haue spoke so be it to their soules :
I hope the poyson'd flowers will worke anon. 2045
⟨*Aside.*⟩ *Exit.*

Enter Mater.

Mater. Was my *Mathias* murder'd by the Iew ?
Ferneze, 'twas thy sonne that murder'd him.
Gov. Be patient, gentle Madam, it was he,
He forged the daring challenge made them fight
Mat. Where is the Iew, where is that murderer ? 2050
Gov. In prison till the Law has past on him.

Enter Officer.

Offi. My Lord, the Curtezane and her man are dead ;
So is the Turke, and *Barabas* the Iew.
Gov. Dead ?
Offi. Dead, my Lord, and here they bring his body.
Bosco. This sudden death of his is very strange. 2056
Gov. Wonder not at it, Sir, the heauens are iust :
Their deaths were like their liues, then think not of 'em.
Since they are dead, let them be buried.
For the Iewes body, throw that o're the wals, 2060
To be a prey for Vultures and wild beasts.
So, now away and fortifie the Towne. *Exeunt.*
Bar. What, all alone ? well fare sleepy drinke.
I'le be reueng'd on this accursed Towne ;

2043 I] I'll *Dyce* S.D. *add. Dyce* 2045 S.D. Aside *add. Dyce* Exit] Exeunt Officers with Barabas ; Ithamore, Bellamira, and Pilia-Borza *Dyce* 2056+S.D. Re-enter Officers carrying Barabas as dead *add. Dyce* 2062+S.D. Exeunt all, leaving Barabas on the floor *Dyce, Bull.* Scene II *add. Ellis* S.D. Barabas discovered rising *add. Ellis* 2063 *Prefix* Bara. [rising] *Dyce to Bull.*

For by my meanes *Calymath* shall enter in. 2065
I'le helpe to slay their children and their wiues,
To fire the Churches, pull their houses downe.
Take my goods too, and seize vpon my lands:
I hope to see the Gouernour a slaue,
And, rowing in a Gally, whipt to death. 2070

Enter Calymath, Bashawes, Turkes.

Caly. Whom haue we there, a spy?
Bar. Yes, my good Lord, one that can spy a place
Where you may enter, and surprize the Towne:
My name is *Barabas*; I am a Iew.
Caly. Art thou that Iew whose goods we heard were sold
For Tribute-mony? 2076
Bar. The very same, my Lord:
And since that time they haue hir'd a slaue my man
To accuse me of a thousand villanies:
I was imprison'd, but scap'd their hands. 2080
Caly. Didst breake prison?
Bar. No, no:
I dranke of Poppy and cold mandrake juyce;
And being asleepe, belike they thought me dead,
And threw me o're the wals: so, or how else, 2085
The Iew is here, and rests at your command.
Caly. 'Twas brauely done: but tell me, *Barabas*,
Canst thou, as thou reportest, make *Malta* ours?
Bar. Feare not, my Lord, for here against the Sluice,
The rocke is hollow, and of purpose digg'd, 2090
To make a passage for the running streames
And common channels of the City.
Now whilst you giue assault vnto the wals,
I'le lead 500 souldiers through the Vault,
And rise with them i'th middle of the Towne, 2095
Open the gates for you to enter in,
And by this meanes the City is your owne.
Caly. If this be true, I'le make thee Gouernor.
Iew. And if it be not true, then let me dye. 2099
Caly. Thou'st doom'd thy selfe, assault it presently.
Exeunt.

2071 there] here *Bull.* 2089 sluice *conj. Coll., Cunn., Bull. etc.*: Truce *1633*: trench *Dyce*: turret *or* tower *conj. Mitford* 2092 City] Citadel *Wag.* 2100+Scene II *add. Cunn., Bull.*: Scene III *Ellis*

Alarmes. *Enter Turkes, Barabas, Gouernour, and Knights prisoners.*

Caly. Now vaile your pride you captiue Christians,
And kneele for mercy to your conquering foe :
Now where's the hope you had of haughty *Spaine* ?
Ferneze, speake, had it not beene much better
To ⟨have⟩ kept thy promise then be thus surpriz'd ? 2105
Gov. What should I say ? we are captiues and must yeeld.
Caly. I, villains, you must yeeld, and vnder Turkish yokes
Shall groning beare the burthen of our ire ;
And *Barabas*, as erst we promis'd thee,
For thy desert we make thee Gouernor. 2110
Vse them at thy discretion.
Bar. Thankes, my Lord.
Gov. Oh fatall day, to fall into the hands
Of such a Traitor and vnhallowed Iew !
What greater misery could heauen inflict ? 2115
Caly. 'Tis our command : and *Barabas* we giue
To guard thy person, these our Ianizaries :
Intreat them well, as we haue vsed thee.
And now, braue Bashawes, come, wee'll walke about
The ruin'd Towne, and see the wracke we made : 2120
Farewell braue Iew, farewell great *Barabas*. *Exeunt.*
Bar. May all good fortune follow *Calymath*.
And now, as entrance to our safety,
To prison with the Gouernour and these
Captaines, his consorts and confederates. 2125
Gov. Oh villaine, Heauen will be reueng'd on thee.
Exeunt.
Bar. Away, no more, let him not trouble me.
Thus hast thou gotten, by thy policie,
No simple place, no small authority,
I now am Gouernour of *Malta* ; true, 2130
But *Malta* hates me, and in hating me
My life's in danger, and what boots it thee
Poore *Barabas*, to be the Gouernour,
When as thy life shall be at their command ?
No, *Barabas*, this must be look'd into ; 2135

2105 To kept *1633 to Dyce* : To've kept *Cunn.*, *Bull.* : To keepe *Wag.* have *add. T.B.* 2107 villains *om. Wag.* 2121 + S.D. Exeunt Calymath and Bassoes *Dyce*, *after* 2122 2126 + S.D. Exeunt Turks with Ferneze and Knights *Dyce*, *after* 2127

And since by wrong thou got'st Authority,
Maintaine it brauely by firme policy,
At least vnprofitably lose it not:
For he that liueth in Authority,
And neither gets him friends, nor fils his bags, 2140
Liues like the Asse that *Æsope* speaketh of,
That labours with a load of bread and wine,
And leaues it off to snap on Thistle tops:
But *Barabas* will be more circumspect.
Begin betimes, Occasion's bald behind, 2145
Slip not thine oportunity, for feare too late
Thou seek'st for much, but canst not compasse it.
Within here.

Enter Gouernor with a guard.

Gov. My Lord?
Bar. I, Lord, thus slaues will learne. 2150
Now Gouernor—stand by there, wait within.
⟨*Exeunt Guard.*⟩
This is the reason that I sent for thee;
Thou seest thy life, and *Malta's* happinesse,
Are at my Arbitrament; and *Barabas*
At his discretion may dispose of both: 2155
Now tell me, Gouernor, and plainely too,
What thinkst thou shall become of it and thee?
Gov. This; *Barabas*, since things are in thy power,
I see no reason but of *Malta's* wracke,
Nor hope of thee but extreme cruelty, 2160
Nor feare I death, nor will I flatter thee.
Bar. Gouernor, good words, be not so furious;
'Tis not thy life which can auaile me ought,
Yet you doe liue, and liue for me you shall:
And as for *Malta's* ruine, thinke you not 2165
'Twere slender policy for *Barabas*
To dispossesse himselfe of such a place?
For sith, as once you said, within this Ile
In *Malta* here, that I haue got my goods,
And in this City still haue had successe, 2170
And now at length am growne your Governor,
Your selues shall see it shall not be forgot:
For as a friend not knowne, but in distresse,
I'le reare vp *Malta* now remedilesse.

2151 S.D. *add. Dyce*: To the Guard *add. Reed, Coll.* 2168 within] 'tis in *Cunn.*, *Bull.*

Gov. Will *Barabas* recouer *Malta's* losse? 2175
Will *Barabas* be good to Christians?
Bar. What wilt thou giue me, Gouernor, to procure
A dissolution of the slauish Bands
Wherein the Turke hath yoak'd your land and you?
What will you giue me if I render you 2180
The life of *Calymath*, surprize his men,
And in an out-house of the City shut
His souldiers, till I haue consum'd 'em all with fire?
What will you giue him that procureth this?
Gov. Doe but bring this to passe which thou pretendest,
Deale truly with vs as thou intimatest, 2186
And I will send amongst the Citizens
And by my letters priuately procure
Great summes of mony for thy recompence:
Nay more, doe this, and liue thou Gouernor still. 2190
Bar. Nay, doe thou this, *Ferneze*, and be free;
Gouernor, I enlarge thee, liue with me,
Goe walke about the City, see thy friends:
Tush, send not letters to 'em, goe thy selfe,
And let me see what mony thou canst make; 2195
Here is my hand that I'le set *Malta* free:
And thus we cast it: To a solemne feast
I will inuite young *Selim-Calymath*,
Where be thou present onely to performe
One stratagem that I'le impart to thee, 2200
Wherein no danger shall betide thy life,
And I will warrant *Malta* free for euer.
Gov. Here is my hand, beleeue me, *Barabas*,
I will be there, and doe as thou desirest;
When is the time? 2205
Bar. Gouernor, presently.
For *Callymath*, when he hath view'd the Towne,
Will take his leaue and saile toward *Ottoman.*
Gov. Then will I, *Barabas*, about this coyne,
And bring it with me to thee in the euening. 2210
Bar. Doe so, but faile not; now farewell *Ferneze*:
And thus farre roundly goes the businesse:
Thus louing neither, will I liue with both,
Making a profit of my policie;
And he from whom my most aduantage comes, 2215
Shall be my friend.

2183 His . . till] Until *Wag.* 2212+S.D. Exit Governor *add.* *Reed*

This is the life we Iewes are vs'd to lead;
And reason too, for Christians doe the like.
Well, now about effecting this deuice:
First to surprize great *Selims* souldiers, 2220
And then to make prouision for the feast,
That at one instant all things may be done.
My policie detests preuention:
To what euent my secret purpose driues,
I know; and they shall witnesse with their liues. 2225
Exit.

Enter Calymath, Bashawes.

Caly. Thus haue we view'd the City, seene the sacke,
And caus'd the ruines to be new repair'd,
Which with our Bombards shot and Basiliske,
We rent in sunder at our entry:
And now I see the Scituation, 2230
And how secure this conquer'd Iland stands
Inuiron'd with the mediterranean Sea,
Strong contermin'd with other petty Iles;
And toward *Calabria*, back'd by *Sicily*,
Where *Siracusian Dionisius* reign'd, 2235
Two lofty Turrets that command the Towne.
I wonder how it could be conquer'd thus?

Enter a messenger.

Mess. From *Barabas*, *Malta's* Gouernor, I bring
A message vnto mighty *Calymath*;
Hearing his Soueraigne was bound for Sea, 2240
To saile to *Turkey*, to great *Ottamon*,
He humbly would intreat your Maiesty
To come and see his homely Citadell,
And banquet with him e're thou leau'st the Ile.
Caly. To banquet with him in his Citadell? 2245
I feare me, Messenger, to feast my traine
Within a Towne of warre so lately pillag'd,
Will be too costly and too troublesome:
Yet would I gladly visit *Barabas*,
For well has *Barabas* deseru'd of vs. 2250
Mess. *Selim*, for that, thus saith the Gouernor,
That he hath in store a Pearle so big,

2225 + Scene III *add. Cunn., Bull.*: Scene IV *Ellis* 2228 basilisks *Dyce etc.* 2233 contermin'd] countermured *conj. Deighton* 2235, 2236 *Transposed 1633*: *corr. Rob. etc.* 2235 Where *Rob. etc.*: When *1633, Reed, Coll.* 2252 in] in his *Dyce*[2] *etc.*

So precious, and withall so orient,
As be it valued but indifferently,
The price thereof will serue to entertaine 2255
Selim and all his souldiers for a month;
Therefore he humbly would intreat your Highnesse
Not to depart till he has feasted you.
Caly. I cannot feast my men in *Malta* wals,
Except he place his Tables in the streets. 2260
Mess. Know, *Selim,* that there is a monastery
Which standeth as an out-house to the Towne;
There will he banquet them, but thee at home,
With all thy *Bashawes* and braue followers.
Caly. Well, tell the Gouernor we grant his suit, 2265
Wee'll in this Summer Euening feast with him.
Mess. I shall, my Lord. *Exit.*
Caly. And now, bold *Bashawes,* let vs to our Tents,
And meditate how we may grace vs best
To solemnize our Gouernors great feast. *Exeunt.*

Enter Gouernor, Knights, Del-bosco.

Gov. In this, my Countrimen, be rul'd by me, 2271
Haue speciall care that no man sally forth
Till you shall heare a Culuerin discharg'd
By him that beares the Linstocke, kindled thus;
Then issue out and come to rescue me, 2275
For happily I shall be in distresse,
Or you released of this seruitude.
1 *Kni.* Rather then thus to liue as Turkish thrals,
What will we not aduenture?
Gov. On then, begone. 2280
Kni: Farewell graue Gouernor.

Enter ⟨Barabas⟩ with a Hammar aboue, very busie.

Bar. How stand the cords? How hang these hinges, fast?
Are all the Cranes and Pulleyes sure?
Serv. All fast.
Bar. Leaue nothing loose, all leueld to my mind. 2285
Why now I see that you haue Art indeed.
There, Carpenters, diuide that gold amongst you:

2270+Scene IV. *add. Cunn., Bull.*: Scene V. *Ellis* 2281+S.D. Exeunt, on one side, Knights and Martin Del Bosco; on the other, Ferneze *add. Dyce* Scene V. *add. Bull.*: Scene VI. *Ellis* Enter above Barabas *Dyce* busie] busy; and Carpenters *Dyce* 2287+S.D. Giving money *add. Dyce*

Goe swill in bowles of Sacke and Muscadine:
Downe to the Celler, taste of all my wines.
Carp. We shall, my Lord, and thanke you. 2290
Exeunt.
Bar. And if you like them, drinke your fill and dye:
For so I liue, perish may all the world.
Now *Selim-Calymath*, returne me word
That thou wilt come, and I am satisfied.
Now sirra, what, will he come? 2295

Enter Messenger.

Mess. He will; and has commanded all his men
To come ashore, and march through *Malta* streets,
That thou maist feast them in thy Citadell.
Bar. Then now are all things as my wish wud haue 'em,
There wanteth nothing but the Gouernors pelfe, 2300
And see he brings it:
Now, Gouernor, the summe.

Enter Gouernour.

Gou. With free consent a hundred thousand pounds.
Bar. Pounds saist thou, Gouernor? wel since it is no more
I'le satisfie my selfe with that; nay, keepe it still, 2305
For if I keepe not promise, trust not me.
And Gouernour, now partake my policy:
First, for his Army, they are sent before,
Enter'd the Monastery, and vnderneath
In seuerall places are field-pieces pitch'd, 2310
Bombards, whole Barrels full of Gunpowder,
That on the sudden shall disseuer it,
And batter all the stones about their eares,
Whence none can possibly escape aliue:
Now as for *Calymath* and his consorts, 2315
Here haue I made a dainty Gallery,
The floore whereof, this Cable being cut,
Doth fall asunder; so that it doth sinke
Into a deepe pit past recouery.
Here, hold that knife, and when thou seest he comes,
And with his Bashawes shall be blithely set, 2321
A warning-peece shall be shot off from the Tower,

2295 S.D. *follows* 2294 *Dyce* 2302 S.D. *follows* 2301 *Dyce etc.* 2307 partake] take *Cunn.*, *Bull.* 2320+S.D. Throws down a knife *add. Dyce* 2322 shot off] shot *conj. Dyce*

To giue thee knowledge when to cut the cord,
And fire the house; say, will not this be braue?
Gov. Oh excellent! here, hold thee, *Barabas,* 2325
I trust thy word, take what I promis'd thee.
Bar. No, Gouernor, I'le satisfie thee first,
Thou shalt not liue in doubt of any thing.
Stand close, for here they come: why, is not this
A kingly kinde of trade to purchase Townes 2330
By treachery, and sell 'em by deceit?
Now tell me, worldlings, vnderneath the sunne,
If greater falshood euer has bin done.

Enter Calymath and Bashawes.

Caly. Come, my Companion-Bashawes, see I pray
How busie *Barrabas* is there aboue 2335
To entertaine vs in his Gallery;
Let vs salute him. Saue thee, *Barabas.*
Bar. Welcome great *Calymath.*
Gov. How the slaue jeeres at him?
Bar. Will't please thee, mighty *Selim-Calymath,* 2340
To ascend our homely stayres?
Caly. I, *Barabas,* come Bashawes, attend.
Gov. Stay, *Calymath*;
For I will shew thee greater curtesie
Then *Barabas* would haue affoorded thee. 2345
Kni. Sound a charge there.
{*A charge, the cable cut,*
{*A Caldron discouered.*
Cal. How now, what means this?
Bar. Helpe, helpe me, Christians, helpe.
Gov. See *Calymath,* this was deuis'd for thee.
Caly. Treason, treason! Bashawes, flye. 2350
Gov. No, *Selim,* doe not flye;
See his end first, and flye then if thou canst.
Bar. Oh helpe me, *Selim,* helpe me, Christians.
Gouernour, why stand you all so pittilesse?
Gov. Should I in pitty of thy plaints or thee, 2355
Accursed *Barabas,* base Iew, relent?

2329 *After* come S.D. Ferneze retires *add. Dyce* 2332 sun *Reed etc.*: summe *1633* 2339+S.D. Aside *add. Dyce* 2342 attend] ascend *Dyce, Wag.* 2346 *Prefix* Knight [within] *Dyce* 2346+ S.D. A charge sounded within: Ferneze cuts the cord; the floor of the gallery gives way, and Barabas falls into a caldron placed in a pit *Dyce* S.D. Enter Knights and Martin Del Bosco *add. Dyce*

No, thus I'le see thy treachery repaid,
But wish thou hadst behau'd thee otherwise.
Bar. You will not helpe me then?
Gov. No, villaine, no. 2360
Bar. And villaines, know you cannot helpe me now.
Then *Barabas* breath forth thy latest fate,
And in the fury of thy torments, striue
To end thy life with resolution:
Know, Gouernor, 'twas I that slew thy sonne; 2365
I fram'd the challenge that did make them meet:
Know, *Calymath,* I aym'd thy ouerthrow,
And had I but escap'd this stratagem,
I would haue brought confusion on you all,
Damn'd Christians, dogges, and Turkish Infidels; 2370
But now begins the extremity of heat
To pinch me with intolerable pangs:
Dye life, flye soule, tongue curse thy fill and dye.
Caly. Tell me, you Christians, what doth this portend?
Gov. This traine he laid to haue intrap'd thy life; 2375
Now *Selim* note the vnhallowed deeds of Iewes:
Thus he determin'd to haue handled thee,
But I haue rather chose to saue thy life.
Caly. Was this the banquet he prepar'd for vs?
Let's hence, lest further mischiefe be pretended. 2380
Gov. Nay, *Selim,* stay, for since we haue thee here,
We will not let thee part so suddenly:
Besides, if we should let thee goe, all's one,
For with thy Gallyes couldst thou not get hence,
Without fresh men to rigge and furnish them. 2385
Caly. Tush, Gouernor, take thou no care for that,
My men are all aboord,
And doe attend my comming there by this.
Gov. Why, hardst thou not the trumpet sound a charge?
Caly. Yes, what of that? 2390
Gov. Why, then the house was fir'd,
Blowne vp, and all thy souldiers massacred.
Caly. Oh monstrous treason!
Gov. A Iewes curtesie:
For he that did by treason worke our fall, 2395
By treason hath deliuered thee to vs:
Know therefore, till thy father hath made good
The ruines done to *Malta* and to vs,

2362 fate] hate *Cunn.*, *Bull.* 2370 Christian *Dyce*, *Cunn.*, *Wag.* 2373+S.D. Dies *add. Reed*

Thou canst not part : for *Malta* shall be freed.
Or *Selim* ne're returne to *Ottamen.* 2400
Caly. Nay rather, Christians, let me goe to Turkey,
In person there to meditate your peace ;
To keepe me here will nought aduantage you.
Gov. Content thee, *Calymath*, here thou must stay,
And liue in *Malta* prisoner ; for come all the world 2405
To rescue thee, so will we guard vs now,
As sooner shall they drinke the Ocean dry,
Then conquer *Malta*, or endanger vs.
So march away, and let due praise be giuen
Neither to Fate nor Fortune, but to Heauen. 2410

FINIS.

2402 meditate] mediate *conj. Coll., Dyce etc.* 2405 in Malta] here *Wag.* all *Reed etc.* : call *1633* 2410+S.D. Exeunt *add. Dyce*

EDWARD II

Date. *Edward II* is generally agreed to be the maturest and, with the possible exception of the *Massacre at Paris*, the latest of Marlowe's plays. There is, however, very little external evidence by which to determine the precise year of composition. Henslowe makes no mention of the acting of this piece, as it was in the possession of a rival company—the Earl of Pembroke's—to which we may conclude that Marlowe transferred his services after the completion of the *Jew of Malta* (? 1590), the latter play having been certainly, like its predecessors, *Tamburlaine* and *Doctor Faustus*, one of Henslowe's repertoire.[1]

On July 6, 1593, one month after Marlowe's death, William Jones registered the play under the following designation: 'A booke Intituled *The troublesom Reign and Lamentable Death of* EDWARD *the* SECOND, *king of England, with the tragicall fall of proud* MORTYMER.' As the editions of Jones, the earliest of which probably belongs to 1593,[2] declare on the title-page that the play had been 'sondry times publiquely acted in the honorable Cittie of London, By the right honorable the Earle of Pembroke his Seruants,'[3] we must assume, what in any case would be probable, that the tragedy had been known on the stage for a considerable time before it came into the hands of the printer. The year 1591, or the early part of 1592, seems then the most likely date for the completion of *Edward II* and its first theatrical presentation.

Editions. *Edward II* survives in quarto editions, dated 1594, 1598, 1612, 1622, the first two having been published by William Jones. I have elsewhere[4] given my reasons

[1] If the *Massacre at Paris* is later than *Edward II*, the poet would seem to have renewed his connexion with Henslowe, for the *Diary* records the acting of the former tragedy as a 'new play' on January 30, 1593.

[2] Cf. *infra*.

[3] Quoted from the MS. title-page of ed. ?1593. The statement is repeated on the title-pages of 1594, 1598, and 1612.

[4] Cf. *Modern Language Notes*, March, 1909.

for believing that Jones had already, before the end of the year 1593, issued a version of the play, of which no copy is now known to exist. An eighteenth-century manuscript in the South Kensington Museum purports, however, to reproduce the title-page and the first seventy lines of this edition. The quarto of 1594 has itself been known only during the last two generations, and its text, superior in a great many details to that of 1598, is here for the first time reprinted. Two copies of this 1594 edition have so far been discovered, of which my text follows that preserved in the *Landesbibliothek* of Cassel, Germany.

Concerning the stage history of *Edward II* there appears to be no information except that given on the title-pages of the early editions, namely, that the play was acted by the Earl of Pembroke's men, and, as we learn from the edition of 1622, that it was revived 'by the late Queenes Maiesties Seruants at the Red Bull in S. Johns streete'.[1] Henslowe's *Diary* makes casual mention of two lost plays, which may or may not have borne some relation to ours. In March, 1588/9 he notes the payment of £6 to the dramatists Chettle and Porter for a work called 'the Spencers', and in September, 1602, he expends £6 18*s*. on properties for the 'playe of mortymore'.

Text. Marlowe's authorship of *Edward II* is stated on all the early title-pages and has never been questioned. Publication followed so close on composition in the case of this play that there is no reason to suspect the presence of alien matter, and the text is probably purer than that of any other of Marlowe's dramatic works, though small printers' errors are common enough in the last three editions. As the best preserved of the poet's tragedies, and much the most perfect in all matters of technical skill; as the first considerable history play in the English language; and as the textbook from which Shakespeare undoubtedly learned many lessons of dramatic art, later to be used in *Richard II* and in *Henry IV*, this play of *Edward II* makes a special appeal to the student of dramatic evolution. It is no injustice to these high merits to add that many lovers of Marlowe will turn rather less often to *Edward II* than to *Tamburlaine*, *Doctor Faustus*, or *Hero and Leander*. To the very end there appears in Marlowe's writing no sign

[1] Queen Anne's men played at the Red Bull between 1609 and the death of their patroness in 1619. Cf. Fleay, *History of the London Stage*, pp. 191, 270.

of league or compromise between the hostile forces of lyric and dramatic inspiration. In the earlier plays dramatic fitness is often sacrificed to the craving for poetic self-expression. In *Edward II* the attention to stage requirements and dramatic structure tends frequently to banish some of the subtler and sweeter qualities of Marlowe's verse; or if the lyric vein finds here and there an outlet, it bursts forth as unsubdued as ever, throwing off the restrictions of dramatic propriety and launching into declamation as eloquent and as uncritical as that of *Tamburlaine* itself. In his last great tragedy Marlowe shows no more than in his first an ability to fuse these two main elements of dramatic poetry. The incapacity to do so is doubtless fundamental, and it explains better than anything else why Marlowe's genius could never have developed as that of Shakespeare did.

Source. The main source of *Edward II* is Holinshed's Chronicle, from which Marlowe has selected the material for his tragedy with the imaginative freedom characteristic of Shakespeare's use of the same historian. Chronological accuracy is not attempted, but the true meaning of history is faithfully represented. The Scottish jig (ll. 990–997) is derived from the Chronicles of Fabyan, and one or two other incidents, unrecorded in Holinshed, have been traced to the General Chronicle of John Stowe. The relation of the play to each of these three works has been worked out with some elaborateness by C. Tzschaschel[1] in a Halle dissertation, and the same general results are recorded independently in the introductions to the editions of Tancock and Fleay.

[1] *Marlowe's Edward II und seine Quellen*, 1902.

The troublesome

raigne and lamentable death of Edward *the second,* King *of* England: with the tragicall *fall of proud* Mortimer:

As it was sundrie times publiquely acted *in the honourable citie of London, by the* right honourable the Earle of Pembrooke *his seruants.*

Written by Chri. Marlow *Gent.*

Imprinted at London for *William Iones,*
dwelling neere Holbourne conduit at the
signe of the Gunne. 1594

?1593 = Readings of MS. fragment in South Kensington Museum (6209), purporting to represent edition of that year.
1594 = Quarto edition of that year.
1598 = ,, ,, ,, ,, ,,
1612 = ,, ,, ,, ,, ,,
1622 = ,, ,, ,, ,, ,,
Dod.[1] = Text oi play in Dodsley's *Old Plays*, ed. 1744, vol. ii.
Dod.[2] = ,, ,, ,, ,, ed. 1780, vol. ii.
Dod.[3] = ,, ,, ,, ,, ed. 1825, vol. ii.
ed. 1810 = ,, ,, *Ancient British Drama*, vol. i.
Dilke = ,, ,, *Old English Plays*, 1814, 1815.
Rob. = Robinson's edition of Marlowe, 1826.
Dyce { *Dyce*[1] = Dyce's first ,, ,, 1850.
Dyce { *Dyce*[2] = Dyce's revised ,, ,, 1858, etc.
Cunn. = Cunningham's ,, ,, 1870, etc.
Keltie. = Text of the play in *Works of the British Dramatists*, 1870.
Wag. = W. Wagner's edition of the play, 1871.
Fleay = F. G. F.'s ,, ,, 1877.
Tan. = Tancock's ,, ,, 1879, etc.
Bull. = Bullen's edition of Marlowe, 1885.
Verity = *Temple Dramatists'* edition of the play, 1896.
T. B. = The present editor.
Broughton = J. B's conjectures in copy of *Rob.* (Brit. Mus. 11771 d).
Coll. = J. P. Collier's conjectures in copy of *Dyce*[1] (Brit. Mus. 11771 bbb 6).

⟨DRAMATIS PERSONÆ

KING EDWARD THE SECOND.
PRINCE EDWARD, his son, afterwards KING EDWARD THE THIRD.
KENT, brother to KING EDWARD THE SECOND.
GAVESTON.
ARCHBISHOP OF CANTERBURY
BISHOP OF COVENTRY.
BISHOP OF WINCHESTER.
WARWICK.
LANCASTER.
PEMBROKE.
ARUNDEL.
LEICESTER.
BERKELEY (spelled 'Bartley').
MORTIMER the elder.
MORTIMER the younger, his nephew.
SPENSER the elder.
SPENSER the younger, his son.
BALDOCK.
BEAUMONT.
TRUSSEL.
GURNEY.
MATREVIS.
LIGHTBORN.
SIR JOHN OF HAINAULT.
LEVUNE.
RICE AP HOWEL.
Abbot.
Monks.
Heralds.
Lords, Poor Men, JAMES, Mower, Champion, Messengers, Soldiers, and Attendants.
QUEEN ISABELLA, wife to KING EDWARD THE SECOND.
Niece to KING EDWARD THE SECOND, daughter to the DUKE OF GLOUCESTER.
Ladies.⟩[1]

The troublesome raigne and lamentable death of Edward the second, king of England : with the tragicall fall of proud Mortimer.

Enter Gauestone reading on a letter that was brought him from the king.

My father is deceast, come *Gaueston,*
And share the kingdom with thy deerest friend.
Ah words that make me surfet with delight :
What greater blisse can hap to *Gaueston,*
Then liue and be the fauorit of a king ?
Sweete prince I come, these these thy amorous lines,

[1] *Add. Dyce.*

Heading The troublesome . . Mortimer *om. 1598 etc.* Act I. Scene I, *add. Rob.* S.D. reading on] reading of ?*1593* 6 these these] these ?*1593*

Might haue enforst me to haue swum from France,
And like *Leander* gaspt vpon the sande,
So thou wouldst smile and take me in thy armes.
The sight of London to my exiled eyes, 10
Is as Elizium to a new come soule,
Not that I loue the citie or the men,
But that it harbors him I hold so deare,
The king, vpon whose bosome let me die,
And with the world be still at enmitie: 15
What neede the artick people loue star-light,
To whom the sunne shines both by day and night?
Farewell base stooping to the lordly peeres,
My knee shall bowe to none but to the king.
As for the multitude that are but sparkes, 20
Rakt vp in embers of their pouertie,
Tanti: Ile faune first on the winde,
That glaunceth at my lips and flieth away:
But how now, what are these?

Enter three poore men.

Poore men. Such as desire your worships seruice. 25
Gauest. What canst thou doe?
1. *poore.* I can ride.
Gauest. But I haue no horses. What art thou?
2. *poore.* A traueller.
Gauest. Let me see, thou wouldst do well 30
To waite at my trencher, & tell me lies at dinner time,
And as I like your discoursing, ile haue you.
And what art thou?
3. *poore.* A souldier, that hath seru'd against the Scot.
Gauest. Why, there are hospitals for such as you, 35
I haue no warre, and therefore sir be gone.
Sold. Farewell, and perish by a souldiers hand,
That wouldst reward them with an hospitall.
Gau. I, I, these wordes of his moue me as much,
As if a Goose should play the Porpintine, 40
And dart her plumes, thinking to pierce my brest:
But yet it is no paine to speake men faire,
Ile flatter these, and make them liue in hope.

9 thy *1594*: thine *?1593, 1598 etc.* 14 die] lie *ed. 1810 etc. exc. Keltie, Fleay, Bull.* 19 knees *1622* 20 As] Its *?1593* 21 Rakt] bakt *?1593* 22 tantum *?1593* fawn *Rob. etc.*: fanne *Qq* 28 horse *1598 etc.* 31 time *om. ?1593* 40 Porpintine *1594, ?1593*: Porcupine *1598 etc.* 41 dart] eate *?1593* 43 these] them *?1593* 43+S.D. Aside *add. Dyce*

You know that I came lately out of France,
And yet I haue not viewd my Lord the king, 45
If I speed well, ile entertaine you all.
Omnes. We thanke your worship.
Gauest. I haue some busines, leaue me to my selfe.
Omnes. We will wait heere about the court. *Exeunt.*
Gauest. Do: these are not men for me, 50
I must haue wanton Poets, pleasant wits,
Musitians, that with touching of a string
May draw the pliant king which way I please:
Musicke and poetrie is his delight,
Therefore ile haue Italian maskes by night, 55
Sweete speeches, comedies, and pleasing showes,
And in the day when he shall walke abroad,
Like *Syluan* Nimphes my pages shall be clad,
My men like Satyres grazing on the lawnes,
Shall with their Goate feete daunce an antick hay. 60
Sometime a louelie boye in *Dians* shape,
With haire that gilds the water as it glides,
Crownets of pearle about his naked armes,
And in his sportfull hands an Oliue tree,
To hide those parts which men delight to see, 65
Shall bathe him in a spring, and there hard by,
One like *Actæon* peeping through the groue,
Shall by the angrie goddesse be transformde,
And running in the likenes of an Hart,
By yelping hounds puld downe, and seeme to die, 70
Such things as these best please his maiestie,
My lord. Heere comes the king and the nobles
From the parlament, ile stand aside.

Enter the King, Lancaster, Mortimer senior, Mortimer iunior, Edmund Earle of Kent, Guie Earle of Warwicke, &c

Edward. Lancaster.
Lancast. My Lorde. 75
Gauest. That Earle of Lancaster do I abhorre.
Edw. Will you not graunt me this? in spight of them

49 We] I ?*1593* 54 is] are ?*1593* 58 Syluan ?*1593*, *Dod.*, *Dyce*, *Cunn.*: Siluian *1594–1622* 60 Goates ?*1593* an] the *1598 etc.* 61 Sometimes *Dod.* 65 which] as ?*1593* 70 and] shall *Dod. etc. exc. Fleay*, *Bull.* 72 My . . comes] Here comes *Dod.*[1]: By'r lord! here comes *Rob.*, *Cunn.*, *Wag.*: But soft! here comes *conj. Broughton*: Here comes my lord *Dyce*, *Fleay*, *Tan.*, *Bull.* and] and here *Bull.* 73+S.D. Retires *add. Dyce* 76+S.D. Aside *add. Dyce*

Ile haue my will, and these two *Mortimers*,
That crosse me thus, shall know I am displeasd.
Mor. se. If you loue vs my lord, hate *Gaueston*. 80
Gauest. That villaine *Mortimer*, ile be his death.
Mor. iu. Mine vnckle heere, this Earle, & I my selfe,
Were sworne to your father at his death,
That he should nere returne into the realme:
And know my lord, ere I will breake my oath, 85
This sword of mine that should offend your foes,
Shall sleepe within the scabberd at thy neede,
And vnderneath thy banners march who will,
For *Mortimer* will hang his armor vp.
Gauest. Mort dieu. 90
Edw. Well *Mortimer*, ile make thee rue these words,
Beseemes it thee to contradict thy king?
Frownst thou thereat, aspiring Lancaster?
The sworde shall plane the furrowes of thy browes,
And hew these knees that now are growne so stiffe. 95
I will haue *Gaueston*, and you shall know,
What danger tis to stand against your king.
Gauest. Well doone, *Ned*.
Lan. My lord, why do you thus incense your peeres,
That naturally would loue and honour you: 100
But for that base and obscure *Gaueston*,
Foure Earldomes haue I besides Lancaster,
Darbie, Salsburie, Lincolne, Leicester,
These will I sell to giue my souldiers paye,
Ere *Gaueston* shall stay within the realme, 105
Therefore if he be come, expell him straight.
Edm. Barons & Earls, your pride hath made me mute,
But now ile speake, and to the proofe I hope:
I do remember in my fathers dayes,
Lord *Percie* of the North being highly mou'd, 110
Brau'd *Mowberie* in presence of the king,
For which, had not his highnes lou'd him well,
He should haue lost his head, but with his looke,
The vndaunted spirit of *Percie* was appeasd,
And *Mowberie* and he were reconcild: 115
Yet dare you braue the king vnto his face.
Brother reuenge it, and let these their heads,
Preach vpon poles for trespasse of their tongues.
Warwicke. O our heads.

81 + S.D. Aside *add. Dyce* 83 to] unto *Dod., ed. 1810, Cunn.*
90 + S.D. Aside *add. Dyce* 98 + S.D. Aside *add. Dyce*

Edw. I yours, and therefore I would wish you graunt. 120
Warw. Bridle thy anger, gentle *Mortimer*,
Mor. iu. I cannot, nor I will not, I must speake,
Cosin, our hands I hope shall fence our heads,
And strike off his that makes you threaten vs.
Come vnckle, let vs leaue the brainsick king, 125
And henceforth parle with our naked swords.
Mor. se. Wilshire hath men enough to saue our heads.
Warw. All Warwickshire will loue him for my sake.
Lanc. And Northward *Gaueston* hath many friends.
Adew my Lord, and either change your minde, 130
Or looke to see the throne where you should sit,
To floate in bloud, and at thy wanton head,
The glozing head of thy base minion throwne.

Exeunt Nobiles.

Edw. I cannot brooke these hautie menaces:
Am I a king and must be ouer rulde? 135
Brother displaie my ensignes in the field,
Ile bandie with the Barons and the Earles,
And eyther die, or liue with *Gaueston*.
Gau. I can no longer keepe me from my lord.
Edw. What *Gaueston*, welcome: kis not my hand, 140
Embrace me *Gaueston* as I do thee:
Why shouldst thou kneele, knowest thou not who I am?
Thy friend, thy selfe, another *Gaueston*.
Not *Hilas* was more mourned of *Hercules*,
Then thou hast beene of me since thy exile. 145
Gau. And since I went from hence, no soule in hell
Hath felt more torment then poore *Gaueston*.
Edw. I know it, brother welcome home my friend.
Now let the treacherous *Mortimers* conspire,
And that high minded earle of Lancaster: 150
I haue my wish, in that I ioy thy sight,
And sooner shall the sea orewhelme my land,
Then beare the ship that shall transport thee hence:
I heere create thee Lord high Chamberlaine,
Cheefe Secretarie to the state and me, 155
Earle of Cornewall, king and lord of Man.

128 loue] leave *Dyce, Cunn., Wag.* 29 Gaueston] Lancaster *Rob., Dyce, Cunn., Wag.* 133 S.D. Nobiles] Nobles *1612 etc.* 139+S.D. Comes forward *add. Dyce* 144 of *1594, Rob., Cunn., Bull., Fleay, Wag.*: for *1598, Dod., ed. 1810*: for of *1612, 1622, Dyce, Tan.*

Gauest. My lord, these titles far exceed my worth.
Kent. Brother, the least of these may well suffice
For one of greater birth then *Gaueston.*
Edw. Cease brother, for I cannot brooke these words. 160
Thy woorth sweet friend is far aboue my guifts,
Therefore to equall it receiue my hart.
If for these dignities thou be enuied,
Ile giue thee more, for but to honour thee,
Is *Edward* pleazd with kinglie regiment. 165
Fearst thou thy person ? thou shalt haue a guard :
Wants thou gold ? go to my treasurie,
Wouldst thou be loude and fearde ? receiue my seale,
Saue or condemne, and in our name commaund,
What so thy minde affectes or fancie likes. 170
Gaue. It shall suffice me to enioy your loue,
Which whiles I haue, I thinke my selfe as great,
As *Cæsar* riding in the Romaine streete,
With captiue kings at his triumphant Carre.

Enter the Bishop of Couentrie.

Edw. Whether goes my Lord of Couentrie so fast ? 175
Bish. To celebrate your fathers exequies,
But is that wicked *Gaueston* returnd ?
Edw. I priest, and liues to be reuengd on thee,
That wert the onely cause of his exile.
Gaue. Tis true, and but for reuerence of these robes, 180
Thou shouldst not plod one foote beyond this place.
Bish. I did no more then I was bound to do,
And *Gaueston* vnlesse thou be reclaimd,
As then I did incense the parlement,
So will I now, and thou shalt back to France. 185
Gaue. Sauing your reuerence, you must pardon me.
Edw. Throwe of his golden miter, rend his stole,
And in the channell christen him anew.
Kent. Ah brother, lay not violent hands on him,
For heele complaine vnto the sea of Rome. 190
Gaue. Let him complaine vnto the sea of hell,
Ile be reuengd on him for my exile.
Edw. No, spare his life, but seaze vpon his goods,
Be thou lord bishop, and receiue his rents,
And make him serue thee as thy chaplaine. 195
I giue him thee, here vse him as thou wilt.
Gaue. He shall to prison, and there die in boults.
Edw. I, to the tower, the fleete, or where thou wilt.

Bish. For this offence be thou accurst of God.
Edw. Whose there ? conueie this priest to the tower. 200
Bish. True, true.
Edw. But in the meane time *Gaueston* away,
And take possession of his house and goods.
Come follow me, and thou shalt haue my guarde,
To see it done, and bring thee safe againe. 205
Gaue. What should a priest do with so faire a house ?
A prison may beseeme his holinesse.

Enter both the Mortimers, Warwicke, and Lancaster.

War. Tis true, the Bishop is in the tower,
And goods and body giuen to *Gaueston.*
Lan. What ? will they tyrannize vpon the Church ? 210
Ah wicked king, accurssed *Gaueston,*
This ground which is corrupted with their steps,
Shall be their timeles sepulcher, or mine.
Mor. iu. Wel, let that peeuish Frenchman guard him sure.
Vnlesse his brest be sword proofe he shall die. 215
Mor. se. How now, why droops the earle of Lancaster ?
Mor. iu. Wherfore is *Guy* of Warwicke discontent ?
Lan. That villaine *Gaueston* is made an Earle.
Mortim. sen. An Earle !
War. I, and besides, lord Chamberlaine of the realme, 220
And secretary to, and lord of Man.
Mor. se. We may not, nor we will not suffer this.
Mor. iu. Why post we not from hence to leuie men ?
Lan. My lord of Cornewall now at euery worde,
And happie is the man, whom he vouchsafes 225
For vailing of his bonnet one good looke.
Thus arme in arme, the king and he dooth marche :
Nay more, the guarde vpon his lordship waites :
And all the court begins to flatter him.
War. Thus leaning on the shoulder of the king, 230
He nods, and scornes, and smiles at those that passe.
Mor. se. Doth no man take exceptions at the slaue ?
Lan. All stomack him, but none dare speake a word.
Mor. iu. Ah that bewraies their basenes, Lancaster,
Were all the Earles and Barons of my minde, 235
We'de hale him from the bosome of the king,

200 to] unto *conj. Coll.* 201 True, true] Do, do *Dod., Rob.* : Prut, prut *conj. Dyce* : Tut, tut *conj. Coll.* 207 may] may best *1612, 1622* 207 + S.D. Exeunt *add. Dyce* Scene II *add. Rob.* 236 We'd *Rob. etc.* : Weele *Qq*

And at the court gate hang the pessant vp,
Who swolne with venome of ambitious pride,
Will be the ruine of the realme and vs.

Enter the Bishop of Canterburie.

War. Here comes my lord of Canterburies grace. 240
Lan. His countenance bewraies he is displeasd.
Bish. First were his sacred garments rent and torne,
Then laide they violent hands vpon him next,
Himselfe imprisoned, and his goods asceasd.
This certifie the Pope, away, take horsse. 245
Lan. My lord, will you take armes against the king?
Bish. What neede I, God himselfe is vp in armes,
When violence is offered to the church.
Mor. iu. Then wil you ioine with vs that be his peeres
To banish or behead that *Gaueston*? 250
Bish. What els my lords, for it concernes me neere,
The Bishoprick of Couentrie is his.

Enter the Queene.

Mor. iu. Madam, whether walks your maiestie so fast?
Que. Vnto the forrest, gentle *Mortimer*,
To liue in greefe and balefull discontent, 255
For now my lord the king regardes me not,
But dotes vpon the loue of *Gaueston*.
He claps his cheekes, and hanges about his neck,
Smiles in his face, and whispers in his eares,
And when I come, he frownes, as who should say, 260
Go whether thou wilt seeing I haue Gaueston.
Mor. se. Is it not straunge, that he is thus bewitcht?
Mor. iu. Madam, returne vnto the court againe:
That slie inueigling Frenchman weele exile,
Or lose our liues: and yet ere that day come, 265
The king shall lose his crowne, for we haue power,
And courage to, to be reuengde at full.
Bish. But yet lift not your swords against the king.
Lan. No, but weele lift *Gaueston* from hence.
War. And war must be the meanes, or heele stay stil.
Queen. Then let him stay, for rather then my lord 271
Shall be opprest by ciuill mutinies,
I wil endure a melancholie life,
And let him frollick with his minion.

239 S.D. Bishop] Archbishop *Dod.*[2] *etc.* (*so passim*) 272 by] with *1598 etc.*

Bish. My lords, to eaze all this, but heare me speake : 275
We and the rest that are his counsellers,
Will meete, and with a generall consent
Confirme his banishment with our handes and seales.
Lan. What we confirme the king will frustrate.
Mor. iu. Then may we lawfully reuolt from him. 280
War. But say my lord, where shall this meeting bee ?
Bish. At the new temple.
Mor. iu. Content :
And in the meane time ile intreat you all,
To crosse to Lambeth, and there stay with me. 285
Lan. Come then, lets away.
Mor. iu. Madam farewell.
Qu. Farewell sweet *Mortimer*, and for my sake,
Forbeare to leuie armes against the king.
Mor. iu. I, if words will serue, if not, I must. 290

Enter Gaueston *and the earle of Kent.*

Gau. *Edmund* the mightie prince of Lancaster,
That hath more earldomes then an asse can beare,
And both the *Mortimers* two goodly men,
With *Guie* of Warwick that redoubted knight,
Are gone towards Lambeth, there let them remaine. 295
Exeunt.

Enter Nobiles.

Lan. Here is the forme of *Gauestons* exile :
May it please your lordship to subscribe your name.
Bish. Giue me the paper.
Lan. Quick quick my lorde, I long to write my name.
War. But I long more to see him banisht hence. 300
Mor. iu. The name of *Mortimer* shall fright the king,
Vnlesse he be declinde from that base pesant.

Enter the King and Gaueston.

Edw. What ? are you mou'd that *Gaueston* sits heere ?
It is our pleasure, we will haue it so.
Lan. Your grace doth wel to place him by your side, 305
For no where else the new earle is so safe.

290 + Scene III. *add. Rob.* 295 + Scene IV. *add. Rob.* S.D. Nobiles] Nobles *1612 etc.* 302 S.D. Enter King Edward, Gaveston and Kent *Dyce*

Mor. se. What man of noble birth can brooke this sight ?
Quam male conueniunt :
See what a scornfull looke the pesant casts.
Penb. Can kinglie Lions fawne on creeping Ants ? 310
War. Ignoble vassaile that like *Phaeton,*
Aspir'st vnto the guidance of the sunne.
Mor. iu. Their downfall is at hand, their forces downe,
We will not thus be facst and ouerpeerd.
Edw. Lay hands on that traitor *Mortimer.* 315
Mor. se. Lay hands on that traitor *Gaueston.*
Kent. Is this the dutie that you owe your king ?
War. We know our duties, let him know his peeres.
Edw. Whether will you beare him ? stay or ye shall die.
Mor. se. We are no traitors, therefore threaten not. 320
Gau. No, threaten not my lord, but pay them home.
Were I a king—
Mor. iu. Thou villaine, wherfore talkes thou of a king,
That hardly art a gentleman by birth ?
Edw. Were he a peasant, being my minion, 325
Ile make the prowdest of you stoope to him.
Lan. My lord, you may not thus disparage vs,
Away I say with hatefull *Gaueston.*
Mort. se. And with the earle of Kent that fauors him.
Edw. Nay, then lay violent hands vpon your king, 330
Here *Mortimer*, sit thou in *Edwards* throne,
Warwicke and *Lancaster*, weare you my crowne.
Was euer king thus ouerrulde as I ?
Lan. Learne then to rule vs better and the realme.
Mor. iu. What we haue done, our hart bloud shall maintaine. 335
War. Think you that we can brooke this vpstart pride ?
Edw. Anger and wrathfull furie stops my speech.
Bish. Why are you moou'd, be patient my lord,
And see what we your councellers haue done.
Mor. iu. My lords, now let vs all be resolute, 340
And either haue our wils, or lose our liues.
Edw. Meete you for this, proud ouerdaring peeres ?
Ere my sweete *Gaueston* shall part from me,
This Ile shall fleete vpon the Ocean,
And wander to the vnfrequented Inde. 345
Bish. You know that I am legate to the Pope,

315 on] upon *conj. Coll.* 329+S.D. Attendants remove Gaveston and Kent *add. Dyce*

On your allegeance to the sea of Rome,
Subscribe as we haue done to his exile.
Mor. iu. Curse him, if he refuse, and then may we
Depose him and elect an other king. 350
Edw. I, there it goes, but yet I will not yeeld,
Curse me, depose me, doe the worst you can.
Lan. Then linger not my lord, but do it straight.
Bish. Remember how the Bishop was abusde,
Either banish him that was the cause thereof, 355
Or I will presentlie discharge these lords
Of dutie and allegeance due to thee.
Edw. It bootes me not to threat, I must speake faire,
The Legate of the Pope will be obayd:
My lord, you shalbe Chauncellor of the realme, 360
Thou Lancaster, high admirall of our fleete,
Yong *Mortimer* and his vnckle shalbe earles,
And you lord Warwick, president of the North,
And thou of Wales: if this content you not,
Make seuerall kingdomes of this monarchie, 365
And share it equally amongst you all,
So I may haue some nooke or corner left,
To frolike with my deerest *Gaueston.*
Bish. Nothing shall alter vs, wee are resolu'd.
Lan. Come, come, subscribe. 370
Mor. iu. Why should you loue him, whome the world hates so?
Edw. Because he loues me more then all the world;
Ah none but rude and sauage minded men,
Would seeke the ruine of my *Gaueston,*
You that be noble borne should pitie him. 375
Warwicke. You that are princely borne should shake him off,
For shame subscribe, and let the lowne depart.
Mor. se. Vrge him, my lord.
Bish. Are you content to banish him the realme?
Edw. I see I must, and therefore am content. 380
In steede of inke, ile write it with my teares.
Mor. iu. The king is loue-sick for his minion.
Edw. Tis done, and now accursed hand fall off.
Lan. Giue it me, ile haue it published in the streetes.
Mor. iu. Ile see him presently dispatched away. 385
Bish. Now is my heart at ease.

359+S.D. Aside *add. Dyce* 360 you] ye *1612, 1622* 375 be] are *1612, 1622* 381+S.D. Subscribes *add. Dyce*

Warw. And so is mine.
Penb. This will be good newes to the common sort.
Mor. se. Be it or no, he shall not linger here.
Exeunt Nobiles.
Edw. How fast they run to banish him I loue, 390
They would not stir, were it to do me good :
Why should a king be subiect to a priest ?
Proud Rome, that hatchest such imperiall groomes,
For these thy superstitious taperlights,
Wherewith thy antichristian churches blaze, 395
Ile fire thy crased buildings, and enforce
The papall towers to kisse the lowlie ground,
With slaughtered priests make *Tibers* channell swell,
And bankes raisd higher with their sepulchers :
As for the peeres that backe the cleargie thus, 400
If I be king, not one of them shall liue.

Enter Gaueston.

Gau. My lord, I heare it whispered euery where,
That I am banishd, and must flie the land.
Edw. Tis true sweete *Gaueston*, oh were it false.
The Legate of the Pope will haue it so, 405
And thou must hence, or I shall be deposd,
But I will raigne to be reueng'd of them,
And therefore sweete friend, take it patiently,
Liue where thou wilt, ile send thee gould enough,
And long thou shalt not stay, or if thou doost, 410
Ile come to thee, my loue shall neare decline.
Gaue. Is all my hope turnd to this hell of greefe.
Edw. Rend not my hart with thy too piercing words
Thou from this land, I from my selfe am banisht.
Gau. To go from hence, greeues not poore *Gaueston*, 415
But to forsake you, in whose gratious lookes
The blessednes of *Gaueston* remaines,
For no where else seekes he felicitie.
Edw. And onely this torments my wretched soule,
That whether I will or no thou must depart : 420
Be gouernour of Ireland in my stead,
And there abide till fortune call thee home.
Here take my picture, and let me weare thine.

389 S.D. Nobles *1612 etc.* 394 For] With *Dod.*,[1] *Rob.*, *Dyce*, *Cunn.* 397 The] Thy *Rob.* 398 make *Dod.*,[1] *Rob. etc.* : may *Qq* 399 raisd *Qq*, *Dyce*, *Bull.* : raise *Dod.*, *Rob.* : rise *ed. 1810*, *Cunn.*, *Fleay* 423+S.D. They exchange pictures *add. Dyce*

O might I keepe thee heere, as I doe this,
Happie were I, but now most miserable. 425
Gauest. Tis something to be pitied of a king.
Edw. Thou shalt not hence, ile hide thee *Gaueston.*
Gau. I shal be found, and then twil greeue me more.
Edwa. Kinde wordes, and mutuall talke, makes our greefe greater.
Therefore with dum imbracement let vs part. 430
Stay *Gaueston,* I cannot leaue thee thus.
Gau. For euery looke, my lord drops downe a teare,
Seeing I must go, do not renew my sorrow.
Edwa. The time is little that thou hast to stay,
And therefore giue me leaue to looke my fill, 435
But come sweete friend, ile beare thee on thy way.
Gau. The peeres will frowne.
Edw. I passe not for their anger, come lets go,
O that we might as well returne as goe.

Enter Edmund and Queen Isabell.

Qu. Whether goes my lord? 440
Edw. Fawne not on me French strumpet, get thee gone.
Qu. On whom but on my husband should I fawne?
Gau. On *Mortimer,* with whom vngentle Queene—
I say no more, iudge you the rest my lord.
Qu. In saying this, thou wrongst me *Gaueston,* 445
Ist not enough, that thou corrupts my lord,
And art a bawd to his affections,
But thou must call mine honor thus in question?
Gau. I meane not so, your grace must pardon me.
Edw. Thou art too familiar with that *Mortimer,* 450
And by thy meanes is *Gaueston* exilde,
But I would wish thee reconcile the lords,
Or thou shalt nere be reconcild to me.
Qu. Your highnes knowes, it lies not in my power.
Edw. Away then, touch me not: come, *Gaueston.* 455
Qu. Villaine, tis thou that robst me of my lord.
Gau. Madam, tis you that rob me of my lord.
Edw. Speake not vnto her, let her droope and pine.
Qu. Wherein my lord, haue I deserud these words?
Witnesse the teares that *Isabella* sheds, 460
Witnesse this hart, that sighing for thee breakes,
How deare my lord is to poore *Isabell.*

432 lord] love *Dod., Dyce*[2], *Cunn.* 439 S.D. Enter Queen Isabella *Dyce*

Edw. And witnesse heauen how deere thou art to me.
There weepe, for till my *Gaueston* be repeald,
Assure thy selfe thou comst not in my sight. 465

Exeunt Edward and Gaueston.

Qu. O miserable and distressed Queene!
Would when I left sweet France and was imbarkt,
That charming *Circes* walking on the waues,
Had chaungd my shape, or at the mariage day
The cup of *Hymen* had beene full of poyson, 470
Or with those armes that twind about my neck,
I had beene stifled, and not liued to see
The king my lord thus to abandon me:
Like frantick *Iuno* will I fill the earth,
With gastlie murmure of my sighes and cries, 475
For neuer doted *Ioue* on *Ganimed*
So much as he on cursed *Gaueston*.
But that will more exasperate his wrath,
I must entreat him, I must speake him faire,
And be a meanes to call home *Gaueston*: 480
And yet heele euer dote on *Gaueston*,
And so am I for euer miserable.

Enter the Nobles to the Queene.

Lanc. Looke where the sister of the king of Fraunce,
Sits wringing of her hands, and beats her brest.
Warw. The king I feare hath ill intreated her. 485
Pen. Hard is the hart, that iniures such a saint.
Mor. iu. I know tis long of *Gaueston* she weepes.
Mor. se. Why? he is gone.
Mor. iu. Madam, how fares your grace?
Qu. Ah *Mortimer*! now breaks the kings hate forth, 490
And he confesseth that he loues me not.
Mor. iu. Crie quittance Madam then, & loue not him.
Qu. No, rather will I die a thousand deaths,
And yet I loue in vaine, heele nere loue me.
Lan. Feare ye not Madam, now his minions gone, 495
His wanton humor will be quicklie left.
Qu. O neuer, Lancaster! I am inioynde,
To sue vnto you all for his repeale:
This wils my lord, and this must I performe,
Or else be banisht from his highnesse presence. 500

468 Circe *Dod. etc.* 469 at] that *1612*, *1622*, *Rob.*, *Cunn.* 483 sister] daughter *conj. Dod.*[2] 486 iniuries *1598*, *Bull.*, *Fleay*

Lan. For his repeale? Madam, he comes not back,
Vnlesse the sea cast vp his shipwrack body.
War. And to behold so sweete a sight as that,
Theres none here, but would run his horse to death.
Mor. iu. But madam, would you haue vs cal him home?
Qu. I *Mortimer*, for till he be restorde, 506
The angrie king hath banished me the court:
And therefore as thou louest and tendrest me,
Be thou my aduocate vnto these peeres.
Mor. iu. What, would ye haue me plead for *Gaueston*?
Mor. se. Plead for him he that will, I am resolude. 511
Lan. And so am I my lord, diswade the Queene.
Qu. O *Lancaster*, let him diswade the king,
For tis against my will he should returne.
War. Then speake not for him, let the pesant go. 515
Qu. Tis for my selfe I speake, and not for him.
Pen. No speaking will preuaile, and therefore cease.
Mor. iu. Faire Queene forbeare to angle for the fish,
Which being caught, strikes him that takes it dead,
I meane that vile *Torpedo*, *Gaueston*, 520
That now I hope flotes on the Irish seas.
Qu. Sweete *Mortimer*, sit downe by me a while,
And I will tell thee reasons of such waighte,
As thou wilt soone subscribe to his repeale.
Mor. iu. It is impossible, but speake your minde. 525
Qu. Then thus, but none shal heare it but our selues.
Lanc. My Lords, albeit the Queen winne *Mortimer*,
Will you be resolute and hold with me?
Mor. se. Not I against my nephew.
Pen. Feare not, the queens words cannot alter him. 530
War. No, doe but marke how earnestly she pleads.
Lan. And see how coldly his lookes make deniall.
War. She smiles, now for my life his mind is changd.
Lanc. Ile rather loose his friendship I, then graunt.
Mor. iu. Well of necessitie it must be so. 535
My Lords, that I abhorre base *Gaueston*,
I hope your honors make no question,
And therefore though I pleade for his repeall,
Tis not for his sake, but for our auaile:
Nay, for the realms behoofe and for the kings. 540
Lanc. Fie *Mortimer*, dishonor not thy selfe,

502 shipwrackt *1598–1622*: shipwrecked *mod. edd.* 510 ye] you *1598 etc.* 511 he *om. 1598 etc.* 526+S.D. Talks to Y. Mor. apart *add. Dyce*

Can this be true twas good to banish him ?
And is this true to call him home againe ?
Such reasons make white blacke, and darke night day.
Mor. iu. My Lord of Lancaster, marke the respect. 545
Lan. In no respect can contraries be true.
Qu. Yet good my lord, heare what he can alledge.
War. All that he speakes, is nothing, we are resolu'd.
Mor. iu. Do you not wish that *Gaueston* were dead ?
Pen. I would he were. 550
Mor. iu. Why then my lord, giue me but leaue to speak.
Mor. se. But nephew, do not play the sophister.
Mor. iu. This which I vrge, is of a burning zeale,
To mend the king, and do our countrie good :
Know you not *Gaueston* hath store of golde, 555
Which may in Ireland purchase him such friends,
As he will front the mightiest of vs all,
And whereas he shall liue and be beloude,
Tis hard for vs to worke his ouerthrow.
War. Marke you but that my lord of Lancaster. 560
Mor. iu. But were he here, detested as he is,
How easilie might some base slaue be subbornd,
To greet his lordship with a poniard,
And none so much as blame the murtherer,
But rather praise him for that braue attempt, 565
And in the Chronicle, enrowle his name,
For purging of the realme of such a plague.
Pen. He saith true.
Lan. I, but how chance this was not done before ?
Mor. iu. Because my lords, it was not thought vpon : 570
Nay more, when he shall know it lies in vs,
To banish him, and then to call him home,
Twill make him vaile the topflag of his pride,
And feare to offend the meanest noble man.
Mor. se. But how if he do not, Nephew ? 575
Mor. iu. Then may we with some colour rise in armes,
For howsoeuer we haue borne it out,
Tis treason to be vp against the king.
So shall we haue the people of our side,
Which for his fathers sake leane to the king, 580
But cannot brooke a night growne mushrump,
Such a one as my Lord of Cornewall is,
Should beare vs downe of the nobilitie,

564 murther *1612, 1622* 579 of] on *1612, 1622, Dod., Rob., ed. 1810*

And when the commons and the nobles ioyne,
Tis not the king can buckler *Gaueston.* 585
Weele pull him from the strongest hould he hath.
My lords, if to performe this I be slack,
Thinke me as base a groome as *Gaueston* ?
Lan. On that condition Lancaster will graunt.
War. And so will *Penbrooke* and I. 590
Mor. se. And I.
Mor. iu. In this I count me highly gratified,
And *Mortimer* will rest at your commaund.
Qu. And when this fauour *Isabell* forgets,
Then let her liue abandond and forlorne, 595
But see in happie time, my lord the king,
Hauing brought the Earle of Cornewall on his way,
Is new returnd: this newes will glad him much,
Yet not so much as me. I loue him more
Then he can *Gaueston,* would he lou'd me 600
But halfe so much, then were I treble blest.

Enter king Edward moorning.

Edw. Hees gone, and for his absence thus I moorne.
Did neuer sorrow go so neere my heart,
As dooth the want of my sweete *Gaueston* ?
And could my crownes reuenew bring him back, 605
I would freelie giue it to his enemies,
And thinke I gaind, hauing bought so deare a friend.
Qu. Harke how he harpes vpon his minion.
Edw. My heart is as an anuill vnto sorrow,
Which beates vpon it like the Cyclops hammers, 610
And with the noise turnes vp my giddie braine,
And makes me frantick for my *Gaueston* :
Ah had some bloudlesse furie rose from hell,
And with my kinglie scepter stroke me dead,
When I was forst to leaue my *Gaueston.* 615
Lan. Diablo, what passions call you these ?
Qu. My gratious lord, I come to bring you newes.
Edw. That you haue parled with your *Mortimer.*
Qu. That *Gaueston,* my Lord, shalbe repeald.
Edw. Repeald, the newes is too sweet to be true. 620
Qu. But will you loue me, if you finde it so ?
Edw. If it be so, what will not *Edward* do ?
Qu. For *Gaueston,* but not for *Isabell.*
Edw. For thee faire Queene, if thou louest *Gaueston,*

Ile hang a golden tongue about thy neck, 625
Seeing thou hast pleaded with so good successe.
Qu. No other iewels hang about my neck
Then these my lord, nor let me haue more wealth,
Then I may fetch from this ritch treasurie:
O how a kisse reuiues poore *Isabell.* 630
Edw. Once more receiue my hand, and let this be,
A second mariage twixt thy selfe and me.
Qu. And may it prooue more happie then the first.
My gentle lord, bespeake these nobles faire,
That waite attendance for a gratious looke, 635
And on their knees salute your maiestie.
Edw. Couragious Lancaster, imbrace thy king,
And as grosse vapours perish by the sunne,
Euen so let hatred with thy soueraignes smile:
Liue thou with me as my companion. 640
Lan. This salutation ouerioyes my heart.
Edw. Warwick shalbe my chiefest counseller:
These siluer haires will more adorne my court,
Then gaudie silkes, or rich imbrotherie.
Chide me sweete Warwick, if I go astray. 645
War. Slay me my lord, when I offend your grace.
Edw. In sollemne triumphes, and in publike showes,
Penbrooke shall beare the sword before the king.
Pen. And with this sword, *Penbrooke* wil fight for you.
Edw. But wherefore walkes yong *Mortimer* aside? 650
Be thou commaunder of our royall fleete,
Or if that loftie office like thee not,
I make thee heere lord Marshall of the realme.
Mor. iu. My lord, ile marshall so your enemies,
As England shall be quiet, and you safe. 655
Edw. And as for you, lord *Mortimer* of Chirke,
Whose great atchiuements in our forrain warre,
Deserues no common place, nor meane reward:
Be you the generall of the leuied troopes,
That now are readie to assaile the Scots. 660
Mor. se. In this your grace hath highly honoured me,
For with my nature warre doth best agree.
Qu. Now is the king of England riche and strong,
Hauing the loue of his renowned peeres.
Edw. I *Isabell*, nere was my heart so light. 665
Clarke of the crowne, direct our warrant forth

625 thy] my *1612*, *1622* 639 soueraigne *1594*, *1598* 644 embroidery *Dod. etc.* 654 so] all *1612*, *1622*

For *Gaueston* to Ireland : *Beamont* flie,
As fast as *Iris*, or *Ioues Mercurie*.
Beam. It shalbe done my gratious Lord.
Edw. Lord *Mortimer*, we leaue you to your charge: 670
Now let vs in, and feast it roiallie :
Against our friend the earle of Cornewall comes,
Weele haue a generall tilt and turnament,
And then his mariage shalbe solemnized,
For wot you not that I haue made him sure, 675
Vnto our cosin, the earle of Glosters heire ?
Lan. Such newes we heare my lord.
Edw. That day, if not for him, yet for my sake,
Who in the triumphe will be challenger,
Spare for no cost, we will requite your loue. 680
Warwick. In this, or ought, your highnes shall commaund vs.
Edward. Thankes gentle Warwick, come lets in and reuell. *Exeunt.*

Manent Mortimers.

Mor. se. Nephue, I must to Scotland, thou staiest here,
Leaue now to oppose thy selfe against the king,
Thou seest by nature he is milde and calme, 685
And seeing his minde so dotes on *Gaueston*,
Let him without controulement haue his will.
The mightiest kings haue had their minions,
Great *Alexander* loude *Ephestion*,
The conquering *Hercules* for *Hilas* wept, 690
And for *Patroclus* sterne *Achillis* droopt :
And not kings onelie, but the wisest men,
The Romaine *Tullie* loued *Octauius*,
Graue *Socrates*, wilde *Alcibiades* :
Then let his grace, whose youth is flexible, 695
And promiseth as much as we can wish,
Freely enioy that vaine light-headed earle,
For riper yeares will weane him from such toyes.
Mor. iu. Vnckle, his wanton humor greeues not me,
But this I scorne, that one so baselie borne 700
Should by his soueraignes fauour grow so pert,
And riote it with the treasure of the realme.

667 *After* Ireland S.D. Enter Beaumont with warrant *add. Dyce* 669 + S.D. Exit *add. Dyce* 675 wote *1598, 1612* : wrote *1622* 679 the *om. 1612, 1622* 690 Hercules *mod. edd. exc. Dod.*[1] : Hector *Qq* for] did for *1622* : for his *Dod., ed. 1810, Cunn., Bull.* wept] weepe *1622*

While souldiers mutinie for want of paie,
He weares a lords reuenewe on his back,
And *Midas* like he iets it in the court, 705
With base outlandish cullions at his heeles,
Whose proud fantastick liueries make such show,
As if that *Proteus* god of shapes appearde.
I haue not seene a dapper iack so briske,
He weares a short Italian hooded cloake, 710
Larded with pearle, and in his tuskan cap
A iewell of more value then the crowne:
Whiles other walke below, the king and he
From out a window laugh at such as we,
And floute our traine, and iest at our attire: 715
Vnckle, tis this that makes me impatient.

Mor. se. But nephew, now you see the king is changd.

Mor. iu. Then so am I, and liue to do him seruice,
But whiles I haue a sword, a hand, a hart,
I will not yeeld to any such vpstart. 720
You know my minde, come vnckle lets away. *Exeunt.*

Enter Spencer *and* Balduck.

Bald. Spencer, seeing that our Lord th'earle of Glosters dead,
Which of the nobles dost thou meane to serue?

Spen. Not *Mortimer*, nor any of his side,
Because the king and he are enemies. 725
Baldock: learne this of me, a factious lord
Shall hardly do himselfe good, much lesse vs,
But he that hath the fauour of a king,
May with one word aduaunce vs while we liue:
The liberall earle of Cornewall is the man, 730
On whose good fortune *Spencers* hope depends.

Bald. What, meane you then to be his follower?

Spen. No, his companion, for he loues me well,
And would haue once preferd me to the king.

Bald. But he is banisht, theres small hope of him. 735

Spen. I for a while, but *Baldock* marke the end,
A friend of mine told me in secrecie,
That hees repeald, and sent for back againe,
And euen now, a poast came from the court,
With letters to our ladie from the King, 740

707 makes *1622* 713 others *1612*, *1622*, *Dod. to Cunn.* 721+Act the Second. Scene I. *add. Rob.* 722 *Two lines Dyce etc., div. after* Spencer th'] the *Dyce etc.*

And as she red, she smild, which makes me thinke,
It is about her louer *Gaueston.*
Bald. Tis like enough, for since he was exild,
She neither walkes abroad, nor comes in sight:
But I had thought the match had beene broke off, 745
And that his banishment had changd her minde.
Spen. Our Ladies first loue is not wauering,
My life for thine she will haue *Gaueston.*
Bald. Then hope I by her meanes to be preferd,
Hauing read vnto her since she was a childe. 750
Spen. Then *Balduck*, you must cast the scholler off,
And learne to court it like a Gentleman,
Tis not a black coate and a little band,
A Veluet cap'de cloake, fac'st before with Serge,
And smelling to a Nosegay all the day, 755
Or holding of a napkin in your hand,
Or saying a long grace at a tables end,
Or making lowe legs to a noble man,
Or looking downeward, with your eye lids close,
And saying, trulie ant may please your honor, 760
Can get you any fauour with great men,
You must be proud, bold, pleasant, resolute,
And now and then, stab as occasion serues.
Bald. *Spencer*, thou knowest I hate such formall toies,
And vse them but of meere hypocrisie. 765
Mine old lord whiles he liude, was so precise,
That he would take exceptions at my buttons,
And being like pins heads, blame me for the bignesse,
Which made me curate-like in mine attire,
Though inwardly licentious enough, 770
And apt for any kinde of villanie.
I am none of these common pedants I,
That cannot speake without *propterea quod.*
Spen. But one of those that saith *quandoquidem*,
And hath a speciall gift to forme a verbe. 775
Bald. Leaue of this iesting, here my lady comes.

Enter the Ladie.

Lady. The greefe for his exile was not so much,
As is the ioy of his returning home.
This letter came from my sweete *Gaueston.*
What needst thou loue, thus to excuse thy selfe? 780
I know thou couldst not come and visit me.

764 formall *om. 1612, 1622* 765 of] as *1622*

'I will not long be from thee though I die :'
This argues the entire loue of my Lord.
'When I forsake thee, death seaze on my heart,'
But rest thee here where *Gaueston* shall sleepe. 785
Now to the letter of my Lord the King,
He wils me to repaire vnto the court,
And meete my *Gaueston* : why do I stay,
Seeing that he talkes thus of my mariage day ?
Whose there, *Balduck* ? 790
See that my coache be readie, I must hence.

Bald. It shall be done, madam. *Exit.*

Lad. And meete me at the parke pale presentlie :
Spencer, stay you and beare me companie,
For I haue ioyfull newes to tell thee of : 795
My lord of Cornewall is a comming ouer,
And will be at the court as soone as we.

Spen. I knew the King would haue him home againe.

Lad. If all things sort out, as I hope they will,
Thy seruice *Spencer* shalbe thought vpon. 800

Spen. I humbly thanke your Ladieship.

Lad. Come lead the way, I long till I am there.

Enter Edward, the Queene, Lancaster, Mortimer, Warwicke, Penbrooke, Kent, attendants.

Edw. The winde is good, I wonder why he stayes,
I feare me he is wrackt vpon the sea.

Queen. Looke *Lancaster* how passionate he is, 805
And still his minde runs on his minion.

Lan. My Lord.

Edw. How now, what newes, is *Gaueston* arriude ?

Mor. i⟨u⟩. Nothing but *Gaueston*, what means your grace ?
You haue matters of more waight to thinke vpon, 810
The King of Fraunce sets foote in Normandie.

Edw. A trifle, weele expell him when we please :
But tell me *Mortimer*, whats thy deuise,
Against the stately triumph we decreed ?

Mor. A homely one my lord, not worth the telling. 815

Edw. Prethee let me know it.

Mor. iu. But seeing you are so desirous, thus it is :
A loftie Cedar tree faire flourishing,

785 But rest] I put *Dod.*[1] rest *1594* : *om. 1598* : stay *1612, 1622, Dod.*[2] *etc.* 785+S.D. Placing the letter in her bosom *add. Broughton* 802+Scene II. *add. Rob.* 816 Prethee *1594* : Prey thee *1598-1622* : Pray thee *Dod. etc.*

On whose top-branches Kinglie Eagles pearch,
And by the barke a canker creepes me vp, 820
And gets vnto the highest bough of all.
The motto : *Æque tandem.*
Edw. And what is yours, my lord of *Lancaster* ?
Lan. My lord, mines more obscure then *Mortimers* :
Plinie reports, there is a flying Fish, 825
Which all the other fishes deadly hate,
And therefore being pursued, it takes the aire :
No sooner is it vp, but thers a foule,
That seaseth it : this fish, my lord, I beare,
The motto this : *Vndique mors est.* 830
Edw. Proud *Mortimer*, vngentle *Lancaster*,
Is this the loue you beare your soueraigne ?
Is this the fruite your reconcilement beares ?
Can you in words make showe of amitie,
And in your shields display your rancorous minds ? 835
What call you this but priuate libelling,
Against the Earle of Cornewall and my brother ?
Qu. Sweete husband be content, they all loue you.
Edw. They loue me not that hate my *Gaueston*.
I am that Cedar, shake me not too much, 840
And you the Eagles, sore ye nere so high,
I haue the gesses that will pull you downe,
And *Æque tandem* shall that canker crie,
Vnto the proudest peere of Britanie :
Though thou comparst him to a flying Fish, 845
And threatenest death whether he rise or fall,
Tis not the hugest monster of the sea,
Nor fowlest Harpie that shall swallow him.
Mor. iu. If in his absence thus he fauors him,
What will he do when as he shall be present ? 850
Lan. That shall wee see, looke where his lordship comes.

Enter Gaueston.

Edw. My *Gaueston*,
Welcome to *Tinmouth*, welcome to thy friend.
Thy absence made me droope, and pine away,
For as the louers of faire *Danae*, 855
When she was lockt vp in a brasen tower,
Desirde her more, and waxt outragious,

825 a *om. 1598* 831 *Prefix* Edw.] Kent *Dyce etc.* 841 ye] you *1622* 842 jesses *Dyce etc.* : gresses *1594–1622*

So did it sure with me: and now thy sight
Is sweeter farre, then was thy parting hence
Bitter and irkesome to my sobbing heart. 860
Gau. Sweet Lord and King, your speech preuenteth mine,
Yet haue I words left to expresse my ioy:
The sheepeherd nipt with biting winters rage
Frolicks not more to see the paynted springe,
Then I doe to behold your Maiestie. 865
Edw. Will none of you salute my *Gaueston*?
Lan. Salute him? yes: welcome Lord Chamberlaine.
Mor. iu. Welcome is the good Earle of Cornewall.
War. Welcome Lord gouernour of the Ile of Man.
Pen. Welcome maister secretarie. 870
Edm. Brother, doe you heare them?
Edw. Stil wil these Earles and Barrons vse me thus?
Gau. My Lord I cannot brooke these iniuries.
Qu. Aye me poore soule when these begin to iarre.
Edw. Returne it to their throtes, ile be thy warrant.
Gau. Base leaden Earles that glorie in your birth, 876
Goe sit at home and eate your tenants beefe:
And come not here to scoffe at *Gaueston*,
Whose mounting thoughts did neuer creepe so low,
As to bestow a looke on such as you. 880
Lan. Yet I disdaine not to doe this for you.
Edw. Treason, treason: whers the traitor?
Pen. Heere, here.
King: Conuey hence *Gaueston*, thaile murder him.
Gau. The life of thee shall salue this foule disgrace. 885
Mor. iu. Villaine thy life, vnlesse I misse mine aime.
Qu. Ah furious *Mortimer* what hast thou done?
Mor. No more then I would answere were he slaine.
Ed. Yes more then thou canst answer though he liue,
Deare shall you both abie this riotous deede: 890
Out of my presence, come not neere the court.
Mor. iu. Ile not be barde the court for *Gaueston*.
Lan. Weele haile him by the eares vnto the block.
Edw. Looke to your owne heads, his is sure enough.

858 sure *1594–1612*: fare *1622 etc.* 874+S.D. Aside *add. Dyce* 881+S.D. Draws his sword, and offers to stab Gaveston *add. Dyce* 883–4 *One line 1594–1622* Heere .. murder him PEN'S *speech 1594–1622, Rob., Cunn.* Here, here, king! EDW. Convey *Dyce*[1], *Bull., Fleay*: Here, here! K. EDW. Convey *Dyce*[2], *Tancock, Wag.* 886+S.D. Offers to stab him *add. Rob.*: Wounds Gaveston *add. Dyce* 888+S.D. Exit Gaveston with Attendants *add. Dyce* 890 abie *1594*: abide *1598–1622 etc.*

War. Looke to your owne crowne, if you back him thus.
Edm. *Warwicke,* these words do ill beseeme thy years.
Edw. Nay all of them conspire to crosse me thus,
But if I liue, ile tread vpon their heads,
That thinke with high lookes thus to tread me down.
Come *Edmund* lets away, and leuie men, 900
Tis warre that must abate these Barons pride.
Exit the King.
War. Lets to our castels, for the king is mooude.
Mor. iu. Moou'd may he be, and perish in his wrath.
Lan. Cosin it is no dealing with him now,
He meanes to make vs stoope by force of armes, 905
And therefore let vs iointlie here protest,
To prosecute that *Gaueston* to the death.
Mor. iu. By heauen, the abiect villaine shall not liue.
War. Ile haue his bloud, or die in seeking it.
Pen. The like oath *Penbrooke* takes. 910
Lan. And so doth *Lancaster*:
Now send our Heralds to defie the King,
And make the people sweare to put him downe.
Enter a Poast.
Mor. iu. Letters, from whence?
Messen. From Scotland my lord. 915
Lan. Why how now cosin, how fares all our friends?
Mor. iu. My vnckles taken prisoner by the Scots.
Lã. Weel haue him ransomd man, be of good cheere.
Mor. They rate his ransome at fiue thousand pound.
Who should defray the money, but the King, 920
Seeing he is taken prisoner in his warres?
Ile to the King.
Lan. Do cosin, and ile beare thee companie.
War. Meane time my lord of *Penbrooke* and my selfe
Will to Newcastell heere, and gather head. 925
Mor. iu. About it then, and we will follow you.
Lan. Be resolute, and full of secrecie.
War. I warrant you.
Mor. iu. Cosin, and if he will not ransome him,
Ile thunder such a peale into his eares, 930
As neuer subiect did vnto his King.
Lan. Content, ile beare my part. Holla whose there?

901 S.D. Exeunt King Edward, Queen Isabella and Kent *Dyce* 928+S.D. Exit with Pembroke *add. Dyce* 932+S.D. Guard appears. Enter Guard *add. Rob.*

Mor. iu. I marry, such a garde as this dooth well.
Lan. Lead on the way.
Guard. Whither will your lordships? 935
Mor. iu. Whither else but to the King?
Guar. His highnes is disposde to be alone.
Lan. Why, so he may, but we will speake to him.
Guard. You may not in, my lord.
Mor. iu. May we not? 940
Edw. How now, what noise is this?
Who haue we there, ist you?
Mor. Nay, stay my lord, I come to bring you newes,
Mine vnckles taken prisoner by the Scots.
Edw. Then ransome him. 945
Lan. Twas in your wars, you should ransome him.
Mor. iu. And you shall ransome him, or else.
Edm. What *Mortimer*, you will not threaten him?
Edw. Quiet your self, you shall haue the broad seale,
To gather for him thoroughout the realme. 950
Lan. Your minion *Gaueston* hath taught you this.
Mor. iu. My lord, the familie of the *Mortimers*
Are not so poore, but would they sell their land,
Would leuie men enough to anger you.
We neuer beg, but vse such praiers as these. 955
Edw. Shall I still be haunted thus?
Mor. iu. Nay, now you are heere alone, ile speake my minde.
Lan. And so will I, and then my lord farewell.
Mor. The idle triumphes, maskes, lasciuious showes
And prodigall gifts bestowed on *Gaueston*, 960
Haue drawne thy treasure drie, and made thee weake,
The murmuring commons ouerstretched hath.
Lan. Looke for rebellion, looke to be deposde.
Thy garrisons are beaten out of Fraunce,
And lame and poore, lie groning at the gates, 965
The wilde *Oneyle*, with swarmes of Irish Kernes,
Liues vncontroulde within the English pale,
Vnto the walles of Yorke the Scots made rode,
And vnresisted, draue away riche spoiles.

940+S.D. Enter Edward and Kent *add. Rob.* 942+S.D. Going *add. Dyce* 954 Would *1594, 1598*: Twoul'd *1612, 1622, Dyce etc.*: Could *Dod. to Rob.* 956 haunted] taunted *Rob.* 961 treasury *1612, 1622 etc.* 962 hath] break *Dod. etc.* 968 make *Dod. etc.* 969 draue *1594–1622*: draw *Dod. to Rob.*: drive *Dyce etc.*

Mor. iu. The hautie *Dane* commands the narrow seas,
While in the harbor ride thy ships vnrigd. 971
Lan. What forraine prince sends thee embassadors ?
Mor. Who loues thee ? but a sort of flatterers.
Lan. Thy gentle Queene, sole sister to *Valoys*,
Complaines that thou hast left her all forlorne. 975
Mor. Thy court is naked, being bereft of those,
That makes a king seeme glorious to the world,
I meane the peeres, whom thou shouldst dearly loue :
Libels are cast againe thee in the streete,
Ballads and rimes made of thy ouerthrow. 980
Lan. The Northren borderers seeing the houses burnt,
Their wiues and children slaine, run vp and downe,
Cursing the name of thee and *Gaueston*.
Mor. When wert thou in the field with banner spred ?
But once, and then thy souldiers marcht like players, 985
With garish robes, not armor, and thy selfe
Bedaubd with golde, rode laughing at the rest,
Nodding and shaking of thy spangled crest,
Where womens fauors hung like labels downe.
Lan. And thereof came it, that the fleering Scots, 990
To Englands high disgrace, haue made this Iig :
Maids of England, sore may you moorne,
For your lemmons you haue lost at Bannocks borne,
With a heaue and a ho.
What weeneth the king of England, 995
So soone to haue woone Scotland,
With a rombelow.
Mor. *Wigmore* shall flie, to set my vnckle free.
Lan. And when tis gone, our swordes shall purchase more.
If ye be moou'de, reuenge it as you can, 1000
Looke next to see vs with our ensignes spred.
Exeunt Nobiles.
Edwa. My swelling hart for very anger breakes.
How oft haue I beene baited by these peeres ?
And dare not be reuengde, for their power is great :
Yet shall the crowing of these cockerels 1005
Affright a Lion ? *Edward*, vnfolde thy pawes,
And let their liues bloud slake thy furies hunger :

979 againe] against *1612, 1622, Dod., Rob., Cunn.* 981 their houses *1598–1622 etc.* 984 banners *1622* 990 thereof] therefore *1612, 1622* 1000 ye] you *1622, Dyce* as] if *1622* 1001 S.D. Nobles *1612, 1622 etc.* 1002 for] with *1622*

If I be cruell, and growe tyrannous,
Now let them thanke themselues, and rue too late.
Kent. My lord, I see your loue to *Gaueston* 1010
Will be the ruine of the realme and you,
For now the wrathfull nobles threaten warres,
And therefore, brother, banish him for euer.
Edw. Art thou an enemie to my *Gaueston*?
Kent. I, and it greeues me that I fauoured him. 1015
Edw. Traitor be gone, whine thou with *Mortimer.*
Kent. So will I, rather then with *Gaueston.*
Edw. Out of my sight, and trouble me no more.
Kent. No maruell though thou scorne thy noble peeres,
When I thy brother am reiected thus. *Exit.*
Edw. Away. Poore *Gaueston,* that hast no friend but me,
Do what they can, weele liue in *Tinmoth* here,
And so I walke with him about the walles,
What care I though the Earles begirt vs round?
Heere comes she thats cause of all these iarres. 1025

Enter the Queene, Ladies 3, Baldock, and Spencer.

Qu. My lord, tis thought the Earles are vp in armes.
Edw. I, and tis likewise thought you fauour 'em.
Qu. Thus do you still suspect me without cause.
La. Sweet vnckle speake more kindly to the queene.
Gau. My lord, dissemble with her, speake her faire. 1030
Edw. Pardon me sweet, I forgot my selfe.
Qu. Your pardon is quicklie got of *Isabell.*
Edw. The yonger *Mortimer* is growne so braue,
That to my face he threatens ciuill warres.
Gau. Why do you not commit him to the tower? 1035
Edw. I dare not, for the people loue him well.
Gau. Why then weele haue him priuilie made away.
Edw. Would Lancaster and he had both carroust
A bowle of poison to each others health:
But let them go, and tell me what are these. 1040
Lad. Two of my fathers seruants whilst he liu'de,
Mait please your grace to entertaine them now.
Edw. Tell me, where wast thou borne?
What is thine armes?
Bald. My name is *Baldock,* and my gentrie 1045
I fetcht from Oxford, not from Heraldrie.
Edw. The fitter art thou *Baldock* for my turne,
Waite on me, and ile see thou shalt not want.

1027 'em *Dyce, Bull.*: him *1594–1622*: them *Dod., Rob., Cunn.*

Bald. I humblie thanke your maiestie.
Edw. Knowest thou him *Gaueston*? 1050
Gau. I my lord,
His name is *Spencer*, he is well alied.
For my sake let him waite vpon your grace,
Scarce shall you finde a man of more desart.
Edw. Then *Spencer* waite vpon me, for his sake 1055
Ile grace thee with a higher stile ere long.
Spen. No greater titles happen vnto me,
Then to be fauoured of your maiestie.
Edw. Cosin, this day shalbe your mariage feast,
And *Gaueston*, thinke that I loue thee well, 1060
To wed thee to our neece, the onely heire
Vnto the Earle of Gloster late deceased.
Gau. I know, my lord, many will stomack me,
But I respect neither their loue nor hate.
Edw. The head-strong Barons shall not limit me. 1065
He that I list to fauour shall be great:
Come lets away, and when the mariage ends,
Haue at the rebels, and their complices.
Exeunt omnes.

Enter Lancaster, Mortimer, Warwick, Penbrooke, Kent.

Kent. My lords, of loue to this our natiue land,
I come to ioine with you, and leaue the king, 1070
And in your quarrell and the realmes behoofe,
Will be the first that shall aduenture life.
Lan. I feare me you are sent of pollicie,
To vndermine vs with a showe of loue.
Warw. He is your brother, therefore haue we cause 1075
To cast the worst, and doubt of your reuolt.
Edm. Mine honor shalbe hostage of my truth,
If that will not suffice, farewell my lords.
Mor. iu. Stay *Edmund*, neuer was Plantagenet
False of his word, and therefore trust we thee. 1080
Pen. But whats the reason you should leaue him now?
Kent. I haue enformd the Earle of Lancaster.
Lan. And it sufficeth: now my lords know this,
That *Gaueston* is secretlie arriude,
And here in *Tinmoth* frollicks with the king. 1085
Let vs with these our followers scale the walles,
And sodenly surprize them vnawares.
Mor. iu. Ile giue the onset.

1068 + Scene III. *add. Rob.* 1077 shalbe] should be *1622*

War. And ile follow thee.

Mor. iu. This tottered ensigne of my auncesters, 1090
Which swept the desart shore of that dead sea,
Whereof we got the name of *Mortimer*,
Will I aduaunce vpon thes castell walles,
Drums strike alarum, raise them from their sport,
And ring aloude the knell of *Gaueston*. 1095

Lanc. None be so hardie as to touche the King,
But neither spare you *Gaueston*, nor his friends.

Exeunt.

Enter the king and Spencer, to them Gaueston, &c.

Edw. O tell me *Spencer*, where is *Gaueston*?

Spen. I feare me he is slaine my gratious lord.

Edw. No, here he comes, now let them spoile and kill:
Flie, flie, my lords, the earles haue got the holde, 1101
Take shipping and away to Scarborough.
Spencer and I will post away by land.

Gau. O stay my lord, they will not iniure you.

Edw. I will not trust them, *Gaueston* away. 1105

Gau. Farewell my Lord.

Edw. Ladie, farewell.

Lad. Farewell sweete vnckle till we meete againe.

Edw. Farewell sweete *Gaueston*, and farewell Neece.

Qu. No farewell to poore *Isabell*, thy Queene? 1110

Edw. Yes, yes, for *Mortimer* your louers sake.

Exeunt omnes, manet Isabella.

Qu. Heauens can witnesse, I loue none but you.
From my imbracements thus he breakes away,
O that mine armes could close this Ile about,
That I might pull him to me where I would, 1115
Or that these teares that drissell from mine eyes,
Had power to mollifie his stonie hart,
That when I had him we might neuer part.

Enter the Barons, alarums.

Lan. I wonder how he scapt.

Mor. iu. Whose this, the Queene? 1120

Qu. I *Mortimer*, the miserable Queene,
Whose pining heart her inward sighes haue blasted,
And body with continuall moorning wasted:
These hands are tir'd with haling of my lord

1093 thes *T. B.*: this *1594–1622 etc.* castell] castle's *Dod. etc.* 1094 raise] rouse *conj. Coll.* 1096 to *om. 1598, 1612* 1097 + Scene IV. *add. Rob.*

From *Gaueston*, from wicked *Gaueston*, 1125
And all in vaine, for when I speake him faire,
He turnes away, and smiles vpon his minion.
Mor. iu. Cease to lament, and tell vs wheres the king ?
Qu. What would you with the king, ist him you seek ?
Lan. No madam, but that cursed *Gaueston*. 1130
Farre be it from the thought of Lancaster,
To offer violence to his soueraigne,
We would but rid the realme of *Gaueston*.
Tell vs where he remaines, and he shall die.
Qu. Hees gone by water vnto Scarborough, 1135
Pursue him quicklie, and he cannot scape,
The king hath left him, and his traine is small.
War. Forslowe no time, sweet Lancaster, lets march.
Mor. How comes it, that the king and he is parted ?
Qu. That this your armie going seuerall waies, 1140
Might be of lesser force, and with the power
That he intendeth presentlie to raise,
Be easilie supprest : and therefore be gone.
Mor. Heere in the riuer rides a Flemish hoie,
Lets all aboord, and follow him amaine. 1145
Lan. The wind that bears him hence, wil fil our sailes,
Come, come aboord, tis but an houres sailing.
Mor. Madam, stay you within this castell here.
Qu. No *Mortimer*, ile to my lord the king.
Mor. Nay, rather saile with vs to Scarborough. 1150
Qu. You know the king is so suspitious,
As if he heare I haue but talkt with you,
Mine honour will be cald in question,
And therefore gentle *Mortimer* be gone.
Mor. Madam, I cannot stay to answer you, 1155
But thinke of *Mortimer* as he deserues.
Qu. So well hast thou deseru'de sweete *Mortimer*,
As *Isabell* could liue with thee for euer.
In vaine I looke for loue at *Edwards* hand,
Whose eyes are fixt on none but *Gaueston* : 1160
Yet once more ile importune him with praiers.
If he be straunge and not regarde my wordes,
My sonne and I will ouer into France,
And to the king my brother there complaine,
How *Gaueston* hath robd me of his loue : 1165

1139 is] are *Dod., Rob., Cunn.* 1140 this] thus *Dod. etc. exc. Fleay* 1143 and *om. 1622 etc.* 1156 + S.D. Exeunt Barons *add. Rob.* 1161 praiers *1594*: prayer *1598–1622 etc.*

But yet I hope my sorrowes will haue end,
And *Gaueston* this blessed day be slaine. *Exeunt.*

Enter Gaueston *pursued.*

Gau. Yet lustie lords I haue escapt your handes,
Your threats, your larums, and your hote pursutes,
And though deuorsed from king *Edwards* eyes, 1170
Yet liueth *Pierce* of *Gaueston* vnsurprizd,
Breathing, in hope (*malgrado* all your beards,
That muster rebels thus against your king)
To see his royall soueraigne once againe.

Enter the Nobles.

War. Vpon him souldiers, take away his weapons. 1175
Mor. Thou proud disturber of thy countries peace,
Corrupter of thy king, cause of these broiles,
Base flatterer, yeeld, and were it not for shame,
Shame and dishonour to a souldiers name,
Vpon my weapons point here shouldst thou fall, 1180
And welter in thy goare.
Lan. Monster of men,
That like the Greekish strumpet traind to armes
And bloudie warres, so many valiant knights,
Looke for no other fortune wretch then death, 1185
Kind *Edward* is not heere to buckler thee.
War. Lancaster, why talkst thou to the slaue ?
Go souldiers take him hence, for by my sword,
His head shall off: *Gaueston*, short warning
Shall serue thy turne: it is our countries cause, 1190
That here seuerelie we will execute
Vpon thy person: hang him at a bough.
Gau. My Lord.
War. Souldiers, haue him away:
But for thou wert the fauorit of a King, 1195
Thou shalt haue so much honor at our hands.
Gau. I thanke you all my lords, then I perceiue,
That heading is one, and hanging is the other,
And death is all.

Enter earle of Arundell.

Lan. How now my lord of *Arundell* ? 1200

1167 S.D. Exit *Rob. etc.* 1167+Scene V *add. Rob.* 1186 Kind *1594*: King *1598 etc.* 1192 at] upon *Dod.* 1193 Lord] lords *Dod. to Bull. exc. Dyce*

Arun. My lords, king *Edward* greetes you all by me.
War. *Arundell,* say your message.
Aru. His maiesty, hearing that you had taken *Gaueston,*
Intreateth you by me, yet but he may
See him before he dies, for why he saies, 1205
And sends you word, he knowes that die he shall,
And if you gratifie his grace so farre,
He will be mindfull of the curtesie.
Warw. How now ?
Gau. Renowmed *Edward,* how thy name 1210
Reuiues poore *Gaueston.*
War. No, it needeth not.
Arundell, we will gratifie the king
In other matters, he must pardon vs in this,
Souldiers away with him. 1215
Gauest. Why my Lord of Warwicke,
Will not these delaies beget my hopes ?
I know it lords, it is this life you aime at,
Yet graunt king *Edward* this.
Mor. iu. Shalt thou appoint 1220
What we shall graunt ? Souldiers away with him :
Thus weele gratifie the king,
Weele send his head by thee, let him bestow
His teares on that, for that is all he gets
Of *Gaueston,* or else his sencelesse trunck. 1225
Lan. Not so my Lord, least he bestow more cost,
In burying him, then he hath euer earned.
Arun. My lords, it is his maiesties request,
And in the honor of a king he sweares,
He will but talke with him and send him backe. 1230
War. When can you tell ? *Arundell* no, we wot,
He that the care of realme remits,
And driues his nobles to these exigents
For *Gaueston,* will if he zease him once,
Violate any promise to possesse him. 1235
Arun. Then if you will not trust his grace in keepe,
My lords, I will be pledge for his returne.

1203 *Two lines Bull., div. after* majesty that *om Cunn.* 1204 yet but] but that *Dod., Rob., Cunn.* 1217 not *om. Dod., Rob.* : now *Dyce* : not that *Fleay* delaies] short delays *Dyce* my] me any *Dod., Rob.* 1222 Thus weele] Thus far we will *Fleay* 1229 in] on *Dod. to Dyce*[1], *Cunn.* 1232 that] that hath *1612, 1622* Realme-remits *1612, 1622* realme] his realm *Dod. etc. exc. Fleay* : kingly realm *Fleay* 1234 zease *1594* : seaze *1598–1622* : sees *Cunn.*

Mor. iu. It is honourable in thee to offer this,
But for we know thou art a noble gentleman,
We will not wrong thee so, 1240
To make away a true man for a theefe.

Gaue. How meanst thou *Mortimer*? that is ouer base.

Mor. Away base groome, robber of kings renowme,
Question with thy companions and thy mates.

Pen. My lord *Mortimer*, and you my lords each one,
To gratifie the kings request therein, 1246
Touching the sending of this *Gaueston*,
Because his maiestie so earnestlie
Desires to see the man before his death,
I will vpon mine honor vndertake 1250
To carrie him, and bring him back againe,
Prouided this, that you my lord of Arundell
Will ioyne with me.

War. Penbrooke, what wilt thou do?
Cause yet more bloudshed: is it not enough 1255
That we haue taken him, but must we now
Leaue him on had-Iwist, and let him go?

Pen. My lords, I will not ouer wooe your honors,
But if you dare trust *Penbrooke* with the prisoner,
Vpon mine oath I will returne him back. 1260

Arun. My lord of Lancaster, what say you in this?

Lan. Why I say, let him go on *Penbrookes* word.

Pen. And you, lord *Mortimer*?

Mor. iu. How say you, my lord of Warwick?

War. Nay, do your pleasures, I know how twill prooue.

Pen. Then giue him me. 1266

Gau. Sweete soueraigne, yet I come
To see thee ere I die.

Warw. Yet not perhaps,
If Warwickes wit and policie preuaile. 1270

Mor. iu. My lord of Penbrooke, we deliuer him you,
Returne him on your honor, sound away. *Exeunt.*

Manent Penbrooke, Arundel, Gauest. & Penbrookes men, foure souldiers.

Pen. My Lord, you shall go with me,

1238 It is] 'Tis *Dyce etc.* 1244 thy mates *1594*, *Dod.*, *Rob.*: mates *1598–1622*, *Dyce etc.* 1250 mine] my *1612*, *1622* 1270 + S.D. Aside *add. Dyce* 1272 + S.D. Arundel *Dyce etc.*: Mat. *1594–1622* 1273 My Lord] My Lord of Arundel *conj. Dyce*, *Cunn.*, *Bull.*

My house is not farre hence, out of the way
A little, but our men shall go along. 1275
We that haue prettie wenches to our wiues,
Sir, must not come so neare and balke their lips.
Aru. Tis verie kindlie spoke my lord of *Penbrooke,*
Your honor hath an adamant of power
To drawe a prince. 1280
Pen. So my lord: come hether *Iames,*
I do commit this *Gaueston* to thee,
Be thou this night his keeper, in the morning
We will discharge thee of thy charge, be gon.
Gau. Vnhappie *Gaueston,* whether goest thou now. 1285
Exit cum seruis Pen.
Horse boy. My lord, weele quicklie be at *Cobham.*
Exeunt ambo.

Enter Gaueston moorning, and the earle of Penbrookes men.

Gaue. O treacherous Warwicke thus to wrong thy friend!
Iames. I see it is your life these armes pursue.
Gau. Weaponles must I fall and die in bands,
O must this day be period of my life! 1290
Center of all my blisse! and yee be men,
Speede to the king.

Enter Warwicke and his companie.

War. My lord of Penbrookes men,
Striue you no longer, I will haue that *Gaueston.*
Iam. Your lordship doth dishonor to your selfe, 1295
And wrong our lord, your honorable friend.
War. No *Iames,* it is my countries cause I follow.
Goe, take the villaine, soldiers, come away,
Weel make quick worke, commend me to your maister
My friend, and tell him that I watcht it well. 1300
Come, let thy shadow parley with king *Edward.*
Gau. Treacherous earle, shall I not see the king?
War. The king of heauen perhaps, no other king,
Away. *Exeunt Warwike and his men, with Gauest.*
Manet Iames cum cæteris.
⟨*Iam.*⟩ Come fellowes, it booted not for vs to striue,
We will in hast go certifie our Lord. *Exeunt.*

1277 and *1594*: to *1598–1622 etc.* 1286+Act the Third. Scene I. *add. Rob.* 1291 all *om. 1612, 1622* 1305 booteth *1612, 1622, Dod., Rob.* 1306+Scene II. *add. Rob.*

Enter king Edward and Spencer, with Drummes and Fifes.

Edw. I long to heare an answer from the Barons
Touching my friend, my deerest *Gaueston.*
Ah *Spencer,* not the riches of my realme
Can ransome him, ah he is markt to die. 1310
I know the malice of the yonger *Mortimer,*
Warwick I know is roughe, and Lancaster
Inexorable, and I shall neuer see
My louely *Pierce,* my *Gaueston* againe,
The Barons ouerbeare me with their pride. 1315

Spencer. Were I king *Edward* Englands soueraigne,
Sonne to the louelie *Elenor* of Spaine,
Great *Edward Longshankes* issue: would I beare
These braues, this rage, and suffer vncontrowld
These Barons thus to beard me in my land, 1320
In mine owne realme? my lord pardon my speeche,
Did you retaine your fathers magnanimitie,
Did you regard the honor of your name,
You would not suffer thus your maiestie
Be counterbuft of your nobilitie. 1325
Strike off their heads, and let them preach on poles,
No doubt, such lessons they will teach the rest,
As by their preachments they will profit much,
And learne obedience to their lawfull king.

Edw. Yea gentle *Spencer,* we haue beene too milde, 1330
Too kinde to them, but now haue drawne our sword,
And if they send me not my *Gaueston,*
Weele steele it on their crest, and powle their tops.

Bald. This haught resolue becomes your maiestie,
Not to be tied to their affection, 1335
As though your highnes were a schoole boy still,
And must be awde and gouernd like a child.

Enter Hugh Spencer *an old man, father to the yong* Spencer, *with his trunchion, and soldiers.*

Spen. pa. Long liue my soueraigne the noble *Edward,*
In peace triumphant, fortunate in warres.

Edw. Welcome old man, comst thou in *Edwards* aide?
Then tell thy prince, of whence, and what thou art. 1341

Spen. pa. Loe, with a band of bowmen and of pikes,

1314 Pierce, my Gaueston *1594*: Pierce of Gaueston *1598–1622 etc.* 1334 haught] high *Dod.*[1] 1341 thy *1594, Dyce etc.*: the *1598–1622, Dod., Rob.*

Browne bils, and targetiers, 400 strong,
Sworne to defend king *Edwards* royall right,
I come in person to your maiestie, 1345
Spencer, the father of *Hugh Spencer* there,
Bound to your highnes euerlastinglie,
For fauors done in him, vnto vs all.
Edw. Thy father *Spencer*?
Spen. filius. True, and it like your grace, 1350
That powres in lieu of all your goodnes showne,
His life, my lord, before your princely feete.
Edw. Welcome ten thousand times, old man againe.
Spencer, this loue, this kindnes to thy King,
Argues thy noble minde and disposition: 1355
Spencer, I heere create thee earle of Wilshire,
And daily will enrich thee with our fauour,
That as the sun-shine shall reflect ore thee:
Beside, the more to manifest our loue,
Because we heare Lord *Bruse* dooth sell his land, 1360
And that the *Mortimers* are in hand withall,
Thou shalt haue crownes of vs, t'outbid the Barons,
And *Spenser*, spare them not, but lay it on.
Souldiers a largis, and thrice welcome all.
Spen. My lord, here comes the Queene. 1365

Enter the Queene and her sonne, and Levune a Frenchman.

Edw. Madam, what newes?
Qu. Newes of dishonor, lord, and discontent,
Our friend *Levune*, faithfull and full of trust,
Informeth vs, by letters and by words,
That lord *Valoyes* our brother, king of Fraunce, 1370
Because your highnesse hath beene slack in homage,
Hath seazed Normandie into his hands:
These be the letters, this the messenger.
Edw. Welcome *Levune*, tush *Sib*, if this be all,
Valoys and I will soone be friends againe. 1375
But to my *Gaueston*: shall I neuer see,
Neuer behold thee now? Madam in this matter
We will employ you and your little sonne,
You shall go parley with the king of Fraunce.

1348 fauors *1594*: fauour *1598–1622 etc.* 1362 t'] to *1612, 1622* 1363 but *1594, Cunn., Fleay*: *om. 1598–1622, Dod. to Dyce, Bull.*: no *Wag.* 1365 S.D. Levune *Dyce etc. (passim)*: Lewne *Qq* 1368, 1374, 1390 Levune *Dyce etc.*: Lewne *Qq* 1377 now] more *Dod., Rob., Cunn., Fleay*

Boye, see you beare you brauelie to the king, 1380
And do your message with a maiestie.
Prin. Commit not to my youth things of more waight
Then fits a prince so yong as I to beare,
And feare not lord and father, heauens great beames
On *Atlas* shoulder shall not lie more safe, 1385
Then shall your charge committed to my trust.
Qu. A boye, this towardnes makes thy mother feare
Thou art not markt to many daies on earth.
Edw. Madam, we will that you with speed be shipt,
And this our sonne, *Levune* shall follow you 1390
With all the hast we can dispatch him hence.
Choose of our lords to beare you companie,
And go in peace, leaue vs in warres at home.
Qu. Vnnatural wars, where subiects braue their king,
God end them once: my lord I take my leaue, 1395
To make my preparation for Fraunce.

Enter lord Arundel.

Edw. What, lord *Arundel* dost thou come alone?
Arun. Yea my good lord, for *Gaueston* is dead.
Edw. Ah traitors, haue they put my friend to death?
Tell me *Arundel* died he ere thou camst, 1400
Or didst thou see my friend to take his death?
Arun. Neither my lord, for as he was surprizd,
Begirt with weapons, and with enemies round,
I did your highnes message to them all,
Demanding him of them, entreating rather, 1405
And said, vpon the honour of my name,
That I would vndertake to carrie him
Vnto your highnes, and to bring him back.
Edw. And tell me, would the rebels denie me that?
Spen. Proud recreants. 1410
Edw. Yea *Spencer*, traitors all.
Arun. I found them at the first inexorable,
The earle of Warwick would not bide the hearing,
Mortimer hardly, *Penbrooke* and *Lancaster*
Spake least: and when they flatly had denyed, 1415

1396+S.D. Exit with Prince Edward *add. Dyce* S.D. lord Arundel] lord Matre. *1594–1612*: Lord Matreuis *1622*: *corr. Dyce. The mistake is continued throughout the scene* 1397 Arundel *Dyce etc.*: Matre. *1594–1622* 1398 Yea] Yes *1612, 1622* 1398, 1402, 1412, 1424 *Prefix* Mat. *1594–1622*: *corr. Dyce* 1415 Spake] Speake *1598, 1612*

Refusing to receiue me pledge for him,
The earle of *Penbrooke* mildlie thus bespake:
My lords, because our soueraigne sends for him,
And promiseth he shall be safe returnd,
I will this vndertake, to haue him hence, 1420
And see him redeliuered to your hands.
Edw. Well, and how fortunes that he came not?
Spen. Some treason, or some villanie was cause.
Arun. The earle of Warwick seazde him on his way,
For being deliuered vnto *Penbrookes* men, 1425
Their lord rode home, thinking his prisoner safe,
But ere he came, Warwick in ambush laie,
And bare him to his death, and in a trenche
Strake off his head, and marcht vnto the campe.
Spen. A bloudie part, flatly against law of armes. 1430
Edw. O shall I speake, or shall I sigh and die!
Spen. My lord, referre your vengeance to the sword,
Vpon these Barons, harten vp your men,
Let them not vnreuengd murther your friends,
Aduaunce your standard *Edward* in the field, 1435
And marche to fire them from their starting holes.

Edward kneeles, and saith.

By earth, the common mother of vs all,
By heauen, and all the moouing orbes thereof,
By this right hand, and by my fathers sword,
And all the honors longing to my crowne, 1440
I will haue heads, and liues for him as many
As I haue manors, castels, townes, and towers.
Tretcherous *Warwicke*, traiterous *Mortimer*:
If I be Englands king, in lakes of gore
Your headles trunkes, your bodies will I traile, 1445
That you may drinke your fill, and quaffe in bloud,
And staine my roiall standard with the same,
That so my bloudie colours may suggest
Remembrance of reuenge immortallie
On your accursed traiterous progenie: 1450
You villaines that haue slaine my *Gaueston*.
And in this place of honor and of trust,
Spencer, sweet *Spencer*, I adopt thee heere,
And meerely of our loue we do create thee

1416 me] my *1622* 1422 fortunes] fortunes it *Dyce, Cunn., Bull., Wag.* not] not then *Fleay* 1429 Stroke *1612, 1622* 1430 'gainst *1622 etc.* 1442+S.D. Rises *add. Dyce* 1452 this] his *Cunn., Bull.*

Earle of Gloster, and lord Chamberlaine, 1455
Despite of times, despite of enemies.
Spen. My lord, heres a messenger from the Barons,
Desires accesse vnto your maiestie.
Edw. Admit him neere. 1459

Enter the Herald from the Barons, with his coate of armes.

Messen. Long liue king *Edward*, Englands lawful lord.
Edw. So wish not they I wis that sent thee hither,
Thou comst from *Mortimer* and his complices,
A ranker route of rebels neuer was:
Well, say thy message.
Messen. The Barons vp in armes, by me salute 1465
Your highnes, with long life and happines,
And bid me say as plainer to your grace,
That if without effusion of bloud,
You will this greefe haue ease and remedie,
That from your princely person you remooue 1470
This *Spencer*, as a putrifying branche,
That deads the royall vine, whose golden leaues
Empale your princelie head, your diadem,
Whose brightnes such pernitious vpstarts dim,
Say they, and louinglie aduise your grace, 1475
To cherish vertue and nobilitie,
And haue old seruitors in high esteeme,
And shake off smooth dissembling flatterers:
This graunted, they, their honors, and their liues,
Are to your highnesse vowd and consecrate. 1480
Spen. A traitors, will they still display their pride?
Edw. Away, tarrie no answer, but be gon.
Rebels, will they appoint their soueraigne
His sports, his pleasures, and his companie: 1484
Yet ere thou go, see how I do deuorce *Embrace*
Spencer from me: now get thee to thy lords, *Spencer.*
And tell them I will come to chastise them,
For murthering *Gaueston*: hie thee, get thee gone,
Edward with fire and sword, followes at thy heeles.
My lord, perceiue you how these rebels swell: 1490
Souldiers, good harts, defend your soueraignes right,

1457 heers *1612, 1622, Dod.*[1], *Rob., Cunn., Dyce*[2]: heres is *1594, 1598*: here is *Dod.*[2], [3], *Dyce*[1], *Bull.* 1463 route] roote *1598, 1612* 1469 this greefe] of this *1622* 1472 leaue *1598* (*B.M. copy, but the Bodleian copy gives rightly* leaues) 1489 + S.D. Exit Herald *add. Dyce* 1490 lord] lords *Dyce etc.*

For now, euen now, we marche to make them stoope.
Away. *Exeunt.*

Alarums, excursions, a great fight, and a retreate.

Enter the king, Spencer the father, Spencer the sonne, and the noblemen of the kings side.

Edw. Why do we sound retreat? vpon them lords,
This day I shall powre vengeance with my sword 1495
On those proud rebels that are vp in armes,
And do confront and countermaund their king.
Spen. son. I doubt it not my lord, right will preuaile.
Spen. fa. Tis not amisse my liege for eyther part
To breathe a while, our men with sweat and dust 1500
All chockt well neare begin to faint for heate,
And this retire refresheth horse and man.
Spen. son. Heere come the rebels.

Enter the Barons, Mortimer, Lancaster, Warwick, Penbrooke, cum cæteris.

Mor. Looke *Lancaster*, yonder is *Edward* among his flatterers.
Lan. And there let him bee, 1505
Till hee pay deerely for their companie.
War. And shall or *Warwicks* sword shal smite in vaine.
Edw. What rebels, do you shrinke, and sound retreat?
Mor. iu. No Edward, no, thy flatterers faint and flie.
Lan. Th'ad best betimes forsake them and their trains,
For theile betray thee, traitors as they are. 1511
Spen. so. Traitor on thy face, rebellious *Lancaster.*
Pen. Away base vpstart, brau'st thou nobles thus?
Spen. fa. A noble attempt, and honourable deed,
Is it not, trowe ye, to assemble aide, 1515
And leuie armes against your lawfull king?
Edw. For which ere long their heads shall satisfie,
T'appeaze the wrath of their offended king.
Mor. iu. Then *Edward*, thou wilt fight it to the last,
And rather bathe thy sword in subiects bloud, 1520
Then banish that pernicious companie.
Edw. I traitors all, rather then thus be braude,

1493+Scene III. *add. Rob.* 1504 yonder's *Dod.* 'mong *Dod.* 1510 Th'ad] They'd *mod. edd., but the abbreviation probably stands for* thou had them *T. B.*: thee *1594–1622 etc.* 1515 Is it] It is *1598* 1519 wilt] will *1598*

Make Englands ciuill townes huge heapes of stones,
And plowes to go about our pallace gates.
War. A desperate and vnnaturall resolution, 1525
Alarum to the fight,
Saint George for England, and the Barons right.
Edw. S. George for England, and king *Edwards* right.

Enter Edward, with the Barons captiues.

Edw. Now lustie lords, now not by chance of warre,
But iustice of the quarrell and the cause 1530
Vaild is your pride: me thinkes you hang the heads,
But weele aduance them traitors, now tis time
To be auengd on you for all your braues,
And for the murther of my deerest friend,
To whome right well you knew our soule was knit, 1535
Good *Pierce* of *Gaueston* my sweet fauoret.
A rebels, recreants, you made him away.
Edm. Brother, in regard of thee and of thy land,
Did they remooue that flatterer from thy throne. 1539
Edw. So sir, you haue spoke, away, auoid our presence.
Accursed wretches, wast in regard of vs,
When we had sent our messenger to request
He might be spared to come to speake with vs,
And *Penbrooke* vndertooke for his returne,
That thou proud *Warwicke* watcht the prisoner, 1545
Poore *Pierce*, and headed him against lawe of armes,
For which thy head shall ouer looke the rest
As much as thou in rage out wentst the rest?
War. Tyrant, I scorne thy threats and menaces,
Tis but temporall that thou canst inflict. 1550
Lan. The worst is death, and better die to liue,
Then liue in infamie vnder such a king.
Edw. Away with them my lord of Winchester,
These lustie leaders Warwicke and Lancaster,
I charge you roundly off with both their heads. 1555
Away.
War. Farewell vaine worlde.
Lan. Sweete *Mortimer* farewell.
Mor. iu. England, vnkinde to thy nobilitie,
Grone for this greefe, behold how thou art maimed. 1560

1528 S.D. Alarums. Exeunt the two parties severally. Enter King Edward and his followers, with the Barons and Kent captive *Dyce* 1540+S.D. Exit Kent *add. Dyce* 1542 messengers *1612, 1622* 1546 'gainst *1622 etc.*

Edw. Go take that haughtie *Mortimer* to the tower,
There see him safe bestowed, and for the rest,
Do speedie execution on them all.
Be gon.
Mor. iu. What *Mortimer*? can ragged stonie walles 1565
Immure thy vertue that aspires to heauen?
No *Edward*, Englands scourge, it may not be,
Mortimers hope surmounts his fortune farre.
Edw. Sound drums and trumpets, marche with me my friends,
Edward this day hath crownd him king a new. *Exit*

Manent Spencer filius, Levune & Baldock.

Spen. *Levune*, the trust that we repose in thee 1571
Begets the quiet of king *Edwards* land,
Therefore be gon in hast, and with aduice
Bestowe that treasure on the lords of Fraunce,
That therewith all enchaunted like the guarde, 1575
That suffered *Ioue* to passe in showers of golde
To *Danae*, all aide may be denied
To *Isabell* the Queene, that now in France
Makes friends, to crosse the seas with her yong sonne,
And step into his fathers regiment. 1580
Levu. Thats it these Barons and the subtill Queene
Long leueld at.
Bald. Yea, but *Levune* thou seest,
These Barons lay their heads on blocks together,
What they intend, the hangman frustrates cleane. 1585
Levun. Haue you no doubts my lords, ile clap so close
Among the lords of France with Englands golde,
That *Isabell* shall make her plaints in vaine,
And Fraunce shall be obdurat with her teares. 1589
Spen. Then make for Fraunce amaine, *Levune* away,
Proclaime king *Edwards* warres and victories.
Exeunt omnes.

Enter Edmund.

Edm. Faire blowes the winde for Fraunce, blowe gentle gale,

1568 his] hie *1612, 1622* 1568 + S.D. The captive Barons are led off *add. Dyce* 1570 S.D. Levune *Dyce etc.*: Lewne *Qq*: Lecune *Rob.* *So ll.* 1571, 1583, 1590 1575 therewithall *1622* 1582 leveld *conj. Dod.*[3], *Dyce etc.*: leuied *1594–1622* 1586 doubts *1594*: doubte *1598–1622 etc.* clap so *Dod. etc.*: claps *1594–1622* 1591 + Act the Fourth. Scene I. *add. Rob.*

Till *Edmund* be arriude for Englands good,
Nature, yeeld to my countries cause in this.
A brother, no, a butcher of thy friends, 1595
Proud *Edward*, doost thou banish me thy presence?
But ile to Fraunce, and cheere the wronged Queene,
And certifie what *Edwards* loosenes is.
Vnnaturall king, to slaughter noble men
And cherish flatterers: *Mortimer* I stay 1600
Thy sweet escape,
Stand gratious gloomie night to his deuice.

Enter Mortimer disguised.

Mor. iu. Holla, who walketh there, ist you my lord?
Edm. Mortimer tis I,
But hath thy potion wrought so happilie? 1605
Mor. iu. It hath my lord, the warders all a sleepe,
I thanke them, gaue me leaue to passe in peace:
But hath your grace got shipping vnto Fraunce?
Edm. Feare it not. *Exeunt.*

Enter the Queene and her sonne.

Qu. A boye, our friends do faile vs all in Fraunce,
The lords are cruell, and the king vnkinde, 1611
What shall we doe?
Prince. Madam, returne to England,
And please my father well, and then a Fig
For all my vnckles frienship here in Fraunce. 1615
I warrant you, ile winne his highnes quicklie,
A loues me better than a thousand *Spencers.*
Qu. A boye, thou art deceiude at least in this,
To thinke that we can yet be tun'd together,
No, no, we iarre too farre. Vnkinde *Valoys,* 1620
Vnhappie *Isabell,* when Fraunce reiects,
Whether, O whether doost thou bend thy steps?

Enter sir Iohn of Henolt.

S. Ioh. Madam, what cheere?
Qu. A good sir *Iohn* of *Henolt,*
Neuer so cheereles, nor so farre distrest. 1625
S. Ioh. I heare sweete lady of the kings vnkindenes,
But droope not madam, noble mindes contemne
Despaire: will your grace with me to *Henolt*?

1609 + Scene II. *adā Rob.* 1622 doost] must *conj. Dyce:* dar'st *conj. Coll.*

And there stay times aduantage with your sonne?
How say you my Lord, will you go with your friends, 1630
And share of all our fortunes equallie?
Prin. So pleaseth the Queene my mother, me it likes.
The king of England, nor the court of Fraunce,
Shall haue me from my gratious mothers side,
Till I be strong enough to breake a staffe, 1635
And then haue at the proudest *Spencers* head.
Sir Iohn. Well said my lord.
Qu. Oh my sweet hart, how do I mone thy wrongs?
Yet triumphe in the hope of thee my ioye.
Ah sweete sir *Iohn*, euen to the vtmost verge 1640
Of *Europe*, or the shore of *Tanaise*,
Will we with thee to *Henolt*, so we will.
The Marques is a noble Gentleman,
His grace I dare presume will welcome me,
But who are these? 1645

Enter Edmund and Mortimer.

Edm. Madam, long may you liue
Much happier then your friends in England do.
Qu. Lord *Edmund* and lord *Mortimer* aliue?
Welcome to Fraunce: the newes was heere my lord,
That you were dead, or very neare your death. 1650
Mor. iu. Lady, the last was truest of the twaine,
But *Mortimer* reserude for better hap,
Hath shaken off the thraldome of the tower,
And liues t'aduance your standard good my lord.
Prin. How meane you, and the king my father liues?
No my lord *Mortimer*, not I, I trow. 1656
Qu. Not sonne, why not? I would it were no worse,
But gentle lords, friendles we are in Fraunce.
Mor. iu. Mounsier le Grand, a noble friend of yours,
Tould vs at our arriuall all the newes, 1660
How hard the nobles, how vnkinde the king
Hath shewed himself: but madam, right makes roome,
Where weapons want, and though a many friends
Are made away, as Warwick, Lancaster,
And others of our partie and faction, 1665

1631 share of all *T. B.*: shake off all *1594–1622 etc.*: share with us *conj. Broughton* 1632 please *Fleay* 1634 haue] heave *conj. Broughton* 1641 or] on *Dyce* 1654 t'] to *1612, 1622* 1655 and] an *Cunn.*, *Wag.* 1665 partie] part *Dyce, Cunn., Fleay, Tancock, Wag.* faction] our faction *conj. Broughton*

Yet haue we friends, assure your grace, in England
Would cast vp cappes, and clap their hands for ioy,
To see vs there appointed for our foes.
Edm. Would all were well, and *Edward* well reclaimd,
For Englands honor, peace, and quietnes. 1670
Mort. But by the sword, my lord, it must be deseru'd.
The king will nere forsake his flatterers.
S. Ioh. My Lords of England, sith the vngentle king
Of Fraunce refuseth to giue aide of armes
To this distressed Queene his sister heere, 1675
Go you with her to *Henolt*: doubt yee not,
We will finde comfort, money, men, and friends
Ere long, to bid the English king a base.
How say yong Prince, what thinke you of the match ?
Prin. I thinke king *Edward* will out-run vs all. 1680
Qu. Nay sonne, not so, and you must not discourage
Your friends that are so forward in your aide.
Edm. Sir *Iohn* of *Henolt*, pardon vs I pray,
These comforts that you giue our wofull queene,
Binde vs in kindenes all at your commaund. 1685
Qu. Yea gentle brother, and the God of heauen
Prosper your happie motion good sir *Iohn.*
Mor. iu. This noble gentleman forward in armes,
Was borne I see to be our anchor hold.
Sir *Iohn* of *Henolt*, be it thy renowne, 1690
That Englands Queene, and nobles in distresse,
Haue beene by thee restored and comforted.
S. Iohn. Madam along, and you my lord with me,
That Englands peeres may *Henolts* welcome see.

Enter the king, Arundel, the two Spencers, with others.

Edw. Thus after many threats of wrathfull warre, 1695
Triumpheth Englands *Edward* with his friends,
And triumph *Edward* with his friends vncontrould.
My lord of Gloster, do you heare the newes ?
Spen. iu. What newes my lord ?
Edw. Why man, they say there is great execution 1700
Done through the realme: my lord of *Arundell*
You haue the note, haue you not ?

1671 it] 't *Dyce etc.* 1673 the] th' *Dyce etc.* 1678 a base] abase *1622, Dod., Rob.* 1679 How say] How say'st *Dyce*: Now say *conj. Dyce, Cunn., Wag.* yong] you *Rob.* you *om. 1612* 1693 lords *Dyce, Bull.* 1694 + Scene III. *add. Rob.* S.D. Arundel *Dyce etc.*: Matr. (Matreuis) *1594–1622* 1697 with his friends] henceforth *conj. Broughton* his *om. Cunn., Wag.*

Arun. From the lieutenant of the tower my lord.
Edw. I pray let vs see it, what haue we there?
Read it *Spencer.* *Spencer reads their names.*
Why so, they barkt a pace a month agoe, 1706
Now on my life, theile neither barke nor bite.
Now sirs, the newes from Fraunce. Gloster, I trowe
The lords of Fraunce loue Englands gold so well,
As *Isabell* gets no aide from thence. 1710
What now remaines, haue you proclaimed, my lord,
Reward for them can bring in *Mortimer*?
Spen. iu. My lord, we haue, and if he be in England,
A will be had ere long I doubt it not.
Edw. If, doost thou say? *Spencer*, as true as death,
He is in Englands ground, our port-maisters 1716
Are not so careles of their kings commaund.

Enter a Poaste.

How now, what newes with thee, from whence come these?
Post. Letters my lord, and tidings foorth of Fraunce,
To you my lord of Gloster from *Levune.* 1720
Edward. Reade.

Spencer reades the letter.

My dutie to your honor præmised, &c. I haue according to instructions in that behalfe, dealt with the king of Fraunce his lords, and effected, that the Queene all discontented and discomforted, is gone, whither if you aske, with sir *Iohn* of *Henolt*, brother to the Marquesse, into Flaunders: with them are gone lord *Edmund*, and the lord *Mortimer*, hauing in their company diuers of your nation, and others, and as constant report goeth, they intend to giue king *Edward* battell in England sooner then he can looke for them: this is all the newes of import. 1731
Your honors in all seruice, Levune.

Edw. A villaines, hath that *Mortimer* escapt?
With him is *Edmund* gone associate?
And will sir *Iohn* of *Henolt* lead the round? 1735
Welcome a Gods name Madam and your sonne,
England shall welcome you, and all your route,

1703 *Prefix* Matr. *1594–1622*: *corr. Dyce* 1706 a month] not long *1612, 1622* 1710 Isabella *Dyce, Cunn., Bull.* gets] will get *conj. Broughton* no] no more *Fleay* 1720 Levune *Dyce etc.*: Lewne *1594–1622*: Lewen *Dod.*: Lecune *Rob.* *So in l.* 1732 1721 S.D. letter] Letters *1612, 1622* 1722 præmised *1598–1622 etc.*: promised *1594*

Gallop a pace bright *Phœbus* through the skie,
And duskie night, in rustie iron carre,
Betweene you both, shorten the time I pray, 1740
That I may see that most desired day,
When we may meet these traitors in the field.
Ah nothing greeues me but my little boye
Is thus misled to countenance their ils.
Come friends to Bristow, there to make vs strong, 1745
And windes as equall be to bring them in,
As you iniurious were to beare them foorth. ⟨*Exeunt.*⟩

Enter the Queene, her sonne, Edmund, Mortimer, and sir Iohn.

Qu. Now lords, our louing friends and countrimen,
Welcome to England all with prosperous windes,
Our kindest friends in Belgia haue we left, 1750
To cope with friends at home: a heauie case,
When force to force is knit and sword and gleaue
In ciuill broiles makes kin and country men
Slaughter themselues in others and their sides
With their owne weapons gorde, but whats the helpe? 1755
Misgouerned kings are cause of all this wrack,
And *Edward* thou art one among them all,
Whose loosnes hath betrayed thy land to spoyle,
And made the channels ouerflow with blood.
Of thine own people patron shouldst thou be, 1760
But thou—

Mor. iu. Nay madam, if you be a warriar
Ye must not grow so passionate in speeches:
Lords, sith that we are by sufferance of heauen
Arriued and armed in this princes right, 1765
Heere for our countries cause sweare we to him
All homage, fealtie and forwardnes,
And for the open wronges and iniuries
Edward hath done to vs, his Queene and land,
We come in armes to wrecke it with the swords: 1770
That Englands queene in peace may reposesse
Her dignities and honors, and withall
We may remooue these flatterers from the king,
That hauocks Englands wealth and treasurie.

1747 S.D. Exeunt *add. Dod.* Scene IV. *add. Rob.* 1759 channell *1598–1622 etc.* 1763 Ye] You *1622, Dyce, Bull.* 1764 *Two lines Bull., div. after* Lords that *omit conj. Dyce, Cunn., Wag.* 1773 these] those *Rob., Cunn., Wag.*

S. Io. Sound trumpets my lord & forward let vs martch,
Edward will thinke we come to flatter him. 1776
Edm. I would he neuer had bin flattered more. ⟨*Exeunt.*⟩

Enter the King, Baldock, and Spencer the sonne, flying about the stage.

Spe. Fly, fly, my Lord, the Queene is ouer strong,
Her friends doe multiply and yours doe fayle,
Shape we our course to Ireland there to breath. 1780
Edw. What, was I borne to flye and runne away,
And leaue the *Mortimers* conquerers behind ?
Giue me my horse and lets r'enforce our troupes :
And in this bed of honors die with fame.
Bal. O no my lord, this princely resolution 1785
Fits not the time ; away, we are pursu'd.

Edmund alone with a sword and target.

Edm. This way he fled, but I am come too late.
Edward alas my hart relents for thee,
Proud traytor *Mortimer* why doost thou chase
Thy lawfull king thy soueraigne with thy sword ? 1790
Vilde wretch, and why hast thou of all vnkinde,
Borne armes against thy brother and thy king ?
Raigne showers of vengeance on my cursed head,
Thou God to whom in iustice it belongs
To punish this vnnaturall reuolt : 1795
Edward, this *Mortimer* aimes at thy life :
O fly him then, but Edmund calme this rage,
Dissemble or thou diest, for *Mortimer*
And *Isabell* doe kisse while they conspire,
And yet she beares a face of loue forsooth : 1800
Fie on that loue that hatcheth death and hate.
Edmund away, Bristow to Longshankes blood
Is false, be not found single for suspect :
Proud *Mortimer* pries neare into thy walkes.

Enter the Queene, Mortimer, the young Prince and Sir Iohn of Henolt.

Qu. Succesfull battells giues the God of kings 1805
To them that fight in right and feare his wrath :
Since then succesfully we haue preuayled,

1777 S.D. Exeunt *add. Dod.* Scene V. *add. Rob.* 1784 honors *1594* : honor *1598–1622 etc.* 1805 Succesfulls *1598, 1612* battells *1594* : battel *1598–1622 etc.* 1807 succesfully] successiuely *1622*

Thankes be heauens great architect and you.
Ere farther we proceede my noble lordes,
We heere create our welbeloued sonne, 1810
Of loue and care vnto his royall person,
Lord warden of the realme, and sith the fates
Haue made his father so infortunate,
Deale you my lords in this, my louing lords,
As to your wisdomes fittest seemes in all. 1815

Edm. Madam, without offence if I may aske,
How will you deale with *Edward* in his fall?

Prince. Tell me good vnckle, what *Edward* doe you meane?

Edm. Nephew, your father, I dare not call him king.

Mor. My lord of Kent, what needes these questions?
Tis not in her controulment, nor in ours, 1821
But as the realme and parlement shall please,
So shall your brother be disposed of.
I like not this relenting moode in *Edmund*,
Madam, tis good to looke to him betimes. 1825

Qu. My lord, the Maior of Bristow knows our mind.

Mor. Yea madam, and they scape not easilie,
That fled the feeld.

Qu. *Baldock* is with the king,
A goodly chauncelor, is he not my lord? 1830

S. Ioh. So are the *Spencers*, the father and the sonne.

Edm. This *Edward* is the ruine of the realme.

Enter Rice ap Howell, and the Maior of Bristow, with Spencer the father.

Rice. God saue Queene *Isabell*, & her princely sonne.
Madam, the Maior and Citizens of Bristow,
In signe of loue and dutie to this presence, 1835
Present by me this traitor to the state,
Spencer, the father to that wanton *Spencer*,
That like the lawles *Catiline* of Rome,
Reueld in Englands wealth and treasurie.

Qu. We thanke you all. 1840

Mor. iu. Your louing care in this
Deserueth princelie fauors and rewardes,
But wheres the king and the other *Spencer* fled?

1808 Thankes *1594*: Thankt *1598–1622*: Thanked *Dyce to Bull.* heauens] the heavens *Fleay* 1813 vnfortunate *1622*, *Dod.*, *Rob.* 1823+S.D. Aside to the Qu. *add. Dod.* 1827 scape] scapt *1612* 1832 *Prefix* Edm.] Y. Mor. *Dyce*, *Wag.*, *Tan.*

Rice. Spencer the sonne, created earle of Gloster,
Is with that smoothe toongd scholler *Baldock* gone, 1845
And shipt but late for Ireland with the king.
Mort. iu. Some whirle winde fetche them backe, or sincke them all:
They shalbe started thence I doubt it not.
Prin. Shall I not see the king my father yet?
Edmund. Vnhappies *Edward,* chaste from Englands bounds. 1850
S. Ioh. Madam, what resteth, why stand ye in a muse?
Qu. I rue my lords ill fortune, but alas,
Care of my countrie cald me to this warre.
Mort. Madam, haue done with care & sad complaint,
Your king hath wrongd your countrie and himselfe, 1855
And we must seeke to right it as we may,
Meane while, haue hence this rebell to the blocke.
Your lordship cannot priuiledge your head.
Spen. pa. Rebell is he that fights against his prince,
So fought not they that fought in *Edwards* right. 1860
Mort. Take him away, he prates, you *Rice ap Howell,*
Shall do good seruice to her Maiestie,
Being of countenance in your countrey here,
To follow these rebellious runnagates,
We in meane while madam, must take aduise, 1865
How *Baldocke, Spencer,* and their complices,
May in their fall be followed to their end.
Exeunt omnes.

Enter the Abbot, Monkes, Edward, Spencer, and Baldocke.

Abbot. Haue you no doubt my Lorde, haue you no feare,
As silent and as carefull will we be,
To keepe your royall person safe with vs, 1870
Free from suspect, and fell inuasion
Of such as haue your maiestie in chase,
Your selfe, and those your chosen companie,
As daunger of this stormie time requires.
Edwa. Father, thy face should harbor no deceit, 1875
O hadst thou euer beene a king, thy hart
Pierced deeply with sence of my distresse,

1847+S.D. Aside *add. Rob.* 1850 Unhappy *Dod. to Cunn., Wag., Tan.*: Unhappy's *Bull.*: Unhappy is *Fleay* 1850+S.D. Aside *add. Dyce* 1858 *om. 1598–1622 etc.* 1859 his *1594*: the *1598–1622 etc.* 1867+Scene VI. *add. Rob.* 1869 will we *1594*: we will *1598–1622 etc.* 1877 with] with a *Dod. etc. exc. Dyce, Tan.*

Could not but take compassion of my state.
Stately and proud, in riches and in traine,
Whilom I was powerfull and full of pompe, 1880
But what is he, whome rule and emperie
Haue not in life or death made miserable?
Come *Spencer*, come *Baldocke*, come sit downe by me,
Make triall now of that philosophie,
That in our famous nurseries of artes 1885
Thou suckedst from *Plato*, and from *Aristotle*.
Father, this life contemplatiue is heauen,
O that I might this life in quiet lead,
But we alas are chaste, and you my friends,
Your liues and my dishonor they pursue. 1890
Yet gentle monkes, for treasure, golde nor fee,
Do you betray vs and our companie.

Monks. Your grace may sit secure, if none but wee
Doe wot of your abode.

Spen. Not one aliue, but shrewdly I suspect 1895
A gloomie fellow in a meade belowe,
A gaue a long looke after vs my lord,
And all the land I know is vp in armes,
Armes that pursue our liues with deadly hate.

Bald. We were imbarkt for Ireland, wretched we, 1900
With awkward windes and sore tempests driuen,
To fall on shoare, and here to pine in feare
Of *Mortimer* and his confederates.

Edw. *Mortimer*, who talkes of *Mortimer*,
Who wounds me with the name of *Mortimer*, 1905
That bloudy man? good father on thy lap
Lay I this head, laden with mickle care,
O might I neuer open these eyes againe,
Neuer againe lift vp this drooping head,
O neuer more lift vp this dying hart! 1910

Spen. son. Looke vp my lord. *Baldock*, this drowsines
Betides no good, here euen we are betraied.

Enter with Welch hookes, Rice ap Howell, a Mower, and the Earle of Leicester.

Mower. Vpon my life, those be the men ye seeke.

Rice. Fellow enough: my lord I pray be short,
A faire commission warrants what we do. 1915

Lei. The Queenes commission, vrgd by *Mortimer*,

1884 that *om. 1612*: thy *1622* 1901 sore] with sore *1622*, *Dyce*: surly *Dod.*[1] 1908 open] ope *1612*, *1622 etc.*

What cannot gallant *Mortimer* with the Queene?
Alas, see where he sits, and hopes vnseene
T'escape their hands that seeke to reaue his life:
Too true it is, *quem dies vidit veniens superbum,* 1920
Hunc dies vidit fugiens iacentem.
But Leister leaue to growe so passionate,
Spencer and *Baldocke,* by no other names,
I arrest you of high treason here,
Stand not on titles, but obay th'arrest, 1925
Tis in the name of *Isabell* the Queene:
My lord, why droope you thus?

Edw. O day! the last of all my blisse on earth,
Center of all misfortune. O my starres!
Why do you lowre vnkindly on a king? 1930
Comes Leister then in *Isabellas* name,
To take my life, my companie from me?
Here man, rip vp this panting brest of mine,
And take my heart, in reskew of my friends.

Rice. Away with them. 1935

Spen. iu. It may become thee yet,
To let vs take our farewell of his grace.

Abb. My heart with pittie earnes to see this sight,
A king to beare these words and proud commaunds. 1939

Edw. *Spencer,* a sweet *Spencer,* thus then must we part.

Spen. iu. We must my lord, so will the angry heauens.

Edw. Nay so will hell, and cruell *Mortimer,*
The gentle heauens haue not to do in this.

Bald. My lord, it is in vaine to greeue or storme,
Here humblie of your grace we take our leaues, 1945
Our lots are cast, I feare me so is thine.

Edwa. In heauen wee may, in earth neuer shall wee meete,
And Leister say, what shall become of vs?

Leist. Your maiestie must go to Killingworth. 1949

Edw. Must! tis somwhat hard, when kings must go.

Leist. Here is a Litter readie for your grace,
That waites your pleasure, and the day growes old.

Rice. As good be gon, as stay and be benighted.

Edw. A litter hast thou, lay me in a hearse,
And to the gates of hell conuay me hence, 1955

1917 gallant *om. 1612, 1622* with] doe with *1622* 1924 I I do *Rob. etc. exc. Dyce, Tan.* 1931 Comes *1594, Dod. etc.*: Come *1598*: Came *1612, 1622* 1938 earnes] yearns *Dod., Rob., Cunn., Wag.* 1940 a *om. Dod., Rob., Cunn.* 1954 in] on *1612, 1622*

Let *Plutos* bels ring out my fatall knell,
And hags howle for my death at *Charons* shore,
For friends hath *Edward* none, but these, and these,
And these must die vnder a tyrants sword.

Rice. My lord, be going, care not for these, 1960
For we shall see them shorter by the heads.

Edw. Well, that shalbe, shalbe: part we must,
Sweete *Spencer*, gentle *Baldocke*, part we must.
Hence fained weeds, vnfained are my woes.
Father, farewell: Leister, thou staist for me, 1965
And go I must, life farewell with my friends.

Exeunt Edward and Leicester.

Spen. iu. O is he gone! is noble *Edward* gone,
Parted from hence, neuer to see vs more!
Rent sphere of heauen, and fier forsake thy orbe,
Earth melt to ayre, gone is my soueraigne, 1970
Gone, gone alas, neuer to make returne.

Bald. Spencer, I see our soules are fleeted hence,
We are depriude the sun-shine of our life.
Make for a new life man, throw vp thy eyes,
And hart and hand to heauens immortall throne, 1975
Pay natures debt with cheerefull countenance,
Reduce we all our lessons vnto this,
To die sweet *Spencer*, therefore liue wee all,
Spencer, all liue to die, and rise to fall. 1979

Rice. Come, come, keepe these preachments till you come to the place appointed. You, and such as you are, haue made wise worke in England. Will your Lordships away?

Mower. Your worship I trust will remember me?

Rice. Remember thee fellow? what else? 1985
Follow me to the towne. ⟨*Exeunt.*⟩

Enter the king, Leicester, with a Bishop for the crowne.

Lei. Be patient good my lord, cease to lament,
Imagine Killingworth castell were your court,

1958 friend *Rob., Cunn., Fleay, Wag.* Edward] hapless Edward *conj. Dyce, Cunn., Wag.* and these *om. Dyce, Cunn., Wag.* 1959 And these *om Dod., Rob.* 1964+S.D. Throwing off his disguise *add. Dyce* 1966 S.D. Leicester *1594, Dod. etc.*: Lancaster *1598–1622* 1972 fleeted *1594*: fleeting *1598–1622 etc.* 1982 your Lordships] you *Fleay* 1984 worship *1594*: Lordship *1598–1622 etc.* 1986 S.D. Exeunt *add. Dod.*[2] Act the Fifth. Scene I. *add. Rob.* S.D. Enter King Edward, Leicester, the Bishop of Winchester, and Trussel *Dyce*

And that you lay for pleasure here a space,
Not of compulsion or neceissitie. 1990
Edw. Leister, if gentle words might comfort me,
Thy speeches long agoe had easde my sorrowes,
For kinde and louing hast thou alwaies beene:
The greefes of priuate men are soone allayde,
But not of kings, the forrest Deare being strucke 1995
Runnes to an herbe that closeth vp the wounds,
But when the imperiall Lions flesh is gorde,
He rends and teares it with his wrathfull pawe,
⟨And⟩ highly scorning, that the lowly earth
Should drinke his bloud, mounts vp into the ayre: 2000
And so it fares with me, whose dauntlesse minde
The ambitious *Mortimer* would seeke to curbe,
And that vnnaturall Queene false *Isabell*,
That thus hath pent and mu'd me in a prison,
For such outragious passions cloye my soule, 2005
As with the wings of rancor and disdaine,
Full often am I sowring vp to heauen,
To plaine me to the gods against them both:
But when I call to minde I am a king,
Me thinkes I should reuenge me of the wronges, 2010
That *Mortimer* and *Isabell* haue done.
But what are kings, when regiment is gone,
But perfect shadowes in a sun-shine day?
My nobles rule, I beare the name of king,
I weare the crowne, but am contrould by them, 2015
By *Mortimer*, and my vnconstant Queene,
Who spots my nuptiall bed with infamie,
Whilst I am lodgd within this caue of care,
Where sorrow at my elbow still attends,
To companie my hart with sad laments, 2020
That bleedes within me for this strange exchange.
But tell me, must I now resigne my crowne,
To make vsurping *Mortimer* a king?
Bish. Your grace mistakes, it is for Englands good,
And princely *Edwards* right we craue the crowne. 2025
Edw. No, tis for *Mortimer*, not *Edwards* head,
For hees a lambe, encompassed by Woolues,
Which in a moment will abridge his life:
But if proud *Mortimer* do weare this crowne,

1999 And *add. Dod. etc.* 2000 into *1594, Fleay, Wag.*: to *1598–1622 etc. exc. Fleay, Wag.* 2010 the *1594, Dod., Rob.*: my *1598–1622, Dyce etc.*

Heauens turne it to a blaze of quenchelesse fier, 2030
Or like the snakie wreathe of *Tisiphon*,
Engirt the temples of his hatefull head,
So shall not Englands Vine be perished,
But *Edwards* name suruiues, though *Edward* dies.
Lei. My lord, why waste you thus the time away? 2035
They stay your answer, will you yeeld your crowne?
Edw. Ah Leister, way how hardly I can brooke
To loose my crowne and kingdome, without cause,
To giue ambitious *Mortimer* my right,
That like a mountaine ouerwhelmes my blisse. 2040
In which extreame my minde here murthered is:
But what the heauens appoint, I must obaye,
Here, take my crowne, the life of *Edward* too,
Two kings in England cannot raigne at once:
But stay a while, let me be king till night, 2045
That I may gaze vpon this glittering crowne,
So shall my eyes receiue their last content,
My head, the latest honor dew to it,
And ioyntly both yeeld vp their wished right.
Continue euer thou celestiall sunne, 2050
Let neuer silent night possesse this clime,
Stand still you watches of the element,
All times and seasons rest you at a stay,
That *Edward* may be still faire Englands king:
But dayes bright beames dooth vanish fast away, 2055
And needes I must resigne my wished crowne.
Inhumaine creatures, nurst with Tigers milke,
Why gape you for your soueraignes ouerthrow?
My diadem I meane, and guiltlesse life.
See monsters see, ile weare my crowne againe, 2060
What, feare you not the furie of your king?
But haplesse *Edward*, thou art fondly led,
They passe not for thy frownes as late they did,
But seekes to make a new elected king,
Which fils my mind with strange despairing thoughts, 2065
Which thoughts are martyred with endles torments.
And in this torment, comfort finde I none,

2033 Vine *Rob. etc.*: Vines *1594–1622, Dod.* 2034 suruiues *1594, 1598, Bull.*: suruies *1612*: suruiue *1622 etc. exc. Bull.* 2041 extreams *1612, 1622* 2042 what *1594, Dod., Rob., Cunn., Bull.*: that *1598–1622, Dyce, Fleay* 2043 + S.D. Taking off the crown *add. Dyce* 2045 be *om. 1598* 2055 beames *1594*: beame *1598–1622 etc.* 2060 + S.D. He puts on the crown *add. Rob.*

But that I feele the crowne vpon my head,
And therefore let me weare it yet a while.

Tru⟨ssel.⟩ My Lorde, the parlement must haue present newes, 2070
And therefore say, will you resigne or no?

The king rageth.

Edw. Ile not resigne, but whilst I liue, ⟨be king.⟩
Traitors be gon, and ioine you with *Mortimer*,
Elect, conspire, install, do what you will,
Their bloud and yours shall seale these treacheries. 2075

Bish. This answer weele returne, and so farewell.

Leist. Call them againe my lorde, and speake them faire,
For if they goe, the prince shall lose his right

Edward. Call thou them back, I haue no power to speake.

Lei. My lord, the king is willing to resigne. 2080

Bish. If he be not, let him choose.

Edw. O would I might, but heauens & earth conspire
To make me miserable: heere receiue my crowne.
Receiue it? no, these innocent hands of mine
Shall not be guiltie of so foule a crime, 2085
He of you all that most desires my bloud,
And will be called the murtherer of a king,
Take it: what are you mooude, pitie you me?
Then send for vnrelenting *Mortimer*
And *Isabell*, whose eyes being turnd to steele, 2090
Will sooner sparkle fire then shed a teare:
Yet stay, for rather then I will looke on them,
Heere, heere: now sweete God of heauen,
Make me despise this transitorie pompe,
And sit for aye inthronized in heauen, 2095
Come death, and with thy fingers close my eyes,
Or if I liue, let me forget my selfe.

Bish. My lorde.

Edw. Call me not lorde,
Away, out of my sight: ah pardon me, 2100
Greefe makes me lunatick.
Let not that *Mortimer* protect my sonne,

2070 *Prefix* Tru. *1594–1622*: Trusty *Dod. to Rob.*: Bishop *Dilke* 2072 but] not *1612, 1622, Cunn., Wag.* be king *add. Dod. etc. exc. Cunn., Wag.* 2073 and *om. Cunn., Wag.* you *om. Dod. to Rob.* 2074 conspire] confirm *Dod.*[2], *Rob.* 2090 being *1598–1622 etc.*: beene *1594* 2093+S.D. He gives them the crown *add. Rob.* 2097+S.D. Enter Bartley *follows this line 1594–1622, Dod.* 2098 *Prefix* Bartley *1594–1622, Dod.*: Winch. *Rob.*: Bish. of Win. *Dyce*

More safetie is there in a Tigers iawes,
Then his imbrasements. Beare this to the queene,
Wet with my teares, and dried againe with sighes, 2105
If with the sight thereof she be not mooued,
Returne it backe and dip it in my bloud.
Commend me to my sonne, and bid him rule
Better then I, yet how haue I transgrest,
Vnlesse it be with too much clemencie? 2110

Tru. And thus, most humbly do we take our leaue.

Edward. Farewell, I know the next newes that they bring,
Will be my death, and welcome shall it be.
To wretched men death is felicitie.

Enter Bartley.

Leist. An other poast, what newes bringes he? 2115

Edw. Such newes as I expect: come *Bartley*, come,
And tell thy message to my naked brest.

Bart. My lord, thinke not a thought so villanous
Can harbor in a man of noble birth.
To do your highnes seruice and deuoire, 2120
And saue you from your foes, *Bartley* would die.

Leist. My lorde, the counsell of the Queene commaunds,
That I resigne my charge.

Edw. And who must keepe mee now, must you my lorde?

Bart. I, my most gratious lord, so tis decreed. 2125

Edw. By *Mortimer*, whose name is written here.
Well may I rent his name, that rends my hart,
This poore reuenge hath something easd my minde.
So may his limmes be torne as is this paper,
Heare me immortall *Ioue*, and graunt it too. 2130

Bart. Your grace must hence with mee to *Bartley* straight.

Edw. Whether you will: all places are alike,
And euery earth is fit for buriall.

Leist. Fauor him my lord, as much as lieth in you.

Bart. Euen so betide my soule as I vse him. 2135

Edw. Mine enemie hath pitied my estate,
And thats the cause that I am now remooude.

2103 is there *1594*: there is *1598–1622 etc.* 2104+S.D. Gives a handkerchief *add. Dyce* 2111+S.D. Exeunt Bishop and Attendants *add. Rob.* 2114 S.D. *follows line* 2097 *1594–1622, Dod.* Bartley] Berkley *Rob. etc.* (*passim*) 2122 of] and *1612, 1622* 2126 S.D. Taking the paper *add. Dyce after Prefix* 127+S.D. Tears it *add. Dyce*

Bartley. And thinkes your grace that *Bartley* will bee cruell?

Edw. I know not, but of this am I assured,
That death ends all, and I can die but once. 2140
Leicester, farewell.

Leicester. Not yet my lorde, ile beare you on your waye.

Exeunt omnes.

Enter Mortimer, and Queene Isabell.

Mor. iu. Faire *Isabell*, now haue we our desire,
The proud corrupters of the light-brainde king
Haue done their homage to the loftie gallowes, 2145
And he himselfe lies in captiuitie.
Be rulde by me, and we will rule the realme,
In any case, take heed of childish feare,
For now we hould an old Wolfe by the eares,
That if he slip will seaze vpon vs both, 2150
And gripe the sorer being gript himselfe.
Thinke therefore madam that imports vs much,
To erect your sonne with all the speed we may,
And that I be protector ouer him,
For our behoofe will beare the greater sway 2155
When as a kings name shall be vnder writ.

Qu. Sweet *Mortimer*, the life of *Isabell*,
Be thou perswaded, that I loue thee well,
And therefore so the prince my sonne be safe,
Whome I esteeme as deare as these mine eyes, 2160
Conclude against his father what thou wilt,
And I my selfe will willinglie subscribe.

Mort. iu. First would I heare newes that hee were deposde,
And then let me alone to handle him.

Enter Messenger.

Mor. iu. Letters, from whence? 2165

Messen. From Killingworth my lorde.

Qu. How fares my lord the king?

Messen. In health madam, but full of pensiuenes.

Queene. Alas poore soule, would I could ease his greefe.

2142 + Scene II. *add. Rob.* 2152 that] it *Dod.*[1], *Rob.*, *Dyce*[1], *Cunn.*: that it *Bull.*: that 't *Fleay* vs *1612*, *1622*, *Rob. etc.*: as *1594*, *1598*, *Dod.*[2], [3] 2155 will *1594*, *1598*: twill *1612*, *1622*, *Dod.*[2] *etc.* 2163 newes that *1594*, *Cunn.*: newes *1598–1622*, *Dyce*, *Bull.*: the news *Wag.*

⟨*Enter Winchester with the Crown.*⟩

Thankes gentle Winchester: sirra, be gon. 2170

Winchester. The king hath willingly resignde his crowne.

Qu. O happie newes, send for the prince my sonne.

Bish. Further, or this letter was sealed, Lord *Bartley* came,

So that he now is gone from Killingworth,

And we haue heard that *Edmund* laid a plot, 2175

To set his brother free, no more but so.

The lord of *Bartley* is so pitifull,

As Leicester that had charge of him before.

Qu. Then let some other be his guardian.

Mor. iu. Let me alone, here is the priuie seale. 2180

Whose there? call hither *Gurney* and *Matreuis*.

To dash the heauie headed *Edmunds* drift,

Bartley shall be dischargd, the king remooude,

And none but we shall know where he lieth.

Qu. But *Mortimer*, as long as he suruiues 2185

What safetie rests for vs, or for my sonne?

Mort. iu. Speake, shall he presently be dispatch'd and die?

Queene. I would hee were, so it were not by my meanes.

Enter Matreuis and Gurneye.

Mortim. iu. Inough *Matreuis*, write a letter presently

Vnto the Lord of *Bartley* from our selfe, 2190

That he resigne the king to thee and *Gurney*,

And when tis done, we will subscribe our name.

Matr. It shall be done my lord.

Mor. iu. Gurney.

Gurn. My Lorde. 2195

Mort. iu. As thou intendest to rise by *Mortimer*,

Who now makes Fortunes wheele turne as he please,

Seeke all the meanes thou canst to make him droope,

And neither giue him kinde word, nor good looke.

Gurn. I warrant you my lord. 2200

Mort. iu. And this aboue the rest: because we heare

That *Edmund* casts to worke his libertie,

Remooue him still from place to place by night,

2169 S.D. *add. Rob.* 2173 letter *omit conj. Dyce, Cunn., Wag., Fleay* 2177 so] as *Rob., Cunn., Wag.*: *om. ed. 1810* 2180 + S.D. Exit the Bish. of Win. *add. Dyce* 2181 + S.D. To Attendants within *add. Dyce* 2184 And where he lieth none but we shall know *Fleay*

Till at the last, he come to Killingworth,
And then from thence to *Bartley* back againe : 2205
And by the way to make him fret the more,
Speake curstlie to him, and in any case
Let no man comfort him : if he chaunce to weepe,
But amplifie his greefe with bitter words.

Matre. Feare not my Lord, weele do as you commaund.

Mor. iu. So now away, post thitherwards amaine. 2211

Qu. Whither goes this letter, to my lord the king ?
Commend me humblie to his Maiestie,
And tell him, that I labour all in vaine,
To ease his greefe, and worke his libertie : 2215
And beare him this, as witnesse of my loue.

Matre. I will madam.

Exeunt Matreuis and Gurney.
Manent Isabell and Mortimer.

Enter the yong Prince, and the Earle of Kent talking with him.

Mor. iu. Finely dissembled, do so still sweet Queene.
Heere comes the yong prince, with the Earle of Kent.

Qu. Some thing he whispers in his childish eares. 2220

Mort. iu. If he haue such accesse vnto the prince,
Our plots and stratagems will soone be dasht.

Queen. Vse *Edmund* friendly, as if all were well.

Mor. iu. How fares my honorable lord of Kent ? 2224

Edmun. In health sweete *Mortimer*, how fares your grace ?

Queene. Well, if my Lorde your brother were enlargde.

Edm. I heare of late he hath deposde himselfe.

Queen. The more my greefe.

Mortim. iu. And mine.

Edmun. Ah they do dissemble. 2230

Queen. Sweete sonne come hither, I must talke with thee.

Mortim. iu. Thou being his vnckle, and the next of bloud,
Doe looke to be protector ouer the prince.

Edm. Not I my lord : who should protect the sonne,
But she that gaue him life, I meane the Queene ? 2235

Prin. Mother, perswade me not to weare the crowne,
Let him be king, I am too yong to raigne.

Queene. But bee content, seeing it his highnesse pleasure.

2204 Till *1598–1622 etc.* : And *1594* 2216+S.D. Gives ring *add. Dyce* 2230+S.D. Aside *add. Dyce* 2233 o'er *Dyce etc.* 2238 it *1594, 1598, Dod.*[1] : it is *1612, 1622, Dod.*[2] *to Rob.* : 'tis *Dyce etc.*

Prin. Let me but see him first, and then I will.
Edmund. I do sweete Nephew. 2240
Quee. Brother, you know it is impossible.
Prince. Why, is he dead?
Queen. No, God forbid.
Edmun. I would those wordes proceeded from your heart.
Mort. iu. Inconstant *Edmund*, doost thou fauor him,
That wast a cause of his imprisonment? 2246
Edm. The more cause haue I now to make amends.
Mort. iu. I tell thee tis not meet, that one so false
Should come about the person of a prince.
My lord, he hath betraied the king his brother, 2250
And therefore trust him not.
Prince. But hee repents, and sorrowes for it now.
Queen. Come sonne, and go with this gentle Lorde and me.
Prin. With you I will, but not with *Mortimer*.
Mort. iu. Why yongling, s'dainst thou so of *Mortimer*?
Then I will carrie thee by force away. 2256
Prin. Helpe vnckle Kent, *Mortimer* will wrong me.
Quee. Brother *Edmund*, striue not, we are his friends,
Isabell is neerer then the earle of Kent.
Edm. Sister, *Edward* is my charge, redeeme him. 2260
Queen. *Edward* is my sonne, and I will keepe him.
Edmu. *Mortimer* shall know that he hath wrongde mee.
Hence will I haste to Killingworth castle,
And rescue aged *Edward* from his foes,
To be reuengde on *Mortimer* and thee. 2265
Exeunt omnes.

Enter Matreuis and Gurney with the king.

Matr. My lord, be not pensiue, we are your friends.
Men are ordaind to liue in miserie,
Therefore come, dalliance dangereth our liues.
Edw. Friends, whither must vnhappie *Edward* go,
Will hatefull *Mortimer* appoint no rest? 2270
Must I be vexed like the nightly birde,
Whose sight is loathsome to all winged fowles?
When will the furie of his minde asswage?
When will his hart be satisfied with bloud?

2265 + S.D. Aside *add. Dyce* Scene III. *add. Rob.* 2266 pensiue] so pensive *Wag.*

If mine will serue, vnbowell straight this brest, 2275
And giue my heart to *Isabell* and him,
It is the chiefest marke they leuell at.
Gurney. Not so my liege, the Queene hath giuen this charge,
To keepe your grace in safetie,
Your passions make your dolours to increase. 2280
Edw. This vsage makes my miserie increase.
But can my ayre of life continue long,
When all my sences are anoyde with stenche ?
Within a dungeon Englands king is kept,
Where I am steru'd for want of sustenance, 2285
My daily diet is heart breaking sobs,
That almost rents the closet of my heart.
Thus liues old *Edward* not relieu'd by any,
And so must die, though pitied by many.
O water, gentle friends, to coole my thirst, 2290
And cleare my bodie from foule excrements.
Matr. Heeres channell water, as our charge is giuen.
Sit downe, for weele be Barbars to your grace.
Edw. Traitors away, what will you murther me,
Or choake your soueraigne with puddle water ? 2295
Gurn. No, but wash your face, and shaue away your beard,
Least you be knowne, and so be rescued.
Matr. Why striue you thus ? your labour is in vaine.
Edward. The Wrenne may striue against the Lions strength,
But all in vaine: so vainely do I striue, 2300
To seeke for mercie at a tyrants hand.
They wash him with puddle water, and shaue his beard away.
Immortall powers, that knowes the painfull cares,
That waites vpon my poore distressed soule,
O leuell all your lookes vpon these daring men,
That wronges their liege and soueraigne, Englands king.
O *Gaueston*, it is for thee that I am wrongd, 2306
For me both thou and both the *Spencers* died,
And for your sakes, a thousand wronges ile take.
The *Spencers* ghostes, where euer they remaine,
Wish well to mine, then tush, for them ile die. 2310
Matr. Twixt theirs and yours shall be no enmitie.

2279 To] Only to *conj. Dyce, Cunn., Fleay, Wag.* 2280 to *om. 1622* 2304 all *omit conj. Dyce, Cunn., Wag., Fleay*

Come, come, away, now put the torches out,
Weele enter in by darkenes to Killingworth.

Enter Edmund.

Gurn. How now, who comes there?
Matr. Guarde the king sure, it is the earle of Kent. 2315
Edw. O gentle brother, helpe to rescue me.
Matr. Keepe them a sunder, thrust in the king.
Edm. Souldiers, let me but talke to him one worde.
Gur. Lay hands vpon the earle for this assault. 2319
Edmu. Lay downe your weapons, traitors, yeeld the king.
Matr. *Edmund*, yeeld thou thy self, or thou shalt die.
Edmu. Base villaines, wherefore doe you gripe mee thus?
Gurney. Binde him, and so conuey him to the court.
Edm. Where is the court but heere? heere is the king,
And I will visit him, why stay you me? 2325
Matr. The court is where lord *Mortimer* remaines,
Thither shall your honour go, and so farewell.

Exeunt Matr. and Gurney, with the king.

Manent Edmund and the souldiers.

Edm. O miserable is that commonweale, where lords
Keepe courts, and kings are lockt in prison!
Sould. Wherefore stay we? on sirs to the court. 2330
Edm. I, lead me whether you will, euen to my death,
Seeing that my brother cannot be releast.

Exeunt omnes.

Enter Mortimer alone.

Mort. iu. The king must die, or *Mortimer* goes downe,
The commons now begin to pitie him,
Yet he that is the cause of *Edwards* death 2335
Is sure to pay for it when his sonne is of age,
And therefore will I do it cunninglie.
This letter written by a friend of ours
Containes his death, yet bids them saue his life.
Edwardum occidere nolite timere, bonum est: 2340
Feare not to kill the king, tis good he die.
But read it thus, and thats an other sence:
Edwardum occidere nolite, timere bonum est:
Kill not the king, tis good to feare the worst.
Vnpointed as it is, thus shall it goe, 2345
That being dead, if it chaunce to be found,

2319 this *1594*: his *1598–1622 etc.* 2332 + Scene IV. *add. Rob.*

Matreuis and the rest may beare the blame,
And we be quit that causde it to be done:
Within this roome is lockt the messenger,
That shall conueie it, and performe the rest, 2350
And by a secret token that he beares,
Shall he be murdered when the deed is done.
Lightborn,
Come forth, art thou as resolute as thou wast? 2354

Light. What else my lord? and farre more resolute.
Mort. iu. And hast thou cast how to accomplish it?
Light. I, I, and none shall know which way he died.
Mortim. iu. But at his lookes *Lightborne* thou wilt relent.
Light. Relent, ha, ha, I vse much to relent.
Mort. iu. Well, do it brauely, and be secret. 2360
Light. You shall not need to giue instructions,
Tis not the first time I haue killed a man,
I learnde in Naples how to poison flowers,
To strangle with a lawne thrust through the throte,
To pierce the wind-pipe with a needles point, 2365
Or whilst one is a sleepe, to take a quill
And blowe a little powder in his eares,
Or open his mouth, and powre quick siluer downe,
But yet I haue a brauer way then these.
Mort. iu. Whats that? 2370
Light. Nay, you shall pardon me, none shall knowe my trickes.
Mort. iu. I care not how it is, so it be not spide,
Deliuer this to *Gurney* and *Matreuis*,
At euery ten miles end thou hast a horse.
Take this, away, and neuer see me more. 2375
Lightborne. No?
Mort. iu. No, vnlesse thou bring me newes of *Edwards* death.
Light. That will I quicklie do, farewell my lord.
Mor. The prince I rule, the queene do I commaund,
And with a lowly conge to the ground, 2380
The proudest lords salute me as I passe,
I seale, I cancell, I do what I will,

2354 S.D. Enter Lightborn *add. Dyce after* forth as resolute *1594*: so resolute *1598–1622 etc.* 2364 through] downe *1612*, *1622*, *Dyce*, *Cunn.*, *Wag.* 2373+S.D. Gives letter *add. Dyce* 2374 miles *1594*, *1622*: mile *1598*, *1612*, *Dod. etc.* 2375 S.D. Gives money *add. Dyce after* this

Feard am I more then lou'd, let me be feard,
And when I frowne, make all the court looke pale,
I view the prince with *Aristorchus* eyes, 2385
Whose lookes were as a breeching to a boye.
They thrust vpon me the Protectorship,
And sue to me for that that I desire,
While at the councell table, graue enough,
And not vnlike a bashfull puretaine, 2390
First I complaine of imbecilitie,
Saying it is, *onus quam grauissimum,*
Till being interrupted by my friends,
Suscepi that *prouinciam* as they terme it,
And to conclude, I am Protector now. 2395
Now is all sure, the Queene and *Mortimer*
Shall rule the realme, the king, and none rule vs,
Mine enemies will I plague, my friends aduance,
And what I list commaund, who dare controwle?
Maior sum quam cui possit fortuna nocere, 2400
And that this be the coronation day,
It pleaseth me and *Isabell* the Queene.
The trumpets sound, I must go take my place.

Enter the yong King, Bishop, Champion, Nobles, Queene.

Bish. Long liue king *Edward,* by the grace of God
King of England, and lorde of Ireland. 2405
Cham. If any Christian, Heathen, Turke, or Iew,
Dares but affirme, that *Edwards* not true king,
And will auouche his saying with the sworde,
I am the Champion that will combate him.
Mort. iu. None comes, sound trumpets. 2410
King. Champion, heeres to thee.
Qu. Lord *Mortimer,* now take him to your charge.

Enter Souldiers with the Earle of Kent prisoner.

Mor. iu. What traitor haue wee there with blades and billes?
Sould. *Edmund* the Earle of Kent.
King. What hath he done? 2415
Sould. A would haue taken the king away perforce,
As we were bringing him to Killingworth.
Mortimer iu. Did you attempt his rescue, *Edmund* speake?

2390 puretaine] paretaine *1594, 1598* 2397 rule vs] rules vs *1598, 1612, 1622, Dod., Dyce, Cunn.* 2410+S.D. Trumpets *add. Dyce* 2411+S.D. Gives purse *add. Dyce*

Edm. *Mortimer*, I did, he is our king,
And thou compelst this prince to weare the crowne. 2420
Mort. iu. Strike off his head, he shall haue marshall lawe.
Edm. Strike of my head? base traitor I defie thee.
King. My lord, he is my vnckle, and shall liue.
Mor. iu. My lord, he is your enemie, and shall die.
Edmund. Staie villaines. 2425
King. Sweete mother, if I cannot pardon him,
Intreate my lord Protector for his life.
Qu. Sonne, be content, I dare not speake a worde.
King. Nor I, and yet me thinkes I should commaund,
But seeing I cannot, ile entreate for him: 2430
My lord, if you will let my vnckle liue,
I will requite it when I come to age.
Mort. iu. Tis for your highnesse good, and for the realmes.
How often shall I bid you beare him hence? 2434
Edm. Art thou king, must I die at thy commaund?
Mort. iu. At our commaund, once more away with him.
Edm. Let me but stay and speake, I will not go,
Either my brother or his sonne is king,
And none of both them thirst for *Edmunds* bloud,
And therefore soldiers whether will you hale me? 2440
They hale Edmund away, and carie him to be beheaded.
King. What safetie may I looke for at his hands,
If that my Vnckle shall be murthered thus?
Queen. Feare not sweete boye, ile garde thee from thy foes,
Had *Edmund* liu'de, he would haue sought thy death.
Come sonne, weele ride a hunting in the parke. 2445
King. And shall my Vnckle *Edmund* ride with vs?
Queene. He is a traitor, thinke not on him, come.
Exeunt omnes.

Enter Matr. and Gurney.

Matr. *Gurney*, I wonder the king dies not,
Being in a vault vp to the knees in water,
To which the channels of the castell runne, 2450
From whence a dampe continually ariseth,
That were enough to poison any man,
Much more a king brought vp so tenderlie.
Gurn. And so do I, *Matreuis*: yesternight

2435 king] a king *1612, 1622* 2439 none . . them] neither of them *ed. 1810, Rob.* them *1598, 1622, Dod., Dyce etc.*: then *1594, 1612* 2447 + Scene V. *add. Rob.* 2450 runs *1622*

I opened but the doore to throw him meate, 2455
And I was almost stifeled with the sauor.
Matr. He hath a body able to endure
More then we can enflict, and therefore now,
Let vs assaile his minde another while.
Gurn. Send for him out thence, and I will anger him.
Matr. But stay, whose this? 2461

Enter Lightborne.

Light. My lord protector greetes you.
Gurn. Whats heere? I know not how to conster it.
Matr. *Gurney*, it was left vnpointed for the nonce,
Edwardum occidere nolite timere, 2465
Thats his meaning.
Light. Know you this token, I must haue the king?
Matr. I, stay a while, thou shalt haue answer straight.
This villain's sent to make away the king.
Gurney. I thought as much. 2470
Matr. And when the murders done,
See how he must be handled for his labour,
Pereat iste: let him haue the king,
What else? Heere is the keyes, this is the lake,
Doe as you are commaunded by my lord. 2475
Light. I know what I must do, get you away,
Yet be not farre off, I shall need your helpe.
See that in the next roome I haue a fier,
And get me a spit, and let it be red hote.
Matre. Very well. 2480
Gurn. Neede you any thing besides?
Light. What else? a table and a fetherbed.
Gurn. Thats all?
Light. I, I, so when I call you bring it in.
Matre. Feare not you that. 2485
Gurn. Heeres a light to go into the dungeon.
Lightbor. So now must I about this geare: nere was there any
So finely handled as this king shalbe.
Foh, heeres a place in deed with all my hart.
Edward. Whose there, what light is that, wherefore comes thou? 2490

2463 conster *1594*: construe *1598–1622 etc.* 2467 you] ye *Dod. to Rob., Cunn., Bull.* S.D. Gives token *add. Dyce* 2485 you *1594*: thou *1598–1622 etc.* 2486 + S.D. Gives light to Lightborn, and then exit with Matrevis *add. Dyce* 2490 comes *1594*: com'st *1598–1622 etc.*

Light. To comfort you, and bring you ioyfull newes.
Edward. Small comfort findes poore *Edward* in thy lookes,
Villaine, I know thou comst to murther me.
Light. To murther you my most gratious lorde?
Farre is it from my hart to do you harme. 2495
The Queene sent me, to see how you were vsed,
For she relents at this your miserie.
And what eyes can refraine from shedding teares,
To see a king in this most pittious state?
Edw. Weepst thou already? list a while to me, 2500
And then thy heart, were it as *Gurneys* is,
Or as *Matreuis*, hewne from the *Caucasus*,
Yet will it melt, ere I haue done my tale.
This dungeon where they keepe me, is the sincke,
Wherein the filthe of all the castell falles. 2505
Light. O villaines!
Edw. And there in mire and puddle haue I stood,
This ten dayes space, and least that I should sleepe,
One plaies continually vpon a Drum,
They giue me bread and water being a king, 2510
So that for want of sleepe and sustenance,
My mindes distempered, and my bodies numde,
And whether I haue limmes or no, I know not.
O would my bloud dropt out from euery vaine,
As doth this water from my tattered robes: 2515
Tell *Isabell* the Queene, I lookt not thus,
When for her sake I ran at tilt in Fraunce,
And there vnhorste the duke of *Cleremont*.
Light. O speake no more my lorde, this breakes my heart.
Lie on this bed, and rest your selfe a while. 2520
Edw. These lookes of thine can harbor nought but death.
I see my tragedie written in thy browes,
Yet stay a while, forbeare thy bloudie hande,
And let me see the stroke before it comes,
That euen then when I shall lose my life, 2525
My minde may be more stedfast on my God.
Light. What meanes your highnesse to mistrust me thus?
Edwa. What meanes thou to dissemble with me thus?
Light. These handes were neuer stainde with innocent bloud,
Nor shall they now be tainted with a kings. 2530

2525 That] That and *1594–1622* 2528 mean'st *1598*, *Dod. etc.*

Edward. Forgiue my thought, for hauing such a thought,
One iewell haue I left, receiue thou this.
Still feare I, and I know not whats the cause,
But euerie iointe shakes as I giue it thee:
O if thou harborst murther in thy hart, 2535
Let this gift change thy minde, and saue thy soule,
Know that I am a king, oh at that name,
I feele a hell of greefe: where is my crowne?
Gone, gone, and doe I remaine aliue? 2539
Light. Your ouerwatchde my lord, lie downe and rest.
Edw. But that greefe keepes me waking, I shoulde sleepe,
For not these ten daies haue these eyes lids closd.
Now as I speake they fall, and yet with feare
Open againe. O wherefore sits thou heare?
Light. If you mistrust me, ile be gon my lord. 2545
Edw. No, no, for if thou meanst to murther me,
Thou wilt returne againe, and therefore stay.
Light. He sleepes.
Edw. O let me not die yet, stay, O stay a while.
Light. How now my Lorde. 2550
Edw. Something still busseth in mine eares,
And tels me, if I sleepe I neuer wake,
This feare is that which makes me tremble thus,
And therefore tell me, wherefore art thou come?
Light. To rid thee of thy life. *Matreuis* come. 2555
Edw. I am too weake and feeble to resist,
Assist me sweete God, and receiue my soule.
Light. Runne for the table.
Edw. O spare me, or dispatche me in a trice.
⟨*King Edward is murdered.*⟩
Light. So, lay the table downe, and stampe on it, 2560
But not too hard, least that you bruse his body.
Matreuis. I feare mee that this crie will raise the towne,
And therefore let vs take horse and away.
Light. Tell me sirs, was it not brauelie done?
Gurn. Excellent well, take this for thy rewarde. 2565
Then Gurney stabs Lightborne.
Come let vs cast the body in the mote,

2531 my thought] my fau't *Fleay* 2532+S.D. Giving jewel *add. Dyce* 2539 aliue *om. 1612, 1622* 2542 eye-lids *1622* 2549 yet, stay] yet *1622, Dyce* 2555+S.D. Enter Matrevis and Gurney *add. Dyce* 2559 S.D. *add. Rob.*

And beare the kings to *Mortimer* our lord.
Away. *Exeunt omnes.*

Enter Mortimer and Matreuis.

Mortim. iu. Ist done, *Matreuis*, and the murtherer dead?
Matr. I my good Lord, I would it were vndone. 2570
Mort. iu. *Matreuis*, if thou now growest penitent
Ile be thy ghostly father, therefore choose
Whether thou wilt be secret in this,
Or else die by the hand of *Mortimer*.
Matr. *Gurney*, my lord, is fled, and will I feare, 2575
Betray vs both, therefore let me flie.
Mort. iu. Flie to the Sauages.
Matr. I humblie thanke your honour.
Mor. iu. As for my selfe, I stand as *Ioues* huge tree,
And others are but shrubs compard to me, 2580
All tremble at my name, and I feare none,
Lets see who dare impeache me for his death?

Enter the Queene.

Queen. A *Mortimer*, the king my sonne hath news,
His fathers dead, and we haue murdered him. 2584
Mor. iu. What if he haue? the king is yet a childe.
Queene. I, I, but he teares his haire, and wrings his handes,
And vowes to be reuengd vpon vs both,
Into the councell chamber he is gone,
To craue the aide and succour of his peeres.
Aye me, see where he comes, and they with him, 2590
Now *Mortimer* begins our tragedie.

Enter the king, with the lords.

Lords. Feare not my lord, know that you are a king.
King. Villaine.
Mort. iu. How now my lord? 2594
King. Thinke not that I am frighted with thy words.
My father's murdered through thy treacherie,
And thou shalt die, and on his mournefull hearse,
Thy hatefull and accursed head shall lie,
To witnesse to the world, that by thy meanes,
His kingly body was too soone interrde. 2600

2568 + Scene VI. *add. Rob.* 2571 now *om. 1612, 1622* 2586 I, I] Ay *Dyce, Cunn., Fleay*: I *Bull.* 2594 How] Ho *1598, Dyce, Bull.*

Qu. Weepe not sweete sonne.
King. Forbid not me to weepe, he was my father,
And had you lou'de him halfe so well as I,
You could not beare his death thus patiently,
But you I feare, conspirde with *Mortimer*. 2605
Lords. Why speake you not vnto my lord the king?
Mor. iu. Because I thinke scorne to be accusde,
Who is the man dare say I murderedd him?
King. Traitor, in me my louing father speakes,
And plainely saith, twas thou that murdredst him. 2610
Mort. iu. But hath your grace no other proofe then this?
King. Yes, if this be the hand of *Mortimer*.
Mortim. iu. False *Gurney* hath betraide me and himselfe.
Queen. I feard as much, murther cannot be hid.
Mort. iu. Tis my hand, what gather you by this. 2615
King. That thither thou didst send a murtherer.
Mort. iu. What murtherer? bring foorth the man I sent.
King. A *Mortimer*, thou knowest that he is slaine,
And so shalt thou be too: why staies he heere?
Bring him vnto a hurdle, drag him foorth, 2620
Hang him I say, and set his quarters vp,
But bring his head back presently to me.
Queen. For my sake sweete sonne pittie *Mortimer*.
Mort. iu. Madam, intreat not, I will rather die,
Then sue for life vnto a paltrie boye. 2625
King. Hence with the traitor, with the murderer.
Mort. iu. Base fortune, now I see, that in thy wheele
There is a point, to which when men aspire,
They tumble hedlong downe: that point I touchte,
And seeing there was no place to mount vp higher, 2630
Why should I greeue at my declining fall?
Farewell faire Queene, weepe not for *Mortimer*,
That scornes the world, and as a traueller,
Goes to discouer countries yet vnknowne.
King. What, suffer you the traitor to delay? 2635
Queen. As thou receiuedst thy life from me,
Spill not the bloud of gentle *Mortimer*.
King. This argues, that you spilt my fathers bloud,
Els would you not intreate for *Mortimer*.
Queen. I spill his bloud? no. 2640

2607 thinke] think it *conj. Dyce*[2] 2608 dare *1594*: dares *1598–1622 etc.* 2612+S.D. Shewing letter *add. Dyce* 2613+S.D. Aside to Queen Isabella *add. Dyce* 2635+S.D. Mortimer is taken away *add. Cunn.* 2640 no *om. 1612, 1622*

King. I, madam, you, for so the rumor runnes.
Queen. That rumor is vntrue, for louing thee
Is this report raisde on poore *Isabell.*
King. I doe not thinke her so vnnaturall.
Lords. My lord, I feare me it will prooue too true. 2645
King. Mother, you are suspected for his death,
And therefore we commit you to the Tower,
Till further triall may be made thereof.
If you be guiltie, though I be your sonne,
Thinke not to finde me slack or pitifull. 2650
Qu. Nay, to my death, for too long haue I liued,
When as my sonne thinkes to abridge my daies.
King. Awaye with her, her wordes inforce these teares,
And I shall pitie her if she speake againe.
Queen. Shall I not moorne for my beloued lord, 2655
And with the rest accompanie him to his graue?
Lords. Thus madam, tis the kings will you shall hence.
Quee. He hath forgotten me, stay, I am his mother.
Lords. That bootes not, therefore gentle madam goe.
Queen. Then come sweete death, and rid me of this greefe. 2660
Lords. My lord, here is the head of *Mortimer.*
King. Goe fetche my fathers hearse, where it shall lie,
And bring my funerall robes: accursed head,
Could I haue rulde thee then, as I do now,
Thou hadst not hatcht this monstrous treacherie? 2665
Heere comes the hearse, helpe me to moorne my lords:
Sweete father heere, vnto thy murdered ghost,
I offer vp this wicked traitors head,
And let these teares distilling from mine eyes,
Be witnesse of my greefe and innocencie. 2670

FINIS.

⟨Small device.⟩

Imprinted at London for *William*
Ihones, *and are to be solde at his*
shop, neere vnto Houlburne
Conduit. 1594.

2648 may *om.* *1612, 1622* 2656 his] the *1612, 1622*

DIDO

Date and authorship. No question in Marlowe criticism offers greater difficulties than those which concern the date and authorship of the *Tragedy of Dido.* Our only source of information is the title-page of the single early edition, where we learn that the piece had been 'Played by the Children of her Maiesties Chappell', and that the authors were 'Christopher Marlowe and Thomas Nash, Gent.' Nearly all recent critics[1] are agreed in the opinion that the tragedy was probably sketched in its earliest form before Marlowe left Cambridge (1587). After *Tamburlaine*, Marlowe's dramatic career follows a pretty definite line of development, into which it is difficult to fit either the subject-matter or the general structure of *Dido.* On the other hand, the classical story and close dependence on Vergil would naturally point back to the academic period, which seems certainly to have produced the Ovid translations, and which probably inspired the version of Lucan as well. Again, the dramatic looseness of the play would mark it as immature work, while it is significant that a number of lines stand in the apparent relation of earlier and somewhat unfinished drafts of famous passages in *Tamburlaine* or *Doctor Faustus.*[2] Yet it seems pretty clear that the extant text of *Dido* dates from a later period than that of Marlowe's and Nash's residence at Cambridge, for much of the blank verse shows very considerable finish and fluency. Verbal similarities have been pointed out also between this play and *Edward II*, which, though less numerous than those connecting *Dido* with *Tamburlaine* and *Faustus*, are yet so significant as to make it very likely that Marlowe subjected his old Cambridge play to

[1] Knutowski, *Das Dido-Drama von Marlowe und Nash*, Breslau, 1905; Ward, *Eng. Dram. Lit.*; Fleay, *Biog. Chron. Eng. Dr.*; Ingram, *Christopher Marlowe and his Associates.*

[2] Cp. for example *Dido*, 478–82, and *Doctor Faustus*, 1328 ff.; *Dido*, 1062–5, and *Tamburlaine* I, 2075–9.

a complete revision at about the period when he was writing *Edward II* and the not dissimilar *Hero and Leander.*[1]

The connexion of Thomas Nash with our play is very uncertain, and on the evidence of style would seem to be slight. There is no discernible resemblance between Nash's only other extant dramatic work, *Summer's Last Will and Testament,* and any part of *Dido,* whereas the peculiar style of Marlowe can be recognized in almost every scene. Lines 1549–1600, which occur within a couple of pages of the end of the drama, are in themselves almost sufficient disproof of the theory that Nash found the tragedy a torso and added the conclusion. Marlowe perhaps never wrote more characteristic verses than these:

> So thou wouldst proue as true as *Paris* did,
> Would, as faire *Troy* was, *Carthage* might be sackt,
> And I be calde a second *Helena.*
> . . . .
> Thy mother was no Goddesse periurd man,
> Nor *Dardanus* the author of thy stocke:
> But thou art sprung from *Scythian Caucasus,*
> And Tygers of *Hircania* gaue thee sucke.[2]

In no other case can Marlowe be shown to have collaborated with a fellow dramatist during his London career, unless with Shakespeare in the Henry VI plays, and the conclusion would at first seem almost unavoidable that *Dido* is the product of an old college partnership between two Cambridge contemporaries. There is much which is attractive in this view, and I should be reluctant to abandon it entirely; yet reasons exist which make it probable, if not certain, that Nash was in some way connected with the play at a period subsequent to 1587. In the first place Marlowe's name on the title-page of a tragedy was certainly of much more value in 1594 than Nash's, and it is unlikely that the publisher of the quarto, even if he had been himself aware of the fact, would have called the reader's attention to the minor dramatist's ancient concern in a work which had been recently revised and renovated by the more celebrated author. The fact may be added, for what it is worth, that Nash's introductory epistle to *Menaphon* in 1589 suggests a dislike for Marlowe's dramatic

[1] Cf. Knutowski, *op. cit.*

[2] ll. 1554–6, 1564–7.

methods hardly in consonance with the theory of recent joint authorship, whereas his later allusions to the poet indicate regard and admiration.

There exists a third rather mysterious bit of evidence tending to connect Nash with *Dido* at a period which can only very shortly have antedated the play's publication. It is an Elegy on Marlowe's death, which both Bishop Tanner[1] and Warton, the literary historian,[2] declare to be affixed to the 1594 edition of *Dido,* but which is not found in any of the three known copies. Tanner and Warton appear to have written independently on the subject; the latter furnished Malone with certain details not specified by the former. It can hardly be doubted, therefore, that this elegy really occurred in at least one copy of the tragedy, and since Nash is definitely mentioned as the author, we can perhaps infer that it was a printed addition to the play, inserted by way of dedication or prologue, and not a mere manuscript note on a fly-leaf. Nash's connexion with *Dido* may therefore be analogous to Heywood's connexion with the *Jew of Malta*: he may merely have prepared the play for the printers by introducing a few superficial changes and writing a prefatory elegy which through negligence of the printer or late arrival found its way into only a part of the edition. This assumption does not necessarily contradict the theory that Nash had an earlier and more fundamental concern in the play, but it leaves the theory without any sort of confirmation. In any case it appears to be probable that *Dido* is in its present form mainly the work of Marlowe and that the play represents two stages in that poet's development.

Stage history. The only early edition of *Dido* was published by Thomas Woodcocke in 1594, apparently without registration. Only three copies are certainly known to exist,[3] and they appear to agree in every respect; the present text follows the Bodleian copy. From the title-page we learn that the tragedy had been acted by the 'Children of the Chapel'. The one ascertained fact concerning the history of this company during the ten years previous to 1594 seems to be that they acted before the

[1] *Bibliotheca Britannico-Hibernica*, 1748, p. 512.

[2] *Hist. Eng. Poetry*, iii. p. 433, note.

[3] Hazlitt's *Handbook*, p. 373, says four, but probably inaccurately; one of the three copies seems here to have been counted twice.

Queen at Croydon in 1591, under the direction of N. Giles, and Mr. Fleay assumes,[1] apparently with no further evidence, that *Dido* was presented on this occasion. Henslowe's *Diary*, from which we should, of course, have no right to expect information regarding a play of the Chapel Children, does contain two allusions to a possibly related drama on the same subject. On January 3, 1597, Henslowe expended 29 shillings for furnishings 'a geanste the playe of dido & enevs', and two entries below he adds the memorandum: 'Lent vnto the company when they fyrst played dido at nyght the some of thirtishillynges wch wasse the 8 of Jenewary 1597.' (i.e., 1598)

Source. The primary source of *Dido* is found in the first, second, and fourth books of the *Aeneid*. Knutowski [2] has exerted himself to show that the play is also influenced in various passages by Ovid's works. A comparison of the tragedy with the Vergilian original throws interesting light on the structure of the former. Parts of the play follow the corresponding lines of the *Aeneid* with schoolboy slavishness, whereas the borrowed material is elsewhere altered with a freedom and insight which evidence a mature judgement and no small dramatic skill. In this respect, as in others, the text of *Dido* appears to be a composite of elements dating from two rather widely separated periods.

There is no evidence that the play of Marlowe and Nash was directly influenced by any of the earlier dramas on the same subject, though it is not unlikely that Halliwell's Latin play of *Dido*, performed at Cambridge in 1564, or Gager's Oxford play (1583) in the same language, may have offered the original suggestion for our tragedy.

[1] *Biog. Chron. Eng. Dr.* ii. 147.

[2] *Op. cit.*, p. 61 ff.

THE
Tragedie of Dido
Queene of Carthage:
Played by the Children of her *Maiesties Chappell.*

Written by Christopher Marlowe, and *Thomas Nash. Gent.*

Actors

Iupiter.	*Ascanius.*
Ganimed.	*Dido.*
Venus.	*Anna.*
Cupid.	*Achates.*
Iuno.	*Ilioneus.*
Mercurie, or Hermes.	*Iarbas.*
Æneas.	*Cloanthes.*
	Sergestus.

AT LONDON,
Printed, by the Widdowe *Orwin*, for *Thomas Woodcocke*, and are to be solde at his shop, in Paules Church-yeard, at the signe of the blacke Beare. 1594.

1594 = Quarto edition of that year.

Hurst = Text of the play in vol. ii of *Old English Drama*, published by Hurst, Robinson & Co., 1825.

Rob. = Robinson's edition of Marlowe, 1826.

Dyce { *Dyce*[1] = Dyce's first edition of Marlowe, 1850.
Dyce[2] = Dyce's revised edition of Marlowe, 1858, etc. }

Cunn. = Cunningham's edition of Marlowe, 1870, etc.

Bull. = Bullen's edition of Marlowe, 1885.

Gros. = Text of the play in Grosart's edition of Nash (vol. vi), vol. ii, 1885.

McK. = Text of the play in McKerrow's edition of Nash (vol. ii), 1904.

T. B. = The present editor.

Broughton = J. B.'s MS. notes in copy of *Rob.* (Brit. Mus. 11771 d).

Coll. = J. P. Collier's MS. notes in copy of *Dyce*[1] (Brit. Mus. 11771 bbb 6).

Deighton = Conjectural emendations in *The Old Dramatists*, 1896.

Elze = Conjectural emendations in *Notes on Elizabethan Dramatists*, 1889.

Mitford = J. M.'s conjectures, quoted by Dyce.

The Tragedie of *Dido* Queene *of Carthage.*

⟨*Actus* I. *Scena* I.⟩

Here the Curtaines draw, there is discouered Iupiter *dandling*
Ganimed *vpon his knee, and* Mercury
lying asleepe.

Iup. Come gentle *Ganimed* and play with me,
I loue thee well, say *Iuno* what she will.
Gan. I am much better for your worthles loue,
That will not shield me from her shrewish blowes:
To day when as I fild into your cups, 5
And held the cloath of pleasance whiles you dranke,
She reacht me such a rap for that I spilde,
As made the bloud run downe about mine eares.
Iup. What? dares she strike the darling of my thoughts?
By *Saturnes* soule, and this earth threatning haire, 10
That shaken thrise, makes Natures buildings quake,
I vow, if she but once frowne on thee more,
To hang her meteor like twixt heauen and earth,
And bind her hand and foote with golden cordes,
As once I did for harming *Hercules*. 15
Gan. Might I but see that pretie sport afoote,
O how would I with *Helens* brother laugh,
And bring the Gods to wonder at the game:
Sweet *Iupiter*, if ere I pleasde thine eye,
Or seemed faire walde in with Egles wings, 20
Grace my immortall beautie with this boone,
And I will spend my time in thy bright armes.
Iup. What ist sweet wagge I should deny thy youth?
Whose face reflects such pleasure to mine eyes,
As I exhal'd with thy fire darting beames, 25
Haue oft driuen backe the horses of the night,

Act I. Scene I. *add. Hurst* S.D. Mercury] Hermes *Dyce to Bull.*
10 haire *Dyce etc.*: aire *1594, Hurst, Rob.*

When as they would haue hal'd thee from my sight:
Sit on my knee, and call for thy content,
Controule proud Fate, and cut the thred of time.
Why are not all the Gods at thy commaund, 30
And heauen and earth the bounds of thy delight?
Vulcan shall daunce to make thee laughing sport,
And my nine Daughters sing when thou art sad,
From *Iunos* bird Ile pluck her spotted pride,
To make thee fannes wherewith to coole thy face, 35
And *Venus* Swannes shall shed their siluer downe,
To sweeten out the slumbers of thy bed:
Hermes no more shall shew the world his wings,
If that thy fancie in his feathers dwell,
But as this one Ile teare them all from him, 40
⟨*Plucks a feather from Hermes' wings.*⟩
Doe thou but say their colour pleaseth me:
Hold here my little loue, these linked gems, ⟨*Gives jewels.*⟩
My *Iuno* ware vpon her marriage day,
Put thou about thy necke my owne sweet heart,
And tricke thy armes and shoulders with my theft. 45

Gan. I would haue a iewell for mine eare,
And a fine brouch to put in my hat,
And then Ile hugge with you an hundred times.

Iup. And shall haue *Ganimed*, if thou wilt be my loue.

Enter Venus.

Venus. I, this is it, you can sit toying there, 50
And playing with that female wanton boy,
Whiles my *Æneas* wanders on the Seas,
And rests a pray to euery billowes pride.
Iuno, false *Iuno* in her Chariots pompe,
Drawne through the heauens by Steedes of *Boreas* brood, 55
Made *Hebe* to direct her ayrie wheeles
Into the windie countrie of the clowdes,
Where finding *Æolus* intrencht with stormes,
And guarded with a thousand grislie ghosts,
She humbly did beseech him for our bane, 60
And charg'd him drowne my sonne with all his traine.
Then gan the windes breake ope their brazen doores,
And all *Æolia* to be vp in armes:
Poore *Troy* must now be sackt vpon the Sea,

40+S.D. *add. Dyce* 42+S.D. *add. Dyce* 46 haue] have too *conj. Dyce* 47 in] into *Hurst, Cunn., Bull.* 49 shall] shalt *Hurst to Cunn.* 59 ghosts] gusts *conj. Coll.*

And *Neptunes* waues be enuious men of warre, 65
Epeus horse, to *Ætnas* hill transformd,
Prepared stands to wracke their woodden walles,
And *Æolus* like *Agamemnon* sounds
The surges, his fierce souldiers, to the spoyle:
See how the night *Vlysses*-like comes forth, 70
And intercepts the day as *Dolon* erst:
Ay me! the Starres supprisde like *Rhesus* Steedes,
Are drawne by darknes forth *Astræus* tents.
What shall I doe to saue thee my sweet boy?
When as the waues doe threat our Chrystall world, 75
And *Proteus* raising hils of flouds on high,
Entends ere long to sport him in the skie.
False *Iupiter*, rewardst thou vertue so?
What? is not pietie exempt from woe?
Then dye *Æneas* in thine innocence, 80
Since that religion hath no recompence.

Iup. Content thee *Cytherea* in thy care,
Since thy *Æneas* wandring fate is firme,
Whose wearie lims shall shortly make repose
In those faire walles I promist him of yore: 85
But first in bloud must his good fortune bud,
Before he be the Lord of *Turnus* towne,
Or force her smile that hetherto hath frownd:
Three winters shall he with the Rutiles warre,
And in the end subdue them with his sword, 90
And full three Sommers likewise shall he waste,
In mannaging those fierce barbarian mindes:
Which once performd, poore *Troy* so long supprest,
From forth her ashes shall aduance her head,
And flourish once againe that erst was dead: 95
But bright *Ascanius*, beauties better worke,
Who with the Sunne deuides one radiant shape,
Shall build his throne amidst those starrie towers,
That earth-borne *Atlas* groning vnderprops:
No bounds but heauen shall bound his Emperie, 100
Whose azured gates enchased with his name
Shall make the morning hast her gray vprise,
To feede her eyes with his engrauen fame.
Thus in stoute *Hectors* race three hundred yeares,
The Romane Scepter royall shall remaine, 105
Till that a Princesse priest conceau'd by *Mars*,

72 Ay] Ah *Hurst* 73 Astraea's *Hurst*, *Dyce*[1], *Cunn.*

Shall yeeld to dignitie a dubble birth,
Who will eternish *Troy* in their attempts.
Venus. How may I credite these thy flattering termes,
When yet both sea and sands beset their ships, 110
And *Phœbus* as in Stygian pooles, refraines
To taint his tresses in the Tyrrhen maine?
Iup. I will take order for that presently:
Hermes awake, and haste to *Neptunes* realme,
Whereas the Wind-god warring now with Fate, 115
Besiege the ofspring of our kingly loynes.
Charge him from me to turne his stormie powers,
And fetter them in *Vulcans* sturdie brasse,
That durst thus proudly wrong our kinsmans peace.
⟨*Exit Hermes.*⟩
Venus farewell, thy sonne shall be our care: 120
Come *Ganimed*, we must about this geare.
Exeunt Iupiter cum Ganimed.
Venus. Disquiet Seas lay downe your swelling lookes,
And court *Æneas* with your calmie cheere,
Whose beautious burden well might make you proude,
Had not the heauens conceau'd with hel-borne clowdes, 125
Vaild his resplendant glorie from your view.
For my sake pitie him *Oceanus*,
That erst-while issued from thy watrie loynes,
And had my being from thy bubling froth:
Triton I know hath fild his trumpe with *Troy*, 130
And therefore will take pitie on his toyle,
And call both *Thetis* and *Cymothoe*,
To succour him in this extremitie.

Enter Æneas with Ascanius, with one or two more.

What? doe I see my sonne now come on shoare?
Venus, how art thou compast with content, 135
The while thine eyes attract their sought for ioyes:
Great *Iupiter*, still honourd maist thou be,
For this so friendly ayde in time of neede.
Here in this bush disguised will I stand,
Whiles my *Æneas* spends himselfe in plaints, 140
And heauen and earth with his vnrest acquaints.

108 eternize *Hurst, Cunn.* 115 wind-gods *Cunn.* 116 Besieges *Dyce, Bull., Gros.* 119+S.D. *add. Dyce* 132 Cymothoe *conj. Dyce, Bull. etc.*: Cimodoæ *1594*: Cymodoce *Hurst, Dyce, Cunn.* 133+S.D. Enter Aeneas, Ascanius, Achates, and others *Dyce* 136 attrect *conj. Gros.*

Æn. You sonnes of care, companions of my course,
Priams misfortune followes vs by sea,
And *Helens* rape doth haunt ye at the heeles.
How many dangers haue we ouer past? 145
Both barking *Scilla*, and the sounding Rocks,
The *Cyclops* shelues, and grim *Ceranias* seate
Haue you oregone, and yet remaine aliue?
Pluck vp your hearts, since fate still rests our friend,
And chaunging heauens may those good daies returne, 150
Which *Pergama* did vaunt in all her pride.
Acha. Braue Prince of *Troy*, thou onely art our God,
That by thy vertues freest vs from annoy,
And makes our hopes suruiue to coming ioyes:
Doe thou but smile, and clowdie heauen will cleare, 155
Whose night and day descendeth from thy browes:
Though we be now in extreame miserie,
And rest the map of weatherbeaten woe:
Yet shall the aged Sunne shed forth his haire,
To make vs liue vnto our former heate, 160
And euery beast the forrest doth send forth,
Bequeath her young ones to our scanted foode.
Asca. Father I faint, good father giue me meate.
Æn. Alas sweet boy, thou must be still a while,
Till we haue fire to dresse the meate we kild: 165
Gentle *Achates*, reach the Tinder boxe,
That we may make a fire to warme vs with,
And rost our new found victuals on this shoare.
Venus. See what strange arts necessitie findes out,
How neere my sweet *Æneas* art thou driuen? 170
Æn. Hold, take this candle and goe light a fire,
You shall haue leaues and windfall bowes enow
Neere to these woods, to rost your meate withall:
Ascanius, goe and drie thy drenched lims,
Whiles I with my *Achates* roaue abroad, 175
To know what coast the winde hath driuen vs on,
Or whether men or beasts inhabite it.
Acha. The ayre is pleasant, and the soyle most fit
For Cities, and societies supports:

144 ye *Dyce*, *Gros.*, *McK.*: thee *1594*: us *Hurst*, *Bull.*: that *conj. McK.* 147 Ceraunia's *Dyce* 153 annoys *conj. Dyce* 154 mak'st *Hurst*, *Dyce*, *Gros.* coming *Dyce etc.*: cunning *1594*, *Hurst*, *Rob.* 159 aged . . shed] azur'd . . spread *conj. Coll.* hair *conj. Mitford*, *Dyce etc.*: aire *1594*, *Hurst* 170+S.D. Aside *add. Dyce* 175 roaue] roam *Hurst*, *Cunn.* 177+S.D. Exeunt Ascanius and others *add. Dyce*

Yet much I maruell that I cannot finde 180
No steps of men imprinted in the earth.
Venus. Now is the time for me to play my part:
Hoe yong men, saw you as you came
Any of all my Sisters wandring here?
Hauing a quiuer girded to her side, 185
And cloathed in a spotted Leopards skin.
Æn. I neither saw nor heard of any such:
But what may I faire Virgin call your name?
Whose lookes set forth no mortall forme to view,
Nor speech bewraies ought humaine in thy birth, 190
Thou art a Goddesse that delud'st our eyes,
And shrowdes thy beautie in this borrowd shape:
But whether thou the Sunnes bright Sister be,
Or one of chast *Dianas* fellow Nimphs,
Liue happie in the height of all content, 195
And lighten our extreames with this one boone,
As to instruct vs vnder what good heauen
We breathe as now, and what this world is calde,
On which by tempests furie we are cast,
Tell vs, O tell vs that are ignorant, 200
And this right hand shall make thy Altars crack
With mountaine heapes of milke white Sacrifize.
Venus. Such honour, stranger, doe I not affect:
It is the vse for Turen maides to weare
Their bowe and quiuer in this modest sort, 205
And suite themselues in purple for the nonce,
That they may trip more lightly ore the lawndes,
And ouertake the tusked Bore in chase.
But for the land whereof thou doest enquire,
It is the Punick kingdome rich and strong, 210
Adioyning on *Agenors* stately towne,
The kingly seate of Southerne *Libia*,
Whereas Sidonian *Dido* rules as Queene.
But what are you that aske of me these things?
Whence may you come, or whither will you goe? 215
Æn. Of *Troy* am I, *Æneas* is my name,
Who driuen by warre from forth my natiue world,
Put sailes to sea to seeke out *Italy*:
And my diuine descent from sceptred *Ioue*.
With twise twelue Phrigian ships I plowed the deepe, 220

183 came] came along *conj. Dyce, Cunn.* 190 betrays *Cunn.* 192 shroud'st *Hurst, Dyce* 198 as] us *conj. Coll., Gros.* 204 Turen] Tyrian *Hurst to Bull.*

And made that way my mother *Venus* led:
But of them all scarce seuen doe anchor safe,
And they so wrackt and weltred by the waues,
As euery tide tilts twixt their oken sides:
And all of them vnburdened of their loade, 225
Are ballassed with billowes watrie weight.
But haples I, God wot, poore and vnknowne,
Doe trace these Libian deserts all despisde,
Exild forth *Europe* and wide *Asia* both,
And haue not any couerture but heauen. 230
Venus. Fortune hath fauord thee what ere thou be,
In sending thee vnto this curteous Coast:
A Gods name on and hast thee to the Court,
Where *Dido* will receiue ye with her smiles:
And for thy ships which thou supposest lost, 235
Not one of them hath perisht in the storme,
But are ariued safe not farre from hence:
And so I leaue thee to thy fortunes lot,
Wishing good lucke vnto thy wandring steps. *Exit.*
Æn. Achates, tis my mother that is fled, 240
I know her by the mouings of her feete:
Stay gentle *Venus*, flye not from thy sonne,
Too cruell, why wilt thou forsake me thus?
Or in these shades deceiu'st mine eye so oft?
Why talke we not together hand in hand? 245
And tell our griefes in more familiar termes:
But thou art gone and leau'st me here alone,
To dull the ayre with my discoursiue moane. *Exit.*

⟨*Scena* 2.⟩

Enter ⟨*Iarbas, followed by*⟩ *Illioneus, and Cloanthus* ⟨*and Sergestus.*⟩

Illio. Follow ye Troians, follow this braue Lord,
And plaine to him the summe of your distresse. 250
Iar. Why, what are you, or wherefore doe you sewe?
Illio. Wretches of *Troy*, enuied of the windes,
That craue such fauour at your honors feete,

226 balasted *Hurst* 233 A] A' *Dyce*: In *Hurst, Cunn.* 244 shades] shapes *conj. Cunn.* deceive *Cunn.* eye] eyes *Hurst to Bull.* 245 talke] walk *Cunn.* 248 + Scene II. *add. Hurst* S.D. Bracketed words *add. Hurst*

As poore distressed miserie may pleade:
Saue, saue, O saue our ships from cruell fire, 255
That doe complaine the wounds of thousand waues,
And spare our liues whom euery spite pursues.
We come not we to wrong your Libian Gods,
Or steale your houshold Lares from their shrines:
Our hands are not prepar'd to lawles spoyle, 260
Nor armed to offend in any kind:
Such force is farre from our vnweaponed thoughts,
Whose fading weale of victorie forsooke,
Forbids all hope to harbour neere our hearts.
Iar. But tell me Troians, Troians if you be, 265
Vnto what fruitfull quarters were ye bound,
Before that *Boreas* buckled with your sailes?
Cloan. There is a place *Hesperia* term'd by vs,
An ancient Empire, famoused for armes,
And fertile in faire *Ceres* furrowed wealth, 270
Which now we call *Italia* of his name,
That in such peace long time did rule the same:
Thither made we,
When suddenly gloomie *Orion* rose,
And led our ships into the shallow sands, 275
Whereas the Southerne winde with brackish breath,
Disperst them all amongst the wrackfull Rockes:
From thence a fewe of vs escapt to land,
The rest we feare are foulded in the floods.
Iar. Braue men at armes, abandon fruitles feares, 280
Since Carthage knowes to entertaine distresse.
Serg. I but the barbarous sort doe threat our ships,
And will not let vs lodge vpon the sands:
In multitudes they swarme vnto the shoare,
And from the first earth interdict our feete. 285
Iar. My selfe will see they shall not trouble ye,
Your men and you shall banquet in our Court,
And euery Troian be as welcome here,
As *Iupiter* to sillie *Baucis* house:
Come in with me, Ile bring you to my Queene, 290
Who shall confirme my words with further deedes.
Serg. Thankes gentle Lord for such vnlookt for grace.
Might we but once more see *Æneas* face,
Then would we hope to quite such friendly turnes,
As shall surpasse the wonder of our speech. 295

277 wreckful *Hurst, Dyce*[2] *to Bull.* 289 Baucis *Hurst etc.*: Vausis *1594* 295 shall] all *conj. Dyce*[2]: still *conj. McK.*

Actus 2. ⟨*Scena* 1.⟩

Enter Æneas, Achates, and Ascanius.

Æn. Where am I now? these should be Carthage walles.
Acha. Why stands my sweete *Æneas* thus amazde?
Æn. O my *Achates*, Theban *Niobe*,
Who for her sonnes death wept out life and breath,
And drie with griefe was turnd into a stone, 300
Had not such passions in her head as I.
Me thinkes that towne there should be *Troy*, yon *Idas* hill,
There *Zanthus* streame, because here's *Priamus*,
And when I know it is not, then I dye.
Ach. And in this humor is *Achates* to, 305
I cannot choose but fall vpon my knees,
And kisse his hand: O where is *Hecuba*?
Here she was wont to sit, but sauing ayre
Is nothing here, and what is this but stone?
Æn. O yet this stone doth make *Æneas* weepe, 310
And would my prayers (as *Pigmalions* did)
Could giue it life, that vnder his conduct
We might saile backe to *Troy*, and be reuengde
On these hard harted Grecians, which reioyce
That nothing now is left of *Priamus*: 315
O *Priamus* is left and this is he,
Come, come abourd, pursue the hatefull Greekes.
Acha. What meanes *Æneas*?
Æn. *Achates* though mine eyes say this is stone,
Yet thinkes my minde that this is *Priamus*: 320
And when my grieued heart sighes and sayes no,
Then would it leape out to giue *Priam* life:
O were I not at all so thou mightst be.
Achates, see King *Priam* wags his hand,
He is aliue, *Troy* is not ouercome. 325
Ach. Thy mind *Æneas* that would haue it so
Deludes thy eye sight, *Priamus* is dead.
Æn. Ah *Troy* is sackt, and *Priamus* is dead,
And why should poore *Æneas* be aliue?
Asca. Sweete father leaue to weepe, this is not he: 330
For were it *Priam* he would smile on me.
Acha. *Æneas* see, here come the Citizens.
Leaue to lament lest they laugh at our feares.

Scene I. *add. Hurst* 302 towne there *omit conj. Mitford* 303+S.D. pointing to a statue *add. Gros.* 333 feares] tears *conj. Coll., conj. Bull.*

Enter Cloanthus, Sergestus, Illioneus ⟨*and others*⟩.

Æn. Lords of this towne, or whatsoeuer stile
Belongs vnto your name, vouchsafe of ruth 335
To tell vs who inhabits this faire towne,
What kind of people, and who gouernes them:
For we are strangers driuen on this shore,
And scarcely know within what Clime we are.
Illio. I heare *Æneas* voyce, but see him not, 340
For none of these can be our Generall.
Acha. Like *Illioneus* speakes this Noble man,
But *Illioneus* goes not in such robes.
Serg. You are *Achates*, or I deciu'd.
Acha. *Æneas* see, *Sergestus* or his ghost. 345
Illio. He names *Æneas*, let vs kisse his feete.
Cloan. It is our Captaine, see *Ascanius*.
Serg. Liue long *Æneas* and *Ascanius*.
Æn. *Achates*, speake, for I am ouerioyed.
Acha. O *Illioneus*, art thou yet aliue? 350
Illio. Blest be the time I see *Achates* face.
Cloan. Why turnes *Æneas* from his trustie friends?
Æn. *Sergestus*, *Illioneus* and the rest,
Your sight amazde me, O what destinies
Haue brought my sweete companions in such plight? 355
O tell me, for I long to be resolu'd.
Illio. Louely *Æneas*, these are Carthage walles,
And here Queene *Dido* weares th' imperiall Crowne,
Who for *Troyes* sake hath entertaind vs all,
And clad vs in these wealthie robes we weare. 360
Oft hath she askt vs vnder whom we seru'd,
And when we told her she would weepe for griefe,
Thinking the sea had swallowed vp thy ships,
And now she sees thee how will she reioyce?
Serg. See where her seruitors passe through the hall 365
Bearing a banket, *Dido* is not farre.
Illio. Looke where she comes: *Æneas* viewe her well.
Æn. Well may I view her, but she sees not me.

Enter Dido and her traine.

Dido. What stranger art thou that doest eye me thus?
Æn. Sometime I was a Troian, mightie Queene: 370
But *Troy* is not, what shall I say I am?

S.D. and others *add. Dyce* 344 I] I am *Dyce to McK.* 346 names *Hurst etc.*: meanes *1594* 367 view *Hurst etc.*: viewd *1594* 368 S.D. Enter Dido, Anna, Iarbas, and train *Dyce*

Illio. Renowmed *Dido,* tis our Generall:
Warlike *Æneas.*
Dido. Warlike *Æneas,* and in these base robes?
Goe fetch the garment which *Sicheus* ware: 375
Braue Prince, welcome to Carthage and to me,
Both happie that *Æneas* is our guest:
Sit in this chaire and banquet with a Queene,
Æneas is *Æneas,* were he clad
In weedes as bad as euer *Irus* ware. 380
Æn. This is no seate for one thats comfortles,
May it please your grace to let *Æneas* waite:
For though my birth be great, my fortunes meane,
Too meane to be companion to a Queene.
Dido. Thy fortune may be greater then thy birth, 385
Sit downe *Æneas,* sit in *Didos* place,
And if this be thy sonne as I suppose,
Here let him sit, be merrie louely child.
Æn. This place beseemes me not, O pardon me.
Dido. Ile haue it so, *Æneas,* be content. 390
Asca. Madame, you shall be my mother.
Dido. And so I will sweete child: be merrie man,
Heres to thy better fortune and good starres. (*Drinks.*)
Æn. In all humilitie I thanke your grace.
Dido. Remember who thou art, speake like thy selfe, 395
Humilitie belongs to common groomes.
Æn. And who so miserable as *Æneas* is?
Dido. Lyes it in *Didos* hands to make thee blest,
Then be assured thou art not miserable.
Æn. O *Priamus,* O *Troy,* oh *Hecuba*! 400
Dido. May I entreate thee to discourse at large,
And truely to, how *Troy* was ouercome:
For many tales goe of that Cities fall,
And scarcely doe agree vpon one poynt:
Some say *Antenor* did betray the towne, 405
Others report twas *Sinons* periurie:
But all in this that *Troy* is ouercome,
And *Priam* dead, yet how we heare no newes.
Æn. A wofull tale bids *Dido* to vnfould,
Whose memorie like pale deaths stony mace, 410
Beates forth my senses from this troubled soule,
And makes *Æneas* sinke at *Didos* feete.
Dido. What faints *Æneas* to remember *Troy*?

375 + S.D. Exit an Attendant who brings in the garment, which Aeneas puts on *add. Dyce* 393 S.D. *add. Dyce*

In whose defence he fought so valiantly:
Looke vp and speake. 415

Æn. Then speake *Æneas* with *Achilles* tongue,
And *Dido* and you Carthaginian Peeres
Heare me, but yet with *Mirmidons* harsh eares,
Daily inur'd to broyles and Massacres,
Lest you be mou'd too much with my sad tale. 420
The Grecian souldiers tired with ten yeares warre,
Began to crye, let vs vnto our ships,
Troy is inuincible, why stay we here?
With whose outcryes *Atrides* being apal'd,
Summoned the Captaines to his princely tent, 425
Who looking on the scarres we Troians gaue,
Seeing the number of their men decreast,
And the remainder weake and out of heart,
Gaue vp their voyces to dislodge the Campe,
And so in troopes all marcht to *Tenedos*: 430
Where when they came, *Vlysses* on the sand
Assayd with honey words to turne them backe:
And as he spoke to further his entent,
The windes did driue huge billowes to the shoare,
And heauen was darkned with tempestuous clowdes: 435
Then he alleag'd the Gods would haue them stay,
And prophecied *Troy* should be ouercome:
And therewithall he calde false *Sinon* forth,
A man compact of craft and periurie,
Whose ticing tongue was made of *Hermes* pipe, 440
To force an hundred watchfull eyes to sleepe:
And him, *Epeus* hauing made the horse,
With sacrificing wreathes vpon his head,
Vlysses sent to our vnhappie towne:
Who groueling in the mire of *Zanthus* bankes, 445
His hands bound at his backe, and both his eyes
Turnd vp to heauen as one resolu'd to dye,
Our Phrigian shepherds haled within the gates,
And brought vnto the Court of *Priamus*:
To whom he vsed action so pitifull, 450
Lookes so remorcefull, vowes so forcible,
As therewithall the old man ouercome,
Kist him, imbrast him, and vnloosde his bands,
And then—O *Dido*, pardon me.

Dido. Nay leaue not here, resolue me of the rest. 455

Æn. O th' inchaunting words of that base slaue,

448 shepherds *Hurst etc.*: shepherd *1594* 456 th'] the *Hurst*

Made him to thinke *Epeus* pine-tree Horse
A sacrifize t'appease *Mineruas* wrath:
The rather for that one *Laocoon*
Breaking a speare vpon his hollow breast, 460
Was with two winged Serpents stung to death.
Whereat agast, we were commanded straight
With reuerence to draw it into *Troy*.
In which vnhappie worke was I employd,
These hands did helpe to hale it to the gates, 465
Through which it could not enter twas so huge.
O had it neuer entred, *Troy* had stood.
But *Priamus* impatient of delay,
Inforst a wide breach in that rampierd wall,
Which thousand battering Rams could neuer pierce, 470
And so came in this fatall instrument:
At whose accursed feete as ouerioyed,
We banquetted till ouercome with wine,
Some surfetted, and others soundly slept.
Which *Sinon* viewing, causde the Greekish spyes 475
To hast to *Tenedos* and tell the Campe:
Then he vnlockt the Horse, and suddenly
From out his entrailes, *Neoptolemus*
Setting his speare vpon the ground, leapt forth,
And after him a thousand Grecians more, 480
In whose sterne faces shin'd the quenchles fire,
That after burnt the pride of *Asia*.
By this the Campe was come vnto the walles,
And through the breach did march into the streetes,
Where meeting with the rest, kill, kill they cryed. 485
Frighted with this confused noyse, I rose,
And looking from a turret, might behold
Yong infants swimming in their parents bloud,
Headles carkasses piled vp in heapes,
Virgins halfe dead dragged by their golden haire, 490
And with maine force flung on a ring of pikes,
Old men with swords thrust through their aged sides,
Kneeling for mercie to a Greekish lad,
Who with steele Pol-axes dasht out their braines.
Then buckled I mine armour, drew my sword, 495
And thinking to goe downe, came *Hectors* ghost
With ashie visage, blewish sulphure eyes,
His armes torne from his shoulders, and his breast
Furrowd with wounds, and that which made me weepe,
Thongs at his heeles, by which *Achilles* horse 500

Drew him in triumph through the Greekish Campe,
Burst from the earth, crying, *Æneas* flye,
Troy is afire, the Grecians haue the towne.
Dido. O *Hector* who weepes not to heare thy name?
Æn. Yet flung I forth, and desperate of my life, 505
Ran in the thickest throngs, and with this sword
Sent many of their sauadge ghosts to hell.
At last came *Pirrhus* fell and full of ire,
His harnesse dropping bloud, and on his speare
The mangled head of *Priams* yongest sonne, 510
And after him his band of Mirmidons,
With balles of wilde fire in their murdering pawes,
Which made the funerall flame that burnt faire *Troy*:
All which hemd me about, crying, this is he.
Dido. Ah, how could poore *Æneas* scape their hands? 515
Æn. My mother *Venus* iealous of my health,
Conuaid me from their crooked nets and bands:
So I escapt the furious *Pirrhus* wrath:
Who then ran to the pallace of the King,
And at *Ioues* Altar finding *Priamus,* 520
About whose withered necke hung *Hecuba,*
Foulding his hand in hers, and ioyntly both
Beating their breasts and falling on the ground,
He with his faulchions poynt raisde vp at once,
And with *Megeras* eyes stared in their face, 525
Threatning a thousand deaths at euery glaunce.
To whom the aged King thus trembling spoke:
Achilles sonne, remember what I was,
Father of fiftie sonnes, but they are slaine,
Lord of my fortune, but my fortunes turnd, 530
King of this Citie, but my *Troy* is fired,
And now am neither father, Lord, nor King:
Yet who so wretched but desires to liue?
O let me liue, great *Neoptolemus.*
Not mou'd at all, but smiling at his teares, 535
This butcher whil'st his hands were yet held vp,
Treading vpon his breast, strooke off his hands.
Dido. O end *Æneas,* I can heare no more.
Æn. At which the franticke Queene leapt on his face,
And in his eyelids hanging by the nayles, 540
A little while prolong'd her husbands life:
At last the souldiers puld her by the heeles,
And swong her howling in the emptie ayre,
Which sent an eccho to the wounded King:

Whereat he lifted vp his bedred lims, 545
And would haue grappeld with *Achilles* sonne,
Forgetting both his want of strength and hands,
Which he disdaining whiskt his sword about,
And with the wind thereof the King fell downe:
Then from the nauell to the throat at once, 550
He ript old *Priam*: at whose latter gaspe
Ioues marble statue gan to bend the brow,
As lothing *Pirrhus* for this wicked act:
Yet he vndaunted tooke his fathers flagge,
And dipt it in the old Kings chill cold bloud, 555
And then in triumph ran into the streetes,
Through which he could not passe for slaughtred men:
So leaning on his sword he stood stone still,
Viewing the fire wherewith rich *Ilion* burnt.
By this I got my father on my backe, 560
This yong boy in mine armes, and by the hand
Led faire *Creusa* my beloued wife,
When thou *Achates* with thy sword mad'st way,
And we were round inuiron'd with the Greekes:
O there I lost my wife: and had not we 565
Fought manfully, I had not told this tale:
Yet manhood would not serue, of force we fled,
And as we went vnto our ships, thou knowest
We sawe *Cassandra* sprauling in the streetes,
Whom *Aiax* rauisht in *Dianas* Fane, 570
Her cheekes swolne with sighes, her haire all rent,
Whom I tooke vp to beare vnto our ships:
But suddenly the Grecians followed vs,
And I alas, was forst to let her lye.
Then got we to our ships, and being abourd, 575
Polixena cryed out, *Æneas* stay,
The Greekes pursue me, stay and take me in.
Moued with her voyce, I lept into the sea,
Thinking to beare her on my backe abourd:
For all our ships were launcht into the deepe, 580
And as I swomme, she standing on the shoare,
Was by the cruell Mirmidons surprizd,
And after by that *Pirrhus* sacrifizde.

Dido. I dye with melting ruth, *Æneas* leaue.

Anna. O what became of aged *Hecuba*? 585

549 wind *conj. Coll.*: wound *1594, Hurst* 568+S.D. to Achates *add. Gros.* 570 fane *Hurst etc.*: Fawne *1594* 583 by that] that by *conj. Dyce*[1], *Dyce*[2]

Iar. How got *Æneas* to the fleete againe?
Dido. But how scapt *Helen,* she that causde this warre?
Æn. *Achates* speake, sorrow hath tired me quite.
Acha. What happened to the Queene we cannot shewe,
We heare they led her captiue into Greece. 590
As for *Æneas* he swomme quickly backe,
And *Helena* betraied *Diiphobus*
Her Louer, after *Alexander* dyed,
And so was reconcil'd to *Menelaus.*
Dido. O had that ticing strumpet nere been borne! 595
Troian, thy ruthfull tale hath made me sad:
Come let vs thinke vpon some pleasing sport,
To rid me from these melancholly thoughts.
Exeunt omnes.

Enter Venus ⟨*with Cupid*⟩ *at another doore, and takes Ascanius by the sleeue.*

Venus. Faire child stay thou with *Didos* waiting maide.
Ile giue thee Sugar-almonds, sweete Conserues, 600
A siluer girdle, and a golden purse,
And this yong Prince shall be thy playfellow.
Asca. Are you Queene *Didos* sonne?
Cupid. I, and my mother gaue me this fine bow.
Asca. Shall I haue such a quiuer and a bow? 605
Venus. Such bow, such quiuer, and such golden shafts,
Will *Dido* giue to sweete *Ascanius*:
For *Didos* sake I take thee in my armes,
And sticke these spangled feathers in thy hat,
Eate Comfites in mine armes, and I will sing. ⟨*Sings.*⟩
Now is he fast asleepe, and in this groue 611
Amongst greene brakes Ile lay *Ascanius,*
And strewe him with sweete smelling Violets,
Blushing Roses, purple *Hyacinthe*:
These milke white Doues shall be his Centronels: 615
Who if that any seeke to doe him hurt,
Will quickly flye to *Cythereas* fist.
Now *Cupid* turne thee to *Ascanius* shape,
And goe to *Dido,* who in stead of him
Will set thee on her lap and play with thee: 620

598 S.D. Exeunt all except Ascanius, whom Venus, entering with Cupid at another door, takes by the sleeve as he is going off *Dyce* 610 S.D. *add Dyce* 614 Blushing] With blushing *conj. Mitford, Cunn.* hyacinths *Dyce* 617 Cytherea's *Hurst etc.*: Citheidas *1594*

Then touch her white breast with this arrow head,
That she may dote vpon *Æneas* loue :
And by that meanes repaire his broken ships,
Victuall his Souldiers, giue him wealthie gifts,
And he at last depart to *Italy*, 625
Or els in *Carthage* make his kingly throne.
Cupid. I will faire mother, and so play my part,
As euery touch shall wound Queene *Didos* heart.
Venus. Sleepe my sweete nephew in these cooling shades,
Free from the murmure of these running streames, 630
The crye of beasts, the ratling of the windes,
Or whisking of these leaues, all shall be still,
And nothing interrupt thy quiet sleepe,
Till I returne and take thee hence againe. *Exeunt.*

Actus 3. *Scena* 1.

Enter Cupid solus, ⟨as Ascanius⟩.

Cupid. Now *Cupid* cause the Carthaginian Queene, 635
To be inamourd of thy brothers lookes,
Conuey this golden arrowe in thy sleeue,
Lest she imagine thou art *Venus* sonne :
And when she strokes thee softly on the head,
Then shall I touch her breast and conquer her. 640

Enter Iarbus, Anna, and Dido.

Iar. How long faire *Dido* shall I pine for thee ?
Tis not enough that thou doest graunt me loue,
But that I may enioy what I desire :
That loue is childish which consists in words.
Dido. *Iarbus*, know that thou of all my wooers 645
(And yet haue I had many mightier Kings)
Hast had the greatest fauours I could giue :
I feare me *Dido* hath been counted light,
In being too familiar with *Iarbus* :
Albeit the Gods doe know no wanton thought 650
Had euer residence in *Didos* breast.
Iar. But *Dido* is the fauour I request.
Dido. Feare not *Iarbus*, *Dido* may be thine.
Anna. Looke sister how *Æneas* little sonne
Playes with your garments and imbraceth you 655

634 S.D. as Ascanius *add. Dyce* 640 S.D. Iarbas *Dyce etc.* (*so passim*)

Cupid. No *Dido* will not take me in her armes,
I shall not be her sonne, she loues me not.
Dido. Weepe not sweet boy, thou shalt be *Didos* sonne,
Sit in my lap and let me heare thee sing. ⟨*Cupid sings.*⟩
No more my child, now talke another while, 660
And tell me where learnst thou this pretie song?
Cupid. My cosin *Helen* taught it me in *Troy.*
Dido. How louely is *Ascanius* when he smiles?
Cupid. Will *Dido* let me hang about her necke?
Dido. I wagge, and giue thee leaue to kisse her to. 665
Cupid. What will you giue me? now Ile haue this Fanne.
Dido. Take it *Ascanius*, for thy fathers sake.
Iar. Come *Dido*, leaue *Ascanius*, let vs walke.
Dido. Goe thou away, *Ascanius* shall stay.
Iar. Vngentle Queene, is this thy loue to me? 670
Dido. O stay *Iarbus*, and Ile goe with thee.
Cupid. And if my mother goe, Ile follow her.
Dido. Why staiest thou here? thou art no loue of mine.
Iar. *Iarbus* dye, seeing she abandons thee.
Dido. No, liue *Iarbus*, what hast thou deseru'd, 675
That I should say thou art no loue of mine?
Something thou hast deseru'd. Away I say,
Depart from *Carthage*, come not in my sight.
Iar. Am I not King of rich *Getulia*?
Dido. *Iarbus* pardon me, and stay a while. 680
Cupid. Mother, looke here.
Dido. What telst thou me of rich *Getulia*?
Am not I Queene of *Libia*? then depart.
Iar. I goe to feed the humour of my Loue,
Yet not from *Carthage* for a thousand worlds. 685
Dido. *Iarbus.*
Iar. Doth *Dido* call me backe?
Dido. No, but I charge thee neuer looke on me.
Iar. Then pull out both mine eyes, or let me dye.
Exit Iarb.
Anna. Wherefore doth *Dido* bid *Iarbus* goe? 690
Dido. Because his lothsome sight offends mine eye,
And in my thoughts is shrin'd another loue:
O *Anna*, didst thou know how sweet loue were,
Full soone wouldst thou abiure this single life.

659 S.D. *add. Hurst* 661 learn'dst *Dyce to Bull.* 666 me? now] me now? *Dyce, Bull.* 672 And] An *Dyce*[2], *Bull.* 691 eyes *Cunn.* 692 loue *Dyce to McK. exc. Gros.*: Ioue *1594, Hurst, Gros.*

Anna. Poore soule I know too well the sower of loue.
O that *Iarbus* could but fancie me. 696
Dido. Is not *Æneas* faire and beautifull?
Anna. Yes, and *Iarbus* foule and fauourles.
Dido. Is he not eloquent in all his speech?
Anna. Yes, and *Iarbus* rude and rusticall. 700
Dido. Name not *Iarbus*, but sweete *Anna* say,
Is not *Æneas* worthie *Didos* loue?
Anna. O sister, were you Empresse of the world,
Æneas well deserues to be your loue,
So louely is he that where ere he goes, 705
The people swarme to gaze him in the face.
Dido. But tell them none shall gaze on him but I,
Lest their grosse eye-beames taint my louers cheekes:
Anna, good sister *Anna* goe for him,
Lest with these sweete thoughts I melt cleane away. 710
Anna. Then sister youle abiure *Iarbus* loue?
Dido. Yet must I heare that lothsome name againe?
Runne for *Æneas*, or Ile flye to him. *Exit Anna.*
Cupid. You shall not hurt my father when he comes.
Dido. No, for thy sake Ile loue thy father well. 715
O dull conceipted *Dido*, that till now
Didst neuer thinke *Æneas* beautifull:
But now for quittance of this ouersight,
Ile make me bracelets of his golden haire,
His glistering eyes shall be my looking glasse, 720
His lips an altar, where Ile offer vp
As many kisses as the Sea hath sands:
In stead of musicke I will heare him speake,
His lookes shall be my only Librarie,
And thou *Æneas*, *Didos* treasurie, 725
In whose faire bosome I will locke more wealth,
Then twentie thousand Indiaes can affoord:
O here he comes, loue, loue, giue *Dido* leaue
To be more modest then her thoughts admit,
Lest I be made a wonder to the world. 730

⟨*Enter Æneas, Achates, Sergestus, Illioneus, and Cloanthus.*⟩

Achates, how doth *Carthage* please your Lord?
Acha. That will *Æneas* shewe your maiestie.
Dido. *Æneas*, art thou there?
Æn. I vnderstand your highnesse sent for me.

695 sowerl] power *Hurst* 730 S.D. *add. Hurst*

Dido. No, but now thou art here, tell me in sooth 735
In what might *Dido* highly pleasure thee.
Æn. So much haue I receiu'd at *Didos* hands,
As without blushing I can aske no more:
Yet Queene of *Affricke*, are my ships vnrigd,
My Sailes all rent in sunder with the winde, 740
My Oares broken, and my Tackling lost,
Yea all my Nauie split with Rockes and Shelfes:
Nor Sterne nor Anchor haue our maimed Fleete,
Our Masts the furious windes strooke ouer bourd:
Which piteous wants if *Dido* will supplie, 745
We will account her author of our liues.
Dido. *Æneas*, Ile repaire thy Troian ships,
Conditionally that thou wilt stay with me,
And let *Achates* saile to *Italy*:
Ile giue thee tackling made of riueld gold, 750
Wound on the barkes of odoriferous trees,
Oares of massie Iuorie full of holes,
Through which the water shall delight to play:
Thy Anchors shall be hewed from Christall Rockes,
Which if thou lose shall shine aboue the waues: 755
The Masts whereon thy swelling sailes shall hang,
Hollow Pyramides of siluer plate:
The sailes of foulded Lawne, where shall be wrought
The warres of *Troy*, but not *Troyes* ouerthrow:
For ballace, emptie *Didos* treasurie, 760
Take what ye will, but leaue *Æneas* here.
Achates, thou shalt be so meanly clad,
As Seaborne Nymphes shall swarme about thy ships,
And wanton Mermaides court thee with sweete songs,
Flinging in fauours of more soueraigne worth, 765
Then *Thetis* hangs about *Apolloes* necke,
So that *Æneas* may but stay with me.
Æn. Wherefore would *Dido* haue *Æneas* stay?
Dido. To warre against my bordering enemies:
Æneas, thinke not *Dido* is in loue, 770
For if that any man could conquer me,
I had been wedded ere *Æneas* came:
See where the pictures of my suiters hang,
And are not these as faire as faire may be?
Acha. I saw this man at *Troy* ere *Troy* was sackt. 775

750+S.D. To Achates *add. Gros.* 755 loose *Cunn.* 762 Meantime, Achates, thou shalt be so clad *conj. Mitford* meanly] seemly *Dyce, Bull.*: meetly *conj. Dyce*: newly *conj. Coll., Cunn.*

Æn. I this in *Greece* when *Paris* stole faire *Helen.*
Illio. This man and I were at *Olympus* games.
Serg. I know this face, he is a Persian borne,
I traueld with him to *Ætolia.*
Cloan. And I in *Athens* with this gentleman, 780
Vnlesse I be deceiu'd disputed once.
Dido. But speake *Æneas*, know you none of these ?
Æn. No Madame, but it seemes that these are Kings.
Dido. All these and others which I neuer sawe,
Haue been most vrgent suiters for my loue, 785
Some came in person, others sent their Legats :
Yet none obtaind me, I am free from all,
And yet God knowes intangled vnto one.
This was an Orator, and thought by words
To compasse me, but yet he was deceiu'd : 790
And this a Spartan Courtier vaine and wilde,
But his fantastick humours pleasde not me :
This was *Alcion*, a Musition,
But playd he nere so sweet, I let him goe :
This was the wealthie King of *Thessaly*, 795
But I had gold enough and cast him off :
This *Meleagers* sonne, a warlike Prince,
But weapons gree not with my tender yeares :
The rest are such as all the world well knowes,
Yet now I sweare by heauen and him I loue, 800
I was as farre from loue, as they from hate.
Æn. O happie shall he be whom *Dido* loues.
Dido. Then neuer say that thou art miserable,
Because it may be thou shalt be my loue :
Yet boast not of it, for I loue thee not, 805
And yet I hate thee not : O if I speake
I shall betray my selfe. *Æneas* speake,
We too will goe a hunting in the woods,
But not so much for thee, thou art but one,
As for *Achates*, and his followers. *Exeunt.*

776 *Prefix* Æn.] Serg. *Dyce*[2] : A Lord *Gros.* 777 Olympia's *Dyce to Bull.* 798 gree] greed *Gros.* 800 now *Dyce etc. exc. Cunn.* : how *1594* : here *Hurst, Cunn.* 807 S.D. Aside *add. Dyce after* selfe speake] come *or* hark *conj. Dyce*[1], *Dyce*[2], *Bull.* 807–8 my selfe. . . We too] my selfe : Aeneas— AEN. Speake ! DIDO. We two *conj. McK.*

⟨Scena 2.⟩

Enter Iuno to Ascanius asleepe.

Iuno. Here lyes my hate, *Æneas* cursed brat, 811
The boy wherein false destinie delights,
The heire of furie, the fauorite of the fates,
That vgly impe that shall outweare my wrath,
And wrong my deitie with high disgrace : 815
But I will take another order now,
And race th'eternall Register of time :
Troy shall no more call him her second hope,
Nor *Venus* triumph in his tender youth :
For here in spight of heauen Ile murder him, 820
And feede infection with his let out life :
Say *Paris*, now shall *Venus* haue the ball ?
Say vengeance, now shall her *Ascanius* dye ?
O no, God wot, I cannot watch my time,
Nor quit good turnes with double fee downe told : 825
Tut, I am simple, without mind to hurt,
And haue no gall at all to grieue my foes :
But lustfull *Ioue* and his adulterous child,
Shall finde it written on confusions front,
That onely *Iuno* rules in *Rhamnuse* towne. 830

Enter Venus.

Venus. What should this meane ? my Doues are back returnd,
Who warne me of such daunger prest at hand,
To harme my sweete *Ascanius* louely life.
Iuno, my mortall foe, what make you here ?
Auaunt old witch and trouble not my wits. 835
Iuno. Fie *Venus*, that such causeles words of wrath,
Should ere defile so faire a mouth as thine :
Are not we both sprong of celestiall rase,
And banquet as two Sisters with the Gods ?
Why is it then displeasure should disioyne 840
Whom kindred and acquaintance counites ?

Scene II. *add. Hurst* 813 The . . furie, the] Heir of the Furies *conj. Deighton* furie] Troy *Cunn.* : furies *Gros.* the fauorite] favourite *conj. Mitford* Fates *Hurst etc.* : face *1594* 817 raze *Hurst to Bull.* the *Cunn.* 821 let-out *Hurst etc.* : left out *1594* 826 without *1594 etc.* : with ought *conj. McK.* mind *Dyce etc.* : made *1594* : might *Hurst, Rob.* : 832 such] some *conj. Cunn.*

'*Venus.* Out hatefull hag, thou wouldst haue slaine my sonne,
Had not my Doues discou'rd thy entent:
But I will teare thy eyes fro forth thy head,
And feast the birds with their bloud-shotten balles, 845
If thou but lay thy fingers on my boy.
Iuno. Is this then all the thankes that I shall haue,
For sauing him from Snakes and Serpents stings,
That would haue kild him sleeping as he lay?
What though I was offended with thy sonne, 850
And wrought him mickle woe on sea and land,
When for the hate of Troian *Ganimed*,
That was aduanced by my *Hebes* shame,
And *Paris* iudgement of the heauenly ball,
I mustred all the windes vnto his wracke, 855
And vrg'd each Element to his annoy:
Yet now I doe repent me of his ruth,
And wish that I had neuer wrongd him so:
Bootles I sawe it was to warre with fate,
That hath so many vnresisted friends: 860
Wherefore I chaunge my counsell with the time,
And planted loue where enuie erst had sprong.
Venus. Sister of *Ioue*, if that thy loue be such,
As these thy protestations doe paint forth,
We two as friends one fortune will deuide: 865
Cupid shall lay his arrowes in thy lap,
And to a Scepter chaunge his golden shafts,
Fancie and modestie shall liue as mates,
And thy faire peacockes by my pigeons pearch:
Loue my *Æneas*, and desire is thine, 870
The day, the night, my Swannes, my sweetes are thine.
Iuno. More then melodious are these words to me,
That ouercloy my soule with their content:
Venus, sweete *Venus*, how may I deserue
Such amourous fauours at thy beautious hand? 875
But that thou maist more easilie perceiue,
How nighly I doe prize this amitie,
Harke to a motion of eternall league,
Which I will make in quittance of thy loue:
Thy sonne thou knowest with *Dido* now remaines, 880
And feedes his eyes with fauours of her Court,
She likewise in admyring spends her time,

844 from *Hurst, Cunn.*: frõ *Gros.* 855 wreck *Hurst, Dyce*[2], *Bull.* 861 chang'd *Dyce etc.*

And cannot talke nor thinke of ought but him :
Why should not they then ioyne in marriage,
And bring forth mightie Kings to Carthage towne, 885
Whom casualtie of sea hath made such friends ?
And *Venus*, let there be a match confirmd
Betwixt these two, whose loues are so alike,
And both our Deities conioynd in one,
Shall chaine felicitie vnto their throne. 890

Venus. Well could I like this reconcilements meanes,
But much I feare my sonne will nere consent,
Whose armed soule alreadie on the sea,
Darts forth her light to *Lauinias* shoare.

Iuno. Faire Queene of loue, I will deuorce these doubts,
And finde the way to wearie such fond thoughts : 896
This day they both a hunting forth will ride
Into these woods, adioyning to these walles,
When in the midst of all their gamesome sports,
Ile make the Clowdes dissolue their watrie workes, 900
And drench *Siluanus* dwellings with their shewers.
Then in one Caue the Queene and he shall meete,
And interchangeably discourse their thoughts,
Whose short conclusion will seale vp their hearts,
Vnto the purpose which we now propound. 905

Venus. Sister, I see you sauour of my wiles,
Be it as you will haue ⟨it⟩ for this once,
Meane time, *Ascanius* shall be my charge,
Whom I will beare to *Ida* in mine armes,
And couch him in *Adonis* purple downe. *Exeunt.*

⟨*Scena* 3.⟩

Enter Dido, Æneas, Anna, Iarbus, Achates, ⟨Cupid as Ascanius,⟩ and followers.

Dido. *Æneas*, thinke not but I honor thee, 911
That thus in person goe with thee to hunt :
My princely robes thou seest are layd aside,
Whose glittering pompe *Dianas* shrowdes supplies,

894 light to] lightning to *or* light unto *conj. Dyce* : light unto *Cunn., Bull.* to] to the *Gros.* : unto *conj. Gros.* Lavinian *conj. Dyce, Gros.* : Lavinium's *conj. Gros.* 898 the woods *Dyce etc.* 901 showers *Hurst etc.* 907 it *add. Hurst, Dyce[2] etc.* Scene III. *add. Hurst* 914 shroud *Hurst to Bull.*

All fellowes now disposde alike to sporte. 915
The woods are wide, and we haue store of game:
Faire Troian, hold my golden bowe awhile,
Vntill I gird my quiuer to my side:
Lords goe before, we two must talke alone.
Iar. Vngentle, can she wrong *Iarbus* so? 920
Ile dye before a stranger haue that grace:
We two will talke alone, what words be these?
Dido. What makes *Iarbus* here of all the rest?
We could haue gone without your companie.
Æn. But loue and duetie led him on perhaps, 925
To presse beyond acceptance to your sight.
Iar. Why, man of *Troy*, doe I offend thine eyes?
Or art thou grieude thy betters presse so nye?
Dido. How now Getulian, are ye growne so braue,
To challenge vs with your comparisons? 930
Pesant, goe seeke companions like thy selfe,
And meddle not with any that I loue:
Æneas, be not moude at what he sayes,
For otherwhile he will be out of ioynt.
Iar. Women may wrong by priuiledge of loue: 935
But should that man of men (*Dido* except)
Haue taunted me in these opprobrious termes,
I would haue either drunke his dying bloud,
Or els I would haue giuen my life in gage.
Dido. Huntsmen, why pitch you not your toyles apace,
And rowse the light foote Deere from forth their laire. 941
Anna. Sister, see, see *Ascanius* in his pompe,
Bearing his huntspeare brauely in his hand.
Dido. Yea little sonne, are you so forward now?
Asca. I mother, I shall one day be a man, 945
And better able vnto other armes.
Meane time these wanton weapons serue my warre,
Which I will breake betwixt a Lyons iawes.
Dido. What, darest thou looke a Lyon in the face?
Asca. I, and outface him to, doe what he can. 950
Anna. How like his father speaketh he in all?
Æn. And mought I liue to see him sacke rich *Thebes*,
And loade his speare with Grecian Princes heads,
Then would I wish me with *Anchises* Tombe,
And dead to honour that hath brought me vp. 955
Iar. And might I liue to see thee shipt away,

915 fellowes] follow us *Cunn.* 922 + S.D. Aside *add. Dyce*
952 might *Hurst*

And hoyst aloft on *Neptunes* hideous hilles,
Then would I wish me in faire *Didos* armes,
And dead to scorne that hath pursued me so.

Æn. Stoute friend *Achates*, doest thou know this wood?

Acha. As I remember, here you shot the Deere, 961
That sau'd your famisht souldiers liues from death,
When first you set your foote vpon the shoare,
And here we met faire *Venus* virgine like,
Bearing her bowe and quiuer at her backe. 965

Æn. O how these irksome labours now delight,
And ouerioy my thoughts with their escape:
Who would not vndergoe all kind of toyle,
To be well stor'd with such a winters tale?

Dido. *Æneas*, leaue these dumpes and lets away, 970
Some to the mountaines, some vnto the soyle,
You to the vallies, thou ⟨*to Iarbas*⟩ vnto the house.

Exeunt omnes: manet ⟨*Iarbas*⟩.

Iar. I, this it is which wounds me to the death,
To see a Phrigian far fet o' the sea,
Preferd before a man of maiestie: 975
O loue, O hate, O cruell womens hearts,
That imitate the Moone in euery chaunge,
And like the Planets euer loue to raunge:
What shall I doe thus wronged with disdaine?
Reuenge me on *Æneas*, or on her: 980
On her? fond man, that were to warre gainst heauen,
And with one shaft prouoke ten thousand darts:
This Troians end will be thy enuies aime,
Whose bloud will reconcile thee to content,
And make loue drunken with thy sweete desire: 985
But *Dido* that now holdeth him so deare,
Will dye with very tidings of his death:
But time will discontinue her content,
And mould her minde vnto newe fancies shapes.
O God of heauen, turne the hand of fate 990
Vnto that happie day of my delight,
And then, what then? *Iarbus* shall but loue:
So doth he now, though not with equall gaine,
That resteth in the riuall of thy paine,
Who nere will cease to soare till he be slaine. *Exit.*

959 + S.D. Aside *add. Dyce to Bull.* 972 S.D. to Iarbas *add. Gros., McK.* 972 S.D. manet Iarbas *Gros.*: manent *1594* 974 far . . sea] o' the farthest sea *conj. Mitford* far fet] far set *Hurst*: forfeit *conj. Broughton* o' *T. B.*: to *1594*: o'er *Dyce etc.*

⟨Scena 4.⟩

The storme. Enter Æneas and Dido in the Caue at seuerall times.

Diao. *Æneas.* 996
Æn. *Dido.*
Dido. Tell me deare loue, how found you out this Caue?
Æn. By chance sweete Queene, as *Mars* and *Venus* met.
Dido. Why, that was in a net, where we are loose,
And yet I am not free, oh would I were. 1001
Æn. Why, what is it that *Dido* may desire
And not obtaine, be it in humaine power?
Dido. The thing that I will dye before I aske,
And yet desire to haue before I dye. 1005
Æn. It is not ought *Æneas* may atchieue?
Dido. *Æneas* no, although his eyes doe pearce.
Æn. What, hath *Iarbus* angred her in ought?
And will she be auenged on his life?
Dido. Not angred me, except in angring thee 1010
Æn. Who then of all so cruell may he be,
That should detaine thy eye in his defects?
Dido. The man that I doe eye where ere I am,
Whose amorous face like *Pean* sparkles fire,
When as he buts his beames on *Floras* bed. 1015
Prometheus hath put on *Cupids* shape,
And I must perish in his burning armes:
Æneas, O *Æneas*, quench these flames.
Æn. What ailes my Queene, is she falne sicke of late?
Dido. Not sicke my loue, but sicke, I must conceale
The torment, that it bootes me not reueale, 1021
And yet Ile speake, and yet Ile hold my peace,
Doe shame her worst, I will disclose my griefe:
Æneas, thou art he. What did I say?
Something it was that now I haue forgot. 1025
Æn. What meanes faire *Dido* by this doubtfull speech?
Dido. Nay, nothing, but *Æneas* loues me not.
Æn. *Æneas* thoughts dare not ascend so high
As *Didos* heart, which Monarkes might not scale.
Dido. It was because I sawe no King like thee, 1030

Scene IV. *add. Hurst* S.D. A storm *Hurst, Cunn.* 1000 where] here *Hurst, Cunn.* 1002 it *om. Hurst, Cunn.* 1009 revenged *Cunn.* 1014 Paean's *Hurst* 1016 hath] now hath *Gros.*

Whose golden Crowne might ballance my content:
But now that I haue found what to effect,
I followe one that loueth fame for me,
And rather had seeme faire ⟨to⟩ *Sirens* eyes,
Then to the Carthage Queene that dyes for him. 1035
Æn. If that your maiestie can looke so lowe,
As my despised worths, that shun all praise,
With this my hand I giue to you my heart,
And vow by all the Gods of Hospitalitie,
By heauen and earth, and my faire brothers bowe, 1040
By *Paphos*, *Capys*, and the purple Sea,
From whence my radiant mother did descend,
And by this Sword that saued me from the Greekes,
Neuer to leaue these newe vpreared walles,
Whiles *Dido* liues and rules in *Iunos* towne, 1045
Neuer to like or loue any but her.
Dido. What more then Delian musicke doe I heare,
That calles my soule from forth his liuing seate,
To moue vnto the measures of delight:
Kind clowdes that sent forth such a curteous storme,
As made disdaine to flye to fancies lap! 1051
Stoute loue in mine armes make thy *Italy*,
Whose Crowne and kingdome rests at thy commande:
Sicheus, not *Æneas* be thou calde:
The King of *Carthage*, not *Anchises* sonne: 1055
Hold, take these Iewels at thy Louers hand,
These golden bracelets, and this wedding ring,
Wherewith my husband woo'd me yet a maide,
And be thou king of *Libia*, by my guift.
Exeunt to the Caue.

Actus 4. *Scena* 1.

Enter Achates, ⟨Cupid as⟩ Ascanius, Iarbus, and Anna.

Acha. Did euer men see such a sudden storme? 1060
Or day so cleere so suddenly orecast?
Iar. I thinke some fell Inchantresse dwelleth here,
That can call them forth when as she please,

1032 affect *Hurst to Gros.* 1033 for me] 'fore me *Dyce to Gros.*: foreign *conj. Coll.* 1034 seeme] seen *Hurst, Rob.* to *add. Cunn.*: in *add. Dyce, Bull. etc.* 1042 descend] ascend *Bull.* 1056+S.D. Giving jewels *add. Dyce* Actus 4. Scena 1. S.D. Cupid as *add. Hurst* 1063 That] One that *conj. Mitford, Gros., conj. Deighton* them forth] forth the winds *conj. Bull.*

And diue into blacke tempests treasurie,
When as she meanes to maske the world with clowdes.
Anna. In all my life I neuer knew the like, 1066
It haild, it snowde, it lightned all at once.
Acha. I thinke it was the diuels reuelling night,
There was such hurly burly in the heauens:
Doubtles *Apollos* Axeltree is crackt, 1070
Or aged *Atlas* shoulder out of ioynt,
The motion was so ouer violent.
Iar. In all this coyle, where haue ye left the Queene?
Asca. Nay, where is my warlike father, can you tell?
Anna. Behold where both of them come forth the Caue.
Iar. Come forth the Caue: can heauen endure this sight?
Iarbus, curse that vnreuenging *Ioue,* 1077
Whose flintie darts slept in *Tiphous* den,
Whiles these adulterors surfetted with sinne:
Nature, why mad'st me not some poysonous beast, 1080
That with the sharpnes of my edged sting,
I might haue stakte them both vnto the earth,
Whil'st they were sporting in this darksome Caue?

⟨*Enter Æneas and Dido.*⟩

Æn. The ayre is cleere, and Southerne windes are whist,
Come *Dido,* let vs hasten to the towne, 1085
Since gloomie *Æolus* doth cease to frowne.
Dido. *Achates* and *Ascanius,* well met.
Æn. Faire *Anna,* how escapt you from the shower?
Anna. As others did, by running to the wood.
Dido. But where were you *Iarbus* all this while? 1090
Iar. Not with *Æneas* in the vgly Caue.
Dido. I see *Æneas* sticketh in your minde,
But I will soone put by that stumbling blocke,
And quell those hopes that thus employ your cares.
Exeunt.

⟨*Scena* 2.⟩

Enters Iarbus to Sacrifize.

Iar. Come seruants, come bring forth the Sacrifize,
That I may pacifie that gloomie *Ioue,* 1096

1074 where's *Hurst to Gros.* 1078 Tiphoeus *Hurst etc.* 1079 While *Hurst* 1083 + S.D. Aside *add. Bull.* S.D. Enter .. Dido *add. Hurst* 1094 cares *Hurst etc.*: eares *1594* Scene II. *add. Hurst*

Whose emptie Altars haue enlarg'd our illes.
Eternall *Ioue*, great master of the Clowdes,
Father of gladnesse, and all frollicke thoughts,
That with thy gloomie hand corrects the heauen, 1100
When ayrie creatures warre amongst themselues :
Heare, heare, O heare *Iarbus* plaining prayers,
Whose hideous ecchoes make the welkin howle,
And all the woods *Eliza* to resound :
The woman that thou wild vs entertaine, 1105
Where straying in our borders vp and downe,
She crau'd a hide of ground to build a towne,
With whom we did deuide both lawes and land,
And all the fruites that plentie els sends forth,
Scorning our loues and royall marriage rites, 1110
Yeelds vp her beautie to a strangers bed,
Who hauing wrought her shame, is straight way fled :
Now if thou beest a pitying God of power,
On whom ruth and compassion euer waites,
Redresse these wrongs, and warne him to his ships, 1115
That now afflicts me with his flattering eyes.

Enter Anna.

Anna. How now *Iarbus*, at your prayers so hard ?
Iar. I, *Anna*, is there ought you would with me ?
Anna. Nay, no such waightie busines of import,
But may be slackt vntill another time : 1120
Yet if you would partake with me the cause
Of this deuotion that detaineth you,
I would be thankfull for such curtesie.
Iar. *Anna*, against this Troian doe I pray,
Who seekes to rob me of thy Sisters loue, 1125
And diue into her heart by coloured lookes.
Anna. Alas poore King that labours so in vaine,
For her that so delighteth in thy paine :
Be rul'd by me, and seeke some other loue,
Whose yeelding heart may yeeld thee more reliefe. 1130
Iar. Mine eye is fixt where fancie cannot start.
O leaue me, leaue me to my silent thoughts,
That register the numbers of my ruth,
And I will either moue the thoughtles flint,

1097 + S.D. Servants bring in the sacrifice, and then exeunt *add. Dyce* 1106 Where] When *conj. Coll.* 1116 eyes] lips *conj. Coll.* 1133 number *Hurst*

Or drop out both mine eyes in drisling teares, 1135
Before my sorrowes tide haue any stint.
Anna. I will not leaue *Iarbus* whom I loue,
In this delight of dying pensiuenes:
Away with *Dido*, *Anna* be thy song,
Anna that doth admire thee more then heauen. 1140
Iar. I may nor will list to such loathsome chaunge,
That intercepts the course of my desire:
Seruants, come fetch these emptie vessels here,
For I will flye from these alluring eyes,
That doe pursue my peace where ere it goes. *Exit.*
Anna. *Iarbus* stay, louing *Iarbus* stay, 1146
For I haue honey to present thee with:
Hard hearted, wilt not deigne to heare me speake?
Ile follow thee with outcryes nere the lesse,
And strewe thy walkes with my discheueld haire. *Exit.*

⟨*Scena* 3.⟩

Enter Æneas alone.

Æn. *Carthage*, my friendly host, adue, 1151
Since destinie doth call me from the shoare:
Hermes this night descending in a dreame,
Hath summond me to fruitfull *Italy*:
Ioue wils it so, my mother wils it so: 1155
Let my Phenissa graunt, and then I goe:
Graunt she or no, *Æneas* must away,
Whose golden fortunes clogd with courtly ease,
Cannot ascend to Fames immortall house,
Or banquet in bright honors burnisht hall, 1160
Till he hath furrowed *Neptunes* glassie fieldes,
And cut a passage through his toples hilles:
Achates come forth, *Sergestus*, *Illioneus*,
Cloanthus, haste away, *Æneas* calles. 1164

Enter Achates, Cloanthus, Sergestus, and Illioneus.

Acha. What willes our Lord, or wherefore did he call?
Æn. The dreames (braue mates) that did beset my bed,
When sleepe but newly had imbrast the night,

1145 goes] flies *conj. Coll.* S.D. Exit. Servants re-enter and carry out the vessels, etc. *Dyce, Bull.* 1150 + Scene III. *add. Hurst* 1152 the *1594*: thy *Hurst etc.* 1158 fortune *Hurst, Cunn.* 1166 dream *Hurst to Cunn.*

Commaunds me leaue these vnrenowmed reames,
Whereas Nobilitie abhors to stay,
And none but base *Æneas* will abide: 1170
Abourd, abourd, since Fates doe bid abourd,
And slice the Sea with sable coloured ships,
On whom the nimble windes may all day waight,
And follow them as footemen through the deepe:
Yet *Dido* casts her eyes like anchors out, 1175
To stay my Fleete from loosing forth the Bay:
Come backe, come backe, I heare her crye a farre,
And let me linke thy bodie to my lips,
That tyed together by the striuing tongues,
We may as one saile into *Italy*. 1180

Acha. Banish that ticing dame from forth your mouth,
And follow your foreseeing starres in all;
This is no life for men at armes to liue,
Where daliance doth consume a Souldiers strength,
And wanton motions of alluring eyes 1185
Effeminate our mindes inur'd to warre.

Illio. Why, let vs build a Citie of our owne,
And not stand lingering here for amorous lookes:
Will *Dido* raise old *Priam* forth his graue,
And build the towne againe the Greekes did burne? 1190
No no, she cares not how we sinke or swimme,
So she may haue *Æneas* in her armes.

Cloan. To *Italy*, sweete friends, to *Italy*,
We will not stay a minute longer here.

Æn. Troians abourd, and I will follow you, 1195
⟨*Exeunt all except Æneas.*⟩
I faine would goe, yet beautie calles me backe:
To leaue her so and not once say farewell
Were to transgresse against all lawes of loue:
But if I vse such ceremonious thankes,
As parting friends accustome on the shoare, 1200
Her siluer armes will coll me round about,
And teares of pearle, crye stay, *Æneas*, stay:
Each word she sayes will then containe a Crowne,
And euery speech be ended with a kisse:
I may not dure this female drudgerie, 1205
To sea *Æneas*, finde out *Italy*. *Exit.*

1168 reams *Dyce*[1], *Gros.*, *McK.*: realms *Dyce*[2] *to Bull.*: beames *1594*, *Hurst* 1178 thy . . my *Dyce etc.*: my . . my *1594*: my . . thy *Hurst* 1195 S.D. *add. Dyce* 1201 coll] coil *Hurst*, *Cunn.* 1206 S.D. exeunt *Hurst*, *Cunn.*

⟨*Scena* 4.⟩

Enter Dido and Anna.

Dido. O *Anna*, runne vnto the water side,
They say *Æneas* men are going abourd,
It may be he will steale away with them:
Stay not to answere me, runne *Anna* runne. ⟨*Exit Anna.*⟩
O foolish Troians that would steale from hence, 1211
And not let *Dido* vnderstand their drift:
I would haue giuen *Achates* store of gold,
And *Illioneus* gum and Libian spice,
The common souldiers rich imbrodered coates, 1215
And siluer whistles to controule the windes,
Which *Circes* sent *Sicheus* when he liued:
Vnworthie are they of a Queenes reward:
See where they come. How might I doe to chide?

Enter Anna, with Æneas, Achates, Illioneus, and Sergestus.

Anna. Twas time to runne, *Æneas* had been gone. 1220
The sailes were hoysing vp, and he abourd.
Dido. Is this thy loue to me?
Æn. O princely *Dido*, giue me leaue to speake,
I went to take my farewell of *Achates.*
Dido. How haps *Achates* bid me not farewell? 1225
Acha. Because I feard your grace would keepe me here.
Dido. To rid thee of that doubt, abourd againe,
I charge thee put to sea and stay not here.
Acha. Then let *Æneas* goe abourd with vs.
Dido. Get you abourd, *Æneas* meanes to stay. 1230
Æn. The sea is rough, the windes blow to the shoare.
Dido. O false *Æneas*, now the sea is rough,
But when you were abourd twas calme enough.
Thou and *Achates* ment to saile away.
Æn. Hath not the Carthage Queene mine onely sonne?
Thinkes *Dido* I will goe and leaue him here? 1236
Dido. *Æneas* pardon me, for I forgot
That yong *Ascanius* lay with me this night:
Loue made me iealous, but to make amends,
Weare the emperiall Crowne of *Libia*, 1240
⟨*Giving him her crown and sceptre.*⟩

1206+Scene IV. *add. Hurst* 1210 S.D. *add. Dyce* 1217 Circe *Hurst to Bull.* 1231 wind blows *Hurst, Cunn.* 1240 S.D. *add. Dyce*

Sway thou the Punike Scepter in my steede,
And punish me *Æneas* for this crime.
Æn. This kisse shall be faire *Didos* punishment.
Dido. O how a Crowne becomes *Æneas* head!
Stay here *Æneas*, and commaund as King. 1245
Æn. How vaine am I to weare this Diadem,
And beare this golden Scepter in my hand?
A Burgonet of steele, and not a Crowne,
A Sword, and not a Scepter fits *Æneas*.
Dido. O keepe them still, and let me gaze my fill: 1250
Now lookes *Æneas* like immortall *Ioue*,
O where is *Ganimed* to hold his cup,
And *Mercury* to flye for what he calles?
Ten thousand *Cupids* houer in the ayre,
And fanne it in *Æneas* louely face. 1255
O that the Clowdes were here wherein thou fleest,
That thou and I vnseene might sport our selues:
Heauen enuious of our ioyes is waxen pale,
And when we whisper, then the starres fall downe,
To be partakers of our honey talke. 1260
Æn. O *Dido*, patronesse of all our liues,
When I leaue thee, death be my punishment.
Swell raging seas, frowne wayward destinies,
Blow windes, threaten ye Rockes and sandie shelfes,
This is the harbour that *Æneas* seekes, 1265
Lets see what tempests can anoy me now.
Dido. Not all the world can take thee from mine armes,
Æneas may commaund as many Moores,
As in the Sea are little water drops:
And now to make experience of my loue, 1270
Faire sister *Anna* leade my louer forth,
And seated on my Gennet, let him ride
As *Didos* husband through the Punicke streetes,
And will my guard with Mauritanian darts,
To waite vpon him as their soueraigne Lord. 1275
Anna. What if the Citizens repine thereat?
Dido. Those that dislike what *Dido* giues in charge
Commaund my guard to slay for their offence:
Shall vulgar pesants storme at what I doe?
The ground is mine that giues them sustenance, 1280
The ayre wherein they breathe, the water, fire,

1248 *Before this line* S.D. Aside *add. Hurst* 1249 + S.D. Offers to return them *add. Gros.* 1256 fled'st *Dyce, Bull., Gros.* 1258 Heaven *Hurst to Gros.*: Heauens *1594*

All that they haue, their lands, their goods, their liues,
And I the Goddesse of all these, commaund
Æneas ride as Carthaginian King.
Acha. *Æneas* for his parentage deserues 1285
As large a kingdome as is *Libia.*
Æn. I, and vnlesse the destinies be false,
I shall be planted in as rich a land.
Dido. Speake of no other land, this land is thine,
Dido is thine, henceforth Ile call thee Lord: 1290
Doe as I bid thee. Sister, leade the way,
And from a turret Ile behold my loue.
Æn. Then here in me shall flourish *Priams* race,
And thou and I *Achates,* for reuenge,
For *Troy,* for *Priam,* for his fiftie sonnes, 1295
Our kinsmens loues, and thousand guiltles soules,
Will leade an hoste against the hatefull Greekes,
And fire proude *Lacedemon* ore their heads.
Exit ⟨*with Trojans*⟩.
Dido. Speakes not *Æneas* like a Conqueror?
O blessed tempests that did driue him in, 1300
O happie sand that made him runne aground:
Henceforth you shall be our Carthage Gods:
I, but it may be he will leaue my loue,
And seeke a forraine land calde *Italy*:
O that I had a charme to keepe the windes 1305
Within the closure of a golden ball,
Or that the Tyrrhen sea were in mine armes,
That he might suffer shipwracke on my breast,
As oft as he attempts to hoyst vp saile.
I must preuent him, wishing will not serue. 1310
Goe, bid my Nurse take yong *Ascanius,*
And beare him in the countrey to her house.
Æneas will not goe without his sonne:
Yet lest he should, for I am full of feare,
Bring me his oares, his tackling, and his sailes: 1315
⟨*Exit a Lord.*⟩
What if I sinke his ships? O heele frowne:
Better he frowne, then I should dye for griefe:
I cannot see him frowne, it may not be:
Armies of foes resolu'd to winne this towne,

1296 loues] lives *Dyce etc.* 1298 S.D. with Trojans *add. McK.* 1302 our] 'mong our *conj. Dyce*: of our *Bull., Gros.* 1315 S.D. *add. Gros.*: One of the Attendants goes out *add. Rob., Cunn.* 1316 heele] he will *Hurst to Gros.*

Or impious traitors vowde to haue my life, 1320
Affright me not, onely *Æneas* frowne
Is that which terrifies poore *Didos* heart:
Not bloudie speares appearing in the ayre,
Presage the downfall of my Emperie,
Nor blazing Commets threatens *Didos* death, 1325
It is *Æneas* frowne that ends my daies:
If he forsake me not, I neuer dye,
For in his lookes I see eternitie,
And heele make me immortall with a kisse.

Enter a Lord.

⟨*Lord.*⟩ Your Nurse is gone with yong *Ascanius*, 1330
And heres *Æneas* tackling, oares and sailes.
Dido. Are these the sailes that in despight of me,
Packt with the windes to beare *Æneas* hence?
Ile hang ye in the chamber where I lye,
Driue if you can my house to *Italy*: 1335
Ile set the casement open that the windes
May enter in, and once againe conspire
Against the life of me poore Carthage Queene:
But though he goe, he stayes in Carthage still,
And let rich Carthage fleete vpon the seas, 1340
So I may haue *Æneas* in mine armes.
Is this the wood that grew in Carthage plaines,
And would be toyling in the watrie billowes,
To rob their mistresse of her Troian guest?
O cursed tree, hadst thou but wit or sense, 1345
To measure how I prize *Æneas* loue,
Thou wouldst haue leapt from out the Sailers hands,
And told me that *Æneas* ment to goe:
And yet I blame thee not, thou art but wood.
The water which our Poets terme a Nimph, 1350
Why did it suffer thee to touch her breast,
And shrunke not backe, knowing my loue was there?
The water is an Element, no Nimph,
Why should I blame *Æneas* for his flight?
O *Dido*, blame not him, but breake his oares, 1355
These were the instruments that launcht him forth.
Theres not so much as this base tackling too,

1329 S.D. Re-enter First Lord with Attendants carrying tackling, etc., *Dyce, Bull.* 1330 *Prefix* Lord *add. Hurst* 1335 + S.D. tears the sails *add. Gros.* 1339 he goe] ye go *Dyce to Bull.* 1355 + S.D. breaks them *add. Gros.*

But dares to heape vp sorrowe to my heart:
Was it not you that hoysed vp these sailes?
Why burst you not, and they fell in the seas? 1360
For this will *Dido* tye ye full of knots,
And sheere ye all asunder with her hands:
Now serue to chastize shipboyes for their faults,
Ye shall no more offend the Carthage Queene.
Now let him hang my fauours on his masts, 1365
And see if those will serue in steed of sailes:
For tackling, let him take the chaines of gold,
Which I bestowd vpon his followers:
In steed of oares, let him vse his hands,
And swim to *Italy*, Ile keepe these sure: 1370
Come beare them in. *Exit.*

⟨*Scena* 5.⟩

Enter the Nurse with Cupid for Ascanius.

Nurse. My Lord *Ascanius*, ye must goe with me.
Cupid. Whither must I goe? Ile stay with my mother.
Nurse. No, thou shalt goe with me vnto my house.
I haue an Orchard that hath store of plums, 1375
Browne Almonds, Seruises, ripe Figs and Dates,
Dewberries, Apples, yellow Orenges,
A garden where are Bee hiues full of honey,
Musk-roses, and a thousand sort of flowers,
And in the midst doth run a siluer streame, 1380
Where thou shalt see the red gild fishes leape,
White Swannes, and many louely water fowles:
Now speake *Ascanius*, will ye goe or no?
Cupid. Come, come, Ile goe, how farre hence is your house?
Nurse. But hereby child, we shall get thither straight.
Cupid. Nurse I am wearie, will you carrie me? 1386
Nurse. I, so youle dwell with me and call me mother
Cupid. So youle loue me, I care not if I doe.
Nurse. That I might liue to see this boy a man!
How pretilie he laughs, goe ye wagge, 1390
Youle be a twigger when you come to age.
Say *Dido* what she will I am not old,

1362 + S.D. knots and cuts them *add. Gros.* 1371 + Scene V. *add. Hurst* 1383 ye] you *Dyce, Bull.* 1390 S.D. He toys with her *add. Gros. after* laughs goe] go, go *conj. Mitford*: go to *Bull.* 1391 trigger *conj. Coll.*

Ile be no more a widowe, I am young.
Ile haue a husband, or els a louer.
Cupid. A husband and no teeth! 1395
Nurse. O what meane I to haue such foolish thoughts!
Foolish is loue, a toy. O sacred loue,
If there be any heauen in earth, tis loue:
Especially in women of your yeares.
Blush, blush for shame, why shouldst thou thinke of loue?
A graue, and not a louer fits thy age: 1401
A graue, why? I may liue a hundred yeares,
Fourescore is but a girles age, loue is sweete.
My vaines are withered, and my sinewes drie,
Why doe I thinke of loue now I should dye? 1405
Cupid. Come Nurse.
Nurse. Well, if he come a wooing he shall speede,
O how vnwise was I to say him nay! *Exeunt.*

Actus 5. 〈*Scena* 1.〉

Enter Æneas with a paper in his hand, drawing the platforme of the citie, with him Achates, 〈*Sergestus,*〉 *Cloanthus, and Illioneus.*

Æn. Triumph my mates, our trauels are at end,
Here will *Æneas* build a statelier *Troy*, 1410
Then that which grim *Atrides* ouerthrew:
Carthage shall vaunt her pettie walles no more,
For I will grace them with a fairer frame,
And clad her in a Chrystall liuerie,
Wherein the day may euermore delight: 1415
From golden *India Ganges* will I fetch,
Whose wealthie streames may waite vpon her towers,
And triple wise intrench her round about:
The Sunne from Egypt shall rich odors bring,
Wherewith his burning beames like labouring Bees, 1420
That loade their thighes with *Hyblas* honeys spoyles,
Shall here vnburden their exhaled sweetes,
And plant our pleasant suburbes with her fumes.
Acha. What length or bredth shal this braue towne containe?

1399–1401 *Spoken by Cupid conj. Coll.* 1399 your] our *conj. Deighton* Scene I *add. Hurst* S.D. Sergestus *add. Dyce, Bull. etc.* 1421 honey-spoils *Hurst to Bull.* 1423 plant] scent *conj. Elze* her] their *conj. Dyce*[1], *Dyce*[2], *Bull.* her fumes] perfumes *conj. Elze.*

Æn. Not past foure thousand paces at the most. 1425
Illio. But what shall it be calde, *Troy* as before?
Æn. That haue I not determinde with my selfe.
Cloan. Let it be term'd *Ænea* by your name.
Serg. Rather *Ascania* by your little sonne.
Æn. Nay, I will haue it calde *Anchisæon*, 1430
Of my old fathers name.

Enter Hermes with Ascanius.

Hermes. *Æneas* stay, *Ioues* Herald bids thee stay.
Æn. Whom doe I see, *Ioues* winged messenger?
Welcome to *Carthage* new erected towne.
Hermes. Why cosin, stand you building Cities here,
And beautifying the Empire of this Queene, 1436
While *Italy* is cleane out of thy minde?
To, too forgetfull of thine owne affayres,
Why wilt thou so betray thy sonnes good hap?
The king of Gods sent me from highest heauen, 1440
To sound this angrie message in thine eares.
Vaine man, what Monarky expectst thou here?
Or with what thought sleepst thou in *Libia* shoare?
If that all glorie hath forsaken thee,
And thou despise the praise of such attempts: 1445
Yet thinke vpon *Ascanius* prophesie,
And yong *Iulus* more then thousand yeares,
Whom I haue brought from *Ida* where he slept,
And bore yong *Cupid* vnto *Cypresse* Ile.
Æn. This was my mother that beguild the Queene,
And made me take my brother for my sonne: 1451
No maruell *Dido* though thou be in loue,
That daylie danlest *Cupid* in thy armes:
Welcome sweet child, where hast thou been this long?
Asca. Eating sweet Comfites with Queene *Didos* maide,
Who euer since hath luld me in her armes. 1456
Æn. *Sergestus*, beare him hence vnto our ships,
Lest *Dido* spying him keepe him for a pledge.
⟨*Exit Sergestus with Ascanius.*⟩
Hermes. Spendst thou thy time about this little boy,
And giuest not eare vnto the charge I bring? 1460
I tell thee thou must straight to *Italy*,
Or els abide the wrath of frowning *Ioue*. ⟨*Exit.*⟩
Æn. How should I put into the raging deepe,

1443 on Lybia's *Hurst, Cunn.* 1458 spying him] spying *Hurst* S.D. *add. Dyce* 1462 S.D. *add Dyce*

Who haue no sailes nor tackling for my ships ?
What, would the Gods haue me, *Deucalion* like, 1465
Flote vp and downe where ere the billowes driue ?
Though she repairde my fleete and gaue me ships,
Yet hath she tane away my oares and masts,
And left me neither saile nor sterne abourd.

Enter to them Iarbus.

Iar. How now *Æneas*, sad, what meanes these dumpes ?
Æn. *Iarbus*, I am cleane besides my selfe. 1471
Ioue hath heapt on me such a desperate charge,
Which neither art nor reason may atchieue,
Nor I deuise by what meanes to contriue.
Iar. As how I pray, may I entreate you tell. 1475
Æn. With speede he bids me saile to *Italy*,
When as I want both rigging for my fleete,
And also furniture for these my men.
Iar. If that be all, then cheare thy drooping lookes,
For I will furnish thee with such supplies : 1480
Let some of those thy followers goe with me,
And they shall haue what thing so ere thou needst.
Æn. Thankes good *Iarbus* for thy friendly ayde,
Achates and the rest shall waite on thee,
Whil'st I rest thankfull for this curtesie. 1485
Exit Iarbus and Æneas traine.
Now will I haste vnto *Lauinian* shoare,
And raise a new foundation to old *Troy*,
Witnes the Gods, and witnes heauen and earth,
How loth I am to leaue these *Libian* bounds,
But that eternall *Iupiter* commands. 1490

Enter Dido and Æneas ⟨*severally*⟩.

Dido. I feare I sawe *Æneas* little sonne,
Led by *Achates* to the Troian fleete :
If it be so, his father meanes to flye :
But here he is, now *Dido* trie thy wit.
Æneas, wherefore goe thy men abourd ? 1495
Why are thy ships new rigd ? or to what end
Launcht from the hauen, lye they in the Rhode ?
Pardon me though I aske, loue makes me aske.

1471 beside *Hurst, Cunn.* 1490 S.D. severally *add. Gros.* Scene II *begins here Rob., Cunn.* 1492 Achates] Sergestus *conj. Dyce* 1494 + S.D. Aside *add. Dyce, Bull.* : S.D. Enter Aeneas *add. Hurst. Cunn.*

Æn. O pardon me, if I resolue thee why:
Æneas will not faine with his deare loue. 1500
I must from hence: this day swift *Mercury*
When I was laying a platforme for these walles,
Sent from his father *Ioue*, appeard to me,
And in his name rebukt me bitterly
For lingering here, neglecting *Italy*. 1505
Dido. But yet *Æneas* will not leaue his loue.
Æn. I am commaunded by immortall *Ioue*,
To leaue this towne and passe to *Italy*,
And therefore must of force.
Dido. These words proceed not from *Æneas* heart. 1510
Æn. Not from my heart, for I can hardly goe,
And yet I may not stay. *Dido* farewell.
Dido. Farewell: is this the mends for *Didos* loue?
Doe Troians vse to quit their Louers thus?
Fare well may *Dido*, so *Æneas* stay, 1515
I dye, if my *Æneas* say farewell.
Æn. Then let me goe and neuer say farewell.
Dido. Let me goe, farewell, I must from hence.
These words are poyson to poore *Didos* soule,
O speake like my *Æneas*, like my loue: 1520
Why look'st thou toward the sea? the time hath been
When *Didos* beautie chaind thine eyes to her:
Am I lesse faire then when thou sawest me first?
O then *Æneas*, tis for griefe of thee:
Say thou wilt stay in *Carthage* with thy Queene, 1525
And *Didos* beautie will returne againe:
Æneas, say, how canst thou take thy leaue?
Wilt thou kisse *Dido*? O thy lips haue sworne
To stay with *Dido*: canst thou take her hand?
Thy hand and mine haue plighted mutuall faith, 1530
Therefore vnkind *Æneas*, must thou say,
Then let me goe, and neuer say farewell.
Æn. O Queene of *Carthage*, wert thou vgly blacke,
Æneas could not choose but hold thee deare,
Yet must he not gainsay the Gods behest. 1535
Dido. The Gods, what Gods be those that seeke my death?

1518 *Prefix* Dido *precedes l.* 1519, *1594 etc. The change is a conjecture of McK.* Let] O let *Gros.* goe] go is *Cunn.*: forgo *conj. Deighton* farewell] farewell none *Dyce*[2]: farewell or none *conj. Gros.* 1522 chaind *Rob. etc.*: chaungd *1594*, *Hurst*: *Qy.* charmed eye *Hurst, Cunn.* 1525 thy *Hurst etc.*: my *1594* 1527+S.D. He kisses her *add. Gros.*

Wherein haue I offended *Iupiter*,
That he should take *Æneas* from mine armes?
O no, the Gods wey not what Louers doe,
It is *Æneas* calles *Æneas* hence, 1540
And wofull *Dido* by these blubbred cheekes,
By this right hand, and by our spousall rites,
Desires *Æneas* to remaine with her:
Si bene quid de te merui, fuit aut tibi quidquam
Dulce meum, miserere domus labentis: & istam 1545
Oro, si quis adhuc precibus locus, exue mentem.

Æn. Desine meque tuis incendere teque querelis,
Italiam non sponte sequor.

Dido. Hast thou forgot how many neighbour kings
Were vp in armes, for making thee my loue? 1550
How *Carthage* did rebell, *Iarbus* storme,
And all the world calles me a second *Helen*,
For being intangled by a strangers lookes:
So thou wouldst proue as true as *Paris* did,
Would, as faire *Troy* was, *Carthage* might be sackt, 1555
And I be calde a second *Helena*.
Had I a sonne by thee, the griefe were lesse,
That I might see *Æneas* in his face:
Now if thou goest, what canst thou leaue behind,
But rather will augment then ease my woe? 1560

Æn. In vaine my loue thou spendst thy fainting breath,
If words might moue me I were ouercome.

Dido. And wilt thou not be mou'd with *Didos* words?
Thy mother was no Goddesse periurd man,
Nor *Dardanus* the author of thy stocke: 1565
But thou art sprung from *Scythian Caucasus*,
And Tygers of *Hircania* gaue thee sucke:
Ah foolish *Dido* to forbeare this long!
Wast thou not wrackt vpon this *Libian* shoare,
And cam'st to *Dido* like a Fisher swaine? 1570
Repairde not I thy ships, made thee a King,
And all thy needie followers Noblemen?
O Serpent that came creeping from the shoare,
And I for pitie harbord in my bosome,
Wilt thou now slay me with thy venomed sting, 1575
And hisse at *Dido* for preseruing thee?
Goe, goe and spare not, seeke out *Italy*,

1542 rites] rights *Hurst* 1546 adhuc *Hurst etc.*: ad hæc *1594* 1552 call'd *Hurst to Cunn.* 1568 this] thus *Rob.* 1569 wreck'd *Hurst, Dyce to Bull.*

I hope that that which loue forbids me doe,
The Rockes and Sea-gulfes will performe at large,
And thou shalt perish in the billowes waies, 1580
To whom poore *Dido* doth bequeath reuenge.
I traytor, and the waues shall cast thee vp,
Where thou and false *Achates* first set foote:
Which if it chaunce, Ile giue ye buriall,
And weepe vpon your liueles carcases, 1585
Though thou nor he will pitie me a whit.
Why star'st thou in my face? if thou wilt stay,
Leape in mine armes, mine armes are open wide:
If not, turne from me, and Ile turne from thee:
For though thou hast the heart to say farewell, 1590
I haue not power to stay thee. ⟨*Exit Æneas.*⟩ Is he gone?
I but heele come againe, he cannot goe,
He loues me to too well to serue me so:
Yet he that in my sight would not relent
Will, being absent, be abdurate still. 1595
By this is he got to the water side,
And, see the Sailers take him by the hand,
But he shrinkes backe, and now remembring me,
Returnes amaine: welcome, welcome my loue:
But wheres *Æneas*? ah hees gone, hees gone! 1600

⟨*Enter Anna.*⟩

Anna. What meanes my sister thus to raue and crye?
Dido. O *Anna*, my *Æneas* is abourd,
And leauing me will saile to *Italy*.
Once didst thou goe, and he came backe againe,
Now bring him backe, and thou shalt be a Queene, 1605
And I will liue a priuate life with him.
Anna. Wicked *Æneas*.
Dido. Call him not wicked, sister, speake him faire,
And looke vpon him with a Mermaides eye,
Tell him, I neuer vow'd at *Aulis* gulfe 1610
The desolation of his natiue *Troy*,
Nor sent a thousand ships vnto the walles,
Nor euer violated faith to him:
Request him gently (*Anna*) to returne,
I craue but this, he stay a tide or two, 1615
That I may learne to beare it patiently.

1579 sea-gulls *Hurst, Cunn.* 1585 lifeless *Hurst to Bull.*
1591 S.D. *add. Hurst* 1600 S.D. *add. Hurst.*

If he depart thus suddenly, I dye :
Run *Anna*, run, stay not to answere me.
Anna. I goe faire sister, heauens graunt good successe.
Exit Anna

Enter the Nurse.

Nurse. O *Dido*, your little sonne *Ascanius* 1620
Is gone ! he lay with me last night,
And in the morning he was stolne from me,
I thinke some Fairies haue beguiled me.
Dido. O cursed hagge and false dissembling wretch !
That slayest me with thy harsh and hellish tale, 1625
Thou for some pettie guift hast let him goe,
And I am thus deluded of my boy :
Away with her to prison presently,
Traytoresse too keend and cursed Sorceresse.
Nurse. I know not what you meane by treason, I, 1630
I am as true as any one of yours.
Exeunt the Nurse ⟨and Attendants⟩.
Dido. Away with her, suffer her not to speake.
My sister comes, I like not her sad lookes.

Enter Anna.

Anna. Before I came, *Æneas* was abourd,
And spying me, hoyst vp the sailes amaine : 1635
But I cride out, *Æneas*, false *Æneas* stay.
Then gan he wagge his hand, which yet held vp,
Made me suppose he would haue heard me speake :
Then gan they driue into the Ocean,
Which when I viewd, I cride, *Æneas* stay, 1640
Dido, faire *Dido* wils *Æneas* stay :
Yet he whose heart of adamant or flint,
My teares nor plaints could mollifie a whit :
Then carelesly I rent my haire for griefe,
Which seene to all, though he beheld me not, 1645
They gan to moue him to redresse my ruth,
And stay a while to heare what I could say,
But he clapt vnder hatches saild away.
Dido. O *Anna*, *Anna*, I will follow him.
Anna. How can ye goe when he hath all your fleete ?
Dido. Ile frame me wings of waxe like *Icarus*, 1651

1628+S.D. Enter Attendants *add. Dyce, Bull.* 1629 too keend] to kind *conj. Coll., conj. Deighton* keend] keen *Hurst* : kind *conj. Gros.* : kenn'd *Cunn., Bull.* 1636 stay *omit conj. Mitford* 1642 heart *1594* : heart's *Hurst etc.*

And ore his ships will soare vnto the Sunne,
That they may melt and I fall in his armes:
Or els Ile make a prayer vnto the waues,
That I may swim to him like *Tritons* neece: 1655
O *Anna*, fetch *Orions* Harpe,
That I may tice a Dolphin to the shoare,
And ride vpon his backe vnto my loue:
Looke sister, looke, louely *Æneas* ships,
See see, the billowes heaue him vp to heauen, 1660
And now downe falles the keeles into the deepe:
O sister, sister, take away the Rockes,
Theile breake his ships. O *Proteus, Neptune, Ioue*,
Saue, saue *Æneas, Didos* leefest loue!
Now is he come on shoare safe without hurt: 1665
But see, *Achates* wils him put to sea,
And all the Sailers merrie make for ioy,
But he remembring me shrinkes backe againe:
See where he comes, welcome, welcome my loue.
Anna. Ah sister, leaue these idle fantasies, 1670
Sweet sister cease, remember who you are.
Dido. *Dido* I am, vnlesse I be deceiu'd,
And must I raue thus for a runnagate?
Must I make ships for him to saile away?
Nothing can beare me to him but a ship, 1675
And he hath all my fleete, what shall I doe
But dye in furie of this ouersight?
I, I must be the murderer of my selfe:
No but I am not, yet I will be straight.
Anna be glad, now haue I found a meane 1680
To rid me from these thoughts of Lunacie:
Not farre from hence
There is a woman famoused for arts,
Daughter vnto the Nimphs *Hesperides*,
Who wild me sacrifize his ticing relliques: 1685
Goe *Anna*, bid my seruants bring me fire. *Exit Anna.*

Enter Iarbus.

Iar. How long will *Dido* mourne a strangers flight,
That hath dishonord her and *Carthage* both?

1652 ship *Hurst, Cunn.* 1656 Anna *repeat conj. Dyce, Cunn. to Gros.* Arions *Dyce to Gros.* 1660 him] 'em *Dyce*[2]: them *Cunn.* 1676 my *Hurst etc.*: thy *1594* 1678 I, I] Aye, I *Hurst to Bull.* 1679+S.D. Aside *add. Dyce*[2], *Bull.* 1682 Not . . hence *omit conj. Mitford* 1682–3 *One line 1594*: *div. Dyce* 1684 Daughter] Guardian *conj. Bull.*: Drugster *conj. Deighton*

How long shall I with griefe consume my daies,
And reape no guerdon for my truest loue? 1690
Dido. *Iarbus,* talke not of *Æneas,* let him goe,
Lay to thy hands and helpe me make a fire,
That shall consume all that this stranger left,
For I entend a priuate Sacrifize,
To cure my minde that melts for vnkind loue. 1695
Iar. But afterwards will *Dido* graunt me loue?
Dido. I, I, *Iarbus,* after this is done,
None in the world shall haue my loue but thou:
So, leaue me now, let none approach this place.
Exit Iarbus.
Now *Dido,* with these reliques burne thy selfe, 1700
And make *Æneas* famous through the world,
For periurie and slaughter of a Queene:
Here lye the Sword that in the darksome Caue
He drew, and swore by to be true to me,
Thou shalt burne first, thy crime is worse then his: 1705
Here lye the garment which I cloath'd him in,
When first he came on shoare, perish thou to:
These letters, lines, and periurd papers all,
Shall burne to cinders in this pretious flame.
And now ye Gods that guide the starrie frame, 1710
And order all things at your high dispose,
Graunt, though the traytors land in *Italy,*
They may be still tormented with vnrest,
And from mine ashes let a Conquerour rise,
That may reuenge this treason to a Queene, 1715
By plowing vp his Countries with the Sword:
Betwixt this land and that be neuer league,
Littora littoribus contraria, fluctibus vndas
Imprecor: arma armis: pugnent ipsiq; nepotes:
Liue false *Æneas,* truest *Dido* dyes, 1720
Sic sic iuuat ire sub vmbras.
⟨*Stabs herself and throws herself into the flames.*⟩

Enter Anna.

Anna. O helpe *Iarbus, Dido* in these flames
Hath burnt her selfe, aye me, vnhappie me!

1690+S.D. Enter Attendants with wood and torches *add. Dyce* 1691 Iarbus] Oh *conj. Mitford* 1698+S.D. They make a fire *add. Dyce* 1703, 1706 lies *Hurst, Dyce* 1721 S.D. *add. Gros.* 1723, 1726 aye] ah *Hurst, Cunn.*

Enter Iarbus running.

Iar. Cursed *Iarbus*, dye to expiate
The griefe that tires vpon thine inward soule, 1725
Dido I come to thee, aye me, *Æneas.* ⟨*Kills himself.*⟩
Anna. What can my teares or cryes preuaile me now?
Dido is dead, *Iarbus* slaine, *Iarbus* my deare loue.
O sweet *Iarbus, Annas* sole delight,
What fatall destinie enuies me thus, 1730
To see my sweet *Iarbus* slay himselfe?
But *Anna* now shall honor thee in death,
And mixe her bloud with thine, this shall I doe,
That Gods and men may pitie this my death,
And rue our ends senceles of life or breath: 1735
Now sweet *Iarbus* stay, I come to thee. ⟨*Kills herself.*⟩

FINIS.

1726 S.D. *add. Hurst* 1736 S.D *add. Hurst*

V. i. 1724–1736

THE MASSACRE AT PARIS

Date. The play of *The Massacre at Paris* or *The Guise*, as Henslowe sometimes terms it with rather more propriety, must have been composed between August 2, 1589, and January 30, 1593. On the first of these dates occurred the event with which the tragedy closes, the death of Henri III of France; on the latter occasion the play was performed at Henslowe's theatre by the company of the Lord Strange. Since Henslowe marks 'the tragedey of the gvyes' as a new play on January 30, 1593, it was probably composed pretty shortly before, and is therefore to be reckoned one of the latest of Marlowe's dramatic works. Crude as the play undoubtedly is, there is nothing to indicate that it was written very immediately after the assassination of the French king, for that event, which in a contemporary 'topical' drama would naturally have formed the mainstay of the plot, is here given very little importance, while the principal interest centres about the ancient history of St. Bartholomew and the animosities of Guise and Navarre.

Stage history. In addition to the single performance by Lord Strange's servants already mentioned, which produced the large sum of £3 14*s*., Henslowe records ten representations by the Admiral's company between June 19 and September 25, 1594. Notes of expenditure for stage properties show that *The Guise* was revived in 1598, and again in 1601, and a further memorandum records the disbursement of £6 'pd at the apoyntment of the companye the 18 of Janeway 1601 [1602, N.S.] vnto E. Alleyn for iij. boockes wch were played', second on the list being 'the massaker of france'. Mr. Greg is no doubt correct in his opinion[1] that the manuscript of our play had been brought to the Admiral's company by Alleyn, when that famous actor left Lord Strange's men to join the other troupe.

Text. *The Massacre at Paris* does not appear to have

[1] *Henslowe's Diary*, II, 157.

been registered for publication. There exists, however, a single early edition 'printed by E. A. for Edward White, dwelling . . . at the signe of the Gun'. The title-page bears no date and the publication has been conjecturally ascribed to various years between 1594 and 1600. I believe that the edition is somewhat later and that it rather follows than precedes the last revival of the play in 1601. In the first place, the very full character of the stage directions[1] indicates that the text is based on a theatre copy, and such a copy would certainly have been more easily obtainable after it was no longer of immediate use to the company. Moreover, Edward White, though he is known to have published a book as early as 1577, was connected with only one other edition of a work by Marlowe—the *Tamburlaine* of 1605/6, where on the title-pages of both parts there is the same mention of White's name with the notice of his shop 'at the signe of the Gunne', and in the case of the second part 'E. A.' is again particularly named as the printer. Such evidence is of no great weight, but it is borne out by the general similarity in typographical details between the 1605/6 *Tamburlaine* and the undated edition of *The Massacre.*

Of all the extant plays of Marlowe this of *The Massacre at Paris* is in its present state much the least meritorious. There can hardly be any doubt that our text is shockingly garbled; it would seem to represent a theatrical abridgement, in which the poet's language and versification have been corrupted on nearly every page, while the very sense of the original can in several passages be only imperfectly preserved. We have no reason to suppose that the play ever possessed in a high degree either coherence or artistic finish; it appears to have been the result of a somewhat ill-digested conception hastily and carelessly worked out. There is nothing to indicate collaboration or methodical revision. Throughout the play, to the very end, occur lines of the most characteristically Marlovian quality,[2] and there appears no trace of any second hand except that of the theatrical adapter. The fallacy of the theory, several times suggested, that Marlowe left the play to be completed by another is evident from the indisputable genuineness of the French king's last speeches (ll. 1205–1221, 1241–1257), while the final words of Navarre, with which the piece

[1] Cf., for instance, those after ll. 592, 1185.

[2] e.g. ll. 91–166, 390–421, 582–588, 686–703, 854–871, 976–1027.

closes, are as convincing in their swing and melody as the poet's autograph :

> And then I vow for to reuenge his death,
> As Rome and all those popish Prelates there,
> Shall curse the time that ere *Nauarre* was King,
> And rulde in France by *Henries* fatall death.

Source. It is not probable that Marlowe derived the subject-matter of his play from any one book. The period of the action covers seventeen years (1572–89), and while the earlier events, such as the Massacre of St. Bartholomew, had already found their way into historical chronicles when the play was written, the later incidents must still have been matter for rumour and journalistic report. Mr. Bullen has pointed out several parallels between Marlowe's treatment of the massacre and that found in Book X of *The Three Partes of Commentaries containing the whole and perfect discourse of the Civill Wars of France*, &c. (1574). Much of Marlowe's information concerning the later occurrences, which are lightly treated in the play, must have been picked up from broadsides or word of mouth gossip.

THE MASSACRE AT PARIS:

With the Death of the Duke of Guise.

As it was plaide by the right honourable the Lord high *Admirall* his Seruants.

Written by *Christopher Marlow.*

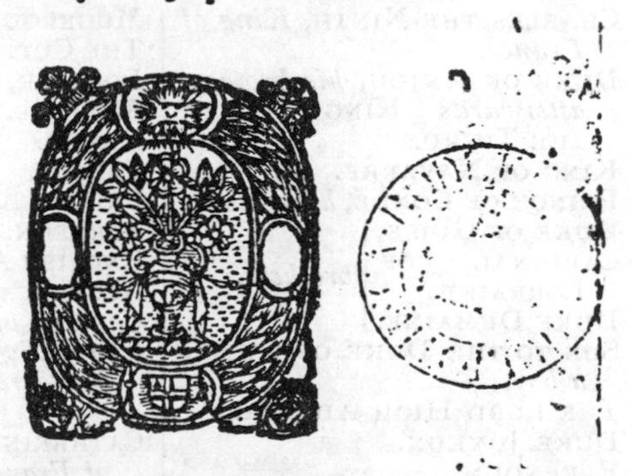

AT LONDON

Printed by *E. A.* for *Edward White*, dwelling neere the little North doore of S. Paules Church, at the signe of the Gun.

O = The undated octavo.
Rob. = Robinson's edition of Marlowe, 1826.
Dyce { *Dyce*[1] = Dyce's first edition of Marlowe, 1850.
Dyce[2] = Dyce's revised edition of Marlowe, 1858, etc. }
Cunn. = Cunningham's edition of Marlowe, 1870, etc.
Bull. = Bullen's edition of Marlowe, 1885.
T. B. = The present editor.

Brereton = Conjectures by J. L. G. B., *Anglia*, *Beiblatt*, xvi. 206.
Coll. = Conjectures by J. P. Collier (Brit. Mus. 11771 bbb 6).
Malone = MS. corrections, probably by M., in Bodleian copy of *O*.
Mitford = Conjectures by J. M., quoted by Dyce.

⟨DRAMATIS PERSONÆ

CHARLES THE NINTH, *King of France.*
DUKE OF ANJOU, *his brother, afterwards* KING HENRY THE THIRD.
KING OF NAVARRE.
PRINCE OF CONDÉ, *his brother.*
DUKE OF GUISE, }
CARDINAL OF LORRAINE, } *brothers.*
DUKE DUMAINE, }
SON TO THE DUKE OF GUISE, *a boy.*
THE LORD HIGH ADMIRAL.
DUKE JOYEUX.
EPERNOUN.
PLESHÈ.
BARTUS.
TWO LORDS OF POLAND.
GONZAGO.
RETES.
MOUNTSORRELL.
MUGEROUN.
THE CUTPURSE.
LOREINE, *a preacher.*
SEROUNE.
RAMUS.
TALEUS.
FRIAR.
SURGEON.
ENGLISH AGENT.
APOTHECARY.
Captain of the Guard, Protestants, Schoolmasters, Soldiers, Murderers, Attendants, &c.

CATHERINE, *the Queen-Mother of France.*
MARGARET, *her daughter, wife to the* KING OF NAVARRE.
THE OLD QUEEN OF NAVARRE.
DUCHESS OF GUISE.
WIFE TO SEROUNE.
Maid to the Duchess of Guise.⟩[1]

[1] *Add. Dyce.*

THE MASSACRE AT PARIS.

With the Death of the Duke of *Guise*.

Enter Charles *the French King, the Queene Mother, the King of* Nauarre, *the Prince of* Condye, *the Lord high Admirall, and the Queene of* Nauarre, *with others.*

Charles.

Prince of *Nauarre* my honourable brother,
Prince *Condy*, and my good Lord Admirall,
I wishe this vnion and religious league,
Knit in these hands, thus ioyn'd in nuptiall rites,
May not desolue, till death desolue our liues, 5
And that the natiue sparkes of princely loue,
That kindled first this motion in our hearts,
May still be feweld in our progenye.
Nauar. The many fauours which your grace hath showne,
From time to time, but specially in this, 10
Shall binde me euer to your highnes will
In what Queen Mother or your grace commands.
Old Qu. Thanks sonne *Nauarre*, you see we loue you well,
That linke you in mariage with our daughter heer:
And as you know, our difference in Religion 15
Might be a meanes to crosse you in your loue.
Charles. Well Madam, let that rest:

Heading Act the First. Scene I. *add. Rob., Cunn.*: Scene I. *Bull.*

And now my Lords the mariage rites perfourm'd,
We think it good to goe and consumate
The rest, with hearing of a holy Masse: 20
Sister, I think your selfe will beare vs company.

Q. Mar. I will my good Lord.

Charles. The rest that will not goe (my Lords) may stay:
Come Mother,
Let vs goe to honor this solemnitie. 25

Old Q. Which Ile desolue with bloud and crueltie.

Exit the King, Q. Mother, *and the* Q. *of* Nauar, *and manet* Nauar, *the Prince of* Condy, *and the Lord high* Admirall.

Nauar. Prince Condy and my good L⟨ord⟩ Admiral,
Now *Guise* may storme but doe vs little hurt:
Hauing the King, Qu⟨een⟩ Mother on our sides,
To stop the mallice of his enuious heart, 30
That seekes to murder all the Protestants:
Haue you not heard of late how he decreed,
If that the King had giuen consent thereto,
That all the protestants that are in Paris,
Should haue been murdered the other night? 35

Ad. My Lord I meruaile that th'aspiring *Guise*
Dares once aduenture without the Kings consent,
To meddle or attempt such dangerous things.

Con. My L⟨ord⟩ you need not meruaile at the *Guise*,
For what he doth the Pope will ratifie: 40
In murder, mischeefe, or in tiranny.

Na. But he that sits and rules aboue the clowdes,
Doth heare and see the praiers of the iust:
And will reuenge the bloud of innocents,
That *Guise* hath slaine by treason of his heart, 45
And brought by murder to their timeles ends.

Ad. My Lord, but did you mark the Cardinall,
The *Guises* brother and the Duke *Dumain*:
How they did storme at these your nuptiall rites,
Because the house of *Burbon* now comes in, 50
And ioynes your linnage to the crowne of France?

Na. And thats ye cause that *Guise* so frowns at vs,
And beates his braines to catch vs in his trap,
Which he hath pitcht within his deadly toyle.

19 *Ends* rest *O*: *corr. Dyce* 20, 21 *Prose O*: *corr. Dyce* 24, 25 *One line O*: *div. Dyce* 26+S.D. Aside *add. Dyce* 29 King, Qu. Mother *O*: king, Queen-Mother *Dyce, Bull.*: king-Queen Mother *Cunn.*

Come my Lords lets go to the Church and pray, 55
That God may still defend the right of France:
And make his Gospel flourish in this land. *Exeunt.*

Enter the Duke of Guise.

Guise. If euer *Hymen* lowr'd at marriage rites,
And had his alters deckt with duskie lightes:
If euer sunne stainde heauen with bloudy clowdes, 60
And made it look with terrour on the worlde:
If euer day were turnde to vgly night,
And night made semblance of the hue of hell,
This day, this houre, this fatall night,
Shall fully shew the fury of them all. 65
Apothecarie.

Enter the Pothecarie.

Pothe. My Lord.
Guise. Now shall I proue and guerdon to the ful
The loue thou bear'st vnto the house of *Guise*:
Where are those perfumed gloues which I sent 70
To be poysoned, hast thou done them? speake,
Will euery sauour breed a pangue of death?
Pothe. See where they be my good Lord,
And he that smelles but to them, dyes.
Guise. Then thou remainest resolute. 75
Pothe. I am my Lord, in what your grace commaundes
Till death.
Guise. Thankes my good freend, I wil requite thy loue.
Goe then, present them to the Queene *Nauarre*:
For she is that huge blemish in our eye, 80
That makes these vpstart heresies in Fraunce:
Be gone my freend, present them to her straite.
Souldyer. Exit *Pothe.*

Enter a Souldier.

Soul. My Lord.
Guise. Now come thou forth and play thy tragick part, 85
Stand in some window opening neere the street,
And when thou seest the Admirall ride by,
Discharge thy musket and perfourme his death:
And then Ile guerdon thee with store of crownes.
Soul. I will my Lord. Exit *Souldi.*

57 + Scene II. *add. Cunn., Bull.* 64 houre] hour and *conj. Dyce, Cunn.* 70 which] which late *Rob., Cunn., Bull.*

Guise. Now *Guise* begins those deepe ingendred thoughts
To burst abroad those neuer dying flames, 92
Which cannot be extinguisht but by bloud.
Oft haue I leueld, and at last haue learnd,
That perill is the cheefest way to happines, 95
And resolution honors fairest aime.
What glory is there in a common good,
That hanges for euery peasant to atchiue?
That like I best that flyes beyond my reach.
Set me to scale the high Peramides, 100
And thereon set the Diadem of Fraunce,
Ile either rend it with my nayles to naught,
Or mount the top with my aspiring winges,
Although my downfall be the deepest hell.
For this, I wake, when others think I sleepe, 105
For this, I waite, that scornes attendance else:
For this, my quenchles thirst whereon I builde
Hath often pleaded kindred to the King.
For this, this head, this heart, this hand and sworde,
Contriues, imagines and fully executes 110
Matters of importe, aimde at by many,
Yet vnderstoode by none.
For this, hath heauen engendred me of earth,
For this, this earth sustaines my bodies waight,
And with this wait Ile counterpoise a Crowne, 115
Or with seditions weary all the worlde:
For this, from Spaine the stately Catholickes
Sends Indian golde to coyne me French ecues:
For this haue I a largesse from the Pope,
A pension and a dispensation too: 120
And by that priuiledge to worke vpon,
My policye hath framde religion.
Religion: *O Diabole.*
Fye, I am ashamde, how euer that I seeme,
To think a word of such a simple sound 125
Of so great matter should be made the ground.
The gentle King whose pleasure vncontrolde,
Weakneth his body, and will waste his Realme,
If I repaire not what he ruinates:
Him as a childe I dayly winne with words, 130
So that for proofe he barely beares the name:
I execute, and he sustaines the blame.

111 aimèd *Dyce etc.* 115 wait] wiat *O*: weight *Rob. etc.*
117 Catholic *Cunn.*

The Mother Queene workes wonders for my sake,
And in my loue entombes the hope of Fraunce :
Rifling the bowels of her treasurie, 135
To supply my wants and necessitie.
Paris hath full fiue hundred Colledges,
As Monestaries, Priories, Abbyes and halles,
Wherein are thirtie thousand able men,
Besides a thousand sturdy student Catholicks, 140
And more, of my knowledge in one cloyster keeps
Fiue hundred fatte Franciscan Fryers and priestes—
All this and more, if more may be comprisde,
To bring the will of our desires to end.
Then *Guise,* 145
Since thou hast all the Cardes within thy hands
To shuffle or cut, take this as surest thing :
That right or wrong, thou deale thy selfe a King
I but, *Nauarre, Nauarre.* Tis but a nook of France,
Sufficient yet for such a pettie King : 150
That with a rablement of his hereticks
Blindes Europs eyes and troubleth our estate :
Him will we—— *Pointing to his Sworde.*
But first lets follow those in France,
That hinder our possession to the crowne : 155
As *Cæsar* to his souldiers, so say I :
Those that hate me will I learn to loath.
Giue me a look, that when I bend the browes,
Pale death may walke in furrowes of my face :
A hand, that with a graspe may gripe the world, 160
An eare, to heare what my detractors say,
A royall seate, a scepter and a crowne :
That those which doe beholde, they may become
As men that stand and gase against the Sunne.
The plot is laide, and things shall come to passe, 165
Where resolution striues for victory. *Exit.*

Enter the King of Nauar *and Queen, and his Mother Queen, the Prince of* Condy, *the* Admirall, *and the* Pothecary *with the gloues, and giues them to the olde Queene.*

Pothe. Maddame, I beseech your grace to accept this simple gift.

144 To] Do *Cunn.* 145–7 *Two lines O, div after* Cardes : *corr. Dyce* 149 Navarre *once Dyce etc.* 155 possession] procession *conj. Brereton* 163 behold them may *Dyce, Cunn.* 166 +Scene III. *add. Cunn., Bull.* 167 accept *Rob. etc.* : except O

Old Qu. Thanks my good freend, holde, take thou this reward. 170

Pothe. I humbly thank your Maiestie. *Exit.* Po.

Old Qu. Me thinkes the gloues haue a very strong perfume,
The sent whereof doth make my head to ake.

Nauar. Doth not your grace know the man that gaue them you? 175

Old Qu. Not wel, but do remember such a man.

Ad. Your grace was ill aduisde to take them then,
Considering of these dangerous times.

Old Qu. Help sonne *Nauarre,* I am poysoned.

Q. Mar. The heauens forbid your highnes such mishap.

Nauar. The late suspition of the Duke of *Guise* 181
Might well haue moued your highnes to beware
How you did meddle with such dangerous giftes.

Q. Mar. Too late it is my Lord if that be true
To blame her highnes, but I hope it be 185
Only some naturall passion makes her sicke.

Old Qu. O no, sweet *Margret,* the fatall poyson
Workes within my head, my brain pan breakes,
My heart doth faint, I dye. *She dyes.*

Nauar. My Mother poysoned heere before my face:
O gracious God, what times are these? 191
O graunt sweet God my daies may end with hers,
That I with her may dye and liue againe.

Q. Mar. Let not this heauy chaunce my dearest Lord,
(For whose effects my soule is massacred) 195
Infect thy gracious brest with fresh supply,
To agrauate our sodaine miserie.

Ad. Come my Lords, let vs beare her body hence,
And see it honoured with iust solemnitie.

As they are going, the Souldier dischargeth his Musket at the Lord Admirall.

Condy. What are you hurt my L⟨ord⟩ high Admiral?

Admi. I my good Lord shot through the arme. 201

Nauar. We are betraide, come my Lords, and let vs
Goe tell the King of this.

Admi. These are
The cursed *Guisians* that doe seeke our death. 205
Oh fatall was this mariage to vs all.

They beare away the Queene *and goe out.*

188 Workes] Doth work *Rob.*: Worketh *conj. Dyce, Cunn.*
204–5 *One line O*: *corr. Dyce*

Enter the King, Queene Mother, *Duke of* Guise, *Duke* Anioy, *Duke* Demayne.

Queene Mother.

My noble sonne, and princely Duke of *Guise*,
Now haue we got the fatall stragling deere
Within the compasse of a deadly toyle,
And as we late decreed we may perfourme. 210
King. Madam, it wilbe noted through the world,
An action bloudy and tirannicall :
Cheefely since vnder safetie of our word,
They iustly challenge their protection :
Besides my heart relentes that noble men, 215
Onely corrupted in religion,
Ladies of honor, Knightes and Gentlemen,
Should for their conscience taste such rutheles ends.
Anioy. Though gentle mindes should pittie others paines,
Yet will the wisest note their proper greefes : 220
And rather seeke to scourge their enemies,
Then be themselues base subiects to the whip.
Guise. Me thinkes my Lord, *Anioy* hath well aduisde,
Your highnes to consider of the thing,
And rather chuse to seek your countries good, 225
Then pittie or releeue these vpstart hereticks.
Queene. I hope these reasons may serue my princely Sonne,
To haue some care for feare of enemies.
King. Well Madam, I referre it to your Maiestie,
And to my Nephew heere the Duke of *Guise* : 230
What you determine, I will ratifie.
Queene. Thankes to my princely sonne: then tell me *Guise*,
What order wil you set downe for the Massacre ?
Guise. Thus Madame.
They that shalbe actors in this Massacre, 235
Shall weare white crosses on their Burgonets,
And tye white linnen scarfes about their armes.
He that wantes these, and is suspected of heresie,
Shall dye, be he King or Emperour. Then Ile haue

206+Scene IV. *add. Rob., Cunn., Bull.* 216 *Ends* honor *O* : *corr. Dyce* 217–18 Knightes . . ends] *Prose O* : *corr. Dyce* 238 suspect *Dyce etc.* 239–41 *Lines end* Emperour, tower, streetes *O* : *corr. Dyce*

A peale of ordinance shot from the tower, at which 240
They all shall issue out and set the streetes.
And then the watchword being giuen, a bell shall ring,
Which when they heare, they shall begin to kill,
And neuer cease vntill that bell shall cease,
Then breath a while. 245

Enter the Admirals *man.*

King. How now fellow, what newes?
Man. And it please your grace the Lord high Admirall,
Riding the streetes was traiterously shot,
And most humbl⟨i⟩e intreates your Maiestie
To visite him sick in his bed. 250
King. Messenger, tell him I will see him straite.
Exit Messenger.
What shall we doe now with the Admirall?
Qu. Your Maiesty were best goe visite him,
And make a shew as if all were well.
King. Content, I will goe visite the Admirall. 255
Guise. And I will goe take order for his death.
Exeunt.

Enter the Admirall *in his bed.*

King. How fares it with my Lord high Admiral,
Hath he been hurt with villaines in the street?
I vow and sweare as I am King of France,
To finde and to repay the man with death: 260
With death delay'd and torments neuer vsde,
That durst presume for hope of any gaine,
To hurt the noble man their soueraign loues.
Ad. Ah my good Lord, these are the *Guisians*,
That seeke to massacre our guiltles liues. 265
King. Assure your selfe my good Lord Admirall,
I deepely sorrow for your trecherous wrong:
And that I am not more secure my selfe,
Then I am carefull you should be preserued.
Cosin, take twenty of our strongest guarde, 270
And vnder your direction see they keep
All trecherous violence from our noble freend,
Repaying all attempts with present death
Vpon the cursed breakers of our peace.

241 'set (= beset) *Cunn.* 247 And] An *Dyce etc.* 256 S.D. Exeunt *Cunn.*: Exit Guise *O* Scene V. *add. Rob., Cunn., Bull.* 263 their] his *Dyce, Cunn.*

And so be pacient good Lord Admirall, 275
And euery hower I will visite you.
Admi. I humbly thank your royall Maiestie.
Exeunt omnes.

Enter Guise, Anioy, Dumaine, Gonzago, Retes, Montsorrell, *and Souldiers to the massacre.*

Guise.

Anioy, Dumaine, Gonzago, Retes, sweare
By the argent crosses in your burgonets,
To kill all that you suspect of heresie. 280
Dumain. I sweare by this to be vnmercifull.
Anioy. I am disguisde and none knows who I am,
And therfore meane to murder all I meet.
Gonza. And so will I.
Retes. And I. 285
Guise. Away then, break into the Admirals house.
Retes. I let the Admirall be first dispatcht.
Guise. The Admirall,
Cheefe standard bearer to the Lutheranes,
Shall in the entrance of this Massacre, 290
Be murdered in his bed. *Gonzago*
Conduct them thither, and then
Beset his house that not a man may liue.
Anioy. That charge is mine. Swizers keepe you the streetes,
And at ech corner shall the Kings garde stand. 295
Gonzago. Come sirs follow me.
Exit Gonzago *and others with him.*
Anioy. Cosin, the Captaine of the Admirals guarde,
Plac'd by my brother, will betray his Lord:
Now *Guise* shall catholiques flourish once againe,
The head being of, the members cannot stand. 300
Retes. But look my Lord, ther's some in the Admirals house.

Enter into the Admirals *house, and he in his bed.*

Anioy. In lucky time, come let vs keep this lane,
And slay his seruants that shall issue out.

277+Scene VI. *add. Rob., Cunn., Bull.* 278 *Ends* Retes *O: corr. Dyce* 288–9 *One line O: corr. Dyce* 291–3 *Two lines O, div. after* thither: *corr. Dyce* 301 S.D. The Admiral discovered in bed; Gonzago and others in the house *Dyce* Scene VII. *add. Cunn.*

Gonza. Where is the Admirall ?
Admi. O let me pray before I dye. 305
Gonza. Then pray vnto our Ladye, kisse this crosse.
Stab him.
Admi. O God forgiue my sins.
Guise. *Gonzago*, what, is he dead ?
Gonza. I my Lord.
Guise. Then throw him down. 310
Anioy. Now cosin view him well,
It may be it is some other, and he escapte.
Guise. Cosin tis he, I know him by his look.
See where my Souldier shot him through the arm.
He mist him neer, but we haue strook him now. 315
Ah base Shatillian and degenerate,
Cheef standard bearer to the Lutheranes,
Thus in despite of thy Religion,
The Duke of *Guise* stampes on thy liueles bulke.
Anioy. Away with him, cut of his head and handes,
And send them for a present to the Pope : 321
And when this iust reuenge is finished,
Vnto mount Faucon will we dragge his coarse :
And he that liuing hated so the crosse,
Shall being dead, be hangd thereon in chaines. 325
Guise. *Anioy, Gonzago, Retes*, if that you three
Will be as resolute as I and *Dumaine* :
There shall not a Hugonet breath in France.
Anioy. I sweare by this crosse, wee'l not be partiall,
But slay as many as we can come neer. 330
Guise. *Mountsorrell*, goe shoote the ordinance of,
That they which haue already set the street
May know their watchword, then tole the bell,
And so lets forward to the Massacre. 334
Mount. I will my Lord. *Exit* Mount.
Guise. And now my Lords let vs closely to our busines.
Anioy. *Anioy* will follow thee.
Du. And so will *Dumaine.*
The ordinance being shot of, the bell tolles.
Guise. Come then, lets away. *Exeunt.*

307+S.D. Dies *add. Dyce* 308 What, is he dead, Gonzago *Cunn.* 310+S.D. The body of the Admiral is thrown down *add. Dyce* 311–12 *Prose O* : *corr. Dyce etc.* 312 it is] 'tis *Dyce etc.* 316–17 *One line O* : *corr. Dyce* 319 lifeless *Dyce etc.* 332 set] 'set *Cunn.* 333 tole] go toll *Cunn.* 336 let vs] let's *Dyce etc.*

The Guise *enters againe, with all the rest, with their Swords drawne, chasing the Protestants.*

Guise.

Tue, tue, tue, 340
Let none escape, murder the Hugonets.
Anioy. Kill them, kill them. *Exeunt.*

Enter Loreine *running, the* Guise *and the rest pursuing him.*

Guise. *Loreine, Loreine,* follow *Loreine.* Sirra,
Are you a preacher of these heresies?
Loreine. I am a preacher of the word of God, 345
And thou a traitor to thy soule and him.
Guise. Dearely beloued brother, thus tis written.
He stabs him.
Anioy. Stay my Lord, let me begin the psalme.
Guise. Come dragge him away and throw him in a ditch.
Exeunt.

Enter Mountsorrell *and knocks at* Serouns *doore.*

Serouns wife. Who is that which knocks there? 350
Mount. *Mountsorrell* from the Duke of *Guise.*
Wife. Husband come down, heer's one would speak with you
From the Duke of *Guise.*

Enter Seroune.

Seroune.

To speek with me from such a man as he?
Mount. I, I, for this *Seroune,* and thou shalt hate. 355
Shewing his dagger.
Seroune. O let me pray before I take my death.
Mount. Despatch then quickly.
Seroune. O Christ my Sauiour.
Mount. Christ, villaine?
Why darst thou presume to call on Christ, 360
Without the intercession of some Saint?
Sanctus Iacobus hee was my Saint, pray to him.

339+Scene VII. *add. Bull.*: Scene VIII. *add. Cunn.* 340 Tuez, tuez, tuez *Dyce etc.* 340–1 *One line O*: *corr. Dyce etc.* 349+Scene VIII. *add. Bull.* 350, 352 S.D. within *add. Dyce after Prefix* 352–3 *Prose O*: *corr. Dyce etc.* 355 hate] ha't *Dyce etc.* 359–62 *Prose O*: *corr. Dyce* 362 Sancta *O*: *corr. Dyce etc.* hee was] he is *conj. Dyce*[1]: he's *Dyce*[2], *Bull.*

Seroune. O let me pray vnto my God.
Mount. Then take this with you. *Stab him.*
Exit.

Enter Ramus *in his studie.*

Ramus. What fearfull cries comes from the riuer Sene,
That frightes poore *Ramus* sitting at his book ? 366
I feare the *Guisians* haue past the bridge,
And meane once more to menace me.

Enter Taleus.

Taleus. Flye *Ramus* flye, if thou wilt saue thy life.
Ramus. Tell me *Taleus*, wherfore should I flye ? 370
Taleus. The *Guisians* are
Hard at thy doore, and meane to murder vs :
Harke, harke they come, Ile leap out at the window.
Ramus. Sweet *Taleus* stay.

Enter Gonzago *and* Retes.

Gonzago.

Who goes there ? 375
Retes. Tis *Taleus*, *Ramus* bedfellow.
Gonza. What art thou ?
Tal. I am as *Ramus* is, a Christian.
Ret. O let him goe, he is a catholick.
Exit Taleus.

Enter Ramus.

Gon. Come *Ramus*, more golde, or thou shalt haue the stabbe. 380
Ramus. Alas
I am a scholler, how should I haue golde ?
All that I haue is but my stipend from the King,
Which is no sooner receiu'd but it is spent.

Enter the Guise *and* Anioy.

Anioy.

Who haue you there ? 385
Ret. Tis *Ramus*, the Kings professor of Logick.
Guise. Stab him.
Ramus. O good my Lord,
Wherein hath *Ramus* been so offencious ?

364+Scene IX. *add. Bull.* 365 Sene] Rene *O* : Seine *Dyce etc.* 371–3 *Prose O* : *corr. Dyce* 381–2 *One line O to Bull.* 388–9 *One line O* : *corr. Dyce*

Guise. Marry sir, in hauing a smack in all, 390
And yet didst neuer sound anything to the depth.
Was it not thou that scoftes the Organon,
And said it was a heape of vanities?
He that will be a flat dicotamest,
And seen in nothing but Epitomies: 395
Is in your iudgment thought a learned man.
And he forsooth must goe and preach in Germany:
Excepting against Doctors axioms,
And *ipse dixi* with this quidditie,
Argumentum testimonii est inartificiale. 400
To contradict which, I say *Ramus* shall dye:
How answere you that? your *nego argumentum*
Cannot serue, sirra: kill him.

Ra. O good my Lord, let me but speak a word.

Anioy. Well, say on. 405

Ramus. Not for my life doe I desire this pause,
But in my latter houre to purge my selfe,
In that I know the things that I haue wrote,
Which as I heare one *Shekius* takes it ill,
Because my places being but three, contains all his: 410
I knew the Organon to be confusde,
And I reduc'd it into better forme.
And this for *Aristotle* will I say,
That he that despiseth him can nere
Be good in Logick or Philosophie. 415
And thats because the blockish Sorbonests
Attribute as much vnto their workes
As to the seruice of the eternall God.

Guise. Why suffer you that peasant to declaime?
Stab him I say and send him to his freends in hell. 420

Anioy. Nere was there Colliars sonne so full of pride.
Kill him.

Guise. My Lord of *Anioy*, there are a hundred Protestants,
Which we haue chaste into the riuer Sene,
That swim about and so preserue their liues:
How may we doe? I feare me they will liue. 425

Dumaine. Goe place some men vpon the bridge,

392 scoftes] scoff'dst *Dyce etc.* 398 axioms *Dyce*[2], *Bull.*: actions *O* 400 testimonii . . inartificiale *conj. Mitford*, *Dyce etc.*: testimonis . . in arte fetialis *O* 402–3 *Prose O* 416 Sorbonnists *Dyce etc.*: thorbonest *O* 417 their] their own *Dyce etc.* 422 My Lord Anjou *Cunn.* 423 Sene] Rene *O*

With bowes and dartes to shoot at them they see,
And sinke them in the riuer as they swim.
Guise. Tis well aduisde *Dumain*, goe see it strait be done.
And in the mean time my Lord, could we deuise, 430
To get those pedantes from the King *Nauarre*,
That are tutors to him and the prince of *Condy*.
Anioy. For that let me alone, Cousin: stay you heer,
And when you see me in, then follow hard.

He knocketh, and enter the King of Nauarre *and Prince of* Condy, *with their scholmaisters*.

How now my Lords, how fare you? 435
Nauar. My Lord, they say
That all the protestants are massacred.
Anioy. I, so they are, but yet what remedy:
I haue done what I could to stay this broile.
Nauarr. But yet my Lord the report doth run, 440
That you were one that made this Massacre.
An. Who I? you are deceiued, I rose but now.

Enter Guise.

Guise. Murder the Hugonets, take those pedantes hence.
Na. Thou traitor *Guise*, lay of thy bloudy hands. 444
Condy. Come let vs goe tell the King. *Exeunt*.
Guise. Come sirs, Ile whip you to death with my punniards point. *He kils them*.
An. Away with them both. *Exit* Anioy.
Guise. And now sirs for this night let our fury stay.
Yet will we not that the Massacre shall end:
Gonzago poste you to Orleance, *Retes* to Deep, 450
Mountsorrell vnto Roan, and spare not one
That you suspect of heresy. And now stay
That bel that to yͤ deuils mattins rings.
Now euery man put of his burgonet, 454
And so conuey him closely to his bed. *Exeunt*.

Enter Anioy, *with two Lords of Poland*.

Anioy.

My Lords of Poland I must needs confesse

429+S.D. Exit Dumaine *add. Dyce etc.* 430 And *om. Cunn.* 433 you *om. Cunn.* 436–7 *Prose O*: *corr. Dyce* 450–3 *Div. after* Orleance, Roan, heresy *O*: *after* Orleans, Rouen, heresy, stay *Dyce* 450 Deep] Dieppe *Dyce etc.* 451 Roan] Rouen *Dyce etc.* 452 *Ends* bell *Cunn.* 453 mattins] midnight matins *Cunn.* 455+Act the Second. Scene I. *add. Rob., Cunn.*: Scene X *add. Bull.*

The offer of your Prince Electors farre
Beyond the reach of my desertes:
For Poland is as I haue been enformde,
A martiall people, worthy such a King, 460
As hath sufficient counsaile in himselfe,
To lighten doubts and frustrate subtile foes:
And such a King whom practise long hath taught,
To please himselfe with mannage of the warres,
The greatest warres within our Christian bounds, 465
I meane our warres against the Muscouites:
And on the other side against the Turke,
Rich Princes both, and mighty Emperours:
Yet by my brother *Charles* our King of France,
And by his graces councell it is thought, 470
That if I vndertake to weare the crowne
Of Poland, it may preiudice their hope
Of my inheritance to the crowne of France:
For if th'almighty take my brother hence,
By due discent the Regall seat is mine. 475
With Poland therfore must I couenant thus,
That if by death of *Charles*, the diadem
Of France be cast on me, then with your leaues
I may retire me to my natiue home.
If your commission serue to warrant this, 480
I thankfully shall vndertake the charge
Of you and yours, and carefully maintaine
The wealth and safety of your kingdomes right.
Lord. All this and more your highnes shall commaund,
For Polands crowne and kingly diadem. 485
Anioy. Then come my Lords, lets goe. *Exeunt.*

Enter two with the Admirals *body.*

1. Now sirra, what shall we doe with the Admirall?
2. Why let vs burne him for an heretick.
1. O no, his bodye will infect the fire, and the fire the aire, and so we shall be poysoned with him. 490
2. What shall we doe then?
1. Lets throw him into the riuer.
2. Oh twill corrupt the water, and the water the fish, and by the fish our selues when we eate them.
1. Then throw him into the ditch. 495

486+⟨Act II⟩. Scene II. *add. Rob., Cunn.*: Scene XI. *add. Bull.*
494 by *om. Dyce etc.*

2. No, no, to decide all doubts, be rulde by me, lets hang him heere vpon this tree.

1. Agreede. *They hang him.*

Enter the Duke of Guise, *and* Queene Mother, *and the* Cardinall.

Guise. Now Madame, how like you our lusty Admirall?
Queene. Beleeue me *Guise* he becomes the place so well,
As I could long ere this haue wisht him there. 501
But come lets walke aside, thair's not very sweet.
Guise. No by my faith Madam.
Sirs, take him away and throw him in some ditch.
Carry away the dead body.
And now Madam as I vnderstand, 505
There are a hundred Hugonets and more,
Which in the woods doe holde their synagogue:
And dayly meet about this time of day,
And thither will I to put them to the sword.
Qu. Doe so sweet *Guise*, let vs delay no time, 510
For if these straglers gather head againe,
And disperse themselues throughout the Realme of France,
It will be hard for vs to worke their deaths.
Be gone, delay no time sweet *Guise*.
Guise. Madam 515
I goe as whirl-windes rage before a storme. *Exit Guise.*
Qu. My Lord of Loraine haue you markt of late,
How *Charles* our sonne begins for to lament
For the late nights worke which my Lord of *Guise*
Did make in Paris amongst the Hugonites? 520
Card. Madam, I haue heard him solemnly vow,
With the rebellious King of *Nauarre*,
For to reuenge their deaths vpon vs all.
Qu. I, but my Lord let me alone for that,
For *Katherine* must haue her will in France: 525
As I doe liue, so surely shall he dye,
And *Henry* then shall weare the diadem.
And if he grudge or crosse his Mothers will,
Ile disinherite him and all the rest:
For Ile rule France, but they shall weare the crowne: 530

498 S.D. They hang up the body on a tree, and then exeunt *Dyce* 502 thair's *O*: th' air's *Dyce*[1]: the air's *Dyce*[2] *etc.* 509 And *om. Cunn.* 515–16 *One line O*: *corr. Dyce* 520 amongst] 'mongst *Malone, Cunn.*: among *Bull.*

And if they storme, I then may pull them downe.
Come my Lord let vs goe. *Exeunt.*

Enter fiue or sixe Protestants with bookes, and kneele to-gether. Enter also the Guise.

Guise. Downe with the Hugonites, murder them.
Protestant. O *Mounser de Guise,* heare me but speake.
Guise. No villain, that toung of thine, 535
That hath blasphemde the holy Church of Rome,
Shall driue no plaintes into the *Guises* eares,
To make the iustice of my heart relent:
Tue, tue, tue, let none escape: *Kill them.*
So, dragge them away. *Exeunt.*

Enter the King of France, Nauar *and* Epernoune *staying him: enter* Qu. Mother, *and the* Cardinall.

King.

O let me stay and rest me heer a while, 541
A griping paine hath ceasde vpon my heart:
A sodaine pang, the messenger of death.
Qu. O say not so, thou kill'st thy mothers heart.
King. I must say so, paine forceth me complaine. 545
Na. Comfort your selfe my Lord and haue no doubt,
But God will sure restore you to your health.
King. O no, my louing brother of *Nauarre.*
I haue deseru'd a scourge I must confesse,
Yet is there pacience of another sort, 550
Then to misdoe the welfare of their King:
God graunt my neerest freends may proue no worse.
O holde me vp, my sight begins to faile,
My sinnewes shrinke, my braines turne vpside downe, 554
My heart doth break, I faint and dye. *He dies.*
Queene. What art thou dead, sweet sonne? speak to thy Mother.
O no, his soule is fled from out his breast,
And he nor heares, nor sees vs what we doe:
My Lords, what resteth there now for to be done?
But that we presently despatch Embassadours 560
To Poland, to call *Henry* back againe,

532 let] lets *O* 532+⟨Act II.⟩ Scene III. *add. Rob., Cunn.*: Scene XII. *add. Bull.* 539 Tuez, tuez, tuez *Dyce etc.* 540 +Scene XIII. *add. Bull.* 550 there] their *Cunn., Bull.* 554 brain turns *Cunn.* 559 there now for] now for *Cunn.*: there now *Bull.*

To weare his brothers crowne and dignity.
Epernoune, goe see it presently be done,
And bid him come without delay to vs. 564
Eper. Madam, I will. *Exit* Eper.
Queene. And now my Lords after these funerals be done,
We will with all the speed we can prouide
For *Henries* coronation from Polonie:
Come let vs take his body hence.
All goe out, but Nauarre *and* Pleshe.
Nauar. And now *Pleshé* whilste that these broiles doe last, 570
My opportunity may serue me fit,
To steale from France, and hye me to my home.
For heers no saftie in the Realme for me,
And now that *Henry* is cal'd from Polland,
It is my due by iust succession: 575
And therefore as speedily as I can perfourme,
Ile muster vp an army secretly,
For feare that *Guise* ioyn'd with the K⟨ing⟩ of Spaine,
Might seeke to crosse me in mine enterprise.
But God that alwaies doth defend the right, 580
Will shew his mercy and preserue vs still.
Pleshe. The vertues of our true Religion
Cannot but march with many graces more:
Whose army shall discomfort all your foes,
And at the length in Pampelonia crowne, 585
In spite of Spaine and all the popish power,
That holdes it from your highnesse wrongfully:
Your Maiestie her rightfull Lord and Soueraigne.
Nauar. Truth *Pleshe*, and God so prosper me in all,
As I entend to labour for the truth, 590
And true profession of his holy word:
Come *Pleshe*, lets away whilste time doth serue. *Exeunt*.
Sound Trumpets within, and then all crye viue le Roy *two or three times*.

Enter Henry crownd: Queene, Cardinall, *Duke of* Guise, Epernoone, *the kings Minions, with others, and the Cutpurse*.

All. Viue le Roy, viue le Roy. *Sound Trumpets*.

566 *Two lines, div. after* now *Bull. Qy. omit* be? 570 now Pleshé *Dyce*[2] *etc.*: now Nauarre *O*, *Dyce*[1]: Pleshé now *conj. Dyce*[1] 579 seek *Dyce etc.*: seeme *O* 584 discomfit *Dyce* 585 Pampeluna *Dyce* 592+⟨Act II.⟩ Scene IV. *Rob.*, *Cunn.*: Scene XIV. *add. Bull.* S.D. viue la Roy *O*: *corr. Rob.* *So in ll.* 593, 603

Qu. Welcome from Poland *Henry* once agayne,
Welcome to France thy fathers royall seate, 595
Heere hast thou a country voide of feares,
A warlike people to maintaine thy right,
A watchfull Senate for ordaining lawes,
A louing mother to preserue thy state,
And all things that a King may wish besides: 600
All this and more hath *Henry* with his crowne.
Car. And long may *Henry* enioy all this & more.
All. Viue le Roy, viue le Roy. *Sound trumpets.*
Henry. Thanks to you al. The guider of all crownes
Graunt that our deeds may wel deserue your loues: 605
And so they shall, if fortune speed my will,
And yeeld your thoughts to height of my desertes.
What saies our Minions, think they *Henries* heart
Will not both harbour loue and Maiestie?
Put of that feare, they are already ioynde, 610
No person, place, or time, or circumstance,
Shall slacke my loues affection from his bent.
As now you are, so shall you still persist,
Remooueles from the fauours of your King.
Mugeroun. We know that noble mindes change not their thoughts 615
For wearing of a crowne, in that your grace
Hath worne the Poland diadem, before
You were inuested in the crowne of France.
Henry. I tell thee *Mugeroun* we will be freends,
And fellowes to, what euer stormes arise. 620
Mugeroun. Then may it please your Maiestie to giue me leaue,
To punish those that doe prophane this holy feast.
He cuts of the Cutpurse eare, for cutting of the golde buttons off his cloake.
Henry. How meanst thou that?
Cutpurse. O Lord, mine eare.
Mugeroun. Come sir, giue me my buttons and heers your eare. 625
Guise. Sirra, take him away.
Henry. Hands of good fellow, I will be his baile
For this offence: goe sirra, worke no more,
Till this our Coronation day be past:
And now, 630

622 S.D. *follows* 623 *Dyce etc.* 630–1 *One line O: corr. Dyce etc.*

Our solemne rites of Coronation done,
What now remaines, but for a while to feast,
And spend some daies in barriers, tourny, tylte,
And like disportes, such as doe fit the Court?
Lets goe my Lords, our dinner staies for vs. 635

Goe out all, but the Queene *and the* Cardinall.

Queene.

My Lord Cardinall of Loraine, tell me,
How likes your grace my sonnes pleasantnes?
His minde you see runnes on his minions,
And all his heauen is to delight himselfe:
And whilste he sleepes securely thus in ease, 640
Thy brother *Guise* and we may now prouide
To plant our selues with such authoritie,
As not a man may liue without our leaues.
Then shall the Catholick faith of Rome
Flourish in France, and none deny the same. 645

Car. Madam, as in secrecy I was tolde,
My brother *Guise* hath gathered a power of men,
Which are he saith, to kill the Puritans,
But tis the house of *Burbon* that he meanes.
Now Madam must you insinuate with the King, 650
And tell him that tis for his Countries good,
And common profit of Religion.

Qu. Tush man, let me alone with him,
To work the way to bring this thing to passe:
And if he doe deny what I doe say, 655
Ile dispatch him with his brother presently,
And then shall *Mounser* weare the diadem:
Tush, all shall dye vnles I haue my will,
For while she liues *Katherine* will be Queene.
Come my Lord, let vs goe seek the *Guise*, 660
And then determine of this enterprise. *Exeunt.*

Enter the Duchesse of Guise, *and her Maide.*

Duch. Goe fetch me pen and inke.

Maid. I will Madam. *Exit* Maid.

Duch. That I may write vnto my dearest Lord.
Sweet *Mugeroune*, tis he that hath my heart, 665
And *Guise* vsurpes it, cause I am his wife:
Faine would I finde some means to speak with him

648 are *Dyce etc.*: as *O* 660 lord *Dyce etc.*: Lords *O*
661 +⟨Act II.⟩ Scene V. *add. Rob., Cunn.*: Scene XV. *add. Bull.*
663 S.D. *follows* 664 *Dyce, Bull.*

But cannot, and therfore am enforst to write,
That he may come and meet me in some place,
Where we may one inioy the others sight. 670

Enter the Maid *with Inke and Paper.*

So, set it down and leaue me to my selfe. *She writes.*
O would to God this quill that heere doth write,
Had late been pluckt from out faire *Cupids* wing:
That it might print these lines within his heart.

Enter the Guise.

Guise. What, all alone my loue, and writing too: 675
I prethee say to whome thou writes?
Duch. To such a one my Lord, as when she reads
My lines,
Will laugh I feare me at their good aray.
Guise. I pray thee let me see. 680
Duch. O no my Lord, a woman only must
Partake the secrets of my heart.
Guise. But Madam I must see. *He takes it.*
Are these your secrets that no man must know?
Duch. O pardon me my Lord. 685
Guise. Thou trothles and vniust, what lines are these?
Am I growne olde, or is thy lust growne yong,
Or hath my loue been so obscurde in thee,
That others needs to comment on my text?
Is all my loue forgot which helde thee deare? 690
I, dearer then the apple of mine eye?
Is *Guises* glory but a clowdy mist,
In sight and iudgement of thy lustfull eye?
Mor d⟨ie⟩u, were not the fruit within thy wombe,
Of whose encrease I set some longing hope: 695
This wrathfull hand should strike thee to the hart.
Hence strumpet, hide thy head for shame,
And fly my presence if thou looke to liue. *Exit ⟨Duchess⟩.*
O wicked sexe, periured and vniust,
Now doe I see that from the very first, 700
Her eyes and lookes sow'd seeds of periury,
But villaine he to whom these lines should goe,
Shall buy her loue euen with his dearest bloud. *Exit.*

676 writ'st *Dyce etc.* 677–9 *Prose O*: *div. after* such, lines *Dyce, Bull.*: *after* lines *Cunn.* 677 my Lord *om. Cunn.* 694 were *Dyce etc.*: wert *O* 695 Of] On *Cunn.*

Enter the King of Nauarre, Pleshe *and* Bartus, *and their train, with drums and trumpets.*

Nauarre.

My Lords, sith in a quarrell iust and right,
We vndertake to mannage these our warres 705
Against the proud disturbers of the faith,
I meane the *Guise*, the Pope, and King of Spaine,
Who set themselues to tread vs vnder foot,
And rent our true religion from this land ;
But for you know our quarrell is no more, 710
But to defend their strange inuentions,
Which they will put vs to with sword and fire :
We must with resolute mindes resolue to fight,
In honor of our God and countries good.
Spaine is the counsell chamber of the pope, 715
Spaine is the place where he makes peace and warre,
And *Guise* for Spaine hath now incenst the King,
To send his power to meet vs in the field.
Bartus. Then in this bloudy brunt they may beholde,
The sole endeuour of your princely care, 720
To plant the true succession of the faith,
In spite of Spaine and all his heresies.
Nauarre. The power of vengeance now incampes it selfe
Vpon the hauty mountains of my brest :
Plaies with her goary coulours of reuenge, 725
Whom I respect as leaues of boasting greene,
That change their coulour when the winter comes,
When I shall vaunt as victor in reuenge.

Enter a Messenger.

How now sirra, what newes ?
Mes. My Lord, as by our scoutes we vnderstande, 730
A mighty army comes from France with speed :
Which are already mustered in the land,
And meanes to meet your highnes in the field.
Na. In Gods name, let them come.
This is the *Guise* that hath incenst the King, 735
To leauy armes and make these ciuill broyles :
But canst thou tell who is their generall ?
Mes. Not yet my Lord, for thereon doe they stay :
But as report doth goe, the Duke of *Ioyeux*
Hath made great sute vnto the King therfore. 740

703+Scene XVI. *add. Bull.* 739 Duke of] Duke *Cunn.*

Na. It will not counteruaile his paines I hope.
I would the *Guise* in his steed might haue come,
But he doth lurke within his drousie couch,
And makes his footstoole on securitie :
So he be safe he cares not what becomes 745
Of King or Country, no not for them both.
But come my Lords, let vs away with speed,
And place our selues in order for the fight. *Exeunt.*

Enter the King of France, Duke of Guise, Epernoune,
and Duke Ioyeux.

King. My sweet *Ioyeux*, I make thee Generall
Of all my army now in readines 750
To march against the rebellious King *Nauarre.*
At thy request I am content thou goe,
Although my loue to thee can hardly suffer,
Regarding still the danger of thy life.
Ioyeux. Thanks to your Maiestie, and so I take my
leaue. 755
Farwell to my Lord of *Guise* and *Epernoune.*
Guise. Health and harty farwell to my Lord *Ioyeux.*
Exit Ioyeux.
King. So kindely Cosin of *Guise* you and your wife
Doe both salute our louely Minions.
He makes hornes at the Guise.
Remember you the letter gentle sir, 760
Which your wife writ
To my deare Minion, and her chosen freend ?
Guise. How now my Lord, faith this is more then need,
Am I thus to be iested at and scornde ?
Tis more then kingly or Emperious. 765
And sure if all the proudest Kings
In Christendome should beare me such derision,
They should know how I scornde them and their mockes
I loue your Minions? dote on them your selfe,
I know none els but holdes them in disgrace : 770
And heer by all the Saints in heauen I sweare,
That villain for whom I beare this deep disgrace :
Euen for your words that haue incenst me so,
Shall buy that strumpets fauour with his blood,

748 + Scene XVII. *add. Bull.* 751 'gainst *Dyce*[2], *Bull.* 753 suffer *O* : suffer't *Dyce*, *Bull.* : suffer it *Cunn.* 756 to *om. Cunn.* 758–62 *Prose O* : *corr. Dyce* 759 S.D. *follows* 762 *Dyce etc.* 766 Kings] kings beside *Cunn.* 766–7 *Div. after* In *O*

Whether he haue dishonoured me or no. 775
Par la mor d⟨ie⟩u, Il mo⟨ur⟩ra. *Exit.*

King. Beleeue me this iest bites sore.

Eper. My Lord, twere good to make them frends
For his othes are seldome spent in vaine.

Enter Mugeroun.

King. How now *Mugeroun*, metst thou not the *Guise* at the doore? 780

Muge. Not I my Lord, what if I had?

King. Marry if thou hadst, thou mightst haue had the stab,
For he hath solemnely sworne thy death.

Muge. I may be stabd, and liue till he be dead,
But wherfore beares he me such deadly hate? 785

King. Because his wife beares thee such kindely loue.

Muge. If that be all, the next time that I meet her,
Ile make her shake off loue with her heeles.
But which way is he gone? Ile goe make a walk
On purpose from the Court to meet with him. *Exit.*

King. I like not this, come *Epernoune* 791
Lets goe seek the Duke and make them freends. *Exeunt.*

Alarums within. The Duke Ioyeux *slaine.*
Enter the King of Nauarre *and his traine.*

Nauarre.

The Duke is slaine and all his power dispearst,
And we are grac'd with wreathes of victory:
Thus God we see doth euer guide the right, 795
To make his glory great vpon the earth.

Bar. The terrour of this happy victory,
I hope will make the King surcease his hate:
And either neuer mannage army more,
Or else employ them in some better cause. 800

Na. How many noble men haue lost their liues,
In prosecution of these cruell armes,
Is ruth and almost death to call to minde:
But God we know will alwaies put them downe,
That lift themselues against the perfect truth, 805

776 Par la mort de Dieu, il mourra *Dyce etc.* 777 me] me, Epernoune *Cunn.* 789–90 *Prose O* 791–2 *Prose O*: *corr. Dyce etc.* 792 Lets] Let us *Dyce, Bull.* 792+⟨Act II.⟩ Scene VI. *add. Rob., Cunn.* Scene XVIII. *add. Bull.* S.D. Alarums within and a cry 'The Duke Joyeux is slain' *Dyce*

Which Ile maintaine so long as life doth last,
And with the Q⟨ueen⟩ of England ioyne my force
To beat the papall Monarck from our lands,
And keep those relicks from our countries coastes.
Come my Lords, now that this storme is ouerpast, 810
Let vs away with triumph to our tents. *Exeunt.*

Enter a Souldier.

Soul. Sir, to you sir, that dares make the Duke a cuckolde, and vse a counterfeite key to his priuie Chamber doore: And although you take out nothing but your owne, yet you put in that which displeaseth him and so forestall his market, and set vp your standing where you should not: and whereas hee is your Landlord, you will take vpon you to be his, and tyll the ground that he himself should occupy, which is his own free land. If it be not too free there's the question: and though I come not to take possession (as I would I might) yet I meane to keepe you out, which I will if this geare holde: what are ye come so soone? haue at ye sir.

Enter Mugeroun.
He shootes at him and killes him.

Enter the Guise.

Guise. Holde thee tall Souldier, take thee this and flye.
Exit Soul.
Lye there the Kings delight, and *Guises* scorne. 825
Reuenge it *Henry* as thou list or dare,
I did it only in despite of thee.
Take him away.

Enter the King *and* Epernoune.

King.

My Lord of *Guise*, we vnderstand
That you haue gathered a power of men.
What your intent is yet we cannot learn, 830
But we presume it is not for our good.

Guise. Why I am no traitor to the crowne of France.
What I haue done tis for the Gospell sake.

Eper. Nay for the Popes sake, and thine owne benefite.
What Peere in France but thou (aspiring *Guise*) 835

811+Scene XIX. *add. Bull.* 812–27 *For Collier's version of this scene, probably a forgery, see* p. 483–4 823 S.D. Enter Mugeroun *follows* holde *in* 822 *Dyce etc.* 824 *Prefix* Guise [Giving a purse] *Dyce, Bull.* 828–31 *Prose O*: *corr. Dyce etc.*

Durst be in armes without the Kings consent ?
I challenge thee for treason in the cause.
Guise. Ah base *Epernoune*, were not his highnes heere,
Thou shouldst perceiue the D⟨uke⟩ of *Guise* is mou'd.
King. Be patient *Guise* and threat not *Epernoune*, 840
Least thou perceiue the King of France be mou'd.
Guise. Why ? I am a Prince of the *Valoyses* line,
Therfore an enemy to the *Burbonites*.
I am a iuror in the holy league,
And therfore hated of the Protestants. 845
What should I doe but stand vpon my guarde ?
And being able, Ile keep an hoast in pay.
Epernoune. Thou able to maintaine an hoast in pay,
That liuest by forraine exhibition.
The Pope and King of Spaine are thy good frends, 850
Else all France knowes how poor a Duke thou art.
King. I those are they that feed him with their golde,
To countermaund our will and check our freends.
Guise. My Lord, to speak more plainely, thus it is :
Being animated by Religious zeale, 855
I meane to muster all the power I can,
To ouerthrow those sexious Puritans :
And know my Lord, the Pope will sell his triple crowne,
I, and the catholick *Philip* King of Spaine,
Ere I shall want, will cause his Indians 860
To rip the golden bowels of America.
Nauarre that cloakes them vnderneath his wings,
Shall feele the house of *Lorayne* is his foe :
Your highnes needs not feare mine armies force,
Tis for your safetie and your enemies wrack. 865
King. *Guise*, weare our crowne, and be thou King of France,
And as Dictator make or warre or peace,
Whilste I cry *placet* like a Senator.
I cannot brook thy hauty insolence,
Dismisse thy campe or else by our Edict 870
Be thou proclaimde a traitor throughout France.
Guise. The choyse is hard, I must dissemble.
My Lord, in token of my true humilitie,
And simple meaning to your Maiestie :
I kisse your graces hand, and take my leaue, 875
Intending to dislodge my campe with speed.

857 sexious *O* : factious *conj. Malone, conj. Coll., Dyce*[2] *etc.* 872 +S.D. Aside *add. Dyce*

King. Then farwell *Guise*, the King and thou are freends.
Exit Guise.

Eper. But trust him not my Lord,
For had your highnesse seene with what a pompe
He entred Paris, and how the Citizens 880
With gifts and shewes did entertaine him,
And promised to be at his commaund:
Nay, they fear'd not to speak in the streetes,
That the *Guise* durst stand in armes against the King,
For not effecting of his holines will. 885

King. Did they of Paris entertaine him so?
Then meanes he present treason to our state.
Well, let me alone; whose within there?

Enter one with a pen and inke.

Make a discharge of all my counsell straite,
And Ile subscribe my name and seale it straight. 890
My head shall be my counsell, they are false:
And *Epernoune* I will be rulde by thee.

Eper. My Lord,
I think for safety of your royall person,
It would be good the *Guise* were made away, 895
And so to quite your grace of all suspect.

King. First let vs set our hand and seale to this,
(*He writes.*
And then Ile tell thee what I meane to doe.
So, conuey this to the counsell presently. *Exit one.*
And *Epernoune* though I seeme milde and calme, 900
Thinke not but I am tragicall within:
Ile secretly conuay me vnto Bloyse,
For now that Paris takes the *Guises* parte,
Heere is no staying for the King of France,
Vnles he meane to be betraide and dye: 905
But as I liue, so sure the *Guise* shall dye. *Exeunt.*

Enter the King of Nauarre *reading of a letter, and* Bartus.

Nauarre.

My Lord, I am aduertised from France,

878–82 *Four lines O, div. after* highnesse, Paris, shewes: *corr. T. B.*: *different division in Dyce etc.* 883 speak] speak it *Bull.* 890+S.D. Attendant writes *add. Dyce* 893–4 *One line O*: *corr. Dyce²*, *Bull.* 894 royall *om. Cunn.* 906+Act the Third. Scene I. *add. Rob., Cunn.*: Scene XX. *add. Bull.*

That the *Guise* hath taken armes against the King,
And that Paris is reuolted from his grace.
Bar. Then hath your grace fit oportunitie, 910
To shew your loue vnto the King of France:
Offering him aide against his enemies,
Which cannot but be thankfully receiu'd.
Nauarre. Bartus, it shall be so, poast then to Fraunce,
And there salute his highnesse in our name, 915
Assure him all the aide we can prouide,
Against the *Guisians* and their complices.
Bartus be gone, commend me to his grace,
And tell him ere it be long, Ile visite him. 919
Bar. I will my Lord. *Exit.*

Enter Pleshe.

Nauarre. Pleshe.
Pleshe. My Lord.
Na. Pleshe, goe muster vp our men with speed,
And let them march away to France amaine:
For we must aide the King against the *Guise.* 925
Be gone I say, tis time that we were there.
Pleshe. I goe my Lord.
Nauar. That wicked *Guise* I feare me much will be
The ruine of that famous Realme of France:
For his aspiring thoughts aime at the crowne, 930
And takes his vantage on Religion,
To plant the Pope and popelings in the Realme,
And binde it wholy to the Sea of Rome:
But if that God doe prosper mine attempts,
And send vs safely to arriue in France: 935
Wee'l beat him back, and driue him to his death,
That basely seekes the ruine of his Realme. *Exeunt.*

Enter the Captaine of the guarde, and three murtherers.

Captaine.

Come on sirs, what, are you resolutely bent,
Hating the life and honour of the *Guise*?
What, will you not feare when you see him come? 940
1. Feare him said you? tush, were he heere, we would kill him presently.

908 the Guise] Guise *Cunn.* 920 S.D. Enter Pleshè *follows* 921 *Dyce, Bull.* 931 And] 'A *Dyce*: He *Cunn.* 937 S.D. Exit *Dyce etc.* ⟨Act III.⟩ Scene II. *add. Rob., Cunn.*: Scene XXI. *add. Bull.*

2. O that his heart were leaping in my hand.
3. But when will he come that we may murther him?
Cap. Well, then I see you are resolute. 945
1. Let vs alone, I warrant you.
Cap. Then sirs take your standings within this Chamber,
For anon the *Guise* will come.
All. You will giue vs our money?
Cap. I, I, feare not: stand close, so, be resolute: 950
Now fals the star whose influence gouernes France,
Whose light was deadly to the Protestants:
Now must he fall and perish in his height.

Enter the King *and* Epernoune.
King.

Now Captain of my guarde, are these murtherers ready?
Cap. They be my good Lord. 955
King. But are they resolute and armde to kill,
Hating the life and honour of the *Guise*?
Cap. I warrant ye my Lord.
King. Then come proud *Guise* and heere disgordge thy brest,
Surchargde with surfet of ambitious thoughts: 960
Breath out that life wherein my death was hid,
And end thy endles treasons with thy death.

Enter the Guise *and knocketh.*
Guise.

Holla verlete, hey: *Epernoune*, where is the King?
Eper. Mounted his royall Cabonet.
Guise. I prethee tell him that the *Guise* is heere. 965
Eper. And please your grace the Duke of *Guise* doth craue
Accesse vnto your highnes.
King. Let him come in.
Come *Guise* and see thy traiterous guile outreacht,
And perish in the pit thou mad'st for me. 970
The Guise *comes to the King.*
Guise. Good morrow to your Maiestie.
King. Good morrow to my louing Cousin of *Guise*
How fares it this morning with your excellence?

950+S.D. Exeunt Murderers *add. Dyce etc.* 958+S.D. Exit *add. Dyce* 963, 965 *Prefix* Guise [within] *Dyce, Bull.* 966–7 *Prose O*: *corr. Dyce* 970+S.D. Aside *add. Cunn.*

Guise. I heard your Maiestie was scarsely pleasde,
That in the Court I bare so great a traine. 975
King. They were to blame that said I was displeasde,
And you good Cosin to imagine it.
Twere hard with me if I should doubt my kinne,
Or be suspicious of my deerest freends:
Cousin, assure you I am resolute, 980
Whatsoeuer any whisper in mine eares,
Not to suspect disloyaltye in thee,
And so sweet Cuz farwell. *Exit* King.
Guise. So,
Now sues the King for fauour to the *Guise*, 985
And all his Minions stoup when I commaund:
Why this tis to haue an army in the fielde.
Now by the holy sacrament I sweare,
As ancient Romanes ouer their Captiue Lords,
So will I triumph ouer this wanton King, 990
And he shall follow my proud Chariots wheeles.
Now doe I but begin to look about,
And all my former time was spent in vaine:
Holde Sworde,
For in thee is the Duke of *Guises* hope. 995

Enter one of the Murtherers.

Villaine, why dost thou look so gastly? speake.
Mur. O pardon me my Lord of *Guise*.
Guise. Pardon thee, why what hast thou done?
Mur. O my Lord, I am one of them that is set to murder you. 1000
Guise. To murder me villaine?
Mur. I my Lord, the rest haue taine their standings in the next roome, therefore good my Lord goe not foorth.
Guise. Yet *Cæsar* shall goe forth. 1005
Let mean consaits, and baser men feare death,
But they are pesants, *I* am Duke of *Guise*:
And princes with their lookes ingender feare.
1. Stand close, he is comming, I know him by his voice. 1010

984–5 *One line O*: *div. Dyce etc.* 989 o'er *Dyce etc.* 994–5 *One line O, Cunn.* 995 Duke of *om. Cunn.* 1005–8 *Prose O*: *corr. Malone, Dyce* 1009 *Prefix* First Murd. [within] *Dyce*

Guise. As pale as ashes, nay then tis time
To look about.

All. Downne with him, downe with him.

They stabbe him.

Guise. Oh I haue my deaths wound, giue me leaue to speak. 1015

2. Then pray to God, and aske forgiuenes of the King.

Guise. Trouble me not, I neare offended him,
Nor will I aske forgiuenes of the King.
Oh that I haue not power to stay my life,
Nor immortalitie to be reueng'd: 1020
To dye by Pesantes, what a greefe is this?
Ah *Sextus*, be reueng'd vpon the King,
Philip and Parma, I am slaine for you:
Pope excommunicate, Philip depose,
The wicked branch of curst *Valois* his line. 1025
Viue la messa, perish Hugonets,
Thus *Cæsar* did goe foorth, and thus he dyed. *He dyes.*

Enter Captaine of the Guarde.

Captaine.

What, haue you done?
Then stay a while and Ile goe call the King,
But see where he comes. 1030
My Lord, see where the *Guise* is slaine.

King. Ah this sweet sight is phisick to my soule,
Goe fetch his sonne for to beholde his death:
Surchargde with guilt of thousand massacres,
Mounser of *Loraine* sinke away to hell. 1035
And in remembrance of those bloudy broyles,
To which thou didst alure me being aliue:
And heere in presence of you all I sweare,
I nere was King of France vntill this houre:
This is the traitor that hath spent my golde 1040
In making forraine warres and ciuile broiles.
Did he not draw a sorte of English priestes
From Doway to the Seminary at Remes,

1011–12 *Prose O*: *div. Dyce*[2], *Bull.* 1011 tis] it is *Dyce*[2], *Bull.* 1012+S.D. Enter First and Second Murderers *add. Dyce* 1013 *Prefix* All] First and Sec. Murderers *Dyce* 1014 I haue] I've *Cunn.* death-wound *Cunn.* 1026 messe *Dyce etc.* 1027 dyed] dies *Cunn.* 1028–30 *Prose O*: *corr. Dyce* 1030 + S.D. Enter King Henry, Epernoun, and Attendants *add. Dyce etc.* 1033+S.D. Exit an Attendant *add. Dyce etc.*

To hatch forth treason gainst their naturall Queene?
Did he not cause the King of Spaines huge fleete 1045
To threaten England and to menace me?
Did he not iniure *Mounser* thats deceast?
Hath he not made me in the Popes defence,
To spend the treasure that should strength my land
In ciuill broiles between *Nauarre* and me? 1050
Tush, to be short, he meant to make me Munke,
Or else to murder me, and so be King.
Let Christian princes that shall heare of this,
(As all the world shall know our *Guise* is dead)
Rest satisfied with this that heer I sweare, 1055
Nere was there King of France so yoakt as I.

Eper. My Lord heer is his sonne.

Enter the Guises *sonne.*

King.

Boy, look where your father lyes.

Yong Guise. My father slaine, who hath done this deed?

King. Sirra twas I that slew him, and will slay 1060
Thee too, and thou proue such a traitor.

Yong Guise. Art thou King, and hast done this bloudy deed?
Ile be reuengde.

He offereth to throwe his dagger.

King. Away to prison with him, Ile clippe his winges
Or ere he passe my handes: away with him. *Exit* Boy.
But what auaileth that this traitors dead, 1066
When Duke *Dumaine* his brother is aliue,
And that young Cardinall that is growne so proud?
Goe to the Gouernour of Orleance,
And will him in my name to kill the Duke. 1070
Get you away and strangle the Cardinall.
These two will make one entire Duke of *Guise*,
Especially with our olde mothers helpe.

Eper. My Lord, see where she comes, as if she droupt
To heare these newes. 1075

Enter Queene Mother.

King. And let her droup, my heart is light enough.

1060–1 *Prose O*: *corr. Dyce* 1064–5 *Prose O*: *corr. Dyce*: *div. after* him, handes *Malone* 1070+S.D. To the Captain of the Guard *add. Dyce etc.* 1071+S.D. To the Murderers. Exeunt Captain of the Guard and Murderers *add. Dyce etc.* 1074–5 *Prose O*: *corr. Malone, Dyce*

Mother, how like you this deuice of mine?
I slew the *Guise*, because I would be King.
Queene. King, why so thou wert before.
Pray God thou be a King now this is done. 1080
King. Nay he was King and countermanded me,
But now I will be King and rule my selfe,
And make the *Guisians* stoup that are aliue.
Queene. I cannot speak for greefe: when thou wast borne,
I would that I had murdered thee my sonne. 1085
My sonne? thou art a changeling, not my sonne.
I curse thee and exclaime thee miscreant,
Traitor to God, and to the realme of France.
King. Cry out, exclaime, houle till thy throat be hoarce,
The *Guise* is slaine, and I reioyce therefore: 1090
And now will I to armes: come *Epernoune*,
And let her greeue her heart out if she will.
Exit the King *and* Epernoune.
Queene. Away, leaue me alone to meditate.
Sweet *Guise*, would he had died so thou wert heere:
To whom shall I bewray my secrets now, 1095
Or who will helpe to builde Religion?
The Protestants will glory and insulte,
Wicked *Nauarre* will get the crowne of France,
The Popedome cannot stand, all goes to wrack,
And all for thee my *Guise*: what may I doe? 1100
But sorrow seaze vpon my toyling scule,
For since the *Guise* is dead, I will not liue. *Exit.*
Enter two dragging in the Cardenall.
Car. Murder me not, I am a Cardenall.
1. Wert thou the Pope thou mightst not scape from vs.
Car. What will you fyle your handes with Churchmens bloud? 1105
2. Shed your bloud, O Lord no: for we entend to strangle you.
Car. Then there is no remedye but I must dye.
1. No remedye, therefore prepare your selfe.
Car. Yet liues 1110
My brother Duke *Dumaine*, and many moe:
To reuenge our deaths vpon that cursed King,
Vpon whose heart may all the furies gripe,
And with their pawes drench his black soule in hell.

1093+S.D. Exeunt Attendants *add. Dyce etc.* 1102+⟨Act III.⟩ Scene III. *add. Rob., Cunn.*: Scene XXII *add. Bull.* 1110–11 *One line O etc.*

1. Yours my Lord Cardinall, you should haue saide. 1115

Now they strangle him.

So, pluck amaine,
He is hard hearted, therfore pull with violence.
Come take him away. *Exeunt.*

Enter Duke Dumayn *reading of a letter, with others.*

Dumaine.

My noble brother murthered by the King,
Oh what may I doe, for to reuenge thy death? 1120
The Kings alone, it cannot satisfie.
Sweet Duke of *Guise* our prop to leane vpon,
Now thou art dead, heere is no stay for vs:
I am thy brother, and ile reuenge thy death,
And roote *Valoys* his line from forth of France, 1125
And beate proud *Burbon* to his natiue home,
That basely seekes to ioyne with such a King,
Whose murderous thoughts will be his ouerthrow.
Hee wild the Gouernour of Orleance in his name,
That I with speed should haue beene put to death. 1130
But thats preuented, for to end his life,
And all those traitors to the Church of Rome,
That durst attempt to murder noble *Guise.*

Enter the Frier.

Frier.

My Lord, I come to bring you newes, that your brother the Cardinall of Loraine by the Kings consent is lately strangled vnto death. 1136

Dumaine. My brother Cardenall slaine and I aliue?
O wordes of power to kill a thousand men.
Come let vs away and leauy men,
Tis warre that must asswage this tyrantes pride. 1140

Frier. My Lord, heare me but speak,
I am a Frier of the order of the Iacobyns,
That for my conscience sake will kill the King.

Dumaine. But what doth moue thee aboue the rest to doe the deed? 1145

Frier. O my Lord, I haue beene a great sinner in my dayes, and the deed is meritorious.

1116–17 *Prose O, Cunn.*: *corr. Dyce, Bull.* 1118+Scene XXIII. *add. Bull.* 1120 for *om. Cunn.* 1132 And all *Malone, Dyce etc.*: His life, and all *O* 1137 Cardenall] the Cardinal *Dyce, Cunn.* 1139 vs] us straight *Cunn.*

Dumaine. But how wilt thou get opportunitye ?
Frier. Tush my Lord, let me alone for that.
Dumaine. Frier come with me, 1150
We will goe talke more of this within. *Exeunt.*

Sound Drumme and Trumpets, and enter the King of France, and Nauarre, Epernoune, Bartus, Pleshe, *and Souldiers.*

King.

Brother of *Nauarre* I sorrow much,
That euer I was prou'd your enemy,
And that the sweet and princely minde you beare
Was euer troubled with iniurious warres: 1155
I vow as I am lawfull King of France,
To recompence your reconciled loue
With all the honors and affections,
That euer I vouchsafte my dearest freends.
Nauarre. It is enough if that *Nauarre* may be 1160
Esteemed faithfull to the King of France,
Whose seruice he may still commaund till death.
King. Thankes to my Kingly Brother of *Nauarre.*
Then heere wee'l lye before Lutecia walles,
Girting this strumpet Cittie with our siege, 1165
Till surfeiting with our afflicting armes,
She cast her hatefull stomack to the earth.

Enter a Messenger.

Messenger.

And it please your Maiestie heere is a Frier of the order of the Iacobins, sent from the President of Paris, that craues accesse vnto your grace. 1170
King. Let him come in.

Enter Frier with a Letter.

Epernoune.

I like not this Friers look.
Twere not amisse my Lord, if he were searcht.
King. Sweete *Epernoune,* our Friers are holy men,
And will not offer violence to their King, 1175
For all the wealth and treasure of the world.
Frier, thou dost acknowledge me thy King ?
Frier. I my good Lord, and will dye therein.

1151+⟨Act III.⟩ Scene IV. *add. Rob., Cunn.*: Scene XXIV *add. Bull.* 1164 Lutetia-walls *Dyce, Bull.*: Lucrecia walles *O*: Lutetia's walls *Cunn.*

King. Then come thou neer, and tell what newes thou bringst.
Frier. My Lord, 1180
The President of Paris greetes your grace,
And sends his dutie by these speedye lines,
Humblye crauing your gracious reply.
King. Ile read them Frier, and then Ile answere thee.
Frier. *Sancte Iacobus*, now haue mercye vpon me. 1185

He stabs the King with a knife as he readeth the letter, and then the King getteth the knife and killes him.

Epernoune.

O my Lord, let him liue a while.
King. No, let the villaine dye, and feele in hell
Iust torments for his trechery.
Nauarre. What, is your highnes hurt?
King. Yes *Nauarre*, but not to death I hope. 1190
Nauarre. God shield your grace from such a sodaine death:
Goe call a surgeon hether strait.
King. What irreligeous Pagans partes be these,
Of such as holde them of the holy church?
Take hence that damned villaine from my sight. 1195
Eper. Ah, had your highnes let him liue,
We might haue punisht him to his deserts.
King. Sweet *Epernoune* all Rebels vnder heauen,
Shall take example by his punishment
How they beare armes against their soueraigne. 1200
Goe call the English Agent hether strait,
Ile send my sister England newes of this,
And giue her warning of her trecherous foes.
Nauarre. Pleaseth your grace to let the Surgeon search your wound.
King. The wound I warrant ye is deepe my Lord, 1205
Search Surgeon and resolue me what thou seest.

The Surgeon searcheth.

Enter the English Agent.

Agent for England, send thy mistres word,

1180–3 *Prose O*: *corr. Dyce etc.* 1183+S.D. Gives letter *add. Dyce, Bull.* 1185 Jacobe *Dyce etc.* 1187–8 *Prose O*: *corr. Dyce etc.* 1192+S.D. Exit an Attendant *add. Dyce etc.* 1195 +S.D. Attendants carry out the Friar's body *add. Dyce etc.* 1199–1200 *Prose O*: *corr. Dyce etc.* 1199 his *Dyce etc.*: their *O* 1201+S.D. Exit an Attendant *add. Dyce, Bull.* 1203 +S.D. Enter a Surgeon *add. Dyce etc.*

What this detested Iacobin hath done.
Tell her for all this that I hope to liue,
Which if I doe, the Papall Monarck goes 1210
To wrack and antechristian kingdome falles.
These bloudy hands shall teare his triple Crowne,
And fire accursed Rome about his eares.
Ile fire his crased buildings and inforse
The papall towers to kisse the holy earth. 1215
Nauarre, giue me thy hand, I heere do sweare
To ruinate that wicked Church of Rome,
That hatcheth vp such bloudy practises,
And heere protest eternall loue to thee,
And to the Queene of England specially, 1220
Whom God hath blest for hating Papestry.

Nauarre. These words reuiue my thoughts and comforts me,
To see your highnes in this vertuous minde.

King. Tell me Surgeon, shall I liue?

Sur. Alas my Lord, the wound is dangerous, 1225
For you are stricken with a poysoned knife.

King. A poysoned knife, what shall the French king dye,
Wounded and poysoned, both at once?

Eper. O that that damned villaine were aliue againe,
That we might torture him with some new found death. 1230

Bar. He died a death too good, the deuill of hell
Torture his wicked soule.

King. Ah curse him not sith he is dead. O,
The fatall poyson workes within my brest,
Tell me Surgeon and flatter not, may I liue? 1235

Sur. Alas my Lord, your highnes cannot liue.

Nauarre. Surgeon, why saist thou so? the King may liue.

King. Oh no *Nauarre*, thou must be King of France.

Nauarre. Long may you liue, and still be King of France.

Eper. Or else dye *Epernoune*. 1240

King. Sweet *Epernoune* thy King must dye. My Lords
Fight in the quarrell of this valiant Prince,
For he is your lawfull King and my next heire:
Valoyses lyne ends in my tragedie.

1210 *Ends* wrack *O*: *corr. Malone* 1211 and] and th' *Dyce*[2], *Cunn.* 1214 enforce *conj. Dyce*[1], *Dyce*[2], *etc.*: incense *O* 1215 holy] lowly *Dyce etc.* 1221 Papestry] popery *Cunn.* 1225–6 *Prose O*: *corr. Dyce etc.* 1231–2 *Prose O*: *div. after* good *Dyce etc.* 1233–5 *Prose O*: *div. after* dead, breast *Dyce etc.* 1241 *Ends* dye *O*: *corr. Dyce*

Now let the house of *Bourbon* weare the crowne, 1245
And may it neuer end in bloud as mine hath done.
Weep not sweet *Nauarre,* but reuenge my death.
Ah *Epernoune,* is this thy loue to me?
Henry thy King wipes of these childish teares,
And bids thee whet thy sword on *Sextus* bones, 1250
That it may keenly slice the Catholicks.
He loues me not ⟨the most⟩ that sheds most teares,
But he that makes most lauish of his bloud.
Fire Paris where these trecherous rebels lurke.
I dye *Nauarre,* come beare me to my Sepulchre. 1255
Salute the Queene of England in my name,
And tell her *Henry* dyes her faithfull freend. *He dyes.*

Nauarre. Come Lords, take vp the body of the King,
That we may see it honourably interde:
And then I vow for to reuenge his death, 1260
As Rome and all those popish Prelates there,
Shall curse the time that ere *Nauarre* was King,
And rulde in France by *Henries* fatall death.

They march out with the body of the King, lying on foure mens shoulders with a dead march, drawing weapons on the ground.

FINIS.

1246 may't *Cunn.* ne'er *Dyce etc.* 1252 the most *add.* *Dyce*[2], *etc.*: the best *add.* *Rob.*, *Dyce*[1] 1260 for to *O*: so to *Dyce etc.*

APPENDIX TO THE MASSACRE AT PARIS

ll. 812-827. In place of this passage, as given in the quarto, Collier published an amplified version which he claims to have derived from a manuscript source. The first allusion to the matter occurs in the introduction to Collier's edition of *The Jew of Malta* in the Dodsley of 1825, vol. viii, pp. 244, 245, where the editor says, alluding to the *Massacre at Paris*:

'A curious MS. fragment of one quarto leaf of this tragedy came into the hands of Mr. Rodd of Newport-street not long since, which, as it very materially differs from the printed edition, is here inserted *literatim*: it perhaps formed part of a copy belonging to the theatre at the time it was first acted, and it would be still more valuable should any accident hereafter shew that it is in the original handwriting of Marlow.'

He then inserts the following version of the scene:

'*Enter a* SOULDIER *w*[th] *a muskett.*

Souldier. Now, ser, to you y[t] dares make a duke a cuckolde, and use a counterfeyt key to his privie chamber: thoughe you take out none but yo[r] owne treasure, yet you put in y[t] displeases him, and fill up his rome y[t] he shold occupie. Herein, ser, you forestalle the markett, and sett upe yo[r] standinge where you shold not. But you will say you leave him rome enoughe besides: that's no answere: he's to have the choyce of his owne freeland, yf it be not to free, there's the questione. Now for where he is your landlorde, you take upon you to be his, and will needs enter by defaulte. What thoughe you weere once in possession yett comminge upon you once unawares, he frayde you out againe: therefore your entrye is mere intrusion: this is against the law, ser. And thoughe I come not to keep possessione as I wolde I mighte, yet I come to keepe you out, ser,

Enter MINION.

You are welcome, ser! have at you. [*He kills him.*

Minion. Trayterous Guise ah, thou has morthered me!

Enter GUISE.

Guise. Hold thee, tale soldier: take thee this and flye. [*Exit.*

Thus falls imperfett exhalation,
Which our great sonn of France cold not effecte;
A fyery meteor in the fermament.
Lye there, the kinge's delyght and Guise's scorne!
Revenge it, Henry, if thou list or dar'st;

I did it onely in dispight of thee.
Fondly hast thou incest (*sic*) the Guise's sowle
That if (*sic*) it self was hote enoughe to worke
Thy just degestion wth extreamest shame,
The armye I have gathered now shall ayme:
Now at thie end thine exterpatione:
And when thou think'st I have forgotten this,
And that thou most reposest one my faythe,
Than will I wake thee from thy foolishe dreame,
And lett thee see thie self my prysoner. [*Exeunt.*'

In Collier's *Annals of the Stage*, 1831 (iii. 133–5) the same passage is inserted with a slightly varying explanation of its origin. The spelling is absolutely different and many phrases are entirely changed. As the MS. has apparently been seen by no one else, and as the wording of the expanded passage is very suspicious, Collier's statement should be received with caution.

HERO AND LEANDER

Hero and Leander is probably the latest of Marlowe's writings. Left a fragment at the poet's death, it was licensed a few months later (September 28, 1593) by John Wolf, as 'a booke intituled HERO *and* LEANDER beinge an amorous poem devised by CHRISTOPHER MARLOW'. There is no evidence that Wolf actually published an edition; the earliest known to exist was issued in 1598 by Edward Blount, to whom Wolf seems in the meantime to have transferred his right in both this poem and in the translation of Lucan.[1]

On March 2, 1597/8, Edward Blount assigned over to Paul Linley 'A booke in Englishe called HERO *and* LEANDER', and the latter published in 1598 at least one[2] complete version of the poem, including Chapman's continuation. Blount's right, derived from Wolf, seems to have extended only to Marlowe's portion of the poem; the rest Linley had probably secured from another source. The precise nature of the transaction between Blount and Linley is obscure. At the time that the former apparently gave up his interest in *Hero and Leander*—on what was by Elizabethan reckoning March 2, 1597—his own 1598 edition of the first two sestiads can obviously not have been published. It may have been in type, and there may have been an agreement with Linley, permitting its publication before Linley himself brought out the complete work, but the probability is that Blount did not entirely abandon his copyright in the poem. It is certain that he was later connected with the publication of the 1609 and 1613 editions.

In 1600 Paul Linley died (cf. McKerrow, *Dict. of Printers*, 177) and the *Stationers' Register* contains the following entry for June 26 of that year: 'John flasket Entred for his

[1] Cf. Introduction to *Lucan's First Book*, p. 642. The *Stationers' Register* does not, however, record any such transfer.

[2] Probably there were two 1598 editions which include the entire poem, besides Blount's edition of Marlowe's fragment.

copies by consent of our Maister and Master Man Warden these bookes and partes of Bookes folowynge whiche were Paule Lynlayes.' Then follow the titles of twenty-four works, one of which is 'HERO *and* LEANDER with the j. booke of LUCAN by MARLOWE'. Flasket published *Hero and Leander* in this same year (1600), and again in 1606. Strangely enough the title-page of the 1600 edition makes no mention of Chapman's continuation, which it contains, and advertises the presence of the Lucan translation, which, notwithstanding, does not appear in this book, but was published separately the same year by Thomas Thorpe with acknowledgements to Blount as former holder of the copyright.[1] Flasket had his head quarters at Linley's old place of business, the sign of the Black Bear in Paul's Churchyard, and Blount advertises the sale of his 1609 and 1613 editions at the same place. Possibly the most reasonable explanation of the puzzle is to assume that some kind of loose partnership existed between Blount and Linley and later between Blount and Flasket in regard to *Hero and Leander*. In any case it would seem clear that Blount's 1598 edition, containing only Marlowe's portion of the poem without Chapman's Arguments and division into Sestiads, is the oldest chronologically and the most authoritative.[2] My text follows this edition as far as it goes, the supplementary matter being given from the British Museum copy of Linley's 1598 edition.

The popularity of *Hero and Leander* with the Elizabethan public was enormous. The literature of the time abounds in allusions to the poem, and the list of early editions is a most impressive one. There were probably three separate editions in 1598, others in 1600, 1606, 1609, 1613, 1616, 1617, 1622, 1629, and 1637. Of these I have been unable so far to collate the third 1598 edition, the existence of which is not quite certainly established, or the unique copies of the 1616, 1617, and 1622 versions.

From lines 183–198 of the third sestiad it seems probable that Chapman's conclusion was undertaken by the authority of Marlowe himself, though such an interpretation may easily be a straining of the vague hints of the lines in

[1] Cf. Introduction to *Lucan's First Book*, p. 643, and p. 647, l. 9.

[2] The relatively small value of the later editions is shown by the fact that none of them corrects the evidently incorrect succession of lines at the end of the second sestiad. Cf. note to ll. 279–300, p. 511.

question. During the year 1598, which was otherwise so important for the poem, there appeared another attempt at completing the torso. This continuation, which is of no poetic value, was the work of a feeble young poet, Henry Petowe, and was licensed April 14, 1598, by Andrew Harris, the publisher of the only edition. A ballad of Hero and Leander was entered on the *Stationers' Register* by John White on July 2, 1614.

Though *Hero and Leander* has often been called, and partly purports to be, a translation of the short Greek poem of the ' pseudo-Musaeus ', it is almost entirely original throughout, except as regards the bare outline of the story. Chapman's completion of the poem seems, as has been said, to have been more or less authorized, and his supplementary cantos have been printed in every edition except the first. There is, however, very little cohesion as regards the plot between Marlowe's fragment and Chapman's, while in tone there is no resemblance whatever. The continuation has all the rhetorical stateliness of Chapman's best verse, and in places—notably in the tale of Teras [1]—it possesses real poetic feeling and grace, but in general Chapman's part of the poem is confused, obscure, and dull. The eight hundred lines written by Marlowe show a lucidity and an artistic mastery of detail, both in structure and in expression, which no other narrative poem in English literature perhaps can equal. We here see Marlowe's genius at its very best—certainly in its most complete and rounded development. It is doubtful whether the English heroic couplet through all its varied and honourable history from the time of Chaucer to that of John Keats, has ever been used with more perfect melody or more wonderful understanding of its peculiar capabilities than in the first two sestiads of *Hero and Leander*. The verses have all the polish of Pope, and they have in addition a richness in sound and sense which finds its closest parallel in a work of the poet otherwise perhaps most nearly akin to Marlowe, the *Endymion* of Keats.

[1] Cf. pp. 534-42.

HERO AND LEANDER.

By Christopher Marloe.

LONDON,
Printed by Adam Islip,
for Edward Blunt.
1598.

HERO AND LEANDER:

Begun by *Christopher Marloe*; and *finished by* George Chapman.

Ut Nectar, Ingenium.

At London

Printed by *Felix Kingston*, for *Paule Linley*, and are to be solde in Paules Church-yard, at the signe of the Blacke-beare.

1598.

1598 { *1598*[1] = Blount's quarto edition of that year, containing only Marlowe's part.
1598[2] = Linley's quarto edition of that year (Brit. Mus. C. 40. e. 68). }

1600 = Quarto edition of that year.
1606 = ,, ,, ,, ,, ,,
1609 = ,, ,, ,, ,, ,,
1613 = ,, ,, ,, ,, ,,
1616 = Edition of that year.
1617 = ,, ,, ,, ,, ,,
1622 = Quarto edition of that year.
1629 = ,, ,, ,, ,, ,,
1637 = ,, ,, ,, ,, ,,

Singer = *Select English Poets*, ed. S. W. Singer, No. VIII, 1821.
Rob. = Robinson's edition of Marlowe, 1826.
Dyce { *Dyce*[1] = Dyce's first edition of Marlowe, 1850.
Dyce[2] = Dyce's revised edition of Marlowe, 1858, etc. }
Cunn. = Cunningham's edition of Marlowe, 1870, etc.
Bull. = Bullen's edition of Marlowe, 1885.
T. B. = The present editor.

Broughton = Conjectures of J. B. in copy of *Rob.* (Brit. Mus. 11771 d).
E. P. = Quotations from *Hero and Leander* in *England's Parnassus*, 1600.

To the Right Worshipfull, Sir Thomas Walsingham, Knight.

Sir, wee thinke not our selues discharged of the dutie wee owe to our friend, when wee haue brought the breathlesse bodie to the earth: for albeit the eye there taketh his euer farwell of that beloued obiect, yet the impression of the man, that hath beene deare vnto vs, liuing an after life in our memory, there 5 *putteth vs in mind of farther obsequies due vnto the deceased. And namely of the performance of whatsoeuer we may iudge shal make to his liuing credit, and to the effecting of his determinations preuented by the stroke of death. By these meditations (as by an intellectuall will) I suppose my selfe executor to* 10 *the vnhappily deceased author of this Poem, vpon whom knowing that in his life time you bestowed many kind fauors, entertaining the parts of reckoning and woorth which you found in him, with good countenance and liberall affection: I cannot but see so far into the will of him dead, that what-* 15 *soeuer issue of his brain should chance to come abroad, that the first breath it should take might be the gentle aire of your liking: for since his selfe had ben accustomed thervnto, it would prooue more agreeable and thriuing to his right children, than any other foster countenance whatsoeuer. At this time* 20 *seeing that this vnfinished Tragedy happens vnder my hands to be imprinted; of a double duty, the one to your selfe, the other to the deceased, I present the same to your most fauourable allowance, offring my vtmost selfe now and euer to bee readie, At your* 25 *Worships disposing:*

Edward Blunt.

(Ep. Ded.) 1 not *om. 1629, 1637* 3 euer *om. 1637* 6 farther] other *1629, 1637* 11 vnhappily *1598*[1], [2], *1600*: vnhappie *1606–37* 12 that *om. 1629, 1637* 18 thervnto] thereto *1613–37* 22 a *om. 1637* adouble *1629* *Signature* Edward Blunt *1598*[1]: E. B. *1598*[2] *etc.*

Hero and Leander.

⟨THE ARGUMENT OF THE FIRST SESTYAD.

Heros *description and her Loues,*
The Phane of Venus ; *where he moues*
His worthie Loue-suite, and attaines ;
Whose blisse the wrath of Fates restraines,
For Cupids *grace to* Mercurie,
Which tale the Author doth implie.⟩[1]

On *Hellespont* guiltie of True-loues blood,
In view and opposit two citties stood,
Seaborderers, disioin'd by *Neptunes* might :
The one *Abydos,* the other *Sestos* hight.
At *Sestos, Hero* dwelt ; *Hero* the faire, 5
Whom young *Apollo* courted for her haire,
And offred as a dower his burning throne,
Where she should sit for men to gaze vpon.
The outside of her garments were of lawne,
The lining purple silke, with guilt starres drawne, 10
Her wide sleeues greene, and bordered with a groue,
Where *Venus* in her naked glory stroue,
To please the carelesse and disdainfull eies
Of proud *Adonis* that before her lies.
Her kirtle blew, whereon was many a staine, 15
Made with the blood of wretched Louers slaine.
Vpon her head she ware a myrtle wreath,
From whence her vaile reacht to the ground beneath.
Her vaile was artificiall flowers and leaues,
Whose workmanship both man and beast deceaues. 20
Many would praise the sweet smell as she past,
When t'was the odour which her breath foorth cast,
And there for honie bees haue sought in vaine,
And beat from thence, haue lighted there againe.
About her necke hung chaines of peble stone, 25
Which lightned by her necke, like Diamonds shone.

[1] *Add. 1598*[2] 3 Seaborders *1598–1613* : *corr. 1629, 1637* 4 th'other *1629, 1637* 9 were] was *Rob.* 10 lining] linnen *1637* 17 wore *1637*

She ware no gloues, for neither sunne nor wind
Would burne or parch her hands, but to her mind,
Or warme or coole them, for they tooke delite
To play vpon those hands, they were so white. 30
Buskins of shels all siluered vsed she,
And brancht with blushing corall to the knee;
Where sparrowes pearcht, of hollow pearle and gold,
Such as the world would woonder to behold:
Those with sweet water oft her handmaid fils, 35
Which as shee went would cherupe through the bils.
Some say, for her the fairest *Cupid* pyn'd,
And looking in her face, was strooken blind.
But this is true, so like was one the other,
As he imagyn'd *Hero* was his mother. 40
And oftentimes into her bosome flew,
About her naked necke his bare armes threw,
And laid his childish head vpon her brest,
And with still panting rockt, there tooke his rest.
So louely faire was *Hero*, *Venus* Nun, 45
As nature wept, thinking she was vndone;
Because she tooke more from her than she left,
And of such wondrous beautie her bereft:
Therefore in signe her treasure suffred wracke,
Since *Heroes* time, hath halfe the world beene blacke. 50
Amorous *Leander*, beautifull and yoong,
(Whose tragedie diuine *Musæus* soong)
Dwelt at *Abidus*: since him dwelt there none,
For whom succeeding times make greater mone.
His dangling tresses that were neuer shorne, 55
Had they beene cut, and vnto *Colchos* borne,
Would haue allur'd the vent'rous youth of *Greece*
To hazard more than for the golden Fleece.
Faire *Cinthia* wisht his armes might be her spheare,
Greefe makes her pale, because she mooues not there. 60
His bodie was as straight as *Circes* wand,
Ioue might haue sipt out *Nectar* from his hand.
Euen as delicious meat is to the tast,
So was his necke in touching, and surpast
The white of *Pelops* shoulder. I could tell ye, 65
How smooth his brest was, & how white his bellie,
And whose immortall fingars did imprint
That heauenly path, with many a curious dint,

40 his] her *1613* 44 rockt *1598*[1]: rocke *1598*[2] *etc.* 54 make *1598*, *1637*, *Dyce etc.*: may *1600–29*, *Rob.* 55 dandling *1629*, *1637*

That runs along his backe, but my rude pen
Can hardly blazon foorth the loues of men, 70
Much lesse of powerfull gods: let it suffise,
That my slacke muse sings of *Leanders* eies,
Those orient cheekes and lippes, exceeding his
That leapt into the water for a kis
Of his owne shadow, and despising many, 75
Died ere he could enioy the loue of any.
Had wilde *Hippolitus Leander* seene,
Enamoured of his beautie had he beene,
His presence made the rudest paisant melt,
That in the vast vplandish countrie dwelt, 80
The barbarous *Thratian* soldier moou'd with nought,
Was moou'd with him, and for his fauour sought.
Some swore he was a maid in mans attire,
For in his lookes were all that men desire,
A pleasant smiling cheeke, a speaking eye, 85
A brow for loue to banquet roiallye,
And such as knew he was a man would say,
Leander, thou art made for amorous play:
Why art thou not in loue, and lou'd of all?
Though thou be faire, yet be not thine owne thrall. 90
 The men of wealthie *Sestos*, euerie yeare,
(For his sake whom their goddesse held so deare,
Rose-cheekt *Adonis*) kept a solemne feast.
Thither resorted many a wandring guest,
To meet their loues; such as had none at all, 95
Came louers home from this great festiuall.
For euerie street like to a Firmament
Glistered with breathing stars, who where they went,
Frighted the melancholie earth, which deem'd
Eternall heauen to burne, for so it seem'd, 100
As if another *Phaeton* had got
The guidance of the sunnes rich chariot.
But far aboue the loueliest *Hero* shin'd,
And stole away th'inchaunted gazers mind,
For like Sea-nimphs inueigling harmony, 105
So was her beautie to the standers by.
Nor that night-wandring pale and watrie starre
(When yawning dragons draw her thirling carre
From *Latmus* mount vp to the glomie skie,
Where crown'd with blazing light and maiestie, 110

72 sings] must sing *1613–37* 73 Those] These *1613–37* 94 wandring] wandered *1606–37* 108 drew *1637* thirling] whirling *Rob.*

She proudly sits) more ouer-rules the flood,
Than she the hearts of those that neere her stood.
Euen as, when gawdie Nymphs pursue the chace,
Wretched *Ixions* shaggie footed race,
Incenst with sauage heat, gallop amaine 115
From steepe Pine-bearing mountains to the plaine:
So ran the people foorth to gaze vpon her,
And all that view'd her, were enamour'd on her.
And as in furie of a dreadfull fight,
Their fellowes being slaine or put to flight, 120
Poore soldiers stand with fear of death dead strooken,
So at her presence all surpris'd and tooken,
Await the sentence of her scornefull eies:
He whom she fauours liues, the other dies.
There might you see one sigh, another rage, 125
And some (their violent passions to asswage)
Compile sharpe satyrs, but alas too late,
For faithfull loue will neuer turne to hate.
And many seeing great princes were denied,
Pyn'd as they went, and thinking on her died. 130
On this feast day, O cursed day and hower,
Went *Hero* thorow *Sestos*, from her tower
To *Venus* temple, w⟨h⟩ere vnhappilye,
As after chaunc'd, they did each other spye.
So faire a church as this, had *Venus* none, 135
The wals were of discoloured *Iasper* stone,
Wherein was *Proteus* carued, and o'rehead,
A liuelie vine of greene sea agget spread;
Where by one hand, light headed *Bacchus* hoong,
And with the other, wine from grapes out wroong. 140
Of Christall shining faire the pauement was,
The towne of *Sestos* cal'd it *Venus* glasse.
There might you see the gods in sundrie shapes,
Committing headdie ryots, incest, rapes:
For know, that vnderneath this radiant floure 145
Was *Danaes* statue in a brazen tower,
Ioue slylie stealing from his sisters bed,
To dallie with *Idalian Ganimed*,
And for his loue *Europa* bellowing loud,
And tumbling with the Rainbow in a cloud: 150
Blood-quaffing *Mars* heauing the yron net,
Which limping *Vulcan* and his *Cyclops* set:

119 in furie of a] in a furie of *1609* 137 ouer head *1598*[a] *etc.*

Loue kindling fire, to burne such townes as *Troy*,
Syluanus weeping for the louely boy
That now is turn'd into a *Cypres* tree, 155
Vnder whose shade the Wood-gods loue to bee.
And in the midst a siluer altar stood;
There *Hero* sacrificing turtles blood,
Vaild to the ground, vailing her eie-lids close,
And modestly they opened as she rose: 160
Thence flew Loues arrow with the golden head,
And thus *Leander* was enamoured.
Stone still he stood, and euermore he gazed,
Till with the fire that from his count'nance blazed,
Relenting *Heroes* gentle heart was strooke, 165
Such force and vertue hath an amorous looke.
It lies not in our power to loue, or hate,
For will in vs is ouer-rul'd by fate.
When two are stript long ere the course begin,
We wish that one should loose, the other win; 170
And one especiallie doe we affect
Of two gold Ingots like in each respect.
The reason no man knowes, let it suffise,
What we behold is censur'd by our eies.
Where both deliberat, the loue is slight, 175
Who euer lov'd, that lov'd not at first sight?
He kneel'd, but vnto her deuoutly praid;
Chast *Hero* to her selfe thus softly said:
Were I the saint hee worships, I would heare him,
And as shee spake those words, came somewhat nere
him. 180
He started vp, she blusht as one asham'd;
Wherewith *Leander* much more was inflam'd.
He toucht her hand, in touching it she trembled,
Loue deepely grounded, hardly is dissembled.
These louers parled by the touch of hands, 185
True loue is mute, and oft amazed stands.
Thus while dum signs their yeelding harts entangled,
The aire with sparkes of liuing fire was spangled,
And night deepe drencht in mystie *Acheron*
Heau'd vp her head, and halfe the world vpon 190
Breath'd darkenesse forth (darke night is *Cupids* day).
And now begins *Leander* to display

A periphrasis of night.

159 Vaild *1598*[1], *Dyce etc.*: Taild *1598*[2]–*1637*: Kneel'd *Rob.* 180 those] these *1637* somewhat] something *1629*, *1637* 184 ground *1637* 189–91 *Marginal note om. 1600–37.*

Loues holy fire, with words, with sighs and teares,
Which like sweet musicke entred *Heroes* eares,
And yet at euerie word shee turn'd aside, 195
And alwaies cut him off as he replide.
At last, like to a bold sharpe Sophister,
With chearefull hope thus he accosted her.
 Faire creature, let me speake without offence,
I would my rude words had the influence, 200
To lead thy thoughts as thy faire lookes doe mine,
Then shouldst thou bee his prisoner who is thine.
Be not vnkind and faire, mishapen stuffe
Are of behauiour boisterous and ruffe.
O shun me not, but heare me ere you goe, 205
God knowes I cannot force loue, as you doe.
My words shall be as spotlesse as my youth,
Full of simplicitie and naked truth.
This sacrifice (whose sweet perfume descending,
From *Venus* altar to your footsteps bending) 210
Doth testifie that you exceed her farre,
To whom you offer, and whose Nunne you are.
Why should you worship her? her you surpasse,
As much as sparkling Diamonds flaring glasse.
A Diamond set in lead his worth retaines, 215
A heauenly Nimph, belov'd of humane swaines,
Receiues no blemish, but oft-times more grace,
Which makes me hope, although I am but base,
Base in respect of thee, diuine and pure,
Dutifull seruice may thy loue procure, 220
And I in dutie will excell all other,
As thou in beautie doest exceed loues mother.
Nor heauen, nor thou, were made to gaze vpon,
As heauen preserues all things, so saue thou one.
A stately builded ship, well rig'd and tall, 225
The Ocean maketh more maiesticall:
Why vowest thou then to liue in *Sestos* here,
Who on Loues seas more glorious wouldst appeare?
Like vntun'd golden strings all women are,
Which long time lie vntoucht, will harshly iarre. 230
Vessels of Brasse oft handled, brightly shine,
What difference betwixt the richest mine
And basest mold, but vse? for both, not vs'de,
Are of like worth. Then treasure is abus'de,

204 behauiours *1613* 227 to] no *1606* 232 betwixt] betweene *1637*

When misers keepe it; being put to lone, 235
In time it will returne vs two for one.
Rich robes themselues and others do adorne,
Neither themselues nor others, if not worne.
Who builds a pallace and rams vp the gate,
Shall see it ruinous and desolate. 240
Ah simple *Hero*, learne thy selfe to cherish,
Lone women like to emptie houses perish.
Lesse sinnes the poore rich man that starues himselfe,
In heaping vp a masse of drossie pelfe,
Than such as you: his golden earth remains, 245
Which after his disceasse, some other gains.
But this faire iem, sweet in the losse alone,
When you fleet hence, can be bequeath'd to none.
Or if it could, downe from th'enameld skie
All heauen would come to claime this legacie, 250
And with intestine broiles the world destroy,
And quite confound natures sweet harmony.
Well therefore by the gods decreed it is,
We humane creatures should enioy that blisse
One is no number, mayds are nothing then, 255
Without the sweet societie of men.
Wilt thou liue single still? one shalt thou bee,
Though neuer-singling *Hymen* couple thee.
Wild sauages, that drinke of running springs,
Thinke water farre excels all earthly things: 260
But they that dayly tast neat wine, despise it.
Virginitie, albeit some highly prise it,
Compar'd with marriage, had you tried them both,
Differs as much as wine and water doth.
Base boullion for the stampes sake we allow, 265
Euen so for mens impression do we you,
By which alone, our reuerend fathers say,
Women receaue perfection euerie way.
This idoll which you terme *Virginitie*,
Is neither essence subiect to the eie, 270
No, nor to any one exterior sence,
Nor hath it any place of residence,
Nor is't of earth or mold celestiall,
Or capable of any forme at all.
Of that which hath no being doe not boast, 275
Things that are not at all are neuer lost.

242 Lone] Loue *1598²–1600* 243 sinnes] since *1598²–1606*
261 neat] sweet *1637* 266 impressions *1637*

Men foolishly doe call it vertuous,
What vertue is it that is borne with vs ?
Much lesse can honour bee ascrib'd thereto,
Honour is purchac'd by the deedes wee do. 280
Beleeue me *Hero*, honour is not wone,
Vntill some honourable deed be done.
Seeke you for chastitie, immortall fame,
And know that some haue wrong'd *Dianas* name ?
Whose name is it, if she be false or not, 285
So she be faire, but some vile toongs will blot ?
But you are faire (aye me) so wondrous faire,
So yoong, so gentle, and so debonaire,
As *Greece* will thinke, if thus you liue alone,
Some one or other keepes you as his owne. 290
Then *Hero* hate me not, nor from me flie,
To follow swiftly blasting infamie.
Perhaps, thy sacred Priesthood makes thee loath,
Tell me, to whom mad'st thou that heedlesse oath ?
  To *Venus*, answered shee, and as shee spake, 295
Foorth from those two tralucent cesternes brake
A streame of liquid pearle, which downe her face
Made milk-white paths, wheron the gods might trace
To *Ioues* high court. Hee thus replide : The rites
In which Loues beauteous Empresse most delites, 300
Are banquets, Dorick musicke, midnight-reuell,
Plaies, maskes, and all that stern age counteth euill.
Thee as a holy Idiot doth she scorne,
For thou in vowing chastitie hast sworne
To rob her name and honour, and thereby 305
Commit'st a sinne far worse than periurie,
Euen sacrilege against her Deitie,
Through regular and formall puritie.
To expiat which sinne, kisse and shake hands,
Such sacrifice as this *Venus* demands. 310
  Thereat she smild, and did denie him so,
As put thereby, yet might he hope for mo.
Which makes him quickly re-enforce his speech,
And her in humble manner thus beseech.
  Though neither gods nor men may thee deserue, 315
Yet for her sake whom you haue vow'd to serue,
Abandon fruitlesse cold Virginitie,
The gentle queene of Loues sole enemie.
Then shall you most resemble *Venus* Nun,

294 mad'st thou] thou mad'st *1637*   304 hast] hath *1609*

When *Venus* sweet rites are perform'd and done. 320
Flint-brested *Pallas* ioies in single life,
But *Pallas* and your mistresse are at strife.
Loue *Hero* then, and be not tirannous,
But heale the heart, that thou hast wounded thus,
Nor staine thy youthfull years with auarice, 325
Faire fooles delight to be accounted nice.
The richest corne dies, if it be not reapt,
Beautie alone is lost, too warily kept.
These arguments he vs'de, and many more,
Wherewith she yeelded, that was woon before. 330
Heroes lookes yeelded, but her words made warre,
Women are woon when they begin to iarre.
Thus hauing swallow'd *Cupids* golden hooke,
The more she striv'd, the deeper was she strooke.
Yet euilly faining anger, stroue she still, 335
And would be thought to graunt against her will.
So hauing paus'd a while, at last shee said:
Who taught thee Rhethoricke to deceiue a maid?
Aye me, such words as these should I abhor,
And yet I like them for the Orator. 340
With that *Leander* stoopt, to haue imbrac'd her,
But from his spreading armes away she cast her,
And thus bespake him: Gentle youth forbeare
To touch the sacred garments which I weare.
Vpon a rocke, and vnderneath a hill, 345
Far from the towne (where all is whist and still,
Saue that the sea playing on yellow sand,
Sends foorth a ratling murmure to the land,
Whose sound allures the golden *Morpheus*
In silence of the night to visite vs.) 350
My turret stands, and there God knowes I play
With *Venus* swannes and sparrowes all the day.
A dwarfish beldame beares me companie,
That hops about the chamber where I lie,
And spends the night (that might be better spent) 355
In vaine discourse, and apish merriment.
Come thither. As she spake this, her toong tript,
For vnawares (*Come thither*) from her slipt,
And sodainly her former colour chang'd,
And here and there her eies through anger rang'd. 360

326 nice] wise *E. P.* 327 richest] ripest *E. P.* 328 warily] early *E. P.* 347 on] upon *1637* 353 beares] keepes *1637* 358 thither] hither *1629, 1637*

And like a planet, mouuing seuerall waies,
At one selfe instant, she poore soule assaies,
Louing, not to loue at all, and euerie part
Stroue to resist the motions of her hart.
And hands so pure, so innocent, nay such, 365
As might haue made heauen stoope to haue a touch,
Did she vphold to *Venus*, and againe
Vow'd spotlesse chastitie, but all in vaine.
Cupid beats downe her praiers with his wings,
Her vowes aboue the emptie aire he flings: 370
All deepe enrag'd, his sinowie bow he bent,
And shot a shaft that burning from him went,
Wherewith she strooken look'd so dolefully,
As made Loue sigh, to see his tirannie.
And as she wept, her teares to pearle he turn'd, 375
And wound them on his arme, and for her mourn'd.
Then towards the pallace of the destinies,
Laden with languishment and griefe he flies,
And to those sterne nymphs humblie made request,
Both might enioy ech other, and be blest. 380
But with a ghastly dreadfull countenaunce,
Threatning a thousand deaths at euerie glaunce,
They answered Loue, nor would vouchsafe so much
As one poore word, their hate to him was such.
Harken a while, and I will tell you why: 385
Heauens winged herrald, *Ioue-borne Mercury*,
The selfe-same day that he asleepe had layd
Inchaunted Argus, spied a countrie mayd,
Whose carelesse haire, in stead of pearle t'adorne it,
Glist'red with deaw, as one that seem'd to skorne it: 390
Her breath as fragrant as the morning rose,
Her mind pure, and her toong vntaught to glose.
Yet prowd she was, (for loftie pride that dwels
In tow'red courts, is oft in sheapheards cels.)
And too too well the faire vermilion knew, 395
And siluer tincture of her cheekes, that drew
The loue of euerie swaine: On her, this god
Enamoured was, and with his snakie rod,
Did charme her nimble feet, and made her stay,
The while vpon a hillocke downe he lay, 400
And sweetly on his pipe began to play,
And with smooth speech her fancie to assay,

370 aboue] about *conj.* *Dyce*[1], *Dyce*[2] 377 toward *1629* 389 pearles *1637* 400 a] the *1600–37*

Till in his twining armes he lockt her fast,
And then he woo'd with kisses, and at last,
As sheap-heards do, her on the ground hee layd, 405
And tumbling in the grasse, he often strayd
Beyond the bounds of shame, in being bold
To eie those parts, which no eie should behold.
And like an insolent commaunding louer,
Boasting his parentage, would needs discouer 410
The way to new *Elisium*: but she,
Whose only dower was her chastitie,
Hauing striu'ne in vaine, was now about to crie,
And craue the helpe of sheap-heards that were nie.
Herewith he stayd his furie, and began 415
To giue her leaue to rise: away she ran,
After went *Mercurie*, who vs'd such cunning,
As she to heare his tale, left off her running.
Maids are not woon by brutish force and might,
But speeches full of pleasure and delight. 420
And knowing *Hermes* courted her, was glad
That she such louelinesse and beautie had
As could prouoke his liking, yet was mute,
And neither would denie, nor graunt his sute.
Still vowd he loue, she wanting no excuse 425
To feed him with delaies, as women vse,
Or thirsting after immortalitie,—
All women are ambitious naturallie,—
Impos'd vpon her louer such a taske,
As he ought not performe, nor yet she aske. 430
A draught of flowing *Nectar* she requested,
Wherewith the king of Gods and men is feasted.
He readie to accomplish what she wil'd,
Stole some from *Hebe* (*Hebe Ioues* cup fil'd,)
And gaue it to his simple rustike loue, 435
Which being knowne (as what is hid from *Joue*?)
He inly storm'd, and waxt more furious
Than for the fire filcht by *Prometheus*,
And thrusts him down from heauen: he wandring here,
In mournfull tearmes, with sad and heauie cheare 440
Complaind to *Cupid*. *Cupid* for his sake,
To be reueng'd on Ioue did vndertake,
And those on whom heauen, earth, and hell relies,
I mean the Adamantine Destinies,

406 in] on *1629, 1637* 420 pleasure *1598*[1], *1629, 1637, Rob.. Dyce*: pleasures *1598*[2]–*1613, Cunn., Bull.*

He wounds with loue, and forst them equallie 445
To dote vpon deceitfull *Mercurie.*
They offred him the deadly fatall knife,
That sheares the slender threads of humane life,
At his faire feathered feet the engins layd,
Which th'earth from ougly *Chaos* den vp-wayd: 450
These he regarded not, but did intreat,
That Ioue, vsurper of his fathers seat,
Might presently be banisht into hell,
And aged *Saturne* in *Olympus* dwell.
They granted what he crau'd, and once againe 455
Saturne and *Ops* began their golden raigne.
Murder, rape, warre, lust and trecherie,
Were with *Ioue* clos'd in *Stigian* Emprie.
But long this blessed time continued not:
As soone as he his wished purpose got, 460
He recklesse of his promise did despise
The loue of th'euerlasting Destinies.
They seeing it, both Loue and him abhor'd,
And *Iupiter* vnto his place restor'd.
And but that Learning, in despight of Fate, 465
Will mount aloft, and enter heauen gate,
And to the seat of *Ioue* it selfe aduaunce,
Hermes had slept in hell with ignoraunce,
Yet as a punishment they added this,
That he and *Pouertie* should alwaies kis. 470
And to this day is euerie scholler poore,
Grosse gold from them runs headlong to the boore.
Likewise the angrie sisters thus deluded,
To venge themselues on *Hermes*, haue concluded
That *Midas* brood shall sit in Honors chaire, 475
To which the *Muses* sonnes are only heire:
And fruitfull wits that in aspiring are,
Shall discontent run into regions farre;
And few great lords in vertuous deeds shall ioy,
But be surpris'd with euery garish toy; 480
And still inrich the loftie seruile clowne,
Who with incroching guile keepes learning downe
Then muse not *Cupids* sute no better sped,
Seeing in their loues the Fates were iniured.

⟨*The end of the first Sestyad.*

447 deadly fatall] fatall deadly *1637* 457 warre, lust] war and lust *Rob. etc.* 465 but that] that but *1629, 1637* 477 inaspiring *Dyce etc.*: high-aspiring *conj. Bull.*

THE ARGUMENT OF THE SECOND SESTYAD.

Hero *of loue takes deeper sence,*
And doth her loue more recompence.
Their first nights meeting, where sweet kisses
Are th' only crownes of both their blisses.
He swims t' Abydus, *and returnes ;*
Cold Neptune *with his beautie burnes,*
Whose suite he shuns, and doth aspire
Heros *faire towre, and his desire.)*[1]

By this, sad *Hero*, with loue vnacquainted,
Viewing *Leanders* face, fell downe and fainted.
He kist her, and breath'd life into her lips,
Wherewith as one displeas'd, away she trips.
Yet as she went, full often look'd behind, 5
And many poore excuses did she find
To linger by the way, and once she stayd,
And would haue turn'd againe, but was afrayd,
In offring parlie, to be counted light.
So on she goes, and in her idle flight, 10
Her painted fanne of curled plumes let fall,
Thinking to traine *Leander* therewithall.
He being a nouice, knew not what she meant,
But stayd, and after her a letter sent,
Which ioyfull *Hero* answerd in such sort, 15
As he had hope to scale the beauteous fort,
Wherein the liberall graces lock'd their wealth,
And therefore to her tower he got by stealth.
Wide open stood the doore, hee need not clime,
And she her selfe before the pointed time 20
Had spread the boord, with roses strowed the roome,
And oft look't out, and mus'd he did not come.
At last he came, O who can tell the greeting
These greedie louers had at their first meeting.
He askt, she gaue, and nothing was denied, 25
Both to each other quickly were affied.
Looke how their hands, so were their hearts vnited,
And what he did she willingly requited.
(Sweet are the kisses, the imbracements sweet,
When like desires and affections meet, 30
For from the earth to heauen is *Cupid* rais'd,
Where fancie is in equall ballance pais'd)

[1] *Add. 1598² etc.* 17 lock *1629, 1637* 30 and] and like *1629, 1637, Rob. to Bull.*

Yet she this rashnesse sodainly repented,
And turn'd aside, and to her selfe lamented,
As if her name and honour had beene wrong'd, 35
By being possest of him for whom she long'd:
I, and shee wisht, albeit not from her hart,
That he would leaue her turret and depart.
The mirthfull God of amorous pleasure smil'd,
To see how he this captiue Nymph beguil'd. 40
For hitherto hee did but fan the fire,
And kept it downe that it might mount the hier.
Now waxt she iealous, least his loue abated,
Fearing her owne thoughts made her to be hated.
Therefore vnto him hastily she goes, 45
And like light *Salmacis*, her body throes
Vpon his bosome, where with yeelding eyes
She offers vp her selfe a sacrifice,
To slake his anger if he were displeas'd.
O what god would not therewith be appeas'd? 50
Like *Æsops* cocke, this iewell he enioyed,
And as a brother with his sister toyed,
Supposing nothing else was to be done,
Now he her fauour and good will had wone.
But know you not that creatures wanting sence 55
By nature haue a mutuall appetence,
And wanting organs to aduaunce a step,
Mou'd by Loues force, vnto ech other lep?
Much more in subiects hauing intellect,
Some hidden influence breeds like effect. 60
Albeit *Leander* rude in loue, and raw,
Long dallying with *Hero*, nothing saw
That might delight him more, yet he suspected
Some amorous rites or other were neglected.
Therefore vnto his bodie hirs he clung, 65
She, fearing on the rushes to be flung,
Striu'd with redoubled strength: the more she striued,
The more a gentle pleasing heat reuiued,
Which taught him all that elder louers know,
And now the same gan so to scorch and glow, 70
As in plaine termes (yet cunningly) he crau'd it,
Loue alwaies makes those eloquent that haue it.

55 you] ye *1613* 58 lep] leap *1629, 1637, Rob., Cunn.* 68 pleasing] pleasant *1600* 71 he crau'd] he'd crave *Rob.*: he crave *Dyce*[2] *etc.*

Shee, with a kind of graunting, put him by it,
And euer as he thought himselfe most nigh it,
Like to the tree of *Tantalus* she fled, 75
And seeming lauish, sau'de her maydenhead.
Ne're king more sought to keepe his diademe,
Than Hero this inestimable gemme.
Aboue our life we loue a stedfast friend,
Yet when a token of great worth we send, 80
We often kisse it, often looke thereon,
And stay the messenger that would be gon:
No maruell then, though *Hero* would not yeeld
So soone to part from that she deerely held.
Iewels being lost are found againe, this neuer, 85
T'is lost but once, and once lost, lost for euer.
Now had the morne espy'de her louers steeds,
Whereat she starts, puts on her purple weeds,
And red for anger that he stayd so long,
All headlong throwes her selfe the clouds among, 90
And now *Leander* fearing to be mist,
Imbrast her sodainly, tooke leaue, and kist.
Long was he taking leaue, and loath to go,
And kist againe, as louers vse to do.
Sad *Hero* wroong him by the hand, and wept, 95
Saying, let your vowes and promises be kept.
Then standing at the doore, she turnd about,
As loath to see *Leander* going out.
And now the sunne that through th'orizon peepes,
As pittying these louers, downeward creepes, 100
So that in silence of the cloudie night,
Though it was morning, did he take his flight.
But what the secret trustie night conceal'd
Leanders amorous habit soone reueal'd,
With *Cupids* myrtle was his bonet crownd, 105
About his armes the purple riband wound,
Wherewith she wreath'd her largely spreading heare,
Nor could the youth abstaine, but he must weare
The sacred ring wherewith she was endow'd,
When first religious chastitie she vow'd: 110
Which made his loue through *Sestos* to bee knowne,
And thence vnto *Abydus* sooner blowne
Than he could saile, for incorporeal Fame,
Whose waight consists in nothing but her name,

85 being] beene *1613–37* 94 vsde *1600* 100 downwards *1629, 1637* 103 what] when *1637* 113 incorporall *1598*[2], *1600*

Is swifter than the wind, whose tardie plumes 115
Are reeking water and dull earthlie fumes.
Home when he came, he seem'd not to be there,
But like exiled aire thrust from his sphere,
Set in a forren place, and straight from thence,
Alcides like, by mightie violence 120
He would haue chac'd away the swelling maine,
That him from her vniustly did detaine.
Like as the sunne in a Dyameter,
Fires and inflames obiects remooued farre,
And heateth kindly, shining lat'rally; 125
So beautie, sweetly quickens when t'is ny,
But being separated and remooued,
Burnes where it cherisht, murders where it loued.
Therefore euen as an Index to a booke,
So to his mind was yoong *Leanders* looke. 130
O none but gods haue power their loue to hide,
Affection by the count'nance is descride.
The light of hidden fire itselfe discouers,
And loue that is conceal'd, betraies poore louers.
His secret flame apparantly was seene, 135
Leanders Father knew where hee had beene,
And for the same mildly rebuk't his sonne,
Thinking to quench the sparckles new begonne.
But loue resisted once, growes passionate,
And nothing more than counsaile louers hate. 140
For as a hote prowd horse highly disdaines
To haue his head control'd, but breakes the raines,
Spits foorth the ringled bit, and with his houes
Checkes the submissiue ground: so hee that loues,
The more he is restrain'd, the woorse he fares. 145
What is it now, but mad *Leander* dares?
O *Hero, Hero,* thus he cry'de full oft,
And then he got him to a rocke aloft,
Where hauing spy'de her tower, long star'd he on't,
And pray'd the narrow toyling *Hellespont* 150
To part in twaine, that hee might come and go,
But still the rising billowes answered no.
With that hee stript him to the yu'rie skin,
And crying, Loue I come, leapt liuely in.

115 windes *1637* 126 sweetly] quickly *1637* t'is] it's *1609–37* 128 it's cherisht *E. P.* 131 but gods haue power] haue power but Gods *1613–37*

Whereat the saphir visag'd god grew prowd, 155
And made his capring *Triton* sound alowd,
Imagining that *Ganimed* displeas'd,
Had left the heauens; therefore on him hee seaz'd.
Leander striu'd, the waues about him wound,
And puld him to the bottome, where the ground 160
Was strewd with pearle, and in low corrall groues
Sweet singing Meremaids, sported with their loues
On heapes of heauie gold, and tooke great pleasure
To spurne in carelesse sort the shipwracke treasure.
For here the stately azure pallace stood, 165
Where kingly *Neptune* and his traine abode.
The lustie god imbrast him, cald him loue,
And swore he neuer should returne to Ioue.
But when he knew it was not *Ganimed*,
For vnder water he was almost dead, 170
He heau'd him vp, and looking on his face,
Beat downe the bold waues with his triple mace,
Which mounted vp, intending to haue kist him,
And fell in drops like teares, because they mist him.
Leander being vp, began to swim, 175
And looking backe, saw *Neptune* follow him,
Whereat agast, the poore soule gan to crie,
O let mee visite *Hero* ere I die.
The god put *Helles* bracelet on his arme,
And swore the sea should neuer doe him harme. 180
He clapt his plumpe cheekes, with his tresses playd,
And smiling wantonly, his loue bewrayd.
He watcht his armes, and as they opend wide,
At euery stroke, betwixt them would he slide,
And steale a kisse, and then run out and daunce, 185
And as he turnd, cast many a lustfull glaunce,—
And threw him gawdie toies to please his eie,—
And diue into the water, and there prie
Vpon his brest, his thighs, and euerie lim,
And vp againe, and close beside him swim, 190
And talke of loue: *Leander* made replie,
You are deceau'd, I am no woman I.
Thereat smilde *Neptune*, and then told a tale,
How that a sheapheard sitting in a vale
Playd with a boy so faire and kind, 195
As for his loue both earth and heauen pyn'd;

164 shipwrackt *1629*: shipwreck *Rob.*, *Dyce*[2] *etc.* 181 claps *1629*, *1637* 187 throw *Dyce etc.* 191 talkt *1600* 195 faire] louely faire *1629*, *1637*, *Rob. etc.*

That of the cooling riuer durst not drinke,
Least water-nymphs should pull him from the brinke.
And when hee sported in the fragrant lawnes,
Gote-footed Satyrs and vp-staring Fawnes 200
Would steale him thence. Ere halfe this tale was done,
Aye me, *Leander* cryde, th'enamoured sunne,
That now should shine on *Thetis* glassie bower,
Descends vpon my radiant *Heroes* tower.
O that these tardie armes of mine were wings! 205
And as he spake, vpon the waues he springs
Neptune was angrie that hee gaue no eare,
And in his heart reuenging malice bare:
He flung at him his mace, but as it went,
He cald it in, for loue made him repent. 210
The mace returning backe his owne hand hit,
As meaning to be veng'd for darting it.
When this fresh bleeding wound *Leander* viewd,
His colour went and came, as if he rewd
The greefe which *Neptune* felt. In gentle brests, 215
Relenting thoughts, remorse and pittie rests.
And who haue hard hearts, and obdurat minds,
But vicious, harebraind, and illit'rat hinds?
The god seeing him with pittie to be moued,
Thereon concluded that he was beloued. 220
(Loue is too full of faith, too credulous,
With follie and false hope deluding vs.)
Wherefore *Leanders* fancie to surprize,
To the rich *Ocean* for gifts he flies.
'Tis wisedome to giue much, a gift preuailes, 225
When deepe perswading Oratorie failes.
By this *Leander* being nere the land,
Cast downe his wearie feet, and felt the sand.
Breathlesse albeit he were, he rested not,
Till to the solitarie tower he got, 230
And knockt and cald, at which celestiall noise
The longing heart of *Hero* much more ioies
Then nymphs & sheapheards, when the timbrell rings,
Or crooked Dolphin when the sailer sings;
She stayd not for her robes, but straight arose, 235
And drunke with gladnesse, to the dore she goes,
Where seeing a naked man, she scriecht for feare,
Such sights as this to tender maids are rare,

200 vp-starting *1609–37*, *Rob.* 201 Ere halfe this] ere halfe his *1629*, *1637*: Ere half his *Rob.*

And ran into the darke herselfe to hide.
Rich iewels in the darke are soonest spide. 240
Vnto her was he led, or rather drawne,
By those white limmes, which sparckled through the lawne.
The neerer that he came, the more she fled,
And seeking refuge, slipt into her bed.
Whereon *Leander* sitting, thus began, 245
Through numming cold all feeble, faint and wan:
If not for loue, yet, loue, for pittie sake,
Me in thy bed and maiden bosome take,
At least vouchsafe these armes some little roome,
Who hoping to imbrace thee, cherely swome. 250
This head was beat with manie a churlish billow,
And therefore let it rest vpon thy pillow.
Herewith afrighted *Hero* shrunke away,
And in her luke-warme place *Leander* lay,
Whose liuely heat like fire from heauen fet, 255
Would animate grosse clay, and higher set
The drooping thoughts of base declining soules,
Then drerie *Mars* carowsing *Nectar* boules.
His hands he cast vpon her like a snare,
She ouercome with shame and sallow feare, 260
Like chast *Diana*, when *Acteon* spyde her,
Being sodainly betraide, dyu'd downe to hide her.
And as her siluer body downeward went,
With both her hands she made the bed a tent,
And in her owne mind thought her selfe secure, 265
O'recast with dim and darksome couerture.
And now she lets him whisper in her eare,
Flatter, intreat, promise, protest and sweare,
Yet euer as he greedily assayd
To touch those dainties, she the *Harpey* playd, 270
And euery lim did as a soldier stout,
Defend the fort, and keep the foe-man out.
For though the rising yu'rie mount he scal'd,
Which is with azure circling lines empal'd,
Much like a globe, (a globe may I tearme this, 275
By which loue sailes to regions full of blis,)
Yet there with *Sysiphus* he toyld in vaine,
Till gentle parlie did the truce obtaine.

246 Through] Though *1598*[2], *1600* 257 dropping *1629, 1637* 260 sallow] shallow *1629, 1637* 267 now *om. 1637* 269 euer] euer after *1613* 270 daintie *1613* 272 foe-men *1609–37*

Wherein *Leander* on her quiuering brest,
Breathlesse spoke some thing, and sigh'd out the rest; 280
Which so preuail'd, as he with small ado
Inclos'd her in his armes and kist her to.
And euerie kisse to her was as a charme,
And to *Leander* as a fresh alarme,
So that the truce was broke, and she alas, 285
(Poore sillie maiden) at his mercie was.
Loue is not ful of pittie (as men say)
But deaffe and cruell, where he meanes to pray.
Euen as a bird, which in our hands we wring,
Foorth plungeth, and oft flutters with her wing, 290
She trembling stroue, this strife of hers (like that
Which made the world) another world begat
Of vnknowne ioy. Treason was in her thought,
And cunningly to yeeld her selfe she sought.
Seeming not woon, yet woon she was at length, 295
In such warres women vse but halfe their strength.
Leander now like Theban *Hercules*,
Entred the orchard of *Th'esperides*,
Whose fruit none rightly can describe but hee
That puls or shakes it from the golden tree: 300
And now she wisht this night were neuer done,
And sigh'd to thinke vpon th'approching sunne,
For much it greeu'd her that the bright day-light
Should know the pleasure of this blessed night,
And them like *Mars* and *Ericine* display, 305
Both in each others armes chaind as they lay.
Againe she knew not how to frame her looke,
Or speake to him who in a moment tooke
That which so long so charily she kept,
And faine by stealth away she would haue crept, 310
And to some corner secretly haue gone,
Leauing *Leander* in the bed alone.
But as her naked feet were whipping out,
He on the suddaine cling'd her so about,

279–300 *Owing probably to the displacement of a leaf in Marlowe's lost MS. these lines are given in wrong sequence in all previous editions. The early quartos all insert ll. 279–90 between 300 and 301, which cannot be right. Singer in his edition of 1821 shifted ll. 289, 290 to a position between 278 and 291, and this order (278, 289–300, 279–88, 301) has been retained by all subsequent editors.* 280 some things *1598*[2], *1600* 281 he *om. 1637* 287 pittie] mercy. 304 this] the *1600* 305 them *conj. Broughton, Dyce etc.*: then *Qq* display *Singer etc.*: displayd *Qq* 306 others] other *1600* lay *Singer etc.*: layd *Qq* 308 who] whom *1600*

That Meremaid-like vnto the floore she slid, 315
One halfe appear'd, the other halfe was hid.
Thus neere the bed she blushing stood vpright,
And from her countenance behold ye might
A kind of twilight breake, which through the heare,
As from an orient cloud, glymse here and there. 320
And round about the chamber this false morne
Brought fooerth the day before the day was borne.
So *Heroes* ruddie cheeke *Hero* betrayd,
And her all naked to his sight displayd,
Whence his admiring eyes more pleasure tooke 325
Than *Dis,* on heapes of gold fixing his looke.
By this *Apollos* golden harpe began
To sound foorth musicke to the *Ocean,*
Which watchfull *Hesperus* no sooner heard,
But he the day bright-bearing Car prepar'd, 330
And ran before, as Harbenger of light,
And with his flaring beames mockt ougly night,
Till she o'recome with anguish, shame, and rage,
Dang'd downe to hell her loathsome carriage.

Desunt nonnulla.

316 One] And *1598*[2], *1600* 319 heare] haire *1629*, *1637*: air *Singer etc.* hair *is probably meant* 320 glymse] glimse *1629*, *1637*: glimps'd *Singer, etc.* *The word intended is doubtless* gleams. 330 day bright-bearing] Day's bright-bearing *conj.* *Broughton*: bright Day-bearing *Dyce etc.* 334 Dang'd] Hurld *1598*[2], *1600* Desunt nonnulla *1598*[1]: The end of the second Sestyad *1598*[2]–*1637*. *The edition 1598*[1] *ends here. The rest of the poem, Chapman's work, appeared first in ed. 1598*[2], *the text of which is from this point followed.*

TO MY BEST ESTEEMED
AND WORTHELY HONORED
LADY, THE LADY WALSINGHAM,

one of the Ladies of her Maiesties
Bed-chamber.

I present your Ladiship with the last affections of the first two Louers that euer Muse *shrinde in the Temple of* Memorie ; *being drawne by strange instigation to employ some of my serious time in so trifeling a subiect, which yet made the first Author, diuine* Musæus, *eternall. And were it not that wee must subiect our accounts of these common receiued conceits to seruile custome ; it goes much against my hand to signe that for a trifling subiect, on which more worthines of soule hath been shewed, and weight of diuine wit, than can vouchsafe residence in the leaden grauitie of any* Mony-Monger ; *in whose profession all serious subiects are concluded. But he that shuns trifles must shun the world ; out of whose reuerend heapes of substance and austeritie, I can, and will, ere long, single, or tumble out as brainles and passionate fooleries, as euer panted in the bosome of the most ridiculous Louer. Accept it therfore* (*good Madam*) *though as a trifle, yet as a serious argument of my affection : for to bee thought thankefull for all free and honourable fauours, is a great summe of that riches my whole thrift intendeth.*

Such vncourtly and sillie dispositions as mine, whose contentment hath other obiects than profit or glorie ; are as glad, simply for the naked merit of vertue, to honour such as aduance her, as others that are hired to commend with deepeliest politique bountie.

It hath therefore adioynde much contentment to my desire of your true honour to heare men of desert in Court adde to mine owne knowledge of your noble disposition, how gladly you doe your best to preferre their desires ; and haue as absolute respect to their meere good parts, as if they came perfumed and charmed with golden incitements. And this most sweet inclination, that flowes from the truth and eternitie of Nobles, assure your Ladiship doth more suite your other Ornaments, and makes more to the aduancement of your Name, and happines of your proceedings, then if (*like others*) *you displaied Ensignes of state and sowrenes in your forehead, made smooth with nothing but sensualitie and presents.*

This poore Dedication (*in figure of the other vnitie betwixt*

Sir Thomas *and your selfe) hath reioynd you with him, my honoured best friend, whose continuance of ancient kindnes to my still-obscured estate, though it cannot encrease my loue to him, which hath euer been entirely circulare; yet shall it encourage my deserts to their vtmost requitall, and make my hartie gratitude speake; to which the vnhappines of my life hath hetherto been vncomfortable and painfull dumbnes.*

By your Ladiships vowd in most wished seruice:

George Chapman.

THE ARGVMENT OF THE

THIRD SESTYAD.

Leander *to the enuious light*
Resignes his night-sports with the night,
And swims the Hellespont *againe ;*
Thesme *the Deitie soueraigne*
Of Customes and religious rites 5
Appeares, reprouing his delites
Since Nuptiall honors he neglected ;
Which straight he vowes shall be effected.
Faire Hero *left Deuirginate*
Waies, and with furie wailes her state : 10
But with her loue and womans wit
She argues, and approueth it.

New light giues new directions, Fortunes new
To fashion our indeuours that ensue,
More harsh (at lest more hard) more graue and hie
Our subiect runs, and our sterne *Muse* must flie.
Loues edge is taken off, and that light flame, 5
Those thoughts, ioyes, longings, that before became
High vnexperienst blood, and maids sharpe plights
Must now grow staid, and censure the delights,
That being enioyd aske iudgement ; now we praise,
As hauing parted : Euenings crowne the daies. 10
And now ye wanton loues, and yong desires,
Pied vanitie, the mint of strange Attires ;
Ye lisping Flatteries, and obsequious Glances,
Relentfull Musicks, and attractiue Dances,
And you detested Charmes constraining loue, 15
Shun loues stolne sports by that these Louers proue.
By this the Soueraigne of Heauens golden fires,
And yong *Leander*, Lord of his desires,
Together from their louers armes arose :
Leander into *Hellespontus* throwes 20
His *Hero*-handled bodie, whose delight
Made him disdaine each other Epethite.
And as amidst the enamourd waues he swims,
The God of gold of purpose guilt his lims,
That this word guilt, including double sence, 25
The double guilt of his *Incontinence*,

He cals Phœbus the God of Gold,

Argument. 6 reproving *Dyce etc.* : improuing *Qq*

since the vertue of his beams creates it.

Might be exprest, that had no stay t'employ
The treasure which the Loue-god let him ioy
In his deare *Hero*, with such sacred thrift,
As had beseemd so sanctified a gift: 30
But like a greedie vulgar Prodigall
Would on the stock dispend, and rudely fall
Before his time, to that vnblessed blessing,
Which for lusts plague doth perish with possessing.
Joy grauen in sence, like snow in water wasts; 35
Without preserue of vertue nothing lasts.
What man is he that with a welthie eie
Enioyes a beautie richer than the skie,
Through whose white skin, softer then soundest sleep,
With damaske eyes, the rubie blood doth peep, 40
And runs in branches through her azure vaines,
Whose mixture and first fire, his loue attaines;
Whose both hands limit both Loues deities,
And sweeten humane thoughts like Paradise;
Whose disposition silken is and kinde, 45
Directed with an earth-exempted minde;
Who thinks not heauen with such a loue is giuen?
And who like earth would spend that dower of heauen,
With ranke desire to ioy it all at first?
What simply kils our hunger, quencheth thirst, 50
Clothes but our nakednes, and makes vs liue,
Praise doth not any of her fauours giue:
But what doth plentifully minister
Beautious apparell and delicious cheere,
So orderd that it still excites desire, 55
And still giues pleasure freenes to aspire
The palme of *Bountie*, euer moyst preseruing:
To loues sweet life this is the courtly caruing.
Thus *Time*, and all-states-ordering *Ceremonie*
Had banisht all offence: *Times* golden Thie 60
Vpholds the flowrie bodie of the earth
In sacred harmonie, and euery birth
Of men, and actions makes legitimate,
Being vsde aright; *The vse of time is Fate.*
Yet did the gentle flood transfer once more 65
This prize of Loue home to his fathers shore;
Where he vnlades himselfe of that false welth
That makes few rich, treasures composde by stelth;
And to his sister kinde *Hermione*,
(Who on the shore kneeld, praying to the sea 70
For his returne) he all Loues goods did show
In *Hero* seasde for him, in him for *Hero*.
His most kinde sister all his secrets knew,
And to her singing like a shower he flew,
Sprinkling the earth, that to their tombs tooke in 75
Streames dead for loue to leaue his iuorie skin,

Which yet a snowie fome did leaue aboue,
As soule to the dead water that did loue;
And from thence did the first white Roses spring,
(For loue is sweet and faire in euery thing) 80
And all the sweetned shore as he did goe,
Was crownd with odrous roses white as snow.
Loue-blest *Leander* was with loue so filled,
That loue to all that toucht him he instilled.
And as the colours of all things we see, 85
To our sights powers communicated bee:
So to all obiects that in compasse came
Of any sence he had, his sences flame
Flowd from his parts with force so virtuall,
It fir'd with sence things weere insensuall. 90
 Now (with warme baths and odours comforted)
When he lay downe he kindly kist his bed,
As consecrating it to *Heros* right,
And vowd thereafter that what euer sight
Put him in minde of *Hero*, or her blisse, 95
Should be her Altar to prefer a kisse.
 Then laid he forth his late inriched armes,
In whose white circle Loue writ all his charmes,
And made his characters sweet *Heros* lims,
When on his breasts warme sea she sideling swims. 100
And as those armes (held vp in circle) met,
He said: See sister *Heros* Carquenet,
Which she had rather weare about her neck,
Then all the iewels that doth *Iuno* deck.
 But as he shooke with passionate desire, 105
To put in flame his other secret fire,
A musick so diuine did pierce his eare,
As neuer yet his rauisht sence did heare:
When suddenly a light of twentie hews
Brake through the roofe, and like the Rainbow views 110
Amazd *Leander*; in whose beames came downe
The Goddesse *Ceremonie*, with a Crowne
Of all the stars, and heauen with her descended.
Her flaming haire to her bright feete extended,
By which hung all the bench of Deities; 115
And in a chaine, compact of eares and eies,
She led Religion; all her bodie was
Cleere and transparent as the purest glasse:
For she was all presented to the sence;
Deuotion, Order, State, and Reuerence 120
Her shadowes were; Societie, Memorie;
All which her sight made liue, her absence die.
A rich disparent Pentackle she weares,
Drawne full of circles and strange characters:

90 were *T. B.*: meere *Qq*, *Dyce etc.*

Her face was changeable to euerie eie ; 125
One way lookt ill, another graciouslie ;
Which while men viewd, they cheerfull were & holy :
But looking off, vicious and melancholy :
The snakie paths to each obserued law
Did *Policie* in her broad bosome draw : 130
One hand a Mathematique Christall swayes,
Which gathering in one line a thousand rayes
From her bright eyes, *Confusion* burnes to death,
And all estates of men distinguisheth.
By it *Morallitie* and *Comelinesse* 135
Themselues in all their sightly figures dresse.
Her other hand a lawrell rod applies,
To beate back *Barbarisme*, and *Auarice*,
That followd eating earth, and excrement
And humane lims ; and would make proud ascent 140
To seates of Gods, were *Ceremonie* slaine ;
The *Howrs* and *Graces* bore her glorious traine,
And all the sweetes of our societie
Were Spherde, and treasurde in her bountious eie.
Thus she appeard, and sharply did reproue 145
Leanders bluntnes in his violent loue ;
Tolde him how poore was substance without rites,
Like bils vnsignd, desires without delites ;
Like meates vnseasond ; like ranke corne that growes
On Cottages, that none or reapes or sowes : 150
Not being with ciuill forms confirm'd and bounded,
For humane dignities and comforts founded :
But loose and secret all their glories hide,
Feare fils the chamber, darknes decks the Bride.
She vanisht, leauing pierst *Leanders* hart 155
With sence of his vnceremonious part,
In which with plaine neglect of Nuptiall rites,
He close and flatly fell to his delites :
And instantly he vowd to celebrate
All rites pertaining to his maried state. 160
So vp he gets and to his father goes,
To whose glad eares he doth his vowes disclose :
The Nuptials are resolu'd with vtmost powre,
And he at night would swim to *Heros* towre.
From whence he ment to *Sestus* forked Bay 165
To bring her couertly, where ships must stay,
Sent by her father throughly rigd and mand,
To waft her safely to *Abydus* Strand.
There leaue we him, and with fresh wing pursue
Astonisht *Hero*, whose most wished view 170
I thus long haue forborne, because I left her
So out of countnance, and her spirits bereft her.
To looke of one abasht is impudence,
When of sleight faults he hath too deepe a sence.

Her blushing het her chamber: she lookt out, 175
And all the ayre she purpled round about,
And after it a foule black day befell,
Which euer since a red morne doth foretell,
And still renewes our woes for *Heros* wo,
And foule it prou'd, because it figur'd so 180
The next nights horror, which prepare to heare;
I faile if it prophane your daintiest eare.
Then thou most strangely-intellectuall fire,
That proper to my soule hast power t'inspire
Her burning faculties, and with the wings 185
Of thy vnspheared flame visitst the springs
Of spirits immortall; Now (as swift as Time
Doth follow Motion) finde th'eternall Clime
Of his free soule, whose liuing subiect stood
Vp to the chin in the Pyerean flood, 190
And drunke to me halfe this Musean storie,
Inscribing it to deathles Memorie:
Confer with it, and make my pledge as deepe,
That neithers draught be consecrate to sleepe.
Tell it how much his late desires I tender, 195
(If yet it know not) and to light surrender
My soules darke ofspring, willing it should die
To loues, to passions, and societie.
Sweet *Hero* left vpon her bed alone,
Her maidenhead, her vowes, *Leander* gone, 200
And nothing with her but a violent crew
Of new come thoughts that yet she neuer knew,
Euen to her selfe a stranger; was much like
Th' *Iberian* citie that wars hand did strike
By English force in princely *Essex* guide, 205
When peace assur'd her towres had fortifide;
And golden-fingred *India* had bestowd
Such wealth on her, that strength and Empire flowd
Into her Turrets; and her virgin waste
The wealthie girdle of the Sea embraste: 210
Till our *Leander* that made *Mars* his *Cupid*,
For soft loue-sutes, with iron thunders chid:
Swum to her Towers, dissolu'd her virgin zone;
Lead in his power, and made Confusion
Run through her streets amazd, that she supposde 215
She had not been in her owne walls inclosde,
But rapt by wonder to some forraine state,
Seeing all her issue so disconsolate:
And all her peacefull mansions possest
With wars iust spoyle, and many a forraine guest 220
From euery corner driuing an enioyer,
Supplying it with power of a destroyer.
So far'd fayre *Hero* in th'expugned fort
Of her chast bosome, and of euery sort

183 thou *T. B.*: how *Qq*: now *Rob.*, *Cunn.*: no *Dyce*, *Bull.*

Strange thoughts possest her, ransacking her brest 225
For that that was not there, her wonted rest.
She was a mother straight and bore with paine
Thoughts that spake straight and wisht their mother slaine;
She hates their liues, & they their own & hers:
Such strife still growes where sin the race prefers. 230
Loue is a golden bubble full of dreames,
That waking breakes, and fils vs with extreames.
She mus'd how she could looke vpon her Sire,
And not shew that without, that was intire.
For as a glasse is an inanimate eie, 235
And outward formes imbraceth inwardlie:
So is the eye an animate glasse that showes
In-formes without vs. And as *Phœbus* throwes
His beames abroad, though he in clowdes be closde,
Still glancing by them till he finde opposde 240
A loose and rorid vapour that is fit
T'euent his searching beames, and vseth it
To forme a tender twentie-coloured eie,
Cast in a circle round about the skie.
So when our firie soule, our bodies starre, 245
(That euer is in motion circulare)
Conceiues a forme; in seeking to display it
Through all our clowdie parts, it doth conuey it
Forth at the eye, as the most pregnant place,
And that reflects it round about the face. 250
And this euent vncourtly *Hero* thought
Her inward guilt would in her lookes haue wrought:
For yet the worlds stale cunning she resisted
To beare foule thoughts, yet forge what lookes she listed,
And held it for a very sillie sleight, 255
To make a perfect mettall counterfeit,
Glad to disclaime her selfe, proud of an Art,
That makes the face a Pandar to the hart.
Those be the painted Moones, whose lights prophane
Beauties true Heauen, at full still in their wane. 260
Those be the Lapwing faces that still crie,
Here tis, when that they vow is nothing nie.
Base fooles, when euery moorish fowle can teach
That which men thinke the height of humane reach.
But custome that the Apoplexie is 265
Of beddred nature and liues led amis,
And takes away all feeling of offence:
Yet brazde not *Heros* brow with impudence;
And this she thought most hard to bring to pas,
To seeme in countnance other then she was, 270
As if she had two soules; one for the face,
One for the hart; and that they shifted place
As either list to vtter, or conceale
What they conceiu'd: or as one soule did deale

With both affayres at once, keeps and eiects 275
Both at an instant contrarie effects:
Retention and eiection in her powrs
Being acts alike: for this one vice of ours,
That forms the thought, and swaies the countenance,
Rules both our motion and our vtterance. 280
  These and more graue conceits toyld *Heros* spirits:
For though the light of her discoursiue wits
Perhaps might finde some little hole to pas
Through all these worldly cinctures; yet (alas)
There was a heauenly flame incompast her; 285
Her Goddesse, in whose Phane she did prefer
Her virgin vowes; from whose impulsiue sight
She knew the black shield of the darkest night
Could not defend her, nor wits subtilst art:
This was the point pierst *Hero* to the hart. 290
Who heauie to the death, with a deep sigh
And hand that languisht, tooke a robe was nigh,
Exceeding large, and of black Cypres made,
In which she sate, hid from the day in shade,
Euen ouer head and face downe to her feete; 295
Her left hand made it at her bosome meete;
Her right hand leand on her hart-bowing knee,
Wrapt in vnshapefull foulds twas death to see:
Her knee stayd that, and that her falling face
Each limme helpt other to put on disgrace. 300
No forme was seene, where forme held all her sight:
But like an Embrion that saw neuer light:
Or like a scorched statue made a cole
With three-wingd lightning: or a wretched soule
Muffled with endles darknes, she did sit: 305
The night had neuer such a heauie spirit.
Yet might an imitating eye well see,
How fast her cleere teares melted on her knee
Through her black vaile, and turnd as black as it,
Mourning to be her teares: then wrought her wit 310
With her broke vow, her Goddesse wrath, her fame,
All tooles that enginous despayre could frame:
Which made her strow the floore with her torne haire,
And spread her mantle peece-meale in the aire.
Like *Ioues* sons club, strong passion strook her downe, 315
And with a piteous shrieke inforst her swoune:
Her shrieke made with another shrieke ascend
The frighted Matron that on her did tend:
And as with her owne crie her sence was slaine,
So with the other it was calde againe. 320
She rose and to her bed made forced way,
And layd her downe euen where *Leander* lay:
And all this while the red sea of her blood
Ebd with *Leander:* but now turnd the flood,

And all her fleete of sprites came swelling in 325
With childe of saile, and did hot fight begin
With those seuere conceits, she too much markt,
And here *Leanders* beauties were imbarkt.
He came in swimming painted all with ioyes,
Such as might sweeten hell: his thought destroyes 330
All her destroying thoughts: she thought she felt
His heart in hers with her contentions melt,
And chid her soule that it could so much erre,
To check the true ioyes he deseru'd in her.
Her fresh heat blood cast figures in her eyes, 335
And she supposde she saw in *Neptunes* skyes
How her star wandred, washt in smarting brine
For her loues sake, that with immortall wine
Should be embath'd, and swim in more hearts ease,
Than there was water in the Sestian seas. 340
Then said her *Cupid* prompted spirit: Shall I
Sing mones to such delightsome harmony?
Shall slick-tongde fame patcht vp with voyces rude,
The drunken bastard of the multitude,
(Begot when father Iudgement is away, 345
And gossip-like, sayes because others say,
Takes newes as if it were too hot to eate,
And spits it slauering forth for dog-fees meate)
Make me for forging a phantastique vow,
Presume to beare what makes graue matrons bow? 350
Good vowes are neuer broken with good deedes,
For then good deedes were bad: vowes are but seedes,
And good deeds fruits; euen those good deedes that grow
From other stocks than from th'obserued vow.
That is a good deede that preuents a bad: 355
Had I not yeelded, slaine my selfe I had.
Hero Leander is, Leander Hero:
Such vertue loue hath to make one of two.
If then *Leander* did my maydenhead git,
Leander being my selfe I still retaine it. 360
We breake chast vowes when we liue loosely euer:
But bound as we are, we liue loosely neuer.
Two constant louers being ioynd in one,
Yeelding to one another, yeeld to none.
We know not how to vow, till loue vnblinde vs, 365
And vowes made ignorantly neuer binde vs.
Too true it is that when t'is gone men hate
The ioyes as vaine they tooke in loues estate:
But that's since they haue lost the heauenly light
Should shew them way to iudge of all things right. 370
When life is gone death must implant his terror,
As death is foe to life, so loue to error.
Before we loue how range we through this sphere,
Searching the sundrie fancies hunted here:

Now with desire of wealth transported quite 375
Beyond our free humanities delight:
Now with ambition climing falling towrs,
Whose hope to scale our feare to fall deuours:
Now rapt with pastimes, pomp, all ioyes impure;
In things without vs no delight is sure. 380
But loue with all ioyes crownd, within doth sit;
O Goddesse pitie loue and pardon it.
This spake she weeping: but her Goddesse eare
Burnd with too sterne a heat, and would not heare.
Aie me, hath heauens straight fingers no more graces 385
For such as *Hero*, then for homeliest faces?
Yet she hopte well, and in her sweet conceit
Waying her arguments, she thought them weight:
And that the logick of *Leanders* beautie,
And them together would bring proofes of dutie. 390
And if her soule, that was a skilfull glance
Of Heauens great essence, found such imperance
In her loues beauties; she had confidence
Ioue lou'd him too, and pardond her offence.
Beautie in heauen and earth this grace doth win, 395
It supples rigor, and it lessens sin.
Thus, her sharpe wit, her loue, her secrecie,
⟨Trouping together, made her wonder why
She should not leaue her bed, and to the Temple?
Her health said she must liue; her sex, dissemble. 400
She viewd *Leanders* place, and wisht he were
Turnd to his place, so his place were *Leander*.
Aye me (said she) that loues sweet life and sence
Should doe it harme! my loue had not gone hence,
Had he been like his place. O blessed place, 405
Image of Constancie. Thus my loues grace
Parts no where but it leaues some thing behinde
Worth obseruation: he renownes his kinde.
His motion is like heauens Orbiculer:
For where he once is, he is euer there. 410
This place was mine: *Leander* now t'is thine;
Thou being my selfe, then it is double mine:
Mine, and *Leanders* mine, *Leanders* mine.
O see what wealth it yeelds me, nay yeelds him:
For I am in it, he for me doth swim. 415
Rich, fruitfull loue, that doubling selfe estates
Elixer-like contracts, though separates.
Deare place, I kisse thee, and doe welcome thee,
As from *Leander* euer sent to mee.

The end of the Third Sestyad.⟩

383 she *Rob. etc.*: he *Qq* 398 ff. *By a mistake of the printer the page containing the conclusion of the third sestiad is omitted in the British Museum copy of ed.* 1598[2]. *Lines 398–419 are therefore here given from the edition of 1600.*

THE ARGVMENT OF THE
FOVRTH SESTYAD

Hero, *in sacred habit deckt,*
Doth priuate sacrifice effect.
Her Skarfs description wrought by fate,
Ostents *that threaten her estate.*
The strange, yet Phisicall euents, 5
Leanders *counterfeit presents.*
In thunder Ciprides *descends,*
Presaging both the louers ends.
Ecte *the Goddesse of remorce,*
With vocall and articulate force 10
Inspires Leucote, Venus *swan,*
T' excuse the beautious Sestian.
Venus, *to wreake her rites abuses,*
Creates the monster Eronusis ;
Enflaming Heros *Sacrifice,* 15
With lightning darted from her eyes :
And thereof springs the painted beast,
That euer since taints euery breast.

Eronusis, Dissi-⟨mu⟩la-tion.

Now from *Leanders* place she rose, and found
Her haire and rent robe scattred on the ground :
Which taking vp, she euery peece did lay
Vpon an Altar ; where in youth of day
She vsde t'exhibite priuate Sacrifice : 5
Those would she offer to the Deities
Of her faire Goddesse, and her powerfull son,
As relicks of her late-felt passion :
And in that holy sort she vowd to end them,
In hope her violent fancies that did rend them, 10
Would as quite fade in her loues holy fire,
As they should in the flames she ment t'inspire.
Then put she on all her religious weedes,
That deckt her in her secret sacred deedes :
A crowne of Isickles, that sunne nor fire 15
Could euer melt, and figur'd chast desire.
A golden star shinde in her naked breast,
In honour of the Queene-light of the East.
In her right hand she held a siluer wand,
On whose bright top *Peristera* did stand, 20

Argument. 14–16 *The marginal note is partially clipped away in the British Museum copy of ed. 1598*[2]

Who was a Nymph, but now transformd a Doue,
And in her life was deare in *Venus* loue:
And for her sake she euer since that time,
Chusde Doues to draw her Coach through heauens blew clime.
Her plentious haire in curled billowes swims 25
On her bright shoulder: her harmonious lims
Sustainde no more but a most subtile vaile
That hung on them, as it durst not assaile
Their different concord: for the weakest ayre
Could raise it swelling from her bewties fayre 30
Nor did it couer, but adumbrate onelie
Her most heart-piercing parts, that a blest eie
Might see (as it did shadow) fearfullie
All that all-loue-deseruing Paradise:
It was as blew as the most freezing skies, 35
Neere the Seas hew, for thence her Goddesse came:
On it a skarfe she wore of wondrous frame;
In midst whereof she wrought a virgins face,
From whose each cheeke a firie blush did chace
Two crimson flames, that did two waies extend, 40
Spreading the ample skarfe to either end,
Which figur'd the diuision of her minde,
Whiles yet she rested bashfully inclinde,
And stood not resolute to wed *Leander*.
This seru'd her white neck for a purple sphere, 45
And cast it selfe at full breadth downe her back.
There (since the first breath that begun the wrack
Of her free quiet from *Leanders* lips)
She wrought a Sea in one flame full of ships:
But that one ship where all her wealth did passe 50
(Like simple marchants goods) *Leander* was:
For in that Sea she naked figured him;
Her diuing needle taught him how to swim,
And to each thred did such resemblance giue,
For ioy to be so like him, it did liue. 55
Things senceles liue by art, and rationall die,
By rude contempt of art and industrie.
Scarce could she work but in her strength of thought,
She feard she prickt *Leander* as she wrought:
And oft would shrieke so, that her Guardian frighted, 60
Would staring haste, as with some mischiefe cited.
They double life that dead things griefs sustayne:
They kill that feele not their friends liuing payne.
Sometimes she feard he sought her infamie,
And then as she was working of his eie, 65
She thought to pricke it out to quench her ill:
But as she prickt, it grew more perfect still.
Trifling attempts no serious acts aduance;
The fire of loue is blowne by dalliance.
In working his fayre neck she did so grace it, 70
She still was working her owne armes t'imbrace it:

That, and his shoulders, and his hands were seene
Aboue the streame, and with a pure Sea greene
She did so queintly shadow euery lim,
All might be seene beneath the waues to swim. 75
In this conceited skarfe she wrought beside
A Moone in change, and shooting stars did glide
In number after her with bloodie beames,
Which figur'd her affects in their extreames,
Pursuing Nature in her Cynthian bodie, 80
And did her thoughts running on change implie:
For maids take more delights when they prepare
And thinke of wiues states, than when wiues they are.
Beneath all these she wrought a Fisherman,
Drawing his nets from forth that Ocean; 85
Who drew so hard ye might discouer well,
The toughned sinewes in his neck did swell:
His inward straines draue out his blood-shot eyes,
And springs of sweat did in his forehead rise:
Yet was of nought but of a Serpent sped, 90
That in his bosome flew and stung him dead.
And this by fate into her minde was sent,
Not wrought by meere instinct of her intent.
At the skarfs other end her hand did frame,
Neere the forkt point of the deuided flame, 95
A countrie virgin keeping of a Vine,
Who did of hollow bulrushes combine
Snares for the stubble-louing Grashopper,
And by her lay her skrip that nourisht her.
Within a myrtle shade she sate and sung, 100
And tufts of wauing reedes about her sprung:
Where lurkt two Foxes, that while she applide
Her trifling snares, their theeueries did deuide:
One to the vine, another to her skrip,
That she did negligently ouerslip: 105
By which her fruitfull vine and holesome fare
She suffred spoyld to make a childish snare.
These omenous fancies did her soule expresse,
And euery finger made a Prophetesse,
To shew what death was hid in loues disguise, 110
And make her iudgement conquer destinies.
O what sweet formes fayre Ladies soules doe shrowd,
Were they made seene & forced through their blood,
If through their beauties like rich work through lawn,
They would set forth their minds with vertues drawn, 115
In letting graces from their fingers flie,
To still their yas thoughts with industrie:
That their plied wits in numbred silks might sing
Passions huge conquest, and their needels leading
Affection prisoner through their own-built citties, 120
Pinniond with stories and Arachnean ditties.

Proceed we now with *Heros* sacrifice ;
She odours burnd, and from their smoke did rise
Vnsauorie fumes, that ayre with plagues inspired,
And then the consecrated sticks she fired, 125
On whose pale flame an angrie spirit flew,
And beate it downe still as it vpward grew.
The virgin Tapers that on th'altar stood,
When she inflam'd them burnd as red as blood :
All sad ostents of that too neere successe, 130
That made such mouing beauties motionlesse.
Then *Hero* wept ; but her affrighted eyes
(She quickly wrested from the sacrifice :
Shut them, and inwards for *Leander* lookt,
Searcht her soft bosome, and from thence she pluckt 135
His louely picture : which when she had viewd,
Her beauties were with all loues ioyes renewd.
The odors sweetned, and the fires burnd cleere,
Leanders forme left no ill obiect there.
Such was his beautie that the force of light, 140
Whose knowledge teacheth wonders infinite,
The strength of number and proportion,
Nature had plaste in it to make it knowne
Art was her daughter, and what humane wits
For studie lost, intombd in drossie spirits. 145
After this accident (which for her glorie
Hero could not but make a historie)
Th' inhabitants of *Sestus*, and *Abydus*
Did euerie yeare with feasts propitious
To faire *Leanders* picture sacrifice, 150
And they were persons of especiall prize
That were allowd it, as an ornament
T' inrich their houses ; for the continent
Of the strange vertues all approu'd it held :
For euen the very looke of it repeld 155
All blastings, witchcrafts, and the strifes of nature
In those diseases that no hearbs could cure.
The woolfie sting of Auarice it would pull,)
And make the rankest miser bountifull.
It kild the feare of thunder and of death ; 160
The discords that conceits ingendereth
Twixt man and wife it for the time would cease :
The flames of loue it quencht, and would increase :
Held in a princes hand it would put out
The dreadfulst Comet : it would ease all doubt 165
Of threatned mischiefes : it would bring asleepe
Such as were mad : it would enforce to weepe
Most barbarous eyes : and many more effects
This picture wrought, and sprung *Leandrian* sects,

132 *Here again a page is omitted in the British Museum copy of ed. 1598*[2]. *Lines 133-58 follow the edition of 1600.*

Of which was *Hero* first: For he whose forme 170
(Held in her hand) cleerd such a fatall storme,
From hell she thought his person would defend her,
Which night and *Hellespont* would quickly send her.
With this confirmd, she vowd to banish quite
All thought of any check to her delite: 175
And in contempt of sillie bashfulnes,
She would the faith of her desires professe:
Where her Religion should be Policie,
To follow loue with zeale her pietie:
Her chamber her Cathedrall Church should be, 180
And her *Leander* her chiefe Deitie.
For in her loue these did the gods forego;
And though her knowledge did not teach her so,
Yet did it teach her this, that what her hart
Did greatest hold in her selfe greatest part, 185
That she did make her god; and t'was lesse nought
To leaue gods in profession and in thought,
Than in her loue and life: for therein lies
Most of her duties, and their dignities;
And raile the brain-bald world at what it will, 190
Thats the grand Atheisme that raignes in it still.
Yet singularitie she would vse no more,
For she was singular too much before:
But she would please the world with fayre pretext;
Loue would not leaue her conscience perplext. 195
Great men that will haue lesse doe for them still,
Must beare them out though th'acts be nere so ill.
Meannes must Pandar be to Excellencie,
Pleasure attones Falshood and Conscience:
Dissembling was the worst (thought *Hero* then) 200
And that was best now she must liue with men.
O vertuous loue that taught her to doe best,
When she did worst, and when she thought it lest.
Thus would she still proceed in works diuine,
And in her sacred state of priesthood shine, 205
Handling the holy rites with hands as bold,
As if therein she did *Ioues* thunder hold;
And need not feare those menaces of error,
Which she at others threw with greatest terror.
O louely *Hero*, nothing is thy sin, 210
Wayd with those foule faults other Priests are in;
That hauing neither faiths, nor works, nor bewties,
T'engender any scuse for slubberd duties,
With as much countnance fill their holie chayres,
And sweat denouncements gainst prophane affayres, 215
As if their liues were cut out by their places,
And they the only fathers of the Graces.
Now as with setled minde she did repaire
Her thoughts to sacrifice her rauisht haire

And her torne robe which on the altar lay, 220
And only for Religions fire did stay;
She heard a thunder by the Cyclops beaten,
In such a volley as the world did threaten,
Giuen *Venus* as she parted th'ayrie Sphere,
Discending now to chide with *Hero* here: 225
When suddenly the Goddesse waggoners,
The Swans and Turtles that in coupled pheres
Through all worlds bosoms draw her influence,
Lighted in *Heros* window, and from thence
To her fayre shoulders flew the gentle Doues, 230
Gracefull *Ædone* that sweet pleasure loues,
And ruffoot *Chreste* with the tufted crowne,
Both which did kisse her, though their Goddes frownd.
The Swans did in the solid flood, her glasse,
Proyne their fayre plumes; of which the fairest was 235
Ioue-lou'd *Leucote*, that pure brightnes is;
The other bountie-louing *Dapsilis*.
All were in heauen, now they with *Hero* were:
But *Venus* lookes brought wrath, and vrged feare.
Her robe was skarlet, black her heads attire, 240
And through her naked breast shinde streames of fire,
As when the rarefied ayre is driuen
In flashing streames, and opes the darkned heauen.
In her white hand a wreath of yew she bore,
And breaking th'icie wreath sweet *Hero* wore, 245
She forst about her browes her wreath of yew,
And sayd: Now minion to thy fate be trew,
Though not to me, indure what this portends;
Begin where lightnes will, in shame it ends.
Loue makes thee cunning; thou art currant now 250
By being counterfeit: thy broken vow
Deceit with her pide garters must reioyne,
And with her stampe thou countnances must coyne:
Coynes and pure deceits for purities,
And still a mayd wilt seeme in cosoned eies, 255
And haue an antike face to laugh within,
While thy smooth lookes make men digest thy sin.
But since thy lips (lest thought forsworne) forswore,
Be neuer virgins vow worth trusting more.
When Beauties dearest did her Goddesse heare 260
Breathe such rebukes gainst that she could not cleare,
Dumbe sorrow spake alowd in teares and blood
That from her griefe-burst vaines in piteous flood,
From the sweet conduits of her fauor fell:
The gentle Turtles did with moanes make swell 265
Their shining gorges: the white black-eyde Swans
Did sing as wofull Epicedians,
As they would straightwaies dye: when pities Queene
The Goddesse *Ecte*, that had euer beene

264 fauor] sauor *1598*[2]

Hid in a watrie clowde neere *Heros* cries, 270
Since the first instant of her broken eies,
Gaue bright *Leucote* voyce, and made her speake,
To ease her anguish, whose swolne breast did breake
With anger at her Goddesse, that did touch
Hero so neere for that she vsde so much. 275
And thrusting her white neck at *Venus*, sayd:
Why may not amorous *Hero* seeme a mayd,
Though she be none, as well as you suppresse
In modest cheekes your inward wantonnesse?
How often haue wee drawne you from aboue, 280
T'exchange with mortals rites for rites in loue?
Why in your preist then call you that offence
That shines in you, and is your influence?
With this the furies stopt *Leucotes* lips,
Enioynd by *Venus*, who with Rosie whips 285
Beate the kind Bird. Fierce lightning from her eyes
Did set on fire faire *Heros* sacrifice,
Which was her torne robe, and inforced hayre;
And the bright flame became a mayd most faire
For her aspect: her tresses were of wire, 290
Knit like a net, where harts all set on fire
Strugled in pants and could not get releast:
Her armes were all with golden pincers drest,
And twentie fashiond knots, pullies, and brakes,
And all her bodie girdled with painted Snakes. 295
Her doune parts in a Scorpions taile combinde,
Freckled with twentie colours; pyed wings shinde
Out of her shoulders; Cloth had neuer die,
Nor sweeter colours neuer viewed eie,
In scorching *Turkie, Cares, Tartarie*, 300
Than shinde about this spirit notorious;
Nor was *Arachnes* web so glorious.
Of lightning and of shreds she was begot;
More hold in base dissemblers is there not.
Her name was *Eronusis*. *Venus* flew 305
From *Heros* sight, and at her Chariot drew
This wondrous creature to so steepe a height,
That all the world she might command with sleight
Of her gay wings: and then she bad her hast,
Since *Hero* had dissembled, and disgrast 310
Her rites so much, and euery breast infect
With her deceits; she made her Architect
Of all dissimulation, and since then
Neuer was any trust in maides nor men.
O it spighted 315
Fayre *Venus* hart to see her most delighted,
And one she chusde for temper of her minde,
To be the only ruler of her kinde,
So soone to let her virgin race be ended;
Not simply for the fault a whit offended, 320

Description and creation of Dissimulation.

But that in strife for chastnes with the Moone,
Spitefull *Diana* bad her shew but one,
That was her seruant vowd, and liu'd a mayd,
And now she thought to answer that vpbrayd,
Hero had lost her answer; who knowes not 325
Venus would seeme as farre from any spot
Of light demeanour, as the very skin
Twixt *Cynthias* browes? Sin is asham'd of Sin.
Vp *Venus* flew, and scarce durst vp for feare
Of *Phœbes* laughter, when she past her Sphere: 330
And so most vgly clowded was the light,
That day was hid in day; night came ere night,
And *Venus* could not through the thick ayre pierce,
Till the daies king, god of vndanted verse,
Because she was so plentifull a theame 335
To such as wore his Lawrell *Anademe*,
Like to a firie bullet made descent,
And from her passage those fat vapours rent,
That being not throughly rarefide to raine,
Melted like pitch as blew as any vaine, 340
And scalding tempests made the earth to shrinke
Vnder their feruor, and the world did thinke
In euery drop a torturing Spirit flew,
It pierst so deeply, and it burnd so blew.
Betwixt all this and *Hero*, *Hero* held 345
Leanders picture as a Persian shield:
And she was free from feare of worst successe;
The more ill threats vs, we suspect the lesse:
As we grow haples, violence subtle growes,
Dumb, deafe, & blind, & comes when no man knowes. 350

The end of the fourth Sestyad.

THE ARGVMENT OF THE FIFT SESTYAD.

Day doubles her accustomd date,
As loth the night, incenst by fate,
Should wrack our louers; Heros *plight,*
Longs for Leander, *and the night:*
Which ere her thirstie wish recouers, 5
She sends for two betrothed louers,
And marries them, that (with their crew,
Their sports and ceremonies due)
She couertly might celebrate
With secret ioy her owne estate. 10
She makes a feast, at which appeares
The wilde Nymph Teras, *that still beares*
An Iuory Lute, tels Omenous tales,
And sings at solemne festiuales.

Now was bright *Hero* weary of the day,
Thought an Olympiad in *Leanders* stay.
Sol, and the soft-foote *Howrs* hung on his armes,
And would not let him swim, foreseeing his harmes:
That day *Aurora* double grace obtainde 5
Of her loue *Phœbus*; she his Horses rainde,
Set on his golden knee, and as she list
She puld him back; and as she puld, she kist
To haue him turne to bed; he lou'd her more,
To see the loue *Leander Hero* bore. 10
Examples profit much; ten times in one,
In persons full of note, good deedes are done.
Day was so long, men walking fell asleepe,
The heauie humors that their eyes did steepe,
Made them feare mischiefs. The hard streets were beds 15
For couetous churles, and for ambitious heads,
That spight of Nature would their busines plie.
All thought they had the falling *Epilepsie*,
Men groueld so vpon the smotherd ground,
And pittie did the hart of heauen confound. 20
The Gods, the Graces, and the Muses came
Downe to the Destinies, to stay the frame
Of the true louers deaths, and all worlds teares:
But death before had stopt their cruell eares.
All the Celestials parted mourning then, 25
Pierst with our humane miseries more then men.
Ah, nothing doth the world with mischiefe fill,
But want of feeling one anothers ill.
With their descent the day grew something fayre,
And cast a brighter robe vpon the ayre. 30

Hero to shorten time with merriment,
For yong *Alcmane*, and bright *Mya* sent,
Two louers that had long crau'd mariage dues
At *Heros* hands: but she did still refuse,
For louely *Mya* was her consort vowd 35
In her maids state, and therefore not allowd
To amorous Nuptials: yet faire *Hero* now
Intended to dispence with her cold vow,
Since hers was broken, and to marrie her:
The rites would pleasing matter minister 40
To her conceits, and shorten tedious day.
They came; sweet Musick vsherd th'odorous way,
And wanton Ayre in twentie sweet forms danst
After her fingers; Beautie and Loue aduanst
Their ensignes in the downles rosie faces 45
Of youths and maids, led after by the Graces.
For all these *Hero* made a friendly feast,
Welcomd them kindly, did much loue protest,
Winning their harts with all the meanes she might,
That when her fault should chance t'abide the light, 50
Their loues might couer or extenuate it,
And high in her worst fate make pittie sit.
  She married them, and in the banquet came
Borne by the virgins: *Hero* striu'd to frame
Her thoughts to mirth. Aye me, but hard it is 55
To imitate a false and forced blis.
Ill may a sad minde forge a merrie face,
Nor hath constrained laughter any grace.
Then layd she wine on cares to make them sinke;
Who feares the threats of fortune, let him drinke. 60
  To these quick Nuptials entred suddenly
Admired *Teras* with the Ebon Thye,
A Nymph that haunted the greene *Sestyan* groues,
And would consort soft virgins in their loues,
At gaysome Triumphs, and on solemne dayes, 65
Singing prophetike Elegies and Layes:
And fingring of a siluer Lute she tide
With black and purple skarfs by her left side.
Apollo gaue it, and her skill withall,
And she was term'd his Dwarfe she was so small. 70
Yet great in vertue, for his beames enclosde
His vertues in her: neuer was proposde
Riddle to her, or Augurie, strange or new,
But she resolu'd it: neuer sleight tale flew
From her charmd lips without important sence, 75
Shewne in some graue succeeding consequence.
  This little Siluane with her songs and tales
Gaue such estate to feasts and Nuptiales,
That though oft times she forewent Tragedies,
Yet for her strangenes still she pleasde their eyes, 80

And for her smalnes they admir'd her so,
They thought her perfect borne and could not grow
All eyes were on her: *Hero* did command
An Altar deckt with sacred state should stand,
At the Feasts vpper end close by the Bride, 85
On which the pretie Nymph might sit espide.
Then all were silent; euery one so heares,
As all their sences climbd into their eares:
And first this amorous tale that fitted well
Fayre *Hero* and the Nuptials she did tell: 90

The tale of Teras.

Hymen that now is god of Nuptiall rites,
And crownes with honor loue and his delights,
Of *Athens* was a youth so sweet of face,
That many thought him of the femall race:
Such quickning brightnes did his cleere eyes dart, 95
Warme went their beames to his beholders hart.
In such pure leagues his beauties were combinde,
That there your Nuptiall contracts first were signde.
For as proportion, white and crimsine, meet
In Beauties mixture, all right cleere, and sweet; 100
The eye responsible, the golden haire,
And none is held without the other faire:
All spring together, all together fade;
Such intermixt affections should inuade
Two perfect louers: which being yet vnseene, 105
Their vertues and their comforts copied beene,
In Beauties concord, subiect to the eie;
And that, in *Hymen*, pleasde so matchleslie,
That louers were esteemde in their full grace,
Like forme and colour mixt in *Hymens* face; 110
And such sweete concord was thought worthie then
Of torches, musick, feasts, and greatest men:
So *Hymen* lookt, that euen the chastest minde
He mou'd to ioyne in ioyes of sacred kinde:
For onely now his chins first doune consorted 115
His heads rich fleece, in golden curles contorted;
And as he was so lou'd, he lou'd so too,
So should best bewties, bound by Nuptialls doo.
Bright *Eucharis*, who was by all men saide
The noblest, fayrest, and the richest maide 120
Of all th' *Athenian* damzels, *Hymen* lou'd
With such transmission, that his heart remou'd
From his white brest to hers, but her estate
In passing his was so interminate
For wealth and honor, that his loue durst feede 125
On nought but sight and hearing, nor could breede
Hope of requitall, the grand prise of loue;
Nor could he heare or see but he must proue

How his rare bewties musick would agree
With maids in consort: therefore robbed he 130
His chin of those same few first fruits it bore,
And clad in such attire as Virgins wore,
He kept them companie, and might right well,
For he did all but *Eucharis* excell
In all the fayre of Beautie: yet he wanted 135
Vertue to make his owne desires implanted
In his deare *Eucharis*; for women neuer
Loue beautie in their sex, but enuie euer.
His iudgement yet (that durst not suite addresse,
Nor past due meanes presume of due successe) 140
Reason gat fortune in the end to speede
To his best praye⟨r⟩s: but strange it seemd indeede,
That fortune should a chast affection blesse,
Preferment seldome graceth bashfulnesse.
Nor grast it *Hymen* yet; but many a dart 145
And many an amorous thought enthrald his hart,
Ere he obtaind her; and he sick became,
Forst to abstaine her sight, and then the flame
Rag'd in his bosome. O what griefe did fill him:
Sight made him sick, and want of sight did kill him. 150
The virgins wondred where *Diætia* stayd,
For so did *Hymen* terme himselfe a mayd.
At length with sickly lookes he greeted them:
Tis strange to see gainst what an extreame streame
A louer striues; poore *Hymen* lookt so ill, 155
That as in merit he increased still,
By suffring much, so he in grace decreast.
Women are most wonne when men merit least:
If merit looke not well, loue bids stand by,
Loues speciall lesson is to please the eye. 160
And *Hymen* soone recouering all he lost,
Deceiuing still these maids, but himselfe most.
His loue and he with many virgin dames,
Noble by birth, noble by beauties flames,
Leauing the towne with songs and hallowed lights, 165
To doe great *Ceres Eleusina* rites
Of zealous Sacrifice, were made a pray
To barbarous Rouers that in ambush lay,
And with rude hands enforst their shining spoyle,
Farre from the darkned Citie, tir'd with toyle. 170
And when the yellow issue of the skie
Came trouping forth, ielous of crueltie
To their bright fellowes of this vnder heauen,
Into a double night they saw them driuen,
A horride Caue, the theeues black mansion, 175
Where wearie of the iourney they had gon,
Their last nights watch, and drunke with their sweete gains,
Dull *Morpheus* entred, laden with silken chains,

142 prayers *Dyce etc.*

Stronger then iron, and bound the swelling vaines
And tyred sences of these lawles Swaines. 180
But when the virgin lights thus dimly burnd;
O what a hell was heauen in! how they mournd
And wrung their hands, and wound their gentle forms
Into the shapes of sorrow! Golden storms
Fell from their eyes: As when the Sunne appeares, 185
And yet it raines, so shewd their eyes their teares.
And as when funerall dames watch a dead corse,
Weeping about it, telling with remorse
What paines he felt, how long in paine he lay,
How little food he eate, what he would say; 190
And then mixe mournfull tales of others deaths,
Smothering themselues in clowds of their owne breaths;
At length, one cheering other, call for wine,
The golden boale drinks teares out of their eine,
As they drinke wine from it; and round it goes, 195
Each helping other to relieue their woes:
So cast these virgins beauties mutuall raies,
One lights another, face the face displaies;
Lips by reflexion kist, and hands hands shooke,
Euen by the whitenes each of other tooke. 200
But *Hymen* now vsde friendly *Morpheus* aide,
Slew euery theefe, and rescude euery maide.
And now did his enamourd passion take
Hart from his hartie deede, whose worth did make
His hope of bounteous *Eucharis* more strong; 205
And now came *Loue* with *Proteus*, who had long
Inggl'd the little god with prayers and gifts,
Ran through all shapes, and varied all his shifts,
To win *Loues* stay with him, and make him loue him:
And when he saw no strength of sleight could moue him 210
To make him loue, or stay, he nimbly turnd
Into *Loues* selfe, he so extreamely burnd.
And thus came *Loue* with *Proteus* and his powre,
T'encounter *Eucharis*: first like the flowre
That *Iunos* milke did spring, the siluer Lillie, 215
He fell on *Hymens* hand, who straight did spie
The bounteous Godhead, and with wondrous ioy
Offred it *Eucharis*. She wondrous coy
Drew back her hand: the subtle flowre did woo it,
And drawing it neere, mixt so you could not know it. 220
As two cleere Tapers mixe in one their light,
So did the Lillie and the hand their white:
She viewd it, and her view the forme bestowes
Amongst her spirits: for as colour flowes
From superficies of each thing we see, 225
Euen so with colours formes emitted bee:
And where Loues forme is, loue is, loue is forme;
He entred at the eye, his sacred storme

Rose from the hand, loues sweetest instrument :
It stird her bloods sea so, that high it went, 230
And beate in bashfull waues gainst the white shore
Of her diuided cheekes ; it rag'd the more,
Because the tide went gainst the haughtie winde
Of her estate and birth : And as we finde
In fainting ebs, the flowrie Zephire hurles 235
The greene-hayrd *Hellespont*, broke in siluer curles,
Gainst *Heros* towre : but in his blasts retreate,
The waues obeying him, they after beate,
Leauing the chalkie shore a great way pale,
Then moyst it freshly with another gale : 240
So ebd and flowde the blood in *Eucharis* face,
Coynesse and Loue striu'd which had greatest grace.
Virginitie did fight on Coynesse side ;
Feare of her parents frownes, and femall pride,
Lothing the lower place more then it loues 245
The high contents desert and vertue moues.
With loue fought *Hymens* beautie and his valure,
Which scarce could so much fauour yet allure
To come to strike, but fameles idle stood,
Action is firie valours soueraigne good. 250
But Loue once entred, wisht no greater ayde
Then he could find within ; thought thought betrayd,
The bribde, but incorrupted Garrison
Sung *Io Hymen* ; there those songs begun,
And Loue was growne so rich with such a gaine, 255
And wanton with the ease of his free raigne,
That he would turne into her roughest frownes
To turne them out ; and thus he *Hymen* crownes
King of his thoughts, mans greatest Emperie :
This was his first braue step to deitie. 260
Home to the mourning cittie they repayre,
With newes as holesome as the morning ayre
To the sad parents of each saued maid :
But *Hymen* and his *Eucharis* had laid
This plat, to make the flame of their delight 265
Round as the Moone at full, and full as bright.
Because the parents of chast *Eucharis*
Exceeding *Hymens* so, might crosse their blis ;
And as the world rewards deserts, that law
Cannot assist with force : so when they saw 270
Their daughter safe, take vantage of their owne,
Praise *Hymens* valour much, nothing bestowne :
Hymen must leaue the virgins in a Groue
Farre off from *Athens*, and go first to proue
If to restore them all with fame and life, 275
He should enioy his dearest as his wife.
This told to all the maids, the most agree :
The riper sort knowing what t'is to bee

The first mouth of a newes so farre deriu'd,
And that to heare and beare newes braue folks liu'd, 280
As being a carriage speciall hard to beare
Occurrents, these occurrents being so deare,
They did with grace protest, they were content
T'accost their friends with all their complement
For *Hymens* good: but to incurre their harme, 285
There he must pardon them. This wit went warme
To *Adoleshes* braine, a Nymph borne hie,
Made all of voyce and fire, that vpwards flie:
Her hart and all her forces nether traine
Climbd to her tongue, and thither fell her braine, 290
Since it could goe no higher, and it must go:
All powers she had, euen her tongue, did so.
In spirit and quicknes she much ioy did take,
And lou'd her tongue, only for quicknes sake,
And she would hast and tell. The rest all stay, 295
Hymen goes on⟨e⟩, the Nymph another way:
And what became of her Ile tell at last:
Yet take her visage now: moyst lipt, long fa'st,
Thin like an iron wedge, so sharpe and tart,
As twere of purpose made to cleaue *Loues* hart. 300
Well were this louely Beautie rid of her,
And *Hymen* did at *Athens* now prefer
His welcome suite, which he with ioy aspirde:
A hundred princely youths with him retirde
To fetch the Nymphs: Chariots and Musick went, 305
And home they came: heauen with applauses rent.
The Nuptials straight proceed, whiles all the towne
Fresh in their ioyes might doe them most renowne.
First gold-lockt *Hymen* did to Church repaire,
Like a quick offring burnd in flames of haire. 310
And after, with a virgin firmament,
The Godhead-prouing Bride attended went
Before them all; she lookt in her command,
As if forme-giuing *Cyprias* siluer hand
Gripte all their beauties, and crusht out one flame, 315
She blusht to see how beautie ouercame
The thoughts of all men. Next before her went
Fiue louely children deckt with ornament
Of her sweet colours, bearing Torches by,
For light was held a happie Augurie 320
Of generation, whose efficient right
Is nothing else but to produce to light.
The od disparent number they did chuse,
To shew the vnion married loues should vse,
Since in two equall parts it will not seuer. 325
But the midst holds one to reioyne it euer,
As common to both parts: men therfore deeme,
That equall number Gods doe not esteeme,

289 nether] neither *1598*[2]

Being authors of sweet peace and vnitie,
But pleasing to th'infernall Emperie, 330
Vnder whose ensignes Wars and Discords fight,
Since an euen number you may disunite
In two parts equall, nought in middle left,
To reunite each part from other reft:
And fiue they hold in most especiall prise, 335
Since t'is the first od number that doth rise
From the two formost numbers vnitie
That od and euen are; which are two, and three,
For one no number is: but thence doth flow
The powerfull race of number. Next did go 340
A noble Matron that did spinning beare
A huswifes rock and spindle, and did weare
A Weathers skin, with all the snowy fleece,
To intimate that euen the daintiest peece,
And noblest borne dame should industrious bee: 345
That which does good disgraceth no degree.
  And now to *Iunos* Temple they are come,
Where her graue Priest stood in the mariage rome.
On his right arme did hang a skarlet vaile,
And from his shoulders to the ground did traile. 350
On either side, Ribands of white and blew;
With the red vaile he hid the bashfull hew
Of the chast Bride, to shew the modest shame,
In coupling with a man should grace a dame.
Then tooke he the disparent Silks, and tide 355
The Louers by the wasts, and side to side,
In token that thereafter they must binde
In one selfe sacred knot each others minde.
Before them on an Altar he presented
Both fire and water: which was first inuented, 360
Since to ingenerate euery humane creature,
And euery other birth produ'st by Nature,
Moysture and heate must mixe: so man and wife
For humane race must ioyne in Nuptiall life.
Then one of *Iunos* Birds, the painted Iay, 365
He sacrifisde, and tooke the gall away.
All which he did behinde the Altar throw,
In signe no bitternes of hate should grow
Twixt maried loues, nor any least disdaine.
Nothing they spake, for twas esteemd too plaine 370
For the most silken mildnes of a maid,
To let a publique audience heare it said
She boldly tooke the man: and so respected
Was bashfulnes in *Athens*: it erected
To chast *Agneia*, which is Shamefastnesse, 375
A sacred Temple, holding her a Goddesse.
And now to Feasts, Masks, and triumphant showes,
The shining troupes returnd, euen till earths throwes

Brought forth with ioy the thickest part of night,
When the sweet Nuptiall song that vsde to cite 380
All to their rest, was by *Phemonoe* sung,
First *Delphian* Prophetesse, whose graces sprung
Out of the *Muses* well: she sung before
The Bride into her chamber: at which dore
A Matron and a Torch-bearer did stand; 385
A painted box of Confits in her hand
The Matron held, and so did other some
That compast round the honourd Nuptiall rome.
The custome was that euery maid did weare,
During her maidenhead, a silken Sphere 390
About her waste, aboue her inmost weede,
Knit with *Mineruas* knot, and that was freede
By the faire Bridegrome on the mariage night,
With many ceremonies of delight:
And yet eternisde *Hymens* tender Bride, 395
To suffer it dissolu'd so sweetly cride.
The maids that heard so lou'd, and did adore her,
They wisht with all their hearts to suffer for her.
So had the Matrons, that with Confits stood
About the chamber, such affectionate blood, 400
And so true feeling of her harmeles paines,
That euery one a showre of Confits raines.
For which the Brideyouths scrambling on the ground,
In noyse of that sweet haile her cryes were drownd.
And thus blest *Hymen* ioyde his gracious Bride, 405
And for his ioy was after deifide.

The Saffron mirror by which *Phœbus* loue,
Greene *Tellus* decks her, now he held aboue
The clowdy mountaines: and the noble maide,
Sharp-visag'd *Adolesche*, that was straide 410
Out of her way, in hasting with her newes,
Not till this houre th' *Athenian* turrets viewes,
And now brought home by guides, she heard by all
That her long kept occurrents would be stale,
And how faire *Hymens* honors did excell 415
For those rare newes, which she came short to tell.
To heare her deare tongue robd of such a ioy
Made the well-spoken Nymph take such a toy,
That downe she sunke: when lightning from aboue
Shrunk her leane body, and for meere free loue, 420
Turnd her into the pied-plum'd *Psittacus*,
That now the Parrat is surnam'd by vs,
Who still with counterfeit confusion prates
Nought but newes common to the commonst mates.
This tolde, strange *Teras* toucht her Lute and sung 425
This dittie, that the Torchie euening sprung.

404 her *Dyce etc.*: their *Qq* 412 this *1598*[2], *Dyce etc.*: his *1600–37*

Epithalamion Teratos.

Come, come deare night, Loues Mart of kisses,
Sweet close of his ambitious line,
The fruitfull summer of his blisses,
Loues glorie doth in darknes shine. 430
O come soft rest of Cares, come night,
Come naked vertues only tire,
The reaped haruest of the light,
Bound vp in sheaues of sacred fire.
Loue cals to warre, 435
Sighs his Alarmes,
Lips his swords are,
The field his Armes.
Come Night and lay thy veluet hand
On glorious Dayes outfacing face; 440
And all thy crouned flames command
For Torches to our Nuptiall grace.
Loue cals to warre,
Sighs his Alarmes,
Lips his swords are, 445
The field his Armes.
No neede haue we of factious Day,
To cast in enuie of thy peace
Her bals of Discord in thy way:
Here beauties day doth neuer cease, 450
Day is abstracted here,
And varied in a triple sphere.
Hero, Alcmane, Mya so outshine thee,
Ere thou come here let *Thetis* thrice refine thee.
Loue cals to warre, 455
Sighs his Alarmes,
Lips his swords are,
The field his Armes.
The Euening starre I see:
Rise youths, the Euening starre 460
Helps Loue to summon warre,
Both now imbracing bee.
Rise youths, loues right claims more then banquets, rise.
Now the bright Marygolds that deck the skies,
Phœbus celestiall flowrs, that (contrarie 465
To his flowers here) ope when he shuts his eie,
And shuts when he doth open, crowne your sports:
Now loue in night, and night in loue exhorts
Courtship and Dances: All your parts employ,
And suite nights rich expansure with your ioy, 470
Loue paints his longings in sweet virgins eyes:
Rise youths, loues right claims more then banquets, rise.
Rise virgins, let fayre Nuptiall loues enfolde
Your fruitles breasts: the maidenheads ye holde

Are not your owne alone, but parted are ; 475
Part in disposing them your Parents share,
And that a third part is : so must ye saue
Your loues a third, and you your thirds must haue.
Loue paints his longings in sweet virgins eyes :
Rise youths, loues right claims more then banquets, rise.

Herewith the amorous spirit that was so kinde 481
To *Teras* haire, and combd it downe with winde,
Still as it Comet-like brake from her braine,
Would needes haue *Teras* gone, and did refraine
To blow it downe : which staring vp, dismaid 485
The timorous feast, and she no longer staid :
But bowing to the Bridegrome and the Bride,
Did like a shooting exhalation glide
Out of their sights : the turning of her back
Made them all shrieke, it lookt so ghastly black. 490
O haples *Hero*, that most haples clowde
Thy soone-succeeding Tragedie foreshowde.
Thus all the Nuptiall crew to ioyes depart,
But much-wrongd *Hero* stood Hels blackest dart :
Whose wound because I grieue so to display, 495
I vse digressions thus t'encrease the day.

The end of the fift Sestyad.

THE ARGVMENT OF THE SIXT SESTYAD.

Leucote *flyes to all the windes,*
And from the fates their outrage bindes,
That Hero *and her loue may meete.*
Leander (*with* Loues *compleate Fleete*
Mand in himselfe) *puts forth to Seas,* 5
When straight the ruthles Destinies
With Ate *stirre the windes to warre*
Vpon the Hellespont : *Their iarre*
Drownes poore Leander. Heros *eyes,*
Wet witnesses of his surprise, 10
Her Torch blowne out, Griefe casts her downe
Vpon her loue, and both doth drowne.
In whose iust ruth the God of Seas
Transformes them to th' Acanthides.

No longer could the day nor Destinies
Delay the night, who now did frowning rise
Into her Throne ; and at her humorous brests
Visions and Dreames lay sucking : all mens rests

Fell like the mists of death vpon their eyes, 5
Dayes too long darts so kild their faculties.
The windes yet, like the flowrs to cease began:
For bright *Leucote*, *Venus* whitest Swan,
That held sweet *Hero* deare, spread her fayre wings,
Like to a field of snow, and message brings 10
From *Venus* to the Fates, t'entreate them lay
Their charge vpon the windes their rage to stay,
That the sterne battaile of the Seas might cease,
And guard *Leander* to his loue in peace.
The Fates consent, (aye me dissembling Fates) 15
They shewd their fauours to conceale their hates,
And draw *Leander* on, least Seas too hie
Should stay his too obsequious destinie:
Who like a fleering slauish Parasite,
In warping profit or a traiterous sleight, 20
Hoopes round his rotten bodie with deuotes,
And pricks his descant face full of false notes,
Praysing with open throte (and othes as fowle
As his false heart) the beautie of an Owle,
Kissing his skipping hand with charmed skips, 25
That cannot leaue, but leapes vpon his lips
Like a cock-sparrow, or a shameles queane
Sharpe at a red-lipt youth, and nought doth meane
Of all his antick shewes, but doth repayre
More tender fawnes, and takes a scattred hayre 30
From his tame subiects shoulder; whips, and cals
For euery thing he lacks; creepes gainst the wals
With backward humblesse, to giue needles way:
Thus his false fate did with *Leander* play.
First to black *Eurus* flies the white *Leucote*, 35
Borne mongst the *Negros* in the *Leuant* Sea,
On whose curld head the glowing Sun doth rise,
And shewes the soueraigne will of Destinies,
To haue him cease his blasts, and downe he lies.
Next, to the fennie *Notus* course she holds, 40
And found him leaning with his armes in folds
Vpon a rock, his white hayre full of showres,
And him she chargeth by the fatall powres,
To hold in his wet cheekes his clowdie voyce.
To *Zephire* then that doth in flowres reioyce. 45
To snake-foote *Boreas* next she did remoue,
And found him tossing of his rauisht loue,
To heate his frostie bosome hid in snow,
Who with *Leucotes* sight did cease to blow.
Thus all were still to *Heros* harts desire, 50
Who with all speede did consecrate a fire
Of flaming Gummes, and comfortable Spice,
To light her Torch, which in such curious price
She held, being obiect to *Leanders* sight,
That nought but fires perfum'd must giue it light. 55

She lou'd it so, she grieu'd to see it burne,
Since it would waste and soone to ashes turne:
Yet if it burnd not, twere not worth her eyes,
What made it nothing, gaue it all the prize.
Sweet Torch, true Glasse of our societie; 60
What man does good, but he consumes thereby?
But thou wert lou'd for good, held high, giuen show:
Poore vertue loth'd for good, obscur'd, held low.
Doe good, be pinde; be deedles good, disgrast:
Vnles we feede on men, we let them fast. 65
Yet *Hero* with these thoughts her Torch did spend.
When Bees makes waxe, Nature doth not intend
It shall be made a Torch: but we that know
The proper vertue of it make it so,
And when t'is made we light it: nor did Nature 70
Propose one life to maids, but each such creature
Makes by her soule the best of her free state,
Which without loue is rude, disconsolate,
And wants loues fire to make it milde and bright,
Till when, maids are but Torches wanting light. 75
Thus gainst our griefe, not cause of griefe we fight,
The right of nought is gleande, but the delight.
Vp went she, but to tell how she descended,
Would God she were not dead, or my verse ended.
She was the rule of wishes, summe and end 80
For all the parts that did on loue depend:
Yet cast the Torch his brightnes further forth;
But what shines neerest best, holds truest worth.
Leander did not through such tempests swim
To kisse the Torch, although it lighted him: 85
But all his powres in her desires awaked,
Her loue and vertues cloth'd him richly naked.
Men kisse but fire that only shewes pursue,
Her Torch and *Hero*, figure shew and vertue.
Now at opposde *Abydus* nought was heard, 90
But bleating flocks, and many a bellowing herd,
Slaine for the Nuptials, cracks of falling woods,
Blowes of broad axes, powrings out of floods.
The guiltie *Hellespont* was mixt and stainde
With bloodie Torrents, that the shambles raind; 95
Not arguments of feast, but shewes that bled,
Foretelling that red night that followed.
More blood was spilt, more honors were addrest,
Then could haue graced any happie feast.
Rich banquets, triumphs, euery pomp employes 100
His sumptuous hand: no misers nuptiall ioyes.
Ayre felt continuall thunder with the noyse,
Made in the generall mariage violence:
And no man knew the cause of this expence,
But the two haples Lords, *Leanders* Sire, 105

And poore *Leander*, poorest where the fire
Of credulous loue made him most rich surmisde.
As short was he of that himselfe he prisde,
As is an emptie Gallant full of forme,
That thinks each looke an act, each drop a storme, 110
That fals from his braue breathings; most brought vp
In our *Metropolis*, and hath his cup
Brought after him to feasts; and much Palme beares,
For his rare iudgement in th'attire he weares,
Hath seene the hot Low Countries, not their heat, 115
Obserues their rampires and their buildings yet.
And for your sweet discourse with mouthes is heard,
Giuing instructions with his very beard.
Hath gone with an Ambassadour, and been
A great mans mate in trauailing, euen to *Rhene*, 120
And then puts all his worth in such a face,
As he saw braue men make, and striues for grace
To get his newes forth; as when you descrie
A ship with all her sayle contends to flie
Out of the narrow Thames with windes vnapt, 125
Now crosseth here, then there, then this way rapt,
And then hath one point reacht; then alters all,
And to another crooked reach doth fall
Of halfe a burdbolts shoote; keeping more coyle,
Then if she danst vpon the Oceans toyle: 130
So serious is his trifling companie,
In all his swelling ship of vacantrie.
And so short of himselfe in his high thought.
Was our *Leander* in his fortunes brought
And in his fort of loue that he thought won, 135
But otherwise he skornes comparison.
O sweet *Leander*, thy large worth I hide
In a short graue; ill fauourd stormes must chide
Thy sacred fauour; I in floods of inck
Must drowne thy graces, which white papers drink, 140
Euen as thy beauties did the foule black Seas:
I must describe the hell of thy disease,
That heauen did merit: yet I needes must see
Our painted fooles and cockhorse Pessantrie
Still still vsurp, with long liues, loues, and lust, 145
The seates of vertue, cutting short as dust
Her deare bought issue; ill to worse conuerts,
And tramples in the blood of all deserts.
Night close and silent now goes fast before
The Captaines and their souldiers to the shore, 150
On whom attended the appointed Fleete
At *Sestus* Bay, that should *Leander* meete,
Who fainde he in another ship would passe:
Which must not be, for no one meane there was
To get his loue home, but the course he tooke. 155
Forth did his beautie for his beautie looke,

And saw her through her Torch, as you beholde
Sometimes within the Sunne a face of golde,
Form'd in strong thoughts, by that traditions force,
That saies a God sits there and guides his course. 160
His sister was with him, to whom he shewd
His guide by Sea: and sayd: Oft haue you viewd
In one heauen many starres, but neuer yet
In one starre many heauens till now were met.
See louely sister, see, now *Hero* shines 165
No heauen but her appeares: each star repines,
And all are clad in clowdes, as if they mournd,
To be by influence of Earth out-burnd.
Yet doth she shine, and teacheth vertues traine,
Still to be constant in Hels blackest raigne, 170
Though euen the gods themselues do so entreat them
As they did hate, and Earth as she would eate them.
Off went his silken robe, and in he leapt;
Whom the kinde waues so licorously cleapt,
Thickning for haste one in another so, 175
To kisse his skin, that he might almost go
To *Heros* Towre, had that kind minuit lasted.
But now the cruell fates with *Ate* hasted
To all the windes, and made them battaile fight
Vpon the *Hellespont*, for eithers right 180
Pretended to the windie monarchie.
And forth they brake, the Seas mixt with the skie,
And tost distrest *Leander*, being in hell,
As high as heauen; Blisse not in height doth dwell.
The Destinies sate dancing on the waues, 185
To see the glorious windes with mutuall braues
Consume each other: O true glasse to see,
How ruinous ambitious Statists bee
To their owne glories! Poore *Leander* cried
For help to Sea-borne *Venus*; she denied: 190
To *Boreas*, that for his *Atthæas* sake,
He would some pittie on his *Hero* take,
And for his owne loues sake, on his desires:
But Glorie neuer blowes cold Pitties fires.
Then calde he *Neptune*, who through all the noise 195
Knew with affright his wrackt *Leanders* voice:
And vp he rose, for haste his forehead hit
Gainst heauens hard Christall; his proud waues he smit
With his forkt scepter, that could not obay,
Much greater powers then *Neptunes* gaue them sway. 200
They lou'd *Leander* so, in groanes they brake
When they came neere him; and such space did take
Twixt one another, loth to issue on,
That in their shallow furrowes earth was shone,
And the poore louer tooke a little breath: 205
But the curst Fates sate spinning of his death

On euery waue, and with the seruile windes
Tumbled them on him: And now *Hero* findes
By that she felt her deare *Leanders* state.
She wept and prayed for him to euery fate, 210
And euery winde that whipt her with her haire
About the face she kist and spake it faire,
Kneeld to it, gaue it drinke out of her eyes
To quench his thirst: but still their cruelties
Euen her poore Torch enuied, and rudely beate 215
The bating flame from that deare foode it eate:
Deare, for it nourisht her *Leanders* life,
Which with her robe she rescude from their strife:
But silke too soft was, such hard hearts to breake,
And she deare soule, euen as her silke, faint, weake 220
Could not preserue it: out, O out it went.
Leander still cald *Neptune*, that now rent
His brackish curles, and tore his wrinckled face
Where teares in billowes did each other chace,
And (burst with ruth) he hurld his marble Mace 225
At the sterne Fates: it wounded *Lachesis*
That drew *Leanders* thread, and could not misse
The thread it selfe, as it her hand did hit,
But smote it full and quite did sunder it.
The more kinde *Neptune* rag'd, the more he raste 230
His loues liues fort, and kild as he embraste.
Anger doth still his owne mishap encrease;
If any comfort liue, it is in peace.
O theeuish Fates, to let Blood, Flesh, and Sence
Build two fayre Temples for their Excellence, 235
To rob it with a poysoned influence.
Though soules gifts starue, the bodies are held dear
In vgliest things; Sence-sport preserues a Beare.
But here nought serues our turnes; O heauen & earth,
How most most wretched is our humane birth? 240
And now did all the tyrannous crew depart,
Knowing there was a storme in *Heros* hart,
Greater then they could make, & skornd their smart.
She bowd her selfe so low out of her Towre,
That wonder twas she fell not ere her howre, 245
With searching the lamenting waues for him;
Like a poore Snayle, her gentle supple lim
Hung on her Turrets top so most downe right,
As she would diue beneath the darknes quite,
To finde her Iewell; Iewell, her *Leander*, 250
A name of all earths Iewels pleasde not her,
Like his deare name: *Leander*, still my choice,
Come nought but my *Leander*; O my voice
Turne to *Leander*: hence-forth be all sounds,
Accents, and phrases that shew all griefes wounds, 255
Analisde in *Leander*. O black change!
Trumpets doe you with thunder of your clange,

Driue out this changes horror, my voyce faints:
Where all ioy was, now shrieke out all complaints.
Thus cryed she, for her mixed soule could tell 260
Her loue was dead: And when the morning fell
Prostrate vpon the weeping earth for woe,
Blushes that bled out of her cheekes did show
Leander brought by *Neptune*, brusde and torne
With Citties ruines he to Rocks had worne, 265
To filthie vsering Rocks that would haue blood,
Though they could get of him no other good.
She saw him, and the sight was much much more,
Then might haue seru'd to kill her; should her store
Of giant sorrowes speake? Burst, dye, bleede, 270
And leaue poore plaints to vs that shall succeede.
She fell on her loues bosome, hugg'd it fast,
And with *Leanders* name she breath'd her last.
Neptune for pittie in his armes did take them,
Flung them into the ayre, and did awake them. 275
Like two sweet birds surnam'd th' *Acanthides*,
Which we call Thistle-warps, that neere no Seas
Dare euer come, but still in couples flie,
And feede on Thistle tops, to testifie
The hardnes of their first life in their last: 280
The first in thornes of loue, and sorrowes past,
And so most beautifull their colours show,
As none (so little) like them: her sad brow
A sable veluet feather couers quite,
Euen like the forehead cloths that in the night, 285
Or when they sorrow, Ladies vse to weare:
Their wings blew, red and yellow mixt appeare,
Colours, that as we construe colours paint
Their states to life; the yellow shewes their saint,
The deuill *Venus*, left them; blew their truth, 290
The red and black, ensignes of death and ruth.
And this true honor from their loue-deaths sprung,
They were the first that euer Poet sung.

FINIS.

LYRIC POEMS

APART from the translation of Ovid's Elegies, the only lyric poems which can reasonably be attributed to Marlowe are the two here printed. It is not unlikely that others may have perished or may still exist in some of the anonymous miscellanies of the Elizabethan age.

The famous song of 'The passionate Shepherd to his love' has come down to us in four different versions, none of which seems to be entirely accurate. I follow that given in the popular anthology, *England's Helicon* (1600),[1] but print, of course, all the variant readings in the notes. The text of the recently discovered Thornborough Commonplace Book (MS.) is very interesting and probably corrects the printed versions in one or two particulars, though it was almost certainly written down from memory. There is no evidence for the date of this poem, except that it would seem to be older than the parody of it in *The Jew of Malta*.[2]

The fragment printed on page 552 occurs on p. 480 f. of *England's Parnassus*. Nothing further is known of it. Mr. Charles Crawford[3] has evolved the theory that Marlowe wrote a long poem in imitation of 'Come live with me', of which this fragment is the only extant portion, and that the poem so written was later drawn upon for descriptive material in *Dido* and other plays. The fragment begins one of the divisions in which the editor of *England's Parnassus* (1600) groups his selections, and the heading 'Description of Seas, Waters, Riuers, &c.' refers naturally to the entire group and not to the individual poem.

[1] Signatures ⟨A a 1^{v}⟩ and A a 2. [2] Cf. p. 289, *l.* 1816.
[3] Cf. *Collectanea*, First Series, 1906, pp. 1–16.

The passionate Sheepheard to his loue.

Come liue with mee, and be my loue,
And we will all the pleasures proue,
That Vallies, groues, hills and fieldes,
Woods, or steepie mountaine yeeldes.

And wee will sit vpon the Rocks,
Seeing the Sheepheards feede theyr flocks
By shallow Riuers, to whose falls
Melodious byrds sings Madrigalls. 5

And I will make thee beds of Roses,
And a thousand fragrant poesies, 10
A cap of flowers, and a kirtle,
Imbroydred all with leaues of Mirtle.

A gowne made of the finest wooll,
Which from our pretty Lambes we pull,
Fayre lined slippers for the cold, 15
With buckles of the purest gold.

A belt of straw and Iuie buds,
With Corall clasps and Amber studs,
And if these pleasures may thee moue,
Come liue with mee, and be my loue. 20

The Sheepheards Swaines shall daunce & sing
For thy delight each May-morning.
If these delights thy minde may moue,
Then liue with mee, and be my loue.

FINIS.

Chr. Marlow.

Title The passionate Sheepheard to his loue *E.H.* : *om. P.P., MS.* : The Milk maids Song *C.A.* 1 Come *om. P.P.* 3 Vallies, groues] hilles and vallies *P.P.* : hills and *E.H.* : dales and *P.P.* : or hils, or *C.A.* : and woodes or *MS.* 4 Woods, or steepie *E.H.* : And all the craggy *P.P.* : and craggie Rockes or *MS.* : mountains *P.P., C.A., MS.* yeeld *P.P.* 5 And *E.H.* : There *P.P.* : Where *C.A., MS.* 6 Seeing] And see *P.P., C.A., MS.* theyr] our *C.A.* 7 to] by *P.P.* 8 sing *P.P., C.A.* 9 And I will] There will I *P.P.* : Where wee *MS.* beds] a bed *P.P., MS.* 10 And *E.H.* : With *P.P.* : And then *C.A.* a thousand] thowsande other *MS.* 13–16 *om. P.P.* : *follows l. 20 MS.* 14 pretty] little *MS.* 15 Fayre lined slippers *E.H.* : Slippers lin'd choicely *C.A.* 17 and] with *MS.* 19 And . . thee] if theise delightes thy mynde may *MS.* 20 Come] Then *P.P., MS.* *Before l. 21 MS. add. the stanza* : Thy dyshes shal be filde with meate | such as the gods doe use to eate | shall one and everye table bee | preparde eache daye for thee and mee 21–24 *om. P.P.* 21 shepparde *MS.* 22 May] faire *MS.* Finis *and signature om.* *P.P., C.A., MS.*

⟨*E.H.* = Version of the poem in *England's Helicon*, 1600.
P.P. = Version of the poem in *The Passionate Pilgrim*, 1599.
C.A. = Version of the poem in Walton's *Compleat Angler*, 1653.
MS. = Version of the poem in Thornborough Commonplace Book, quoted by Ingram, *Christopher Marlowe and his Associates*, 1904, p. 222, 225.⟩

Description of Seas, Waters, Riuers, &c.

I walkt along a streame for purenesse rare,
Brighter then sun-shine, for it did acquaint
The dullest sight with all the glorious pray,
That in the pibble paued chanell lay.
No molten Christall, but a richer mine, 5
Euen natures rarest alchumie ran there,
Diamonds resolud, and substance more diuine,
Through whose bright gliding current might appeare
A thousand naked Nymphes, whose yuorie shine,
Enameling the bankes, made them more deare 10
Then euer was that glorious *Pallas* gate,
Where the day-shining sunne in triumph sate.
Vpon this brim the Eglantine and Rose,
The Tamoriscke, Oliue, and the Almond tree,
As kind companions in one vnion growes, 15
Folding their twindring armes as oft we see
Turtle-taught louers either other close,
Lending to dulnesse feeling Sympathie.
And as a costly vallance ore a bed,
So did their garland tops the brooke orespred : 20
Their leaues that differed both in shape and showe,
(Though all were greene) yet difference such in greene,
Like to the checkered bent of *Iris* bowe,
Prided the running maine as it had beene—

Ch. Marlowe.

OVID'S ELEGIES

Early editions. Marlowe's translation of the Elegies of Ovid survives in at least six early editions. All are undated and all claim—with probable untruth—to have been printed at Middleburgh in Holland. There is no mention of the work in the *Stationers' Register*, and, indeed, none could be expected, for everything indicates that it was published surreptitiously and with the express disapprobation of the authorities. Copies of one edition were publicly burned at Stationers' Hall on June 4, 1599, by order of the Archbishop of Canterbury and the Bishop of London.[1]

In the absence of all the usual criteria for date and provenance, it is a matter of some difficulty to distinguish the various editions from one another and to decide the question of their sequence. The six which I have been able to identify fall into three groups. Two (*Ish.* and *Bind.*) are incomplete; they represent a mere selection from the elegies. Two others (*Mal.* 368 and *Mal.* 133) are shown by their typography, in such matters, for example, as the use of 'u' and 'v', to be half a century later than Marlowe's time; these editions, which can hardly have been printed earlier than 1640, are practically of no value whatever. Two other versions (*Mas.* and *Douce*) give a complete text and appear to date from the close of the sixteenth century.

It has generally been assumed that the abridged editions (*Ish., Bind.*), containing only ten of the most licentious elegies, are more ancient than the others, but we have no proof of this. As far as the evidence at hand goes, they may equally well be cheap pirated reprints of such portions of the work as would find readiest acceptance among the vulgar. All the texts are marred by the numerous blunders which one would expect to find in hasty and surreptitious

[1] Cf. Arber, *Transcript Stationers' Register*, iii. 677–8. The wrath of the authorities appears to have been directed rather against Davies's *Epigrams* than against the *Elegies* themselves.

productions. None can be received as the *editio princeps*, but that on which I have in general based my text (*Mas.*) appears to be certainly the best and not improbably the oldest.

Date of composition and general character. Whatever may be the date of the extant editions, there would seem to be little doubt as to the period of composition of the poems. No difference in style or method is observable between the elegies included in the abridged editions and the rest. All are characterized alike by boyish stiffness of expression, by metrical inexperience, and defective scholarship. The one example of mature versification to be found in the collection is the second rendering of Elegy I. 15 on pp. 581, 582, where Ben Jonson seems to have filed and polished Marlowe's crude version (pp. 579, 580) before inserting it as his own into the *Poetaster*.[1] The translation of the elegies is almost certainly the work of Marlowe's Cambridge period, and is very probably the earliest of his extant writings. Laughable mistranslations of the original, which a mature poet, however bad a Latinist, could never have admitted into his verse, are here quite common. Two famous ones have been noted by nearly all the editors: the rendering of 'Carmine dissiliunt, abruptis faucibus, angues' by 'Snakes leape by verse *from caues of broken mountaines*' (II. 1, 25), and the translation of 'cānēbat frugibus' as '*did sing* with corne' (III. 9, 39). Very often also the young poet, though understanding the sense of the original, is unable to find an idiomatic equivalent, and in excess of piety produces an English paraphrase which until compared with the Latin is wholly unintelligible. A third fault of the work cannot be justly charged to the account of the translator. It is evident that Marlowe's text of Ovid was in many points inferior to that of modern editions, and its bad readings have naturally found their way into the translation. A single line will illustrate at once all three of the defects just referred to. In I. 7, ll. 39, 40 (p. 568), we read:

Let the sad captiue formost with lockes spred
On her white necke but for hurt cheekes be led.

Here the second line, which in itself is utterly meaningless, receives no elucidation from the Latin of modern texts of

[1] There is no apparent ground for the assumption of Gifford, Dyce, and others, that both versions are by Jonson.

Ovid, 'Si sinerent laesae, candida tota, genae,' but the occurrence of the nonsense is at least rendered explicable when we find that a 1568 edition of the *Amores* substitutes *colla* for *tota*.

Judged by absolute standards, Marlowe's *Elegies* must be agreed to be a failure both as poetry and as a rendering of the Latin. When considered, however, as a very early metrical exercise, the translation shows decided promise. The most striking merit is probably the enthusiasm with which the dull work is performed; though many lines are flat and pointless to the reader, there is none which seems to have been tame in the writing. Through all his rather disastrous struggles with an unmastered art and a very imperfectly mastered language, the translator has manifestly been supported by a real poetic fervour. Occasionally the lines have a very melodious cadence, and there is prevailingly a richness of vocabulary and epithet which promise much. Finally, these poems display a facility in riming which in a young poet is extraordinary, and which more perhaps than anything else in the work presages the incomparable melody of the first and second books of *Hero and Leander*.

The text of Sir John Davies's *Epigrams* is affixed to that of the *Elegies* in all known editions, and is here reprinted from *Mas.* In accordance with my rule for the treatment of 'Spuria', variant readings are recorded only where the text of *Mas.* appears to be corrupt. The twenty-ninth epigram is twice referred to by Th. Bastard in his *Chrestoleros*, 1598.[1] Malone regards this as establishing a posterior limit for the publication of the *Elegies and Epigrams*, but the evidence is of little value, since Bastard may well have known the epigram in question before it appeared in a printed book.

[1] Bk. II, Epigram 15; Bk. III, Epigram 3. Bastard's work has been reprinted, *Publications Spenser Society*, 47, 1888.

ALL
OVIDS ELEGIES:
3. BOOKES.

By C. M.

Epigrams by *J. D.*

[***]
[***]

At Middlebourgh.

Mas. = Octavo edition (Bodley, Mason AA 207).

Douce = Octavo edition (Bodley, Douce O 31).

Ish. = Isham copy, reprinted by Ch. Edmonds, 1870. Small fours. 'Certaine elegies.'

Bind. = British Museum copy (C 34 a 57). Formerly J. Bindley's. 'Certaine Elegies.'

Mal. { *Mal. 368* = Octavo edition so numbered in Bodley (also Brit. Mus. 11388 aa 25).
Mal. 133 = Octavo edition so numbered in Bodley (also Brit. Mus. $\frac{1068 \text{ g } 20}{2}$)

MS. = Manuscript version of Davies' Epigrams, quoted by Dyce.

Rob. = Robinson's edition of Marlowe, 1826.

Dyce { *Dyce*^{1} = Dyce's first edition of Marlowe, 1850.
Dyce^2 = Dyce's revised edition of Marlowe, 1858, etc.

Cunn. = Cunningham's edition of Marlowe, 1870, etc.

Bull. = Bullen's edition of Marlowe, 1885.

T. B. = The present editor.

Malone = Conjectures by M. in MS. transcript of a copy of ? Bind. (Bodley, Mal. 133).

P. Ouidij Nasonis Amorum,
Liber primus.

ELEGIA. I.

Quemadmodum a Cupidine pro bellis amores scribere coactus sit.

We which were *Ouids* fiue bookes now are three,
For these before the rest preferreth he.
If reading fiue thou plainst of tediousnesse,
Two tane away, thy labour will be lesse.
With Muse prepar'd I meant to sing of Armes, 5
Choosing a subiect fit for fierce alarmes.
Both verses were a like till loue (men say)
Began to smile and tooke one foote away.
Rash boy, who gaue thee power to change a line?
We are the Muses Prophets, none of thine. 10
What if thy mother take *Dianas* bowe?
Shall *Dian* fanne, when loue begins to glowe?
In wooddie groues ist meete that *Ceres* raigne,
And quiuer-bearing *Dian* till the plaine?
Who'le set the faire trest sunne in battell ray 15
While *Mars* doth take the *Aonian* Harpe to play?
Great are thy kingdomes, ouer strong and large,
Ambitious impe, why seekst thou further charge?
Are all things thine? the Muses *Tempe* thine?
Then scarse can *Phœbus* say, this Harpe is mine. 20
When in this workes first verse I trode aloft,
Loue slackt my Muse, and made my numbers soft.
I haue no mistresse, nor no fauorit,
Being fittest matter for a wanton wit.
Thus I complain'd, but loue vnlockt his quiuer, 25
Tooke out the shaft, ordain'de my heart to shiuer:

4 thy] the *Bind.* 5 prepar'd] vpreard *Ish.*, *Bind.* meane *Ish.*, *Bind.* Armes] ames *Bind.* 8 take *Ish.*, *Bind.* 11 What] That *Ish.*, *Bind.* 19 Tempe *Ish.*, *Bind.*: Temple *Mas.*, *Douce*, *Mal.* 21 worke *Ish.*, *Bind.* 22 Loue] I *Ish.*, *Bind.* number *Ish.*, *Bind.*

And bent his sinewie bowe vpon his knee,
Saying, Poet heere's a worke beseeming thee.
Oh woe is mee, hee neuer shootes but hits,
I burne, loue in my idle bosome sits. 30
Let my first verse be sixe, my last fiue feete,
Fare-well sterne warre, for blunter Poets meete.
Elegian Muse, that warblest amorous laies,
Girt my shine browe with Sea-banke Mirtle sprays.

ELEGIA. 2.

Quod primo amore correptus, in triumphum duci se a cupidine patiatur.

What makes my bed seeme hard seeing it is soft?
Or why slips downe the couerlet so oft?
Although the nights be long, I sleepe not tho,
My sides are sore with tumbling too and fro.
Were loue the cause, it's like I should descry him, 5
Or lyes he close, and shootes where none can spie him?
'Twas so, hee strooke mee with a slender dart,
'Tis cruell loue turmoyles my captiue heart.
Yeelding or strugling do we giue him might,
Lets yeeld, a burthen easly borne is light. 10
I saw a brandisht fire encrease in strength,
Which being not shakt, I saw it dye at length.
Young Oxen newly yoakt are beaten more
Then Oxen which haue drawne the plough before.
And rough Iades mouthes with stuborne bits are torne, 15
But managde horses heads are lightly borne.
Vnwilling louers loue doth more torment
Then such as in their bondage feele content.
Loe I confesse, I am thy captiue I,
And hold my conquer'd hands for thee to tie. 20
What needst thou warre? I sue to thee for grace,
With armes to conquer armelesse men is base.
Yoake *Venus* Doues, put Mirtle on thy haire,
Vulcan will giue thee chariots rich and faire.

34 sprays *Dyce etc.*: praise *old edd.* 34 + *Signature* C. Marlowe *add. Ish., Bind.*

Elegia 2] *This elegy comes last of all in Ish., Bind.* 1 soft] so soft *Bind.* 7 slender] tẽder *Bind.* 9 strugling] striuing *Ish., Bind.* 12 shakt *Ish., Bind., Dyce etc.*: slackt *Mas., Douce, Mal.* 14 which] that *Mal.*

The people thee applauding thou shalt stand, 25
Guiding the harmelesse Pigeons with thy hand.
Yong men, and women shalt thou lead as thrall,
So will thy triumph seeme magnificall.
I lately caught, will haue a new made wound,
And captiue like be manacled and bound. 30
Good meaning shame, and such as seeke loues wracke,
Shall follow thee their hands tyed at their backe.
Thee all shall feare, and worship as a King,
Io Triumphe shall thy people sing.
Smooth speeches, feare, and rage shall by thee ride, 35
Which troopes haue alwayes beene on *Cupids* side;
Thou with these souldiours conquerest gods and men,
Take these away, where is thine honour then?
Thy mother shall from heauen applaud this showe,
And on their faces heapes of Roses strowe. 40
With beautie of thy wings thy faire haire guilded,
Ride golden loue in chariots richly builded.
Vnlesse I erre, full many shalt thou burne,
And giue wounds infinite at euery turne.
In spite of thee forth will thine arrowes flye, 45
A scortching flame burnes all the standers by.
So hauing conquer'd *Inde* was *Bacchus* hew,
Thee pompous Birds, and him two Tygers drew.
Then seeing I grace thy show in following thee,
Forbeare to hurt thy selfe in spoiling me. 50
Behold thy kinsmans *Cæsars* prosperous bands,
Who guards the conquered with his conquering hands.

ELEGIA. 3.

Ad amicam.

I aske but right: let hir that caught me late,
Either loue, or cause that I may neuer hate.
I aske too much, would she but let me loue her!
Loue knowes with such like praiers I daily moue her.

26 thy *om. Bind.* 28 triumphs *Ish., Bind.* 34 Triumphe *T. B.*: triumphing *old edd. etc.* 36 haue] hath *Ish.* 38 thine] thy *Ish., Bind.* 44 wounds] wordes *Bind.* 45 thine] thy *Ish., Bind.* 51 kinsman *Dyce etc.* 52 the] thee *Mas.*
Elegia 3. amicam] amicum *Ish., Bind.* 1 hir *Ish., Bind.*: hc *Mas.*: he *Douce, Mal. 368*: him *Mal. 133* 2 neuer *om. Bind.* 3 aske] craue *Bind., Dyce* 4 Loue *Ish.. Bind.*: Ioue *Mas. to Mal., Dyce etc.*

Accept him that wil serue thee all his youth, 5
Accept him that will loue with spotlesse truth
If loftie titles cannot make me thine,
That am descended but of Knightly line,
(Soone may you plow the little land I haue,
I gladly grant my parents giuen to saue) 10
Apollo, Bacchus and the Muses may,
And *Cupid* who hath markt me for thy pray;
My spotlesse life, which but to Gods giues place,
Naked simplicitie, and modest grace.
I loue but one, and her I loue, change neuer, 15
If men haue faith, Ile liue with thee for euer.
The yeares that fatall destinie shall giue
Ile liue with thee, and dye, ere thou shall grieue.
Be thou the happy subiect of my bookes,
That I may write things worthy thy faire lookes. 20
By verses horned *Io* got her name,
And she to whom in shape of Swanne *Ioue* came,
And she that on a fain'd Bull swamme to land,
Griping his false hornes with her virgin hand.
So likewise we will through the world be rung, 25
And with my name shall thine be alwayes sung.

ELEGIA. 4.

Amicam, qua arte, quibusue nutibus in cæna, præsente viro vti debeat, admonet.

Thy husband to a banquet goes with me,
Pray God it may his latest supper be.
Shall I sit gazing as a bashfull guest,
While others touch the damsell I loue best?
Wilt lying vnder him his bosome clippe? 5
About thy neck shall he at pleasure skippe?
Marueile not, though the faire Bride did incite
The drunken *Centaures* to a sodaine fight.
I am no halfe horse, nor in woods I dwell,
Yet scarse my hands from thee containe I well. 10

6 with] thee with *Bind.* 7 make me] cause me to be *Bind.* 9 lands *Ish., Bind.* 15 her] he *Bind.* 18 ere] or *Ish., Bind.* shalt *Ish., Bind., Douce, Mal.* 133 21 horned] honored *Mal.* 22 Swanne] Bull *Ish., Bind.*: bird *conj. Malone.*
Elegia 4. *om. Ish., Bind.* 5 Wilt] With *Douce*

But how thou shouldst behaue thy selfe now know:
Nor let the windes away my warnings blowe.
Before thy husband come, though I not see
What may be done, yet there before him bee.
Lie with him gently, when his limbes he spread 15
Vpon the bed, but on my foote first tread.
View me, my becks, and speaking countenance;
Take, and receiue each secret amorous glaunce.
Words without voyce shall on my eye browes sit,
Lines thou shalt read in wine by my hand writ. 20
When our lasciuious toyes come in thy minde,
Thy Rosie cheekes be to thy thombe inclinde.
If ought of me thou speak'st in inward thought,
Let thy soft finger to thy eare be brought,
When I (my light) do or say ought that please thee, 25
Turne round thy gold-ring, as it were to ease thee.
Strike on the boord like them that pray for euiil,
When thou doest wish thy husband at the deuill.
What wine he fills thee wisely will him drinke,
Aske thou the boy what thou enough doest thinke. 30
When thou hast tasted, I will take the cup,
And where thou drinkst, on that part I will sup.
If hee giues thee what first himselfe did tast,
Euen in his face his offered Goblets cast.
Let not thy necke by his vile armes be prest, 35
Nor leane thy soft head on his boistrous brest.
Thy bosomes Roseat buds let him not finger,
Chiefely on thy lips let not his lips linger.
If thou giuest kisses, I shall all disclose,
Say they are mine, and hands on thee impose. 40
Yet this Ile see, but if thy gowne ought couer,
Suspitious feare in all my veines will houer.
Mingle not thighes, nor to his legge ioyne thine,
Nor thy soft foote with his hard foote combine.
I haue beene wanton, therefore am perplext, 45
And with mistrust of the like measure vext.
I and my wench oft vnder clothes did lurke,
When pleasure mou'd vs to our sweetest worke.
Do not thou so, but throw thy mantle hence,
Least I should thinke thee guilty of offence. 50

12 warning *Mal.* 16 feete *Douce* 18 receiue] return *Dyce to Bull.* 21 in] to *Cunn.*, *Bull.* 22 thombe] tombe *Mal.* 34 Goblets] gobbets *Dyce to Bull.* 36 leaue *Mas.*, *Douce*

Entreat thy husband drinke, but do not kisse,
And while he drinkes, to adde more do not misse,
If hee lyes downe with Wine and sleepe opprest,
The thing and place shall counsell vs the rest.
When to go homewards we rise all along, 55
Haue care to walke in middle of the throng.
There will I finde thee, or be found by thee,
There touch what euer thou canst touch of mee.
Aye me, I warne what profits some few howers,
But we must part, when heau'n with black night lowers. 60
At night thy husband clippes thee, I will weepe
And to the dores sight of thy selfe keepe:
Then will he kisse thee, and not onely kisse
But force thee giue him my stolne honey blisse.
Constrain'd against thy will giue it the pezant, 65
Forbeare sweet wordes, and be your sport vnpleasant.
To him I pray it no delight may bring,
Or if it do, to thee no ioy thence spring:
But though this night thy fortune be to trie it,
To me to morrow constantly deny it. 70

ELEGIA. 5.

Corinnæ Concubitus.

In summers heate and mid-time of the day
To rest my limbes vpon a bed I lay,
One window shut, the other open stood,
Which gaue such light as twincles in a wood,
Like twilight glimps at setting of the Sunne 5
Or night being past, and yet not day begunne.
Such light to shamefast maidens must be showne,
Where they may sport, and seeme to bee vnknowne.
Then came *Corinna* in a long loose gowne,
Her white neck hid with tresses hanging downe: 10
Resembling fayre *Semiramis* going to bed
Or *Layis* of a thousand wooers sped.
I snacht her gowne, being thin, the harme was small,
Yet striu'd she to be couered there withall.

59 warne] warme *Mal.* 61 thee *om. Douce* 62 keepe] will keep *Dyce to Bull.* 66 be] in *Mal.*
Elegia 5. 7 shame-fac'd *Mal. 133* 10 tresses] trells *Bind.* 12 wooers] louers *Ish., Bind., Dyce* sped] spread *Ish., Bind.*

And striuing thus as one that would be cast, 15
Betray'd her selfe, and yelded at the last.
Starke naked as she stood before mine eye,
Not one wen in her body could I spie.
What armes and shoulders did I touch and see,
How apt her breasts were to be prest by me? 20
How smooth a belly vnder her wast saw I?
How large a legge, and what a lustie thigh?
To leaue the rest, all lik'd me passing well,
I cling'd her naked body, downe she fell,
Iudge you the rest: being tirde she bad me kisse, 25
Ioue send me more such after-noones as this.

ELEGIA. 6.

Ad Ianitorem, vt fores sibi aperiat.

Vnworthy porter, bound in chaines full sore.
On mooued hookes set ope the churlish dore.
Little I aske, a little entrance make:
The gate halfe ope my bent side in will take.
Long loue my body to such vse makes slender 5
And to get out doth like apt members render.
He shewes me how vnheard to passe the watch,
And guides my feete least stumbling falles they catch.
But in times past I fear'd vaine shades, and night,
Wondring if any walked without light. 10
Loue hearing it laug'd with his tender mother
And smiling sayed, be thou as bold as other.
Forth-with loue came: no darke night-flying spright,
Nor hands prepar'd to slaughter, me affright.
Thee feare I too much: only thee I flatter, 15
Thy lightning can my life in pieces batter.
Why enuiest me this hostile denne vnbarre?
See how the gates with my teares wat'red are.
When thou stood'st naked ready to be beate,
For thee I did thy mistris faire entreate. 20
But what entreates for thee some-times tooke place,
(O mischiefe) now for me obtaine small grace.

23 lik'd] pleasde *Bind.* 24 naked] faire white *Bind.* 25 tirde] tride *Mas., Douce, Mal.*

Elegia 6. *om. Ish., Bind.* 5 makes *Dyce etc.*: make *Mas. to Mal.* 17 denne] dende *Mas. to Mal. 368*: dend *Mal. 133*: *Qy.* den t'?

Gratis thou maiest be free, giue like for like.
Night goes away: the dores barre backeward strike.
Strike, so againe hard chaines shall binde thee neuer, 25
Nor seruile water shalt thou drinke for euer.
Hard-hearted *Porter* doest and wilt not heare?
With stiffe oake propt the gate doth still appeare.
Such rampierd gates beseiged Cittyes ayde,
In midst of peace why art of armes afraide? 30
Excludst a louer, how wouldst vse a foe?
Strike backe the barre, night fast away doth goe.
With armes or armed men I come not guarded,
I am alone, were furious loue discarded.
Although I would, I cannot him cashiere 35
Before I be diuided from my geere.
See loue with me, wine moderate in my braine,
And on my haires a crowne of flowers remaine.
Who feares these armes? who wil not go to meete them?
Night runnes away; with open entrance greete them? 40
Art carelesse? or ist sleepe forbids thee heare
Giuing the windes my words running in thine eare?
Well I remember when I first did hire thee
Watching till after mid-night did not tire thee.
But now perchaunce thy wench with thee doth rest. 45
Ah howe thy lot is aboue my lot blest:
Though it be so, shut me not out therefore.
Night goes away: I pray thee ope the dore.
Erre we? or do the turned hinges sound,
And opening dores with creaking noyse abound? 50
We erre: a strong blast seem'd the gates to ope:
Aie me, how high that gale did lift my hope!
If *Boreas* beares *Orithyas* rape in minde,
Come breake these deafe dores with thy boysterous wind.
Silent the Cittie is: nights deawie hoast 55
March fast away: the barre strike from the poast,
Or I more sterne then fire or sword will turne,
And with my brand these gorgeous houses burne.
Night, loue, and wine to all extreames perswade:
Night shamelesse, wine and loue are fearelesse made. 60
All haue I spent: no threats or prayers moue thee,
O harder then the dores thou gardest I proue thee.

34 were] we *Mal. 133* 50 abound] rebound *conj. Bull.* 53 beares] beare *Mal. 133*: bear'st *Dyce, Cunn.* 58 these] the *Mal.* 61 haue I] I have *Mal. 133*

No pritty wenches keeper maist thou bee:
The carefull prison is more meete for thee.
Now frosty night her flight beginnes to take, 65
And crowing Cocks poore soules to worke awake.
But thou my crowne, from sad haires tane away,
On this hard threshold till the morning lay.
That when my mistresse there beholds thee cast,
She may perceiue how we the time did wast: 70
What ere thou art, farewell, be like me paind,
Carelesse, farewell, with my falt not distaind.
And farewell cruell posts, rough thresholds block,
And dores conioynd with an hard iron lock.

ELEGIA. 7.

Ad pacandam amicam, quam verberauerat.

Binde fast my hands, they haue deserued chaines,
While rage is absent, take some friend the paynes.
For rage against my wench mou'd my rash arme,
My Mistresse weepes whom my mad hand did harme.
I might haue then my parents deare misus'd, 5
Or holy gods with cruell strokes abus'd.
Why? *Aiax* maister of the seuen-fould shield,
Butcherd the flocks he found in spatious field,
And he who on his mother veng'd his sire
Against the destinies durst sharpe darts require. 10
Could I therefore her comely tresses teare?
Yet was she graced with her ruffled hayre.
So fayre she was, *Atalanta* she resembled,
Before whose bow *th' Arcadian* wild beasts trembled.
Such *Ariadne* was, when she bewayles 15
Her periur'd *Theseus* flying vowes and sayles,
So chast *Minerua* did *Cassandra* fall
Deflowr'd except, within thy Temple wall.
That I was mad, and barbarous all men cried,
She nothing said, pale feare her tongue had tyed. 20
But secretlie her lookes with checks did trounce mee,
Her teares, she silent, guilty did pronounce me.
Would of mine armes, my shoulders had beene scanted,
Better I could part of my selfe haue wanted.

66 soules *om. Mal. 133* 69 thee] the *Mal.* 72 disdaind *Mal.*
Elegia 7. *om. Ish., Bind.* 4 hand] arme *Mal. 133* 10 sharpe *omit conj. Bull.* 13 Atalanta] Atlante *Mal. 133* 18 thy] the *Mal. 133* 20 tyed] died *Mal. 133*

To mine owne selfe haue I had strength so furious? 25
And to my selfe could I be so iniurious?
Slaughter and mischiefs instruments, no better,
Deserued chaines these cursed hands shall fetter,
Punisht I am, if I a *Romaine* beat,
Ouer my Mistris is my right more great? 30
Tydides left worst signes of villanie,
He first a Goddesse strooke; an other I.
Yet he harm'd lesse, whom I profess'd to loue
I harm'd: a foe did *Diomedes* anger moue.
Go now thou Conqueror, glorious triumphs raise, 35
Pay vowes to *Ioue*, engirt thy hayres with baies,
And let the troupes which shall thy Chariot follow,
Io, a strong man conquerd this Wench, hollow.
Let the sad captiue formost with lockes spred
On her white necke but for hurt cheekes be led. 40
Meeter it were her lips were blewe with kissing
And on her necke a wantons marke not missing.
But though I like a swelling floud was driuen,
And as a pray vnto blinde anger giuen,
Wa'st not enough the fearefull Wench to chide? 45
Nor thunder in rough threatings haughty pride?
Nor shamefully her coate pull ore her crowne,
Which to her wast her girdle still kept downe,
But cruelly her tresses hauing rent
My nayles to scratch her louely cheekes I bent. 50
Sighing she stood, her bloodlesse white lookes shewed
Like marble from the *Parian* Mountaines hewed.
Her halfe dead ioynts, and trembling limmes I sawe,
Like *Popler* leaues blowne with a stormy flawe,
Or slender eares, with gentle *Zephire* shaken, 55
Or waters tops with the warme south-winde taken.
And downe her cheekes, the trickling teares did flow,
Like water gushing from consuming snowe.
Then first I did perceiue I had offended,
My bloud the teares were that from her descended. 60
Before her feete thrice prostrate downe I fell,
My feared hands thrice back she did repell.
But doubt thou not (reuenge doth griefe appease)
With thy sharpe nayles vpon my face to seaze.

36 hayres] haire *Mal. 133* 42 wanton *Douce, Mal.* 46 threatnings *Mal., Dyce to Bull.* 51 lookes] locks *Mal. 133* 56 waters] water *Mal. 368*: water- *Mal. 133* 62 repell] expell *Mal.*

Bescratch mine eyes, spare not my lockes to breake, 65
(Anger will helpe thy hands though nere so weake.)
And least the sad signes of my crime remaine,
Put in their place thy keembed haires againe.

ELEGIA. 8.

Exæcratur lenam, quæ puellam suam meretricia arte instituebat.

There is, who ere will knowe a bawde aright
Giue eare, there is an old trot *Dipsas* hight.
Her name comes from the thing: she being wise
Sees not the morne on rosie horses rise.
She magick arts and *Thessale* charmes doth know, 5
And makes large streams back to their fountaines flow.
She knows with gras, with thrids on wrõg wheeles spun,
And what with Mares ranck humour may be done.
When she will, cloudes the darckned heau'n obscure,
When she will, day shines euery where most pure. 10
(If I haue faith) I sawe the starres drop bloud,
The purple moone with sanguine visage stood.
Her I suspect among nights spirits to fly,
And her old body in birdes plumes to lie.
Fame saith as I suspect, and in her eyes 15
Two eye-balles shine, and double light thence flies.
Great grand-sires from their antient graues she chides
And with long charmes the solide earth diuides.
She drawes chast women to incontinence,
Nor doth her tongue want harmefull eloquence. 20
By chaunce I heard her talke, these words she sayd
While closely hid betwixt two dores I layed:
Mistris, thou knowest thou hast a blest youth pleas'd
He staide, and on thy lookes his gazes seaz'd.
And why shouldst not please? none thy face exceedes. 25
Aye me, thy body hath no worthy weedes.
As thou art faire, would thou wert fortunate,
Wert thou rich, poore should not be my state.
Th'opposed starre of *Mars* hath done thee harme,
Now *Mars* is gone: *Venus* thy side doth warme, 30

67 crimes *Mal. 133* 68 thy] the *Cunn.* kembed *Dyce to Bull.*
Elegia 8. *om. Ish., Bind.* meretricia] meretricis *Dyce to Bull.* 7 wrõg] wrung *Dyce to Bull.* 13 night *Mal. 133* 28 state] estate *conj. Dyce*

And brings good fortune: a rich louer plants
His loue on thee, and can supply thy wants.
Such is his forme as may with thine compare,
Would he not buy thee thou for him shouldst care.—
She blusht.—Red shame becomes white cheekes, but this
If feigned, doth well; if true it doth amisse. 36
When on thy lappe thine eyes thou dost deiect
Each one according to his gifts respect.
Perhaps the *Sabines* rude, when *Tatius* raignde,
To yeeld their loue to more then one disdainde. 40
Now *Mars* doth rage abroad without all pitty,
And *Venus* rules in her *Æneas* Citty.
Faire women play, shee's chast whom none will haue,
Or, but for bashfulnesse her selfe would craue.
Shake off these wrinckles that thy front assault, 45
Wrinckles in beauty is a grieuous fault.
Penelope in bowes her youths strength tride,
Of horne the bowe was that approu'd their side.
Time flying slides hence closely, and deceaues vs,
And with swift horses the swift yeare soone leaues vs. 50
Brasse shines with vse; good garments would be worne,
Houses not dwelt in are with filth forlorne.
Beauty not exercisde with age is spent,
Nor one or two men are sufficient.
Many to rob is more sure, and lesse hatefull, 55
From dog-kept flocks come preys to woolues most gratefull.
Behold what giues the Poet but new verses?
And thereof many thousand he rehearses.
The Poets God arayed in robes of gold,
Of his gilt Harpe the well tun'd strings doth hold. 60
Let *Homer* yeeld to such as presents bring
(Trust me) to giue, it is a witty thing.
Nor, so thou maist obtaine a wealthy prize,
The vaine name of inferiour slaues despize.
Nor let the armes of antient lines beguile thee, 65
Poore louer with thy gransires I exile thee.
Who seekes, for being faire, a night to haue?
What he will giue, with greater instance craue.
Make a small price, while thou thy nets doest lay,
Least they should fly, being tane, the tirant play. 70
Dissemble so, as lou'd he may be thought,
And take heed least he gets that loue for nought.

31 fortunes *Mal.* 133 65 lines *Dyce to Bull.*: liues *Mas. to Mal.*

Deny him oft, feigne now thy head doth ake:
And *Isis* now will shew what scuse to make.
Receiue him soone, least patient vse he gaine, 75
Or least his loue oft beaten backe should waine:
To beggers shut, to bringers ope thy gate.
Let him within heare bard out louers prate.
And as first wrongd the wronged some-times banish,
Thy fault with his fault so repuls'd will vanish: 80
But neuer giue a spatious time to ire,
Anger delaide doth oft to hate retire.
And let thine eyes constrained learne to weepe,
That this, or that man may thy cheekes moist keepe.
Nor, if thou couzenst one, dread to for-sweare, 85
„ *Venus* to mockt men lendes a sencelesse eare.
Seruants fit for thy purpose thou must hire
To teach thy louer, what thy thoughts desire.
Let them aske some-what, many asking little,
Within a while great heapes grow of a tittle. 90
And sister, Nurse, and mother spare him not,
By many hands great wealth is quickly got.
When causes fale thee to require a gift,
By keeping of thy birth make but a shift.
Beware least he vnriual'd loues secure, 95
Take strife away, loue doth not well endure.
On all the bed mens tumbling let him viewe
And thy neck with lasciuious markes made blew.
Chiefely shew him the gifts, which others send:
If he giues nothing, let him from thee wend. 100
When thou hast so much as he giues no more,
Pray him to lend what thou maist nere restore.
Let thy tongue flatter, while thy minde harme-workes:
Vnder sweete hony deadly poison lurkes.
If this thou doest to me by long vse knowne, 105
Nor let my words be with the windes hence blowne,
Oft thou wilt say, liue well, thou wilt pray oft,
That my dead bones may in their graue lie soft.
As thus she spake, my shadow me betraide.
With much ado my hands I scarsely staide 110
But her bleare eyes, balde scalpes thin hoary flieces
And riueld cheekes I would haue puld a pieces.

77 thy] the *Mal.* 86 mocke *Mal. 133* 90 tittle] little *Douce* 93 When causes fale] What were it for *Douce* 97 bed mens' *Dyce to Bull.*: beds men *Mas. to Mal.* 111 thin *Dyce to Bull.*: thine *Mas. to Mal.* 112 a] in *Mal. 133*

The gods send thee no house, a poore old age,
Perpetuall thirst, and winters lasting rage.

ELEGIA. 9.

Ad Atticum, amantem non oportere desidiosum esse, sicuti nec militem.

All Louers warre, and *Cupid* hath his tent,
Atticke, all louers are to warre farre sent.
What age sits *Mars*, with *Venus* doth agree,
Tis shame for eld in warre or loue to be.
What yeares in souldiours Captaines do require 5
Those in their louers, pretty maydes desire.
Both of them watch: each on the hard earth sleepes:
His Mistris dores this; that his Captaines keepes.
Souldiers must trauaile farre: the wench forth send,
Her valliant louer followes without end. 10
Mounts, and raine-doubled flouds he passeth ouer,
And treades the deserts snowy heapes do couer.
Going to sea, *East* windes he doth not chide
Nor to hoist saile attends fit time and tyde.
Who but a souldiour or a louer is bould 15
To suffer storme mixt snowes with nights sharpe cold?
One as a spy doth to his enemies goe,
The other eyes his riuall as his foe.
He Citties greate, this thresholds lies before:
This breakes Towne gates, but he his Mistris dore. 20
Oft to inuade the sleeping foe tis good
And arm'd to shed vnarmed peoples bloud.
So the fierce troupes of *Thracian Rhesus* fell
And Captiue horses bad their Lord fare-well.
Sooth Louers watch till sleepe the hus-band charmes, 25
Who slumbring, they rise vp in swelling armes.
The keepers hands and corps-dugard to passe
The souldiours, and poore louers worke ere was.
Doubtfull is warre and loue, the vanquisht rise
And who thou neuer think'st should fall downe lies. 30
Therefore who ere loue sloathfulnesse doth call,
Let him surcease: loue tries wit best of all.
Achilles burnd *Briseis* being tane away:
Troianes destroy the *Greeke* wealth, while you may.

Elegia 9. *om. Ish., Bind.* 4 eld] old *Mal.* 12 desert *Cunn., Bull.* do *Dyce to Bull.*: to *Mas. to Mal. 133* 14 fit] full *Douce* 25 Sooth] Such *Mal.* 27 hands] armes *Mal. 133*

Hector to armes went from his wiues embraces, 35
And on *Andromache* his helmet laces.
Great *Agamemnon* was, men say, amazed,
On *Priams* loose-trest daughter when he gazed.
Mars in the deed the black-smithes net did stable,
In heauen was neuer more notorious fable. 40
My selfe was dull, and faint, to sloth inclinde,
Pleasure, & ease had mollifide my minde.
A faire maides care expeld this sluggishnesse,
And to her tentes wild me my selfe addresse.
Since maist thou see me watch and night warres moue:
He that will not growe slothfull let him loue. 46

ELEGIA. 10.

Ad puellam, ne pro amore præmia poscat.

Such as the cause was of two husbands warre,
Whom *Troiane* ships fecht from *Europa* farre;
Such as was *Leda,* whom the God deluded
In snowe-white plumes of a false swanne included;
Such as *Amimone* through the drie fields strayed 5
When on her head a water pitcher laied:
Such wert thou, and I fear'd the Bull and Eagle
And what ere loue made *Ioue* should thee inuegle.
Now all feare with my mindes hot loue abates,
No more this beauty mine eyes captiuates. 10
Ask'st why I chaunge? because thou crau'st reward:
This cause hath thee from pleasing me debard.
While thou wert plaine, I lou'd thy minde and face:
Now inward faults thy outward forme disgrace.
Loue is a naked boy, his yeares saunce staine 15
And hath no cloathes, but open doth remaine.
Will you for gaine haue *Cupid* sell himselfe?
He hath no bosome, where to hide base pelfe.
Loue and Loues sonne are with fierce armes to oddes;
To serue for pay beseemes not wanton gods. 20
The whore stands to be bought for each mans mony
And seekes vild wealth by selling of her Cony,
Yet greedy Bauds command she curseth still,
And doth constraind, what you do of good will.

35 wife's *Rob. etc.* 36 Adromache *Mas. to Mal.*
Elegia 10. *om. Ish., Bind.* 11 Ask't *Mal.* 19 to] at *Dyce to Bull.*

Take from irrationall beasts a president, 25
Tis shame their wits should be more excelent.
The Mare askes not the Horse, the Cowe the Bull,
Nor the milde Ewe gifts from the Ramme doth pull.
Only a Woman gets spoiles from a Man,
Farmes out her-self on nights for what she can, 30
And lets what both delight, what both desire,
Making her ioy according to her hire.
The sport being such as both alike sweete try it,
Why should one sell it, and the other buy it?
Why should I loose, and thou gaine by the pleasure 35
Which man and woman reape in equall measure?
Knights of the post of periuries make saile,
The vniust Iudge for bribes becomes a stale.
Tis shame sould tongues the guilty should defend
Or great wealth from a iudgement seate ascend. 40
Tis shame to growe rich by bed merchandize,
Or prostitute thy beauty for bad prize.
Thankes worthely are due for things vnbought,
For beds ill hyr'd we are indebted nought.
The hirer payeth al, his rent discharg'd 45
From further duty he rests then inlarg'd.
Faire Dames for-beare rewards for nights to craue,
Ill gotten goods good end will neuer haue.
The Sabine gauntlets were too dearely wunne
That vnto death did presse the holy Nunne. 50
The sonne slew her, that forth to meete him went,
And a rich neck-lace caus'd that punnishment.
Yet thinke no scorne to aske a wealthy churle,
He wants no gifts into thy lap to hurle.
Take clustred grapes from an ore-laden vine, 55
May bounteous loue *Alcinous* fruite resigne.
Let poore men show their seruice, faith, and care:
All for their Mistrisse, what they haue, prepare.
In verse to praise kinde Wenches tis my part,
And whom I like eternize by mine art. 60
Garments do weare, iewells and gold do wast,
The fame that verse giues doth for euer last.
To giue I loue, but to be ask't disdayne,
Leaue asking, and Ile giue what I refraine.

29 Spoyle *Douce* 41 bed] bad *Mal.* 56 May *Dyce etc.*: Many *Mas. to Mal.* 59 verses *Mal. 133* praise] prepare *Douce* 60 mine] my *Mal.*

ELEGIA. 11.

Napen alloquitur, vt paratas tabellas ad Corinnam perferat.

In skilfull gathering ruffled haires in order,
Nape free-borne, whose cunning hath no border,
Thy seruice for nights scapes is knowne commodious
And to giue signes dull wit to thee is odious.
Corinna clips me oft by thy perswasion, 5
Neuer to harme me made thy faith euasion.
Receiue these lines, them to my Mistrisse carry,
Be sedulous, let no stay cause thee tarry.
Nor flint, nor iron, are in thy soft brest
But pure simplicity in thee doth rest. 10
And tis suppos'd loues bowe hath wounded thee:
Defend the ensignes of thy warre in mee.
If, what I do, she askes, say hope for night,
The rest my hand doth in my letters write.
Time passeth while I speake, giue her my writ 15
But see that forth-with shee peruseth it.
I charge thee marke her eyes and front in reading,
By speechlesse lookes we guesse at things succeeding.
Straight being read, will her to write much backe,
I hate faire *Paper* should writte matter lacke. 20
Let her make verses, and some blotted letter,
On the last edge to stay mine eyes the better.
What neede she tire her hand to hold the quill?
Let this word, come, alone the tables fill.
Then with triumphant laurell will I grace them 25
And in the midst of *Venus* temple place them,
Subscribing that to her I consecrate
My faithfull tables being vile maple late.

ELEGIA. 12.

Tabellas quas miserat execratur, quod amica noctem negabat.

Bewaile my chaunce: the sad booke is returned,
This day denyall hath my sport adiourned.

Elegia 11. *om. Ish., Bind.* 4 sighes *Douce* to thee *om. Douce* 23 tire *Dyce etc.*: try *Mas. to Mal.*
Elegia 12. *om. Ish., Bind.*

Presages are not vaine, when she departed
Nape by stumbling on the thre-shold started.
Going out againe passe forth the dore more wisely 5
And som-what higher beare thy foote precisely.
Hence luck-lesse tables, funerall wood, be flying
And thou the waxe stuft full with notes denying,
Which I thinke gather'd from cold hemlocks flower
Wherein bad hony *Corsicke* Bees did power. 10
Yet as if mixt with red leade thou wert ruddy,
That colour rightly did appeare so bloudy.
As euill wood throwne in the high-waies lie,
Be broake with wheeles of chariots passing by.
And him that hew'd you out for needfull vses 15
Ile proue had hands impure with all abuses.
Poore wretches on the tree themselues did strangle,
There sat the hang-man for mens neckes to angle.
To hoarse scrich-owles foule shadowes it allowes,
Vultures and furies nestled in the boughes. 20
To these my loue I foolishly committed
And then with sweete words to my Mistrisse fitted.
More fitly had they wrangling bondes contained
From barbarous lips of some Atturney strained.
Among day bookes and billes they had laine better 25
In which the Merchant wayles his banquerout debter.
Your name approues you made for such like things,
The number two no good diuining bringes.
Angry, I pray that rotten age you wrackes
And sluttish white-mould ouergrowe the waxe. 30

ELEGIA. 13.

Ad Auroram, ne properet.

Now ore the sea from her old Loue comes she
That drawes the day from heauens cold axletree.
Aurora whither slidest thou ? downe againe
And birdes for *Memnon* yearely shal be slaine.
Now in her tender armes I sweetly bide, 5
If euer, now well lies she by my side.

5 more] most *Douce* 23 they *Dyce etc.* : thy *Mas. to Mal.* 27 names *Mal. 133.*
Elegia 13. 1 ore] on *Ish., Bind.* 4 for *Dyce etc.* : from *old edd.*

The aire is cold, and sleepe is sweetest now
And birdes send forth shrill notes from euery bough:
Whither runst thou, that men, and women loue not?
Hold in thy rosy horses that they moue not. 10
Ere thou rise, starres teach sea-men where to saile,
But when thou commest they of their courses faile.
Poore trauailers though tierd, rise at thy sight,
And souldiours make them ready to the fight.
The painefull hinde by thee to field is sent, 15
Slowe Oxen early in the yoake are pent.
Thou cousenst boyes of sleepe, and doest betray them
To *Pedants* that with cruell lashes pay them.
Thou mak'st the surety to the Lawyer runne,
That with one word hath nigh himselfe vndone. 20
The Lawyer and the client hate thy view,
Both whom thou raisest vp to toyle anew.
By thy meanes women of their rest are bard,
Thou setst their labouring hands to spin and card.
All could I beare, but that the wench should rise 25
Who can endure saue him with whom none lyes?
How oft wisht I, night would not giue thee place,
Nor morning starres shunne thy vprising face.
How oft that either winde would breake thy coach,
Or steeds might fall forc'd with thick clouds approach. 30
Whether goest thou hatefull Nimph? *Memnon* the elfe
Receiu'd his cole-black colour from thy selfe.
Say that thy loue with *Cæphalus* were not knowne,
Then thinkest thou thy loose life is not showne?
Would *Tithon* might but talke of thee a while, 35
Not one in heauen should be more base and vile.
Thou leauest his bed, because hee's faint through age,
And early mountest thy hatefull carriage.
But heldst thou in thine armes some *Cephalus*,
Then wouldst thou cry, stay night and runne not thus. 40
Doest punish me, because yeares make him waine?
I did not bid thee wed an aged swaine.
The Moone sleepes with *Endymion* euery day,
Thou art as faire as she, then kisse and play.
Ioue that thou shoulst not hast but waite his leasure, 45
Made two nights one to finish vp his pleasure.

12 courses] course *Bind.*: counsell *Mal. 133* 14 *om. Bind.* 17 coosnest *Ish., Bind., Dyce to Bull.* 21 hate] both do hate *Ish., Bind.* 24 setst] seest *Bind.* 25 All] This *Ish., Bind.* 29 thy] the *Mal. 133* 39 heldst] hadst *Ish., Bind.* 41 Doest punish] Punish ye *Ish., Bind.* 43 with] and *Bind.*

I chid no more, she blusht and therefore heard me,
Yet lingered not the day, but morning scard me.

ELEGIA. 14.

Puellam consolatur cui præ nimia cura
comæ deciderant.

Leaue colouring thy tresses I did cry,
Now hast thou left no haires at all to die.
But what had beene more faire had they beene kept?
Beyond thy robes thy dangling lockes had sweept.
Feardst thou to dresse them being fine and thinne 5
Like to the silke the curious *Seres* spinne,
Or thrids which spiders slender foote drawes out
Fastning her light web some old beame about?
Not black, nor golden were they to our viewe,
Yet although neither mixt of eithers hue, 10
Such as in hilly *Idas* watry plaines,
The Cedar tall spoyld of his barke retaines.
Ad they were apt to curle an hundred waies,
And did to thee no cause of dolour raise.
Nor hath the needle, or the combes teeth reft them, 15
The maide that kembd them euer safely left them.
Oft was she drest before mine eyes, yet neuer,
Snatching the combe, to beate the wench out driue her.
Oft in the morne her haires not yet digested,
Halfe sleeping on a purple bed she rested, 20
Yet seemely like a *Thracian Bacchinall*
That tyr'd doth rashly on the greene grasse fall.
When they were slender, and like downy mosse,
Thy troubled haires, alas, endur'd great losse.
How patiently hot irons they did take 25
In crooked trannells crispy curles to make.
I cryed, tis sinne, tis sinne, these haires to burne,
They well become thee, then to spare them turne.
Farre off be force, no fire to them may reach,
Thy very haires will the hot bodkin teach. 30

47 chid *Ish., Dyce to Bull.*: chide *Mas. to Mal., Bind.*
Elegia 14. *om. Ish., Bind.* 4 lackes *Mas., Douce* 10 neither *Dyce etc.*: either *Mas. to Mal.* 13 Ad] And *Douce to Mal.* 22–33 *The first letter or two of each of these lines is illegible in Mas.* 24 Thy *Dyce etc.*: They *Mas. to Mal.* 26 trammels *Rob., Cunn.*

Lost are the goodly lockes, which from their crowne
Phœbus and *Bacchus* wisht were hanging downe.
Such were they as *Diana* painted stands
All naked holding in her waue-moist hands.
Why doest thy ill kembd tresses losse lament? 35
Why in thy glasse doest looke being discontent?
Bee not to see with wonted eyes inclinde,
To please thy selfe, thy selfe put out of minde.
No charmed herbes of any harlot skathd thee,
No faithlesse witch in *Thessale* waters bath'd thee. 40
No sicknesse harm'd thee, farre be that away,
No enuious tongue wrought thy thicke lockes decay.
By thine owne hand and fault thy hurt doth growe,
Thou mad'st thy head with compound poyson flow.
Now *Germany* shall captiue haire-tyers send thee, 45
And vanquisht people curious dressings lend thee,
Which some admiring, O thou oft wilt blush
And say he likes me for my borrowed bush,
Praysing for me some vnknowne *Guelder* dame,
But I remember when it was my fame. 50
Alas she almost weepes, and her white cheekes,
Died red with shame, to hide from shame she seekes.
She holds, and viewes her old lockes in her lappe,
Aye me, rare gifts vnworthy such a happe.
Cheere vp thy selfe, thy losse thou maiest repaire, 55
And be heereafter seene with natiue haire.

ELEGIA. 15.

Ad inuidos, quod fama poetarum sit perennis.

Enuie why carpest thou my time is spent so ill,
And termst my workes fruites of an idle quill?
Or that vnlike the line from whence I come,
Warres dustie honours are refusd being yong?
Nor that I study not the brawling lawes, 5
Nor set my voyce to sale in euery cause?
Thy scope is mortall, mine eternall fame,
That all the world may euer chaunt my name.

37 see] see thy *Mal. 133*
Elegia 15. 2 tearmes *Ish., Bind.* my] our *Ish., Bind.* 3 come] sprung *Dyce etc.* *Cf. Jonson's version below, l.* 3 4 dustie] rustie *Mas. to Mal.* 8 may] might *Ish., Bind.*

Homer shall liue while *Tenedos* stands and *Ide*,
Or into Sea swift *Simois* doth slide. 10
Ascræus liues, while grapes with new wine swell,
Or men with crooked Sickles corne downe fell.
The world shall of *Callimachus* euer speake,
His Arte excelld, although his witte was weake.
For euer lasts high *Sophocles* proud vaine, 15
With Sunne and Moone *Aratus* shall remaine.
While bond-men cheate, fathers hard, bawds whorish,
And strumpets flatter, shall *Menander* flourish.
Rude *Ennius*, and *Plautus* full of witt,
Are both in fames eternall legend writt. 20
What age of *Varroes* name shall not be tolde,
And *Iasons Argos* and the fleece of golde?
Loftie *Lucretius* shall liue that howre,
That nature shall dissolue this earthly bower.
Æneas warre, and *Tityrus* shall be read, 25
While *Rome* of all the conquered world is head.
Till *Cupids* Bowe and fiery Shafts be broken,
Thy verses sweet *Tibullus* shalbe spoken.
And *Gallus* shall be knowne from East to West,
So shall *Licoris* whom he loued best. 30
Therefore when Flint and Iron weare away,
Verse is immortall, and shall nere decay.
To verse let Kings giue place, and Kingly showes,
And bankes ore which gold-bearing *Tagus* flowes.
Let base conceipted witts admire vilde things, 35
Faire *Phœbus* lead me to the Muses springs.
About my head be quiuering mirtle wound,
And in sad louers heads let me be found.
The liuing, not the dead can enuie bite,
For after death all men receiue their right. 40
Then though death rakes my bones in funerall fire,
Ile liue, and as he puls me downe mount higher.

10 into] to the *Ish.*, *Bind.*, *Bull.* doth] shall *Ish.*, *Bind.*, *Bull.* 13, 14 *om. Ish.*, *Bind.* 16 Aeratus *Ish.*: Eratus *Bind.* 17 hard] hoord *old edd.*: be hard *Dyce to Bull.* *Cf. Jonson's version below, l.* 17 22 Argo *Dyce etc.* 26 conquering *Ish.*, *Bind.* 30 Licorus *Ish.*, *Bind.* 32 nere *om. Bind.* 33 To . . place] Let Kings giue place to verse *Ish.*, *Bind.* 34 And] The *Ish.*, *Bind.* 37 be] the *Mal.* 41 rakes] rackes *Ish.*, *Bull.*: rocks *Bind.*, *Dyce*: takes *Mal.* 133

The same by B. I.

Enuie, why twitst thou me, my Time's spent ill?
And call'st my verse fruites of an idle quill?
Or that (vnlike the line from whence I sprong)
Wars dustie honors I pursue not young?
Or that I studie not the tedious lawes; 5
And prostitute my voyce in euery cause?
Thy scope is mortall; mine eternall Fame,
Which through the world shall euer chaunt my name.
Homer will liue, whil'st *Tenedos* stands, and *Ide*,
Or to the sea, fleete *Simoïs* doth slide: 10
And so shall *Hesiod* too, while vines doe beare,
Or crooked sickles crop the ripened eare,
Callimachus, though in Inuention lowe,
Shall still be sung, since he in Arte doth flowe.
No losse shall come to *Sophocles* proud vaine, 15
With Sunne and Moone *Aratus* shall remaine.
Whil'st Slaues be false, Fathers hard, & Bauds be whorish,
Whilst Harlots flatter, shall *Menander* florish.
Ennius, though rude, and *Accius* high-reard straine,
A fresh applause in euery age shall gaine. 20
Of *Varro's* name, what eare shall not be tolde?
Of *Iasons Argo*? and the *Fleece* of *golde*?
Then shall *Lucretius* loftie numbers die,
When Earth, and Seas in fire and flames shall frie.
Titirus, Tillage, *Æney* shall be read, 25
Whil'st *Rome* of all the conquer'd world is head.
Till *Cupids* fires be out, and his bowe broken,
Thy verses (neate *Tibullus*) shall be spoken.
Our *Gallus* shall be knowne from East to west:
So shall *Licoris*, whom he now loues best. 30
The suffering Plough-share or the flint may weare:
But heauenly *Poësie* no death can feare.
Kings shall giue place to it, and Kingly showes,
The bankes ore which gold-bearing *Tagus* flowes.
Kneele hindes to trash: me let bright Phœbus swell, 35
With cups full flowing from the *Muses* well.
The frost-drad myrtle shall impale my head,
And of sad louers Ile be often read.

Second version om. Ish., Bind. 8 though *Mal. 133* 14 in Arte] Arte in *Mal. 368* 37 The frost-drad] Frost-fearing *Ben Jonson folio 1616.* frost-drad] frost-dead *Mal. 133*

,, Enuy the liuing, not the dead, doth bite.
,, For after death all men receiue their right. 40
Then when this body falls in funeral fire,
My name shall liue, and my best part aspire.

P. Ouidii Nasonis Amorum
Liber Secundus

ELEGIA. I.

Quod pro gigantomachia amores scribere sit coactus

I *Ouid* Poet of my wantonnesse,
Borne at *Peligny*, to write more addresse.
So *Cupid* wills, farre hence be the seuere,
You are vnapt my looser lines to heare.
Let Maydes whom hot desire to husbands leade, 5
And rude boyes toucht with vnknowne loue me reade,
That some youth hurt as I am with loues bowe
His owne flames best aquainted signes may knowe,
And long admiring say, by what meanes learnd
Hath this same Poet my sad chaunce discernd? 10
I durst the great celestiall battells tell,
Hundred-hand *Gyges*, and had done it well,
With earthes reuenge and how *Olimpus* toppe
High *Ossa* bore, mount *Pelion* vp to proppe.
Ioue and Ioues thunderbolts I had in hand 15
Which for his heauen fell on the Gyants band.
My wench her dore shut, Ioues affares I left,
Euen Ioue himselfe out off my wit was reft.
Pardon me Ioue, thy weapons ayde me nought,
Her shut gates greater lightning then thyne brought. 20
Toyes, and light Elegies my darts I tooke,
Quickly soft words hard dores wide open strooke.
Verses reduce the horned bloudy moone
And call the sunnes white horses backe at noone.
Snakes leape by verse from caues of broken mountaines 25
And turned streames run back-ward to their fountaines.

Elegia I. *om. Ish., Bind.* 1 my *Dyce etc.*: thy *Mas. to Mal.* 17 Ioues] loues *Douce* 19 weapon *Mal. 133* 24 backe *Dyce etc.*: blacke *Mas. to Mal.*

Verses ope dores, and lockes put in the poast,
Although of oake, to yeeld to verses boast.
What helpes it me of fierce *Achill* to sing?
What good to me wil either *Aiax* bring? 30
Or he who war'd and wand'red twenty yeare?
Or wofull *Hector* whom wilde iades did teare?
But when I praise a pretty wenches face
Shee in requitall doth me oft imbrace.
A great reward: *Heroes,* O famous names 35
Farewel, your fauour nought my minde inflames.
Wenches apply your faire lookes to my verse
Which golden loue doth vnto me rehearse.

ELEGIA. 2.

Ad Bagoum, vt custodiam puellæ sibi commissæ laxiorem habeat.

Bagous whose care doth thy Mistrisse bridle,
While I speake some fewe, yet fit words be idle.
I sawe the damsell walking yesterday
There where the porch doth *Danaus* fact display
Shee pleas'd me soone, I sent, and did her woo, 5
Her trembling hand writ back she might not doo.
And asking why, this answeare she redoubled,
Because thy care too much thy Mistresse troubled.
Keeper if thou be wise cease hate to cherish,
Beleeue me, whom we feare, we wish to perish. 10
Nor is her husband wise, what needes defence
When vn-protected ther is no expence?
But furiously he follow his loues fire
And thinke her chast whom many doe desire.
Stolne liberty she may by thee obtaine, 15
Which giuing her, she may giue thee againe.
Wilt thou her fault learne, she may make thee tremble,
Feare to be guilty then thou maiest desemble.
Thinke when she reades, her mother letters sent her,
Let him goe forth knowne, that vnknowne did enter, 20

35 O] of *Dyce etc.*
Elegia 2. *om. Ish., Bind.* 1 thy] my *Mal.* 4 fact] pack *conj. Cunn.* 8 they care *Mas., Douce* 12 unprotected *Dyce to Bull.*: vn-protested *Mas. to Mal. 133* 13 followed *Mal., Dyce* 14 thinke *Douce*: thinkes *Mas., Mal., Dyce etc.*

Let him goe see her though she doe not languish
And then report her sicke and full of anguish.
If long she stayes, to thinke the time more short
Lay downe thy forehead in thy lap to snort.
Enquire not what with *Isis* may be done 25
Nor feare least she to th'theater's runne.
Knowing her scapes thine honour shall encrease,
And what lesse labour then to hold thy peace?
Let him please, haunt the house, be kindly vsd,
Enioy the wench, let all else be refusd. 30
Vaine causes faine of him, the true to hide
And what she likes, let both hold ratifide.
When most her husband bends the browes and frownes
His fauning wench with her desire he crownes.
But yet sometimes to chide thee let her fall 35
Counterfet teares: and thee lewd hangman call.
Obiect thou then what she may well excuse,
To staine all faith in truth, by false crimes vse.
Of wealth and honour so shall grow thy heape,
Do this and soone thou shalt thy freedome reape. 40
On tell-tales neckes thou seest the linke-knitt chaines,
The filthy prison faithlesse breasts restraines.
Water in waters, and fruite flying touch
Tantalus seekes, his long tongues gaine is such.
While *Iunos* watch-man *Io* too much eyde, 45
Him timelesse death tooke, she was deifide.
I sawe ones legges with fetters blacke and blewe,
By whom the husband his wiues incest knewe.
More he deseru'd, to both great harme he fram'd,
The man did grieue, the woman was defam'd. 50
Trust me all husbands for such faults are sad
Nor make they any man that heare them glad.
If he loues not, deafe eares thou doest importune,
Or if he loues, thy tale breedes his misfortune.
Nor is it easily prou'd though manifest, 55
She safe by fauour of her iudge doth rest.
Though himselfe see, heele credit her denyall,
Condemne his eyes, and say there is no tryall.
Spying his mistrisse teares, he will lament
And say this blabbe shall suffer punnishment. 60
Why fightst gainst oddes? to thee being cast do happe
Sharpe stripes, she sitteth in the iudges lappe.

22 *different from Latin* 26 the theâtres *Dyce* 29 the] thy *Douce* 48 wife's *Dyce etc.*

To meete for poyson or vilde facts we craue not,
My hands an vnsheath'd shyning weapon haue not
Wee seeke that through thee safely loue we may, 65
What can be easier then the thing we pray?

ELEGIA. 3.

Ad Eunuchum seruantem dominam.

Aye me an *Eunuch* keepes my mistrisse chaste,
That cannot *Venus* mutuall pleasure taste.
Who first depriu'd yong boyes of their best part,
With selfe same woundes he gaue, he ought to smart.
To kinde requests thou wouldst more gentle proue, 5
If euer wench had made luke-warme thy loue:
Thou wert not borne to ride, or armes to beare,
Thy hands agree not with the warlike speare.
Men handle those, all manly hopes resigne,
Thy mistrisse enseignes must be likewise thine. 10
Please her, her hate makes others thee abhorre,
If she discardes thee, what vse seruest thou for?
Good forme there is, yeares apt to play togither,
Vnmeete is beauty without vse to wither.
Shee may deceiue thee, though thou her protect, 15
What two determine neuer wants effect.
Our prayers moue thee to assist our drift,
While thou hast time yet to bestowe that gift.

ELEGIA. 4.

Quod amet mulieres, cuiuscunque formæ sint.

I meane not to defend the scapes of any,
Or iustifie my vices being many.
For I confesse, if that might merite fauour,
Heere I display my lewd and loose behauiour.
I loathe, yet after that I loathe I runne, 5
Oh how the burthen irkes, that we should shunne.
I cannot rule my selfe, but where loue please
Am driuen like a ship vpon rough seas.
No one face likes me best, all faces moue,
A hundred reasons make me euer loue. 10

Elegia 3. *om. Ish., Bind.*
Elegia 4. 8 Am] And *Ish., Bind.* 10 makes *Ish., Bind.*

If any eye me with a modest looke,
I burn, and by that blushfull glance am tooke.
And she thats coy I like for being no clowne,
Me thinkes she would be nimble when shees downe.
Though her sowre lookes a *Sabines* browe resemble, 15
I thinke sheele do, but deepely can dissemble.
If she be learn'd, then for her skill I craue her,
If not, because shees simple I would haue her.
Before *Callimachus* one preferres me farre,
Seeing she likes my bookes why should we iarre? 20
An other railes at me and that I write
Yet would I lie with her if that I might.
Trips she, it likes me well, plods she, what than?
Shee would be nimbler, lying with a man.
And when one sweetely sings, then straight I long 25
To quauer on her lips euen in her song.
Or if one touch the Lute with arte and cunning
Who wold not loue those hands for their swift running?
And her I like that with a maiesty
Folds vp her armes and makes lowe curtesy. 30
To leaue my selfe, that am in loue with all,
Some one of these might make the chastest fall.
If she be tall, shees like an *Amazon*,
And therefore filles the bed she lies vpon.
If short, she lies the rounder: to say troth, 35
Both short and long please me, for I loue both.
I thinke what one vndeckt would be, being drest:
Is she attired, then shew her graces best.
A white wench thralles me, so doth golden yellowe
And nut-browne girles in doing haue no fellowe. 40
If her white necke be shadoed with blacke haire,
Why so was *Lædas*, yet was *Læda* faire.
Amber trest is she, then on the morne thinke I,
My loue alludes to euery history:
A yong wench pleaseth, and an old is good, 45
This for her lookes, that for her woman-hood.
Nay what is she that any *Roman* loues
But my ambitious ranging minde approues?

12 burn *Dyce etc.*: blush *old edd.* I burn, and] And blush, I *conj. Malone* glance] glasse *Ish., Bind.* 14 would] should *Ish., Bind.* nimble] quick *Bind.* shees] she is *Bind.* 22 lie] be *Bind.* 24 would] will *Douce* 28 hands] nimble handes *Bind.* 29 her] she *Ish., Bind.* 35 say] speake *Ish., Bind., Bull.* 37–40 *om Ish., Bind.* 43 Amber] Yellow *Ish., Bind.* 46 that] and that *Douce* 48 ranging] raging *Mal. 133.*

ELEGIA. 5.

Ad amicam corruptam.

No loue is so dere (quiuerd *Cupid* flie)
That my chiefe wish should be so oft to die.
Minding thy fault, with death I wish to reuill,
Alas a wench is a perpetuall euill.
No intercepted lines thy deedes display, 5
No gifts giuen secretly thy crime bewray:
O would my proofes as vaine might be withstood,
Aye me poore soule, why is my cause so good?
He's happy, that his loue dares boldly credit,
To whom his wench can say, I neuer did it. 10
He's cruell, and too much his griefe doth fauour
That seekes the conquest by her loose behauiour.
Poore wretch I sawe when thou didst thinke I slumbred,
Not drunke your faults on the spilt wine I numbred.
I sawe your nodding eye-browes much to speake, 15
Euen from your cheekes parte of a voice did breake.
Not silent were thine eyes, the boord with wine
Was scribled, and thy fingers writ a line.
I knew your speech (what do not louers see?)
And words that seem'd for certaine markes to be. 20
Now many guests were gone, the feast being done,
The youthfull sort to diuers pastimes runne.
I sawe you then vnlawfull kisses ioyne,
(Such with my tongue it likes me to purloyne).
None such the sister giues her brother graue, 25
But such kinde wenches let their louers haue.
Phœbus gaue not *Diana* such, tis thought,
But *Venus* often to her *Mars* such brought.
What doest, I cryed, transportst thou my delight?
My lordly hands ile throwe vpon my right. 30
Such blisse is onely common to vs two,
In this sweete good why hath a third to do?
This, and what grife inforc'd me say I say'd,
A scarlet blush her guilty face arayed.
Euen such as by *Aurora* hath the skie, 35
Or maides that their betrothed husbands spie.

Elegia 5. *om. Ish., Bind.* 3 thy] my *Douce* 9 dare *Mal.* 13 wretch *Dyce, Bull.*: wench *Mas. to Mal., Cunn.* 14 Not] Nor *Mal. 133* 16 your] her *Mal. 133* a] her *Mal. 133* 25 her] the *Mal.* 27 not] to *Mal.*

Such as a rose mixt with a lilly breedes,
Or when the Moone trauailes with charmed steedes,
Or such, as least long yeares should turne the die,
Arachine staynes *Assyrian* iuory. 40
To these, or some of these like was her colour,
By chaunce her beauty neuer shined fuller.
She viewed the earth: the earth to viewe beseem'd her.
She looked sad: sad, comely I esteem'd her.
Euen kembed as they were, her lockes to rend, 45
And scratch her faire soft cheekes I did intend.
Seeing her face, mine vpreard armes discended,
With her owne armor was my wench defended.
I that ere-while was fierce, now humbly sue,
Least with worse kisses she should me indue. 50
She laught, and kissed so sweetely as might make
Wrath-kindled *Ioue* away his thunder shake.
I grieue least others should such good perceiue,
And wish hereby them all vnknowne to leaue.
Also much better were they then I tell, 55
And euer seemed as some new sweete befell.
Tis ill they pleas'd so much, for in my lips,
Lay her whole tongue hid, mine in hers she dips.
This grieues me not, no ioyned kisses spent
Bewaile I onely, though I them lament. 60
No where can they be taught but in the bed,
I know no maister of so great hire sped.

ELEGIA. 6.

In mortem psittaci.

The parrat from east *India* to me sent,
Is dead, al fowles her exequies frequent.
Go goodly birdes, striking your breasts bewaile,
And with rough clawes your tender cheekes assaile.
For wofull haires let piece-torne plumes abound, 5
For long shrild trumpets let your notes resound.
Why *Philomele* doest *Tereus* leudnesse mourne?
All wasting years haue that complaint out worne.

40 Arachne *Douce, Dyce etc.* 50 indue] endure *Mal. 133*
Elegia 6. *om. Ish., Bind.* 3 goodly] godly *Dyce etc.* 8 out *T. B.*: not *Mas. to Mal.*: now *Dyce etc.*

Thy tunes let this rare birdes sad funerall borrowe,
Itis as great, but auntient cause of sorrowe. 10
All you whose pineons in the cleare aire sore,
But most thou friendly turtle-doue, deplore.
Full concord all your liues was you betwixt,
And to the end your constant faith stood fixt.
What *Pylades* did to *Orestes* proue, 15
Such to the parrat was the turtle doue.
But what auailde this faith ? her rarest hue ?
Or voice that howe to change the wilde notes knew ?
What helpes it thou wert giuen to please my wench ?
Birdes haples glory, death thy life doth quench. 20
Thou with thy quilles mightst make greene *Emerald* dark,
And passe our scarlet of red saffrons marke.
No such voice-feigning bird was on the ground,
Thou spokest thy words so well with stammering sound.
Enuy hath rapt thee, no fierce warres thou mouedst, 25
Vaine babling speech, and pleasant peace thou louedst.
Behold how quailes among their battailes liue,
Which do perchance old age vnto them giue.
A little fild thee, and for loue of talke,
Thy mouth to taste of many meates did balke. 30
Nuts were thy food, and Poppie causde thee sleepe,
Pure waters moisture thirst away did keepe.
The rauenous vulture liues, the Puttock houers
Around the aire, the Cadesse raine discouers,
And Crowes suruiues armes-bearing *Pallas* hate, 35
Whose life nine ages scarce bring out of date.
Dead is that speaking image of mans voice,
The Parrat giuen me, the farre worlds best choice.
The greedy spirits take the best things first,
Supplying their voide places with the worst. 40
Thersites did *Protesilaus* suruiue,
And *Hector* dyed his brothers yet aliue.
My wenches vowes for thee what should I show,
Which stormie South-windes into sea did blowe ?
The seuenth day came, none following mightst thou see 45
And the fates distaffe emptie stood to thee,
Yet words in thy benummed palate rung,
Farewell *Corinna* cryed thy dying tongue.

10 Itis as] It is as *Mas. to Mal.* : Itys a *Dyce etc.* 22 Saffron *Mal. 133* 25 warres] waters *Mal. 133* 30 did] didst *Mal. 133* 35 crow *Dyce etc.* 38 world's *Dyce etc.* : words *Mas. to Mal.* 48 Corinda cryed the *Mal. 133*

Elisium hath a wood of holme trees black,
Whose earth doth not perpetuall greene-grasse lacke, 50
There good birds rest (if we beleeue things hidden)
Whence vncleane fowles are said to be forbidden.
There harmelesse Swans feed all abroad the riuer,
There liues the *Phœnix* one alone bird euer.
There *Iunoes* bird displayes his gorgious feather, 55
And louing Doues kisse eagerly together.
The Parrat into wood receiu'd with these,
Turnes all the goodly birdes to what she please.
A graue her bones hides, on her corps great graue
The little stones these little verses haue: 60
This tombe approoues I pleasde my mistresse well,
My mouth in speaking did all birds excell.

ELEGIA. 7.

Amicæ se purgat quod ancillam non amet.

Doost me of new crimes alwayes guilty frame ?
To ouer-come, so oft to fight I shame,
If on the Marble Theater I looke,
One among many is to grieue thee tooke.
If some faire wench me secretly behold, 5
Thou arguest she doth secret markes vnfold.
If I praise any, thy poore haires thou tearest,
If blame, dissembling of my fault thou fearest.
If I looke well, thou thinkest thou doest not moue,
If ill, thou saiest I die for others loue. 10
Would I were culpable of some offence,
They that deserue paine, beare't with patience.
Now rash accusing, and thy vaine beliefe,
Forbid thine anger to procure my griefe.
Loe how the miserable great eared *Asse*, 15
Duld with much beating slowly forth doth passe.
Behold *Cypassis* wont to dresse thy head,
Is charg'd to violate her mistresse bed.
The Gods from this sinne rid me of suspition,
To like a base wench of despisd condition. 20
With *Venus* game who will a seruant grace ?
Or any back made rough with stripes imbrace ?

53 There] The *Mal. 133* abroad] about *Mal. 133* 58 goodly] godly *Dyce etc.*
Elegia 7. *om. Ish., Bind.* 8 fault] heart *Mal. 133*

Adde she was diligent thy locks to braide,
And for her skill to thee a gratefull maide,
Should I sollicit her that is so iust, 25
To take repulse, and cause her shew my lust?
I sweare by *Venus*, and the wingd boyes bowe,
My selfe vnguilty of this crime I know.

ELEGIA. 8.

Ad Cypassim ancillam Corinnæ.

Cypassis that a thousand wayes trimst haire,
Worthy to keembe none but a Goddesse faire,
Our pleasant scapes shew thee no clowne to be,
Apt to thy mistrisse, but more apt to me.
Who that our bodies were comprest bewrayde? 5
Whence knowes *Corinna* that with thee I playde?
Yet blusht I not, nor vsde I any saying,
That might be vrg'd to witnesse our false playing.
What if a man with bond-women offend,
To proue him foolish did I ere contend? 10
Achilles burnt with face of captiue *Briseis*,
Great *Agamemnon* lou'd his seruant *Chriseis*.
Greater then these my selfe I not esteeme,
What graced Kings, in me no shame I deeme.
But when on thee her angry eyes did rush, 15
In both thy cheekes she did perceiue thee blush.
But being present, might that worke the best,
By *Venus* Deity how did I protest.
Thou Goddesse doest command a warme South-blast,
My false oathes in *Carpathian* seas to cast. 20
For which good turne my sweete reward repay,
Let me lie with thee browne *Cypasse* to day.
Vngrate why feignest new feares? and doest refuse;
Well maiest thou one thing for thy Mistresse vse.
If thou deniest foole, Ile our deeds expresse, 25
And as a traitour mine owne fault confesse,
Telling thy mistresse, where I was with thee,
How oft, and by what meanes we did agree.

Elegia 8. *om. Ish., Bind.* 16 thy *Dyce etc.*: my *Mas. to Mal.* thee] the *Mal.* 20 false *T. B.*: selfe *old edd. etc.*: to] do *Mal.*

ELEGIA. 9.

Ad Cupidinem.

O *Cupid* that doest neuer cease my smart,
O boy that lyest so slothfull in my heart.
Why me that alwayes was thy souldiour found,
Doest harme, and in thy tents why doest me wound?
Why burnes thy brand, why strikes thy bow thy friends? 5
More glory by thy vanquisht foes assends.
Did not *Pelides* whom his Speare did grieue,
Being requirde, with speedy helpe relieue?
Hunters leaue taken beasts, pursue the chase,
And then things found do euer further pace. 10
We people wholy giuen thee feele thine armes,
Thy dull hand stayes thy striuing enemies harmes.
Doest ioy to haue thy hooked Arrowes shaked
In naked bones? loue hath my bones left naked.
So many men and maidens without loue, 15
Hence with great laude thou maiest a triumph moue.
Rome if her strength the huge world had not fild,
With strawie cabins now her courts should build.
The weary souldiour hath the conquerd fields,
His sword layed by, safe, though rude places yeelds. 20
The Docke inharbours ships drawne from the floods,
Horse freed from seruice range abroad the woods,
And time it was for me to liue in quiet,
That haue so oft seru'd pretty wenches dyet.
Yet should I curse a God, if he but said, 25
Liue without loue, so sweete ill is a maide.
For when my loathing it of heate depriues me,
I know not whether my mindes whirle-wind driues me.
Euen as a head-strong courser beares away
His rider vainely striuing him to stay, 30
Or as a sodaine gale thrustes into sea
The hauen touching barcke now nere the lea,
So wauering *Cupid* bringes me backe amaine,
And purple loue resumes his dartes againe.
Strike boy, I offer thee my naked brest, 35
Heere thou hast strength, here thy right hand doth rest.
Here of themselues thy shafts come, as if shot,
Better then I their quiuer knowes them not.

Elegia 9. *om. Ish., Bind.* 4 thy] my *Mal.* 20 though] through *Mal. 133*: to *Rob.* 32 hauen] heauen *Mas., Douce*

Haples is he that all the night lies quiet
And slumbring, thinkes himselfe much blessed by it. 40
Foole, what is sleepe but image of cold death?
Long shalt thou rest when Fates expire thy breath,
But me let crafty damsells words deceiue,
Great ioyes by hope I inly shall conceiue.
Now let her flatter me, now chide me hard, 45
Let her enioy me oft, oft be debard.
Cupid by thee, *Mars* in great doubt doth trample,
And thy step-father fights by thy example.
Light art thou, and more windie then thy winges,
Ioyes with vncertaine faith thou takest and brings. 50
Yet loue, if thou with thy faire mother heare,
Within my brest no desert empire beare,
Subdue the wandring wenches to thy raigne,
So of both people shalt thou homage gaine.

ELEGIA. 10.

Ad Græcinum quod eodem tempore duas amet.

Græcinus (well I wot) thou touldst me once,
I could not be in loue with two at once.
By thee deceiued, by thee surpriz'd am I,
For now I loue two women equally.
Both are well fauour'd, both rich in aray, 5
Which is the loueliest it is hard to say.
This seemes the fairest, so doth that to me,
And this doth please me most, and so doth she.
Euen as a boate, tost by contrary winde,
So with this loue, and that, wauers my minde. 10
Venus, why doublest thou my endlesse smart?
Was not one wench enough to grieue my hart?
Why addst thou stars to heauen, leaues to greene woods
And to the vast deepe sea fresh water flouds?
Yet this is better farre then lie alone, 15
Let such as be mine enemies haue none.
Yea let my foes sleepe in an empty bed,
And in the midst their bodies largely spread.
But may soft loue rowse vp my drowsie eyes,
And from my mistris bosome let me rise. 20

46 her . . me] me enjoy her *Dyce to Bull.*
Elegia 10. 5 rich in] in rich *Douce* 8 And *om. Ish., Bind.*
13 wood *Mas.* 14 vast deepe] deep vast *Ish., Bind., Bull.*

Let one wench cloy me with sweete loues delight
If one can doote, if not, two euery night.
Though I am slender, I haue store of pith
Nor want I strength but weight to presse her with.
Pleasure addes fuell to my lust-full fire, 25
I pay them home with that they most desire.
Oft haue I spent the night in wantonnesse,
And in the morne beene liuely nere the lesse.
Hee's happy who loues mutuall skirmish slayes,
And to the Gods for that death *Ouid* prayes. 30
Let souldiours chase their enemies amaine,
And with their bloud eternall honour gaine.
Let Marchants seeke wealth ⟨and⟩ with periured lips
Being wrackt carowse the sea tir'd by their ships.
But when I dye, would I might droupe with doing, 35
And in the midst thereof, set my soule going,
That at my funeralls some may weeping crye,
Euen as he led his life, so did he dye.

ELEGIA. 11

Ad amicam nauigantem.

The lofty Pine from high mount *Pelion* raught
Ill waies by rough seas wõdring waues first taught,
Which rashly twixt the sharpe rocks in the deepe,
Caried the famous golden-fleeced sheepe.
O would that no Oares might in seas haue suncke, 5
The *Argos* wrackt had deadly waters drunke.
Loe country Gods, and known bed to forsake
Corinna meanes, and dangerous wayes to take.
For thee the East and West winds make me pale,
With Icy *Boreas*, and the Southerne gale: 10
Thou shalt admire no woods or Citties there,
The vniust seas all blewish do appeare.
The Ocean hath no painted stones or shelles,
The sucking shore with their aboundance swels.

29 slayes *Ish., Bind., Dyce etc.*: layes *Mas. to Mal.* 31 souldiour *Ish., Bind.* their] his *Ish., Bind.* 32 their] his *Ish., Bind.* 33 and *add. Cunn., Bull.* 34 Being *Cunn., Bull.*: And being *old edd., Dyce* 36 set] let *Bind.*
Elegia 11. *om. Ish., Bind.* 2 wãdring *Mal. 133* 6 Argo Wreck'd *Dyce etc.* 7 known *Dyce etc.*: know *old edd.*

Maides, on the shore with marble white feete tread, 15
So farre 'tis safe, but to go farther dread.
Let others tell how winds fierce battailes wage,
How *Scyllaes* and *Caribdis* waters rage,
And with what rocke the feard *Cerannia* threat,
In what gulfe either *Syrtes* haue their seate. 20
Let others tell this, and what each one speakes
Beleeue, no tempest the beleeuer wreakes.
Too late you looke back, when with anchors weighd,
The crooked Barque hath her swift sailes displayd.
The carefull ship-man now feares angry gusts, 25
And with the waters sees death neere him thrusts.
But if that *Triton* tosse the troubled floud,
In all thy face will be no crimsen bloud.
Then wilt thou *Lædas* noble twinne-starres pray,
And he is happy whom the earth holds, say. 30
It is more safe to sleepe, to read a booke,
The *Thracian* Harpe with cunning to haue strooke,
But if my words with winged stormes hence slip,
Yet *Galatea* fauour thou her ship.
The losse of such a wench much blame will gather, 35
Both to the Sea-nimphes, and the Sea-nimphes father.
Go minding to returne with prosperous winde,
Whose blast may hether strongly be inclinde,
Let *Nereus* bend the waues vnto this shore,
Hether the windes blowe, here the spring-tide rore. 40
Request milde *Zephires* helpe for thy auaile,
And with thy hand assist thy swelling saile.
I from the shore thy knowne ship first will see,
And say it brings her that preserueth me ;
Ile clip and kisse thee with all contentation, 45
For thy returne shall fall the vowd oblation,
And in the forme of beds weele strowe soft sand,
Each little hill shall for a table stand :
There wine being fild, thou many things shalt tell,
How almost wrackt thy ship in maine seas fell, 50
And hasting to me, neither darkesome night,
Nor violent South-windes did thee ought affright.
Ile thinke all true, though it be feigned matter.
Mine owne desires why should my selfe not flatter ?
Let the bright day-starre cause in heauen this day be, 55
To bring that happy time so soone as may be.

19 rocks *Dyce etc.* Ceraunia *Dyce etc.* 23 anchor *Douce*
42 the swelling *Dyce*

ELEGIA. 12.

Exultat, quod amica potitus sit.

About my temples go triumphant bayes,
Conquer'd *Corinna* in my bosome layes.
She whom her husband, guard, and gate as foes,
Least Arte should winne her, firmely did inclose.
That victory doth chiefely triumph merit, 5
Which without bloud-shed doth the pray inherit.
No little ditched townes, no lowlie walles,
But to my share a captiue damsell falles.
When *Troy* by ten yeares battle tumbled downe,
With the *Atrides* many gainde renowne. 10
But I no partner of my glory brooke,
Nor can an other say his helpe I tooke.
I guide and souldiour wunne the field and weare her,
I was both horse-man, foote-man, standard bearer.
Nor in my act hath fortune mingled chance, 15
O care-got triumph hetherwards aduance.
Nor is my warres cause new, but for a Queene
Europe, and *Asia* in firme peace had beene.
The *Lapithes*, and the *Centaures* for a woman,
To cruell armes their drunken selues did summon. 20
A woman forc'd the *Troyanes* new to enter
Warres, iust *Latinus*, in thy kingdomes center:
A woman against late-built *Rome* did send
The *Sabine* Fathers, who sharpe warres intend.
I saw how Bulls for a white Heifer striue, 25
Shee looking on them did more courage giue.
And me with many, but yet me without murther,
Cupid commands to moue his ensignes further.

ELEGIA. 13.

Ad Isidem, vt parientem Corinnam iuuet.

While rashly her wombes burthen she casts out,
Wearie *Corinna* hath her life in doubt.
She secretly with me such harme attempted,
Angry I was, but feare my wrath exempted.

Elegia 12. *om. Ish., Bind.* 2 bosomes *Mal. 368* 12 his] this *Mal. 133* 27 yet me] yet *Mal.*: me *Dyce etc.*
Elegia 13. *om. Ish., Bind.* 3 with] from *Cunn., Bull.*

But she conceiu'd of me, or I am sure 5
I oft haue done, what might as much procure.
Thou that frequents *Canopus* pleasant fields,
Memphis, and *Pharos* that sweete date trees yeelds,
And where swift *Nile* in his large channell slipping,
By seauen huge mouthes into the sea is dipping, 10
By fear'd *Anubis* visage I thee pray,
So in thy Temples shall *Osiris* stay,
And the dull snake about thy offrings creepe,
And in thy pompe hornd *Apis* with thee keepe:
Turne thy lookes hether, and in one spare twaine, 15
Thou giuest my mistris life, she mine againe.
Shee oft hath seru'd thee vpon certaine dayes,
Where the *French* rout engirt themselues with Bayes.
On labouring women thou doest pitty take,
Whose bodies with their heauy burthens ake. 20
My wench *Lucina*, I intreat thee fauour,
Worthy she is, thou shouldst in mercy saue her.
In white, with incense Ile thine Altars greete,
My selfe will bring vowed gifts before thy feete,
Subscribing, *Naso* with *Corinna* sau'd. 25
Do but deserue gifts with this title grau'd,
But if in so great feare I may aduize thee,
To haue this skirmish fought, let it suffice thee.

ELEGIA. 14.

In amicam, quod abortivum ipsa fecerit.

What helpes it Woman to be free from warre?
Nor being arm'd fierce troupes to follow farre,
If without battell selfe-wrought wounds annoy them,
And their owne priuie weapon'd hands destroy them?
Who vnborne infants first to slay inuented 5
Deseru'd thereby with death to be tormented.
Because thy belly should rough wrinckles lacke,
Wilt thou thy wombe-inclosed off-spring wracke?
Had ancient Mothers this vile custome cherisht,
All humaine kinde by their default had perisht, 10

9 slipping] skipping *Cunn.* 10 dipping *T. B.*: slipping *Mas. to Mal., Cunn.*: skipping *Dyce* 23 In . . incense] In wiues, with incest *Douce*
Elegia 14. *om. Ish., Bind.* 1 Woman] women *Dyce etc.* freed *Mal.*

Or stones, our stockes originall, should be hurld
Againe by some in this vnpeopled world.
Who should haue *Priams* wealthy substance wonne,
If watry *Thetis* had her childe fordone?
In swelling wombe her twinnes had *Ilia* kilde, 15
He had not beene that conquering *Rome* did build.
Had *Venus* spoilde her bellies *Troyane* fruite,
The earth of *Cæsars* had beene destitute.
Thou also, that wert borne faire, hadst decayed,
If such a worke thy mother had assayed. 20
My selfe that better dye with louing may
Had seene, my mother killing me, no day.
Why takest increasing grapes from Vine-trees full?
With cruell hand why doest greene Apples pull?
Fruites ripe will fall, let springing things increase, 25
Life is no light price of a small surcease:
Why with hid irons are your bowels torne?
And why dire poison giue you babes vnborne?
At *Cholcis* stain'd with childrens bloud men raile,
And mother-murtherd *Itis* thee bewaile, 30
Both vnkinde parents, but for causes sad,
Their wedlocks pledges veng'd their husbands bad.
What *Tereus*, what *Iason* you prouokes,
To plague your bodies with such harmefull strokes?
Armenian Tygers neuer did so ill, 35
Nor dares the Lyonesse her young whelpes kill.
But tender Damsels do it, though with paine,
Oft dyes she that her paunch-wrapt child hath slaine
Shee dyes, and with loose haires to graue is sent,
And who ere see her, worthily lament. 40
But in the ayre let these words come to nought,
And my presages of no weight be thought.
Forgiue her gratious Gods this one delict,
And on the next fault punishment inflict.

ELEGIA. 15.

Ad annulum, quem dono amicæ dedit.

Thou ring that shalt my faire girles finger binde,
Wherein is seene the giuers louing minde:

11 Or *Dyce etc.*: On *Mas. to Mal. 133* 16 did] bid *Mal. 368* 22 no *Dyce etc.*: to *Mas. to Mal.* 29 At] And *Mal.* 30 thee] they *conj. Dyce, Cunn., Bull.*
Elegia 15. *om. Ish., Bind.*

Be welcome to her, gladly let her take thee,
And her small ioynts incircling round hoope make thee.
Fit her so well, as she is fit for me : 5
And of iust compasse for her knuckles bee.
Blest ring thou in my mistris hand shalt lye.
My selfe poore wretch mine owne gifts now enuie.
O would that sodainly into my gift,
I could my selfe by secret Magicke shift. 10
Then would I wish thee touch my mistris pappe,
And hide thy left hand vnderneath her lappe.
I would get off though straight, and sticking fast,
And in her bosome strangely fall at last.
Then I, that I may seale her priuy leaues, 15
Least to the waxe the hold-fast drye gemme cleaues,
Would first my beautious wenches moist lips touch,
Onely Ile signe nought, that may grieue me much.
I would not out, might I in one place hit,
But in lesse compasse her small fingers knit. 20
My life, that I will shame thee neuer feare,
Or be a loade thou shouldst refuse to beare.
Weare me, when warmest showers thy members wash,
And through the gemme let thy lost waters pash.
But seeing thee, I thinke my thing will swell, 25
And euen the ring performe a mans part well.
Vaine things why wish I ? go small gift from hand,
Let her my faith with thee giuen vnderstand.

ELEGIA. 16.

Ad amicam, vt ad rura sua veniat.

Sulmo, Pelignies third part me containes,
A small, but wholesome soyle with watrie veynes.
Although the sunne to riue the earth incline,
And the *Icarian* froward Dog-starre shine,
Pilignian fields with liqued riuers flowe, 5
And on the soft ground fertile greene grasse growe.
With corne the earth abounds, with vines much more,
And some few pastures *Pallas* Oliues bore.

7 Blest ring thou] Bestring *Douce* hand shalt] armes shall *Douce* 22 be *Dyce etc.* : by *Mas. to Mal.* 23 thy] my *Mal.*
Elegia 16. *om. Ish., Bind.* 5 with] which *Mas., Douce*

And by the rising herbes, where cleare springs slide,
A grassie turffe the moistened earth doth hide. 10
But absent is my fire, lyes ile tell none,
My heate is heere, what moues my heate is gone.
Pollux and *Castor*, might I stand betwixt,
In heauen without thee would I not be fixt.
Vpon the cold earth pensiue let them lay, 15
That meane to trauaile some long irkesome way.
Or els will maidens, yong-mens mates, to go
If they determine to perseuer so.
Then on the rough *Alpes* should I tread aloft,
My hard way with my mistrisse would seeme soft. 20
With her I durst the *Lybian Syrtes* breake through,
And raging Seas in boistrous South-winds plough.
No barking Dogs that *Syllaes* intrailes beare,
Nor thy gulfes crooked *Malea*, would I feare.
No flowing waues with drowned ships forth poured, 25
By cloyed *Charibdis*, and againe deuoured.
But if sterne *Neptunes* windie powre preuaile,
And waters force, force helping Gods to faile,
With thy white armes vpon my shoulders seaze,
So sweete a burthen I will beare with eaze. 30
The youth oft swimming to his *Hero* kinde,
Had then swum ouer, but the way was blinde.
But without thee, although vine-planted ground
Conteines me, though the streames in fields surround,
Though *Hindes* in brookes the running waters bring, 35
And coole gales shake the tall trees leauy spring,
Healthfull *Peligny* I esteeme nought worth,
Nor do I like the country of my birth.
Sythia, *Cilicia*, *Brittaine* are as good,
And rockes dyed crimson with *Prometheus* bloud. 40
Elmes loue the Vines, the Vines with Elmes abide,
Why doth my mistresse from me oft deuide ?
Thou swarest, deuision should not twixt vs rise,
By me, and by my starres, thy radiant eyes.
Maides words more vaine and light then falling leaues, 45
Which as it seemes, hence winde and sea bereaues.
If any godly care of me thou hast,
Adde deeds vnto thy promises at last.

12 heate . . heate] heart . . heat *Mal. 133* 23 dog *Mal. 133* 34 in fields] in field *Mal.* : the fields *Dyce etc.* 43 swarest *T. B.* : swearest *Mas. to Mal.* : swear'd'st *Dyce etc.*

And with swift Naggs drawing thy little Coach,
(Their reines let loose) right soone my house approach. 50
But when she comes, you swelling mounts sinck downe,
And falling vallies be the smooth-wayes crowne.

ELEGIA. 17.

Quod Corinnæ soli sit seruiturus.

To serue a wench if any thinke it shame,
He being Iudge, I am conuinc'd of blame.
Let me be slandered, while my fire she hides,
That *Paphos*, and the floud-beate *Cithera* guides.
Would I had beene my mistresse gentle prey, 5
Since some faire one I should of force obey.
Beauty giues heart, *Corinnas* lookes excell,
Aye me why is it knowne to her so well?
But by her glasse disdainefull pride she learnes,
Nor she her selfe but first trim'd vp discernes. 10
Not though thy face in all things make thee raigne,
(O face most cunning mine eyes to detaine)
Thou oughtst therefore to scorne me for thy mate,
Small things with greater may be copulate.
Loue-snarde *Calypso* is supposde to pray 15
A mortall nimphes refusing Lord to stay.
Who doubts, with *Pelius*, *Thetis* did consort,
Egeria with iust *Numa* had good sport,
Venus with *Vulcan*, though smiths tooles laide by,
With his stumpe-foote he halts ill-fauouredly. 20
This kinde of verse is not alike, yet fit
With shorter numbers the heroicke sit.
And thou my light accept me how so euer,
Lay in the mid bed, there be my law giuer.
My stay no crime, my flight no ioy shall breede, 25
Nor of our loue to be asham'd we need,
For great reuenews I good verses haue,
And many by me to get glory craue.
I know a wench reports her selfe *Corinne*,
What would not she giue that faire name to winne? 30

49 with *om. Mal.* 51 you *Dyce etc.*: your *Mas. to Mal.*
Elegia 17. *om. Ish., Bind.* 4 the *om. Dyce etc.* 19 smiths] some smiths *Mal. 133*

But sundry flouds in one banke neuer go,
Eurotas cold, and poplar bearing *Po.*
Nor in my bookes shall one but thou be writ,
Thou doest alone giue matter to my wit.

ELEGIA. 18.

Ad Macrum, quod de amoribus scribat.

To tragick verse while thou *Achilles* trainst,
And new sworne souldiours maiden armes retainst,
Wee *Macer* sit in *Venus* slothfull shade,
And tender loue hath great things hatefull made.
Often at length, my wench depart I bid, 5
Shee in my lap sits still as earst she did.
I sayd it irkes me: halfe to weping framed,
Aye me, she cries, to loue, why art ashamed?
Then wreathes about my necke her winding armes,
And thousand kisses giues, that worke my harmes: 10
I yeeld, and back my wit from battells bring,
Domesticke acts, and mine owne warres to sing.
Yet tragedies, and scepters fild my lines,
But though I apt were for such high deseignes,
Loue laughed at my cloak, and buskines painted, 15
And rule so soone with priuate hands acquainted.
My Mistris deity also drewe me fro it,
And loue triumpheth ore his buskind Poet.
What lawfull is, or we professe loues art,
(Alas my precepts turne my selfe to smart) 20
We write, or what *Penelope* sends *Vlysses*,
Or *Phillis* teares that her *Domophoon* misses,
What thanklesse *Iason*, *Macareus* and *Paris*,
Phedra, and *Hipolite* may read, my care is,
And what poore *Dido* with her drawne sword sharpe 25
Doth say, with her that lou'd the *Aonian* harpe.
As soone as from strange lands *Sabinus* came,
And writings did from diuerse places frame,
White-cheekt *Penelope* knewe *Vlisses* signe,
The stepdame read *Hyppolitus* lustlesse line. 30
Eneas to *Elisa* answere giues,
And *Phillis* hath to reade; if now she liues.
Iasons sad letter doth *Hipsipile* greete,
Sappho her vowed harpe laies at *Phœbus* feete.

Elegia 18. *om. Ish., Bind.*

Nor of thee *Macer* that resoundst forth armes, 35
Is golden loue hid in *Mars* mid alarmes.
There *Paris* is, and *Helens* crymes record,
With *Laodameia* mate to her dead Lord.
Vnlesse I erre to these thou more incline
Then warres, and from thy tents wilt come to mine. 40

ELEGIA. 19.

Ad riualem, cui vxor curæ non erat.

Foole if to keepe thy wife thou hast no neede,
Keepe her for me, my more desire to breede.
Wee skorne things lawfull, stolne sweetes we affect,
Cruell is he that loues whom none protect.
Let vs both louers hope, and feare alike, 5
And may repulse place for our wishes strike.
What should I do with fortune that nere failes me?
Nothing I loue, that at all times auailes me.
Wily *Corinna* sawe this blemish in me,
And craftily knowes by what meanes to winne me. 10
Ah often, that her haole head aked, she lying,
Wild me, whose slowe feete sought delay be flying.
Ah oft how much she might she feignd offence;
And doing wrong made shew of innocence.
So hauing vext she nourisht my warme fire, 15
And was againe most apt to my desire.
To please me, what faire termes and sweet words ha's shee?
Great gods what kisses, and how many gaue she?
Thou also that late tookest mine eyes away,
Oft couzen me, oft being wooed say nay. 20
And on thy threshold let me lie dispred,
Suffring much cold by hoary nights frost bred.
So shall my loue continue many yeares,
This doth delight me, this my courage cheares.
Fat loue, and too much fulsome me annoyes, 25
Euen as sweete meate a glutted stomacke cloyes.
In brazen tower had not *Danae* dwelt,
A mothers ioy by *Ioue* she had not felt.

39 thou] I *Mal. 133* 40 will *Mal.*
Elegia 19. *om. Ish., Bind.* 2 for] from *Douce* 10 knowes] knew *conj. Dyce* 12 be] by *Douce, Mal.* 18 gaue] ga' *Dyce, Bull.* 20 of being *Mal.*

While *Iuno Io* keepes when hornes she wore,
Ioue liked her better then he did before. 30
Who couets lawfull things takes leaues from woods,
And drinkes stolne waters in surrownding floudes.
Her louer let her mocke, that long will raigne.
Aye me, let not my warnings cause my paine.
What euer haps, by suffrance harme is done, 35
What flies, I followe, what followes me I shunne.
But thou of thy faire damsell too secure,
Beginne to shut thy house at euening sure.
Search at the dore who knocks oft in the darke,
In nights deepe silence why the ban-dogges barke. 40
Whether the subtile maide lines bringes and carries,
Why she alone in empty bed oft tarries.
Let this care some-times bite thee to the quick,
That to deceits it may me forward pricke.
To steale sands from the shore he loues alife, 45
That can effect a foolish wittalls wife.
Now I forewarne, vnlesse to keepe her stronger,
Thou doest beginne, she shall be mine no longer.
Long haue I borne much, hoping time would beate thee
To guard her well, that well I might entreate thee. 50
Thou suffrest what no husband can endure,
But of my loue it will an end procure.
Shall I poore soule be neuer interdicted?
Nor neuer with nights sharpe reuenge afflicted?
In sleeping shall I fearelesse drawe my breath? 55
Wilt nothing do, why I should wish thy death?
Can I but loath a husband growne a baude?
By thy default thou doest our ioyes defraude.
Some other seeke that may in patience striue with thee,
To pleasure me, for-bid me to coriue with thee. 60

46 affect *Dyce etc.* 48 she] he *Mal. 133* 60 pleasure] please *Mal.*

P. Ouidij Nasonis Amorum
Liber tertius.

ELEGIA. I.

Deliberatio poetæ, vtrum elegos pergat scribere an potius tragedias.

An old wood, stands vncut of long yeares space,
Tis credible some godhead haunts the place.
In midst thereof a stone-pau'd sacred spring,
Where round about small birdes most sweetely sing.
Heere while I walke hid close in shadie groue, 5
To finde what worke my muse might moue I stroue.
Elegia came with haires perfumed sweete,
And one, I thinke, was longer of her feete.
A decent forme, thinne robe, a louers looke,
By her footes blemish greater grace she tooke. 10
Then with huge steps came violent *Tragedie*,
Sterne was her front, her cloake on ground did lie.
Her left hand held abroad a regal scepter,
The *Lydian* buskin ⟨in⟩ fit paces kept her.
And first she sayd: when will thy loue be spent? 15
O Poet carelesse of thy argument.
Wine-bibbing banquets tell thy naughtinesse,
Each crosse waies corner doth as much expresse.
Oft some points at the prophet passing by,
And this is he whom fierce loue burnes, they cry. 20
A laughing stocke thou art to all the citty,
While without shame thou singst thy lewdnesse ditty.
Tis time to moue graue things in lofty stile,
Long hast thou loyterd, greater workes compile.
The subiect hides thy wit, mens acts resound, 25
This thou wilt say to be a worthy ground.
Thy muse hath played what may milde girles content,
And by those numbers is thy first youth spent.
Now giue the *Roman* Tragedie a name,
To fill my lawes thy wanton spirit frame. 30

Elegia I. *om. Ish., Bind.* 2 God-head *Dyce etc.*: good head *Mas. to Mal.* 10 she] we *Mal.* 12 cloak *Dyce etc.*: looke *Mas. to Mal.* 14 in *Dyce etc.*: *om. Mas. to Mal.* paces *Dyce etc.*: places *Mas. to Mal.* 15 she *Dyce etc.*: he *Mas. to Mal.*

This saied, she mou'd her buskins gaily varnisht,
And seauen times shooke her head with thicke locks garnisht.
The other smilde, (I wot) with wanton eyes,
Erre I ? or mirtle in her right hand lies.
With lofty wordes stout Tragedie (she sayd) 35
Why treadst me downe ? art thou aye grauely plaied ?
Thou deignst vnequall lines should thee rehearse,
Thou fightst against me vsing mine owne verse.
Thy lofty stile with mine I not compare,
Small doores vnfitting for large houses are. 40
Light am I, and with me, my care, light loue,
Not stronger am I then the thing I moue.
Venus without me should be rusticall,
This goddesse company doth to me befall.
What gate thy stately words cannot vnlocke, 45
My flatt'ring speeches soone wide open knocke.
And I deserue more then thou canst in verity,
By suffring much not borne by thy seuerity.
By me *Corinna* learnes, cousening her guard,
To get the dore with little noise vnbard, 50
And slipt from bed cloth'd in a loose night-gowne,
To moue her feete vnheard in setting downe.
Ah howe oft on hard doores hung I engrau'd,
From no mans reading fearing to be sau'd.
But till the keeper went forth, I forget not, 55
The maide to hide me in her bosome let not.
What gift with me was on her birth day sent,
But cruelly by her was drown'd and rent.
First of thy minde the happy seedes I knewe,
Thou hast my gift, which she would from thee sue. 60
She left; I say'd, you both I must beseech,
To empty aire may go my fearefull speech.
With scepters, & high buskins th'one would dresse me,
So through the world shold bright renown expresse me.
The other giues my loue a conquering name, 65
Come therefore, and to long verse shorter frame.
Graunt Tragedie thy Poet times least tittle,
Thy labour euer lasts, she askes but little.
She gaue me leaue, soft loues in time make hast,
Some greater worke will vrge me on at last. 70

32 time *Mas., Douce* 41 me] thee *Mal. 368* 42 things *Douce* 52 setting *Dyce etc.*: sitting *Mas. to Mal.* 55 keeper *Dyce etc.*: keepes *Mas., Douce*: keepers *Mal.*

ELEGIA. 2.

Ad amicam cursum equorum spectantem.

I sit not here the noble horse to see,
Yet whom thou fauourst, pray may conquerour be.
To sit, and talke with thee I hether came,
That thou maiest know with loue thou mak'st me flame.
Thou viewst the course, I thee: let either heed 5
What please them, and their eyes let either feede.
What horse-driuer thou fauourst most is best,
Because on him thy care doth hap to rest.
Such chaunce let me haue: I would brauely runne,
On swift steedes mounted till the race were done. 10
Now would I slacke the reines, now lash their hide,
With wheeles bent inward now the ring-turne ride.
In running if I see thee, I shall stay,
And from my hands the reines will slip away.
Ah *Pelops* from his coach was almost feld, 15
Hippodameias lookes while he beheld.
Yet he attain'd by her support to haue her,
Let vs all conquer by our mistris fauour.
In vaine why flyest backe? force conioynes vs now:
The places lawes this benefit allowe. 20
But spare my wench thou at her right hand seated,
By thy sides touching ill she is entreated.
And sit thou rounder, that behind vs see,
For shame presse not her backe with thy hard knee.
But on the ground thy cloathes too loosely lie, 25
Gather them vp, or lift them loe will I.
Enuious garments so good legges to hide,
The more thou look'st, the more the gowne enuide.
Swift *Atalantas* flying legges like these,
Wish in his hands graspt did *Hippomenes*. 30
Coate-tuckt *Dianas* legges are painted like them,
When strong wilde beasts she stronger hunts to strike them.
Ere these were seene, I burnt: what will these do?
Flames into flame, flouds thou powrest seas into.
By these I iudge, delight me may the rest, 35
Which lie hid vnder her thinne veile supprest.
Yet in the meane time wilt small windes bestowe,
That from thy fanne, mou'd by my hand may blow?

Elegia 2. *om. Ish., Bind.* 11 their] her *Douce* 28 gown's *Cunn., Bull.*

Or is my heate of minde, not of the skie?
Ist womens loue my captiue brest doth frie? 40
While thus I speake, blacke dust her white robes ray:
Foule dust, from her faire body go away.
Now comes the pompe; themselues let all men cheere:
The shout is nigh; the golden pompe comes heere.
First victory is brought with large spred wing, 45
Goddesse come here, make my loue conquering.
Applaud you *Neptune*, that dare trust his waue,
The sea I vse not: me my earth must haue.
Souldiour applaud thy *Mars*: no warres we moue,
Peace pleaseth me, and in mid peace is loue. 50
With *Augures Phœbus*, *Phœbe* with hunters standes,
To thee *Minerua* turne the craftes-mens hands.
Ceres and *Bacchus* Country-men adore,
Champions please *Pollux*, *Castor* loues horsemen more.
Thee gentle *Venus*, and the boy that flies, 55
We praise: great goddesse ayde my enterprize,
Let my new mistris graunt to be beloued.
She beckt, and prosperous signes gaue as she moued.
What *Venus* promisd, promise thou we pray,
Greater then her, by her leaue th'art, Ile say. 60
The Gods, and their rich pompe witnesse with me,
For euermore thou shalt my mistris be.
Thy legges hang downe, thou maiest, if that be best,
A while thy tiptoes on the foote-stoole rest.
Now greatest spectacles the *Prætor* sends, 65
Fower-chariot horses from the lists euen ends.
I see whom thou affectest: he shall subdue,
The horses seeme, as thy desire they knewe.
Alas he runnes too farre about the ring,
What doest? thy wagon in lesse compasse bring. 70
What doest vnhappy? her good wishes fade,
Let with strong hand the reine to bend be made.
One slowe we fauour, *Romans* him reuoke:
And each giue signes by casting vp his cloake.
They call him backe, least their gownes tosse thy haire, 75
To hide thee in my bosome straight repaire.
But now againe the barriers open lye;
And forth the gay troupes on swift horses flie.

41 spake *Mal. 133* 54 pleace *Mas.*, *Douce*: place *Mal.* 64 A *Dyce etc.*: Or *Mas. to Mal.* 68 thy . . they *Dyce etc.*: they . . they *Mas.*, *Mal.*: they . . thy *Douce*

At last now conquer, and out-runne the rest :
My mistris wish confirme with my request. 80
My mistris hath her wish, my wish remaine :
He holdes the palme : my palme is yet to gaine,
She smilde, and with quicke eyes behight some grace :
Pay it not heere, but in an other place.

ELEGIA. 3.

De amica, quæ periurauerat.

What, are there Gods ? her selfe she hath forswore,
And yet remaines the face she had before.
How long her lockes were, ere her oath she tooke :
So long they be, since she her faith forsooke.
Faire white with rose red was before commixt : 5
Now shine her lookes pure white and red betwixt.
Her foote was small : her footes forme is most fit :
Comely tall was she, comely tall shee's yet.
Sharpe eyes she had : radiant like starres they be,
By which she periurd oft hath lyed by me. 10
Insooth th'eternall powers graunt maides society
Falsely to sweare, their beauty hath some deity.
By her eyes I remember late she swore,
And by mine eyes, and mine were pained sore.
Say gods : if she vnpunisht you deceiue, 15
For others faults why do I losse receiue ?
But did you not so enuy *Cepheus* Daughter,
For her ill-beautious Mother iudgd to slaughter.
Tis not enough, she shakes your record off,
And vnreuengd mockt Gods with me doth scoffe. 20
But by my paine to purge her periuries,
Couzend, I am the couzeners sacrifice.
God is a name, no substance, feard in vaine,
And doth the world in fond beliefe deteine.
Or if there be a God, he loues fine wenches, 25
And all things too much in their sole power drenches.
Mars girts his deadly sword on for my harme :
Pallas launce strikes me with vnconquerd arme.
At me *Apollo* bends his pliant bowe :
At me *Ioues* right-hand lightning hath to throwe. 30

79 last *Douce* : least *Mas., Mal., Dyce etc.*
Elegia 3 *om. Ish., Bind.* 10 by *Mas. to Mal.* : to *Dyce etc.*

The wronged Gods dread faire ones to offend,
And feare those, that to feare them least intend.
Who now will care the Altars to perfume?
Tut, men should not their courage so consume.
Ioue throwes downe woods, and Castles with his fire: 35
But bids his darts from periurd girles retire.
Poore *Semele*, among so many burn'd,
Her owne request to her owne torment turnd.
But when her louer came, had she drawne backe,
The fathers thigh should vnborne *Bacchus* lacke. 40
Why grieue I? and of heauen reproches pen?
The Gods haue eyes, and brests as well as men.
Were I a God, I should giue women leaue,
With lying lips my God-head to deceaue,
My selfe would sweare, the wenches true did sweare, 45
And I would be none of the Gods seuere.
But yet their gift more moderately vse,
Or in mine eyes good wench no paine transfuse.

ELEGIA. 4.

Ad virum seruantem coniugem.

Rude man, 'tis vaine, thy damsell to commend
To keepers trust: their wits should them defend.
Who, without feare, is chaste, is chast in sooth:
Who, because meanes want, doeth not, she doth.
Though thou her body guard, her minde is staind: 5
Nor, least she will, can any be restrainde.
Nor canst by watching keepe her minde from sinne.
All being shut out, th'adulterer is within.
Who may offend, sinnes least; power to do ill
The fainting seedes of naughtinesse doth kill. 10
Forbeare to kindle vice by prohibition,
Sooner shall kindnesse gaine thy wills fruition.
I saw a horse against the bitte stiffe-neckt,
Like lightning go, his strugling mouth being checkt.
When he perceiud the reines let slacke, he stayde, 15
And on his loose mane the loose bridle laide.
How to attaine what is denyed we thinke,
Euen as the sicke desire forbidden drinke.

45 did sheare *Douce*
Elegia 4. *om. Ish., Bind.* 6 least] less *Dyce etc.*

Argus had either way an hundred eyes,
Yet by deceit loue did them all surprize. 20
In stone, and Yron walles *Danae* shut,
Came forth a mother, though a maide there put.
Penelope, though no watch look'd vnto her,
Was not defilde by any gallant wooer.
What's kept, we couet more: the care makes theft: 25
Few loue what others haue vnguarded left.
Nor doth her face please, but her husbands loue;
I know not what men thinke should thee so moue.
She is not chaste, that's kept, but a deare whore:
Thy feare is then her body valued more. 30
Although thou chafe, stolne pleasure is sweet play,
She pleaseth best, I feare, if any say.
A free-borne wench no right 'tis vp to locke:
So vse we women of strange nations stocke.
Because the keeper may come say, I did it, 35
She must be honest to thy seruants credit.
He is too clownish, whom a lewd wife grieues,
And this townes well knowne customes not beleeues,
Where *Mars* his sonnes not without fault did breed,
Remus and *Romulus*, *Ilias* twinne-borne seed. 40
Cannot a faire one, if not chast, please thee?
Neuer can these by any meanes agree.
Kindly thy mistris vse, if thou be wise.
Looke gently, and rough husbands lawes despise.
Honour what friends thy wife giues, sheele giue many: 45
Least labour so shall winne great grace of any,
So shalt thou go with youths to feasts together:
And see at home much that thou nere broughtst thether

ELEGIA. 5.

Ad amnem, dum iter faceret ad amicam.

Floud with redde-growne slime bankes, till I be past
Thy waters stay: I to my mistris hast.

29 that's kept . . whore] that keepes away her loue *Douce* 46 so shall] thou shalt *Douce*
Elegia 5. *om. Ish., Bind. This elegy is in modern texts of Ovid the sixth, that now called the fifth not being found in the edition from which Marlowe translated. The discrepancy in numbering continues to the end of the book.*

Thou hast no bridge, nor boate with ropes to throw,
That may transport me without oares to rowe.
Thee I haue pass'd, and knew thy streame none such, 5
When thy waues brim did scarse my anckles touch.
With snow thaw'd from the next hill now thou rushest,
And in thy foule deepe waters thicke thou gushest.
What helpes my hast: what to haue tane small rest?
What day and night to trauaile in her quest? 10
If standing here I can by no meanes get,
My foote vpon the further banke to set.
Now wish I those wings noble *Perseus* had,
Bearing the head with dreadfull Adders clad,
Now wish the chariot, whence corne seeds were found, 15
First to be throwne vpon the vntill'd ground.
I speake old Poets wonderfull inuentions,
Nere was, nor shall be, what my verse mentions.
Rather thou large banke ouer-flowing riuer,
Slide in thy bounds, so shalt thou runne for euer. 20
(Trust me) land-streame thou shalt no enuie lack,
If I a louer bee by thee held back.
Great flouds ought to assist young men in loue,
Great flouds the force of it do often proue.
In mid *Bithynia* 'tis said *Inachus*, 25
Grew pale, and in cold foords hot lecherous.
Troy had not yet beene ten yeares siege out-stander,
When nimph *Neæra* rapt thy lookes *Scamander.*
What? not *Alpheus* in strange lands to runne
Th' *Arcadian* Virgins constant loue hath wunne? 30
And *Crusa* vnto *Zanthus* first affide,
They say *Peneus* neere *Phthias* towne did hide.
What should I name *Æsope*, that *Thebe* lou'd,
Thebe who Mother of fiue Daughters prou'd?
If *Achelous*, I aske where thy hornes stand, 35
Thou saiest broke with *Alcides* angry hand.
Not *Calydon*, nor *Ætolia* did please:
One *Deianira* was more worth then these.
Rich *Nile* by seauen mouthes to the vast sea flowing,
Who so well keepes his waters head from knowing, 40
Is by *Euadne* thought to take such flame,
As his deepe whirle-pooles could not quench the same.

7 now] how *Mal. 133* rushest] gushest *Dyce etc.* 8 thicke] now *Mal.*: new *Dyce's 'ed. C'*. gushest *T. B.*: rushest *old edd.* 14 adders *Dyce etc.*: Arrowes *Mas. to Mal.* 15 seeds *T. B.*: fields *old edd., etc.* 33 Æsope] Asop *Dyce etc.* 39 vast] west *Douce*

Drye *Enipeus, Tyro* to embrace,
Flye backe his streame chargd, the streame chargd, gaue place.
Nor passe I thee, who hollow rocks downe tumbling, 45
In *Tiburs* field with watry fome art rumbling,
Whom *Ilia* pleasd, though in her lookes griefe reueld,
Her cheekes were scratcht, her goodly haires discheueld.
She wailing *Mars* sinne, and her vncles crime,
Strayd bare-foote through sole places on a time. 50
Her, from his swift waues, the bold floud perceau'd,
And from the mid foord his hoarse voice vpheau'd,
Saying, why sadly treadst my banckes vpon,
Ilia, sprung from *Idæan Laomedon* ?
Where's thy attire ? why wand'rest heere alone ? 55
To stay thy tresses white veyle hast thou none ?
Why weepst ? and spoilst with teares thy watry eyes ?
And fiercely knockst thy brest that open lyes ?
His heart consists of flint, and hardest steele,
That seeing thy teares can any ioy then feele. 60
Feare not : to thee our Court stands open wide,
There shalt be lou'd : *Ilia* lay feare aside.
Thou ore a hundreth Nimphes, or more shalt raigne :
For fiue score Nimphes, or more our flouds conteine.
Nor *Romane* stocke scorne me so much (I craue) 65
Gifts then my promise greater thou shalt haue.
This said he : shee her modest eyes held downe,
Her wofull bosome a warme shower did drowne.
Thrice she prepar'd to flie, thrice she did stay,
By feare depriu'd of strength to runne away. 70
Yet rending with enraged thumbe her tresses,
Her trembling mouth these vnmeete sounds expresses.
O would in my fore-fathers tombe deepe layde,
My bones had beene, while yet I was a maide.
Why being a vestall am I wooed to wed, 75
Deflowr'd and stained in vnlawfull bed ?
Why stay I ? men point at me for a whore,
Shame, that should make me blush, I haue no more.
This said : her coate hood-winckt her fearefull eyes,
And into water desperately she flies. 80
Tis said the slippery streame held vp her brest,
And kindly gaue her, what she liked best.
And I beleeue some wench thou hast affected :
But woods and groues keepe your faults vndetected.

44 his stream *Dyce etc.* : his shame *Mas. to Mal.* 46 fome] some *Douce*

While thus I speake, the waters more abounded: 85
And from the channell all abroad surrounded.
Mad streame, why doest our mutuall ioyes deferre?
Clowne, from my iourney why doest me deterre?
How wouldst thou flowe wert thou a noble floud,
If thy great fame in euery region stood? 90
Thou hast no name, but com'st from snowy mountaines;
No certaine house thou hast, nor any fountaines.
Thy springs are nought but raine and melted snowe:
Which wealth cold winter doth on thee bestowe.
Either th'art muddy in mid winter tide: 95
Or full of dust doest on the drye earth slide.
What thirstie traueller euer drunke of thee?
Who sayd with gratefull voyce perpetuall bee?
Harmefull to beasts, and to the fields thou proues:
Perchance these others, me mine owne losse mooues. 100
To this I fondly loues of flouds told plainly:
I shame so great names to haue vsde so vainly:
I know not what expecting, I ere while
Nam'd *Achelaus*, *Inachus*, and *Nile*,
But for thy merits I wish thee, white streame, 105
Drye winters aye, and sunnes in heate extreame.

ELEGIA. 6.

Quod ab amica receptus, cum ea coire non potuit, conqueritur.

Either she was foule, or her attire was bad,
Or she was not the wench I wisht t'haue had.
Idly I lay with her, as if I lou'd not,
And like a burthen grieu'd the bed that mou'd not.
Though both of vs perform'd our true intent, 5
Yet could I not cast anckor where I meant.
She on my neck her Iuory armes did throwe,
Her armes farre whiter, then the *Sythian* snow.
And eagerly she kist me with her tongue,
And vnder mine her wanton thigh she flung. 10
Yea, and she soothd me vp, and calld me sire,
And vsde all speech that might prouoke, and stirre.

85 Whilst *Mal. 133* 101 floude *Mal.* 104 Nile *Dyce etc.*: Ile *Mas. to Mal.*

Elegia 6] Elegia VII. *Dyce etc.* 3 not] her not *Ish., Bind.* 8 Her . . then] That were as white as *Ish., Bind.*

Yet like as if cold Hemlock I had drunke,
It mocked me, hung downe the head, and sunke.
Like a dull Cipher, or rude block I lay, 15
Or shade, or body was I who can say?
What will my age do, age I cannot shunne,
When in my prime my force is spent and done?
I blush, that being youthfull, hot, and lustie,
I proue neither youth nor man, but old and rustie. 20
Pure rose she, like a Nunne to sacrifice,
Or one that with her tender brother lyes.
Yet boorded I the golden *Chie* twise,
And *Libas*, and the white cheekt *Pitho* thrice.
Corinna crau'd it in a summers night, 25
And nine sweete bowts we had before day-light.
What, wast my limbs through some *Thessalian* charmes?
May spells, and drugges do silly soules such harmes?
With virgin waxe hath some imbast my ioynts?
And pierc'd my liuer with sharpe needles points? 30
Charmes change corne to grasse and make it die.
By charmes are running springs and fountaines dry.
By charmes mast drops from oakes, from vines grapes fal,
And fruite from trees when ther's no winde at all.
Why might not then my sinewes be inchaunted, 35
And I growe faint as with some spirit haunted?
To this adde shame: shame to performe it quaild me
And was the second cause why vigour failde me.
My idle thoughts delighted her no more,
Then did the robe or garment which she wore. 40
Yet might her touch make youthfull *Pylius* fire
And *Tithon* liuelier then his years require.
Euen her I had, and she had me in vaine,
What might I craue more, if I aske againe?
I thinke the great gods grieu'd they had bestow'd 45
The benefit: which lewdly I for-slow'd.
I wisht to be receiu'd in, in I get me,
To kisse, I kisse: to lie with her, she let me.

18 When] Seeing *Ish.*, *Bind.*, *Bull.* 19 that] and *Ish.*, *Bind.* 20 neither] nor *conj. Dyce.*, *Cunn.* 26 we had] had we *Ish.*, *Bind.*, *Bull.* 28 May] Nay *Mal.* drugges] droughs *Ish.*, *Bind.* 30 And] Had *Bind.* needles] needlesse *Douce*: needle *Ish.*, *Bind.*, *Bull.* 31 makes *Ish.* 38 vigour] rigor *Bind.* 40 wore] more *Mas.* 46 The] This *Ish.*, *Bind.*, *Bull.* 47 receiu'd] restored *Bind.* in I get] and in I got *Ish.*, *Bind.* 48 I kiss'd *Dyce*, *Cunn.*

Why was I blest? why made King to refuse it?
Chuffe-like had I not gold and could not vse it? 50
So in a spring thriues he that told so much,
And lookes vpon the fruits he cannot touch.
Hath any rose so from a fresh yong maide,
As she might straight haue gone to church and praide?
Well I beleeue, she kist not as she should, 55
Nor vs'd the sleight and cunning which she could,
Huge oakes, hard adamants might she haue moued,
And with sweet words cause deafe rocks to haue loued.
Worthy she was to moue both gods and men,
But neither was I man nor liued then. 60
Can deafe eare take delight when *Phæmius* sings?
Or *Thamiras* in curious painted things?
What sweete thought is there but I had the same?
And one gaue place still as an other came.
Yet not-withstanding like one dead it lay, 65
Drouping more then a rose puld yester-day.
Now when he should not iette, he boults vpright,
And craues his taske, and seekes to be at fight.
Lie downe with shame, and see thou stirre no more,
Seeing thou wouldst deceiue me as before. 70
Thou cousenest me: by thee surpriz'd am I,
And bide sore losse with endlesse infamy.
Nay more, the wench did not disdaine a whit,
To take it in her hand, and play with it.
But when she sawe it would by no meanes stand, 75
But still droupt downe, regarding not her hand,
Why mockst thou me? she cryed, or being ill
Who bad thee lie downe heere against thy will?
Either th'art witcht with bloud of frogs newe dead
Or iaded camst thou from some others bed. 80
With that her loose gowne on, from me she cast her,
In skipping out her naked feete much grac'd her.
And least her maide should know of this disgrace,
To couer it, spilt water on the place.

49 to refuse] and refusde *Ish.*, *Bind.* 51 a spring] aspiring *Bind.* 52 fruite *Mal.* 56 and] nor *Ish.*, *Bind.* 58 caus'd *Dyce etc.* loued *Ish.*, *Bind.*, *Dyce etc.*: moned *Mas.*, *Douce*: moved *Mal.* 60 nor] ne *Bind.* 61 eare] yeares *Ish.*, *Bind.*: ears *Dyce etc.* 65 it] I *Douce* 66 then] like *Douce* 70 thou] now thou *Ish.*, *Bind.* 71 cousendst *Ish.*, *Bind.* 72 sore losse] great hurt *Bind.* 74 her *om. Douce* 76 dropt *Bind.* 81 that *om. Douce* 84 on] in *Douce*, *Ish.*, *Bind.*, *Bull.*

ELEGIA. 7.

Quod ab amica non recipiatur, dolet.

What man will now take liberall arts in hand,
Or thinke soft verse in any stead to stand?
Wit was some-times more pretious then gold,
Now pouerty great barbarisme we hold.
When our bookes did my mistris faire content, 5
I might not go whether my papers went.
She prais'd me, yet the gate shutt fast vpon her,
I heere and there go witty with dishonour.
See a rich chuffe whose wounds great wealth inferr'd,
For bloudshed knighted, before me preferr'd. 10
Foole canst thou him in thy white armes embrace?
Foole canst thou lie in his enfolding space?
Knowest not this head a helme was wont to beare,
This side that serues thee, a sharpe sword did weare.
His left hand whereon gold doth ill alight, 15
A target bore: bloud sprinckled was his right.
Canst touch that hand wherewith some one lies dead?
Ah whether is thy brests soft nature fled?
Behold the signes of antient fight, his skarres,
What ere he hath his body gaind in warres. 20
Perhaps he'ele tell howe oft he slewe a man,
Confessing this, why doest thou touch him than?
I the pure priest of *Phœbus* and the muses,
At thy deafe dores in verse sing my abuses.
Not what we slouthfull knowe, let wise men learne, 25
But follow trembling campes, and battailes sterne,
And for a good verse drawe the first dart forth,
Homer without this shall be nothing worth.
Ioue being admonisht gold had soueraigne power,
To winne the maide came in a golden shewer. 30
Till then, rough was her father, she seuere,
The posts of brasse the walles of iron were.
But when in gifts the wise adulterer came,
She held her lap ope to receiue the same.
Yet when old *Saturne* heauens rule possest 35
All gaine in darknesse the deepe earth supprest.

Elegia 7. om. Ish., Bind.: Elegia VIII. *Dyce etc.* 13 this] his *Mal.* 17 lies *Dyce etc.*: lie *old edd.* 18 thy] they *Mas.* fled] sled *Mas.* 25 know *Dyce etc.*: knewe *old edd.* 27 darts *Mal.*

Gold, siluer, irons heauy weight, and brasse,
In hell were harbourd, here was found no masse.
But better things it gaue, corne without ploughes,
Apples, and hony in oakes hollow boughes. 40
With strong plough shares no man the earth did cleaue,
The ditcher no markes on the ground did leaue.
Nor hanging oares the troubled seas did sweepe,
Men kept the shoare, and sailde not into deepe.
Against thy selfe, mans nature, thou wert cunning, 45
And to thine owne losse was thy wit swift running.
Why gird'st thy citties with a towred wall?
Why letst discordant hands to armour fall?
What doest with seas? with th' earth thou wert content,
Why seek'st not heau'n the third realme to frequent? 50
Heauen thou affects, with *Romulus*, temples braue
Bacchus, *Alcides*, and now *Cæsar* haue.
Gold from the earth in steade of fruits we pluck,
Souldiours by bloud to be inricht haue lucke.
Courts shut the poore out; wealth giues estimation, 55
Thence growes the Iudge, and knight of reputation.
All they possesse: they gouerne fieldes, and lawes,
They manadge peace, and rawe warres bloudy iawes,
Onely our loues let not such rich churles gaine,
Tis well, if some wench for the poore remaine. 60
Now, *Sabine*-like, though chast she seemes to liue,
One her commands, who many things can giue.
For me, she doth keeper, and husband feare.
If I should giue, both would the house forbeare.
If of scornd louers god be venger iust, 65
O let him change goods so ill got to dust.

ELEGIA. 8.

Tibulli mortem deflet.

If *Thetis*, and the morne their sonnes did waile,
And enuious fates great goddesses assaile,
Sad *Elegia* thy wofull haires vnbinde:
Ah now a name too true thou hast, I finde.

43 Sea *Mal. 133* 46 thine owne] thy one *Mal.* 49 th' *om. Mal. 133* 57 All they] All thee *Douce* 62 her *Dyce etc.*: she *Mas. to Mal.*

Elegia 8. *om. Ish., Bind.*: Elegia IX. *Dyce etc.* 3 Elegia *Mal.*: Eeliga *Mas., Douce*: Elegy *Dyce etc.*

Tibullus, thy workes Poet, and thy fame, 5
Burnes his dead body in the funerall flame.
Loe *Cupid* brings his quiuer spoyled quite,
His broken bowe, his fire-brand without light.
How piteously with drouping wings he stands,
And knocks his bare brest with selfe-angry hands. 10
The locks spred on his necke receiue his teares,
And shaking sobbes his mouth for speeches beares.
So at *Æneas* buriall men report,
Faire-fac'd *Iulus*, he went forth thy court.
And *Venus* grieues, *Tibullus* life being spent, 15
As when the wilde boare *Adons* groine had rent.
The gods care we are cald, and men of piety,
And some there be that thinke we haue a deity.
Outrageous death profanes all holy things
And on all creatures obscure darcknesse brings. 20
To *Thracian Orpheus* what did parents good ?
Or songs amazing wilde beasts of the wood ?
Where *Linus* by his father *Phœbus* layed
To sing with his vnequald harpe is sayed.
See *Homer* from whose fountaine euer fild, 25
Pierian deawe to Poets is distild.
Him the last day in black *Auerne* hath drownd,
Verses alone are with continuance crown'd.
The worke of Poets lasts *Troyes* labours fame,
And that slowe webbe nights falshood did vnframe. 30
So *Nemesis*, so *Delia* famous are,
The one his first loue, th'other his new care.
What profit to vs hath our pure life bred ?
What to haue laine alone in empty bed ?
When bad fates take good men, I am forbod 35
By secreat thoughts to thinke there is a god.
Liue godly, thou shalt die, though honour heauen,
Yet shall thy life be forcibly bereauen.
Trust in good verse, *Tibullus* feeles deaths paines,
Scarse rests of all what a small vrne conteines. 40
Thee sacred Poet could sad flames destroy ?
Nor feared they thy body to annoy ?
The holy gods gilt temples they might fire,
That durst to so great wickednesse aspire.
Eryx bright *Empresse* turnd her lookes aside, 45
And some, that she refrain'd teares, haue deni'd.

16 Adonis *Douce, Mal.* 17 and] the *Mal.* 133 24 vequall *Douce* 34 alone] above *Mal.* 41 Thee] The *Mal.*

Yet better ist, then if *Corcyras Ile*
Had thee vnknowne interr'd in ground most vile.
Thy dying eyes here did thy mother close,
Nor did thy ashes her last offrings lose. 50
Part of her sorrowe heere thy sister bearing,
Comes forth her vnkeembd locks asunder tearing.
Nemesis and thy first wench ioyne their kisses
With thine, nor this last fire their presence misses.
Delia departing, happier lou'd, she saith, 55
Was I: thou liu'dst, while thou esteemdst my faith.
Nemesis answeares, what's my losse to thee?
His fainting hand in death engrasped mee.
If ought remaines of vs but name, and spirit,
Tibullus doth *Elysiums* ioy inherit. 60
Their youthfull browes with Iuie girt to meete him,
With *Caluus* learnd *Catullus* comes and greete him,
And thou, if falsely charged to wrong thy friend,
Gallus that carst not bloud, and life to spend.
With these thy soule walkes, soules if death release, 65
The godly, sweete *Tibullus* doth increase.
Thy bones I pray may in the vrne safe rest,
And may th' earths weight thy ashes nought molest.

ELEGIA. 9.

Ad Cererem, conquerens quod eius sacris cum amica concumbere non permittatur.

Come were the times of *Ceres* sacrifize,
In emptie bed alone my mistris lies.
Golden-hair'd *Ceres* crownd with eares of corne,
Why are our pleasures by thy meanes forborne?
Thee, goddesse, bountifull all nations iudge, 5
Nor lesse at mans prosperity any grudge.
Rude husband-men bak'd not their corne before,
Nor on the earth was knowne the name of floore.
On mast of oakes, first oracles, men fed,
This was their meate, the soft grasse was their bed. 10
First *Ceres* taught the seede in fields to swell,
And ripe-earde corne with sharpe-edg'd sithes to fell.

52 vnkeembe *old edd.* 62 greets *Dyce*[1] 64 carst] car'd'st *Dyce etc.* 65 thy] my *Mal.* 133
Elegia 9. *om. Ish., Bind.*: Elegia XI. *Dyce etc.* 10 there meate *Mas.*

She first constraind bulles necks to beare the yoake,
And vntild ground with crooked plough-shares broake.
Who thinkes her to be glad at louers smart, 15
And worshipt by their paine, and lying apart?
Nor is she, though she loues the fertile fields,
A clowne, nor no loue from her warme brest yeelds.
Be witnesse *Crete* (nor *Crete* doth all things feigne)
Crete proud that *Ioue* her nourcery maintaine. 20
There he who rules the worlds starre-spangled towers,
A little boy druncke teate-distilling showers.
Faith to the witnesse *Ioues* praise doth apply,
Ceres, I thinke, no knowne fault will deny.
The goddesse sawe *Iasion* on *Candyan Ide*, 25
With strong hand striking wild-beasts brist'led hyde.
She sawe, and as her marrowe tooke the flame,
Was diuers waies distract with loue, and shame.
Loue conquer'd shame, the furrowes dry were burnd,
And corne with least part of it selfe returnd. 30
When well-toss'd mattocks did the ground prepare,
Being fit broken with the crooked share,
And seedes were equally in large fields cast,
The plough-mans hopes were frustrate at the last.
The graine-rich goddesse in high woods did stray, 35
Her long haires eare-wrought garland fell away.
Onely was *Crete* fruitfull that plenteous yeare,
Where *Ceres* went each place was haruest there.
Ida the seate of groues did sing with corne,
Which by the wild boare in the woods was shorne. 40
Law-giuing *Minos* did such yeares desire;
And wisht the goddesse long might feele loues fire.
Ceres what sports to thee so grieuous were,
As in thy sacrifize we them forbeare?
Why am I sad, when *Proserpine* is found, 45
And *Iuno* like with *Dis* raignes vnder ground?
Festiuall dayes aske *Venus*, songs, and wine,
These gifts are meete to please the powers diuine.

ELEGIA. 10.

Ad amicam, a cuius amore discedere non potest.

Long haue I borne much, mad thy faults me make:
Dishonest loue my wearied brest forsake,

46 with *om. Mal.*
Elegia 10. *om. Ish., Bind.*: Elegia XI. *Dyce etc.*

Now haue I freed my selfe, and fled the chaine,
And what I haue borne, shame to beare againe.
We vanquish, and tread tam'd loue vnder feete, 5
Victorious wreathes at length my Temples greete.
Suffer, and harden: good growes by this griefe,
Oft bitter iuice brings to the sicke reliefe.
I haue sustainde so oft thrust from the dore,
To lay my body on the hard moist floore. 10
I know not whom thou lewdly didst imbrace,
When I to watch supplyed a seruants place.
I saw when forth a tyred louer went,
His side past seruice, and his courage spent.
Yet this is lesse, then if he had seene me, 15
May that shame fall mine enemies chance to be.
When haue not I fixt to thy side close layed?
I haue thy husband, guard, and fellow plaied.
The people by my company she pleasd,
My loue was cause that more mens loue she seazd. 20
What should I tell her vaine tongues filthy lyes,
And to my losse God-wronging periuries?
What secret becks in banquets with her youths,
With priuy signes, and talke dissembling truths?
Hearing her to be sicke, I thether ranne, 25
But with my riuall sicke she was not than.
These hardned me, with what I keepe obscure,
Some other seeke, who will these things endure,
Now my ship in the wished hauen crownd,
With ioy heares *Neptunes* swelling waters sound. 30
Leaue thy once powerfull words, and flatteries,
I am not as I was before, vnwise.
Now loue, and hate my light brest each way moue;
But victory, I thinke will hap to loue.
Ile hate, if I can; if not, loue gainst my will: 35
Bulles hate the yoake, yet what they hate haue still.
I flie her lust, but follow beauties creature;
I loath her manners, loue her bodies feature.
Nor with thee, nor without thee can I liue,
And doubt to which desire the palme to giue. 40
Or lesse faire, or lesse lewd would thou mightst bee,
Beauty with lewdnesse doth right ill agree.
Her deeds gaine hate, her face entreateth loue:
Ah, she doth more worth then her vices proue.

3 Now] Nor *Mal.* 20 men *Mal.*

Spare me, O by our fellow bed, by all 45
The Gods who by thee to be periurde fall,
And by thy face to me a powre diuine,
And by thine eyes whose radiance burnes out mine.
What ere thou art mine art thou: choose this course,
Wilt haue me willing, or to loue by force? 50
Rather Ile hoist vp saile, and vse the winde,
That I may loue yet, though against my minde.

ELEGIA. II.

Dolet amicam suam ita suis carminibus innotuisse vt riuales multos sibi pararit.

What day was that, which all sad haps to bring,
White birdes to louers did not alwayes sing.
Or is I thinke my wish against the starres?
Or shall I plaine some God against me warres?
Who mine was cald, whom I lou'd more then any, 5
I feare with me is common now to many.
Erre I? or by my bookes is she so knowne?
'Tis so: by my witte her abuse is growne.
And iustly: for her praise why did I tell?
The wench by my fault is set forth to sell. 10
The bawde I play, louers to her I guide:
Her gate by my hands is set open wide.
'Tis doubtfull whether verse auaile, or harme,
Against my good they were an enuious charme.
When *Thebes*, when *Troy*, when *Cæsar* should be writ, 15
Alone *Corinna* moues my wanton wit.
With Muse oppos'd would I my lines had done,
And *Phœbus* had forsooke my worke begun.
Nor, as vse will not Poets record heare,
Would I my words would any credit beare. 20
Scylla by vs her fathers rich haire steales,
And *Scyllaes* wombe mad raging dogs conceales.
Wee cause feete flie, wee mingle haires with snakes,
Victorious *Perseus* a wingd steedes back takes.
Our verse great *Tityus* a huge space out-spreads, 25
And giues the viper curled Dogge three heads.

Elegia II. *om. Ish., Bind.*: Elegia XII. *Dyce etc.* innotuisse] innocuisse *Mal. 133* 3 starre *Mas., Douce* 7 books *Dyce etc.*: lookes *old edd.* 14 they were] there was *Mal. 133* 22 mad] made *Mal. 133*

We make *Enceladus* vse a thousand armes,
And men inthralld by Mermaids singing charmes.
The East winds in *Vlisses* baggs we shut,
And blabbing *Tantalus* in mid-waters put. 30
Niobe flint, *Callist* we make a Beare,
Bird-changed *Progne* doth her *Itys* teare.
Ioue turnes himselfe into a Swanne, or gold,
Or his Bulles hornes *Europas* hand doth hold.
Proteus what should I name? teeth, *Thebes* first seed? 35
Oxen in whose mouthes burning flames did breede,
Heau'n starre *Electra* that bewaild her sisters?
The ships, whose God-head in the sea now glisters?
The Sunne turnd backe from *Atreus* cursed table?
And sweet toucht harpe that to moue stones was able? 40
Poets large power is boundlesse, and immense,
Nor haue their words true histories pretence,
And my wench ought to haue seem'd falsely praisd.
Now your credulity harme to me hath raisd.

ELEGIA. 12.

De Iunonis festo.

When fruite fild *Tuscia* should a wife giue me,
We toucht the walles, *Camillus* wonne by thee.
The Priests to *Iuno* did prepare chaste feasts,
With famous pageants, and their home-bred beasts.
To know their rites, well recompenc'd my stay, 5
Though thether leades a rough steepe hilly way.
There stãds an old wood with thick trees darke clouded.
Who sees it, graunts some deity there is shrowded.
An Altar takes mens incense, and oblation,
An Altar made after the ancient fashion. 10
Here when the Pipe with solemne tunes doth sound,
The annuall pompe goes on the couered ground.
White Heifers by glad people forth are led,
Which with the grasse of *Tuscane* fields are fed.
And calues from whose feard front no threatning flyes, 15
And little Piggs, base Hog-sties sacrifice,
And Rams with hornes their hard heads wreathed back.
Onely the Goddesse hated Goate did lack,

39 Sunne] Sea *Mal. 133*
Elegia 12. *om. Ish., Bind.*: Elegia XIII. *Dyce etc.*

By whom disclosd, she in the high woods tooke,
Is said to haue attempted flight forsooke. 20
Now is the goat brought through the boyes with darts,
And giue to him that the first wound imparts.
Where *Iuno* comes, each youth, and pretty maide,
Shew large wayes with their garments there displayed.
Iewels, and gold their Virgin tresses crowne, 25
And stately robes to their gilt feete hang downe.
As is the vse, the Nunnes in white veyles clad,
Vpon their heads the holy mysteries had.
When the chiefe pompe comes, lowd the people hollow,
And she her vestall virgin Priests doth follow. 30
Such was the *Greeke* pompe, *Agamemnon* dead,
Which fact, and country wealth *Halesus* fled,
And hauing wandred now through sea and land,
Built walles high towred with a prosperous hand.
He to th' *Hetrurians Iunoes* feast commended, 35
Let me, and them by it be aye be-friended.

ELEGIA. 13.

Ad amicam, si peccatura est, vt occulte peccet.

Seeing thou art faire, I barre not thy false playing,
But let not me poore soule know of thy straying.
Nor do I giue thee counsell to liue chaste,
But that thou wouldst dissemble, when 'tis paste.
She hath not trod awry, that doth deny it. 5
Such as confesse haue lost their good names by it.
What madnesse ist to tell nights prancks by day?
And hidden secrets openly to bewray?
The strumpet with the stranger will not doo,
Before the roome be cleere, and dore put too. 10
Will you make ship-wrack of your honest name,
And let the world be witnesse of the same?
Be more aduisde, walke as a puritan,
And I shall thinke you chaste, do what you can.
Slip still, onely deny it, when 'tis done, 15
And before folke immodest speeches shunne.

22 giue] given *Dyce etc.* 27 white] their white *Mal.* 35 th'] the *Mal. 133*
Elegia 13] Elegia XIV. *Dyce etc.* 2 know] wit *Bind.* 7 night *Ish., Bind., Dyce etc.* prancks] sports *Bind.* 8 And] Or *Ish., Bind.* 16 folke] people *Bind.*

The bed is for lasciuious toyings meete,
There vse all tricks, and tread shame vnder feete.
When you are vp, and drest, be sage and graue,
And in the bed hide all the faults you haue. 20
Be not asham'de to strip you being there,
And mingle thighes yours euer mine to beare.
There in your Rosie lips my tongue in-tombe,
Practise a thousand sports when there you come.
Forbeare no wanton words you there would speake, 25
And with your pastime let the bed-stead creake.
But with your robes put on an honest face,
And blush, and seeme as you were full of grace.
Deceiue all, let me erre, and thinke I am right,
And like a Wittall thinke thee voide of slight. 30
Why see I lines so oft receiu'd, and giuen?
This bed and that by tumbling made vneuen?
Like one start vp your haire tost and displac'd,
And with a wantons tooth your neck new rac'd?
Graunt this, that what you doe I may not see, 35
If you weigh not ill speeches, yet weigh mee.
My soule fleetes, when I thinke what you haue done,
And thorough euery veine doth cold bloud runne.
Then thee whom I must loue, I hate in vaine,
And would be dead, but dead with thee remaine. 40
Ile not sift much, but holde thee soone excusde,
Say but thou wert iniuriously accusde.
Though while the deed be dooing you be tooke,
And I see when you ope the two leau'd booke,
Sweare I was blinde, deny, if you be wise, 45
And I will trust your words more then mine eyes.
From him that yeelds the palme is quickly got,
Teach but your tongue to say, I did it not,
And being iustifide by two words thinke,
The cause acquits you not, but I that winke. 50

18 tricks] toyes *Bind.* 22 yours euer mine] mine euer yours *Ish.*, *Bind.* 32 This] And this *Mal.* 38 through *Ish.*, *Bind.* 40 but dead] but dying *Ish.*, *Bind.* 43 deedes *Bind.* 45 deny] yeeld not *Ish.*, *Bind.* 46 mine] my *Mal. 133* 47 palme] garland *Ish.*, *Bind.* 50 I that] that I *Mal.* 50+ *Signature* C. Marlow *add. Ish.*, *Bind.*

ELEGIA. 14.

Ad Venerem, quod elegis finem imponat.

Tender loues Mother a new Poet get,
This last end to my *Elegies* is set,
Which I *Pelignis* foster-child haue framde,
(Nor am I by such wanton toyes defamde)
Heire of an antient house, if helpe that can, 5
Not onely by warres rage made Gentleman.
In *Virgil Mantua* ioyes : in *Catul Verone*,
Of me *Pelignis* nation boasts alone,
Whom liberty to honest armes compeld,
When carefull *Rome* in doubt their prowesse held. 10
And some guest viewing watry *Sulmoes* walles,
Where little ground to be inclosd befalles,
How such a Poet could you bring forth, sayes,
How small so ere, Ile you for greatest praise,
Both loues to whom my heart long time did yeeld, 15
Your golden ensignes plucke out of my field,
Horned *Bacchus* grauer furie doth distill.
A greater ground with great horse is to till.
Weake Elegies, delightfull Muse farewell ;
A worke, that after my death, heere shall dwell. 20

FINIS.

Elegia 14. *om. Ish., Bind.* : Elegia XV. *Dyce etc.* 9 Who *Mal.* 14 so ere] to erre *Mal.* 16 pluck *Dyce etc.* : pluckt *Mas. to Mal.*

Epigrammes

By I. D.

Ad Musam. ⟨1.⟩

Flie merry Muse vnto that merry towne,
Where thou maist playes, reuels, and triumphes see,
The house of Fame, and Theatre of renowne,
Where all good wittes and spirits loue to be.
Fall in betweene their hands, that praise and loue thee, 5
And be to them a laughter and a iest:
But as for them which scorning shall reprooue thee,
Disdaine their wits, and thinke thine owne the best.
But if thou finde any so grose and dull,
That thinke I doe to priuate Taxing leane: 10
Bid him go hang, for he is but a gull,
And knowes not what an Epigramme does meane,
Which taxeth vnder a particular name
A generall vice which merits publique blame.

Of a Gull. ⟨2.⟩

Oft in my laughing rimes, I name a gull,
But this new terme will many questions breede,
Therefore at first I will expresse at full,
Who is a true and perfect Gull indeed.
A Gull is he, who feares a Veluet gowne, 5
And when a wench is braue, dares not speake to her:
A Gull is he which trauerseth the towne,
And is for marriage knowne a common woer.
A Gull is he, which while he proudly weares
A siluer hilted Rapier by his side: 10
Indures the lyes, and knockes about the eares,
Whilst in his sheath his sleeping sword doth bide.
A Gull is he which weares good hansome cloathes:
And stands in presence stroaking vp his hayre,
And filles vp his vnperfect speech with othes, 15
But speaks not one wise word throughout the yeare.
But to define a gull in termes precise,
A gull is he which seemes, and is not wise.

In Rufum. 3.

Rufus the Courtier, at the Theater,
Leauing the best and most conspicuous place,
Doth either to the stage himselfe transferre,
Or through a grate, doth shew his double face,

(1.) 5 praise and love *Dyce* : loue and praise *old edd.*

For that the clamorous fry of Innes of court 5
Fills vp the priuate roomes of greater price:
And such a place where all may haue resort,
He in his singularity doth despise.
Yet doth not his particuler humour shun,
The common stewes and brothells of the towne, 10
Though all the world in troopes do thither run,
Cleane and vncleane, the gentle and the clowne.
Then why should *Rufus* in his pride abhorre
A common seate that loues a common whore.

In Quintum. 4.

Quintus the dauncer vseth euermore,
His feete in measure and in rule to moue.
Yet on a time he cald his mistresse whore,
And thought with that sweete word to win her loue.
Oh had his tongue like to his feete bin taught, 5
It neuer would haue vttered such a thought.

In Plurimos. 5.

Faustinus, Sextus, Cinna, Ponticus,
With *Gella, Lesbia, Thais, Rodope*:
Rode all to Stanes for no cause serious,
But for their mirth, and for their lechery.
Scarse were they fetled in their lodging, when 5
Wenches, with wenches: men with men fell out.
Men with their wenches, wenches with their men,
Which strait dissolues this ill assembled rout.
But since the diuell brought them thus together,
To my discoursing thoughts it is a wonder, 10
Why presently as soone as they came thither,
The selfe same diuell did them part asunder.
Doubtlesse it seemes it was a foolish diuell,
That thus did part them, ere they did some euill.

In Titum. 6.

Titus the braue and valorous yong gallant,
Three years togither in this towne hath beene,
Yet my Lord Chauncellors tombe he hath not seene
Nor the New water worke, nor the Elephant.
I cannot tell the cause without a smile, 5
He hath beene in the Counter all this while.

In Faustum. 7.

Faustus not Lord nor knight, nor wise nor olde,
To euery place about the towne doth ride,
He rides into the fieldes, Playes to behold,
He rides to take boate at the water side.

He rides to Powles, he rides to th' ordinary, 5
He rides vnto the house of bawdery too.
Thither his horse doth him so often carry,
That shortly he will quite forget to go.

In Katam. 8.

Kate being pleas'd, wisht that her pleasure could
Indure as long as a buffe ierkin would.
Content thee *Kate*, although thy pleasure wasteth
Thy pleasures place like a buffe ierkin lasteth.
For no buffe ierkin hath bin oftner worne 5
Nor hath more scrapings, or more dressings borne.

In Librum. 9

Liber doth vaunt how chastly he hath liu'd,
Since he hath bin seauen years in towne and more,
For that he sweares he hath foure only swiude,
A maide, a wife, a widdow and a whore.
Then *Liber* thou hast swiude all women kinde, 5
For a fift sort I know thou canst not finde.

In Medonem. 10.

Great Captaine *Mœdon* weares a chaine of gold,
Which at fiue hundred crownes is vallued,
For that it was his graund-sires chaine of olde
When great King *Henry Bulloigne* conquered.
And weare it *Mœdon* for it may insue 5
That thou by vertue of this Massie chaine
A stronger towne then *Bulloigne* maist subdue
If wise mens sawes be not reputed vaine.
For what said *Philip* King of *Macedon* ?
There is no Castel so well fortified, 10
But if an Asse laden with gold comes on,
The guard will stoope, and gates fly open wide.

In Gellam. 11.

Gella if thou dost loue thy selfe take heede,
Lest thou my rimes vnto thy louer reade.
For straight thou grinst, and then thy louer seeth
Thy canker-eaten gums and rotten teeth.

In Quintum. 12.

Quintus his wit infused into his braine,
Mislikes the place, and fled into his feete,
And there it wanders vp and downe the streetes,
Dabled in the dyrt, and soaked in the raine.
Doubtlesse his wit intendes not to aspire, 5
Which leaues his head to trauell in the mire.

In Seuerum. 13.

The puritan *Seuerus* oft doth reade
This text, that doth pronounce vaine speech a sinne
That thing defiles a man that doth proceede
From out the mouth, not that which enters in
Hence is it, that we seldome heare him sweare, 5
And thereof as a Pharasie he vaunts.
But he deuours more Capons in one yeare,
Then would suffice an hundred protestants.
And sooth those sectaries are gluttons all,
As wel the threed-bare Cobler as the knight. 10
For those poore slaues which haue not wherewithall
Feed on the rich, till they deuour them quite,
  And so as *Pharoes* kine, they eate vp cleane
  Those that be fat, yet still themselues be leane.

In Leucam. 14.

Leuca in presence once a fart did let,
Some laught a little, she refus'd the place,
And mad with shame, did then her gloue forget,
Which she return'd to fetch with bashfull grace:
And when she would haue said ⟨I want⟩ my gloue, 5
My fart (qd. she) which did more laughter moue.

In Macrum. 15.

Thou canst not speake yet *Macer*, for to speake,
Is to distinguish sounds significant.
Thou with harsh noyse the aire dost rudely breake
But what thou vtterest common sence doth want,
Halfe *English* words, with fustian tearmes among, 5
Much like the burden of a Northerne song.

In Faustum. 16.

That youth, saith *Faustus*, hath a Lyon seene,
Who from a dycing-house comes mony-lesse.
But when he lost his haire, where had he beene?
I doubt me he had seene a Lyonesse.

In Cosmum. 17.

Cosmus hath more discoursing in his head,
Then Ioue, when *Pallas* issued from his braine,
And still he striues to be deliuered
Of all his thoughts at once, but all in vaine.
For as we see at all the play-house dores, 5
When ended is the play, the daunce and song:
A thousand townse-men, gentlemen and whores,

(13). 4 the] that *Mas.*
(17). 2 Ioue] loue *Mas.*

Porters and seruing-men togither throng,
So thoughts of drinking, thriuing, wenching, warre,
And borrowing money, raging in his minde, 10
To issue all at once so forward are
As none at all can perfect passage finde.

In Flaccum. 18.

The false knaue *Flaccus* once a bribe I gaue,
The more foole I to bribe so false a knaue.
But he gaue back my bribe: the more foole he,
That for my folly did not cousen me.

In Cineam. 19.

Thou dogged *Cineas* hated like a dogge,
For still thou grumblest like a masty dogge,
Comparst thy selfe to nothing but a dogge.
Thou saist thou art as weary as a dogge,
As angry, sicke, and hungry as a dogge, 5
As dul and melancholy as a dogge,
As lazy, sleepy, and as idle as a dogge.
But why dost thou compare thee to a dogge
In that, for which all men despise a dogge?
I will compare thee better to a dogge. 10
Thou art as faire and comely as a dogge,
Thou art as true & honest as a dogge.
Thou art as kinde and liberall as a dogge,
Thou art as wise and valiant as a dogge.
But *Cineas*, I haue oft heard thee tell, 15
Thou art as like thy father as may be.
Tis like inough, and faith I like it well,
But I am glad thou art not like to me.

In Gerontem. 20.

Gerons mouldie memory corrects
Old *Holinshed* our famous Chronicler
With morall rules, and pollicy collects
Out of all actions done these fourscore yeares.
Accounts the time of euery old euent, 5
Not from Christs birth, nor from the Princes raigne,
But from some other famous accident,
Which in mens generall notice doth remaine.
The sige of *Bulloigne*, and the plaguy sweat,
The going to *Saint Quintines* and *New-hauen*, 10
The rising in the North, the frost so great
That cart wheele printes on *Thamis* face were seene,
The fall of money, and burning of Powles steeple,
The blazing starre and *Spaniards* ouerthrow:
By these euents, notorious to the people, 15
He measures times, and things forepast doth shew.

But most of all, he chiefly reckons by
A priuate chaunce, the death of his curst wiie :
This is to him the dearest memory
And the happyest accident of all his life. 20

In Marcum. 21.

When *Marcus* comes from *Minnes*, hee still doth swear
By come on seauen that al is lost & gone,
But thats not true, for he hath lost his haire,
Onely for that he came too much at one.

In Ciprium. 22.

The fine youth *Ciprius* is more tierse and neate
Then the new garden of the old temple is,
And still the newest fashion he doth get,
And with the time doth chaunge from that to this.
He weares a hat now of the flat crown-blocke, 5
The treble ruffes, long cloake, and doublet French,
He takes tobacco, and doth weare a locke,
And wastes more time in dressing then a wench.
Yet this new fangled youth, made for these times,
Doth aboue all praise old *George Gascoines* rimes. 10

In Cineam. 23.

When *Cineas* comes amongst his friends in morning
He slyly spies who first his cap doth moue,
Him he sallutes, the rest so grimly scorning
As if for euer they had lost his loue.
I seeing how it doth the humour fit 5
Of this fond gull to be saluted first
Catch at my cap, but moue it not a whit
Which to perceiuing he seemes for spite to burst,
But *Cineas*, why expect you more of me,
Then I of you ? I am as good a man, 10
And better too by many a quallity,
For vault, and daunce, and fence and rime I can.
You keepe a whore at your owne charge men tell me.
Indeed friend (*Cineas*) therein you excel me.

In Gallum. 24.

Gallus hath bin this Summer time in *Friesland*,
And now return'd he speakes such warlike wordes
As if I could their *English* vnderstand,
I feare me they would cut my throat like swordes.
He talkes of counterscarffes, and casomates, 5
Of parapets, of curteynes and pallizadois,
Of flankers, rauelings, gabions he prates,

(24). 6 curteneys *old. edd.*

And of false braies, and sallies, and scaladoes.
But to requite such gulling tearmes as these,
With words of my profession I reply: 10
I tell of fourching, vouchers, and counterpleas,
Of withernams, essoynes and champarty.
So neither of vs vnderstanding one an other,
We part as wise, as when we came togither.

In Decium. 25.

Audacious painters haue nine worthies made,
But Poet *Decius* more audacious farre
Making his mistris march with men of warre,
With title of tenth worthy doth her lade.
Me thinks that gull did vse his tearmes as fit 5
Which tearm'd his loue a giant for her wit.

In Gellam. 26.

If *Gellas* beauty be examined
She hath a dull dead eye, a saddle nose,
An ill shapte face with morphew ouerspread,
And rotten teeth which she in laughing showes.
Briefly she is the filthiest wench in towne, 5
Of all that do the art of whoring vse:
But when she hath put on her sattin-gown,
Her cut lawne apron, and her veluet shooes,
Her greene silk stockings, and her petticoat
Of taffaty, with golden friendge a-round, 10
And is withal perfumd with ciuet hot,
Which doth her valiant stinking breath confound:
Yet she with these addicions is no more,
Then a sweet, filthy, fine ill fauored whore.

In Sillam. 27.

Sylla is often challenged to the field,
To answer as a Gentleman his foes;
But then he doth this only answer yeeld,
That he hath liuings and faire lands to lose.
Silla, if none but beggars valiant were, 5
The King of *Spaine* would put vs all in feare.

In Sillam. 28.

Who dares affirme that *Silla* dare not fight,
When I dare sweare he dares aduenture more,
Then the most braue and all-daring wight,
That euer armes with resolution bore?
He that dares touch the most vnholsome whore, 5
That euer was retirde into the Spittle,
And dares court wenches standing at a dore,

(24). 8 braies] baits *Mas. to Mal.* (26). 8 cut *MS., Dyce*: out *old. edd.*

(The portion of his witte being passing little.)
He that dares giue his dearest friends offences,
Which other valiant fooles doe feare to do : 10
And when a feauer doth confound his sences,
Dare eate raw-beefe, and drinke strong wine thereto:
He that dares take Tobacco on the stage,
Dares man a whore at noone-day through the streete,
Dares daunce in Pawles, and in this formall age, 15
Dares say and do what euer is vnmeete,
Whom feare of shame could neuer yet affright,
Who dares affirme that *Silla* dares not fight?

In Haywodum. 29.

Haywood that did in Epigrams excell,
Is now put downe since my light Muse arose :
As Buckets are put downe into a Well,
Or as a schoole boy putteth downe his hose.

In Dacum. 30.

Amongst the Poets *Dacus* numbred is,
Yet could he neuer make an *English* rime,
But some prose speeches I haue heard of his,
Which haue bin spoken many an hundreth time.
The man that keepes the *Eliphant* hath one, 5
Wherein he tels the wonders of the beast.
Another *Bankes* pronounced long a-gon,
When he his curtales qualities exprest :
He first taught him that keepes the monuments
At Westminster, his formall Tale to say. 10
And also him which Puppets represents,
And also him which with the Ape doth play :
Though all his Poetrie be like to this,
Amongst the Poets *Dacus* numbred is.

In Priscum. 31.

When *Priscus* raisde from low to high estate,
Rod through the street in pompous iollitie,
Caius his poore familiar friend of late,
Be-spake him thus : Sir now you know not me.
'Tis likely friend (quoth *Priscus*) to be so : 5
For at this time my selfe I do not know.

In Brunum. 32.

Brunus which deemes himselfe a faire sweet youth,
Is thirtie nine yeeres of age at least :
Yet was he neuer, to confesse the truth,
But a drye starueling when he was at best.
This gull was sick to shew his Night-cap fine,
And his wrought Pillow ouer-spread with lawne,
But hath bin well since his griefes cause hath line
At *Trollups* by Saint *Clements* Church in pawne.

In Francum. 33.

When *Francus* comes to sollace with his whore,
He sends for Rods & strips himselfe stark naked:
For his lust sleepes, and will not rise before,
By whipping of the wench it be awaked.
I enuie him not, but wish I had the powre, 5
To make my selfe his wench but one halfe houre.

In Castorem. 34.

Of speaking well why do we learne the skill?
Hoping thereby honor and wealth to gaine,
Sith rayling *Castor* doth by speaking ill
Opinion of much wit and golde obtaine.

In Septimium. 35.

Septimius liues, and is like Garlicke seene,
For though his head be white, his blade is greene:
This olde mad Coult deserues a Martyres praise,
For he was burned in Queene *Maryes* dayes.

Of Tobbacco. 36.

Homer of *Moly*, and *Nepenthe* sings,
Moly the Gods most soueraigne Hearbe diuine,
Nepenthe Heauens drinke most gladnesse brings,
Hearts griefe expels, and doth the wits refine:
But this our age another world hath found, 5
From whence an hearbe of Heauenly power is brought.
Moly is not so soueraigne for a wound,
Nor hath *Nepenthe* so great wonders wrought.
It is *Tobacco*, whose sweet substantiall fume
The hellish torment of the teeth doth ease, 10
By drawing downe, and drying vp the rewme,
The Mother and the Nurse of each disease.
It is *Tobacco* which doth colde expell,
And cleares the obstructions of the Arteries,
And surfets threatning Death digesteth well, 15
Decocting all the stomackes crudities.
It is *Tobacco* which hath power to clarifie
The clowdie mists before dim eyes appearing,
It is *Tobacco* which hath power to rarifie
The thick grose humour which doth stop the hearing. 20
The wasting Hectique, and the Quartain Feuer,
Which doth of Phisique make a mockerie,
The gowt it cures, and helps ill breaths for euer,
Whether the cause in Teeth or stomacke be.
And though ill breaths were by it but confounded, 25
Yet that Medicine it doth farre excell,
Which by sir *Thomas Moore* hath bin propounded,

For this is thought a Gentleman-like smell.
O that I were one of these mountie-bankes,
Which praise their Oyles, and Powders which they sell, 30
My customers would giue me coyne with thankes,
I for this ware forsooth a Tale would tell.
Yet would I vse none of these tearmes before,
I would but say, that it the Pox will cure:
This were inough, without discoursing more, 35
All our braue gallants in the towne t'allure.

In Crassum. 37.

Crassus his lyes are not pernicious lyes,
But pleasant fictions hurtfull vnto none
But to himselfe, for no man counts him wise,
To tell for truth that which for false is knowne.
He sweares that *Gaunt* is three score miles about, 5
And that the bridge at *Paris* on the *Seyn*,
Is of such thicknesse, length and breadth throughout,
That sixe score Arches can it scarse sustaine.
He sweares he saw so great a dead mans scull,
At *Canterbury* digde out of the ground, 10
That would containe of wheat three bushels full,
And that in *Kent* are twenty yeomen found,
Of which the poorest euery yeare dispends
Fiue thousand pound: these and fiue thousand mo
So oft he hath recited to his friends, 15
That now himselfe perswades himselfe 'tis so.
But why doth *Crassus* tell his lyes so rife
Of Bridges, Townes, and things that haue no life?
He is a Lawyer, and doth well espie,
That for such lyes an action will not lye. 20

In Philonem. 38.

Philo the Lawyer and the Fortune teller,
The Schoole-maister, the Midwife and the Bawd:
The coniurer, the buyer, and the seller
Of painting which with breathing will be thawd,
Doth practise Phisicke, and his credit growes 5
As doth the Ballad singers auditorie,
Which hath at Temple barre his standing chose,
And to the vulgar sings an Ale-house storie.
First stands a Porter, then an Oyster wife
Doth stint her cry, and stay her steps to heare him, 10
Then comes a cut-purse ready with a knife,
And then a countrey clyent passeth neere him.
There stands the Constable, there stands the Whore,
And listning to the song, heed not each other.

There by the Serieant stands the debitor, 15
And doth no more mistrust him then his brother:
Thus *Orpheus* to such hearers giueth Musique,
And *Philo* to such patients giueth Phisicke.

In Fuscum. 39.

Fuscus is free, and hath the world at will,
Yet in the course of life that he doth leade,
He's like a horse which turning rounde a mill,
Doth alwaies in the selfe same circle treade:
First he doth rise at 10. and at eleuen 5
He goes to *Gyls*, where he doth eate till one,
Then sees a play til sixe, and sups at seauen,
And after supper, straight to bed is gone,
And there till tenne next day he doth remaine,
And then he dines, then sees a commedy, 10
And then he suppes, and goes to bed againe:
Thus rounde he runs without variety:
  Saue that sometimes he comes not to the play
  But falls into a whore-house by the way.

In Afrum. 40.

The smell feast *Afer*, trauailes to the burse
Twice euery day the newest newes to heare
Which when he hath no money in his purse,
To rich mens tables he doth often beare:
He tells how *Gronigen* is taken in, 5
By the braue conduct of illustrious *Vere*:
And how the *Spanish* forces *Brest* would win,
But that they do victorious *Norris* feare.
No sooner is a ship at sea surpris'd,
But straight he learnes the newes & doth disclose it. 10
Faire written in a scrowle he hath names
Of all the widowes which the plague hath made,
And persons, times and places still he frames
To euery tale, the better to perswade:
We call him Fame, for that the wide-mouth slaue 15
Will eate as fast as he wil vtter lies,
For Fame is said an hundreth mouthes to haue,
And he eates more then would fiue score suffice.

In Paulum. 41.

By lawfull mart, and by vnlawfull stealth,
Paulus in spite of enuy fortunate,
Deriues out of the Ocean so much wealth,
As he may well maintaine a Lords estate.
  But on the land a little gulfe there is, 5
  Wherein he drowneth all the wealth of his.

(38). 16 more] mure *Mas.* (39). 5 at a eleuen *Mas.*
(40). 5 Grenigen *Mas.*: Groningen *Dyce*

In Licum. 42.

Lycus which lately is to *Venice* gone,
Shall if he do returne, gaine three for one:
But ten to one, his knowledge and his wit,
Will not be bettered or increas'd a whit.

In Publium. 43.

Publius student at the common law,
Oft leaues his bookes, and for his recreation
To Paris-garden doth himselfe withdrawe
Where he is rauisht with such delectation
As downe amongst the Beares and Dogges he goes, 5
Where whilst he skiping cries to head, to head,
His satten doublet and his veluet hose
Are all with spittle from aboue be-spread,
When he is like his fathers country hall,
Stinking with dogges, and muted all with haukes. 10
And rightly too on him this filth doth fall,
Which for such filthy sports his bookes forsakes,
Leauing old *Ployden*, *Dier* and *Brooke* alone,
To see old *Harry Hunkes* and *Sacarson*.

In Sillam. 44.

When I this proposition had defended,
A coward cannot be an honest man,
Thou *Silla* seemest forth-with to be offended:
And holds the contrary and sweares he can.
But when I tell thee that hee will forsake 5
His dearest friend, in perill of his life,
Thou then art chang'd and saist thou didst mistake,
And so we end our argument and strife.
Yet I thinke oft, and thinke I thinke aright,
Thy argument argues thou wilt not fight. 10

In Dacum. 45.

Dacus with some good collour and pretence,
Tearmes his loues beauty silent eloquence:
For she doth lay more collours on her face,
Then euer *Tully* vs'd his speech to grace.

In Marcum. 46.

Why dost thou *Marcus* in thy misery,
Raile and blaspheme, and call the heau'ns vnkind?
The heauens do owe no kindenesse vnto thee,
Thou hast the heauens so little in thy minde,
For in thy life thou neuer vsest prayer, 5
But at primero, to encounter faire.

(43). 9 hall] shall *Mas. to Mal.*

Meditations of a Gull. 47.

See yonder melancholie gentleman,
Which hoode-winked with his hat, alone doth sit,
Thinke what he thinkes and tell me if you can,
What great affaires troubles his little wit.
He thinkes not of the war twixt *France* and *Spaine* 5
Whether it be for Europs good or ill,
Nor whether the Empire can it selfe maintaine
Against the *Turkish* power encroching still.
Nor what great towne in all the Netherlands
The States determine to besiege this spring, 10
Nor how the *Scottish* pollicy now standes,
Nor what becomes of the *Irish* mutining.
But he doth seriously bethinke him whether
Of the guld people he be more esteem'd,
For his long cloake, or his great black feather, 15
By which each gull is now a gallant deem'd.
Or of a Iourney he deliberates,
To Paris-garden, cocke-pit or the play:
Or how to steale a dogge he meditates,
Or what he shall vnto his mistris say: 20
Yet with these thoughts he thinks himselfe most fit
To be of Counsell with a king for wit.

Ad Musam. 48.

Peace idle muse, haue done, for it is time
Since lowsie *Ponticus* enuies my fame,
And sweares the better sort are much to blame
To make me so well knowne for my ill rime.
Yet *Bankes* his horse is better knowne then he, 5
So are the Cammels and the westerne Hog,
And so is *Lepidus* his printed dogge:
Why doth not *Ponticus* their fames enuie?
Besides this muse of mine, and the blacke fether
Grew both together fresh in estimation, 10
And both growne stale, were cast away togither:
What fame is this that scarse lasts out a fashion?
Onely this last in credit doth remaine,
That from hence-forth, ech bastard cast forth rime
Which doth but sauour of a libell vaine 15
Shall call me father, and be thought my crime,
So dull and with so little sence endu'd,
Is my grose headed iudge the multitude.

FINIS. *I. D.*

LUCAN'S PHARSALIA

BOOK I

THE FIRST BOOK OF LUCAN

MARLOWE's translation of Book I of the *Pharsalia* is first mentioned in an entry in the Stationers' Register, dated September 28, 1593: 'John Wolf Entred for his Copye vnder th[e h]andes of Master MURGETROD and bothe the wardens a booke intituled LUCANS *firste booke of the famous Civill warr betwixt* POMPEY *and* CESAR Englished by CHRISTOPHER MARLOW.' The very next entry is that of 'a booke intituled HERO *and* LEANDER beinge an amorous poem devised by CHRISTOPHER MARLOW', likewise registered by John Wolf and on the same day.

There is a curious and unexplained connexion between these two poems in the circumstances of publication. The *First Book of Lucan* exists in a single old quarto issued in 1600 by Thomas Thorpe,[1] who in the Epistle Dedicatory to his fellow stationer, Edward Blount, alludes to the latter's 'old right' in the work. This Edward Blount himself published in 1598 the earliest extant edition of Marlowe's portion of *Hero and Leander*. In 1600 another edition[2] of the latter poem appeared with the puzzling title-page: 'Hero and Leander: Begunne by Christopher Marloe: Whereunto is added the first booke of Lucan translated line for line by the same Author: Printed for John Flasket.' In spite of this plain statement there is no trace that the *Lucan* ever formed a part of the book in question or was printed during the Elizabethan age in any other edition than that of Thorpe.

The most likely conjecture would seem to be that John Wolf, who registered *Lucan* and *Hero and Leander* on the same day—perhaps with the intention of bringing them out together—transferred his right in both to Blount. The latter resigned his property in *Hero and Leander*, and pre-

[1] The famous publisher of Shakespeare's sonnets (1609). It is worthy of note that Thorpe also published in 1614 a complete translation of the *Pharsalia*, the work of Sir Arthur Gorges.

[2] The third (?) edition, at least one other having been issued in 1598 by Paul Linley. Cf. p. 485.

sumably in *Lucan* as well, to Paul Linley on March 2, 1597–8, and Linley certainly made over both works to John Flasket on June 26, 1600.[1] Flasket's 1600 edition of *Hero and Leander* is undoubtedly the result of the transaction last referred to, but it is not easy to account for the misleading allusion to the Lucan translation on the title page or the failure to mention Chapman. Flasket's original design may have been to produce an edition of the Marlovian part of *Hero and Leander*, supplemented by the *Lucan*. Such an intention may have preceded the arrangement with Linley, and would naturally, in that case, have been altered when the possession of Chapman's long continuation of *Hero and Leander* rendered it unnecessary to eke out a thin volume by the insertion of the *Lucan*. The latter work, being then of no immediate consequence to Flasket, would seem to have been acquired and at once printed by Thomas Thorpe. The *Stationers' Register* contains no record, however, of the transfer of the piece from Flasket to Thorpe or to any one else, and the question of the precise origin of this single early edition of the poem is not easily soluble.

Marlowe's translation of Lucan is a work of some curious interest, as being one of the earliest English poems in blank verse. It displays greater maturity than the *Elegies*, both in expression and in metrical skill, but has the same general faults and must, like the other translation, be ascribed to an early period in the poet's career. In his later years Marlowe would hardly have submitted to the tyranny of a line-for-line translation. Erroneous renderings abound on every page, but it is seldom that the reader meets with what is so common in the *Elegies*—lines entirely destitute of sense or coherence. The work has, as a whole, a majestic rhythm, and the choice of words is always that of the born poet. In many of the finer passages we see the author practising, as it were, that peculiarly melodious blank verse of which he shows himself in *Tamburlaine* so complete a master. Such lines as the following have the distinct flavour of Marlowe's developed style:

> *Figulus* more seene in heauenly mysteries,
> Whose like *Aegiptian Memphis* neuer had
> For skill in stars, and tune-full planeting.[2]

[1] For a fuller discussion of these points see Introduction to *Hero and Leander*, pp. 485, 486.

[2] Ll. 638–640.

LVCANS
FIRST BOOKE
TRANSLATED LINE FOR LINE, BY CHR. MARLOVV.

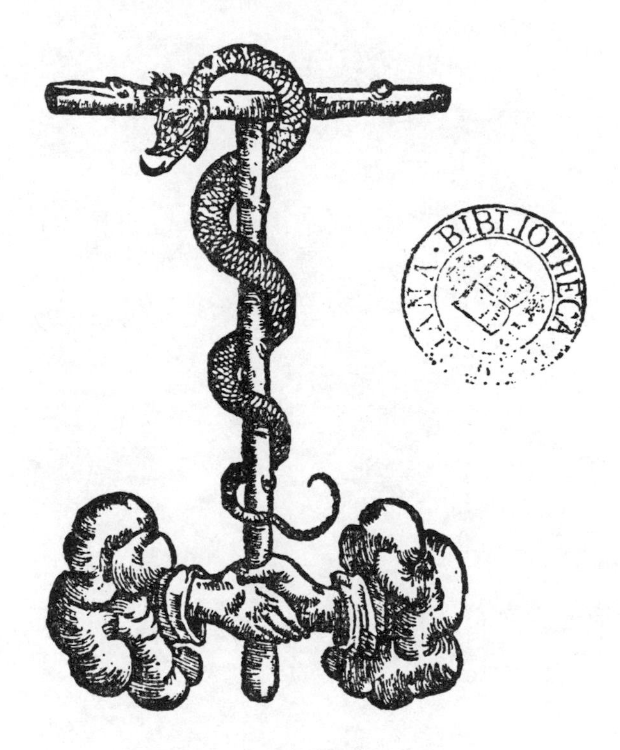

AT LONDON,
Printed by P. Short, and are to be sold by Walter Burre at the Signe of the Flower de Luce in Paules Churchyard, 1600.

1600 = The quarto edition of that year.

Rob. = Robinson's edition of Marlowe, 1826.

Dyce { *Dyce*[1] = Dyce's first edition of Marlowe, 1850.

Dyce { *Dyce*[2] = Dyce's revised edition of Marlowe, 1858, etc.

Cunn. = Cunningham's edition of Marlowe, 1870, etc.

Bull. = Bullen's edition of Marlowe, 1885.

T. B. = The present editor.

TO HIS KIND, AND TRVE FRIEND:
EDWARD BLVNT.

Blount: *I purpose to be blunt with you, & out of my dulnesse to encounter you with a* Dedication *in the memory of that pure Elementall wit* Chr. Marlow; *whose ghoast or* Genius *is to be seene walke the* Churchyard *in (at the least) three or foure sheets. Me thinks you should presently looke wilde now, and* 5
growe humorously frantique vpon the tast of it. Well, least you should, let mee tell you. This spirit was sometime a familiar of your own, Lucans first booke translated; *which (in regard of your old right in it) I haue rais'd in the circle of your Patronage. But stay now* Edward *(if I mistake not)* 10
you are to accommodate your selfe with some fewe instructions, touching the property of a Patron, that you are not yet possest of; and to study them for your better grace as our Gallants do fashions. First you must be proud and thinke you haue merit inough in you, though you are ne're so emptie; then 15
when I bring you the booke take physicke, and keepe state, assigne me a time by your man to come againe, and afore the day be sure to haue chang'd your lodging; in the meane time sleepe little, and sweat with the inuention of some pittiful dry iest or two which you may happen to vtter, with some litle (or 20
not at al) marking of your friends when you haue found a place for them to come in at; or if by chance something has dropt from you worth the taking vp weary all that come to you with the often repetition of it; Censure scornefully inough, and somewhat like a trauailer; commend nothing least you 25
discredit your (that which you would seeme to haue) iudgement. These things if you can mould your selfe to them Ned *I make no question but they will not become you. One speciall vertue in our Patrons of these daies I haue promist my selfe you shall fit excellently, which is to giue nothing; Yes, thy loue I* 30
will challenge as my peculiar Obiect both in this, and (I hope) manie more succeeding offices: Farewell, I affect not the world should measure my thoughts to thee by a scale of this Nature: Leaue to thinke good of me when I fall from thee.

Thine in all rites of perfect friendship, 35

THOM. THORPE.

Ep. Ded. 1 Blount] Blunt *Dyce*

THE FIRST BOOKE OF
LVCAN TRANSLATED
INTO ENGLISH.

Wars worse then ciuill on *Thessalian* playnes,
And outrage strangling law & people strong,
We sing, whose conquering swords their own breasts
launcht,
Armies alied, the kingdoms league vprooted,
Th'affrighted worlds force bent on publique spoile, 5
Trumpets, and drums like deadly threatning other,
Eagles alike displaide, darts answering darts.
Romans, what madnes, what huge lust of warre
Hath made *Barbarians* drunke with *Latin* bloud?
Now Babilon, (proud through our spoile) should stoop, 10
While slaughtred *Crassus* ghost walks vnreueng'd,
Will ye wadge war, for which you shall not triumph?
Ay me, O what a world of land and sea
Might they haue won whom ciuil broiles haue slaine!
As far as *Titan* springs where night dims heauen, 15
I to the *Torrid Zone* where midday burnes,
And where stiffe winter whom no spring resolues,
Fetters the Euxin sea with chaines of yce:
Scythia and wilde *Armenia* had bin yoakt,
And they of *Nilus* mouth (if there liue any.) 20
Roome, if thou take delight in impious warre,
First conquer all the earth, then turne thy force
Against thy selfe: as yet thou wants not foes.
That now the walles of houses halfe rear'd totter,
That rampiers fallen down, huge heapes of stone 25
Lye in our townes, that houses are abandon'd,
And few liue that behold their ancient seats;
Italy many yeares hath lyen vntil'd,

3 launcht] lanc'd *Dyce* 20 mouth] *Qy.* 'source' or 'fount'?
24 rear'd *Dyce etc.*: reafer'd *1600*

And choakt with thorns, that greedy earth wants hinds.
Fierce *Pirhus*, neither thou nor *Hanniball* 30
Art cause, no forraine foe could so afflict vs,
These plagues arise from wreake of ciuill power.
But if for *Nero* (then vnborne) the fates
Would find no other meanes, (and gods not sleightly
Purchase immortal thrones; nor *Ioue* ioide heauen 35
Vntill the cruel Giants war was done.)
We plaine not heauens, but gladly beare these euils
For *Neros* sake: *Pharsalia* grone with slaughter,
And *Carthage* soules be glutted with our blouds;
At *Munda* let the dreadfull battailes ioyne; 40
Adde *Cæsar*, to these illes *Perusian* famine;
The *Mutin* toyles; the fleet at *Leuca* suncke;
And cruel field nere burning *Aetna* fought:
Yet Room is much bound to these ciuil armes,
Which made thee Emperor, thee (seeing thou being old 45
Must shine a star) shal heauen (whom thou louest,)
Receiue with shouts; where thou wilt raigne as King,
Or mount the sunnes plume bearing charriot,
And with bright restles fire compasse the earth,
Vndaunted though her former guide be chang'd. 50
Nature, and euery power shal giue thee place,
What God it please thee be, or where to sway:
But neither chuse the north t'erect thy seat;
Nor yet the aduerse reking southerne pole,
Whence thou shouldst view thy Roome with squinting
beams. 55
If any one part of vast heauen thou swayest,
The burdened axes with thy force will bend;
The midst is best; that place is pure, and bright,
There *Cæsar* may'st thou shine and no cloud dim thee;
Then men from war shal bide in league, and ease, 60
Peace through the world from *Ianus Phane* shal flie,
And boult the brazen gates with barres of Iron
Thou *Cæsar* at this instant art my God,
Thee if I inuocate, I shall not need
To craue *Appoll⟨o⟩es* ayde, or *Bacchus* helpe; 65
Thy power inspires the *Muze* that sings this war.
The causes first I purpose to vnfould
Of these garboiles, whence springs a long discourse,
And what made madding people shake off peace.

42 Leuca] Lucas *Bull. Dyce etc.*: 59 There] Their *1600* 68 a long] along *1600*

The fates are enuious, high seats quickly perish, 70
Vnder great burdens fals are euer greeuous;
Roome was so great it could not beare it selfe:
So when this worlds compounded vnion breakes,
Time ends and to old *Chaos* all things turne;
Confused stars shal meete, celestiall fire 75
Fleete on the flouds, the earth shoulder the sea,
Affording it no shoare, and *Phœbe's* waine
Chace *Phœbus* and inrag'd affect his place,
And striue to shine by day, and ful of strife
Disolue the engins of the broken world. 80
All great things crush themselues, such end the gods
Allot the height of honor, men so strong
By land, and sea, no forreine force could ruine:
O Roome thy selfe art cause of all these euils,
Thy selfe thus shiuered out to three mens shares: 85
Dire league of partners in a kingdome last not.
O faintly ioyn'd friends with ambition blind,
Why ioine you force to share the world betwixt you?
While th' earth the sea, and ayre the earth sustaines;
While *Titan* striues against the worlds swift course; 90
Or *Cynthia* nights Queene waights vpon the day;
Shall neuer faith be found in fellow kings.
Dominion cannot suffer partnership;
This need no forraine proofe, nor far fet story:
Roomes infant walles were steept in brothers bloud; 95
Nor then was land, or sea, to breed such hate,
A towne with one poore church set them at oddes.
Cæsars, and *Pompeys* iarring loue soone ended,
T'was peace against their wils; betwixt them both
Stept *Crassus* in: euen as the slender *Isthmos*, 100
Betwixt the *Aegean* and the *Ionian* sea,
Keepes each from other, but being worne away
They both burst out, and each incounter other:
So when as *Crassus* wretched death who stayd them
Had fild *Assirian Carras* wals with bloud, 105
His losse made way for Roman outrages.
Parthians y'afflict vs more then ye suppose,
Being conquered, we are plaugde with ciuil war.
Swords share our Empire, fortune that made Roome
Gouerne the earth, the sea, the world it selfe 110
Would not admit two Lords: for *Iulia*
Snatcht hence by cruel fates with ominous howles,

94 need] needs *Dyce etc.*

Bare downe to hell her sonne the pledge of peace,
And all bands of that death presaging aliance.
Iulia, had heauen giuen thee longer life 115
Thou hadst restrainde thy headstrong husbands rage,
Yea and thy father to, and swords thrown down,
Made all shake hands as once the *Sabines* did;
Thy death broake amity and trainde to war
These Captaines emulous of each others glory. 120
Thou feard'st (great *Pompey*) that late deeds would dim
Olde triumphs, and that *Cæsars* conquering France
Would dash the wreath thou wearst for Pirats wracke.
Thee wars vse stirde, and thoughts that alwaies scorn'd
A second place; *Pompey* could bide no equall, 125
Nor *Cæsar* no superior, which of both
Had iustest cause vnlawful tis to iudge:
Each side had great partakers; *Cæsars* cause
The gods abetted; *Cato* likt the other.
Both differ'd much, *Pompey* was strooke in yeares, 130
And by long rest forgot to manage armes,
And being popular sought by liberal gifts,
To gaine the light vnstable commons loue,
And ioyed to heare his *Theaters* applause;
He liu'd secure boasting his former deeds, 135
And thought his name sufficient to vphold him,
Like to a tall oake in a fruitfull field,
Bearing old spoiles and conquerors monuments,
Who though his root be weake, and his owne waight
Keepe him within the ground, his armes al bare, 140
His body (not his boughs) send forth a shade;
Though euery blast it nod, and seeme to fal,
When all the woods about stand bolt vp-right,
Yet he alone is held in reuerence.
Cæsars renowne for war was lesse, he restles, 145
Shaming to striue but where he did subdue,
When yre, or hope prouokt, heady, & bould,
At al times charging home, & making hauock;
Vrging his fortune, trusting in the gods,
Destroying what withstood his proud desires, 150
And glad when bloud, & ruine made him way:
So thunder which the wind teares from the cloudes,
With cracke of riuen ayre and hideous sound
Filling the world, leapes out and throwes forth fire,
Affrights poore fearefull men, and blasts their eyes 155
With ouerthwarting flames, and raging shoots

Alongst the ayre and no⟨ugh⟩t resisting it
Falls, and returnes, and shiuers where it lights.
Such humors stirde them vp; but this warrs seed
Was euen the same that wrack's all great dominion. 160
When fortune made vs lords of all, wealth flowed,
And then we grew licencious and rude,
The soldiours pray, and rapine brought in ryot,
Men tooke delight in Iewels, houses, plate,
And scorn'd old sparing diet, and ware robes 165
Too light for women; Pouerty (who hatcht
Roomes greatest wittes) was loath'd, and al the world
Ransackt for golde, which breeds the world decay;
And then large limits had their butting lands,
The ground which *Curius* and *Camillus* till'd, 170
Was stretcht vnto the fields of hinds vnknowne;
Againe, this people could not brooke calme peace,
Them freedome without war might not suffice,
Quarrels were rife, greedy desire stil poore
Did vild deeds, then t'was worth the price of bloud 175
And deem'd renowne to spoile their natiue towne,
Force mastered right, the strongest gouern'd all.
Hence came it that th' edicts were ouerrul'd,
That lawes were broake, *Tribunes* with *Consuls* stroue,
Sale made of offices, and peoples voices 180
Bought by themselues & solde, and euery yeare
Frauds and corruption in the field of *Mars*;
Hence interest and deuouring vsury sprang,
Faiths breach, & hence came war to most men welcom.
Now *Cæsar* ouerpast the snowy *Alpes*. 185
His mind was troubled, and he aim'd at war,
And comming to the foord of *Rubicon*,
At night in dreadful vision fearefull Roome,
Mourning appear'd, whose hoary hayres were torne,
And on her Turret bearing head disperst, 190
And armes all naked, who with broken sighes,
And staring, thus bespoke: What mean'st thou *Cæsar*?
Whether goes my standarde? Romans if ye be,
And beare true harts, stay heare. This spectacle
Stroake *Cæsars* hart with feare, his hayre stoode vp, 195
And faintnes numm'd his steps there on the brincke:
He thus cride out: Thou thunderer that guardst
Roomes mighty walles built on *Tarpeian* rocke,
Ye gods of *Phrigia* and *Iûlus* line,

157 nought *T. B.*: not *1600, Dyce to Bull.*

Quirinus rites and *Latian Ioue* aduanc'd 200
On *Alba* hill, ô *Vestall* flames, ô Roome,
My thoughts sole *goddes*, aide mine enterprise.
I hate thee not, to thee my conquests stoope,
Cæsar is thine, so please it thee, thy soldier;
He, he afflicts Roome that made me Roomes foe. 205
This said, he laying aside all lets of war,
Approcht the swelling streame with drum and ensigne,
Like to a Lyon of scortcht desart *Affricke*,
Who seeing hunters pauseth till fell wrath
And kingly rage increase, then hauing whiskt 210
His taile athwart his backe, and crest heau'd vp,
With iawes wide open ghastly roaring out;
(Albeit the *Moores* light Iauelin or his speare
Sticks in his side) yet runs vpon the hunter.
In summer time the purple *Rubicon*, 215
Which issues from a small spring, is but shallow,
And creepes along the vales deuiding iust
The bounds of *Italy* from *Cisalpin Fraunce*;
But now the winters wrath and wat'ry moone,
Being three daies old inforst the floud to swell, 220
And frozen *Alpes* thaw'd with resoluing winds.
The thunder hou'd horse in a crooked line,
To scape the violence of the streame first waded,
Which being broke the foot had easie passage.
As soone as *Cæsar* got vnto the banke 225
And bounds of Italy; here, here (saith he)
An end of peace; here end polluted lawes;
Hence leagues, and couenants; Fortune thee I follow,
Warre and the destinies shall trie my cause.
This said, the restles generall through the darke 230
(Swifter then bullets throwne from Spanish slinges,
Or darts which *Parthians* backward shoot) marcht on
And then (when *Lucifer* did shine alone,
And some dim stars) he *Arriminum* enter'd:
Day rose and viewde these tumultes of the war; 235
Whether the gods, or blustring south were cause
I know not, but the cloudy ayre did frown;
The soldiours hauing won the market place,
There spred the colours, with confused noise
Of trumpets clange, shril cornets, whistling fifes; 240
The people started; young men left their beds,
And snatcht armes neer their houshold gods hung vp
Such as peace yeelds; wormeaten leatherne targets,

Through which the wood peer'd, headles darts, olde swords
With vgly teeth of blacke rust fouly scarr'd: 245
But seeing white Eagles, & Roomes flags wel known,
And lofty *Cæsar* in the thickest throng,
They shooke for feare, & cold benumm'd their lims,
And muttering much, thus to themselues complain'd:
O wals vnfortunate too neere to France, 250
Predestinate to ruine; all lands else
Haue stable peace, here wars rage first begins,
We bide the first brunt; safer might we dwel
Vnder the frosty beare, or parching East,
Wagons or tents, then in this frontire towne. 255
We first sustain'd the vproares of the *Gaules*,
And furious *Cymbrians* and of *Carthage* Moores,
As oft as Roome was sackt, here gan the spoile.
Thus sighing whispered they, and none durst speake
And shew their feare, or griefe: but as the fields 260
When birds are silent thorough winters rage;
Or sea far from the land, so all were whist.
Now light had quite dissolu'd the mysty night,
And *Cæsars* mind vnsetled musing stood;
But gods and fortune prickt him to this war, 265
Infringing all excuse of modest shame,
And laboring to approue his quarrell good.
The angry Senate vrging *Grachus* deeds,
From doubtfull Roome wrongly expel'd the *Tribunes*,
That crost them; both which now approacht the camp, 270
And with them *Curio*, sometime *Tribune* too,
One that was feed for *Caesar*, and whose tongue
Could tune the people to the Nobles mind.
Cæsar (said he) while eloquence preuail'd,
And I might pleade, and draw the Commons minds 275
To fauour thee against the Senats will,
Fiue yeeres I lengthned thy commaund in France:
But law being put to silence by the wars,
We from our houses driuen, most willingly
Suffered exile: let thy sword bring vs home. 280
Now while their part is weake, and feares, march hence.
,, Where men are ready, lingering euer hurts:
In ten yeares wonst thou France; Roome may be won
With farre lesse toile, and yet the honors more;
Few battailes fought with prosperous successe 285
May bring her downe, and with her all the world.

263 night] might *1600*

Nor shalt thou triumph when thou comst to Roome,
Nor capitall be adorn'd with sacred bayes:
Enuy denies all, with thy bloud must thou
Abie thy conquest past: the sonne decrees 290
To expel the father; share the world thou canst not;
Inioy it all thou maiest. Thus *Curio* spake,
And therewith *Cæsar* prone ennough to warre,
Was so incenst as are *Eleius* steedes
With clamors: who though lockt and chaind in stalls, 295
Souse downe the wals, and make a passage forth.
Straight summon'd he his seuerall companies
Vnto the standard: his graue looke appeasd
The wrastling tumult, and right hand made silence:
And thus he spake: You that with me haue borne 300
A thousand brunts, and tride me ful ten yeeres,
See how they quit our bloudshed in the North,
Our friends death, and our wounds, our wintering
Vnder the Alpes; Roome rageth now in armes
As if the *Carthage Hannibal* were neere; 305
Cornets of horse are mustered for the field;
Woods turn'd to ships; both land and sea against vs.
Had forraine wars ill thriu'd; or wrathful France
Pursu'd vs hither, how were we bestead
When comming conqueror Roome afflicts me thus? 310
Let come their leaders whom long peace hath quail'd
Raw soldiours lately prest, and troupes of gownes;
Brabbling *Marcellus*; *Cato* whom fooles reuerence;
Must *Pompeis* followers with strangers ayde,
(Whom from his youth he bribde) needs make him king?
And shal he triumph long before his time, 316
And hauing once got head still shal he raigne?
What should I talke of mens corne reapt by force,
And by him kept of purpose for a dearth?
Who sees not warre sit by the quiuering Iudge; 320
And sentence giuen in rings of naked swords,
And lawes assailde, and arm'd men in the *Senate*?
Twas his troupe hem'd in *Milo* being accusde;
And now least age might waine his state, he casts
For ciuill warre, wherein through vse he's known 325
To exceed his maister, that arch-traitor *Sylla*.
A brood of barbarous *Tygars* hauing lapt
The bloud of many a heard, whilst with their dams

294 Eleius] Eleus' *Dyce*, *Cunn.*: Elean *Bull.* 311 leader *Dyce etc.* 313 Babbling *Dyce etc.* 327 A *1600*: As *Dyce etc.*

They kennel'd in *Hircania*, euermore
Wil rage and pray: so *Pompey* thou hauing lickt 330
Warme goare from *Syllas* sword art yet athirst,
Iawes flesh'd with bloud continue murderous.
Speake, when shall this thy long vsurpt power end?
What end of mischiefe? *Sylla* teaching thee,
At last learne wretch to leaue thy monarchy. 335
What, now *Scicillian* Pirats are suppresst,
And jaded king of *Pontus* poisoned slaine,
Must *Pompey* as his last foe plume on me,
Because at his commaund I wound not vp
My conquering Eagles? say I merit nought, 340
Yet for long seruice done, reward these men,
And so they triumph, be't with whom ye wil.
Whether now shal these olde bloudles soules repaire?
What seates for their deserts? what store of ground
For seruitors to till? what *Colonies* 345
To rest their bones? say *Pompey*, are these worse
Then Pirats of *Sycillia*? they had houses.
Spead, spread these flags that ten yearsspace haue conquer'd,
Lets vse our tried force, they that now thwart right
In wars wil yeeld to wrong: the gods are with vs. 350
Neither spoile, nor kingdom seeke we by these armes,
But Roome at thraldoms feet to rid from tyrants.
This spoke none answer'd, but a murmuring buz
Th'vnstable people made: their houshold gods
And loue to Room (thogh slaughter steeld their harts 355
And minds were prone) restrain'd them; but wars loue
And *Cæsars* awe dasht all: then *Lalius*
The chiefe *Centurion* crown'd with Oaken leaues,
For sauing of a Romaine Citizen,
Stept forth, and cryde: Chiefe leader of Rooms force, 360
So be I may be bold to speake a truth,
We grieue at this thy patience and delay.
What doubtst thou vs? euen nowe when youthfull bloud
Pricks forth our liuely bodies, and strong armes
Can mainly throw the dart, wilt thou indure 365
These purple groomes? that *Senates* tyranny?
Is conquest got by ciuill war so hainous?
Well, leade vs then to *Syrtes* desart shoare;
Or *Scythia*; or hot *Libiaes* thirsty sands.

332 flesh'd *Dyce etc.*: flesh *1600* 337 jaded king *Dyce etc.*: Jaded, king *1600* 345 seruitors] *Qy.* suruiuors? 357 Lalius] Lælius *Dyce etc.*

This hand that all behind vs might be quail'd, 370
Hath with thee past the swelling Ocean,
And swept the foming brest of *Articks Rhene.*
Loue ouer-rules my will, I must obay thee,
Cæsar, he whom I heare thy trumpets charge
I hould no Romaine; by these ten blest ensignes 375
And all thy seueral triumphs, shouldst thou bid me
Intombe my sword within my brothers bowels;
Or fathers throate; or womens groning wombe;
This hand (albeit vnwilling) should performe it;
Or rob the gods; or sacred temples fire: 380
These troupes should soone pull down the church of *Ioue.*
If to incampe on *Thuscan Tybers* streames,
Ile bouldly quarter out the fields of Rome;
What wals thou wilt be leaueld with the ground,
These hands shall thrust the ram, and make them flie, 385
Albeit the Citty thou wouldst haue so ra'st
Be Roome it selfe. Here euery band applauded,
And with their hands held vp, all ioyntly cryde
They'ill follow where he please: the showts rent heauen,
As when against pine bearing *Ossa's* rocks 390
Beates *Thracian Boreas*; or when trees bowde down,
And rustling swing vp as the wind fets breath
When *Cæsar* saw his army proane to war,
And fates so bent, least sloth and long delay
Might crosse him, he withdrew his troupes from France, 395
And in all quarters musters men for Roome.
They by *Lemannus* nooke forsooke their tents;
They whom the *Lingones* foild with painted speares,
Vnder the rockes by crooked *Vogesus*;
And many came from shallow *Isara,* 400
Who running long, fals in a greater floud,
And ere he sees the sea looseth his name;
The yellow *Ruthens* left their garrisons;
Mild *Atax* glad it beares not Roman boats,
And frontier *Varus* that the campe is farre, 405
Sent aide; so did *Alcides* port, whose seas
Eate hollow rocks, and where the north-west wind
Nor *Zephir* rules not, but the north alone
Turmoiles the coast, and enterance forbids;
And others came from that vncertaine shore, 410

372 Arctic *Dyce etc.* 378 womens groning] groaning women's *conj. Dyce*[1]: groaning woman's *Dyce*[2] 391 bowde] bow *conj. Dyce*[1], *Dyce*[2], *Bull.* 404 boats *Dyce etc.*: bloats *1600*

Which is nor sea, nor land, but oft times both,
And changeth as the Ocean ebbes and flowes:
Whether the sea roul'd alwaies from that point,
Whence the wind blowes stil forced to and fro;
Or that the wandring maine follow the moone; 415
Or flaming *Titan* (feeding on the deepe)
Puls them aloft, and makes the surge kisse heauen,
Philosophers looke you, for vnto me
Thou cause, what ere thou be whom God assignes
This great effect, art hid. They came that dwell 420
By *Nemes* fields, and bankes of *Satirus*,
Where *Tarbels* winding shoares imbrace the sea,
The *Santons* that reioyce in *Cæsars* loue,
Those of *Bituriges* and light *Axon* pikes;
And they of *Rhene* and *Leuca*, cunning darters, 425
And *Sequana* that well could manage steeds;
The *Belgians* apt to gouerne *Brittish* cars;
Th' *Auerni*, too, which bouldly faine themselues
The Romanes brethren, sprung of *Ilian* race;
The stubborne *Neruians* staind with *Cottas* bloud; 430
And *Vangions* who like those of *Sarmata*,
Were open slops: and fierce *Batauians*,
Whome trumpets clang incites, and those that dwel
By *Cyngas* streame, and where swift *Rhodanus*
Driues *Araris* to sea; they neere the hils, 435
Vnder whose hoary rocks *Gebenna* hangs;
And *Treuier*, thou being glad that wars are past thee;
And you late shorne *Ligurians*, who were wont
In large spread heire to exceed the rest of France;
And where to *Hesus*, and fell *Mercury* 440
They offer humane flesh, and where *Ioue* seemes
Bloudy like *Dian*, whom the *Scythians* serue;
And you French *Bardi*, whose immortal pens
Renowne the valiant soules slaine in your wars,
Sit safe at home and chaunt sweet *Poesie*. 445
And *Druides* you now in peace renew
Your barbarous customes, and sinister rites,
In vnfeld woods, and sacred groues you dwell,
And only gods & heauenly powers you know,
Or only know you nothing. For you hold 450
That soules passe not to silent *Erebus*
Or *Plutoes* bloodles kingdom, but else where
Resume a body: so (if truth you sing)

440 Mercury] Mercury (Ioue) *1600* 441 Ioue] it *1600*

Death brings long life. Doubtles these northren men
Whom death the greatest of all feares affright not, 455
Are blest by such sweet error, this makes them
Run on the swords point and desire to die,
And shame to spare life which being lost is wonne.
You likewise that repulst the *Caicke* foe,
March towards Roome ; and you fierce men of *Rhene* 460
Leauing your countrey open to the spoile.
These being come, their huge power made him bould
To mannage greater deeds ; the bordering townes
He garrison'd ; and *Italy* he fild with soldiours.
Vaine fame increast true feare, and did inuade 465
The peoples minds, and laide before their eies
Slaughter to come, and swiftly bringing newes
Of present war, made many lies and tales.
One sweares his troupes of daring horsemen fought
Vpon *Meuanias* plaine, where Buls are graz'd ; 470
Other that *Cæsars* barbarous bands were spread
Along *Nar* floud that into *Tiber* fals,
And that his owne ten ensignes, and the rest
Marcht not intirely, and yet hide the ground,
And that he's much chang'd, looking wild and big, 475
And far more barbarous then the French (his vassals)
And that he lags behind with them of purpose
Borne twixt the *Alpes* & *Rhene*, which he hath brought
From out their Northren parts, and that Roome
He looking on by these men should be sackt. 480
Thus in his fright did each man strengthen Fame,
And without ground, fear'd what themselues had faind :
Nor were the Commons only strooke to heart
With this vaine terror, but the Court, the Senate ;
The fathers selues leapt from their seats ; and flying
Left hateful warre decreed to both the Consuls. 486
Then with their feare, and danger al distract,
Their sway of fleight carries the heady rout
That in chain'd troupes breake forth at euery port ;
You would haue thought their houses had bin fierd 490
Or dropping-ripe, ready to fall with Ruine,
So rusht the inconsiderate multitude
Thorough the Citty hurried headlong on,
As if the only hope (that did remaine
To their afflictions) were t'abandon Roome. 495
Looke how when stormy *Auster* from the breach

474 hide] hid *Dyce*, *Cunn.*

Of *Libian Syrtes* roules a monstrous waue,
Which makes the maine saile fal with hideous sound;
The Pilot from the helme leapes in the sea;
And Marriners, albeit the keele be sound, 500
Shipwracke themselues: euen so the Citty left,
All rise in armes; nor could the bed-rid parents
Keep back their sons, or womens teares their husbands;
They stai'd not either to pray or sacrifice,
Their houshould gods restrain them not, none lingered,
As loath to leaue Roome whom they held so deere: 506
Th'irreuocable people flie in troupes.
O gods that easie grant men great estates,
But hardly grace to keepe them: Roome that flowes
With Citizens and Captiues, and would hould 510
The world (were it together) is by cowards
Left as a pray now *Cæsar* doth approach:
When Romans are besieg'd by forraine foes,
With slender trench they escape night stratagems,
And suddaine rampire raisde of turfe snatcht vp 515
Would make them sleepe securely in their tents.
Thou Roome at name of warre runst from thy selfe,
And wilt not trust thy Citty walls one night:
Wel might these feare, when *Pompey* fear'd and fled.
Now euermore least some one hope might ease 520
The Commons iangling minds, apparant signes arose,
Strange sights appear'd, the angry threatning gods
Fill'd both the earth and seas with prodegies;
Great store of strange and vnknown stars were seene
Wandering about the North, and rings of fire 525
Flie in the ayre, and dreadfull bearded stars,
And Commets that presage the fal of kingdoms.
The flattering skie gliter'd in often flames,
And sundry fiery meteors blaz'd in heauen:
Now spearlike, long; now like a spreading torch 530
Lightning in silence stole forth without clouds,
And from the northren climat snatching fier
Blasted the Capitoll: The lesser stars
Which wont to run their course through empty night
At noone day mustered; *Phœbe* hauing fild 535
Her meeting hornes to match her brothers light,
Strooke with th' earths suddaine shadow waxed pale,
Titan himselfe throand in the midst of heauen,
His burning chariot plung'd in sable cloudes,

510 captiues *Dyce etc.*: Captaines *1600*

And whelm'd the world in darknesse, making men 540
Dispaire of day, as did *Thiestes* towne,
(*Mycenæ*) *Phœbus* flying through the East:
Fierce *Mulciber* vnbarred *Ætna's* gate,
Which flamed not on high; but headlong pitcht
Her burning head on bending *Hespery*. 545
Cole-blacke *Charibdis* whirl'd a sea of bloud;
Fierce Mastiues hould; the vestall fires went out,
The flame in *Alba* consecrate to *Ioue*
Parted in twaine, and with a double point
Rose like the *Theban* brothers funerall fire; 550
The earth went off hir hinges; and the *Alpes*
Shooke the old snow from off their trembling laps.
The Ocean swell'd as high as Spanish *Calpe*,
Or *Atlas* head; their saints and houshold gods
Sweate teares to shew the trauailes of their citty. 555
Crownes fell from holy statues, ominous birds
Defil'd the day, and wilde beastes were seene,
Leauing the woods, lodge in the streetes of Rome.
Cattell were seene that muttered humane speech:
Prodigious birthes with more and vgly iointes, 560
Then nature giues, whose sight appauls the mother,
And dismall Prophesies were spread abroad:
And they whom fierce *Bellonaes* fury moues
To wound their armes, sing vengeance, *Sibils* priests,
Curling their bloudy lockes, howle dreadfull things, 565
Soules quiet and appeas'd sight from their graues,
Clashing of armes was heard in vntrod woods,
Shrill voices schright, and ghoasts incounter men.
Those that inhabited the suburbe fieldes
Fled, fowle *Erinnis* stalkt about the wals, 570
Shaking her snakie haire and crooked pine
With flaming toppe, much like that hellish fiend
Which made the sterne *Lycurgus* wound his thigh,
Or fierce *Agaue* mad; or like *Megæra*
That scar'd *Alcides*, when by *Iunoes* taske 575
He had before lookt *Pluto* in the face.
Trumpets were heard to sound; and with what noise
An armed battaile ioines, such and more strange
Blacke night brought forth in secret: *Sylla's* ghost
Was seene to walke, singing sad Oracles, 580

552 laps] tops *conj. Dyce*[1], *Dyce*[2] 557 Defil'd the day] The day defilèd *conj. Dyce* and] at night *conj. Cunn., Bull.* 564 Sibils] Cybel's *Dyce etc.* 566 sight *1600*: sigh'd *Dyce etc.*

And *Marius* head aboue cold *Tau'ron* peering
(His graue broke open) did affright the Boores.
To these ostents (as their old custome was)
They call th' *Etrurian Augures*, amonst whom
The grauest, *Aruns*, dwelt in forsaken * *Leuca*, * *or Luná.*
Well skild in *Pyromancy*; one that knew 586
The hearts of beasts, and flight of wandring foules.
First he commands such monsters *Nature* hatcht
Against her kind (the barren Mules loth'd issue)
To be cut forth and cast in dismall fiers: 590
Then, that the trembling Citizens should walke
About the City; then the sacred priests
That with diuine lustration purg'd the wals,
And went the round, in, and without the towne.
Next, an inferiour troupe in tuckt vp vestures, 595
After the *Gabine* manner: then the Nunnes
And their vaild Matron, who alone might view
Mineruas statue; then, they that keepe, and read
Sybillas secret works, and washt their saint
In *Almo's* floud: Next learned *Augures* follow, 600
Apolloes southsayers, and *Ioues* feasting priests;
The skipping *Salij* with shields like wedges;
And *Flamins* last, with networke wollen vailes.
While these thus in and out had circled Roome,
Looke, what the lightning blasted *Aruns* takes 605
And it inters with murmurs dolorous,
And cals the place *Bidentall*: on the Altar
He laies a ne're-yoakt Bull, and powers downe wine,
Then crams salt leuin on his crooked knife;
The beast long struggled, as being like to proue 610
An aukward sacrifice, but by the hornes
The quick priest pull'd him on his knees & slew him:
No vaine sprung out but from the yawning gash,
In steed of red bloud wallowed venemous gore.
These direful signes made *Aruns* stand amaz'd, 615
And searching farther for the gods displeasure,
The very cullor scard him; a dead blacknesse
Ranne through the bloud, that turn'd it all to gelly,
And stain'd the bowels with darke lothsome spots;
The liuer swell'd with filth, and euery vaine 620
Did threaten horror from the host of *Cæsar*;
A small thin skinne contain'd the vital parts,
The heart stird not, and from the gaping liuer

599 washt] wash *Dyce etc.*

Squis'd matter through the cal; the intralls pearde,
And which (aie me) euer pretendeth ill, 625
At that bunch where the liuer is, appear'd
A knob of flesh, whereof one halfe did looke
Dead, and discoulour'd; th' other leane and thinne.
By these he seeing what myschiefes must ensue,
Cride out, O gods! I tremble to vnfould 630
What you intend: great *Ioue* is now displeas'd,
And in the brest of this slaine Bull are crept
Th'infernall powers. My feare transcends my words,
Yet more will happen then I can vnfold.
Turne all to good, be *Augury* vaine, and *Tages* 635
Th'arts master falce. Thus in ambiguous tearmes,
Inuoluing all, did *Aruns* darkly sing.
But *Figulus* more seene in heauenly mysteries,
Whose like *Aegiptian Memphis* neuer had
For skill in stars, and tune-full planeting, 640
In this sort spake: The worlds swift course is lawlesse
And casuall; all the starres at randome radge:
Or if *Fate* rule them, Rome thy Cittizens
Are neere some plague: what mischiefe shall insue?
Shall townes be swallowed? shall the thickned aire, 645
Become intemperate? shall the earth be barraine?
Shall water be conieal'd and turn'd to ice?
O Gods what death prepare ye? with what plague
Meane ye to radge? the death of many men
Meetes in one period. If cold noysome *Saturne* 650
Were now exalted, and with blew beames shinde,
Then *Gaynimede* would renew *Deucalions* flood,
And in the fleeting sea the earth be drencht.
O *Phœbus* shouldst thou with thy rayes now sing
The fell *Nemean* beast, th'earth would be fired, 655
And heauen tormented with thy chafing heate,
But thy fiers hurt not; *Mars*, 'tis thou enflam'st
The threatning Scorpion with the burning taile
And fier'st his cleyes. Why art thou thus enrag'd?
Kind *Iupiter* hath low declin'd himselfe; 660
Venus is faint; swift *Hermes* retrograde;
Mars onely rules the heauen: why doe the Planets
Alter their course and vainly dim their vertue?
Sword-girt *Orions* side glisters too bright.
Wars radge draws neare; & to the swords strong hand 665
Let all Lawes yeeld, sinne beare the name of vertue,

642 radge] range *Dyce etc.*

Many a yeare these furious broiles let last,
Why should we wish the gods should euer end them?
War onely giues vs peace, ô Rome continue
The course of mischiefe, and stretch out the date 670
Of slaughter; onely ciuill broiles make peace.
These sad presages were enough to scarre
The quiuering *Romans*, but worse things affright them.
As *Mænus* full of wine on *Pindus* raues,
So runnes a Matron through th'amazed streetes, 675
Disclosing *Phœbus* furie in this sort:
Pean whither am I halde? where shall I fall?
Thus borne aloft I see *Pangeus* hill,
With hoarie toppe, and vnder *Hemus* mount
Philippi plaines; *Phœbus* what radge is this? 680
Why grapples Rome, and makes war, hauing no foes?
Whither turne I now? thou lead'st me toward th'east,
Where *Nile* augmenteth the *Pelusian* sea:
This headlesse trunke that lies on *Nylus* sande
I know: now throughout the aire I flie, 685
To doubtfull *Sirtes* and drie *Affricke*, where
A fury leades the *Emathian* bandes; from thence
To the pine bearing hils, hence to the mounts
Pirene, and so backe to Rome againe.
Se impious warre defiles the Senat house, 690
New factions rise; now through the world againe
I goe; ô *Phœbus* shew me *Neptunes* shore,
And other Regions, I haue seene *Philippi*:
This said, being tir'd with fury she sunke downe.

FINIS

667 furious] firious *1600* 674 Mænas *Dyce etc.* 685 thoroughout *Dyce, Bull.* 688 hence] thence *Dyce etc.*

PRINTED IN GREAT BRITAIN
AT THE UNIVERSITY PRESS, OXFORD
BY VIVIAN RIDLER
PRINTER TO THE UNIVERSITY